PLATO
AND SOCRATES

GARLAND REFERENCE LIBRARY
OF THE HUMANITIES
(VOL. 78)

PLATO
AND SOCRATES
A Comprehensive Bibliography,
1958–1973

Richard D. McKirahan, Jr.

GARLAND PUBLISHING, INC. • NEW YORK & LONDON
1978

Library of Congress Cataloging in Publication Data

McKirahan, Richard D.
   Plato and Socrates.
   (Garland reference library of the humanities; v. 78)
   Includes indexes.
   1. Plato—Bibliography. 2. Socrates—Bibliography. I. Title.
Z8696.M34 [B393]   016.183′2   76-52670
ISBN 0-8240-9895-1

PRINTED IN THE UNITED STATES OF AMERICA

CONTENTS

v

III. THE PLATONIC CORPUS

IV. PLATO AS A WRITER

V. PLATO'S THOUGHT

PREFACE

It has been almost twenty years since Prof. Cherniss published the last complete bibliography on Plato (see below, no. 4554). Since that time, scholarly activity on Plato and Socrates has continued to increase, and the vast amount of material which has been published makes it difficult for even the most diligent to be aware of all the work that has been done, even on particular subjects concerning these two philosophers. The present volume requires no further justification, and my hope is that it will be of value to those doing research on Socrates and Plato.

My intent has been to provide bibliographical information on all scholarly work which was published on Plato and Socrates during the years 1958 through 1973. Of these limits 1958 was selected because Cherniss' work covers the years 1950–1957.[1] My choice of 1973 as the upper limit was due to the availability of bibliographical resources during the time the present bibliography was being compiled. I was able to be confident of a much greater degree of completeness for the years through 1973 than for more recent years.

The work provides bibliographical references to the materials it covers. In this respect it falls short of Cherniss' work, which is a model of a critical bibliography. The decision to omit what would surely have been a valuable feature of the work was determined by considerations of space and time. Even with the basic information I have provided, the book is longer and more expensive than one might wish, and I fear that a thorough bibliography *raisonnée* might easily have been three times as long. Further, there was the obstacle presented by the sheer mass of materials. In 1959 Prof. Cherniss wrote, "It is improbable that any one person, however erudite, alert, and devoted, could read cursorily, not to say critically, all the books, articles, sections of books, and reviews concerned with

Plato which have been published during the last decade."[2] This statement is still more true for the period since 1958, when the annual scholarly output on Plato has doubled (from fewer than 150 items in 1959 to over 300 items[3] by 1970). The evident impossibility of doing an adequate or thorough job of locating, not to mention reading and summarizing, the materials listed (which are written in more than thirty languages) therefore made the present form of the work a necessity.

One of the frequent problems I encountered in working on this project was deciding whether to include or exclude a particular work which dealt with Socrates or Plato only incidentally. My aim was to include all materials primarily concerned with Socrates and Plato, and other works which make a contribution to our understanding of the two philosophers, but these principles (especially the latter) were not easy to apply uniformly.

I somewhat arbitrarily chose to include mention of chapters on Socrates and Plato in histories of ancient philosophy, but to exclude general histories of philosophy or of Western philosophy. Also, I made no effort to locate general histories of ethics, political philosophy or other branches of philosophy, or indeed of other areas of thought (such as mathematics) which might contain chapters on Socrates and Plato, although I have included a few representative examples of such works.

The bibliography is arranged topically. In the selection of topics I have tended to follow Cherniss, with only a few exceptions (principally additional categories) which I did not hesitate to make when the materials at my disposal justified them. Cherniss' observation that "in the study of Plato no neat classification corresponds to the subject-matter, for the treatment of any aspect of Plato's thought is likely to depend upon the interpretation of many other aspects and to affect all these others in turn"[4] should provide sufficient warning to users of the present work. I have attempted to alleviate this difficulty to some degree by cross-references which appear at the end of each section. Further assistance is provided by Special Indices listing the works largely devoted to a number of particular topics within the general areas of Plato's thought that I have identified in Section V.

Since users of this book will be chiefly concerned with locating the books and articles included, I have made an effort to indicate when a book has had more than one edition and when an article has been reprinted. A number of collections of articles and excerpts from books on Socrates and Plato appeared during the period covered, and I have put these in a separate section (XIV) and have located the articles they contain in the appropriate categories throughout the book. A result of this policy has been the inclusion of a number of papers originally published before 1958. I have also included older books which were reprinted during the period covered. It seemed to me that, for example, a person studying the *Sophist* would be interested to learn that Lewis Campbell's 1867 edition of that dialogue was currently available.

The works placed in each category are arranged chronologically and alphabetically (by author) within each year. I have made exceptions to this principle when an author wrote a series of works on a single subject and in some cases where a work provoked one or more discussions, rebuttals, etc. In these cases the latter works are placed immediately after the first one. Further, some subjects (Sections IA, IB, VIIA and XIV) seemed better served by a straight alphabetical arrangement and others (mainly translations of Plato's works) appeared more usefully arranged by language. I have designated books, dissertations and other monographs with an asterisk and have listed as many reviews for these as have come to my attention. I do not claim to have located every review, but have covered the major philosophical and classical journals. I have used the periodical abbreviations found in *L'Année Philologique* wherever possible, and have coined abbreviations for journals not covered by that work. A list of the abbreviations used is provided below.

I would like to take this opportunity to acknowledge my debts of gratitude to Ms. C. L. Claxton for her assistance at the beginning of the project; to Ms. M. Smith and the reference staff at the Honnold Library of the Claremont Colleges for their helpful and patient assistance; to Profs. C. Weber of Kenyon College and T. Mizutani of Tokyo University for generous assistance in locating Japanese materials; to Mr. L. Jones and the consulting staff at the Seaver Computer Center of the Claremont Colleges for the many hours they devoted to giving me advice and instruction and writing programs for use in the project; and to Ms. W. J. Lewis for her efficient and enthusiastic help in the final stages. I would also like to thank Pomona College for the research grant and liberal computer policy without which the present work could not have been completed.

It is almost conventional to apologize for errors a book may be found to contain, and the present case is no exception. I am sure that there are some studies of Socrates and Plato which I failed to locate and errors in some of the entries as they presently stand. The computer I used on the project enabled me to avoid many mistakes and inconsistencies, and proofreading disclosed many more, but in a project of this type and this magnitude I have come to realize that indeed *errare humanum est*. For the remaining mistakes I do apologize.

Claremont, California
September 1977

NOTES

1. It also includes major work done in the decades before 1950 and a few post-1957 items.
2. Cherniss, p. 9.
3. Excluding texts and translations.
4. Cherniss, p. 9.

CORRIGENDA

p. 4	Item 12 should be located on p. 1 between items 3 and 4.
p. 26	Item 135 should be located in section I C.
p. 135	Item 1024 should be located between items 1029 and 1030.
p. 136	Item 1042 should be located between items 1044 and 1045.
p. 165	Item 1295 should be located on p. 166 between items 1307 and 1308.
p. 170	Item 1330 has the following reviews:
	PhilosRdschau VII 1959 70-72 Beierwaltes.
	RPh XXXIV 1960 286 Louis.
	CR X 1960 113-115 Baldry.
	RBPh XXXVIII 1960 934 des Places.
	RFil (La Plata) XI 1962 122-126 Delucchi.
	Gnomon XXXVI 1964 654-658 Koller.
p. 239	Item 2002 belongs with item 2017.
p. 285	Item 2488 belongs in section III C d 30.
p. 286	Items 2491 and 2492 should be grouped together as a single item.
p. 349	Item 3054 should be located between items 3057 and 3058.

INDEX OF PERIODICALS AND ABBREVIATIONS

A&A	Antike und Abendland.
A&R	Atene e Roma.
AAA	Αρχαιολογικὰ Ἀνάλεκτα ἐξ Ἀθηνῶν.
AAAH	Acta ad Archaeologiam et Artium Historiam Pertinentia. Institutum Romanum Norvegiae et Oslo, Universitetsforlag.
AAAPSS	Annals of the American Academy of Political and Social Sciences.
AAHG	Anzeiger fur die Altertumswissenschaft. Hrsg. von der Osterreichischen Humanistischen Gesellschaft.
AAntHung	Acta Antiqua Academiae Scientiarum Hungaricae.
AAP	Atti dell'Accademia Pontaniana.
AASF	Annales Academiae Scientiarum Fennicae.
AAWW	Anzeiger der Oesterreichischen Akademie der Wissenschaften in Wien.
ABG	Archiv fur Begriffsgeschichte.
ABret	Annales de Bretagne.
AC	L'Antiquite Classique.
AClass	Acta Classica.
Acme	Acme.
ACR	American Classical Review.
ACUM	Annales du Centre Universitaire Mediterraneen (Nice).
Aegyptus	Aegyptus.
AEHE, IVe Sect.	Annuaire de l'Ecole Pratique des Hautes Etudes, IVe Section, Sciences historiques et philologiques.
AEHE, Ve Sect.	Annuaire de l'Ecole Pratique des Hautes Etudes, Ve Section, Sciences Religieuses.
AESocCiv	Annales. Economie. Societe. Civilisation (Paris)
Aevum	Aevum.
AFC	Anales de Filologia Clasica (Buenos Aires).
AFLA	Annales de la Faculte des Lettres et Sciences Humaines d'Aix, Serie Classique.
AFLC	Annali della Facolta di Lettere, Filosofia e Magistero della Universita di Cagliari.
AFLN	Annali della Facolta di Lettere e Filosofia della Universita di Napoli.
AFLNice	Annales de la Faculte des Lettres et Sciences Humaines de Nice.
AFUA	Annales Publication. Faculte des Lettres et Sciences Humaines, Universite d'Aix-Marseilles.
AFUN	Anuario filosofico de la Universidad de Navarra.

PERIODICAL INDEX

AGlI	Archivio Glottologico Italiano.
AGM	Sudhoffs Archiv fur Geschichte der Medezin und der Naturwissenschaften.
Agon	Agon.
Agora	Agora (State University of New York at Potsdam).
AGPh	Archiv fur Geschichte der Philosophie.
AHAW	Abhandlungen der Heidelberger Akademie der Wissenschaften.
AHES	Archive for History of Exact Sciences.
AHR	American Historical Review.
AIHM	Archivio Iberoamericano de Historia de la Medicina.
AIHS	Archives Internationales d'Histoire des Sciences.
AIIS	Annali dell'Istituto Italiano per gli Studi Storici.
AIP	Annales de l'Institut de Philosophie, Bruxelles.
ÁIV	Atti dell'Istituto Veneto di Scienze, Lettere ed Arti, Classe di Science morali e Lettere.
AJA	American Journal of Archaeology.
Ajatus	Ajatus.
AJPh	American Journal of Philology.
AK	Antike Kunst.
Akroterion	Akroterion (South Africa).
ALBuc	Analele Universitatea Bucuresti. Acta Logica.
ALFM	Annali della Facolta di Lettere e Filosofia della Universita di Macerata.
ALGP	Annali del Liceo Classico G. Garibaldi di Palermo.
ALing	Archivum Linguisticum.
Altertum	Altertum.
Ambix	Ambix (Cambridge).
AmerAnthropol	American Anthropologist.
America	America (New York).
AmIm	American Imago.
AmSocR	American Sociological Review.
Analecta	Analecta (Egypt).
Analysis	Analysis.
AnCalas	Analecta Calasanctiana (Madrid).
Angelicum	Angelicum (Roma).
AngThR	Anglican Theological Review.
ANQ	American Notes & Queries.
Anregung	Anregung (Munchen).
Antaios	Antaios (Athens).
Antichthon	Antichthon (Sydney).
Antonianum	Antonianum (Roma).
ANTP	Algemeen Nederlands Tijdschrift voor Wijsbegeerte en Psychologie.
AnuFilos	Anuario Filosofico (Pamplona).
Apeiron	Apeiron.
APhFen	Acta Philosophica Fennica.

APQ	American Philosophical Quarterly.
Aquinas	Aquinas (Roma).
Arbor	Arbor (Madrid).
Arcadia	Arcadia (Berlin).
ArchFilos	Archivio di Filosofia.
ArchHistMed	Archiwum Historii Medycyny (Polskie towarzystwo Historii Medycyny).
ArchivPhilos	Archiv fur Philosophie.
ArchMusik	Archiv fur Musikwissenschaft.
ArchPD	Archives de Philosophie du Droit.
ArchPhilos	Archives de Philosophie.
Arctos	Arctos.
Arethusa	Arethusa (Buffalo, N.Y.).
Arguments	Arguments (Paris).
Arion	Arion.
ARSPh	Archiv fur Rechts- und Sozialphilosophie.
Arta	Arta (Romania).
ArtS	Art Sacre (Paris).
AryanPath	Aryan Path (India).
ArzPraxis	Arztliche Praxis.
ASal	Acta Salmanticensia, Filosofia y Letras.
ASchol	American Scholar.
Asclepio	Asclepio (Madrid).
ASHSN	Actes de la Societe Helvetique des Sciences Naturelles.
AsiatStud	Asiatische Studien.
ASNP	Annali della Scuola Normale Superiore di Pisa.
ASSPh	Studia Philosophica. Annuaire de la Societe Suisse de Philosophie.
ASTI	Annual of the Swedish Theological Institute.
Athena	Athena (Athens).
Athenaeum	Athenaeum.
Athene(Chicago)	Athene (Chicago).
AThPsy	Annuaire de Therapeutique Psychiatrique.
Atlantis	Atlantis.
AU	Der altsprachliche Unterricht.
AUBuc	Analele, Universitatea Bucuresti. Stiinte Sociale.
AUBuda	Annales Universitatis Budapestianae de R. Eotvos nominatae, Sectio philologica.
AUChile	Anales de la Universidad de Chile.
AUCPH	Acta Universitatis Carolinae. Philosophica et Historica. (Praha, Universita Karlova).
Augustinianum	Augustinianum.
Augustinus	Augustinus.
AUIJ	Analele Stiintifice ale Universitatii A.I. Cuza din Iasi. Sectiunea 3: Part D: Stiinte Juridice.
AUMLA	Journal of the Australasian Universities Language and Literature Association.
AUP	Annales de l'Universite de Paris.
AUQuito	Anales de la Universidad Central de

	Quito.
AusJP	Australasian Journal of Philosophy.
AUT	Annales Universitatis Turkuensis.
AUToul	Annales publiees trimestriellement par l'Universite de Toulouse-Le Mirail.
AW	Antike Welt.
BA	Books Abroad.
BAB	Bulletin de la Classe des Lettres de l'Academie Royale de Belgique.
BAClLg	Bulletin semestriel de l'Association des classiques de l'Universite de Liege.
BAGB	Bulletin de l'Association Guillaume Bude.
BASP	Bulletin of the American Society of Papyrologists.
BBF	Bulletin des Bibliotheques de France.
BCH	Bulletin de Correspondance Hellenique.
BCO	Bibliotheca Classica Orientalis.
BECh	Bibliotheque de l'Ecole des Chartes, Geneve.
Begegnung	Begegnung. Zeitschrift fur Kultur und Geistesleben.
Belfagor	Belfagor (Firenze).
BFS	Bulletin de la Faculte des Lettres de Strasbourg.
BHM	Bulletin of the History of Medecine.
BHR	Bibliotheque d'Humanisme et Renaissance.
Biblica	Biblica (Roma).
BIBR	Bulletin de l'Institut Historique Belge de Rome.
BICS	Bulletin of the Institute of Classical Studies of the University of London.
BIEH	Boletin del Instituto de Estudios Helenicos (Barcelona).
Bigaku	Bigaku (Japan).
Bijdragen	Bijdragen.
BJ	Bonner Jahrbuch der Rheinischen Landsmuseum in Bonn und des Vereins von Altertumsfreunden im Rheinlande.
BJAes	British Journal of Aesthetics.
BJPS	British Journal for the Philosophy of Science.
BJSoc	British Journal of Sociology.
BO	Bibliotheca Orientalis.
BollFil	Bolletino Filosofico (Roma).
BPEC	Bollettino del Comitato per la Preparazione dell'Edizione nazionale dei Classici greci e latini.
BR	Bucknell Review (Lewisburg, Penn.).
BSEAA	Boletin del Seminario de Estudios de Arte y Arqueologia (Valladolid, Inst. Diego Velazquez).
BSEN	Bulletin de la Societe Francaise d'Etudes Nietzschiennes.
BSL	Bulletin de la Societe de Linguistique de Paris.

BSMB	Bulletin de la Societe Mathematique de Belgique.
BSPh	Bulletin de la Societe Francaise de Philosophie.
BTh	Bulletin de Theologie Ancienne et Medievale (Gembloux).
bThom	Bulletin Thomiste (Paris).
BUJ	Boston University Journal.
BullMur	Bolletino dell'Istituto Storico Italiano per il Medio Evo e Archivio Muratoriano.
Bummei	Bummei (Japan).
Bunka	Bunka (Tokyo).
BW	Book World.
Byzantion	Byzantion.
ByzZ	Byzantinische Zeitschrift.
C&M	Classica et Mediaevalia.
CahAnal	Cahiers pour l'Analyse.
CambRev	Cambridge Review.
CanJPh	Canadian Journal of Philosophy.
CB	Classical Bulletin.
CCHist	Ceskoslovensky Casopis Historicky.
CD	La Ciudad de Dios (Valladolid).
CE	College English.
Centaurus	Centaurus (Kobenhavn).
CF	Classical Folia.
CFC	Cuadernos de Filologia Clasica (Madrid).
ChinCult	Chinese Culture.
CHisp	Cuadernos Hispanoamericanos.
CHL	Commentationes Humanarum Litterarum Societatis Scientiarum Fennicae.
CHR	Catholic Historical Review (Washington).
Christ und Welt	Christ und Welt.
Christengemeinschaft	Die Christengemeinschaft.
CHum	Computers and the Humanities.
Ciceroniana	Ciceroniana (Roma).
CiFe	Ciencia y Fe (Argentina).
CISoc	Cahiers Internationaux de Sociologie.
CISymb	Cahiers Internationaux de Symbolisme.
Cithara	Cithara (St. Bonaventure, N.Y.).
CiTom	La Ciencia Tomista (Salamanca).
CivCatt	Civilta cattolica (Roma).
CJ	Classical Journal.
ClergR	Clergy Review (London).
CollFranc	Collectanea Franciscana (Assisi).
Commentary	Commentary (New York).
CompLit	Comparative Literature.
Comprendre	Comprendre (Venezia).
CompSt	Computer Studies in the Humanities and Verbal Behavior (Univ. of Kansas).
Conceptus	Conceptus (Innsbruck).
Connoisseur	Connoisseur.
ConR	Contemporary Review (London).
ConThM	Concordia Theological Monthly (St. Louis).
Convivium(Barcelona)	Convivium. Filosofia. Psichologia.

PERIODICAL INDEX

DYP	Danish Year-Book of Philosophy.
DZP	Deutsche Zeitschrift fur Philosophie.
EBerg	Les Etudes Bergsoniennes.
EClas	Estudios Clasicos (Madrid).
Economist	Economist.
EdForum	Educational Forum (Menasha, Wisconsin).
Educare	Educare (Messina).
EE	Estudios Eclesiasticos (Madrid).
EEAth	Ἐπιστημονικὴ Ἐπετηρὶς τῆς φιλοσοφικῆς Σχολῆς τοῦ Πανεπιστημίου Ἀθηνῶν.
EEN	Ἐφημερὶς Ἑλλήνων Νομικῶν.
EEThess	Ἐπιστημονικὴ Ἐπετηρὶς τῆς φιλοσοφικῆς Σχολῆς τοῦ Ἀριστοτελείου Πανεπιστημίου Θεσσαλονικῆς.
EHBS	Ἐπετηρὶς Ἑταιρείας Βυζαντινῶν Σπουδῶν.
EHR	English Historical Review.
Eirene	Eirene (Praha).
ELeb	Das Edle Leben.
ELul	Estudios Lulianos (Majorca).
Emerita	Emerita.
Encounter	Encounter (Indianapolis).
EngLangNotes	English Language Notes.
EngSt	English Studies (Amsterdam).
Eos	Eos.
EPh	Etudes Philosophiques.
Episteme(Caracas)	Episteme (Caracas).
Eranos	Eranos.
Eranos-Jb	Eranos-Jahrbuch.
Erasmus	Erasmus.
ErlU	Die Erlanger Universitat.
EstFilos	Estudios Filosoficos (Spain).
Estudos	Estudos (Brazil).
ET	Educational Theory (Danville, Illinois).
Etc.	Etc. (San Francisco).
EtClass	Etudes Classiques (Aix-en-Provence).
EtFr	Etudes Fransiscaines.
Ethica	Ethica (Bologna).
Ethics	Ethics.
EThL	Ephemerides Theologicae Lovanienses.
Euhemer	Euhemer (Warszawa).
Euphrosyne	Euhrosyne (Lisboa).
ExposT	Expository Times (Edinburgh).
F&F	Forschungen und Fortschritte.
FChrist	Freies Christentum (Frankfurt).
FelsefeArk	Felsefe Arkivi (Istanbul).
FilDum	Filosof'ska Dumska (Kiev).
FilLis	Filosofia (Lisboa).
FilNauk	Filosofskie Nauki (Moskva).
Filomata(Krakow)	Filomata (Krakow).
FilosCas	Filosoficky Casopis. Ceskoslovenska Akademie Ved.
FilosMis'l	Filosofska Mis'l (Sophia).
Filosofia	Filosofia (Torino).
FilosUnic	Filosofia dell'Unicita.
FilosV	Filosofia e Vita (Torino).

Filozofia	Filozofia (Slovenska Akademia Vied, Ceskoslovensko).
Filozofija	Filosofija (Beograd).
Finlay	Finlay (Cuba).
FL	Forum der Letteren (Leiden).
FolHum	Folia Humanistica (Barcelona).
FoundLang	Foundations of Language.
FR	Felix Ravenna.
Franciscanum	Franciscanum (Bogota).
FrRev	The French Review.
Futures	Futures.
FZPT	Freiburger Zeitschrift fur Philosophie und Theologie.
G&R	Greece and Rome.
GB	Grazer Beitrage.
GCFI	Giornale critico della Filosofia Italiana.
Gesnerus	Gesnerus (Aarau).
GGA	Gottingische gelehrte Anzeigen.
GIF	Giornale Italiano di Filologia.
GLO	Graecolatina et Orientalia.
Glotta	Glotta.
GM	Giornale di Metafisica.
Gnomon	Gnomon.
GOR	Greek Orthodox Theological Review (Brookline, Massachusetts).
GQ	German Quarterly.
GRBS	Greek, Roman and Byzantine Studies.
Gregorianum	Gregorianum (Roma).
GriechischesBull	Griechisches Bulletin (Bonn).
GWU	Geschichte in Wissenschaft und Unterricht.
Gymnasium	Gymnasium.
Hegel-Jb	Hegel Jahrbuch.
HegelStud	Hegel-Studien.
Helikon	Helikon (Roma).
Hellenica	Ἑλληνικά.
Helmantica	Helmantica (Salamanca).
HER	Harvard Educational Review.
Hermathena	Hermathena.
Hermeneus	Hermeneus.
Hermes	Hermes.
HeythropJ	Heythrop Journal.
HibJ	Hibbert Journal.
HiroshimaUS	Hiroshima University Studies, Literature Department. Philosophy.
Historia	Historia.
History	History.
HistTheor	History and Theory.
HJ	Historisches Jahrbuch.
Hochland	Hochland (Munchen).
Hoko	Hoko (Japan).
HSPh	Harvard Studies in Classical Philology.
HT	History To-day.
HThR	Harvard Theological Review.

HudR	Hudson Review.
Hum(RES)	Humanites. Revue d'Enseignement secondaire et d'Education.
HumAB	Humanities Association Bulletin.
Humanidades	Humanidades (Comillas).
Humanist	The Humanist.
Humanitas	Humanitas (Coimbra).
HZ	Historische Zeitschrift.
IdealStud	Idealistic Studies.
Ideas y Valores	Ideas y Valores. Revista de la Faculdad de Filosofia, Bogota.
IJPR	International Journal for Philosophy of Religion.
IJPsy	Internatinal Journal of Psychoanalysis.
IL	L'Information Litteraire.
IMU	Italia Medioevale e Umanistica.
IncCult	Incontri Culturali (Roma).
Inquiry	Inquiry.
Insan ve dunya	Insan ve dunya (Turkey).
Insikt och Handling	Insikt och Handling (Lund).
Interpretation	Interpretation.
IPQ	International Philosophical Quarterly.
Irenikon	Irenikon (France).
Isis	Isis.
IThQ	Irish Theological Quarterly.
Itinerarium	Itinerarium (Braga, Portugal).
Iura	Iura (Napoli).
Iyyun	Iyyun (Israel).
Izuni	Izuni (Japan Women's Cultural Association).
JAAC	Journal of Aesthetics and Art Criticism.
JAE	Journal of Aesthetic Education.
Janus	Janus.
JAOS	Journal of the American Oriental Society.
JbAC	Jahrbuch fur Antike und Christentum.
JBL	Journal of Biblical Literature.
JBSPhen	Journal of the British Society for Phenomenology.
JCritA	Journal of Critical Analysis.
JCS	Journal of Classical Studies (Japan).
JDAI	Jahrbuch des Deutschen Archaologischen Instituts.
JEconHist	Journal of Economic History.
JEH	Journal of Ecclesiastical History.
JExist	Journal of Existentialism.
JHAW	Jahrbuch der Heidelberger Akademie der Wissenschaften.
JHBS	Journal of the History of the Behavioral Sciences.
JHI	Journal of the History of Ideas.
JHPh	Journal of the History of Philosophy.
JHS	Journal of Hellenic Studies.
Jimbun Ronkyu	Jimbun Ronkyu (Japan).
JNES	Journal of Near Eastern Studies.
JNG	Jahrbuch fur Numismatik und

	Geldgeschichte.
JOEByz	Jahrbuch der Oesterreichischen Byzantinistik.
JPh	Journal of Philosophy.
JPhilosLog	Journal of Philosophical Logic.
JPNP	Journal de Psychologie Normale et Pathologique.
JR	Journal of Religion.
JRGG	Jahrbuch des Real-Gymnasiums Graz.
JRH	Journal of Religious History.
JS	Journal des Savants.
JSL	Journal of Symbolic Logic.
JSS	Jewish Social Studies (New York).
JThought	Journal of Thought.
JThS	Journal of Theological Studies.
JUBA	Journal of the University of Bombay Arts. Humanities and Social Sciences.
JVI	Journal of Value Inquiry.
JWI	Journal of the Warburg and Courtauld Institute.
K&D	Kerygma und Dogma.
Kairos	Kairos (Salzburg).
KakagushiKenkyu	Kakagushi Kenkyu (Japan).
KantStud	Kant-Studien.
Kinesis	Kinesis. A Graduate Journal of Philosophy.
Kleio	Kleio.
Klepzigs	Klepzigs Fachberichte fur die Berg-, Hutten-, Metall-, und Maschinen-Industrie (Dusseldorf).
Kleronomia	Kleronomia (Thessalonike).
Kokalos	Kokalos (Palermo).
Kokoro	Kokoro (Japan).
Kommenden	Die Kommenden. Eine unabhangige Zeitschrift fur geistige und soziale Erneuerung (Freiburg).
Kratylos	Kratylos (Wiesbaden).
Kriterion	Kriterion (Brasil).
Kritik	Kritik (Kobenhavn).
Kultura	Kultura. Szkice, opowiadonia, sprawozdania (Paris).
KunstWerk	Kunst- und Werkerziehung.
L&S	Lingua e Stile.
Labeo	Labeo (Napoli).
Lampadion	Lampadion.
Lampas	Lampas.
LangQ	Language Quarterly.
Language	Language.
Latinitas	Latinitas.
Latomus	Latomus.
LEC	Les Etudes Classiques.
LecNPhys	Lecture Notes in Physics.
Leibeserziehung	Leibeserziehung.
LF	Listy Filologicke (Praha).
Lingua	Lingua (Amsterdam).

PERIODICAL INDEX

Listener	The Listener.
LitNov	Literarni Noviny (Praha).
LJ	Library Journal.
LM	Ludus Magistralis (Bruxelles).
LMS	Letopis Matice Srpske (Novi Sad).
LodskiZN	Uniwersytet Lodski. Zeszyty Naukowe. Seria I. Nauki Humanistyczno-Spoleczne.
LogAn	Logique et Analyse.
Logos	Logos (Napoli).
LThPh	Laval Theologique et Philosophique.
Lustrum	Lustrum.
Lychnos	Lychnos.
M&L	Music & Letters.
M&RS	Medieval and Renaissance Studies (Durham, N.C.).
MAb	Masters Abstracts.
Maia	Maia.
MainCurrents	Main Currents.
Manuscripta	Manuscripta (St. Louis).
ManWorld	Man and World.
MassR	Massachusetts Review.
MCr	Museum Criticum (Bologna).
MDAI(A)	Mitteilungen des Deutschen Archaologischen Instituts (Athen. Abt.).
MDAI(R)	Mitteilungen des Deutschen Archaologischen Instituts (Rom. Abt.).
MDF	Mitteilungen der Deutschen Forschungsgemeinschaft.
MDR	Monatschrift fur Deutsches Recht.
ME	Morale et Enseignement.
Meander	Meander (Warszawa).
MEFR	Melanges d'Archeologie et d'Histoire de l'Ecole Francaise de Rome.
MEJ	Middle East Journal.
Melto	Melto. Recherches Orientales (Universite Saint-Esprit, Kaslik, Lebanon).
MenschS	Mensch und Schicksal (Villach).
Merkur	Merkur.
Metaphilosophy	Metaphilosophy.
Methodos	Methodos. Studies in Classical Philosophy. (Kyoto Univ. Dept. of Literature).
MFS	Magyar Filozofiai Szemle.
MH	Museum Helveticum.
MillNL	Mill News Letter.
Mind	Mind.
MiscCom	Miscelanea Comillas.
MiscFranc	Miscellanea Francescana (Roma).
MKNA	Mededelingen der Koninklijke Nederlandse Akademie van Wetenschappen.
MLQ	Modern Language Quarterly.
Mnemosyne	Mnemosyne.
ModA	Modern Age.
ModLangNotes	Modern Language Notes.
ModLJ	Modern Language Journal.

ModS	Modern Schoolman.
Monatshefte	Monatshefte (Madison, Wisconsin).
Monist	Monist.
Moreana	Moreana (Angers).
MOsaka	Memoirs of Osaka Kyoiku University.
MPh	Museum. Tijdschrift voor Philologie en Geschiedenis (Leiden).
MS	Medieval Studies.
MSR	Melanges de Science Religieuse.
MT	Museum Tusculanum (Kobnhavn).
MTZ	Munchener Theologische Zeitschrift.
MUB	Melanges de l'Universite Saint-Joseph (Beyrouth).
MusAfr	Museum Africum (Ibadan).
MuslW	Muslim World.
MusT	Musical Times.
N&C	Nigeria and the Classics.
N&Q	Notes and Queries (London).
Nacion	La Nacion (Buenos Aires newspaper).
NBfr	New Blackfriars.
NDH	Neue Deutsche Hefte.
NewSt	New Statesman.
NG	Naturaleza y Gracia (Santa Marta, Spain).
NLF	Natural Law Forum.
Nordeste	Nordeste (Argentina).
Nous	Nous.
NouvCom	Le Nouveau Commerce.
NRdschau	Neue Rundschau.
NRP	Nuova Rivista Pedagogica.
NRS	Nuova Rivista Storica.
NRTh	Nouvelle Revue Theologique.
NS	New Scholasticism.
NSam	Neue Sammlung. Gottinger Blatter fur Kultur und Erziehung.
NSt	Nietzsche Studien.
NTS	New Testament Studies.
NTT	Nederlands Theologisch Tijdschrift.
NYRB	New York Review of Books.
NYT	New York Times.
OCP	Orientalia Christiana Periodica (Roma).
OEZOR	Osterreichisches Zeitschrift fur offentliches Recht.
OLME	Δέλτιον Ὁμοσπονδῆς Λειτουργίας μέσης Ἐκπαιδεύσεως.
OLZ	Orientalische Literaturzeitung.
OMF	Otazky marxistickej filozofie (Slovenska Akademia Vied).
Organon	Organon. Revista de Faculdad de Filosofia, Universidad de Rio Grande de Sul, Porte Alegre.
Organon(Wars)	Organon (Warszawa).
Oriens	Oriens (Leiden).
Orientalia	Orientalia (Roma).
Orpheus	Orpheus (Catania).
OUPB	Opera Universitatis Purkynianae

	Brunensis. Facultas philosophica.
P&I	Le Parole e le Idee. Rivista internazionale di varia cultura (Napoli).
PAA	Acts of the Academy of Athens. (Πρακτικὰ τῆς Ἀκαδημίας Ἀθηνῶν.
PAAH	Πρακτικὰ τῆς ἐν Ἀθηναῖς Ἀρχαιολογικῆς Ἑταιρείας (Athens).
PAAPA	Proceedings and Addresses of the American Philosophical Association.
PACA	Proceedings of the African Classical Association.
PACPhA	Proceedings of the American Catholic Philosophical Association.
PaedagRdsch	Padagogische Rundschau.
PaedHist	Paedagogica Historica (Gent).
PaedProv	Padagogische Provinz.
PaedStud	Paedagogische Studien.
Paideia	Paideia (Arona).
PakPJ	Pakistan Philosophical Journal.
PAPhS	Proceedings of the American Philosophical Society.
PAS	Proceedings of the Aristotelian Society.
PASS	Proceedings of the Aristotelian Society, Supplementary volume.
PB	Psychological Bulletin.
PBA	Proceedings of the British Academy.
PCA	Proceedings of the Classical Association (London).
PCP	Pacific Coast Philology.
PCPhS	Proceedings of the Cambridge Philological Society.
PedVit	Pedagogia e Vita (Brescia).
Pegasus	Pegasus (Exeter).
Pensamiento	Pensamiento (Madrid).
Pensiero	Pensiero (Napoli).
Perficit	Perficit (Salamanca).
Personalist	Personalist.
PFMUF	Publicazione della Facolta di Magistero dell'Universita di Ferrara.
Ph&PhenR	Philosophy and Phenomenological Research.
Ph&Rh	Philosophy and Rhetoric.
PhEW	Philosophy East and West.
PhilippSacra	Philippiana Sacra (Manila).
Philologus	Philologus.
PhilosBks	Philosophical Books.
PhilosForum	Philosophical Forum.
PhilosNat	Philosophia Naturalis (Meisenheim).
Philosophia(Argent)	Philosophia (Argentina).
Philosophia(Athens)	Φιλοσοφία (Athens).
Philosophy	Philosophy (London).
Philosophy(Tokyo)	Philosophy (Tokyo).
PhilosQ	Philosophical Quarterly.
PhilosRdschau	Philosophische Rundschau.
PhilosReform	Philosophia Reformata (Amsterdam).
PhilosStud(Irel)	Philosophical Studies (Maynooth,

	Ireland).
PhilosToday	Philosophy Today.
PhilPapers	Philosophical Papers.
PHist	Philosophy and History.
PhJ	Philosophisches Jahrbuch.
Phoenix	Phoenix.
PhQ	Philological Quarterly.
PhR	Philosophical Review.
Phronesis	Phronesis.
Phrontisterion	Phrontisterion (Ibadan).
PhSJap	Philosophical Studies of Japan.
Physis	Physis (Firenze).
PLA	Philosophischer Literaturanzeiger.
Platon	Platon (Athens).
Poetique	Poetique.
PolitTheor	Political Theory.
PP	La Parola del Passato.
PPES	Philosophy of Education Society. Proceedings.
PPol	Il Pensiero Politico (Firenze).
Praxis	Praxis (Zagreb).
PraxMath	Praxis der Mathematik.
Preuves	Preuves.
ProbLog	Probleme de Logica (Bucuresti).
ProcIsraelAcadSciHuman	Proceedings of the Israel Academy of Sciences and Humanities.
Proteus	Proteus (Roma).
Prudentia	Prudentia (Auckland).
PrzegladHuman	Przeglad Humanistyczny (Warszawa).
PSQ	Political Science Quarterly.
Psyche	Psyche.
PsychR	Psychoanalytical Review.
PsyMed	Psychosomatic Medicine.
QIG	Quaderni dell'Istituto di Glottologia (Bologna).
QJS	Quarterly Journal of Speech.
QQ	Queen's Quarterly (Kingston, Ontario).
QUCC	Quaderni Urbinati di Cultura Classica (Roma).
RA	Revue Archeologique.
RAAN	Rendiconti dell'Accademia di Archeologia, Lettere e Belle Arti di Napoli.
RAL	Rendiconti della Classe di Scienze morali, storiche e filologiche dell'Accademia dei Lincei (Roma).
RassFilos	Rassegna di Filosofia.
RassLettItal	Rassegna della Letteratura Italiana.
RassPed	Rassegna di Pedagogia.
Ratio	Ratio.
RB	Revue Benedictine.
RBF	Revista Brasiliera di Filosofia.
RBi	Revue Biblique.
RBPh	Revue Belge de Philologie et d'Histoire.
RCCM	Rivista di Cultura clasica e medioevale.
RD	Revue Historique de Droit Francaise et

RDCC — Etranger. Recherches et Debats du Centre Catholique des Intellectuels Francais.
RDF — Revista Dominicana de Filosofia.
RDPC — Rivista Trimestrale di Diritto e Procedura Civile.
RE — Paulys Real-encyclopadie der classischen Altertumswissenschaft.
REA — Revue des Etudes Anciennes.
REAug — Revue des Etudes Augustiniennes.
REC — Revista de Estudios Clasicos (Mendoza).
REcL — Revue Ecclesiastique de Liege.
RecSR — Recherches de Science Religieuse.
RecTh — Recherches de Theologie ancienne et medievale.
REG — Revue des Etudes Greques.
REL — Revue des Etudes Latines.
RelEduc — Religious Education.
RELO — Revue de l'Organisation internationale pour l'Etude des Langues Anciennes par Ordinateur.
RelStud — Religious Studies.
REngStud — Review of English Studies.
REPh — Revue de l'Enseignement Philosophique.
RESE — Revue des Etudes Sud-est Europeennes (Bucuresti).
Reseaux — Reseaux (Universite de Mons. Centre interdisciplinaire d'etudes philosophiques).
RevE — Revista de Educacion.
RevEsth — Revue d'Esthetique.
RevFacCathOuest — Revue des Facultes Catholiques de l'Ouest (Angers).
RevFiloz — Revista de Filozofie (Bucuresti).
RevFSF — Revista da Faculdade de Letras, Serie de Filosofia (Porto).
RevHum — Revista de Humanidades (Argentina).
RevIE — Revista de Ideas Esteticas (Madrid).
RevNouv — La Revue Nouvelle (Tournai).
RevPol — Review of Politics.
RevUNC — Revista de la Universidad Nacional de Cordoba.
RF — Rivista di Filosofia.
RFIC — Rivista di Filologia e di Istruzione Classica.
RFil(LaPlata) — Revista de Filosofia (La Plata).
RFil(Madrid) — Revista de Filosofia (Madrid).
RFLL — Revista da Faculdade de Letras (Lisboa).
RFNeo — Rivista di Filosofia Neoscholastica.
RFSE — Roczniki filozoficzne, Serie Ethica (Katolicki Uniwersytet Lublin).
RGSPA — Revue Generale des Sciences Pures et Appliquees.
RH — Revue Historique.
RHD — Revue d'Histoire du Droit.

xxxiii

RHE	Revue d'Histoire Ecclesiastique.
RHEF	Revue d'Histoire de l'Eglise de France.
RHLF	Revue d'Histoire litteraire de la France.
RhM	Rheinisches Museum.
RHPharm	Revue d'Histoire de la Pharmacie.
RHPhR	Revue d'Histoire et de Philosophie Religieuses.
RHR	Revue de l'Histoire des Religions.
RHS	Revue d'Histoire des Sciences et de leurs Applications.
RiceUS	Rice University Studies.
RicLing	Ricerche Linguistiche.
RIDA	Revue Internationale des Droits de l'Antiquite.
RIFD	Rivista Internazionale di Filosofia del Diritto.
RIFPS	Rivista Internazionale di Filosofia Politica e Sociale.
RIL	Rendiconti dell'Istituto Lombardo, Classe di Lettere, Scienze morali e storiche.
RIN	Rivista Italiana di Numismatica e Science affini.
Rinascimento	Rinascimento.
RIPh	Revue Internationale de Philosophie.
Riso	Riso (Japan).
RivE	Rivista di Estetica.
RivStCroc	Rivista di Studi Crociani (Napoli).
RLAC	Reallexikon fur Antike und Christentum.
RLT	Rassegna di Letteratura Tomistica.
RM	Review of Metaphysics.
RMF	Revista Mexicana de Filosofia.
RMM	Revue de Metaphysique et de Morale.
ROcc	Revista de Occidente.
Romanitas	Romanitas (Rio de Janeiro).
RP	Research in Phenomenology.
RPAA	Rendiconti della Pontificia Accademia di Archeologia.
RPGA	Revista de Psicologia generale y aplicada (Madrid).
RPh	Revue de Philologie.
RPhilos	Revue Philosophique (de la France et de l'Etranger).
RPhL	Revue Philosophique de Louvain.
RPortFil	Revista Portuguesa de Filosofia.
RPP	Revue de Psychologie des Peuples.
RRFC	Rivista Rosminiana di Filosofia e di Cultura (Pallanza).
RRSS	Revue Roumaine des Sciences Sociales, Serie Philosophie et Logique.
RS	Revue de Synthese.
RSA	Rivista Storica dell'Antichita.
RSC	Rivista di Studi Classici.
RSF	Rivista critica di Storia della Filosofia.
RSFil	Rassegna di Scienze Filosofiche.

RSHum	Revue des Sciences Humaines.
RSI	Rivista Storica Italiana.
RSLR	Rivista di Storia e Letteratura religiosa.
RSPh	Revue des Sciences Philosophiques et Theologiques.
RSR	Revue des Sciences Religieuses.
RThL	Revue Theologique de Louvain.
RThom	Revue Thomiste.
RThPh	Revue de Theologie et de Philosophie.
RUB	Revue de l'Universite de Bruxelles.
RuchFil	Ruch Filozoficzny (Torun).
RUO	Revue de l'Universite d'Ottawa.
RVF	Revista Venezolana de Filosofia (Caracas).
RyF	Razon y Fe (Madrid).
Saeculum	Saeculum.
Salesianum	Salesianum.
Salmanticensis	Salmanticensis.
SaltR	Saltire Review (Edinburgh).
Sapientia(Argentina)	Sapientia (Argentina).
Sapienza	Sapienza (Bologna).
SatR	Saturday Review.
SAWW	Sitzungsberichte der Osterreichischen Akademie der Wissenschaft in Wien.
ScE	Sciences Ecclesiastiques.
Scholastik	Scholastik.
SciAmer	Scientific American.
Scientia	Scientia (Bologna).
SCO	Studi Classici e Orientali.
Scriptorium	Scriptorium.
SDVT	Sbornik pro Dejiny Prirodnich Ved a Techniky (Ceskoslovenska Akademie Ved. Historicky Ustav. Oddeleni pro Dejiny Prirodnich Ved a Techniky).
SEJG	Sacris Erudiri. Jaarboek voor Godsdienstwetenschappen.
SewR	Sewanee Review (Tenn.)
SFBP	Sbornik Filosoficka Faculta Univerzita Komenskeho, Bratislava. Philologica.
SH	Scientiarum Historia (Antwerpen).
SHAW	Sitzungsberichte der Heidelberger Akademie der Wissenschaften.
SicGymn	Siculorum Gymnasium.
SIF	Studi Internazionali di Filosofia.
SIFC	Studi Italiani di Filologia Classica.
SIsl	Studia Islamica (Paris).
Sistematica	Sistematica (Milano).
SJP	Salzburger Jahrbuch der Philosophie.
SJTh	Scottish Journal of Theology.
SKZ	Schweizerisches kaufmannisches Zentrallblatt (Zurich).
SlovPohl	Slovenske Pohlady na Literatura a Umenie (Bratislava).
SMSR	Studi e Materiali di Storia delle

	Religioni.
SO	Symbolae Osloenses.
SocRes	Social Research.
SoJP	Southern Journal of Philosophy.
Sophia	Sophia (Padova).
SozWelt	Soziale Welt.
Spectator	Spectator (London).
Speculum	Speculum.
SPFB	Sbornik Praci Filosoficke Fakulta Brnenske Universita Rada archeologickoklasicka.
SPhG	Studia Philosophica Gandensia.
SpMon	Speech Monographs.
Sprache	Die Sprache.
SprawPTPN	Sprawozdania Poznanskie Towarzystwo Przyjaciol Nauk.
SR	Schweizer Rundschau.
SSJ	Southern Speech Journal.
StimZ	Stimmen der Zeit.
Streven	Streven (Bruxelles).
StudClas	Studii Clasice (Bucuresti).
StudFiloz	Studia Filozoficzne (Warszawa).
StudFr	Studi Francesci.
StudGen	Studium Generale.
StudIsl	Studies in Islam.
Studium	Studium (Avila).
Studium(Italy)	Studium (Italy).
StudMed	Studi Medievali.
StudMon	Studia Monastica.
StudPat	Studia Patavina.
StudPhil	Studies in Philology.
StudRuk	Studie o Rukopisech (Praha, Ceskoslovenska Akademia Ved).
StudUrb	Studi Urbinati di Storia, Filosofia e Letteratura.
SUCPh	Studia Universitatis Babes-Bolyai Series Philologica (Cluj).
Sunrise	Sunrise (Pasadena, Calif.).
Sur	Sur (Argentina).
SwJP	Southwestern Journal of Philosophy.
Symbolon	Symbolon.
Syntheses	Syntheses.
Systematics	Systematics.
SZG	Schweizerische Zeitschrift fur Geschichte.
Tablet	Tablet (London).
TabR	La Table Ronde.
TAPhA	Transactions of the American Philological Association.
TC	Twentieth Century.
TelQuel	Tel Quel.
Teoresi	Teoresi.
TG	Tijdschrift voor Geschiedenis.
Th&Ph	Theologie und Philosophie.
Th-P	(Leiden).

WS	Wiener Studien.
WWeish	Wissenschaft und Weisheit.
WZ	Wiener Zeitschrift fur Philosophie, Psychologie, Padagogik.
WZBer	Wissenschaftliche Zeitschrift der Humboldt-Universitat zu Berlin. Gesellschafts- und Sprachwissenschaftliche Reihe.
WZJena	Wissenschaftliche Zeitschrift der Friedrich-Schiller-Universitat Jena, Gesellschaft und Sprachwissenschaftliche Reihe.
WZLeip	Wissenschaftliche Zeitschrift der Karl Marx Universitat, Leipzig. Gesellschafts und Sprachwissenschaftliche Reihe.
WZPot	Wissenschaftliche Zeitschrift der Padagogische Hochschule Potsdam.
Xenium	Xenium (Cordoba).
Yana	Yana (Utting a. Ammersee).
YClS	Yale Classical Studies.
YLG	Yale University Library Gazette.
ZAnt	Ziva Antika. (Skopje).
ZastMath	Zastosowania Matematyki (Warszawa).
Zeit	Die Zeit. Wochenzeitung fur Politik, Wirtschaft, Handel und Kultur (Hamburg).
ZGF	Zeitschrift fur Ganzheitsforschung (Wien).
ZJKF	Zpravy Jednoty Klasickych Filologu (Praha).
ZKG	Zeitschrift fur Kirchengeschichte.
ZKTh	Zeitschrift fur Katholische Theologie.
Znak	Znak (Krakow).
ZNTW	Zeitschrift fur die Neutestamentliche Wissenschaft und die Kunde der alteren Kirche.
ZNUL	Zeszyty naukowe Katolicki Uniwersytet Lublin.
ZPaed	Zeitschrift fur Padagogik.
ZPE	Zeitschrift fur Papyrologie und Epigraphik.
ZPhF	Zeischrift fur philosophische Forschung.
ZRG	Zeitschrift der Savigny-stiftung fur Rechtsgeschichte (Romanistische Abteilung) (Koln).
ZRGG	Zeitschrift fur Religions- und Geistesgeschichte.
ZWG	Sudhoffs Archiv. Zeitschrift fur Wissenschaftsgeschichte.

I: GENERAL STUDIES ON PLATO

A: BOOKS ON PLATO

This section contains books on Plato generally. It also contains articles dealing directly with those books. These articles are placed immediately after the book they treat. In some cases a book will emphasize one or more areas of Plato's life but still be too broad for inclusion in any single category.

1* AGOGLIA R.M., Platón. Enciclopedia del pensamiento essencial, Buenos Aires, Centro ed. de America Latina 1967 127p.
    Rev. RFil(La Plata) XX 1968 93-95 Presas.

2* ALEXANDRE M., Lecture de Platon. Paris, Bordas 1966 420p.
    Rev. RThPh 1968 201 Schaerer.
    EPh XXII 1967 211 Millet.

3* WESTERINK L.G., Anonymous Prolegomena to Platonic Philosophy, introd., text, transl. and indices by Westerink L.G. Amsterdam, Noord-Holl. Uitg.-Maats. 1962 lii&69p.
    Rev. RecSR L 1962 629-630 des Places.
    CW LV 1962 261 Hoerber.
    EPh 1963 207 Pépin.
    CR XIII 1963 347 Kerferd.
    AC XXXII 1963 633-634 Moraux.
    REG LXXVI 1963 292-294 Trouillard.
    RPh XXXVIII 1964 138 Louis.
    RBPh XLII 1964 256 des Places.
    JHPh I 1963 246-248 Ostwald.

4* BOSSUET J.B., Platon et Aristote, notes de lecture, éd. orig. avec comm. par Goyet T. Études et Commentaires LVI Thèse, Paris, Klincksieck 1965 398p.
    Rev. GIF XVIII 1965 283-284 Pepe.
    REG LXXVIII 1965 735-737 Courcelle.
    Emerita XXXIV 1966 199 Lens.
    RHR CLXIX 1966 199-203 Orcibal.
    AC XXXV 1966 330 Joly.
    AUP XXXVI 1966 223 Goyet.

CR XVI 1966 236 Easterling.
RPh XLI 1967 161 Louis.
RBPh XLV 1967 288-289 des Places.

5* BROECKER W., Platos Gespräche. Frankfurt,
Klostermann 1964 560p. Also 2. erweit. Aufl.
1967 596p.
Rev. Gymnasium LXXII 1965 543-547 Merlan.
PhilosRdschau 1966 156-157 Kuhn.
PhJ LXXIV 1966-1967 177-181 Meinhardt.
DLZ LXXXIX 1968 103-106 Saupe.

6* BRUMBAUGH R.S., Plato for the Modern Age. New York,
Crowell Collier Pr. 1962 256p. 2nd edn. New
York, Collier Books/London, Macmillan 1964 256p.
Rev. Philosophy 1965 249-250 Lacey.
CW LVI 1963 220 Morrow.
LJ 1962 3454 Stevens.
RM XVI 1962-1963 798 A.B.
Ethics LXXIV 1963-1964 310 Sinaiko.
YR 1964 294 Lenz.
Mind LXXV 1966 293 Guthrie.

7* BRUN J., Platon et l'Académie. Coll. Que sais-je?
No. 880, Paris, Presses Universitaires 1960
128p. 2e ed. 1963. Spanish translation,
Platón y la Academía, trad. de Llanos A.
Buenos Aires, Eudeba 1961 62p.
Rev. REA LXIII 1961 149-150 Aubenque.
AC XXX 1961 577-578 Loreau.
RPhL LX 1962 273 Rutten.
Convivium 1961 189-190 J.A.
ME X 1961 56-57 Loreau.
REG LXXIV 1961 509 Weil.
RPhL LIX 1961 522-525 Lefevre.
Sophia XXX 1962 371 Montoneri.
Pensamiento XIX 1963 247-248 Martínez
Gómez.

8* CHAIX-RUY J., La pensée de Platon. Coll. Pour
connaitre, Paris, Bordas 1966 320p.
Rev. ArchPhilos XXX 1967 628 Solignac.
GM XXII 1967 562-563 Sorge.
RSR XLI 1967 260-261 Nedoncelle.
LEC XXXVI 1968 278 Loriaux.
CISymb 1966 99 Witte.

9* CHATELET F., Platon. Coll. Idees LXXXV, Paris,
Gallimard 1965 256p. Also Spanish transl. El
pensamiento de Platon, trad. por Garcia de la
Mora J.M. Madrid, Ed. Labor 1967 181p.
Rev. [of French edn] RSR XLI 1967 260-261

Nedoncelle.
RPhilos CLVIII 1968 283-284 Brunschwig.
Etudes CCCXXIII 1965 718 Morel.
[of Span. edn.] BIEH III,1 1969 87
Corominas.

10* CROMBIE I.M., An Examination of Plato's Doctrines,
I: Plato on Man and Society; II: Plato on
Knowledge and Reality. Internat. Libr. of
Philos. & Scientific Method, London, Routledge
& Kegan Paul 1962 xii&395p.; 1963 x&573p. Vol.
I p.153-155 reprinted as "The Myth of Er",
p.136-139 in Plato's Republic, ed. by Sesonske
A. (see 4614).
Rev. Gnomon XXXV 1963 302-304 Rosenmeyer.
CR XIII 1963 278-280 Guthrie.
CJ LIX 1963 132-133 Hoerber.
PhR LXXII 1963 528-530 Allen.
AmSocR XXVIII 1963 488-489 Bierstedt.
Ph&PhenR XXV 1964 273 Diamadopoulos.
CJ LIX 1964 329 Hoerber.
Thought XXXVIII 1963 620-624; XL 1965
150-152 O'Brien.
TLS 12 Dec. 1963 1036.
Ethics 1963 150.
PhilosBks Jan. 1963 13 Hamlyn.
Personalist XLV 1964 256 O'Neill.
RM XVII 1963-1964 143 R.J.B.
CJ 1964 329 Hoerber.
RM XVII 1963-1964 475 P.S.
CrossCurr 1964 381 Collins.
AusJP 1963 264 Gibson.
PhilosBks Jan. 1964 5 Lloyd.
NS XXXIX 1965 132-134 Crosson.
ModS XLII 1964-1965 214-216 Hassel.
CW LVII 1964 192 Hornsby.
JHS LXXXIV 1964 191-192 Baldry.
G&R XII 1965 97-98 Davis.
CR XV 1965 33-36 Guthrie.
PhilosQ XIV 1964 74-76; XV 1965 358-360
Gulley.
Mind LXXIV 1965 105-116 Gosling.
AESocCiv XIX 1964 1027-1028 Vidal-Naquet.
ModS XLIII 1965-1966 274-277 Brumbaugh.
PhR LXXV 1966 526-530 Vlastos. (reprinted
as "Plato on Knowledge and Reality", p.374-378
in Vlastos G., Platonic Studies (see 4622).)
RBPh XLVI 1968 833-835 de Strycker.
Mind LXXVII 1968 127-130 de Boer.

11* CROMBIE I.M., Plato, the Midwife's Apprentice.
London, Routledge & Kegan Paul 1964, New York,
Barnes & Noble 1965 viii&195p.
Rev. Philosophy XL 1965 267-268 Lacey.
CR XV 1965 285-287 Cross.
CW LIX 1965 130 Hoerber.
Mind LXXV 1966 457-459 Lloyd.
RSF XXI 1966 211-214 Isnardi Parente.
CJ LXI 1966 231 Rist.
PhilosBks May 1965 5 Hamlyn.
PhilosStud(Irel.) XIV 1965 259-260 Watson.
HeythropJ V 1964 233 T.G.
Tablet 1965 41 Armstrong.
ModS XLIII 1965-1966 278-280 Neumann.
RM XIX 1965-1966 150 E.A.R.
NS XLI 1967 122-123 Halton.
BJPS XVII 1966-1967 87-88 Lloyd.
RM XX 1966-1967 648 Owens.

12* BORMANN K., Platon. Kolleg Philosophie, München,
Alber 1973 192p.

13 CARBONARA C., La filosofia greca. Platone. 2a   ed.
Filos. e pedag., Napoli, Libreria scientifica
editrice 1969 168p.

14* DEMOS R., The Philosophy of Plato. New York,
Octagon 1966 406p. Reprint of 1939 edn.

15* DIÈS A., Autour de Platon. Essais de critique et
d'histoire. 2e tir. revu & corr. Coll.
Études anciennes, Paris, Les Belles Lettres 1972
xvi&620p.

16* EGGERS LAN C., Introducción histórica al estudio de
Platón. Buenos Aires, Centro de estudiantes de
Filos. y Letras 1965 108p.
Rev. JHS LXXXVII 1967 166-167 Saunders.

17* FIELD G.C., The Philosophy of Plato. 2nd ed.   with
appendix by Cross R.C. Oxford Paperbacks Univ.
Series XL, Oxford Univ. Pr. 1969   172p.
Original edition 1949.
Rev. REG LXXXIII 1970 259-260 des Places.
AC XXXIX 1970 221 Joly.
CPh LXVI 1971 53 Sprague.
P&I XI 1969 347-349 Janna.

18* FOX A., Plato for Pleasure. Rev. ed. London,
Murray 1962 viii&176p.
Rev. CW LVI 1962 49 Sprague.
TLS 6 April 1962 238.

I A: BOOKS ON PLATO

Augustinus VIII 1963 132-133 Oroz.

19* FRIEDLAENDER P., Platon, I: Seinswahrheit und
Lebenswirklichkeit. 3. durchges. & erg.
Aufl.; II: Die Platonischen Schriften. I.
Periode. 3. verbess. Aufl. Berlin, de
Gruyter 1964 xii&438, vi&353p.

Platon, Bd. III: Die platonischen Schriften, zweite und
dritte Periode. 2. erweiterte und verbesserte
Auflage. Berlin, de Gruyter 1960 vi&532p.
Rev. ASSPh XX 1960 162 Landmann.
Antonianum XXXVI 1961 428 Platzeck.
RPhilos CL 1960 229-236 Schuhl.
StudUrb XXXV 1961 252-253.
Gnomon XXXIV 1962 535-541 Kuhn.
PhilosReform XXVII 1962 77-79 Begemann.
RecSR L 1962 611 des Places.
Bijdragen XXIII 1962 328 Nota.
CollFranc XXXI 1961 678-679 Servus a St.
Anthonius.
Scholastik XXXVIII 1963 126-127 Ennen.
PhilosRdschau X 1962 155 Gadamer.
RUB XIV 1961-1962 238-239 Janssens.
RPortFil XVIII 1962 179-180 Pires.
NG X 1963 179-180 Ventosa.
PhR LXXI 1962 260-261 Ackrill.
Pensamiento XVIII 1962 89 Martínez-Gomez.
Gymnasium LXIX 1962 565-567 Herter.
RPortFil XXII 1966 206-207 Freire.

Plato, I. An Introduction, transl. by Meyerhoff H.:
Bollingen Ser. LIX New York, Pantheon Books
1958 xxiv&424p. 2nd edn. rev. 1969
xxiii&443p.
Rev. LEC XXVI 1958 418 Tilleux.
RPh XXXIII 1959 310 Louis.
CJ LIV 1959 324-326 Minar.
CPh LIV 1959 209-210 Hoerber.
MH XVI 1959 73 Gigon.
CR X 1960 117-118 Bambrough.
RBPh XXXVIII 1960 1218-1220 des Places.
Gnomon XXXIII 1961 216 Kuhn.
PhilosQ XI 1961 87-88 Robinson.
Mnemosyne XVII 1964 191-192 Verdenius.
CPh LXVI 1971 141 Hoerber.

Plato, II: The Dialogues. First Period transl. by
Meyerhoff H. Bollingen Ser. LIX,2, New York,
Pantheon Books 1964 viii&389p.
Rev. P&I VI 1964 311 Garzya.
A&R X 1965 186-187 Lamacchia.

5

LEC XXXIII 1965 439 Loriaux.
RMM LXX 1965 110-114 Wahl.
CPh LXII 1967 54-56 Hoerber.
TLS 20 Jan. 1966 42.
PhilosBks Jan. 1966 18 Hamlyn.
CR XXI 1971 289 Bambrough.

Plato, III, The Dialogues, Second and Third Periods,
transl. by Meyerhoff H. Bollingen Ser. LIX,3,
Princeton Univ. Pr. and London, Routledge &
Kegan Paul 1969 viii&626p.
Rev. P&I X 1968 363 Garzya.
NYRB XIII,8 1969 16-19 Ryle.
Tablet 1969 1262 Armstrong.
PhilosBks May 1970 8 Hamlyn.
Philosophy XLV 1970 251-252 Lacey.
TLS LXIX 1970 105.
RBPh XLVIII 1970 118 des Places.
CPh LXVI 1971 192-193 Hoerber.
CR XXI 1971 289-290 Bambrough.
LEC XL 1972 440-441 Druet.

20* FREIRE A., O pensamento de Platão. Filosofia Estud.
publ. pela Fac. de Filos. de Braga, Braga,
Livr. Cruz 1967 334p.
Rev. RPortFil XXIV 1968 130-131 Losa.

21* FRIIS-JOHANSEN K., Platons Filosofi. Udvikling og
Enhed. Copenhagen, G.E.C. Gad 1966 168p.

22* GAUSS H., Philosophischer Handkommentar zu den
Dialogen Platos. Bern, Lang 4 vols. in 7
parts. I,1: Allgemeine Einleitung in die
platonische Philosophie, 1952 243p.; I,2: Die
Frühdialoge, 1954 215p.; II,1: Die Dialoge der
Uebergangszeit, 1956 229p.; II,2: Die Dialoge
der literarischen Meisterschaft, 1958 272p.;
III: Die Spätdialoge, 1: Theatet, Parmenides,
Sophist und Politicus, 1960 264p.; III: Die
Spätdialoge, 2: Philebus, Timaeus, Critias und
Gesetze, 1961 268p.; Register, 1967 191p.
Rev. RPhL LVI 1958 102-103 Vanhoutte.
MH XV 1958 247 Wehrli.
RecSR XLVII 1959 267 des Places.
Scholastik XXXIV 1959 460 Ennen.
RFil(Madrid) XVIII 1959 505-506 Lledo.
RThPh X 1960 339-341 Lasserre.
Gnomon XXXIII 1961 217 Tarrant.
JCS IX 1961 99-105 Kitajima.
MH XVIII 1961 240 Theiler.
RFil(Madrid) XX 1961 98 Lledo.
RThPh XI 1961 200 Lasserre.

RecSR L 1962 613-614 des Places.
Gnomon XXXIV 1962 415 Tarrant.
RThPh XII 1962 63 Lasserre.
Erasmus XVI 1964 419-427 Gottschalk.
RecSR LVI 1968 619 des Places.

23* GIGON O., Grundprobleme der antiken Philosophie.
Eine Uebersicht uber Inhalt, Absicht und Wesen
der antiken Philosophie und ihre Weiterwirkung
in der Geschichte. Samml. Dalp LXVI, Bern,
Francke 1959 330p. French translation: Les
grands problemes de la philosophie antique,
trad. de Lefevre M. Bibl. scientif., Paris,
Payot 1961 344p.
Rev. [of German edn.] MH XVII 1960 241
Wehrli.
RFil (Madrid) XIX 1960 97 Lledo.
StudUrb XXXIV 1960 194.
RFNeo LII 1960 447-449 Bonetti.
CiFe XVI 1960 86-87.
RF LII 1961 223-228 Isnardi.
FZPT VIII 1961 170-171 Morard.
Convivium 1961 n.11-12 198 J.A.
IPQ I 1961 538 de Strycker.
Bijdragen XXII 1961 107 de Strycker.
Scholastik XXXVI 1961 133 Kern.
ThLZ LXXXVI 1961 934 Wenzl.
RPhL LX 1962 271-272 Rutten.
JCS X 1962 133-136 Tsumura.
Critique XIX 1963 354-357 Sichirollo.
[of French edn.] LEC XXX 1962 127.
AC XXXI 1962 496-497 Joly.
ASSPh XXI 1961 229 Christoff.
RThPh XII 1962 62 Sulliger.
NRTh LXXXIV 1962 992 de Give.
RHPhR XLII 1962 56 Burgelin.
EPh XVII 1962 110-111 Jacob.
RPhilos CLIV 1964 260-262 Galperine.

24* GOSLING J.C.B., Plato. London/Boston, Routledge &
Kegan Paul 1973 319p.

25* GRAF G., Die sokratische Aporie im Denken Platons.
Diss. Basel, Winterthur, Keller 1963 94p.

26* GRUBE G.M.A., Plato's Thought. Boston, Beacon 1958
337p. Reprint of 1935 edn. Also Spanish
transl. El pensamiento de Platón, trad. de
Calvo Martinez T. Bibl. hisp. de filos.
LXXX, Madrid, Ed. Gredos 1973 495p.
Rev. RSF XVI 1961 114-115 Giannantoni.
PhilosRdschau 1961 98-102 Manasse.

RSC XVIII 1970 296-297 d'Agostino.
TPh XXXIII 1971 779 Smets.

27* HAVELOCK E.A., A History of the Greek Mind, I:
Preface to Plato. Oxford, Blackwell/Cambridge,
Mass., Harvard Univ. Pr. 1963 xii&328p.
p.3-15, 20-31 reprinted as "Plato on Poetry",
p.116-136 in Plato's Republic, ed. Sesonske A.
(see 4614). Italian transl. Cultura orale e
civiltà della scrittura. Da Omero a Platone,
trad. Carpitella M., intro. di Gentili B.
Biblioteca di cultura moderna 743, Roma/Bari,
Laterza 1973 xi&351p.
    Rev. TLS 12 Dec. 1963 1036.
    LJ 1963 2014 Schoenheim.
    BJAes III 1963 367-369 Osborne.
    CW LVI 1963 257 Grimaldi.
    NS XXXVIII 1964 526-528 Cleve.
    YR 1964 294 Lenz.
    BA 1964 70 Pritchard.
    CrossCurr 1964 381 Collins.
    RF LV 1964 213-216 Cambiano.
    CPh LIX 1964 70-74 Hoerber.
    Gnomon XXXVI 1964 422-424 Meyerhoff.
    Phoenix XVIII 1964 163-164 Sparshott.
    CR XIV 1964 31-33 Gulley.
    CB XL 1964 80 Rexine.
    CJ LX 1964 78-80 Costas.
    Athene(Chicago) XXV,2 1964 19.
    Manuscripta VIII 1964 179-181 Ong.
    JHS LXXXV 1965 201-202 Baldry.
    Mind LXXIV 1965 147-148 Hicken.
    REG LXXVIII 1965 690-691 Weil.
    AJPh LXXXVII 1966 99-105 Solmsen.
    JCS XIII 1965 172-175 Kitajima.
    Historia XVII 1968 505-507 Thomas.

28 CERRI G., "Il passaggio dalla cultura orale alla
    cultura di comunicazione scritta nell'età di
    Platone". QUCC VIII 1969 119-133.

29* HOFFMANN E., Platon. Eine Einfuhrung in sein
    Philosophieren. Rowohlts Dt. Enzykl. CXLII,
    Hamburg, Rowohlt 1961 171p.
        Rev. DLZ LXXXV 1964 485-486 Nador.

30* HOFFMANN E., Platon. Eine Einfuhrung in sein
    Philosophieren. 2. Aufl. Rowohlts deutsche
    Enzyklopädie CXLII: Sachgebiet Philosophie,
    Reinbek b. Hamburg, Rowohlt 1967 171p.

31 WITZMANN P., "Aspekte platonischen Philosophierens".
    Helikon VII 1967 555-567.

32* HUIT C., La vie et l'oeuvre de Platon, I-II.
    Nachdr. d. Ausg. Paris 1893. Hildesheim/New
    York, Olms 1973 ix&506, 478p.

33* JASPERS K., Plato. Augustin, Kant. Drei Gründer
    des Philosophierens. München, Piper 1961 397p.
    (from Die grossen Philosophen, Bd. I.) Also
    English edn.: Plato and Augustine, [from The
    Great Philosophers] ed. by Arendt H., trans.
    by Manheim R. New York, Harcourt 1962 vii&126p.
    Also French edn.: Les grands philosophes. II:
    Ceux qui fondent la philosophie et ne cessent de
    l'engendrer, Platon, Saint Augustin, trad. sous
    la dir. de Hersch J. Coll. Le monde en 10/18
    Nos.362-363, Paris, Union générale d'éd. 1967
    312p. Also Dutch edn.: Platoon, transl. by
    Zoeterwoude W. Van. Brugge, Desclée de Brouwer
    1958 141p.
        Rev. [of Dutch edn.] Hermeneus XXX 1959
    114 van Straaten.
        Streven XI 1957-1958 1091 vander Kerken.
        CM XLIII 1958 434-435 Jespers.
        Bijdragen XX 1959 109-110 de Strycker.
        RevNouv XXXI 1960 107-108 Van Lier.

34* KOYRÉ A., Introduction à la lecture de Platon.
    Nouv. ed. Coll. Les Essais CVII, Paris,
    Gallimard 1962 231p. Also English transl.:
    Discovering Plato, transl. by Rosenfield L.C.
    New York, Columbia Univ. Pr. 1960 ix&118p.
    Also Spanish transl. Introducción a la lectura
    de Platón, trad. de Sánchez de Zavala V. El
    libro de Bolsillo XVI, Madrid, Alianza Editorial
    1966 198p. Italian transl. Introduzione a
    Platone, a cura di Sichirollo L. Tascabili
    Vallecchi XVI, Firenze, Vallecchi 1973 xi&174p.
        Rev. [of French edn.] RS LXXXIV 1963
    485-487 Rochot.
        [of English edn.] CR XII 1962 134-135
    Bambrough.

35* KRUEGER G., Einsicht und Leidenschaft. Das Wesen
    des platonischen Denkens. 3. durchges. Aufl.
    Frankfurt a.M., Klostermann 1963 xx&336p. 4.
    Aufl. 1973.

36* KUCHARSKI P., Aspects de la spéculation
    platonicienne. Publ. de la Sorbonne Études I,
    Paris, Béatrice-Nauwelaerts 1971 394p.

Rev. DT LXXV 1972 475-478 Cunico.
ArchPhilos XXXV 1972 675-677 Solignac.
TPh XXXIV 1972 365-367 Steel.
EPh 1972 557 Ecole.
Gregorianum LIII 1972 798 González
Caminero.
RS XCIII 1972 296 Mortley.
AC XLII 1973 234 de Ley.

37* LESNIAK K., Platon [in Polish]. Warszawa, Wiedza
Powszechna 1968 246p.

38* MAIRE G., Platon, sa vie, son oeuvre, avec un exposé
de sa philosophie. Coll. Philosophes, Paris,
Presses Universitaires 1966 iv&124p. Also 2e
ed. 1970 128p.
Rev. REG LXXIX 1966 544 Weil.
RPhL LXV 1967 578 Druart.
LEC XXXV 1967 87 Delaunois.
EPh XXII 1967 100 Quoniam.
RPhilos CLVIII 1968 287 Somville.
RS XCI 1970 110 Bernard-Maître.

40* NUNES C.A., Marginalia platonica [in Portuguese].
Belem, Univ. Fed. do Para 1973 255p.

41* NUÑO J.A., El pensamiento de Platón. Col. Temas,
Caracas, Ed. de la Biblioteca, Univ. Central
de Venezuela 1963 172p.

42* OLDEWELT H., Plato. 2e geheel. herz. dr. Helden
van de geest XII, Gravenhage, Kruseman 1964
151p.

43* PERLS H., Plato. Seine Auffassung vom Kosmos,
ubers. vom Franz. Bern/München, Francke 1966
429p.
Rev. TPh XXVIII 1966 734-736 Berger.
CR XVII 1967 394 Gulley.
CPh LXII 1967 201-202 Hoerber.
Th&Ph XLIII 1968 458 Ennen.
RThPh XIX 1968 199-200 Schaerer.
Lychnos 1967-1968 280 Duering.
AAHG XXII 1969 164-167 Vretska.
Helmantica XXII 1971 343-344 Oroz.

44* PONI S., La dottrina di Platone desunta dalle fonte greche. Forli, Società tipografica forlivese 1966 188p.

45* RAEDER H., Platons philosophische Entwicklung. Neudr. d. Augs. Leipzig 1905. Aalen, Scientia-Verl. 1973 435p.

46* RAVEN J.E., Plato's Thought in the Making. A Study of the Development of his Metaphysics. Cambridge Paperback, Cambridge Univ. Pr. 1965 xi&256p. Also Swedish transl. Platons tankevärld. En studie i den platonska metafysikens utveckling, tr. by Söderberg B.G. Stockholm, Prisma 1968 207p.
  Rev. AusJP 1966 122-123 Blaney.
Augustinus 1966 320 Ortall.
AC XXXV 1966 274 des Places.
REG LXXIX 1966 545-546 Moreau.
RThPh XCIX 1966 338 Schaerer.
CPh LXI 1966 264-265 Sprague.
CR XVI 1966 307-309 Crombie.
CW LIX 1966 264 Reesor.
Hermathena CIII 1966 103-105 Luce.
Lychnos 1965-1966 418-419 Duering.
PhilosStud(Irel.) XV 1966 325-326 Bastable.
Dialogue V 1966 267-272 Malcolm.
Crisis XII 1965 412 Ortall.
PhilosBks Oct. 1966 28 Hamlyn.
TLS 20 Jan. 1966 42.
NYRB 18 Aug. 1966 27 Finley.
CrossCurr XVI 1966 168 Collins.
RPortFil XXIII 1967 503 Freire.
CJ LXII 1967 276-277 Berry.
ModS XLIV 1966-1967 295-296 Stack.
Personalist XLVIII 1967 243-244 Beck.
RSF XXII 1967 237-238 Buccellato.
JHPh V 1967 164-165 Frazier.
JCS XV 1967 142-145 Wakabayashi.
RPh XLI 1967 313 Louis.
LEC XXXV 1967 292-293 Moraux.
ArchPhilos XXX 1967 135-136 Solignac.
RF LVIII 1967 90-91 Cambiano.
JHS LXXXVIII 1968 194-195 Robinson.
AJPh LXXXIX 1968 234-237 Neumann.
PhR LXXVII 1968 364-366 Kirwan.
PACA X 1967 58-60 Boyle.
Gnomon XLII 1970 332-335 Ilting.

47* REINHOLD M., A Simplified Approach to Plato and
    Aristotle. Great Neck, N.Y., Barron's Educ.
    Ser. 1964 90p.

48* RITTER C., The Essence of Plato's Philosophy,
    transl. by Alles A. New York, Russell &
    Russell 1968 413p. Reprint of 1933 New York
    edn.

49* ROBIN L., Platon. Nouv. éd. avec bibliogr. mise
    à jour & complétée. Coll. Les grands penseurs,
    Paris, Presses Universitaires 1968 viii&272p.
    Reprint of 1935 Paris edn. with additional
    bibliography. Also Italian transl. Platone,
    trad. di Calabi F. Milano, Lampugnani Nigri
    1971 viii&258p.
        Rev (of French edn.). RSPh LIII 1969 168
    Lemaigre.
        RPhL LXVII 1969 322 Druart.

50 CARBONARA NADDEI M., "Platone nell'interpretazione
    di Leon Robin". Logos III 1971 441-457.

51* RUDBERG G., Platon, En inledning till studiet.
    Lund, Gleerup 1966 164p.

52* RYLE G., Plato's Progress. Cambridge Univ. Pr.
    1966 viii&311p.
        Rev. RM XX 1966-1967 376 E.A.R.
        Hermathena CIII 1966 105-110 Charlton.
        NewSt 9 Sept. 1966 364 Finley.
        Spectator 7 Oct. 1966 454 Flew.
        TLS 8 Sept. 1966 842.
        CW LX 1966 121 Sprague.
        AusJP XLV 1967 104-113 Rankin.
        PhilosBks Jan.1967 23-27 Wasserstein.
        CR XVII 1967 332-336 Easterling.
        CJ LXIII 1967 129-132 Robson.
        RBPh XLV 1967 494-497 Saunders.
        LEC XXXV 1967 200 Ghislain.
        Gnomon XXXIX 1967 230-235 Kuhn.
        Ph&PhenR XXVIII 1967 123-125 Demos.
        CambRev LXXXIX 1967 279-281 O'Brien.
        RM XX 1966-1967 654 Owens.
        DalR 1967 93 Page.
        Aquinas X 1967 99 Giannini.
        Dialogue V 1966-1967 622-626 Rist.
        Augustinus XLII 1967 45-48 Ortall.
        Listener 23 Feb. 1967 267 Burnyeat.
        ModS XLV 1967-1968 343-345 Herx.

UTQ XXXVII 1967-1968 90-102 Robinson.
Phoenix XXII 1968 73-79 Sparshott.
JHS LXXXVIII 1968 195-196 Hicken.
JPh LXV 1968 364-375 Kahn.
JPh LXV 1968 737-742 Randall (comments on Kahn's review).
PhilosQ XVIII 1968 155-165 Allan.
RThPh 1968 201-202 Schaerer.
GGA CCXX 1968 190-201 Sprute.
PhilosRdschau XV 1968 147-148 Gadamer.

JVI I 1967-1968 271-274 Brumbaugh.
NG XV 1968 299-300 Zamora.
PhR LXXXVIII 1969 362-373 Crombie.
ManWorld III 1970 122-134 Gould.
Libes Y.G., "Plato's 'Progress': A review of Gilbert Ryle's new book" [in Hebrew] Iyyun XVIII 1967 22-44 (English summary 111-107).
Cambiano G., "Il Platone di Ryle", RF LIX 1968 316-337.
LaFrance Y., "Le Platon de Gilbert Ryle". RPhL LXIX 1971 337-369.

53 DUBOIS P., "L'évolution chez Platon". RMM LXXIV 1969 446-453.

54 MERLAN P., "Radicalizing Ryle". p.18-27 in The Progress of Plato's Progress (see 4590).

55 HATHAWAY R.F., "Skeptical Maxims about the 'Publication' of Plato's Dialogues". p.28-42 in The Progress of Plato's Progress (see 4590).

56 MALCOLM J., "Ryle on Dialectic". p.43-54 in The Progress of Plato's Progress (see 4590).

57 MATSON W.I., "Ryle on Forms". p.55-62 in The Progress of Plato's Progress (see 4590).

58 SESONSKE A., "Ryle on the Republic". p.63-71 in The Progress of Plato's Progress (see 4590).

59 RYLE G., "Plato's Progress: Counter-Queries". p.72-75 in The Progress of Plato's Progress (see 4590).

60* SAITO N., Plato. Tokyo, Iwanani 1972 207p.

61* SCHLEIERMACHER F., Schleiermacher's Introductions to the Dialogues of Plato, transl. by Dobson W. Reprint of 1836 New York edn. New York, Arno Pr. 1973 432p.

62* SCHUHL P.M., L'oeuvre de Platon. 3e éd. À la re-
cherche de la vérité, Paris, Hachette 1962 228p.
Also 4e éd. Paris, Vrin 1967 230p.
Rev. RecSR LIV 1966 598 des Places.

63* SCHUHL P.M., Études platoniciennes. Bibl. de
Philos. contemporaine, Paris, Presses
Universitaires 1960 180p.
Rev. AUP XXX 1960 192-194 Périgord.
REA LXII 1960 476-477 Moreau.
REG LXXIII 1960 549-552 Weil.
Filosofia XI 1960 780-782 Virieux-Reymond.
RS LXXXI 1960 299-307 Virieux-Reymond.
JHS LXXXI 1961 188 Tarrant.
PhR LXX 1961 425-427 Allen.
Hum(RES) XXXIII 1960-1961,7 31 François.
Convivium 1961 206-207 J.A.
BA 1961 254 Hoerber.
PLA XV 1962 117-119 Geldsetzer.
RecSR XLIX 1961 290-291 des Places.
RivE VI 1961 433-436 Vattimo.
FilLis VIII 1961 90-92 B.A.
Critique XVIII 1962 811-813 Hadot.
ASSPh XXIII 1963 233-234 Voelke.
Gnomon XXXVI 1964 136-144 Kuhn.

64* SCIACCA M.F., Platone. 2a ed. Opere complete di
M.F. Sciacca XXVI & XXVII, Milano, Marzorati
1967 446 & 440p.
Rev. BollFil 1968 132 Chiereghin.
CivCatt III 1968 438 Messineo.
EtFr 1968 190-193 Peteul.
RecSR LVI 1968 619 des Places.
Augustinianum VIII 1968 580.
RSR XLII 1968 346 Menard.
GCFI XLVII 1968 623-625 Plebe.
ArchPhilos XXXI 1968 682-683 Solignac.
REA LXX 1968 461-463 Moreau.
P&I X 1968 123 Pozzo.
RIFD XLV 1968 462-463 Orecchia.
Filosofia XIX 1968 458-462 Bosio.
SC XCVI 1968 528 Biff.
Ethics VII 1968 231-232.
FolHum VI 1968 661 Arasa.
RPortFil XXIV 1968 441-442 Freire.
CD CLXXXI 1968 399-400 Una.
RThPh 1969 136-137 Virieux-Reymond.
Salesianum XXXI 1969 351 Composta.
Gregorianum L 1969 411-414 González
Caminero.
RPhL LXVII 1969 345 Druart.
Sapientia XXIV 1969 235 Bolzán.

FilosV X 1969 87-90 Composta.
Crisis XVI 1969 507 Ruiz Nagore.
Bijdragen XXX 1969 217 Verhaak.
MF LXIX 1969 259-260 Coccia.
Pensamiento XXV 1969 442-444 Martínez
Gómez.
RPhilos CLXX 1970 227 Somville.
ModS XLVII 1969-1970 225-226 Sweeney.
Augustinus XV 1970 95 Ruiz Nagore.
Angelicum   XLVII   1970   243-246
Vansteenkiste.
Logos 1972 157-161 Cosenza.

65* SCIACCA M., Platon, trad. del italiano por Farré
    L., Prol. de Gonzalo Casas M. Buenos Aires,
    Troquel, 1959 406p.

66 GONZÁLEZ-CAMINERO N., "Sciacca platónico". MiscCom
    LI 1969 259-294.

67* SHOREY P., The Unity of Plato's Thought. Chicago
    Reprint Series, Chicago, Univ. of Chicago Pr.
    1960 88p. Also Hamden, Conn., The Shoe String
    Pr. 1968.

68* SHOREY P., What Plato Said. Abridged edn. Chicago,
    Univ. of Chicago Pr. 1965 vi&378p.

69* SLØK J., Platon, with an introd., transl. and notes
    by Sløk J. Copenhagen, Berlingske Forlag 1964
    239p.

70* STOCKHAMMER M., Platons Weltanschauung. Köln,
    Kölner Univ. Verl. 1962 168p.
    Rev. RM XVII 1963-1964 152 J.J.
    PLA XVI 1963 352-357 Marcus.
    RIPh XVIII 1964 142-143 Oedingen.
    PhilosQ XIV 1964 80 Robinson.
    ASSPh XXV 1965 203-205 Wildermuth.
    RPortFil XXI 1965 220 Morão.
    EPh XXII 1967 500-501 Marietti.

71* SUSEMIHL F., Die genetische Entwicklung der
    platonischen Philosophie. Einleitend
    dargestellt. Bd.I-II (Halfte 1/2). Neudr. d.
    Ausg. 1855-1860. Osnabrück, Zeller 1967
    xvi&486, xi&312, xxviii&p.314-696.

72* TAYLOR A.E., Plato, the Man and his Work. New edn.
    University Publications, London, Methuen 1960
    562p. Also Italian transl. Platone, l'uomo e
    l'opera, present. di Pra M. dal, trad. di

Corsi M. Il pensiero filos. V, Firenze, La
Nuova Italia 1968 xviii&862p.
Rev. [of English edn.] SaltR 1961 77
Young.
[of Ital. edn.] RF LX 1969 72-74
Cambiano.
PP XXIII 1968 391-396 Martano.
Problemi della pedag. (Roma Univ.) 1971,2
300-308 Semi.
RFNeo LXI 1969 768-771 Reale.

73 JAEGER W., Rev. of Taylor A.E., Plato, the Man and
his Work. p.401-412 in Jaeger W., Scripta
Minora I (see 4605). Reprinted from Gnomon 1928
1-11.

74* TAYLOR A.E., The Mind of Plato. Ann Arbor
Paperbacks, Ann Arbor, Mich., Univ. of Michigan
Pr. 1960 148p. (first published in 1922 under
the title Plato.) Also reprinted under original
title: Freeport, N.Y., Books for Libraries
1971.

75* THEODORAKOPOULOS N.I., Εἰσαγωγὴ στὸν Πλάτωνα. 4th
edn. Athens, Kollaros 1964. 5th edn. with new
indices. Athens, Institut du Livre M.
Kardamitsa 1970 377p.
Rev. Athene(Chicago) XXV,3 1964 30-31
Anton.

76* THEODORAKOPOULOS J.N., Die Hauptprobleme der
platonischen Philosophie. Heidelberger
Vorlesungen 1969. Den Haag, Nijhoff 1972 95p.
Rev. Philosophia(Athens) III 1973 454-461
Moukanos.

77* TOTSUKA S., Plato [in Japanese]. Tokyo, Maki
Bookstore 1964 226p.

78* TOVAR A., Un libro sobre Platon. 2a ed. Madrid,
Espasa Calpe 1973 157p. Also English transl.
of 1st edn.: An Introduction to Plato, transl.
by Pino F. The Argonaut Libr. of Antiquities,
London/Chicago, Argonaut Pr. 1969 v&147p.
Rev. [of English edn.] CW LXIII 1970 235
Hoerber.
Emerita XXXIX 1971 507 Pinero.

79* VARVARO P., Studi su Platone. 2 vols. Palermo,
Mori 1965 & 1967 xv&2414p. (numbered
consecutively).
Rev. BAGB 1967 248 Trouillard.

Sophia XXXV 1967 134-135 Romano.
Paideia XXII 1967 166-169 Grilli.
FilosV VIII 1967 403-404 Giannini.
Teoresi XXI 1966 162-164 Cristaldi.
GM XXIV 1969 118-119 Guazzoni Foa.

80* VOGEL C.J. DE, Plato, de filosoof van het
transcendente. Wijsger. Monograf., Baarn, Het
Wereldvenster 1968 182p.
Rev. Hermeneus XLI 1970 209 Sinnige.
RBF XX 1970 232-236 van Acker.
REG LXXXIV 1971 211-216 Dandonneau.

81* VOGELIN E., Plato. Baton Rouge, Louisiana State
Univ. Pr. 1966 ix&279p. (Originally publ.
1957 as Order and History, Part I.)

82* VRIES G.J. DE, Inleiding tot het denken van Plato.
4. dr. Hoofdfiguren van het menselijk denken
VI, Amsterdam, Born 1966 95p.
Rev. Hermeneus XXXVII 1966 260.

83* WICHMANN O., Platon. Ideele Gesamtdarstellung und
Studienwerk. Darmstadt, Wiss. Buchges. 1966
ix&703p.
Rev. RFil (La Plata) XVIII 1967 99-101
Maliandi.
Gymnasium LXXIV 1967 364-367 Merlan.
Th&Ph XLIII 1968 267-268 Ennen.
RPortFil XXIV 1968 440 Freire.
RF LIX 1968 222-225 Cambiano.
AAHG XXII 1969 168-170 Vretska.
Helmantica XXII 1971 339 Oroz.

84* WILAMOWITZ-MOELLENDORFF U. VON, Platon. Sein Leben
und seine Werke, 5. Aufl. bearb. & mit einem
Nachw. vers. von Snell B. Berlin, Weidmann
1959 xvi&615p.

85* WILAMOWITZ-MOELLENDORFF U. VON, Platon, II:
Beilagen und Textkritik. 3. Aufl. bearb. von
Stark R. Berlin, Weidmann 1962 460p.
Rev. RBPh XLII 1964 1089-1090
Loicq-Berger.

86 ISNARDI PARENTE M., "Rileggendo il Platon di Ulrich
von Wilamowitz-Moellendorff". ASNP III 1973
147-167.

87* WOODBRIDGE F.J.E., The Son of Apollo. Themes of
Plato. New York, Biblo & Tannen 1971 272p.
Reprint of 1929 edn.

88* WYLLER E.A., Platon. Skrifter utgitt av Det Norske
    Akademi for Sprog og Litteratur, Oslo,
    Universitetsforlaget 1960 39p.

89* WYLLER E.A., Der späte Platon. Tübinger Vorles.
    1965. Hamburg, Meiner 1970 vii&179p.
    Rev. WJb III 1970 276-283 Heintel.
    RIFD XLVII 1970 318-319 d'Agostino.
    CW LXIV 1971 160 Brumbaugh.
    Platon XXIV 1972 392-393 Kostaras.
    CR XXII 1972 198-200 Huby.
    Antonianum XLVII 1972 174 Platzeck.
    Sophia XL 1972 154-157.
    PhilosRdschau XX 1973-1974 205-210
    Schaeffer.
            Solignac A., "Vues nouvelles sur la
    derniere philosophie de Platon". ArchPhilos
    XXXIV 1971 475-493.

90* ZAITEGUI J., Platon, eneko atarian [On Plato's
    Porch] [in Basque]. San Sebastian, Ed. Izarra
    1962 xiv&312p.

91* ZELLER E., Plato and the Older Academy transl. by
    Alleyne S.F. & Goodwin A. Reissue. New York,
    Russell & Russell 1962 629p.

(see 2168, 3715, 4091)

        I B: HISTORIES OF ANCIENT PHILOSOPHY

92* ABBAGNANO N., Storia della filosofia, I: Filosofia
    antica, filosofia patristica, filosofia
    scholastica. Torino, Utet 1963 xx&684p.; 2nd
    edn. revised 1969. (Ch.7 "Socrate"; ch.9
    "Platone".)
            Rev. Mind LXXIV 1965 449 Strawson.
    RFNeo LVI 1964 134-135 A.B.
    RM XIX 1965-1966 578 G.D.D.

93* ABBAGNANO N., La filosofia antica. Bari, Laterza
    1963 472p. (ch.6 "Socrate", p.103-123; ch.8
    "Platone", p.147-207.)
            Rev. GM XIX 1964 224 Bortot.

94* ADORNO F., Storia di filosofia, I: La filosofia
    antica, 1. Milano, Feltrinelli 1961 608p.
    (Socrates, p.137-152; Plato p.171-243; Academy

18

I B: HISTORIES OF ANCIENT PHILOSOPHY

                p.244-258.)
                Rev. Arbor 1963 no. 56 146-147 Bravo
            Lozano.
                GCFI XLII 1963 406-408 Plebe.
                Mnemosyne XVIII 1965 291-293 Mansfeld.
                RF LVII 1966 484-486 Cambiano.

95* ASMUS V.F., Istorija antichnoj filosofii [History of
        ancient Philosophy] [in Russian]. Moskva,
        Vysshaia Skola 1965 320p. (ch.III.1 on Socrates
        and the Socratic schools, p.83-87; ch.IV on
        Plato, p.123-192.)

96* BOAS G., Rationalism in Greek Philosophy.
        Baltimore, Johns Hopkins Univ. Pr. 1961
        xii&488p. (For Socrates see esp. p.76-85; ch.
        3 "The Rationalism of Plato", p.129-187.)
                Rev. LJ 1961 3791 Stevens.
                PhilosBks Oct. 1962 6 Wasserstein.
                CW LV 1962 260 Anton.
                CR XIII 1963 190-192 Gulley.
                HibJ LX 1961-1962 348 Armstrong.
                PhR LXXII 1963 401-405 Morrow.
                EPh XVIII 1963 209-210 Deledalle.
                WHR 1963 90 Gauss.
                AHR LXVII 1961-1962 1058 Hadas.
                PhilosQ XIII 1963 174-175 Smith.
                AESocCiv XIX 1964 1027 Vidal-Naquet.
                JHPh II 1964 87-89 Goheen.

97* BRADY I., A History of Ancient Philosophy.
        Milwaukee, Bruce 1959 xiv&262p. (Ch. 7 "The
        Days of Socrates", p.69-79; ch. 8 "Plato and
        the Academy", p.80-107.)
                Rev. RPhL LIX 1961 110-111 Mansion.
                ThS XXII 1961 696-699 Conway.
                Antonianum XXXVI 1961 126 Platzeck.
                CrossCurr X 1960 163 Collins.
                ModS XXXVIII 1960-1961 78-80 Barth.
                NS XXXIV 1960 364-365 Clark.
                PhilosStud(Irel.) IX 1959 267-268
            Bastable.

98* BRÉHIER E., Histoire de la philosophie, I:
        L'antiquité et le moyen âge. 8e éd., bibliogr.
        mise à jour par Schuhl P.M. Paris, Presses
        Universitaires 1963 268p. Also 9e ed. 1967
        230p. (ch.2 "Socrate"; ch.3 "Platon et
        l'Académie".) Also English transl. History of
        Philosophy. The Hellenic Age, transl. by
        Thomas J. Chicago, Univ. of Chicago Pr. 1963
        242p.

                            19

Rev. (of English transl.) CR XVII 1967
112 Kerferd.
CrossCurr 1964 380 Collins.
RM XVII 1963-1964 625 C.D.
LJ 1964 1248 Debenham.
JHPh II 1964 135.
Dialogue III 1964 326-327 Mamo.
ModS XLII 1964-1965 330 Klubertanz.

99* BRENTANO   F.,   Geschichte   der   griechischen
    Philosophie, aus dem Nachlass hrsg. von
    Mayer-Hillebrand F.   Bern, Francke 1963
    lxiii&396p.   (sec.4   "Sokrates",   p.153-164;
    sec.7 "Platon und die Akademie", p.178-214.)
           Rev. Bijdragen XXV 1964 434-435 de
    Strycker.
           Ideas y Valores VI 1963-1964 361-363
    Gutiérrez Girardot.
           Franciscanum VI 1964 64-65 Herrera.
           RFil(Madrid) XXIII 1964 134-135 Sánchez
    Pasqual.
           PLA XVI 1963 289-293 Hofmann.
           AC XXXIII 1964 259-261 Janssens.
           RBPh XLII 1964 707 Dejans.
           REG LXXVII 1964 612 Aubenque.
           Helmantica XV 1964 429 Flórez.
           NS XXXIX 1965 124-127 Cleve.
           Ph&PhenR 1965-1966 94 Bergman.
           RPh XXXIX 1965 317 Mugler.
           CW LVIII 1965 220 Stewart.
           CPh LX 1965 283 Hoerber.
           AAHG XIX 1966 63-64 Haller.
           RThPh XCVIII 1965 115-116 Schaerer.
           Mnemosyne XIX 1966 64-65 Sassen.
           WZ VIII 1964-1966 52-53 Kraft.
           JHS LXXXVII 1967 164-165 Skemp.
           RFNeo LIX 1967 801 Bausola.

100* BRUMBAUGH R.S., The Philosophers of Greece. New
    York, Crowell 1964 and London, Allen & Unwin
    1966 xi&276p. (Ch.13 "Socrates. The Search for
    the Self", p.123-132;   ch.14 "Plato. Order,
    Fact, and Value", p.133-171.)
           Rev. CW LVIII 1965 256 Fortenbaugh.
           YR 1965 xxiv.
           RM XIX 1965-1966 150 C.D.
           CJ LXI 1966 175-176 De Lucca.
           CPh LXI 1966 65 Sprague.
           TLS 26 Jan. 1967 72.
           PhilosQ XVII 1967 266-267 Huby.
           JHS LXXXVIII 1968 191-192 Kerferd.
           REA LXX 1968 168 Brun.

TPh XXX 1968 174-175 Dhondt.
EPh XXIII 1968 448 Deledalle.
CR LXI 1971 222-224 Morrison.

101* CAPELLE W., Die griechische Philosophie. Bd.I: Von
     Thales bis zum Tode Platons. 3. bearb. Aufl.
     d. 3.   Aufl.   u.d.   Neubearb.   d.
     Literaturverz. von Mueller J. Sammlung Goschen
     Nr.857-857a, Berlin, de Gruyter 1971 301p.
     Rev. BO XXIX 1972 76 Jonkers.

102 CHÂTELET F., "Platon". ch.3, p.72-136 in Histoire
     de la Philosophie., Idées, Doctrines, I: La
     philosophie païenne du VIe siecle avant J.C. au
     IIIe siecle apres J.C., ed. par Châtelet F.
     Paris, Hachette 1972.

103* COPLESTON F., Histoire de la philosophie, I: La
     Grece et Rome [French transl. of English work].
     Paris, Casterman 1964 548p. Also Italian
     transl. Storia della filosofia, I: Grecia e
     Roma. Coll. Paideia, Firenze, La Nuova Italia
     1967 694p.
          Rev. [of French edn.] LEC XXXIII 1965
     430.
          RPhL LXIII 1965 652-654 van Steenberghen.
          EPh XX 1965 84 Delpech.
          RecSR LIV 1966 575 des Places.
          EThL XLII 1966 648 van Steenberghen.
          RevNouv XLI 1965 444-445 Colette.
          NRTh LXXXVIII 1966 319-320 de Give.
          ArchPhilos XXIX 1966 142-144 Solignac.
          Etudes CCCXXII 1965 281-282 Solignac.
          Philosophia 1968 94-95 H.J.P.
          RThom LXX 1970 478-480 Leroy.
          RFil(Mexico) III 1970 107-108 Mansur.
          [of Italian edn.] Studium VII 1967 478-479
     Noriega.
          Sapientia XXIII 1968 71-75 Parica.

104* CORNFORD F.M., Before and After Socrates. Cambridge
     Univ. Pr. 1960 x&113p. Reprint of 1932 edn.
     (Ch.2: "Socrates", p.29-53; ch.3: "Plato",
     p.54-84.)

105* CORNFORD F.M., Sócrates y el pensamiento griego,
     trad. de Gimeno J.M. Madrid, Ed. Norte y Sur
     1964 101p.
          Rev. Perficit II 1970 271-272 Igal.

106* DIANO C., Studi e saggi di filosofia antica. Studia
      aristotelica VI, Padova, Ed. Antenore 1973
      xi&439p. (ch.10 "Socrate", p.75-78; ch.11
      "Platone", p.78-180; "Il problema della materia
      in Platone", p.229-278.)

107* DUMONT J.P., La philosophie antique. Coll. Que
      sais-je? no.250, Paris, Presses Universitaires
      1962 128p. (Ch. 2, "Socrate et les Sophistes";
      ch. 3, "Platon: l'Opinion, les Idées, le
      Bien.")
          Rev. CW LVI 1962 74 Hoerber.
          Hum(RES) XXXVIII 1961-1962,10 33 Guillen.
          RPortFil XVIII 1962 430-431 da Silva.
          EPh XVII 1962 538-539 Quoniam.
          AC XXXII 1963 345 Joly.
          REG LXXVI 1963 270-271 Aubenque.
          Latomus XXII 1963 945-946 Croissant.
          RBPh XLI 1963 667 Dejans.
          RThPh XII 1962 291 Graz.
          RS LXXXV,36 1964 75 Virieux-Reymond.
          Pensamiento XX 1964 106-107 Colomer.

108* FRIES J.F., Die Geschichte der Philosophie, Bd. I.
      (1839). Reprinted as Fries J.F., Sämtliche
      Schriften, Bd.18. Aalen, Scientia-Verl. 1969.
      (p.249-262 on Socrates; p.286-390 on Plato.)

109* FULLER B.A.G., History of Greek Philosophy, vol.
      II: The Sophists, Socrates, Plato. New York,
      Greenwood 1968. Reprint of 1930 edn.

110* GENTILE G., Storia della filosofia (Dalle origini a
      Platone), ed. da Bellezza V.A. Opere complete
      di Giovanni Gentile, vol. X. Firenze, Sansoni
      1964 viii&256p.
          Rev. EPh 1964 608-609 Moreau.
          RIFD XLI 1964 659 Orecchia.
          RFNeo LVI 1964 541-546 Conti.
          RPhL LXII 1964 380-381 Wenin.
          EstFilos XIV 1965 204-205 Montull.
          Pensamiento XXI 1965 187-188 Martínez
      Gómez.
          GCFI XLIX 1965 585-589 Giannantoni.
          GM XXI 1966 372-379 Negri.
          IPQ VI 1966 146-148 Natoli.
          RRCF LX 1966 154-155 Raschini.

111* GEYMONAT L., Storia del pensiero filosofico e
      scientifico, I: L'antichità. Il medioevo.
      Milano, Garzanti 1970 736p. (ch.6 "I sofisti e
      Socrate. L'umanizzazione della cultura",

p.95-121; ch.10 "Platone", p.190-216.)
Rev. AIHS XXIII 1970 232-233 Grmek.
Scientia LXV 1971 115-116 de Murtas.
Belfagor XXVIII 1973 371-378 Timpanaro.

112* GOMPERZ T., Greek Thinkers. A History of Ancient
Philosophy, transl. by Magnus L. & Berry G.G.
Vols. I-IV. London, Murray 1964 1980p.
(Socrates--vol. II p.45-118; Plato--vol. II
p.249-end, vol. III entire.)
Rev. Hermathena CI 1965 71 Luce.
DownsR LXXXIII 1965 381-382 O'Brien.

113* GONZÁLEZ CAMINERO N., Historia philosophiae, I:
Philosophia antiqua, 1: Cyclus colonialis et
cyclus Atheniensis (saec. VII-IV a.Ch.). Roma,
Pontif. Univ. Gregoriana 1960 370p.
(Socrates, p.226-262; Plato, p.263-315.)
Rev. RFil(Madrid) XXIII 1964 132-133
Sánchez Pascual.
Antonianum XXXVI 1961 430 Platzeck.
Augustinianum I 1961 575-576 Kunst.
NRTh LXXXIII 1961 541 Thiry.
Salesianum XXIII 1961 394-395 Composta.
EE XXXVI 1961 505-506 Alejandro.
RPortFil XVII 1961 224 Ribiero.
Scholastik XXXVI 1961 131-132 Kern.
Gregorianum XLII 1961 387-388.
Pensamiento XVIII 1962 101 Alejandro.
Espiritu XI 1962 140 Roig Gironella.

114* GRENET P.B., Histoire de la philosophie ancienne.
Paris, Beauchesne 1960 326p. (Socrates,
p.62-66; Plato, p.70-142.)
Rev. RB LXXI 1961 465.
Sapientia XVI 1961 221-222 Ponferrada.
CiFe XVII 1961 98.
RPhL LIX 1961 515-518 Lefevre.
EstFilos X 1961 317-318 Montull.
ArchPhilos XXIV 1961 370-371 Solignac.
Augustinianum II 1962 236 Mendez.
Scholastik XXXVII 1962 454 Kern.
RPortFil XVIII 1962 427-428 Oliveira.
RThom LXIII 1963 94-97 Dubois.
NRTh LXXXV 1963 314 Thiry.
RS LXXXVII 1966 120 Delpech.

115* GUTHRIE W.K.C., The Greek Philosophers from Thales
to Aristotle. Univ. Paperbacks, London,
Methuen 1967 v&168p. (Ch.4 on Socrates;
chs.5-6 on Plato.) German trans. Die
griechischen Philosophen von Thales bis

Aristoteles,   ubers.   von Raabe G.   Kleine
Vandenhoeck-Reihe XC-XCI, Göttingen, Vandenhoeck
& Ruprecht 1960 125p.
    Rev.   [of German edn.] PhJ LXIX   1961
197-198 Jaeger.
RecSR LII 1964 449 des Places.
[of English edn.] G&R XV 1968 99 Sewter.

116* GUZZO A., Storia della filosofia e della civiltà.
Saggi, Ii: Socrate e Platone. Univ. di Parma,
Ist. di sci. relig., Padova, La Garangola 1973
vii&205p.

117* HACKNEY J., A History of Greek and Roman Philosophy.
New York, Philos. Libr. 1966 ix&269p. (ch.14
p.47-56 on Socrates; chs.17-24 p.63-120 on
Plato.)
    Rev. CW LXI 1967 108 Stewart.
    ModS XLIV 1966-1967 395-397 Kendzierski.

118 HUBY P.M., "Socrates and Plato". Ch. 2, p.14-35 in
O'Connor D.J., A Critical History of Western
Philosophy. New York, Free Press of
Glencoe/London, Collier-Macmillan 1964.

119* JASPERS K., Les grands philosophes. Paris, Plon
1963 980p. (sections on Socrates and Plato)
    Rev. RThPh XCVIII 1965 116 Piguet.
    EPh XIX 1964 611 Jacob.
    RevNouv XLI 1965 180-184 VanderGucht.
    ASSPh XXVI 1966 307-308 Christoff.

120 KLEVE K., "Platon, 427-347 f. Kr.". p.42-63 in
Skard E. et al., Vestens tenkere fra antikken
til våre dager, I: Fra Sokrates til Pascal.
Oslo, Aschehoug 1962.

121* KOJÈVE A., Essai d'une histoire raisonnée de la
philosophie païenne, II: Platon-Aristote.
Bibl. des idees, Paris, Gallimard 1972 405p.
(Part A: "La Parathèse thétique de Platon",
p.7-185.)

122* KRANZ W., Die griechische Philosophie. Zugleich
eine Einfuhrung in die Philosophie uberhaupt.
Bremen, Schünemann 1962 354p. (Part III.1
"Dialektik und Ethik. Sokrates"; III.2 "Die
Idee. Platon".)
    Rev. Sophia XXXII 1964 163.

123* KRANZ W., Historia de la filosofía. vol. II La
filosofía griega, parte 2a, Sócrates y Platón,
trad. por Castaño Piñan A.J. Manuales UTEHA
no.127 sección 7, Filosofía, México, Unión
Tipográfica Editorial Hispano Americana 1962.

124* KUKAVA T., History of Greek Philosophy up to Plato,
I [in Russian]. Tbilisi 1972 412p.

125* LAMANNA E., Storia della filosofia, I: Il pensiero
antico. Firenze, Le Monnier 1961 514 p. (ch.
3 "I Sofisti e Socrate", p.117-142; ch. 4
"Platone", p.143-197.)
Rev. RMM XLIX 1964 230.
RPhL LXIII 1965 474 Wylleman.
EstFilos XI 1962 163-165 Montull.
JHPh 1964 279 Schneider.

126* MACHOVEC D., Dějiny antické filosofie [History of
ancient Philosophy] [in Czech]. Praha, Státní
pedag. naklad. 1962 187p. (includes chapters
on Socrates and Plato.)
Rev. LF XII 1964 185-186 Špaňar.

127* MAYR F.K., Geschichte der Philosophie, I: Antike.
Berckers theol. Grundrisse V,1, Kevelaer,
Butzon & Bercker 1966 352p. (ch.8 "Sokrates",
p.109-120; ch.10 "Platon", p.126-198.)
Rev. ThRev LXV 1969 42-43 Fellermeier.
ThQ CXLVIII 1968 231-232 Dangelmayr.
ZKTh XC 1968 85 Muck.
MTZ XVIII 1967 161-162 Fellermeier.

128* MONDOLFO R., Il pensiero antico. Storia della
filosofia greco-romana. Firenze, La Nuova
Italia, 3rd edn. 1961, 4th edn. 1967
viii&684p.

129* OWENS J., A History of Ancient Western Philosophy.
New York, Appleton-Century-Crofts 1959 xi&434p,
(Socrates, p.165-175; Plato, p.189-280.)

130* PARKER G.F., A Short Account of Greek Philosophy
from Thales to Epicurus. London, Arnold 1967
x&194p. (ch.11 on Socrates; chs.12-14 on
Plato.)

131* REALE G., I problemi del pensiero antico dalle
origini ad Aristotele. Milano, Celuc 1971 639p.
(p.265-305 on Socrates; p.339-442 on Plato.)
Rev. AGPh LV 1973 349 Wagner.

132* ROBIN L., La pensée hellénique des origines à
      Epicure. Questions de méthode, de critique et
      d'histoire, avant-propos de Schuhl P.M.   Paris,
      Presses Universitaires 1967 554p.   Also L'Évol.
      de l'human.-Poche XXXV, Paris, Michel 1973 529p.
      (ch.3 "Socrate"; ch.4 "Platon".) Also in
      English transl. Greek Thought and the Origins
      of the Scientific Spirit, transl. by Dobie M.R.
      New York, Russel & Russell 1967 xx&409p.
      (Reprint of 1928 New York edn.)

133 SCIACCA M.F., "Socrate". p.57-75 in Momenti di
      storia della filosofia, a cura di diversi
      autori. Orientamenti filosofici e pedagogici I,
      Milano, Marzorati 1962.

134* SHIBLES W.A., Models of Ancient Greek Philosophy.
      London, Vision 1971 iii&155p. (for Plato see
      p.90-117.)
            Rev. CW LXVI 1972 168-169 Cooper.
            ACR II 1972 229-230 Epp.

135* SICHIROLLO L., Per una storiografia filosofica.
      Platone. Descartes. Kant. Hegel. Pubbl.
      dell'Univ. di Urbino, Ser. Lett. e Filos
      XXVII, Urbino, Argalia 1970 674p. in 2 vols.
      (part I "Note su Platone e il pensiero antico".)
            Rev. RPhilos CLXII 1972 52 Namer.

136 SKARD E., "Sokrates, 469-399 f.Kr.". p.23-41 in
      Skard E., Winsnes A.H. et al. Vestens tenkere
      fra antikken til våre dager, I: Fra Sokrates
      til Pascal. Oslo, Aschehoug 1962.

137* STRYCKER E. DE, Beknopte geschiedenis van de
      antieke filosofie. Antwerpen, Nederl.
      Boekhandel 1967 215p. (p.64-78 on Socrates;
      p.83-125 on Plato.)
            Rev. ANTP LIX 1967 265-266 Sinnige.
            TPh XXIX 1967 643 de Petter.
            RBPh XLVII 1969 642-643 Pinnoy.
            Mnemosyne XXIII 1970 198-199 Mansfeld.

138* TATARKIEWICZ W., Historia filozofii, I: Filozofia
      starozytna i średniowieczna. New edn. revised
      & enlarged. Warszawa PWN 1958 436p.
            Rev. BCO VI 1961 56-58.

139* THOMSON G., The First Philosophers. 2nd edn.
      London, Lawrence & Wishart 1961. French transl.
      Les premiers philosophes, trad. de Charlot M.
      Coll. Ouvertures, Paris, Ed. sociales 1973

400p. Italian transl. I primi filosofi, trad.
di Innocenti P. Firenze, Vallecchi 1973 390p.

140* VOGELIN E., Order and History, Vol. III: Plato and
Aristotle. Baton Rouge, Lousiana State Univ.
Pr. 1958 xvii&383p.
Rev. TPh XX 1958 358-363 Walgrave.
Thought XXXIII 1958 273-278 Berry.
JHI XIX 1958 442-444 Hadas.
RM XII 1958-1959 257-276 Rosen.
AHR LXIII 1957-1958 939-941 Robinson.
CR LXXIII 1959 251-252 Kerferd.
ARSPh XLV 1959 303-307 Topitsch.
REG LXXIII 1960 546-548 Weil.
CJ LVI 1960 90-92 Oates.
EHR LXXV 1960 288-290 Porteous.
PhilosRdschau 1961 220-230 Manasse.
JHS LXXXI 1961 192 Adkins.
CHR 1962 410 McGuire.

141 WAHL J., "Platon". p.464-607 in Histoire de la
Philosophie, I, sous la dir. de Parain B.
Encyclopedie de la Pleiade XXVI, Paris,
Gallimard 1969.

142* WERNER C., La philosophie grecque. Petite Bibl.
Payot XIV, Paris, Payot 1962 255p; new edn.
1972 250p. (Ch. 2 "La sagesse: Socrate"; ch.
3 "L'Idée: Platon".) Also German transl., Die
Philosophie der Griechen, übers. von Scheier W.
Freiburg, Herder 1966 252p.
Rev. [of French edn.] RPhilos CLV 1965
505-506 Caujolle.
LEC XXX 1962 449 Walbrecq.
EPh XVII 1962 575-576 Moreau.
CW LVI 1963 257 Feldman.
AC XXXII 1963 345 Joly.
JHPh II 1964 137-138.
[of German edn.] DLZ LXXXVIII 1967 4-7
Albrecht.

143* ZELLER E., Die Philosophie der Griechen in ihrer
geschichtlichen Entwicklung. T.II, Abt.1:
Sokrates und die Sokratiker. Plato und die alte
Akademie. appendix "Der gegenwärtige Stand der
Platonforschung" von Hoffmann E. (unveränd.
Nachdr. d. 5. Aufl. 1922) Hildesheim, Olms
1963 xii&1105p.

I C: SECTIONS ON PLATO IN OTHER WORKS

144* ALAIN [pseud.], Idées. Introduction a la
philosophie: Platon--Descartes--Hegel--Comte.
Paris, Club Francais du Livre 1961 xxii&352p.
Also Paris, U.G.E. (Soc. nouvelle Sequana)
1964 384p. New edition: Paris, Flammarion 1967
369p.

145 LANDMANN M., "Platon". p.69-79 in De Homine. Der
Mench im Spiegel seines Gedankens, hrsg. von
Landmann M. u.a. Freiburg Alber 1962.

146 RYLE G., "Plato". p.314-333 in Encyclopedia of
Philosophy., ed. by Edwards P. New
York/London, Collier Macmillan 1967, vol. VI.

147* VALENSIN A., Profili: Platone, Cartesio, Pascal,
Bergson, Blondel, trad. di Marchetti A. Studi
e opinioni XV, Milano, IPL 1968 343p.
Rev. Humanitas XXIV 1969 722-723
Rebuzzini.

148 GOLDSCHMIDT V., "Platon". p.63-76 in Goldschmidt
V., Questions platoniciennes (see 4598).
Reprinted from Les philosophes célèbres, ed.
par Mazenod L. 1956 p.64ff.

149 ROBINSON R. & DENNISTON J.D., "Plato". p.1-15 in
Plato I, ed. by Vlastos G. (see 4619).
Reprint of the article on Plato in The Oxford
Classical Dictionary 1st edn. 1949.

150 SCHMALZRIEDT E., "Platon". p.604-623 in Enzykl.
Die Grossen der Weltgesch. Bd. I. Zürich,
Kindler 1971.

I D: GENERAL ARTICLES ON PLATO

151 CARROLL K.M., "Plato for the uninitiated. An
Account for non-classical Pupils". G&R V 1958
144-158.

152 DURANT W., "Platon". Insan ve dünya 1958 I,1 42-44
& I,2 47-49.

I D: GENERAL ARTICLES ON PLATO

153 GUITTON J., "Portrait de Platon". TabR CL 1960
     34-41.

154 GARCÍA BACCA J.D., "Pensar, amor y verdad (Platon).
     Comentarios a un terceto de A. Machado". Ideas
     y Valores IV 1962 no.14 5-11.

155 PIEPER J., "'Billigkeit' in der Interpretation".
     p.241-255 in Pieper J., Tradition als
     Herausforderung. Aufsätze und Reden. München,
     Kosel 1963. Reprinted from Karl Arnold
     Festschrift, Köln, Opladen 1955.

156 PEURSEN C.A. VAN, "Plato's filosofie--Ideologie of
     rollenspel". WPMW III 1962-1963 20-32.

157 VOLLENHOVEN D.H., "Plato's realisme". PhilosReform
     XXVIII 1963 97-133.

158 SCIACCA M.F., "Attualità di Platone". p.265-277 in
     Sciacca M.F., Platone II (see 64). Reprinted
     from Sciacca M.F., Problemi di filosofia. 2a
     ed. Roma, Perrella 1944.

159 SCIACCA M.F., "Epitome della 'ricerca' platonica".
     p.79-94 in Sciacca M.F., Platone I (see 64).
     Reprinted from Sciacca M.F., Platone Della
     Repubblica, Libri VI e VII. Napoli, Perrella
     1935.

160 SCIACCA M.F., "La verità di Platone". p.21-73 in
     Sciacca M.F., Platone I (see 64). Reprinted
     from GM I 1946 69-87, 241-259.

161 BOEDER H., "Zu Platons eigener Sache". PhJ LXXVI
     1968-1969 37-66.

162 DERRIDA J., "La pharmacie de Platon". TelQuel XXXII
     1968 3-48, XXXIII 1968 18-59. Reprinted in La
     Dissémination. Coll. Tel Quel, Paris, Ed. du
     Seuil 1972.

163 TOUBEAU H., "Le pharmakon et les aromates".
     Critique XXVIII 1972 681-706.

164 BRAGUE R., "En marge de La pharmacie de Platon de J.
     Derrida". RPhL LXXI 1973 271-277.

165 KRAEMER H.J., "Die platonische Akademie und das
     Problem einer systematischen Interpretation der
     Philosophie Platons". p.198-230 in Das
     Platonbild, hrsg. von Gaiser K. (see 4595).

I D: GENERAL ARTICLES ON PLATO

166* NUCHELMANS G., Plato, inleiding door Nuchelmans G.
     WPMW   IX   n.2   1968-1969.   Amsterdam,
     Meulenhoff-Bruna 1968 p.73-127.

167 SCHLEIERMACHER F., "Einleitung zu 'Platons Werke'".
     p.1-32 in Das Platonbild, hrsg. von Gaiser K.
     (see 4595). Reprinted from Schleiermacher F.,
     Platons Werke, Bd.I des ersten Teils, 3. Aufl.
     Berlin 1855 p.5-36.

168 VOGEL C.J. DE, "Examen critique de l'interpretation
     traditionelle de la philosophie de Platon".
     p.155-175 in Vogel C.J. de, Philosophia I (see
     4624). Reprinted with changes from RMM LVI 1951
     249-268. Also Dutch version, "Plato en het
     moderne denken". p.106-125 in Vogel C.J. de,
     Theoria (see 4623).

169 YAMANO K., "Plato's point of view" [in Japanese with
     English summary]. JCS XIX 1971 58-68.

170* DAMBSKA I., Dwa studia o Platonie [Two Studies on
     Plato]. Wroclaw/Warszawa, Ossolineum 1972 86p.

II: PLATO'S LIFE AND HIS RELATIONS TO OTHERS

A: PLATO'S LIFE (GENERAL)

The following works are devoted principally to Plato's
life and his relations with Athens. In
addition, many of the general treatments of
Plato in sections I A, I B and I C contain
discussion of these subjects. Also see the
works referred to in section II E.

171 HARDER R., "Plato und Athen". p.212-222 in Harder
R., Kleine Schriften (see 4599). Reprinted from
Neue Jahrbücher für Wiss. und Jugendbildung,
Leipzig/Berlin, Teubner, X 1934 492-500.

172* PAASSEN C.R. VAN, Platon in den Augen der
Zeitgenossen. Köln, Westdeutscher Verl. 1960
44p.
Rev. ArchPhilos XXVIII 1965 156 Solignac.

173* WINSPEAR A.D., The Genesis of Plato's Thought. 2nd
ed. rev. New York, Russell & Russell 1960
390p.
Rev. PhilosRdschau 1961 188-197 Manasse.

174 LLANOS A., "El fondo historico en la filosofia
social de Platon". Humanitas X 1962 89-133.

175 NOVOTNY F., "Die antiken Platon-Legenden.
Verherrlichung und Verleumdung". OUPB XCII 1964
161-179.

176 FINLEY M.I., "Athenische Demagogen". Altertum XI
1965 67-79.

177 VOURVERIS K.I., "Τὸ φίλον καὶ τὸ κοινὸν ἐν τῇ πόλει".
p.153-165 in Χαριστήριον A.K. Orlandos, I.
Athens, Soc. Archaeol. 1965.

178 PERETTI M.M., "Su alcuni passi della 'Vita di
Platone' di Diogene Laerzio". RFIC XCIII 1965
446-449.

31

179 SODIPO J.O., "The Lighter Side of the ancient Greek
Philosophers". N&C IX 1966 28-37.

180 GÓMEZ ROBLEDO A., "Platon y su epoca". Humanitas
VIII 1967 81-102.

181 RANKIN H.D., "Another Look at Kelsen's View of
Plato". Apeiron II,1 1967 18-26.

182 SCIACCA M.F., "Nota biografica". p.74-78 in Sciacca
M.F., Platone I (see 64). Reprinted from
Sciacca M.F., Platone, Della Repubblica, Libri
VI e VII. Napoli, Perrella 1935.

183* MARTIN G., Platon in Selbstzeugnissen und
Bilddokumenten. Bibliographie von Ferfers D.;
Zeugnisse von Ferfers D. & Lange A. Rowohlts
Monogr. CL, Reinbek b. Hamburg, Rowohlt 1969
157p.

184 CARBONARA NADDEI M., "Platone e Posidonio in Diogene
Laerzio III". Logos I 1970 523-540.

185 NOUSSAN-LETTRY L., "Das Verhaltnis der Texte als
Sache philosophie-geschichtlicher Hermeneutik.
Zu Platons Apologie und Kriton". ZPhF XXV 1971
523-534.

186 DERBOLAV J., "Platon, Philosoph der kritischen
Aufklärung". PaedRdsch XXVI 1972 295-313. Also
in WissWelt XXV 1972 9-25.

187* SANDVOSS E., Platon. Künstler, Politiker,
Philosoph, Theologe. Personlichkeit & Gesch.
LXVI-LXVII, Göttingen, Munsterschmidt 1972 126p.

188 URMENETA F. DE, "Sobre estética testamentaria".
RevIE XXX 1972 307-330.

189 DOERRIE H., "Platons Reisen zu fernen Völkern. Zur
Geschichte eines Motivs der Platon-Legende und
zu seiner Neuwendung durch Lactanz". p.99-118
in Romanitas et Christianitas. Studia J.H.
Waszink a.d. VI kal. Nov. a. MCMLXXIII XIII
lustra complenti oblata hrsg. von Boer W. den
et al. Amsterdam, North Holland Publ. 1973.

190 GAISER K., "Die Platon-Referate des Alkimos bei
Diogenes Laertios (III,9-17)". p.61-79 in
Zetesis (see 4579).

II A: PLATO'S LIFE (GENERAL)

191 GIORGIANTONIO M., "Dove si annida secondo Platone il problema filosofico". Sophia XLI 1973 54-59.

192 PLASS P., "A Fragment of Plato in Diogenes Laertius". ModS LI 1973 29-46.

193 WENDER D., "Plato. Misogynist, Paedophile, and Feminist". Arethusa VI 1973 75-90.

(For further works on this subject see 326, 526, 1290, 1458, 1478, 1853, 1957, 2120, 2416, 3638, 3662, 3693, 3728, 4122)

II B: PLATO AND SYRACUSE

194 MEYER E., "Dionysios II. Dion, Platon und der Reformversuch". p.487-498 in Meyer E., Geschichte des Altertums, 4. Aufl. Bd. 5. Stuttgart 1958.

195* STROHEKER K.F., Dionysius I. Gestalt und Geschichte des Tyrannen von Syrakus. Wiesbaden 1958 262p.

196* BREITENBACH H., Platon und Dion. Skizze eines idealpolitischen Reformversuches im Altertum. Zürich, Artemis-Verl 1960 101p.
Rev. Gnomon XXXV 1963 375-377 Berve.
Helikon III 1963 707-715 von Scheliha.

197* SORDI M., Timoleonte. Palermo, Flaccovio 1961 vi&119p.

198 RANKIN H.D., "Plato's lost Pupil and the Banausic Education". Apeiron I 1966 32.

199* FRITZ K. VON, Platon in Sizilien und das Problem der Philosophenherrschaft. Berlin, de Gruyter 1968 xiv&147p.
Rev. BIEH III,1 1969 83 Alsina.
CW LXII 1969 326 Day.
RF LX 1969 223-224.
REA LXXI 1969 150-151 Moreau.
Salesianum XXXI 1969 348 Composta.
RPh XLIV 1970 128 Louis.
RSC XVII 1969 384-385 d'Agostino.
Phoenix XXIV 1970 79-84 Morrow.
AHR LXXV 1970 1088 Thayer.
ArchPhilos XXXIII 1970 146-148 Solignac.

II B: PLATO AND SYRACUSE

ZPhF XXIV 1970 144-145 Niebergall.
CJ LXVI 1970-1971 188-189 Wassermann.
Helmantica XXII 1971 195 Barcenilla.
CR XXI 1971 26-28 Skemp.
Sophia XXXIX 1971 116-117 Hoefer.
Eirene IX 1971 119-121 Frolikova.
JCS XX 1972 166-169 Amagasaki.
GGA CCXXIV 1972 9-25 Mueller.
PHist V 1972 138-140 Sprute.
AC XLII 1973 238 Loicq-Berger.
BAGB 1973 508ff.

200* MARCUSE L., Plato und Dionys, Geschichte einer
Demokratie und einer Diktatur. Neuausg.
Berlin, Blanvalet 1968 308p. (The former edn.
was entitled Der Philosoph und der Diktator.)

201 ISNARDI PARENTE M., "Platon politico e la VII
epistola. (A proposito di un libro recente)".
RSI LXXXI 1969 261-285. Reprinted p.169-204 in
Isnardi Parente M., Filosofia e politica nelle
Lettere di Platone (see 4603).

202 RIZZO F.P., "Problemi costituzionali sicelioti".
Kokalos XIV-XV 1968-1969 365-396.

203 STROHEKER K.F., "Sizilien und die Magna Graecia zur
Zeit der beiden Dionysii". Kokalos XIV-XV
1968-1969 119-134.

204 SPRUTE J., "Dions syrakusanische Politik und die
politischen Ideale Platons". Hermes C 1972
294-313.

205 MERANTE V., "La Sicilia e Cartagine dal V secolo
alla conquista romana". Kokalos XVIII-XIX
1972-1973 77-107.

(For further discussion of this topic see 401, 1444, 1685)

34

II C: PLATO AND HIS PREDECESSORS AND CONTEMPORARIES
a: PLATO AND SOCRATES

The following works are devoted to the relationship
between Plato and Socrates. The reader should
also consult section IX B as well as I A and I
B. In addition, many works dealing with
particular early works of Plato will be found to
contain material relevant to this subject.

206   DAROS J., "Plato and his Relationship with
      Socrates". Athene XXIV,3 1963 60-61.

207   PATZER H., "Die philosophische Bedeutung der
      Sokratesgestalt in den platonischen Dialogen".
      p.21-43 in Parusia, hrsg. von Flasch K. (see
      4588).

208   ALSINA J., "Sócrates, Platón y la verdad". BIEH I
      1967 39-43.

209   ELLIOTT R.K., "Socrates and Plato's Cave". KantStud
      LVIII 1967 137-157.

210   MEYERHOFF H., "From Socrates to Plato". p.187-201
      in The Critical Spirit. Essays in Honor of
      Herbert Marcuse, ed. by Wolff K.H. & Moore B.
      Boston, Beacon Pr. 1967.

211   VIVES J., "De la intransigencia socrática a la
      intolerancia platónica". p.121-133 in Δώρῳ σὺν
      ὀλίγῳ. Homenatge a Josep Alsina, present. de
      Bejarano V., dir Miralles C. Barcelona, Ed.
      Ariel 1969.

212* CAPIZZI A., Socrate e i personaggi filosofici di
      Platone. Uno studio sulle strutture della
      testimonianza platonica e un'edizione delle
      testimonianze contenute nei dialoghi. Bibl.
      Athena VIII, Roma, Ed. dell'Ateneo 1970 276p.
         Rev. REA LXXIII 1971 451-452 Moreau.
         ERASMUS XXIV 1972 751-753 Lasserre.
         LEC XL 1972 439-440 Druet.
         Sophia XL 1972 154-157.
         Maia XXV 1973 247-248 Guazzoni Foà.
         GM XXVIII 1973 237-241 Sorge.
         CR XXIII 1973 145-147 Gulley.
         AC XLII 1973 618 Bastaits.
         RPh XLVII 1973 334 Louis.

213   JACKSON B.D., "The Prayers of Socrates". Phronesis
      XVI 1971 14-37.

II C a: PLATO AND SOCRATES

214 NAKAMURA K., "Plato's Basic Thought. Something
    common to Socrates and Plato as seen in
    Socrates' Mission in the Apology and the
    so-called Socrates' Biographical Account in
    Phaedo 95e-102a" [in Japanese]. Hokkaido Univ.
    Dept. of Literature Bulletin XIX 1971.

215 MONTUORI M., "I Presocratici e Socrate nella
    testimonianza platonica". GCFI L 1971 452-467.

216* BEAMER E.M., The Socratic Image in Plato. Diss.
    Syracuse Univ. 1972 417p. [microfilm].
    Summary in DA XXXIII 1972 1193A.

217 ROSSETTI L., "Platone biografo di Socrate. Un
    riesame". Proteus IV 1973 63-101.

218* OGGIONI E., Socrate e Platone. Scienze filosofiche,
    Bologna, Patron 1963 137p.
    Rev. RPortFil XXI 1965 220-221 Morao.

(For further works on this subject see 161, 252, 326,
    1060, 1062, 1073, 1075, 1233, 1244, 1245, 1249,
    1251, 1252, 1349, 1478, 1479, 1677, 1931, 1951,
    1954, 2046, 2471, 2550, 2568, 2643, 2711, 2747,
    2761, 2771, 2798, 2806, 2828, 2943, 3104, 3401,
    3435, 3451, 3475, 3501, 3601, 3695, 3737, 3832,
    3833, 3923, 4271, 4275, 4279, 4305, 4406, 4458)

II C b: PLATO AND THE SOPHISTS

The following works are devoted to Plato's relation and
    reactions to the Sophistic movement and
    particular Sophists. Other sections relevant to
    this topic are IX C, V L, V A and those on
    various dialogues such as the Euthydemus,
    Protagoras, Gorgias, Hippias Minor, and Sophist.

219 ELTHEN P., "Les Sophistes et Platon". Arguments IV
    1960 n.20.

220 PIEPER J., "Der Verderb des Wortes und die Macht.
    Platons Kampf gegen die Sophistik". MDF III
    1964 22-38. Also appeared in Hochland LVII 1964
    12-25. Also in Spanish: "Corrupción en las

palabras y en el poder. La lucha de Platón
contra la sofística". FolHum V 1967 203-219.

221 SESONSKE A., "To Make the Weaker Argument defeat the
Stronger". JHPh VI 1968 217-231.

222 CASERTANO G., "Considerazioni introduttive ad uno
studio sui sofisti". Logos II 1971 183-226.

223 FLEISCHER M., "Manipulation und Freiheit. Platons
Auseinandersetzung mit der Sophistik". ZPhF
XXVII 1973 165-189.

For additional discussions see 161, 212, 326, 1054, 1932,
1947, 2058, 2062, 2125, 2173, 2226, 2416, 2623,
2673, 2743, 2780, 2784, 2854, 3149, 3199, 3435,
3643, 3651, 3737, 4154.

GORGIAS

224 HARRISON E.L., "Was Gorgias a Sophist?". Phoenix
XVIII 1964 183-192.

225 SCIACCA M.F., "Gorgia e Platone". p.277-296 in
Sciacca M.F., Platone I (see 64). Reprinted
from Sciacca M.F., Studi sulla filos. antica.
Napoli, Perrella 1935.

For additional discussions see 231, 2552, 4016.

HIPPIAS

226 KERFERD G.B., "Plato and Hippias". Summary in PCA
LX 1963 35-36.

227 CLASSEN C.J., "Bemerkungen zu zwei griechischen
Philosophiehistorikern". Philologus CIX 1965
175-181.

228 JOHANN H.T., "Hippias von Elis und der
Physis-Nomos-Gedanke". Phronesis XVIII 1973
15-25.

II C b: PLATO AND THE SOPHISTS

For additional discussion see 1319, 1960.

PROTAGORAS

229 GIANNANTONI G., "Il frammento 1 di Protagora in una nuova testimonianza platonica". RSF XV 1960 226-237.

230 HEINIMANN F., "Eine vorplatonische Theorie der τέχνη". MH XVIII 1961 105-130.

231 RAMNOUX C., "Nouvelle réhabilitation des sophistes". RMM LXXIII 1968 1-15.

232 DYE J.W., "Plato and Protagoras. Two Ideals of Culture". p.485-489 in Akten XIV. Intern. Kongr. Philos. Wien, 2.-9. September 1968. Vol. IV. Wien, Herder 1968.

233 HEITSCH E., "Ein Buchtitel des Protagoras". Hermes XCVII 1969 292-296.

234 KULLMANN W., "Zur Nachwirkung des homo-mensura-Satzes des Protagoras bei Demokrit und Epikur". AGPh LI 1969 128-144.

235 MORTLEY R.J., "Plato and the Sophistic Heritage of Protagoras". Eranos LXVII 1969 24-32.

236 KOCH H.A., "Protagoras bei Platon, Aristoteles und Sextus Empiricus". Hermes XCIX 1971 278-282.

237 ROSEMAN N., "Protagoras and the Foundations of his educational Thought". PaedHist XI 1971 75-89.

238 COLE A.T., "The Relativism of Protagoras". YClS XXII 1972 19-45.

For additional discussions see 1929, 1931, 1946, 1949, 1957, 1961, 1963, 2438, 2443, 2448, 2775

38

II C b: PLATO AND THE SOPHISTS
           SOPHISTIC WRITINGS

239 COLE A.T. Jr., "The Anonymus Iamblichi and his
     Place in Greek Political Theory". HSPh LXV 1961
     127-163.

240 SPRAGUE R.K., "A Platonic Parallel in the Dissoi
     Logoi". JHPh VI 1968 160-161.

           II C c: PLATO AND THE PRESOCRATICS

The following works are devoted to Plato's relation to the
     thinkers in the Presocratic traditions. They
     include not only discussions of Plato's
     testimonia about these figures and of their part
     in his philosophical development and his
     reactions to them, but also comparisons between
     his views and those of the Presocratics.

                        GENERAL

241 MONDOLFO R., "Sul valore storico delle testimonianze
     di Platone". Filosofia XV 1964 583-601.

242 CHIEREGHIN F., "Le metologia della storiografia
     filosofica di Platone nel Sofista". RAL XXIV
     1969 205-223.

243* PFLAUMER   R.,   Wissen   und   Warheit.   Zur
     Auseinandersetzung   Platons   mit   dem
     vorsokratischen Denken. Diss. Heidelberg 1959
     xiv&373p.

244 SCHAERER R., "Sur la continuité de l'homme antique".
     REG LXXIII 1960 15-26.

245 GADAMER H.G., "Platon und die Vorsokratiker".
     p.127-142 in Epimeleia. Festschrift für Helmut
     Kuhn. München, Pustet 1964. Reprinted p.14-26
     in Gadamer H.G., Kleine Schriften III (see
     4593).

246 PAISSE J.M., "Les rapports de Platon et de la
     philosophie presocratique". LEC XXXIV 1966
     321-339.

                          39

II C c: PLATO AND THE PRESOCRATICS

247* TACCONE GALLUCCI N., Le fonti misteriosofiche del
      pensiero platonico. Bari, Ciccolella [1966?]
      125p.

For additional discussions see 44, 212, 215, 461, 2805,
      2935, 3118, 3236, 3358, 3975.

ANAXAGORAS

248 FRITZ K. VON, "Der νοῦς des Anaxagoras". ABG IX
     1964 87-102.

249 LANZA D., "Anassagora μάλα φιλόσοφος ". Athenaeum
     XLII 1964 548-559.

250 KATO H., "Nous in Anaxagoras with special reference
     to Plato's Critique" [in Japanese]. Philosophy
     (Tokyo) XVI 1966.

251 MUGLER C., "Le κένον de Platon et le πάντα όμοῦ
     d'Anaxagore". REG LXXX 1967 210-219.

252 CARBONARA NADDEI M., "Il ricordo di Anassagora nel
     Fedone platonico". Sophia XL 1972 82-87.

For additional discussion see 1070.

ARCHYTAS

253 THESLEFF H., "Okkelos, Archytas and Plato". Eranos
     LX 1962 8-36.

254 CORDANO F., "Sui frammenti politici attribuiti ad
     Archita in Stobeo". PP XXVI 1971 290-300.

CRATYLUS

255 ESLICK L.J., "The two Cratyluses: the Problem of
     Identity of Indiscernibles". p.81-87 in Atti
     XII Congresso Internazionale di Filosofia.

Venezia, 12-18 settembre 1958. Vol. XI: Storia della Filosofia antica e medievale. Firenze, Sansoni 1960.

256 SCHADEWALDT W., "Platon und Kratylos. Ein Hinweis". p.3-11 in Philomathes. Studies and Essays in the Humanities in Memory of Philip Merlan, ed. by Palmer R.B. & Hamerton-Kelly R. Den Haag, Nijhoff 1971.

DAMON

For discussion of Damon see 3852.

DEMOCRITUS

257 LLEDO E., "Democrito, fr. 18". p.327-333 in Actas primer Congr. Espanol de Estud. classicos (Madrid 15-19 Abril 1956). Madrid 1958.

258 SAMBURSKY S., "A Democritean Metaphor in Plato's Kratylos". Phronesis IV 1959 1-4.

259 SOKOLOV L.P., "Bor'ba mezhdu Demokritom i Platonom po voprosy o kategoriiakh edinichnovo, osobennovo i vseobshchevo [The Battle between Democritus and Plato on the Question of Categorial Unities, particular and universal]" [in Russian]. UZ III 1959 56-124.

260 MARICKI K., "Platon i Demokrit" [in Serbo-Croatian with German summary]. Filozofija VII 1963 89-96.

261 BOLLACK J., "Un silence de Platon (Diogène Laërce IX,40 = Aristoxène fr.131 Wehrli)". RPh XLI 1967 242-246.

262 FERGUSON J., "Plato, Protagoras and Democritus". BR XV 1967 49-58.

263 MUGLER C., "Démocrite et les postulats cosmologiques du Démiurge". REA LXIX 1967 50-58.

II C c: PLATO AND THE PRESOCRATICS

264 FERWERDA R., "Democritus and Plato". Mnemosyne XXV 1972 337-378.

265 GIGON O., "Platon und Demokrit". MH XXIX 1972 153-166.

For additional discussions see 375, 1207, 2890, 3234, 3240, 3260, 3402, 3429.

EMPEDOCLES

266 BOOTH N.B., "Empedocles' Account of Breathing". JHS LXXX 1960 10-15.

267 O'BRIEN D., "The Effect of a Simile. Empedocles' Theories of Seeing and Breathing". JHS XC 1970 140-179.

268 SPRAGUE R.K., "Empedocles, Hera, and Cratylus 404c". CR XXII 1972 169.

For additional discussion see 3079.

HERACLITUS AND HERACLITEANS (Cf. CRATYLUS)

269 MONDOLFO R., "Evidence of Plato and Aristotle relating to the ekpyrosis in Heraclitus". Phronesis III 1958 75-82.

270 SICHIROLLO L., "Per una interpretazione della dossografia platonica. Eraclito in Platone". Pensiero IV 1959 313-327.

271 MONDOLFO R., "Testimonianze su Eraclito anteriori a Platone". RSF XVI 1961 399-424.

272 MONDOLFO R., "La testimonianza di Platone su Eraclito". DeHomine 1967 no.22-23 51-82.

273 LOGOTHETES K., "Ὁ Πλατωνικὸς Θεαίτητος καὶ οἱ Ἡρακλεύτειοι". Platon XXI 1969 3-25.

II C c: PLATO AND THE PRESOCRATICS

274 LOGOTHETES K.I., "Το πᾶν κίνησις ἦν". Platon XXIV
1972 332-334.

For additional discussions see 228, 703, 1695, 2435, 2438,
2725, 2832, 2833, 3019.

HIPPOCRATES AND THE HIPPOCRATIC SCHOOL

275 JOLY R., "La question hippocratique et le témoinage
du Phèdre". REG LXXIV 1961 69-92.

276 JOUANNA J., "La théorie de l'intelligence et de
l'âme dans le traité hippocratique Du régime.
Ses rapports avec Empédocle et le Timée du
Platon". Summary in REG LXXIX 1966 p.xv-xviii.

For additional discussions see 1831, 1841, 2763, 3182,
3387, 3389, 3394, 3401, 3405, 3412, 3414.

ORPHICS

For discussion of the Orphics see 1690, 1837.

PARMENIDES

277* BREUNINGER A., Parmenides und der frühe Platon.
Diss. Tübingen 1958 303p.
Rev. Gnomon XXXIII 1961 87-89 Kerferd.
Gymnasium LXIX 1962 109 Vretska.

278 FALUS R., "Parmenides-Interpretationen". AAntHung
VIII 1960 267-294.

279 GIGANTE M., "Velina gens". PP XIX 1964 135-137.

280 BICKNELL P.J., "Dating the Eleatics". p.1-14 in For
Service to Classical Studies. Essays in honor
of Francis Letters, ed. by Kelly M. Melbourne,
Cheshire 1966.

43

II C c: PLATO AND THE PRESOCRATICS

281 RIVIERE S., "The Path of Truth in Parmenides'
     Teaching and Plato's and Aristotle's Criticism
     of it". Iyyun XVIII 1967 169-182.

282* SUHR M., Platons Kritik an den Eleaten. Vorschläge
     zur Interpretation d. platonischen Dialogs
     Parmenides. Diss. Hamburg Univ. 1970 iv&147p.

283 DUBARLE D., "Le poème de Parménide, doctrine du
     savoir et premier état d'une doctrine de
     l'être". RSPh LVII 1973 3-34, 397-432.

For additional discussions see 1574, 1576, 1841, 2367,
        2383, 2391, 2392, 2515, 2726, 2749, 2775, 2832,
        2833, 2943, 3013, 3019, 3195, 3360, 4042, 4063.

PYTHAGORAS AND THE PYTHAGOREANS

284 DETIENNE M., "Sur la démonologie de l'ancien
     pythagorisme". RHR CLV 1959 17-32.

285 KUCHARSKI P., "Les principes des Pythagoriciens et
     la Dyade de Platon". ArchPhilos XXII 1959
     175-191, 385-431.

286* BURKERT W., Weisheit und Wissenschaft. Studien zu
     Pythagoras, Philolaos und Platon. Erlanger
     Beitr. zur Sprach- & Kunstwiss. X, Nürnberg,
     Carl 1962 xvi&496p.
          Rev. AC XXXII 1963 627-630 Janssens.
          RPh XXXVIII 1964 137 Louis.
          CR XIV 1964 28-29 Gulley.
          CW LVIII 1964 120 Minar.
          Mnemosyne XVII 1964 306-308 Wiersma.
          RecSR LII 1964 456 des Places.
          Isis LV 1964 459-461 von Fritz.
          Scholastik XXXIX 1964 253-256 Ennen.
          DLZ LXXXV 1964 390-391 Szabó.
          RFIC XCII 1964 102-117 Maddalena.
          Gnomon XXXVII 1965 344-354 Morrison.
          RF LVI 1965 219-221 Cambiano.
          AGM XLVIII 1964 367-369 Krafft.
          Mind LXXV 1966 293-295 Guthrie.
          Lychnos 1963-1964 327-331 Duering.
          PLA XVII 1964 245-249 Hennemann.
          Gymnasium LXXVII 1970 69-71 de Vogel.

44

287* FRANK E., Plato und die sogenannten Pythagoreer, Ein
Kapitel aus der Geschichte des griechischen
Geistes. Tübingen, Max Niemeyer 1962 xii&400p.
Reprint of 1923 edn.
Rev. PLZ XVII 1964 345-346 Niebergall.

288 NIEBEL E., "Platon, Aristoteles und der
pythagoreische Gedanke. Zu Oskar Beckers neuen
Werken [Grösse und Grenze der mathematischen
Denkweise and Die Aktualität des pythagoreischen
Gedankens]". KantStud LIII 1961-1962 100-106.

289 ILTING K.H., "Zur Philosophie der Pythagoreer". ABG
IX 1964 103-132.

290 NEBEL G., "Pythagoras". Antaios VII 1966 556-572.

291 WAERDEN B.L. VANDER, "Platon et les sciences
exactes des Pythagoriciens". BSMB XXI 1969
115-123.

292 JOLY R., "Platon ou Pythagore? Héraclide Pontique,
fr. 87-88 Wehrli". p.136-148 in Hommages à M.
Delcourt. Coll. Latomus CXIV, Bruxelles 1970.

293* BERNHARDT J., Platon et le matérialisme ancien. La
théorie de l'âme-harmonie dans la philosophie de
Platon. Bibl. scientif. Science de l'homme,
Paris, Payot 1971 244p.
Rev. RPhilos CLXII 1972 42-43 Trouillard.
EPh 1972 430-433 Lassègue.
BollFil VI 1972 17-18 Cavarero Porceddu.
RIPh XXVII 1973 541 Somville.

294 LAMPROPOULOU S., "Τὸ Πυθαγορικὸν στοιχεῖον παρὰ
Πλάτονι. Ἄμεσοι μαρτυρίαι" [in Greek with
English summary]. Platon XXIV 1972 275-289.

For additional discussions see 36, 223, 1431, 1690, 1837,
2631, 2883, 3002, 3079, 3180, 3206, 3299, 3308,
3314, 3326, 3332, 3356, 3363, 3430, 3529, 3935.

XENOPHANES

295 GUAZZONI FOA V., "Senofane e Parmenide in Platone".
GM XVI 1961 467-476.

II C c: PLATO AND THE PRESOCRATICS

296   EBNER P., "Senofane a Velia".   GM XIX 1964 797-812.

297   MONDOLFO R., "Platon y la interpretación de
      Jenófanes".   RevUNC V 1964 79-90.

298   STEINMETZ P., "Xenophanesstudien".   RhM CIX 1966
      13-73.

ZENO (Cf. PARMENIDES)

299   SOLMSEN F., "The Tradition about Zeno of Elea
      re-examined".   Phronesis XVI 1971 116-141.

For additional discussions see 2749, 2920, 2943.

II C d: PLATO AND OTHER GREEK LITERARY FIGURES

ALCMEON

For discussion of Alcmeon see 3383.

ANACREON

For discussion of Anacreon see 1842.

ANTIPHANES

300   CARLINI A., "Appunti di lettura".   Maia XXI 1969
      273-279.

II C d: PLATO AND OTHER GREEK LITERARY FIGURES

ARISTOPHANES

For discussions of Aristophanes see 1307, 2373, 2380, 3462.

EURIPIDES

301 VYSOKÝ Z.K., "The Antiope of Euripides" [in Czech with German summary]. LF XCI 1968 371-400.

302 CLAUS D., "Phaedra and the Socratic Paradox". YC1S XXII 1972 223-238.

For additional discussion see 3822.

HESIOD

303 SOLMSEN F., "Hesiodic Motifs in Plato". p.171-211 in Hésiode et son influence. Entretiens sur l'antiquité classique VII, Genève-Vandoeuvres, Fond. Hardt 1962.

304* MERENTITIS K.I., Ὁ Ἡσίοδος παρὰ Πλάτονι. Athens 1968 61p.
Rev. CJ LXVI 1970-1971 179-180 Rexine.
JHS XC 1970 202 Walcot.
Maia XXIV 1972 386-389 Valgiglio.

For additional discussions see 2121, 2383, 3645.

HOMER

305 KLEINKNECHT H., "Platonisches im Homer". Gymnasium LXV 1958 59-75.

306 HUXLEY G.L., "Homerica". GRBS III 1960 17-30.

307* LOHSE G., Untersuchungen über Homerzitate bei Platon. Diss. Hamburg 1960 148p.

308 BENARDETE S., "Some Misquotations of Homer in Plato". Phronesis XVIII 1963 173-178.

309 LOHSE G., "Untersuchungen über Homerzitate bei Platon". Helikon IV 1964 3-28, V 1965 248-295.

310 LOHSE G., "Untersuchungen über Homerzitate bei Platon". Helikon VII 1967 223-231.

311 KATO H., "Plato's View of Homer" [in Japanese]. Akita Univ. Bulletin XV 1965.

312 COLONNA A., "La tradizione del testo omerico in Origene". BPEC XVII 1969 61-65.

For additional discussions see 1847, 2173.

ISOCRATES

313* RIES K., Isokrates und Platon im Ringen um die Philosophia. Diss. München 1959 vii&175p.
Rev. Gnomon XXXIII 1961 349-354 Burkert.

314 COULTER J.A., "Phaedrus 279a. The Praise of Isocrates". GRBS VIII 1967 225-236.

315 ERBSE H., "Platons Urteil über Isokrates". Hermes XCIX 1971 183-197.

316 VRIES G.J. DE, "Isocrates in the Phaedrus. A Reply". Mnemosyne XXIV 1971 387-390.

For additional discussions see 1481, 1853.

MUSAEUS

317 GELZER T., "Bemerkungen zu Sprache und Text des Epikers Musaios". MH XXV 1968 11-47.

II C d: PLATO AND OTHER GREEK LITERARY FIGURES

PINDAR

318 ALDERISIO F., "Il nomos di Pindaro nel Gorghias e
nei Nomoi di Platone". RSFil XIII 1960 22-46,
123-148.

For additional discussions see 1160, 3029, 3873.

SAPPHO

For discussion of Sappho see 2373.

SIMONIDES

319 GENTILI B., "Studi su Simonide". Maia XVI 1964
278-306.

320 PARRY H., "An Interpretation of Simonides 4
(Diehl)". TAPhA XCVI 1965 297-320.

For additional discussion see 1929, 1954.

SOLON

321 OLIVA P., "Solon im Wandel der Jahrhunderte".
Eirene XI 1973 31-65.

SOPHOCLES

322 GOULD T., "The Innocence of Oedipus. The
Philosophers on Oedipus the King". Arion IV
1965 363-386, 582-611; V 1966 478-525.

II C d: PLATO AND OTHER GREEK LITERARY FIGURES

323   FUNKE H., "Κρέων ἄπολις". A&A XII 1966 29-50.

SOPHRON

For discussion of Sophron see 2665.

THEOGNIS

324   CARAMELLA S., "Il sigillo di Teognide".   Orpheus   VI
         1959 139-147.

THUCYDIDES

325   MacDONALD C., "Plato, Laws 704a-707c and   Thucydides
         II,35-46".   CR IX 1959 108-109.

XENOPHON

For discussion of Xenophon see 3695.

GENERAL

For discussion of Plato and the Poets see 3814.

GENERAL

326* FIELD G.C., <u>Plato and his Contemporaries.</u> <u>A Study</u>
<u>in fourth-century Life and Thought.</u> 3rd edn.
London, Methuen 1967 xii&242p. (Reprint of 1930
edn. with brief preface.)
Rev. Helmantica XX 1969 164-165 Ortall.
Thomist 1968 277-278 Taylor.
RM XXIII 1969-1970 129 E.A.R.

327 KAYSER J.R. & MOORS K.F., "Ten in the Piraeus.
Neglected Recipients of Socratic Education".
Cithara XII,2 1972 23-32.

AESCHINES OF SPHETTUS

For discussion of Aeschines of Sphettus see 1097.

ALCIBIADES

328 MORI S., "Alcibiades" [in Japanese with English
summary]. JCS IX 1961 34-52.

ARISTIDES

329 CALABI LIMENTANI I., "Aristide il Giusto. Fortuno
di un nome". RIL XCIV 1960 43-67.

II C e: PLATO AND OTHER FIGURES

CALLISTRATUS

For discussion of Callistratus see 1458.

HERODICUS OF SELYMBRIA

330   MOUKANIS D.D., "Ἡρόδικος ὁ Σηλυμβριανὸς ἐν ἀρχαίᾳ
      ἑλληνικῇ γραμματείᾳ". Thrakika XLIV 1970 15-19.

LYCURGUS

331   RENEHAN R., "The Platonism of Lycurgus".   GRBS   XI
      1970 219-231.

MENO

332   ROUSSOS E.N., "Μένων, ὁ μαθητὴς τοῦ Γοργία" [with
      German summary].   Philosophia(Athens)   I   1971
      227-251.

PHAEDO

333   ROSSETTI L., "Socratica in Fedone   di   Elide".
      StudUrb XLVII 1973 364-381.

PITTACUS

For discussion of Pittacus see 3427.

52

II C e: PLATO AND OTHER FIGURES

THEODORUS OF CYRENE

For discussion of Theodorus see 3335.

II D: PLATO AND THE ACADEMY

In addition to a number of works in sections I A and I B
which treat Plato and the Academy, the reader
should also consult section V N on Plato's
"Unwritten Doctrines".

334 LESKY A., "Platon und die Akademie". p.477-508 in
Lesky A., Geschichte der griechischen Literatur:
Bern, 1958.

335 SCHUHL P.M., "Une ecole des sciences politiques".
RPhilos CXLIX 1959 101-103.

336 WIKARJAK J., "Akademia i Lykeion". Filomata(Krakow)
1959 No.133 171-179.

337 FRIEDLAENDER P., "Akademische Randglossen". p.317
in Die Gegenwart der Griechen im neueren Denken.
Festschrift für H.G. Gadamer zum 60.
Geburtstag. Tübingen, Mohr 1960. Reprinted
p.212 in Friedlaender P., Studien zur antiken
Literatur und Kunst (see 4589).

338 DAMBSKA I., "Under the Protection of the Muses" [in
Polish]. Filomata 1961 no.150 23-29.

339* CHERNISS H.F., The Riddle of the Early Academy. New
York, Russell & Russell 1962 103p. Reprint of
1945 edn. Also in German: Die ältere Akademie.
Ein historisches Rätsel und seine Lösung, übers.
von Derbolav J. Bibl. der klass.
Altertumswiss. N.F. 2. Reihe, Heidelberg,
Winter 1966 128p.
        Rev. [of German edn.] Gymnasium LXXIV
1967 362-364 Mansfeld.
        AC XXXVI 1967 320 Joly.
        Th&Ph XLII 1967 113-114 Ennen.
        REA LXXI 1969 144-145 Brunschwig.

Also an excerpt "Speusippos, Xenokrates und die polemische Methode des Aristoteles". p.3-40 in Das Problem der ungeschriebenen Lehre Platons, hrsg. von Wippern J. (see 4626).

340 RYLE G., "Dialectic in the Academy". p.39-68 in New Essays on Plato and Aristotle, ed. by Bambrough R. (see 4582). Reprinted as "The Academy and Dialectic", p.89-115 in Ryle G., Collected Papers, I: Critical Essays. London, Hutchinson & New York, Barnes & Noble 1971.

341 CHROUST A.H., "Plato's Academy; the first Organized School of Political Science in Antiquity". RevPol XXIX 1967 25-40.

342* DOENT E., Platons Spätphilosophie und die Akademie. Untersuchungen zu den platonischen Briefen, zu Platons 'ungeschriebenen Lehre' und zur Epinomis des Philipp von Opus. SAWW CCLI,3, Wien, Boehlau 1967 84p.
Rev. Gnomon XL 1968 329-333 Hager.
AAHG XXI 1968 221-225 Kraemer.
CW LXIV 1971 159 Long.

343 ISNARDI PARENTE M., "Per l'interpretazione della dottrina delle idee nella prima Accademia platonica". AIIS I 1967-1968 9-33.

344 KAPP E., "Platon und die Akademie". p.151-166 in Kapp E., Ausgewählte Schriften (see 4606). Reprinted from Mnemosyne III 1936 227-246.

345 RYLE G., "Dialectic in the Academy". p.69-79 in Aristotle on Dialectic. The Topics, ed. by Owen G.E.L. (see 4611). Reprinted p.116-125 in Ryle G., Collected Papers, I: Critical Essays. London, Hutchinson & New York, Barnes & Noble 1971.

346 SAFFREY H.D., "Ἀγεωμέτρητος μηδεὶς εἰσίτω. Une inscription légendaire". REG LXXXI 1968 67-87.

347 BRUN J., "L'Académie". p.608-619 in Histoire de la Philosophie, I, sous la direction de Parain B. Encyclopedie de la Pleiade XXVI, Paris, Gallimard 1969.

348 ISNARDI PARENTE M., "L'Accademia e le lettere platoniche". p.9-45 in Isnardi Parente M., Filosofia e politica nelle lettere di platone (see 4624). Reprinted from PP XLIII 1955.

349 CHROUST A.H., "Speusippus Succeeds Plato in the
     Scholarchate of the Academy". REG LXXXIV 1971
     338-341.

350* STACHOWIAK H., Rationalismus im Ursprung. Die
     Genesis des axiomatischen Denkens. Libr. of
     Exact Philos. IV, Wien, Springer 1971 xvi&348p.
     (ch.4 "Die Ausbildung der deduktiven Methode in
     der Schule Platons", p.44-120.)
         Rev. Mind LXXXII 1973 292-293 Barnes.
         ModS L 1972-1973 245-246 Rice.

351 BRINGMANN K., "Platons Philebos und Herakleides
     Pontikos' Dialog Περὶ ἡδονῆς". Hermes C 1972
     523-530.

352 TANAKA H., "On Plato's Academy" [in Japanese].
     Kokoro 1972.

For further discussion of the Academy see 165, 286, 340,
     376, 397, 413, 1104, 1120, 1206, 1208, 1406,
     1507, 1590, 1911, 2359, 2459, 2856, 2905, 3086,
     3318, 3387, 3429, 3532, 3670, 4063, 4065, 4067,
     4069, 4073, 4077, 4081, 4555, 4564.

EUDOXUS

For discussion of Eudoxus see 1590, 3306.

THEAETETUS

353 HELLER S., "Theaetets Bedeutung als Mathematiker".
     AGM LI 1967 54-78.

For additional discussion of Theaetetus see 2284, 3289,
     3316, 3324.

II E: INFLUENCE OF PLATO'S BACKGROUND ON HIS THOUGHT

The number of works on Plato containing discussions of his
    cultural background was large enough to warrant
    a list of cross references. It is restricted to
    those dealing primarily with this aspect of his
    thought, since an exhaustive index would include
    too many items to be usefully selective. For
    other studies relevant to this area see in
    particular sections II A and II C.

For works on this subject see 450, 1209, 1210, 1354, 1379,
    1468, 1508, 1819, 1824, 1957, 2634, 2985, 3040,
    3079, 3083, 3220, 3251, 3252, 3272, 3432, 3545,
    3559, 3610, 3611, 3638, 3751, 3762, 3923, 3933,
    3965, 4486.

II F: PLATO AND ARISTOTLE

354 COSENZA P., "Aristotele e la dottrina della
    partecipazione secondo il Sofista platonico".
    AASNap LXIX 1958, 40p.

355 TURNBULL R.G., "Aristotle's Debt to the natural
    Philosophy of the Phaedo". PhilosQ VIII 1958
    131-143.

356 EGERMANN F., "Platonische Spätphilosophie und
    Platonismen bei Aristoteles". Hermes LXXXVII
    1959 133-142.

357 MOREAU J., "L'éloge de la biologie chez Aristote".
    REA LXI 1959 57-64.

358 ALLAN D.J., "Aristotle and the Parmenides".
    p.133-144 in Aristotle and Plato in the
    mid-fourth century, (see 4586).

359* CELARIER J.LeR., Aristotle's Physica and Plato's
    Parmenides. Diss. Univ. of Pennsylvania 1960
    211p. [microfilm]. Summary in DA XXI 1960
    924-925.

360 JAEGER W., Rev. of Werner C., Aristote et l'idéalisme platonicien. p.39-40 in Jaeger, W., Scripta Minora I (see 4605). Reprinted from DLZ 1911 Sp. 2961-2963.

361 JAEGER W., "Aristotle's Verses in Praise of Plato". p.339-345 in Jaeger W., Scripta Minora I (see 4605). reprinted from CQ XXI 1927 13-17.

362 MORROW G.R., "Aristotle's Comments on Plato's Laws". p.145-162 in Aristotle and Plato in the mid-fourth Century (see 4586).

363 SOLMSEN F., "Platonic Influences in the Formation of Aristotle's Physical System". p.213-235 in Aristotle and Plato in the mid-fourth Century (see 4586).

364 VOGEL C.J. DE, "The Legend of the Platonizing Aristotle". p.248-256 in Aristotle and Plato in the mid-fourth Century (see 4586).

365 DUERING I., "Aristotle's Method in Biology. A Note on De Part. An. I,2 639b30-640a2". p.213-221 in Aristote et les Problèmes de méthode. Communications présentées au Symposium Aristotelicum tenu à Louvain du 24 aout au 1 septembre 1960. Aristote, Trad. & Études Coll. publ. par l'Inst. sup. de Phlos. de Louvain, Paris, Nauwelaerts 1961.

366 HAMLYN D.W., "Aristotle on Predication". Phronesis VI 1961 110-126.

367 KEYT D., "Aristotle on Plato's Receptacle". AJPh LXXXII 1961 291-300.

368 OWEN G.E.L., "Τιθέναι τὰ φαινόμενα ". p.84-103 in Aristote et les problèmes de méthode. Communications présentées au Symposium Aristotelicum tenu à Louvain du 24 aout au 1 sept. 1960. Louvain, Publ. Univ. de Louvain & Paris, Béatrice-Nauwelaerts 1961. Reprinted p.167-190 in Aristotle. A Collection of Critical Essays, ed. by Moravcsik J.M.E. Modern Studies in Philosophy, Garden City, N.Y., Doubleday Anchor 1967.

369 ROSEN S.H., "Thought and Touch. A Note on Aristotle's De anima". Phronesis VI 1961 127-137.

II F: PLATO AND ARISTOTLE

370 BERGER H.H., "Aristoteles' formulering van het voorwerp van de metafysiek". TPh XXIV 1962 215-241.

371* CHERNISS H.F., Aristotle's Criticism of Plato and the Academy. New York, Russell & Russell 1962 xxvi&610p. Reprint of 1944 edn.

372 CROMBIE I.M., "An Exegetical Point in Aristotle's Nicomachean Ethics". Mind LXXI 1962 539-540.

373 GOLDEN L., "Catharsis". TAPhA XCIII 1962 51-60.

374 MATSUNAGA Y., "Phaedo 102b3 ff., an Aspect of Plato's Formula 'The one and the Many' with special Reference to 'the Substance and the Attribute' in Aristotle" [in Japanese with English summary]. JCS X 1962 73-87.

375 FEIBLEMAN J.K., "Plato versus the Atomists in Aristotle". Sophia XXXI 1963 68-75.

376 GIGANTE M., "Poesia e critica letteraria nell'Accademia antica". p.234-248 in Miscellanea di studi alessandrini in memoria di A. Rostagni. Torino, Bottega d'Erasmo 1963.

377 JACQUES A., "Acerca de la doctrina platónica de las ideas de acuerdo con el testimonio de Aristóteles y de lo que éste le censura" con un estudio preliminar sobre "Amadeo Jacques (1813-1865) y su tesis latina leída en la Sorbona en 1837", por Roig A.A. REC VIII 1963 7-54.

378 SICHIROLLO L., "Giustificazioni della dialettica in Aristotele (ontologia, storia, politica)". StudUrb XXXVII 1963 65-114, 279-313.

379 SODANO A.R., "Una polemica di Aristotele sulla concezione platonica della materia". RSF XVIII 1963 77-88.

380 ALLAN D.J., "Aristotle's Criticism of Platonic Doctrine concerning Goodness and the Good". PAS LXIV 1963-1964 273-286.

381 BAERTHLEIN K., "Der ὀρθὸς λόγος und das ethische Grundprinzip in den Platonischen Schriften". AGPh XLVI 1964 129-173.

382 CHEN C.H., "From Plato's Receptacle to Aristotle's Matter". p.269-276 in XIII Congreso Internacional de Filosofía. México, D.F., 7-14 de Setiembre de 1963. Comunicaciones Libres, sección XI: Historia de la Filosofía: Vol. IX. Mexico City, Univ. Nac. Aut. de Mexico 1964.

383 CHROUST A.H., "Brevia Aristotelica". ModS XLI 1964 165-167.

384 CHROUST A.H., "Aristotle's earliest 'Course of Lectures on Rhetoric'". AC XXXIII 1964 58-72.

385 CLARK M., "Platonic Justice in Aristotle and Augustine". DownsR LXXXII 1964 25-35.

386 DUERING I., "Aristotle and the Heritage from Plato". Eranos LXII 1964 84-99.

387 GANTAR K., "Wohin deuten die Σωκρατικοί λόγοι in Aristoteles Poetik 1447b11?" Hermes XCII 1964 125-128.

388 KAWADA S., "Aristotle's Interpretation of Plato in his early Works" [in Japanese]. PhSJap no.491 1964.

389 LYKOS K., "Aristotle and Plato on 'Appearing'". Mind LXXIII 1964 496-514.

390 CHROUST A.H., "Aristotle's first literary Effort. The Gryllus, a lost Dialogue on the Nature of Rhetoric". REG LXXVIII 1965 576-591.

391* ELDERS L., Aristotle's Cosmology. A Commentary on the De Caelo. Assen, Van Gorcum 1965 370p.

392 FLASHAR H., "Die Kritik der platonischen Ideenlehre in der Ethik des Aristoteles". p.223-246 in Synusia. Festgabe für Wolfgang Schadewaldt zum 15. Marz 1965, hrsg. von Flashar H. & Gaiser K. Pfullingen, Neske 1965.

393* GEORGIUS TRAPEZUNTIUS, Comparatio phylosophorum Aristotelis et Platonis. Unveränd. Nachdr. d. Ausg. Venetiis 1528. Frankfurt a.M., Minerva-Verl. 1965 169p.

394 ILTING K.H., "Aristoteles über Platons philosophische Entwicklung". ZPhF XIX 1965 377-392.

II F: PLATO AND ARISTOTLE

395 LACEY A.R., "The Eleatics and Aristotle on some
    Problems of Change". JHI XXVI 1965 451-468.

396 NADOR G., "Ueber die Bedeutung der Aristotelischen
    Aesthetik". Altertum XI 1965 143-151.

397 OWEN G.E.L., "The Platonism of Aristotle". PBA LI
    1965 125-150. Reprinted in Studies in the
    Philosophy of Thought and Action. British
    Academy Lectures, sel. & intro. by Strawson
    P.F. Oxford Paperbacks CLV, London, Oxford
    Univ. Pr. 1968; also reprinted as monograph
    The Platonism of Aristotle (British Academy:
    Dawes Hicks Lecture in Philosophy, 1965).
    London, Oxford Univ. Pr. 1965 26p.
    Rev. CR 1968 40-41 Hamlyn.

398 OWEN G.E.L., "A Proof in the Peri Ideon". p.293-312
    in Studies in Plato's Metaphysics, ed. by Allen
    R.E. (see 4580). Reprinted from JHS 1957.

399* PATER W.A. DE, Les Topiques d'Aristote et la
    dialectique platonicienne. La méthodologie de
    la définition. Études thomistes X, Fribourg
    (Suisse), Editions St. Paul 1965 xiv&257p.
    Rev. RSF 1968 243-244 Isnardi Parente.
    PLA 1968 89-91 Lumpe.

400 REICHE H.A.T., "Aristotle on Breathing in the
    Timaeus". AJPh LXXXVI 1965 404-408. Correction
    AJPh LXXXVII 1966 17.

401 RYLE G., "The Timaeus Locrus". Phronesis X 1965
    174-190. Reprinted p.1-17 in The Progress of
    Plato's Progress (see 4590).

402 VOGEL C.J. DE, "Did Aristotle ever accept Plato's
    Theory of Transcendent Ideas? Problems around a
    new Edition of the Protrepticus". AGPh XLVII
    1965 261-298.

403 DUERING I., "Did Aristotle ever accept Plato's
    Theory of Transcendent Ideas?" AGPh XLVIII 1966
    312-316.

404 BLANCHE L., "Les anciens et le mouvement terrestre
    du Timée". REPh XVI 1965-1966 No. 2 1-8.

405 CHROUST A.H., "The Psychology in Aristotle's Lost
    Dialogue Eudemus or On the Soul". AClass IX
    1966 49-62.

406 CHROUST A.H., "Eudemus or On the Soul. A Lost
     Dialogue of Aristotle on the Immortality of the
     Soul". Mnemosyne XIX 1966 17-30.

407 DEWEY E.W., "Aristotle's Aesthetics. A Fulfilment
     of the Platonic Position". Darshana VI 1966
     75-84.

408 DOVATUR A.I., "Plato on Aristotle" [in Russian].
     p.137-144 in Problems of ancient Literature and
     Philology. Moscow 1966.

409 GAISER K., "Die Elegie des Aristoteles an Eudemos".
     MH XXIII 1966 84-106.

410 MERLAN P., "Zum Problem der drei Lebensarten". PhJ
     LXXIV 1966 217-219.

411 THEILER W., "Plato und Eudem". MH XXIII 1966
     192-193.

412 CHROUST A.H., "Aristotle leaves the Academy". G&R
     XIV 1967 39-43.

413* FRAGSTEIN A., VON, Die Diairesis bei Aristoteles.
     Amsterdam, Hakkert 1967 197p.

414 HUBY P.M., "De anima 404b17-27". Apeiron I,2 1967
     14-15.

415 KRAEMER H.J., "Zur geschichtlichen Stelling der
     aristotelischen Metaphysik". KantStud LVIII
     1967 313-354.

416 MERLAN P., "Tò ἀπορῆσαι ἀρχαϊκῶς (Arist. Met. N2,
     1089a1)". Philologus CXI 1967 119-121.

417 MURAJI Y., "Plato and Aristotle" [in Japanese].
     Riso no.409 1967.

418 SALVIAT F., "Aristote et les divisions
     platoniciennes (De Generatione et Corruptione
     II, 330b13-19)". AFLA XLIII 1967 65-84.

419 CHROUST A.H., "Aristotle's Criticism of Plato's
     Philosopher King". RhM CXI 1968 16-22.

420 ELDERS L., "The Topics and the Platonic Theory of
     Principles of Being". p.126-137 in Aristotle on
     Dialectic. The Topics, ed. by Owen, G.E.L.
     (see 4611).

II F: PLATO AND ARISTOTLE

421 GADAMER H.G., "Amicus Plato magis Amica Veritas".
     p.249-268 in Gadamer H.G., Platos dialektische
     Ethik und andere Studien (see 4592).

422 ISNARDI PARENTE M., "A proposito di καθ' αὐτό e
     δυνάμει in Aristotele Phys. A8-9,
     191a23-192a34". RFIC XCVI 1968 129-148.

423 KELLY M.J., "Aristotle as Sophist". JThought III
     1968 253-257.

424 MATTHEWS G.B. & COHEN S.M., "The One and the Many".
     RM XXI 1968 630-655.

425 MERLAN P., "Zwei Bemerkungen zum Aristotelischen
     Plato". RhM CXI 1968 1-15.

426 MOREAU P., "Aristote et la dialectique
     platonicienne". p.80-90 in Aristotle on
     Dialectic. The Topics, ed. by Owen G.E.L.
     (see 4611).

427 OWEN G.E.L., "Dialectic and Eristic in the Treatment
     of the Forms". p.103-125 in Aristotle on
     Dialectic. The Topics, ed. by Owen G.E.L.
     (see 4611).

428* PRANTL C. VON, Über die Entwicklung der
     aristotelischen Logik aus der platonischen
     Philosophie. 2. unveränd. Aufl. Reprograf.
     Nachdr. d. Ausg. 1853. Darmstadt,
     Wissenschaftliche Buchges. 1968 81p.

429 PRAUSS G., "Ding und Eigenschaft bei Platon und
     Aristoteles". KantStud LIX 1968 98-117.

430 SILLITTI G., "Il non ente fra Platone e Aristotele".
     Cultura VI 1968 474-488.

431 SOLMSEN F., "Dialectic without the Forms". p.49-68
     in Aristotle on Dialectic. The Topics, ed. by
     Owen G.E.L. (see 4611).

432 SOLMSEN F., "Aristotle's Syllogism and its Platonic
     Background". p.29-37 in Solmsen F., Kleine
     Schriften II (see 4615). Reprinted from PhR LX
     1951 563-571.

433 STRYCKER E. DE, "Concepts-clés et terminologie dans
     les livres II à VII des Topiques". p.141-163 in
     Aristotle on Dialectic. The Topics, ed. by
     Owen G.E.L. (see 4611).

434 VOGEL C.J. DE, "Aristotle's Attitude to Plato and the Theory of Ideas according to the Topics". p.91-102 in Aristotle on Dialectic. The Topics, ed. by Owen G.E.L. (see 4611).

435 GIGON O., "Zwei Interpretationen zur Eudemischen Ethik". MH XXVI 1969 204-216.

436 ZELLER E., "Die Darstellung der Platonischen Philosophie bei Aristoteles". p.197-300 in Zeller E., Platonische Studien (see 4627).

437 FORTENBAUGH W.W., "On the Antecedents of Aristotle's Bipartite Psychology". GRBS XI 1970 233-250.

438 FORTENBAUGH W.W., "Aristotle's Rhetoric on Emotions". AGPh LII 1970 40-70.

439 FLASHAR H., "Ethik und Politik in der Philosophie des Aristoteles". Gymnasium LXXVIII 1971 278-293.

440 GOTTSCHALK H.B., "Soul as harmonia". Phronesis XVI 1971 179-198.

441* HAPP H., Hyle. Studien zum aristotelischen Materie-Begriff. Berlin, de Gruyter 1971 xv&953p. (p.82-256 on views of matter in Plato and the early Academy.)
Rev. RM XXV 1971-1972 753-754 Sokolowski.
Gregorianum LIII 1972 368-370 Selvaggi.
Angelicum XLIX 1972 280-287 Vansteenkiste.
PhJ LXXIX 1972 415-419 Seidl.
AC XLI 1972 667-668 Byl.
ArchPhilos XXXVI 1973 159-163 Solignac.
DT LXXVI 1973 200-204 Elders.

442 LANZA D., "La critica aristotelica a Platone e i due piani della Politica". Athenaeum XLIX 1971 355-392.

443 MOSS L., "Plato and the Poetics". PhQ L 1971 533-542.

444 REES D.A., "Aristotle's Treatment of φαντασία". p.491-504 in Essays in ancient Greek Philosophy, ed. by Anton J.P. & Kustas G.L. (see 4581).

445* SAFFREY H.D., Le Περὶ φιλοσοφίας d'Aristote et la théorie platonicienne des idées nombres. 2e ed. rev. et accompagnée du compte rendu critique par Cherniss H. Philosophia Antiqua VII,

II F: PLATO AND ARISTOTLE

Leiden, Brill 1971 xiii&93p.
Rev. TPh XXXIV 1972 570-573 van Straaten.

446* SAMARAS C., Die demokratische Theorie bei Aristoteles mit Rücksicht auf Platons Lehre vom Staat. Diss. Salzburg 1971 136p.

447 SCHANKULA H.A.S., "Plato and Aristotle, εὐδαιμονία, ἕξις or ἐνέργεια?". CPh LXVI 1971 244-246.

448 SOLMSEN F., "Plato's First Mover in the eighth book of Aristotle's Physics". p.171-182 in Philomathes. Studies and Essays in the Humanities in Memory of Philip Merlan, ed. by Palmer R.B. & Hamerton-Kelly R. Den Haag, Nijhoff 1971.

449 VERBEKE G., "La critique des Idées dans l'Éthique eudémienne". p.135-156 in Untersuchungen zur Eudemischen Ethik. Akten des 5. Symposium Aristotelicum (Oosterbeck, Niederlande, 21.-29. August 1969), hrsg. von Moraux P. & Harlfinger D. Peripatoi. Philologisch-historische Studien zum Aristotelismus, Bd.I, Berlin, de Gruyter 1971.

450 VIVES J., "La filosofia en el siglo IV". BIEH IV-V 1970-1971 143-153.

451 WHITE N.P., "Aristotle on Sameness and Oneness". PhR LXXX 1971 177-197.

452 ANTON J.P., "On Aristotle's Principle of Contradction. Its ontological Foundations and Platonic Antecedents" [in English with Greek summary]. Philosophia(Athens) II 1972 266-283.

453 BEGEMANN A.W., "Aristote EN 1096a24-28". Mnemosyne XXV 1972 188-189.

454 BYL S., "Un témoinage de Pline l'Ancien sur Aristote?". LM 1972 No.33-35 13-17.

455 JELNICKIJ L.A., "The Role of Slaves and Freedmen in certain types of Greek state Administration in the V & IV Centuries B.C." [in Russian with English summary]. VDI 1972 No.122 100-106.

456 KRAEMER H.J., "Das Verhältnis von Platon und Aristoteles in neuer Sicht". ZPhF XXVI 1972 329-353.

II F: PLATO AND ARISTOTLE

457* O'LEARY J.F., Aristotle's Poetics read as a Reply to
the Platonic Indictment of Poetry. Diss.
Syracuse Univ. 1971 198p. [microfilm].
Summary in DA XXXII 1972 4662A.

458 SPRAGUE R.K., "A parallel with De anima III,5".
Phronesis XVII 1972 250-251.

459* TACK E., Die sogenannten Platonzeugnisse bei
Aristoteles. Diss. Kiel Univ. 1972 425p.

460 BARREAU H., "Le traité aristotelicien du temps,
Physique IV,10-14, 217b29-224a17". RPhilos
CLXIII 1973 401-437.

461 BOLLACK J., "Vom System der Geschichte zur
Geschichte der Systeme". p.11-28 in Geschichte,
Ereignis und Erzählung, hrsg. von Koselleck R.
& Stempel W.D. Poetik und Hermeneutik V,
München, Fink 1973.

462 CHROUST A.H., "Aristotle's alleged 'Revolt' against
Plato". JHPh XI 1973 91-94.

463 FUJISAWA N., "Aristotle's Conception of Philosophy
in the Protrepticus. Comparison with Isocrates,
Plato and Aristotle himself in his later
Treatises" [in Japanese with English summary].
JCS XXI 1973 1-19.

464 HANUS J.G., "Friendship in Aristotelian Ethics". MS
L 1973 351-365.

465 KRAEMER H.J., "Aristoteles und die akademische
Eidoslehre. Zur Geschichte der
Universalienproblems im Platonismus". AGPh LV
1973 119-190.

466 LESZL W., "Alcune osservazioni sulla critica
aristotelica ai Platonici in Met. N2". RFIC CI
1973 70-87.

467 MANSION S., "Deux définitions différentes de la vie
chez Aristote?". RPhL LXXI 1973 425-450.

468 SPRAGUE R.K., "An Anonymous Argument against
Mixture". Mnemosyne XXVI 1973 230-233.

469 SUÁREZ DE LA TORRE E., "El sueño y la fenomenología
onírica en Aristóteles". CFC V 1973 279-311.

65

II F: PLATO AND ARISTOTLE

470 VLASTOS G., "The 'two-level' Paradoxes in
    Aristotle". p.323-334 in Vlastos G., Platonic
    Studies (see 4622).

For further works dealing with Plato and Aristotle see
        165, 251, 288, 322, 389, 628, 688, 785, 1319,
        1370, 1506, 1564, 1616, 2283, 2359, 2472, 2498,
        2706, 2743, 2747, 2751, 2755, 2761, 2770,
        2776, 2784, 2787, 2794, 2856, 2868, 2879, 2883,
        2890, 2891, 2895, 2905, 2908, 2912, 2916, 2917,
        2919, 2931, 2935, 2945, 2971, 2978, 2997, 3009,
        3011, 3012, 3021, 3022, 3044, 3046, 3048, 3049,
        3054, 3055, 3060, 3085, 3096, 3122, 3142, 3148,
        3163, 3165, 3170, 3185, 3195, 3228, 3234, 3245,
        3247, 3261, 3279, 3283, 3299, 3356, 3402, 3412,
        3413, 3433, 3464, 3475, 3476, 3480, 3482, 3484,
        3506, 3533, 3544, 3718, 3741, 3774, 3832, 3835,
        3840, 3846, 3864, 3885, 3898, 3959, 3960, 3978,
        4009, 4040, 4063, 4068, 4094.

II G: PLATO AND LATER FIGURES AND SCHOOLS OF ANCIENT PHILOSOPHY

ARISTOXENUS

471 KUCHARSKI P., "Le Philèbe et les Éléments
    harmoniques d'Aristoxène". RPhilos CXLIX 1959
    41-72.

For additional discussion see 4078, 4086.

THE CYNICS

472* FERNÁNDEZ-GALIANO M., De Platón a Diógenes.   Cuad.
     de la Fundación Pastor VIII, Madrid, Taurus 1964
     77p.
              Rev. Arbor LXIII 1966 507-508 Blázquez.

473 NAKHOV I.M., "The Cynics versus Plato (in the
    Context of the History of the Conflict between
    Materialism and Idealism in Antiquity)" [in
    Russian]. VKF I 1965 97-139.

474 NAKHOV I.M., "The Cynics' Conception of Work" [in Russian with German summary]. p.43-49 in Die Krise der griechischen Polis. Görlitzer Eirene-Tagung 10.-14.10.1967, I, hrsg. von Jurewicz O. & Kuch H. Dt. Akad.-Verl. 1969.

475 FESTUGIÈRE A.J., "Antisthenica". p.283-314 in Festugière A.J., Études de philosophie grecque (see 4587). Reprinted from RSPh 1932 345-375.

476 NICKEL R., "Das Verhältnis von Bedürfnis und Brauchbarkeit in seiner Bedeutung für das kynostoische Ideal der Bedürfnislosigkeit". Hermes C 1972 42-47.

For additional discussion see 2464.

THE EPICUREANS

477 CHILTON C.W., "The Epicurean Theory of the Origin of Language. A Study of Diogenes of Oenoanda, fragments X and XI William". AJPh LXXXIII 1962 159-167.

For additional discussion see 520, 3265.

EUCLID

For discussion of Euclid see 3279.

GALEN

478 BALLESTER L.G., "La utilisación de Platón y Aristóteles en los escritos tardios de Galeno". Episteme(Caracas) V 1971 112-120.

For additional discussion see 3263.

JUSTIN

479 VOGEL C.J. DE, "Plato in de latere en late oudheid,
     bij heidenen en christenen". Lampas VI 1973
     230-254.

THE MEGARIANS

480 KAMIOKA H., "The Megarian School and Plato" [in
     Japanese]. Proceedings of the Dept. of
     Humanities (Tokyo Metropolitan Univ.) XCIV 1973.
For additional discussion see 2227.

PHILO

481 THEILER W., "Philo von Alexandria und der
     hellenisierte Timaeus". p.25-35 in Philomathes.
     Studies and Essays in the Humanities in Memory
     of Philip Merlan, ed. by Palmer R.B. &
     Hamerton-Kelly R. Den Haag, Nijhoff 1971.

482 SCHWARZ W., "A study in Pre-Christian Symbolism:
     Philo de Somniis I.216-218, & Plutarch De Iside
     et Osiride 4 and 77". BICS no.20 1973 104-117.

THE PLATONIC TRADITION INCLUDING PLOTINUS

483 STAMATIS E.S., "Περὶ τῆς θεωρίας τῶν συνόλων παρὰ
     Πλάτωνι". PAA XXXIII 1958 298-303.

484 VOGEL C.J. DE, "La théorie de l'ἄπειρον chez Platon
     et dans la tradition platonicienne". RPhilos
     CXLIX 1959 21-39, Reprinted p.378-395 in Vogel
     C.J. de, Philosophia I (see 4624).

485 HADOT P., "Être, vie pensée chez Plotin et avant Plotin". p.105-157 in Les sources de Plotin. Entretiens sur l'antiquité class. V, Vandoeuvres-Genève, Fond. Hardt 1960.

486 RICH A.N.M., "Plotinus and the Theory of Artistic Imitation". Mnemosyne XIII 1960 233-239.

487* PESCE D., Idea, numero e anima. Primi contributi a una storia del platonismo nell'antichità. Padova, Gregoriana Ed. 1961 103p.
 Rev. Scholastik XXXIX 1964 457 Ennen.

488 PESCE D., "Idea, numero e anima. Primi contributi a una storia del platonismo nell'antichità". StudPat IX 1962 81-129, 315-341.

489 RIST J.M., "Dyad and Intelligible Matter in Plotinus". CQ XII 1962 99-107.

490 RIST J.M., "The Neoplatonic One and Plato's Parmenides". TAPhA XCIII 1962 389-401.

491* KRAEMER H.J., Der Ursprung der Geistmetaphysik. Untersuchungen zur Geschichte des Platonismus zwischen Platon und Plotin. Amsterdam, Schippers 1964 480p.
 Rev. Stromata XXII 1966 162.
 MH XXIII 1966 243 Wehrli.
 RBPh XLIV 1966 579-581 des Places.
 CW LIX 1966 198 Feldman.
 RecSR LIV 1966 296-300 Danielou.
 RCCM VIII 1966 281-283 Simonetti.
 Lychnos 1965-1966 422 Duering.
 ArchPhilos XXX 1967 141-145 Solignac.
 CR XVII 1967 336-338 Blumenthal.
 AAHG XX 1967 225-228 von Ivanka.
 DLZ LXXXVIII 1967 581-583 Schottlaender.
 SJP X-XI 1966-1967 473-475 Beierwaltes.
 PhilosRdschau XV 1968 97-110 Merlan.
 Dialogos V 1968 165-172 Kerkhoff.
 Th&Ph XLIII 1968 268-271 Ennen.
 Gnomon XL 1968 641-653 Oehler (reprinted p.146-161 in Oehler K., Antike Philosophie und Byzantinisches Mittelalter. Aufsätze zur Geschichte der griechischen Denkens, München 1969).
 CJ LXIV 1968 84 Etheridge.
 Mnemosyne XXI 1968 309-310 Westerink.
 Augustinus XIV 1969 416-417 Merino.
 Helmantica XX 1969 165-166 Merino.
 Gymnasium LXXVI 1969 477-479 Oehler.

Latomus XXIX 1970 543-547 Boyancé.
RPhL LXVIII 1970 253-256 Lefèvre.

492* MATTER P.P., Zum Einfluss des Timaios auf das Denken
Plotins. Winterthur, Keller 1964 225p.
Rev. Gnomon XXXVIII 1966 767-770 Page.
RecSR LIV 1966 611 des Places.
AAHG XIX 1966 255-256 von Ivánka.
Gymnasium LXXIV 1967 266 Hoermann.

493 FLASHAR H., "Plato und Aristoteles im Protreptikos
des Jamblichos". AGPh XLVII 1965 53-79.

494 SAMBURSKY S., "Plato, Proclus, and the Limitations
of Science". JHPh III 1965 1-11.

495* VOLKMANN-SCHLUCK K.H., Plotin als Interpret der
Ontologie Platos. 3. erw. Aufl.
Philosophische Abhandlungen X, Frankfurt a.M.,
Klostermann 1966 x&190p.

496 BROECKER W., "Plotin: un platonisme sans Socrate".
AFLA XLIII 1967 107-126.

497 JACKSON B.D., "Plotinus and the Parmenides". JHPh V
1967 315-327.

498 MERLAN P., "Greek Philosophy from Plato to
Plotinus". p.11-132 in The Cambridge History of
Later Greek and Early Medieval Philosophy, ed.
by Armstrong A.H. Cambridge Univ. Pr. 1967.

499 RIST J.M., "Integration and the Undescended Soul in
Plotinus". AJPh LXXXVIII 1967 410-422.

500 SAMBURSKY S., "The Theory of Forms. A Problem and
Four Neoplatonic Solutions". JHPh VI 1968
327-340.

501 SAMBURSKY S., "The Concept of Time in late
Neoplatonism". Proc. Israel Acad. Sci.
Human. II 1968 153-167.

502 DILLON J., "Enn. III 5: Plotinus' Exegesis of the
Symposium Myth". Agon III 1969 29-44.

503 HATHAWAY R.F., "The Neoplatonist Interpretation of
Plato. Remarks on its decisive
Characteristics". JHPh VII 1969 19-26.

504 MANSION S., "Dialectique platonicienne et dialectique plotinienne. Sophiste 254b-256d; Ennéade VI,2,6-8". p.26-28 in La Dialectique. Actes du XIVe Congrès des Societés de Philosophie de Langue française. Nice, 1-4 sept. 1969. Paris, Presses Universitaires 1969.

505* MERLAN P., From Platonism to Neoplatonism. 3rd. ed. rev. Den Haag, Nijhoff 1969 253p.

506 TARAN L., "Plotinus and the ὑπερουράνιος τόπος of the Phaedrus". C&M XXX 1969 258-262.

507 WHITTAKER J., "Ἐπέκεινα νοῦ καὶ οὐσίας". VChr XXIII 1969 91-104. Reprinted ch.9, p.224-254 in Whittaker J., God, Time, Being. Studies in the Transcendental Tradition in Greek Philosophy. Bergen 1970.

508 DOERRIE H., "Der König. Ein platonisches Schlüsselwort, von Plotin mit neuem Sinn erfüllt". RIPh XXIV 1970 217-235.

509 SCHWYZER H.R., "Plotin und Platons Philebus". RIPh XXIV 1970 181-193.

510 TROUILLARD J., "L'âme du Timée et l'un du Parménide dans la perspective néoplatonicienne". RIPh XXIV 1970 236-251.

511 BLUMENTHAL H.J., "Plotinus' Psychology. Aristotle in the Service of Platonism". IPQ XII 1972 340-364.

512 ARMSTRONG A.H., "Elements in the Thought of Plotinus at variance with classical Intellectualism". JHS XCIII 1973 13-22.

513 DOERRIE H., "La doctrine de l'âme dans le néoplatonisme de Plotin à Proclus". RThPh XXIII 1973 116-134.

514 KELESSIDOU-GALANOS A., "Plotin et la dialectique platonicienne de l'absolu" [in French with Greek summary]. Philosophia(Athens) III 1973 307-338.

515 WESTERINK L.G., "Proclus on Plato's three Proofs of Immortality". p.296-306 in Zetesis (see 4579).

For additional discussion see 1000, 1592, 1624, 2283, 2382, 2911, 2984, 2990, 3003, 3230, 3367, 3445, 3473, 3959, 4074.

THE STOICS

516   BALDRY H.C., "Zeno's Ideal State". JHS LXXIX 1959 3-15.

517   WESTMAN R., "Chrysipp III 761 und der Dialog Kleitophon". Eranos LIX 1961 89-100.

518   GARCIA-BORRON J.C., "Los estoicos y Platón, en la obra de los apologetas del s. II. Helenismo y cristianismo". Convivium (Barcelona) 1964 n.17-18, 51-62.

519   DAMBSKA I., "Sur un trait platonicien de la dialectique stoicienne". p.23-25 in La Dialectique. Actes du XIVe Congrès des Societés de Philosophie de Langue française. Nice, 1-4 sept. 1969. Paris, Presses Universitaires 1969.

520* KRAEMER H.J., Platonismus und hellenistische Philosophie. Berlin/New York, de Gruyter 1971 x&396p.
      Rev. ArchPhilos XXXVI 1973 665-666 Solignac.
      LEC XLI 1973 359 Decloux.
      AC XLII 1973 336 Joly.
      FZPT XX 1973 480-483 Wolf.
      PHist VI 1973 39-40 Classen.

521   PEMBROKE S.G., "Oikeiosis". p.114-149 in Problems in Stoicism, ed. by Long A.A. London, Athlone Pr. 1971.

522   JANDA J., "Einige ethisch-soziale Probleme in der Philosophie des Zenon von Kition. Zur Politeia des Zenon". p.99-116 in Soziale Probleme im Hellenismus und im röm. Reich. Akten der Konferenz (Liblice 10. bis 13. Oktober 1972), hrsg. von Oliva P. & Burian J. Praha, Kab. pro Studia řecká, římcká a lat. 1973.

II G: PLATO AND LATER FIGURES AND SCHOOLS OF ANCIENT PHILOSOPHY

For additional discussion see 2813, 2814, 2823, 3420.

THEOPHRASTUS

523 McDIARMID J.B., "Plato in Theophrastus' De
Sensibus". Phronesis IV 1959 59-70.

524 SKEMP J.B., "The Metaphysics of Theophrastus in
relation to the Doctrine of κίνησις in Plato's
Later Dialogues". p.217-223 in Naturphilosophie
bei Aristoteles und Theophrastus. Verhandlungen
des 4. Symposium Aristotelicum, hrsg. von
Duering I. Heidelberg, Stiehm 1969.

ANCIENT COSMOLOGY

525 DOERRIE H., "Divers aspects de la cosmologie de 70
av. J.C. a 20 ap. J.C.". RThPh VI 1972
400-412.

GENERAL

see 526, 3922.

II H: PLATO AND LATER CLASSICAL LITERATURE

GENERAL

526 CHROUST A.H., "Plato's Detractors in Antiquity". RM
XVI 1962-1963 98-118.

II H: PLATO AND LATER CLASSICAL LITERATURE

ANTIPATER

527 DOERRIE H., "Ein Epigramm auf Platons Werke. Anthologia Palatina 9,188". GB I 1973 89-109.

APULEIUS

528 HERRMANN L., "Le dieu-roi d'Apulée". Latomus XVIII 1959 110-116.

529 COURCELLE P., "De Platon à Saint Ambroise par Apulée. Parallèles textuels entre le De excessu fratris et le De Platone". RPh XXXV 1961 15-28.

530 BARRA G., "La biografia di Platone nel De Platone et eius dogmate di Apuleio". RAAN XXXVIII 1963 5-18.

531 THIBAU R., "Les Métamorphoses d'Apulée et la théorie platonicienne de l'Erôs". SPhG III 1965 89-144.

532 SCHLAM C., "Platonica in the Metamorphoses of Apuleius". TAPhA CI 1970 477-487.

533 MORTLEY R., "Apuleius and Platonic Theology". AJPh XCIII 1972 584-590.

CALLIMACHUS

For discussion of Callimachus see 1198.

CICERO

534 LEEMAN A.D., "De Aristotelis Protreptico Somnii Scipionis exemplo". Mnemosyne XI 1958 139-151.

II H: PLATO AND LATER CLASSICAL LITERATURE

535 BRIGNOLI F.M., "L'oscurità del Timeo platonico
    secondo Cicerone e Girolamo". GIF XII 1959
    56-63.

536 KAPP E., "Deum te scito esse?". Hermes LXXXVII 1959
    129-132.

537 BOYANCÉ P., "Cicéron et les semailles d'âmes du
    Timée (De Legibus I,24)". CRAI 1960 283-289.

538 DOUGLAS A.E., "Platonis aemulus? Some reflections
    on Cicero's philosophical writings". Summary in
    PCA LVII 1960 21.

539* GROLLIOS K.C., Κικέρων καὶ Πλατονικὴ ἠθική. Σχόλια
    σὲ μερικὰ χωρία τῶν διαλόγων τοῦ Κικέρωνος De
    Legibus καὶ De Finibus Bonorum et Malorum.
    Athens 1960 164p.
        Rev. CR XVI 1966 119 Adkins.
        CPh LIX 1964 300 Rexine.

540 TRENCSENYI-WALDAPFEL I., "Poésie et réalité
    historique dans la théorie et la pratique
    litteraire de Cicéron". AUBuda II 1960 3-18.

541 BOYANCÉ P., "Cicéron et les semailles d'âmes du
    Timée (De Legibus I,24)". Romanitas III 1961
    111-117.

542 DOUGLAS A.E., "Platonis aemulus?". G&R IX 1962
    41-51.

543 SWOBODA M., "Quid Cicero de poesi et arte
    iudicaverit" [in Polish with summary in Latin].
    Meander XVII 1962 64-85.

544* ZOLL G., Cicero Platonis Aemulus. Untersuchung uber
    die Form von Ciceros Dialogen, besonders von De
    Oratore. Diss. Freiburg i.d. Schw., Zürich,
    Juris-Verl. 1962 160p.

545 BOYANCÉ P., "Cicéron et le Premier Alcibiade". REL
    XLI 1963 210-229.

546 BOYANCÉ P., "Cicéron et le Premier Alcibiade".
    Summary in REL XLII 1964 37-38.

547 KLEIJWEGT A.J., "Philosophischer Gehalt und
    persönliche Stellungnahme in Tusc. I,9-81".
    Mnemosyne XIX 1966 359-388.

II H: PLATO AND LATER CLASSICAL LITERATURE

548 GIOMINI R., "Cicerone. Tim.6,17". RCCM X 1968
59-71.

549 GOERGEMANNS H., "Die Bedeutung der Traumeinkleidung
im Somnium Scipionis". WS N.F. II 1968 46-49.

550 PEPIN J., "Que l'homme n'est rien d'autre que son
âme. Observations sur la tradition du Premier
Alcibiade". Summary in REL XLVI 1968 9-10.

551 ARDLEY G.W.R., "Cicero on Philosophy and History".
Prudentia I 1969 28-41.

552 BOYANCÉ P., "Trois citations de Platon chez
Cicéron". p.126-132 in Hommages à Marcel
Renard, I, éd. par Bibauw J. Coll. Latomus
CI, Bruxelles 1969.

553 COURCELLE P., "Cicéron et le précepte delphique".
GIF XXI 1969 109-120.

554* GOULD R.A., Cicero's Indebtedness to the Platonic
Dialogues in Tusc.Disp. I. Diss. Princeton
Univ. 1968 255p. [microfilm]. Summary in DA
XXIX 1969 2691A-2692A.

555 PÉPIN J., "Que l'homme n'est rien d'autre que son
âme. Observations sur la tradidion du Premier
Alcibiade". REG LXXXII 1969 56-70.

556 GLUCKER J., "Ciceroniana". Eranos LXVIII 1970
231-233.

557 NICOLET C., "Cicéron, Platon et le vote secret".
Historia XIX 1970 39-66.

558 BOYANCÉ P., "Cicéron et les parties de la
philosophie". REL XLIX 1971 127-154. Summary
in REG LXXXIV 1971 p.xxx.

559 HENTSCHKE A., "Zur historischen und literarischen
Bedeutung von Ciceros Schrift De legibus".
Philologus CXV 1971 118-130.

560 TRAGLIA A., "Note su Cicerone traduttore di Platone
e di Epicuro". p.305-340 in Studi filologici e
storici in onore di V. de Falco. Napoli, Libr.
Scient. Ed. 1971.

561 CELENTANO M.S., "Cic. Tim. 13". RCCM XIV 1972
116-121.

II H: PLATO AND LATER CLASSICAL LITERATURE

562 CELENTANO M.S., "Qualche osservazione su due passi
    paralleli di Platone e Cicerone: Plat.
    Tim.29b-Cic. Tim.7". RCCM XV 1973 5-17.

563 FANTHAM E., "Aequabilitas in Cicero's political
    Theory and the Greek Tradition of Proportional
    Justice". CQ XXIII 1973 285-290.

564 FRANZOI A., "Osservazioni sulla traduzione
    ciceroniana del Timeo di Platone" [in Italian
    with summaries in English, French, German].
    PFMUF I No.3 [publ. separately] 47-58.

For additional discussion see 620, 2542, 3907, 4019.

HORACE

565 ALFONSI L., "Orazio, Carm. I,22,1". Aevum XXXVI
    1962 527.

566 PROWSE A.M., "Orazio Serm. II,4 e il Fedro di
    Platone". RFIC XLI 1963 199-202.

567 HELLER J.L., "Horace, Epist. I,1,47-54". AJPh
    LXXXV 1964 297-303.

LUCRETIUS

568 PERELLI L., "Lucrezio contro Epicuro in V, 195-234".
    RFIC XXXIX 1961 239-282.

MARTIAL

569 CARRATELLO U., "Marziale, Canio Rufo e Fedro". GIF
    XVII 1964 122-148.

II H: PLATO AND LATER CLASSICAL LITERATURE

MENANDER

570   WEINSTEIN M.E., "Menander Epitrepontes 44 and 139".
      HSPh LXXV 1971 135-138.

OVID

571   HAMMOND M., "Plato and Ovid's Exile".   HSPh LXIII
      1958 (Stud. Jaeger) 347-361.

572   ROBINSON T.M., "Ovid and the Timaeus".   Athenaeum
      XLVI 1968 256-260.

573   RUCH M., "A propos des origines possibles d'une
      curieuse croyance (Ovide, Mét. XV,389-390)".
      p.666-670 in Hommages à Marcel Renard, I, ed.
      par Bibauw J. Coll. Latomus CI, Bruxelles
      1969.

PETRONIUS

574   CAMERON A., "Petronius and Plato".   CQ XIX 1969
      367-370.

575   SHEY H.J., "Petronius and Plato's Gorgias".   CB
      XLVII 1971 81-84.

PLUTARCH

For discussion of Plutarch see 300, 482, 2383.

II H: PLATO AND LATER CLASSICAL LITERATURE
SALLUST

576 ALFONSI L., "Sul metus Punicus Sallustiano". Athenaeum LI 1973 383-384.

SENECA

577 BICKEL E., "Kant und Seneca. Der bestirnte Himmel über mir und das moralische Gesetz in mir". RhM CII 1959 289-292.

578 USCATESCU J., "Séneca y la idea del hombre". RFil(Madrid) XXIII 1964 313-323.

579 METTE H.J., "Die Funktion des Löwengleichnisses in Senecas Hercules Furens". WS LXXIX 1966 477-489.

TACITUS

580 VOSS B.R., "De Taciti Dialogi quadam cum Protagora Platonis similitudine". Mnemosyne XXVI 1973 293-294.

581 SCHWARZ F.F., "Senecas Tod, imitatio Socratis. Erläuterungen aus Platon und Seneca zu Tacitus (Ann. XV 62-64)". JRGG XCVI 1968 1-14.

THEOCRITUS

582 FROIDEFOND C., "Du Phèdre à l'Idylle XI de Theocrite". EtClass III 1968-1970 279-284.

VERGIL

583 LEACH E.W., "Eclogue IV. Symbolism and Sources". Arethusa IV 1971 167-184.

584* PEPIN J., Mythe et allégorie. Les origines grecques et les contestations judéo-chrétiennes. Paris, Aubier 1958 522p.

585 VRIES G.J. DE, "Ad Clementis Alex. Protrept. VI,67,1 Adnotatiuncula". Mnemosyne XI 1958 253-254.

586* ARMSTRONG A.H. & MARKUS R.A., Christian Faith and Greek Philosophy. London, Darton Longman & Todd 1960 ix&162p.

587 BLUMENBERG H., "Das dritte Höhlengleichnis". Filosofia XI 1960 705-722. Reprinted as a monograph: Studi e ricerche di storia della filos. XXXIX, Torino, Ed. di 'Filosofia' 1961 20p.

588 PALLAS P., "Πλάτων-Παῦλος". Platon XII 1960 162-168.

589 WIKGREN A., "Patterns of Perfection in the Epistle to the Hebrews". NTS VI 1959-1960 159-167.

590 ARMSTRONG A.H., "Platonic Eros and Christian Agape". DownsR LXXIX 1961 105-121. Summary in CJ LVII 1962 179.

591 PALAIOLOGOS G.N., "Ο Πλάτων ὡς φιλόσοφος καὶ παιδαγωγός". Platon XIII 1961 295-298.

592 SAVRAMIS D.S., "The Morality of Plato's Republic compared with the Morality of Paul the Apostle" [in Greek]. Theologia XXXII 1961 91-107, 281-304.

593 UPHOLD W.B. JR., "The fourth Gospel as Platonic Dialectic". Personalist XLII 1961 38-51.

594 ALFONSI L., "Giustino, Apol. I,2-4". VChr XVI 1962 77-78.

595 PRUEMM K., "Reflexiones theologicae et historicae ad usum Paulinum termini εἰκών". VerbumD XL 1962 232-257.

596 COMAN J., "L'immortalité de l'âme dans le Phédon et
     la résurrection des morts dans la littérature
     chrétienne des deux premiers siècles". Helikon
     III 1963 17-40.

597 REFOULE F., "Immortalité de l'âme et résurrection de
     la chair". RHR CLXIII 1963 11-52.

598 SILBERMAN L.H., "Farewell to ὁ ἀμήν. A Note on Rev.
     III,14". JBL LXXXII 1963 213-215.

599 VERDENIUS W.J., "Plato and Christianity". Ratio
     (English edn.) V 1963 15-32; also "Plato und
     das Christentum". Ratio (German edn.) V 1963
     13-28.

600 HOWELL E.B., "St. Paul and the Greek World". G&R
     XI 1964 7-29.

601* IVÁNKA E. VON, Plato christianus. Übernahme und
     Umgestaltung des Platonismus durch die Väter.
     Einsiedeln, Johannes-Verl. 1964 496p.
            Rev. Augustinianum V 1965 433 Folgado
     Flórez.
            RecSR LIII 1965 148-151 Daniélou.
            RSPh XLIX 1965 743-744 Camelot.
            RF LVI 1965 509-510.
            ThQ CXLV 1965 489-491 Moeller.
            REG LXXVIII 1965 715 Courcelle.
            TTQ CXLV 1965 489-493 Seckler.
            DownsR LXXXIII 1965 379-380 Armstrong.
            Augustinus X 1965 252-253 Capánaga.
            MH XXIII 1966 253 Theiler.
            WS LXXIX 1966 625-626 Postl.
            BO XXIII 1966 210-212 Waszink.
            OCP XXXII 1966 279-284 Schultze.
            Aevum XL 1966 194-195 Scazzoso.
            JThS XVII 1966 482 Chadwick.
            PhJ LXXIII 1965-1966 375-377 Beierwaltes.
            Gregorianum XLVII 1966 129 Orbe.
            Irenikon 1966 425-426 M.v.P.
            REA XII 1966 334 Madec.
            Bijdragen XXVII 1966 319 Vanneste.
            Studium VI 1966 354 García.
            Personalist XLVII 1966 449 Reynolds.
            CrossCurr XVI 1966 171 Collins.
            RPortFil XXII 1966 209 Freire.
            RyF CLXXII 1965 125 J.I.
            Speculum XLII 1967 374-375 Kristeller.
            Gymnasium LXXIV 1967 269 Vretska.
            Lychnos 1965-1966 422-425 Duering.
            VChr XXI 1967 66-68 van Winden.

BTh X 1967 239 Botte.
PhilosRdschau XIV 1966-1967 288-291 Seidl.
Kairos IX 1967 134-139 Vereno.
ScE XIX 1967 306 Harvey.
ByzZ LX 1967 318-323 Kuhn.
Pensamiento XXIII 1967 222-224 Martínez
Gómez.
ModS XLIV 1966-1967 381 Sweeney.
ThRev LXIV 1968 319-321 Doerrie.
NG XV 1968 301 Zamora.
JCS XVII 1969 114-116 Nomachi.
MTZ XX 1969 254-255 Gessel.

602 LIBRIZZI C., "Il problema del rapporto
Dante-Platone". Sophia XXXIV 1966 111-115.

603 RIST J.M., "A Note on Eros and Agape in
Pseudo-Dionysius". VChr XX 1966 235-243.

604 WOLFSON H.A., "Plato's pre-existent Matter in
Patristic Philosophy". p.409-420 in The
Classical Tradition. Literary and Historical
Studies in Honor of H. Caplan, ed. by Wallace
L. Ithaca, Cornell Univ. Pr. 1966.

605 CARLINI A., "Appunti sul testo del De mortuis di
Gregorio di Nissa contenuto nel Vaticanus Gr.
2066". ASNP XXXVI 1967 83-92.

606* HOFFMANN E., Platonismo e filosofia cristiana, trad.
Sgarbi G. Collana di studi religiosi, Bologna,
Il Mulino 1967 xxxii&448p.
Rev. RIFD XLV 1968 447-448 L.d'A.
Sistematica II 1969 204-205 A.B.

607 PALLIS P.K., "Η ἀθανασία τῆς ψυχῆς παρὰ Πλάτωνι καὶ
Παύλῳ". Platon XIX 1967 299-314.

608 PLACES E. DES, "La tradition patristique de Platon
(specialement d'après les citations des Lois et
de l'Epinomis dans la Préparation évangélique
d'Eusèbe de Césarée)". REG LXXX 1967 385-394.

609 CILENTO V., "Plato Christianus". RSLR IV 1968
316-328.

610 CULLMANN G.G., "Platone contro Gesù". Sistematica I
1968 37-39.

611 FASCHER E., "Platon und Johannes in ihrem Verhältnis
zu Sokrates und Christus". Altertum XIV 1968
79-86.

612 FREIRE A., "Eros platónico e Ágape cristã".
      RPortFil XXV 1969 No.3-4 19-36.

613 RAMAROSON L., "Contre les temples faits de mains
      d'homme". RPh XLIII 1969 217-238.

614 BOERS H., "Die Theologie des Paulus im Lichte der
      Philosophie Platons". p.57-77 in Quaderni
      Triestini per il lessico della lirica corale
      greca, I, alla memoria di Alfonsina Braun.
      Trieste, Ed. Italo Svevo 1970.

615 FERWERDA R., "Vreemde verleiding, een antwoord aan
      Fiolet". NTT XXVI 1972 345-384.

616 WINDEN J.C.M. VAN, "De verhouding tussen platonisme
      en christelijk geloof bei Justinus" [in Dutch
      with English summary]. Lampas VI 1973 358-364.

For further discussion of this subject see 385, 479, 518,
      529, 535, 799, 1525, 2825, 3063, 3064, 3071,
      3102, 3185, 3196, 3518, 3752, 3922, 3925, 3936,
      3940.

PLATO AND AUGUSTINE

617 THONNARD F.J., "Un texte de Plotin dans la Cité de
      Dieu IX,17". REAug V 1959 447-449.

618 PLINVAL G. DE, "Anticipations de la pensée
      augustinienne dans l'oeuvre de Platon".
      Augustinianum I 1961 310-326.

619 RACHET G., "S. Augustin et les 'Libri
      Platonicorum'". BAGB 1963 336-347.

620 SODANO A.R., "L'interpretazione ciceroniana di Timeo
      41a7-b6 nelle citazioni testuali di Sant'
      Agostino". REAug XI 1965 15-24.

621 BORNHEIM G.A., "Observações sobre a presença da
      metafísica platônica no pensamento de santo
      Agostinho". RBF XVII 1967 434-455.

622 VOSS B.R., "Vernachlässigte Zeugnisse klassischer
      Literatur bei Augustin und Hieronymus".
      p.300-311 in Lemmata. Donum natalicum W.
      Ehlers sexagenario a sodalibus Thesauri Linguae

Latinae oblatum. München, Marstallplatz 8 1968.

623 VOSS B.R., "Vernachlässigte Zeugnisse klassischer
     Literatur bei Augustin und Hieronymus". RhM
     CXII 1969 154-166. (sec.6 "Hieronymus und
     Platons Dialog 'Protagoras'".)

624 VOSS B.R., "Noch einmal Hieronymus und Platons
     Protagoras". RhM CXV 1972 290-291.

625 PICCOLOMINI R., "Platone nel libro VIII del De
     civitate Dei". Augustinianum XI 1971 233-261.

For further discussion see 3049, 3113.

II J: PLATO AND LATER THINKERS

It would be rash to suppose that the following section
contains all studies of Plato's legacy to
medieval and later philosophy, but it should
provide fairly good coverage of material devoted
principally to this subject. I have excluded
material on "Platonism" where that term tends to
lose contact with Plato himself. A certain
amount of this material (e.g. on Hegel and
Nietzsche) might be thought better suited to section II M, but I have preferred to keep it together with other discussions of those thinkers.

ABELARD

626 GREGORY T., "Abélard et Platone (Communicazione
     presentata all'International Conference 'Peter
     Abelard')". StudMed XIII 1972 539-562. Also
     p.38-64 in Peter Abelard. Proceedings of the
     International Conference, Louvain, May 10-12,
     1971, ed. by Buytaert E.M. Medievalia
     Lovaniensia, Ser.I, Studia II, Leuven,
     University Pr. and Den Haag, Nijhoff 1974.

AL-FARABI

627* AL-FARABI, Al-Farabi, Philosophy of Plato and
     Aristotle, transl. with an introd. by Mahdi M.
     New York, Free Pr. of Glencoe 1962 xi&158p.
     Also revised edn. Ithaca, Cornell Univ. Pr.
     1969 xxv& 158p.
     Rev. CW LVI 1963 295 Rosenmeyer.
     JAOS LXXXIII 1963 127 Rescher.
     MEJ 1963 458 Rosenthal.
     RM XVI 1962-1963 578 W.G.E.
     ModS XLI 1963-1964 104 Moore.
     JNES 1965 121 Marmura.
     Speculum XLIV 1969 156-157 Stewart.
     [of revised edn.] Speculum XLIV 1969 158
     Stewart.
     PhEW 1970 196 Izutsu.

628* AL-FARABI, Al-Farabi, Le livre de la conciliation
     des deux sages Platon et Aristote, texte établi
     & annoté par Nader A.N. Beyrouth, Centre docum.
     internat. des Mss. arabes 1965 114p.

629 ALFARABI, "Livre de concordance entre les opinions
     des deux sages, le divin Platon et Aristote",
     intro. and French transl. by Abdel-Massih E.
     Melto V 1969 305-358.

630 ALFARABI, "Concordia entre el Divino Platón y el
     Sabio Aristóteles, por Al-Farabi", trans., pref.
     & notes by Alonso y Alonso P.M. Pensamiento XXV
     1969 21-70.

631 SANKARI F.A., "Plato and Al-Farabi. A Comparison of
     some Aspects of their Political Philosophies".
     Vivarium VIII 1970 1-9. Also appeared in
     MuslWorld LX 1970 218-225, StudIsl VII 1970
     9-18.

632* ROSENTHAL F. & WALZER R., Plato Arabus, vol.II:
     Alfarabius de Platonis philosophia, ed.
     Rosenthal F. & Walzer R. Corpus Platonicum
     Medii Aevi. Nendeln, Liechtenstein, Kraus
     Reprint 1973 xxii&30&23p. Reprint of London
     1943 edn.

II J: PLATO AND LATER THINKERS

AQUINAS

633 BAUER J., "Die Ideenlehre Platons im Urteil des Aquinaten". SJP III 1959 56-74.

634 BAUER J., "Die Ideenlehre Platons im Urteil des Aquinaten". ThJb IV 1961 352-368.

635 OWENS J., "Thomistic common nature and Platonic Idea". MS XXI 1959 211-222.

636 BETTONI E., "La dottrina platonica delle idee nella interpretazione dell'autore della 'Summa philosophiae'". p.211-234 in Studi di filosofia e di storia della filosofia in onore di Francesco Olgiati. Milano, Vita e Pensiero 1962.

637* STRASSER M.W., Saint Thomas' Critique of Platonism in the Liber de Causis. Diss. Univ. of Toronto 1963 299p. [microfilm]. Summary in DA XXIV 1963 2082-2083.

For additional discussion see 3230.

AVICENNA

638 CHAIX-RUY J., "La Sagesse orientale d'Avicenne et les mythes platoniciennes". RMedit XVIII 1958 85-86, 261-307.

For additional discussion see 3990.

BERGSON

639 MOUTSOPOULOS E., "La critique de la philosophie platonicienne chez Bergson". Athena LXVI 1962 192-284.

640 MOUTSOPOULOS E., "La critique du platonisme chez Bergson". EBerg IX 1970 123-156.

II J: PLATO AND LATER THINKERS

641   GIROUX L., "Bergson et la conception du temps chez
      Platon et Aristcte". Dialogue X 1971 479-503.

BLONDEL

642   POLZER G., "Platons Philebos in Blondels Action".
      p.471-485 in Parusia, hrsg. von Flasch K. (see
      4588).

CALVIN

For discussion of Calvin see 3154.

CANTOR

643* FARIS J.A., Plato's Theory of Forms and Cantor's
      Theory of Sets. Belfast, Queen's Univ. 1968
      20p.

CARTAN

For discussion of Cartan see 2867.

COMENIUS

644   NOVOTNY F., "Comenius and Plato" [in Czech with
      German summary]. SPFB XIV 1965 E10 329-333.

CUSANUS

645 HARRIES K., "Cusanus and the Platonic Idea". NS
     XXXVII 1963 188-203.

For additional discussion see 3230.

DANTE

646 PALGEN R., "Das platonische Fundament des Paradiso".
     AAWW CVIII 1971 159-189.

647 DE BONFILS TEMPLER M., "La prima visione della Vita
     Nuova   e   la   dottrina   dei   tre spiriti".
     RassLettItal LXXVI 1972 303-316.

DESCARTES

648 SHAPERE D., "Descartes and Plato". p.275-278 in
     Actes du Xe Congr. Internat. d'Hist. des
     Sci., Ithaca 26 aug.-2 sept. 1962.

649 SHAPERE D., "Descartes and Plato". JHI XXIV 1963
     572-576.

650 GOLDSCHMIDT V., "Le paradigme platonicien et les
     'Regulae'   de   Descartes".   p.231-242 in
     Goldschmidt V., Questions platoniciennes (see
     4598). Reprinted from RPhilos 1951.

For additional discussion see 2935.

DEWEY

651 ANDERSON F.M., "Dewey's Experiment with Greek
     Philosophy". IPQ VII 1967 86-100.

II J: PLATO AND LATER THINKERS

652 HARRINGTON K.W., "John Dewey's Ethics and the
     classical Conception of Man". Diotima I 1973
     125-148.

For additional discussion see 3767.

ECKHART

653 HAAS A.M., "Zur Frage der Selbsterkenntnis bei
     Meister Eckhart". FZPT XV 1968 190-261.

MARSILIO FICINO

654 KRISTELLER P.O., "Marsilio Ficino as a Beginning
     Student of Plato". Scriptorium XX 1966 41-54.

655 ZAMBELLI P., "Platone, Ficino e la magia".
     p.121-142 in Studia humanitatis. Ernesto Grassi
     zum 70. Geburtstag, hrsg. von Hora E. &
     Kessler E. Hum. Bibl. 1. Reihe XVI, München,
     Fink 1973.

FREGE

For discussion of Frege see 4026.

FREUD

656 TOURNEY G., "Eros, Plato and Freud". JHBS II 1966
     256-272.

For additional discussion see 3071, 3203, 3212.

II J: PLATO AND LATER THINKERS

GOETHE

For discussion of Goethe see 1374.

HAMANN

For discussion of Hamann see 2124.

HEGEL

657 GADAMER H.G., "Hegel und die antike Dialektik".
HegelStud I 1961 173-199.

658 BARON R., "Dialectique et humanisme chez Platon et
Hegel". GM XX 1965 142-149.

659 KOJEVE A., "Filosofia e saggezza (Hegel e Platone)".
Differenze 1965 n.5 27-55.

660 WIEHL R., "Platos Ontologie in Hegels Logik des
Seins". HegelStud III 1965 157-180.

661* LASKE O.E., Über die Dialektik Platos und des frühen
Hegel. Diss. Frankfurt 1966 137p.

662 DUSO G., "L'interpretazione hegeliana della
contraddizione nel 'Parmenide', 'Sofista' e
'Filebo'". Pensiero XII 1967 206-220.

663 DUSO G., "Bildung, Politik und Philosophie in der
Hegelschen Interpretation Platons". p.478-485
in Akten XIV. Intern. Kongr. Philos. Wien,
2.-9. September 1968. Vol. IV. Wien, Herder
1968.

664* DUSO G., Hegel interprete di Platone. Padova, Cedam
1969 89p.
Rev. Sophia XXXVIII 1970 109-110
Martorana.
RIFD XLVIII 1971 371-372.
GM XXVI 1971 297-299 Bacchin.

665 TANAKA M., "Hegel and Plato" [in Japanese]. Philosophy (Tokyo) XX 1970.

666 MACHOVEC D., "Hegel und die platonischen Mythen". WJb VI 1973 149-177.

667 MACHOVEC D., "Hegel a Platónovy Mýty [Hegel and the Platonic Myths]". AUCPH V 1971 73-93.

668 MACHOVEC D., "Hegel und die platonischen Mythen". WJb VI 1973 149-177.

669 SEMASKO L.M., "Dialektika Platona i ee interpretacija gegelem [Plato's Dialectic and its Interpretation by Hegel]" [in Russian]. FilNauk 1971 No.4 92-100.

670 ROSEN S., "Σωφροσύνη and Selbstbewusstsein". RM XXXII 1973 617-642.

671 VIEILLARD-BARON J.L., "Les leçons de Hegel sur Platon dans son histoire de la philosophie". RMM LXXVIII 1973 385-419.

For additional discussion see 689, 1076, 2776, 2787, 2801, 2935, 3617.

HEIDEGGER

672 HEIDEGGER M., "La doctrina de Platón acerca de la verdad". RDF V 1959 58-89.

673 REST W., "Platons Lehre von der Padaia. Ein pädagogischer Beitrag zu Martin Heideggers Platon-Deutung". VWP XXXVI 1960 249-261.

674 BECKER O., "Platonische Idee und ontologische Differenz". p.157-191 in Becker O., Dasein und Dawesen. Gesammelte philosophische Aufsätze. Pfullingen, Neske 1963.

675 RICHARDSON W.J., "Heidegger and Plato". HeythropJ IV 1963 273-279.

676 WOLZ H.G., "Plato's Doctrine of Truth: orthotes or aletheia?". Ph&PhenR XXVII 1966 157-182.

677 ROSEN S., "Heidegger's Interpretation of Plato".
JExist VII 1966-1967 477-504.

678* HEIDEGGER M., Questions...II: Qu'est-ce que la
philosophie? Hegel et les Grecs. La thèse de
Kant sur l'être. La doctrine de Platon sur la
vérité. Ce qu'est et comment se determine la
physis, trad. par Axelos K, et alii.
Classiques de la philosophie, Paris, Gallimard
1968 280p.

679 KATES C.A., "Heidegger and the Myth of the Cave".
Personalist L 1969 532-548.

680 VOLLRATH E., "Platons Anamnesislehre und Heideggers
These von der Erinnerung in die Metaphysik".
ZPhF XXIII 1969 349-361.

681 ROSEN S.H., "Heidegger's Interpretation of Plato".
p.51-77 in Essays in Metaphysics by Members of
the Philosophy Department of The Pennsylvania
State University, ed. by Vaught C.G.
University Park, Penn./London, The Penn. State
Univ. Pr. 1970.

682 ALDERMAN H., "Heidegger on the Nature of
Metaphysics". JBSPhen II 1971 12-22.

683 PENEDOS A. DOS, "A interpretação heideggeriana da
alegoria da caverna de Platão". RevFSF I 1971
169-178.

684* BEAUFRET J., Dialogue avec Heidegger I: Philosophie
grecque. Paris, Ed. de Minuit 1973 145p.
("Note sur Platon et Aristote", p.93-121.)

685 GELVEN M., "Eros and Projection: Plato and
Heidegger". SoJP IV 1973 125-136.

HERBART

For discussion of Herbart see 715.

II J: PLATO AND LATER THINKERS

HOBBES

For discussion of Hobbes see 3746, 3755.

IBN KHALDUN

For discussion of Ibn Khaldun see 3736.

KAFKA

For discussion of Kafka see 2081.

KANT

686 HOFFMANN E., "Platon und Kant". p.428-437 in
Hoffmann E., Platonismus und christliche
Philosophie (see 4601).

687 HEIMSOETH H., "Kant und Plato". KantStud LVI
1965-1966 349-372.

688 MARTIN G., "A Lifetime's Study of Kant". 'Kant and
Modern Science' Synthese XXIII 1971 2-17.

689 GAUSS H., "Von Kant uber Hegel zu Plato". p.309-371
in Gauss H., Opuscula Philosophica (see 4596).
Reprinted from ASSPh VII 1947 114-176.

For additional discussion see 3037, 3049, 3089.

II J: PLATO AND LATER THINKERS
                KIERKEGAARD

690 AGOSTINO F. D', "La fenomenologia dell'uomo giusto.
      Un parallelo tra Kierkegaard e Platone". RIFD
      XLIX 1972 153-172.

For additional discussion see 1631, 3784.

                LEVI-STRAUSS

691 ROSEN S., "The Absence of Structure". KantStud LXIV
      1973 246-261.

                 LEIBNIZ

692 MOREAU J., "Ce que Leibniz a recu de Platon".
      p.549-555 in Akten XIV. Intern. Kongr.
      Philos. Wien, 2.-9. September 1968. Vol. V.
      Wien, Herder 1968.

693 MATES B., "Leibniz and the Phaedo". p.135-148 in
      Akten II. Intern. Leibniz-Kongresses.
      Hanover, 17.-22. Juli 1972, Bd.I. Studia
      Leibnitiana, Suppl. XII, Wiesbaden, Steiner
      1973.

For additional discussion see 4034.

                 LINNAEUS

For discussion of Linnaeus see 3413.

              THE LOGICAL ATOMISTS

For discussion of the Logical Atomists see 2454.

                    94

II J: PLATO AND LATER THINKERS

LUTHER

694   FIEDLER R., "Zum Verhältnis Luthers und Melanchthons
      zu Platon. Eine Studie zum Reformationsjubiläum
      1967". Altertum XIII 1967 213-227.

MACHIAVELLI

695   WERNER E., "Machiavel et Platon". RMM LXXVIII 1973
      295-311.

For additional discussion see 3711.

MELANCHTHON

For discussion of Melanchthon see 694.

MILL

696   YAKE J.S., "Mill's Mental Crisis Revisited". MillNL
      IX 1973 16-20.

MORE

697   KERENYI K., "Ursinn und Sinnwandel des Utopischen".
      Eranos-Jb XXXII 1963 9-29.

698   STEINTRAGER J., "Plato and More's Utopia". SocRes
      XXXVI 1969 357-372.

699   JONES J.P., "The Philebus and the Philosophy of
      Pleasure in Thomas More's Utopia". Moreana 1971
      61-69.

NIETZSCHE

700 KLOCH-KORNITZ P. VON, "Der Gorgias Platons und die Philosophie Friedrich Nietzsches". ZPhF XVII 1963 586-603.

701 EBERLEIN E., "Nietzsche und Platon". Gymnasium LXXII 1965 62-71.

702 HAGER F.P., "Nietzsches Opposition gegen Plato und die Frage nach ihrer Berechtigung hinsichtlich der Beziehung zwischen Intellekt und Leben". ASSPh XXV 1965 64-86.

703 DUVAL R., "Le point de départ de la pensée de Nietzsche. Nietzsche et le platonisme". RSPh LIII 1969 601-637.

704 CLEGG J.S., "Nietzsche's Gods in The Birth of Tragedy". JHPh X 1972 431-438.

OCCAM

For discussion of Occam see 4034.

PATER

705 KNOEPFLMACHER U.C., "Pater's Religion of Sanity: 'Plato and Platonism' as a Document of Victorian Unbelief". VicStud VI 1962 151-168.

706* PATER W.H., Plato and Platonism. New York, Greenwood Pr. 1969 282p. Reprint of 1925 edn.

707 SMALL I.C., "Plato and Pater. Fin-de-Siècle Aesthetics". BJAes XII 1972 369-383.

II J: PLATO AND LATER THINKERS

WILLIAM PENN

708 STERN T.N., "Penn's positive Platonism". JThought
     VI 1971 267-274.

POLANYI

709 PROSCH H., "Polanyi's Tacit Knowing in the 'Classic'
     Philosophers". JBSPhen IV 1973 201-216.

PROUDHON

710 DAYAN-HERZBRUN S., "Proudhon, critique de Platon".
     RPhilos CLXII 1972 15-25.

RANDALL

711 MACHLE E.J., "Plato, Aristotle, Salvation and
     Science. Randall's History of Philosophy".
     JHPh X 1972 459-472.

ROUSSEAU

712 HAGER F.P., "Die Beziehungen zwischen Philosophie
     und Erziehung bei Platon und bei Jean-Jacques
     Rousseau". ASSPh XXXII 1972 92-11. Reprinted
     as Sonderausdruck. Basel, Verl. fur Recht und
     Gesellschaft 1973.

For additional discussion see 3711.

RUIBAL

For discussion of Ruibal see 3145.

RUSSELL

713 MARACCHIA S., "Platone e Russell nella definizione
     della   matematica" [with   English transl.].
     Scientia LXV 1971 207-223.

714 MARTIN G., "Bertrand Russell und die platonischen
     Ideen". SIF V 1973 169-180.

For additional discussion see 643, 4026.

SCHLEIERMACHER

715* VORMANN N., Die Bedeutung des Platonismus für der
     Erziehungstheorie bei Schleiermacher und Hebart.
     Beitr. zur Erziehungswiss., Ratingen bei
     Düsseldorf, Henn 1968 169p.

SCHOPENHAUER

716 HEIN H., "Schopenhauer and Platonic Ideas". JHPh IV
     1966 133-144.

For additional discussion see 3037.

SCIACCA

717 MURUZABAL URSUA S., "Acercamiento a la antropología
     filosofico de M.F. Sciacca". AnCalas XXI 1969
     5-63.

II J: PLATO AND LATER THINKERS

SHAW

718 RANKIN H.D., "Plato and Bernard Shaw, Their Ideal
     Communities". Hermathena XCIII 1959 71-77.

SMUTS

719 BRUSCH F.W., "Our Changing World-Views. An Analysis
     of Smuts' 'Holism' and a Comparison of his
     World-View with those of Plato and Dewey".
     p.348-359 in Akten des XIV. Internationalen
     Kongresses fur Philosophie. Wien, 2.-9.
     September 1968. Vol. II. Wien, Herder 1968.

SPINOZA

720 GOULD T., "Four Levels of Reality, in Plato,
     Spinoza, and Blake". Arion VIII 1969 20-50.

THEILHARD DE CHARDIN

721 LIAUZU-BONTEMS J., "La naissance de a civilisation
     d'après Platon et le Père Teilhard de Chardin".
     BAGB 1967 212-220.

DE VIAU

722 MAZZARA R.A., "The Phaedo and Théophile de Viau's
     Traicté de l'immortalité de l'âme". FrRev XL
     1966 329-340.

WHITEHEAD

723 BRENNAN J.G., "Whitehead on Plato's Cosmology".
JHPh IX 1971 67-78.

WINCKELMANN

724* REIN U.G.M., Winckelmanns Begriff der Schönheit.
Über die Bedeutung Platons für Winckelmann.
Diss. Bonn (1971) 1972.

GENERAL

725 WEISSMANN A., "Platonic Ideas in the History of human
Thought". p.1182-1187 in Actes du VIIIe Congrès
International d'Histoire des Sciences,
Firenze-Milano, 3-9 Sett. 1956 (appeared 1958):
Gruppo Italiano di Storia delle Scienze, Vinci
(Firenze), Hermann et Cie., Paris, vol. 3.

726 PATZIG G., "Bemerkungen über den Begriff der Form".
ArchivPhilos IX 1959 93-110.

727 FISCHER P.F., "Plato's Republic and Modern
Utopianism". QQ LXVII 1960 18-27.

728 SCHULZ-FALKENTHAL H., "Die Einschätzung der antiken
Erziehungspraktiker und -theoriker zur Zeit der
Aufklärung und des Neohumanismus". Altertum IX
1963 118-128.

729* TAYLOR A.E., Platonism and its Influence. New York,
Cooper Square Publ. 1963 153p. Reprint of 1932
edn.

730 RALFS G., "Platon und Aristoteles im abendländischen
Bewusstsein." p.56-103 in Lebensformen des
Geistes. Vorträge und Abhandlungen, hrsg. von
Glockner H. Kantstudien Ergänzungshefte LXXXVI,
Köln, Kölner Universitäts-Verl. 1964.

731 OEING-HANHOFF L., "Zur Wirkungsgeschichte der platonischen Anamnesislehre". p.240-271 in Collegium Philosophicum. Studien. Joachim Ritter zum 60. Geburtstag. Basel/Stuttgart, Schwabe 1965.

732 DEMPE H., "Platon und die moderne Philosophie". Gymnasium LXXIV 1967 510-528.

733* MORE P.E., Platonism [Prepared for the Vanuxem Lectures given at Princeton in the autumn of 1917]. 3rd. ed. Reprint of the 1931 ed. New York, AMS Pr. 1969 317p.

734 SODIPO J.O., "Plato and modern Philosophy". N&C XI 1969 6-16.

735* CHYDENIUS J., The Symbolism of Love in Medieval Thought. Commentationes Hum. Litt. Soc. Scient. Fennicae XLIV,1, Helsinki, 1970 68p. Rev. REAug XIX 1973 398 Bleuzen.

736 MOUTSOPOULOS E., "Platon et la philosophie byzantine. Actualité et perspectives". EHBS XXXVII 1969-1970 76-84.

737 CLOSE A.J., "Philosophical Theories of Art and Nature in Classical Antiquity". JHI XXXII 1971 163-184.

738 CLARKE I.F., "Prophets and Predictors. 2. The Primacy of Plato". Futures IV 1972 75-80.

739 WELTY G., "Plato and Delphi". Futures V 1973 281-286.

740 MOCANU T., "Platonic Rigor and our Epoch" [in Rumanian]. Arta XIX 1972 26-27, 40.

For additional discussion see 2978, 3772, 4034.

II K: PLATO AND LATER SCIENCE

The comments prefaced to section II J apply to this section as well. For treatments of Plato's conception of science in general, see section V A.

741 MACCAGNI C., "Riscontri platonici relativi alla matematica in Galileo e Torricelli". Convegno Stud. Torricelliani 1958 65-75.

742 KOYRÉ A. & COHEN I.B., "Newton, Galilée, et Platon". p.111-133 in IX Congr. Intern. Hist. Sci. vol. I 1959. Also in Communications du IX Congr. Intern. Hist. Sci.

743 KOYRÉ A., "Newton, Galilee et Platon". AESocCiv XV 1960 1053-1059.

744 PRESSOUYRE L., "Le cosmos platonicien de la cathédrale d'Anagni". MEFR LXXVIII 1966 551-593.

745 HORSKY Z., "Le Rôle du platonisme dans l'origine de la cosmologie moderne". Organon(Wars) IV 1967 47-54.

746 SOULARD H., "Les signes lapidaires des constructeurs de cathédrales eu égard aux vues de Pythagore et Platon sur le Nombre d'or". BAGB II 1967 221-226.

747 HUNT H.A.K., "Farewell to Plato?" Summary p.49-51 in Australian universities language and literature association, 1969. Proceedings and papers of the twelfth congress, held at the University of Western Australia, 5-11 February 1969, ed. by Treweek A.P. New South Wales, AULLA 1970.

For further discussion see 423, 649.

II L: PLATO AND THE EAST

748 HADAS M., "Plato in Hellenistic Fusion". JHI XIX
1958 3-13.

749 PLACES E. DES, "Un emprunt de la Sagesse aux Lois
de Platon?". Biblica XL 1959 1016-1017.

750 SASTRI K.A. NIKALANTA, "Sur les contacts entre
l'Inde et l'Occident dans l'antiquité". Diogène
1959 no.28 47-74.

751 WAECHTER L., "Der Einfluss platonischen Denkens auf
rabbinische Schöpfungsspekulationen". ZRGG XIV
1962 36-56.

752 KOSMALA H., "Anfang, Mitte und Ende". ASTI II 1963
108-111.

753 CHANG C., "A Comparison of Confucian and Platonic
Ethical Views". PhEW XIII 1964 295-309.

754* AFNAN R.M., Zoroaster's Influence on Greek Thought.
New York, Philos. Libr. 1965 xvi&436p. (ch.6
p.107-116 on Socrates; chs.7-11 p.117-431 on
Plato.)
Rev. CW LIX 1966 196 Fontenrose.
RM XIX 1965-1966 579 P.M.
IPQ VIII 1968 640-645 Cleve.

755* LANDMANN M. Ursprungsbild und Schöpfertat. Zum
platonisch-biblischen Gespräch. Samml. Dialog
VIII, München, Nymphenburg Verl. 1966 352p.
Rev. PLA XX 1967 279-283 Mueller.
DLZ LXXXIX 1968 484-487 Schottlaender
WJb III 1970 320-322 Heintel.

756 LANDMANN M., "Die Weltschöpfung im Timaios und in
der Genesis". Antaios VII 1966 476-500.

757 AVNI A., "Inspiration in Plato and the Hebrew
Prophets". CompLit XX 1968 55-63.

758 KADOWAKI K., "In search of true Dialogue. A
comparative study of Confucius' Lun Yu and
Plato's Dialogues" [in Japanese]. Sophia Univ.
XVIII 1969.

759 PANOUSSI E., "L'origine de la notion de participation chez Zoroastre et chez Platon". p.91-114 in Beiträge zur alten Geschichte und deren Nachleben. Festschrift für Franz Altheim zum 6.10.1968, hrsg. von Stiehl R. & Stier H.E., Bd.I. Berlin, de Gruyter 1969.

760 SATHAYE S.G., "The Aitareya Brāhmaṇa and the Republic". PhEW XIX 1969 435-441.

761 SPENGLER J.J., "Kauṭilya, Plato, Lord Shang. Comparative political Economy". PAPhS CXIII 1969 450-457.

762 FESTUGIÈRE A.J., "Grecs et sages orientaux". p.183-195 in Festugière A.J., Études de philosophie grecque (see 4587). Reprinted from RHR CXXX 1945 29-41.

763 FESTUGIÈRE A.J., "Platon et l'Orient". p.39-79 in Festugière A.J., Études de philosophie grecque (see 4587). Reprinted from RPh 1947 5-45.

764 KURPERSHOEK-SCHERFT T., "Platonisch adversus Boeddhistisch". Hermeneus XLIII 1972 217-224.

765 STEINER E.E. II, "The Hindu Republic". Dialogue XIV 1972 73-82.

766 TONG L.K., "Confucian Jen and Platonic Eros: A Comparative Study". ChinCult XIV 1973 1-8.

For further discussion see 1206, 2133, 230, 2537, 2602, 2692, 3102, 3261, 3283, 3333, 3358, 3476, 3922.

II M: HISTORY OF THE INTERPRETATION OF PLATO

767 TRUEBLOOD A.S., "Plato's Symposium and Ficino's Commentary in Lope de Vega's Dorotea". ModLangNotes LXXIII 506-514.

768 ZACCARIA V., "Pier Candido Decembrio traduttore della Repubblica di Platone (Notizie dall'Epistolario di Decembrio)". IMU II 1959 179-206.

769 JAEGER W., "Der Wandel des Platonbildes im
neunzehnten Jahrhundert". p.129-142 in Jaeger
W., Humanistische Rden und Vorträge (see 4604).

770 WOLFSON H.A., "Extradeical and Intradeical
Interpretation of Platonic Ideas". JHI XXII
1961 3-32. Reprinted p.27-68 in Wolfson H.A.,
Religious Philosophy. A Group of Essays.
Cambridge, Mass., Harvard Univ. Pr. 1961.

771 ISNARDI M., "A proposito di un'interpretazione
cinquecentesca del rapporto teoria-prassi in
Aristotele e Platone". PP no.87 1962 436-447.

772 NOCK A.D., "The Exegesis of Timaeus 28c". VChr XVI
1962 79-86.

773 WYLLER E.A., "Nicolaus Cusanus' 'Om det ikke-andre'
og Platons 'Parmenides" [in Norwegian with
German summary]. Lychnos 1962 43-59.

774 BOYANCÉ P., "Sur l'exégèse hellénistique du Phèdre".
p.45-53 in Miscellanea di studi alessandrini in
memoria di Augusto Rostagni. Torino, Bottega
d'Erasmo 1963.

775 SODANO A.R., "Per un' edizione critica dei frammenti
del commento di Porfirio al Timeo di Platone.
La problematica e la metodologia critica delle
fonti". AAP XII 1963 [47p.].

776 ALSINA CLOTA J., "Interpretaciones de la teología
platónica en el siglo XX". p.274-283 in Actas
II Congr. Esp. de Estud. Clás.
(Madrid-Barcelona, 4-10 de abril de 1961). Publ.
de la Soc. Esp. de Estud. Clás. V, Madrid
1964.

777 CARLINI A., "La traduzione latina del Fedone di
Enrico Aristippo e i codici PW di Platone".
StudMed V 1964 603-612.

778 DELUCCHI A.D., "La problemática en torno del 'Ión'
de Platón". RFil(La Plata) XIV 1964 25-36.

779 RODRÍGUEZ-ADRADOS F., "La interpretación de Platón
en el siglo XX". p.241-273 in Actas del II
Congr. esp. de Estud. clás.
(Madrid-Barcelona, 4-10 de abril de 1961).
Publ. de la Soc. Esp. de Estud. Clás. V,
Madrid 1964.

780* PONI S., Il Fedon e la tesi del dott. E. Munk.
Bologna, Capelli 1965 188p.
Rev. Vichiana II 1965 422 Citti.

781* WILLIAM OF CONCHES, Guillaume de Conches, Glosae
super Platonem, texte crit. avec intro. notes
& tables par Jeauneau E. Textes philos. du
moyen âge XIII, Paris, Vrin 1965 358p.
Rev. REL XLIII 1965 578-579 Munk Olsen.
RPhL LXIII 1965 296-299 Delhaye.
RecSR LIV 1966 613 des Places.
JEH XVII 1966 113 Sheldon-Williams.
Gregorianum XLVII 1966 605-606 Dumeige.
TPh XXVIII 1966 732 Pattin.
RHE LXII 1967 645-64 Silvestre.
RSR XLI 1967 371 Javelet.
Speculum XLII 1967 378-379 O'Donnell.
PhJ LXXIV 1966-1967 182-184 Skovgaard
Jensen.
RPhilos CLVIII 1968 288-289 Trouillard.

782* THEON OF SMYRNA, Exposition des connaissances
mathématiques utiles pour la lecture de Platon,
trad. par Dupuis J. Reprint of 1892 Paris edn.
Bruxelles, Ed. Culture et Civilisation 1966
434p.

783 GUTHRIE W.K.C., "Twentieth Century Approaches to
Plato. I: The Theologian, the Philosopher, the
Sociologist; II: The Historian". p.227-260 in
Lectures in Memory of Louis Taft Semple. First
Series: 1961-1965. University of Cincinnati
Classical Studies I, Princeton, Princeton Univ.
Pr. 1967.

784 BLANCHÉ L., "Les modernes et le mouvement terrestre
du Timée". REPh XVIII 1967-1968,2 1-22.

785* GROSS B., The Great Thinkers on Plato. New York,
Putnam 1968 xxv&323p.

786 MARTANO G., "Il 'Parmenide' e il 'sofista' in
un'interpretazione teologica di Pico della
Mirandola". p.107-120 in Martano G., Studi di
storia del pensiero antico. Coll. Studi
Filos., Napoli, Il Tripode 1968.

787 ZADRO A., "L'insegnamnto della logica attraverso
l'ermeneutica dei testi platonici". RassPed
XXVI 1968 195-227.

788 FESTUGIÈRE A.J., "L'ordre de lecture des dialogues de Platon aux Ve-VIe siècles". MH XXVI 1969 281-296.

789 GADAMER H.G., "Schleiermacher platonicien". ArchivPhilos XXXII 1969 28-39.

790 GIBSON M., "The Study of the Timaeus in the eleventh and twelfth Centuries". Pensamiento XXV 1969 183-194.

791 POUILLOUX J.Y., "Problèmes de traduction. L. Le Roy et le Xe livre de la République". BHR XXXI 1969 47-66.

792 WYLLER E.A., "Die Anthropologie des Nemesius von Emesa und die Alkibiades I-Tradition. Eine Untersuchung zum Platon-Bild in der Schrift "Über die Natur des Menschen' (Kap. I,1)". SO XLIV 1969 126-145.

793 DOENT E., "Schellings Interpretation von Plato, Nomoi 716". Philologus CXIV 1970 150-154.

794 GAETA F., "Giorgio di Trebisonda, le Leggi di Platone e la costituzione di Venezia". BullMur LXXXII 1970 479-501.

795 PARTEE M.H., "Sir Thomas Elyot on Plato's Aesthetics". Viator I 1970 327-335.

796 PARTEE M.H., "Sir Philip Sidney and the Renaissance Knowledge of Plato". EngSt LI 1970 411-424.

797 BERTI E., "Il Critone di Platone nelle edizioni del Cinquecento". SCO XIX-XX 1970-1971 453-460.

798 CAMBIANO G., "La Scuola Megarica nelle interpretazioni moderne". RF LXII 1971 227-253.

799 NOMACHI A., "Some Notes on the History of the Interpretations of the Timaeus (28b7). An Aspect of Interaction between Christianity and Platonism" [in Japanese with English summary]. JCS XIX 1971 69-77.

800 ROUECHE M., "Notes on a Commentary on Plato's Parmenides". GRBS XII 1971 553-556.

801* WEIZSAECKER C.F. VON, Platonische Naturwissenschaft im Laufe der Geschichte. Veröffentlichung der Joachim-Jungius-Gesellschaft der Wiss.

Göttingen, Vandenhoeck & Ruprecht 1971 25p.

802 WESTERINK L.G., "Damascius commentateur de Platon". p.253-260 in Le néoplatonisme (see 4578).

803* CARLINI A., Studi sulla tradizione antica e medievale del Fedone. Bibl. Athena X, Roma, Ed. dell'Ateneo 1972 xvi&219p.
Rev. Durius I 1973 397-398 Gutiérrez.
RFIC CI 1973 358-363 Berti.
AC XLII 1973 234 des Places.

804 FERNÁNDEZ-GALIANO M., "Platón, hoy". EClas XVI 1972 269-291.

805 FRANCO-REPELLINI F., "Note sul Platonbild del terzo umanesimo". Pensiero XVII 1972 91-122.

For further discussion and editions of ancient, medieval and renaissance commentators see 3, 4, 170, 190, 393, 440, 483, 535, 628, 667, 669, 670, 683, 707, 810, 822, 830, 995, 1084, 1284, 1285, 1366, 1539, 1540, 1541, 1542, 1543, 1544, 1668, 1798, 1799, 1800, 1801, 1875, 1876, 2019, 2020, 2021, 2022, 2038, 2332, 2333, 2333, 2334, 2449, 2481, 2482, 2483, 2484, 2485, 2486, 2487, 2488, 2489, 2490, 2491, 2492, 2544, 2545, 2555, 2787, 3367, 3424, 3425, 3913, 3951, 3957, 4562.

III: THE PLATONIC CORPUS

A: TRANSMISSION OF TEXT; INDIRECT TRADITION

806 BRUMBAUGH R.S. & WELLS R., "The Plato Microfilm Project". YLG XXXIV 1959-1960 181-184.

807 BRUMBAUGH R.S., "Logical and Mathematical Symbolism in the Platonic Scholia". JWI XXIV 1961 45-58.

808 BRUMBAUGH R.S., "Logical and Mathematical Symbolism in the Plato Scholia. II. A Thousand Years of Diffusion and Redesign". JWI XXVIII 1965 1-13.

809 BRUMBAUGH R.S., "Symbolism in the Plato Scholia III. A Final Summary". JWI XXXI 1968 1-11.

810 CARLINI A., "I lemmi del commento di Proclo all'Alcibiade I e il codice W di Platone". SCO X 1961 179-187.

811 HUNGER H., "Pseudo-Platonica in einer Ausgabe des 4. Jahrhunderts. Ein neues Fragment in der Papyrussammlung der Oesterreichischen Nationalbibliothek (G39846)". WS LXXIV 1961 40-42.

812 ROMANIUK K., "Le Platon d'Origène. Les citations des Lois, du Phédon, du Phèdre et de la République dans Contra Celse d'Origène". Aegyptus XLI 1961 44-73

813* BRUMBAUGH R.S. et al., A Catalogue of Microfilms in the Plato Microfilm Project, Yale Univ. Library, I: Mss. in Belgium, Denmark, England, Germany and Italy; II: Mss. in Austria, Czechoslovakia, France, Holland and Spain. Post-1600 mss. in Belgium, Denmark, England, Germany and Italy. Addenda to vol. I. New Haven, Yale Univ. Library 1962 v&118&III, iii&64&VI p.

814* WILSON N.G., "A List of Plato Manuscripts". Scriptorium XVI 1962 386-395.

815 DILLER A., "Petrarch's Greek Codex of Plato". CPh LIX 1964 270-272.

109

III A: TRANSMISSION OF TEXT; INDIRECT TRADITION

816 MORESCHINI C., "I lemmi del commento di Proclo al
    Parmenide in rapporto alla tradizione
    manoscritta di Platone". ASNP XXXIII 1964
    251-255.

817 SIJPESTEIJN P.J., "Die Platon-Papyri". Aegyptus
    XLIV 1964 26-33.

818 CHROUST A.H., "The Organization of the Corpus
    Platonicum in Antiquity". Hermes XCIII 1965
    34-46.

819* HOOG I., Der Wert des Phaidon- und Lachespapyrus
    Arsinoe für die Platonüberlieferung. Mit einer
    Neuausgabe der in beiden Papyri erhaltenen Teile
    des Platontextes. Diss. Hamburg 1965 182p.

820 CARLINI A., "Problemi e metodi di critica testuale
    platonica". BPEC XIV 1966 51-64.

821 NICOLL W.S.M., "Problems and Methods in Platonic
    Textual Criticism. A Reply". BPEC XVI 1968
    111-115.

822 SICHERL M., "Platonismus und Textüberlieferung".
    JOEByzG XV 1966 201-229.

823 SIJPESTEIJN P.J., "Ein bisher unveröffentlichter
    Platonpapyrus des Leidener Papyrusinstituts.
    Platon, Phaidon 65a8-c3 und 65e3-66b3".
    Mnemosyne XIX 1966 231-240.

824 VERDENIUS W.J., "Zum Leidener Phaidon-Papyrus".
    Mnemosyne XIX 1966 269.

825* BRUMBAUGH R.S. & WELLS R., The Plato Manuscripts.
    A new Index, prepared by the Plato Microfilm
    Project of the Yale Univ. Library. New Haven,
    Yale Univ. Pr. 1968 163p.
    Rev.Gnomon XLI 1969 615 Wilson.
    BBF XIV 1969 217-218 Parodi.
    CR XX 1970 158-159 Kidd.
    CJ LXV 1970 325-326 Jackson.

826 GAISER K., "Quellenkritische Probleme der indirekten
    Platonüberlieferung". p.31-84 in Idee und Zahl,
    hrsg. von Gadamer H.G. & Schadewaldt W. (see
    4594).

827 KRAEMER H.J., "Die grundsätzlichen Fragen der
    indirekten Platonüberlieferung". p.106-150 in
    Idee und Zahl, hrsg. von Gadamer H.G. &

Schadewaldt W. (see 4594).

828 RYBA B., "De Platonis codice Graeco Olomucensi M531". StudRuk VIII 1969 1-10. Summary in Scriptorium XXVI 1972 414.

829 SANTINELLO G., "Glosse di mano del Cusano alla Repubblica di Platone". Rinascimento IX 1969 117-145.

830 SOLARI R., "La traduzione armena dell'Eutifrone di Platone". RIL CIII 1969 477-499.

831 PHILIP J.A., "The Platonic Corpus". Phoenix XXIV 1970 296-308.

832 KOEBERT R., "Bemerkungen zu den syrischen Zitaten aus Homer und Platon im 5. Buch der Rhetorik des Anton von Tagrit und zum syrischen Περὶ ἀσκήσεως angeblich von Plutarch". Orientalia XL 1971 438-447.

833 WILLIS W.H., "A new Fragment of Plato's Parmenides on Parchment". GRBS XII 1971 539-552.

834 WILLIS W.H., "A Parchment Palimpsest Fragment of Plato at Duke University". Summary in BASP VIII 1971 87-88.

835 IRIGOIN J., "Philologie grecque". AEHE IVe Sect. 1971-1972 175-185.

836 IRIGOIN J., "Philologie grecque". AEHE IVe sect. 1972-1973 197-207.

837 IRIGOIN J., "Philologie grecque". AEHE IVe sect. 1973-1974 205-214.

For further discussions see 55, 608, 810, 1080, 1104, 1191, 1192, 1212, 1306, 1410, 1459, 1637, 1638, 1772, 1773, 1774, 1775, 1776, 1777, 1780, 1863, 1864, 2168, 2211, 2293, 2466, 2544, 2545, 2546, 2571.

III B: AUTHENTICITY AND CHRONOLOGY

838* BOEHME R., Von Sokrates zur Ideenlehre. Beobachtungen zur Chronologie des Platonischen Frühwerks. Diss. Bernenses Ser. 1a IX, Bern, Francke 1959 159p.
Rev. RFIC XXXVII 1959 409-413 Plebe.
RPh XXXlV 1960 284 Louis.
JHS LXXX 1960 229 Tarrant.
Emerita XXIX 1961 168-169 Adrados.
CR XI 1961 32-33 Kerferd.
Ph&PhenR XXI 1960-1961 430-431 Schwarz.
AAHG XIV 1961 173 Vretska.
Gymnasium LXIX 1962 564 Classen.
Sophia XXX 1962 371-372 Montoneri.
Gnomon XL 1968 200-201 Tredennick.

839 COX D.R. & BRANDWOOD L., "On a discriminatory problem connected with the works of Plato". J. Royal Statistical Soc. Ser. B. XXI 1959 195-200.

840 PALEIKAT J., "Métodos científicos para determinar a autenticidade e a ordem de publicação dos diálogos platónicos". Organon, Rev. da Fac. de Filos. Univ. do Rio Grande do Sul, Porto Alegre I,1 Mars. 1956 47-63; III,2 1959 31-40.

841 RIST J.M., "The Order of the Later Dialogues of Plato". Phoenix XIV 1960 207-221.

842 DIAZ TEJERA A., "Ensayo de un metodo linguístico para la cronología de Platón [in Spanish with English summary]". Emerita XXIX 1961 241-286.

843 ROSS W.D., "L'ordinamento dei dialoghi". p.213-225 in Antologia della critica flosofica, ed. da Rossi P. (see 4613). Reprinted from Ross W.D., Plato's Theory of Ideas. Oxford, Clarendon Pr. 1951 p.1-10.

844 DÍAZ TEJERA A., "Die Chronologie der Dialoge Platons". Altertum XI 1965 79-86.

846* MORTON A.Q. & WINSPEAR A.D., It's Greek to the Computer. Montreal, Harvest House 1971 129p. (ch.5 "The Seventh Letter of Plato", p.67-89;

112

ch.6 "The Authorship of the Axiochus", p.91-94;
ch.7 "The Authorship of the Epinomis", p.95-100;
ch.8 "The Authorship of the Timaeus Locrus", p.101-105.)
      Rev. Phoenix XXVI 1972 402 Brandwood.
      CW LXV 1972 119 McDonough.
      HumAB 1973 66 Berry.

847 MICHAELSON S. & MORTON A.Q., "The new Stylometry. A one-word Test of Authorship for Greek Writers". CQ XXII 1972 89-102.

For further discussion see 996, 997, 1001, 1002, 1003, 1104, 1116, 1117, 1195, 1202, 1208, 1212, 1214, 1311, 1312, 1424, 1425, 1426, 1429, 1430, 1433, 1434, 1435, 1436, 1437, 1447, 1449, 1457, 1458, 1465, 1467, 1470, 1496, 1808, 1811, 1812, 1822, 1950, 2199, 2356, 2357, 2367, 2516, 2565, 2715.

III C: EDITIONS, TRANSLATIONS, COMMENTARIES
AND INTERPRETATIONS OF THE WRITINGS THEMSELVES

This section contains texts, translations, commentaries
and scholarly discussions of the Platonic
corpus, including the spurious and doubtful
works. It is divided as follows:
a. Editions and translations of Plato's collected
works. This includes multi-volume sets, whether
complete or incomplete by 1973. The entries are
arranged by language.
b. Anthologies. Typically these are excerpts from
the dialogues on one or more themes. Again,
they are grouped by language.
c. Selected dialogues. These are cross referenced
under the dialogues they contain. Note
exceptions to this policy: works containing the
Apology and Crito (even if they also contain the
Euthyphro and/or the Phaedo) are grouped under
Apology (with cross references under the other
dialogues they contain) and works containing the
Timaeus and Critias are grouped under the
Timaeus and cross referenced under the Critias.
d. Individual works. These are arranged
alphabetically and the entries under them are
grouped into three categories:
   A. Texts and translations (arranged by
language).
   B. Studies of the particular work,
including commentaries, treatments of the work
as a whole, and treatments of particular
passages. The arrangement of this section
varies depending on the nature of the work and
on the number of entries included. As a general
rule, the first items to appear are commentaries
(starting off with the works of ancient,
medieval, and renaissance commentators). Next
come other general treatments of the work as a
whole and finally discussions of particular
issues and passages. In most cases the number
of the writings in the last of these headings
was not large enough to require further
arrangement, but in some cases (especially the
Republic, but also the Parmenides, Phaedo, and a
few others) the arrangement of the work makes it
natural to group the discussions under certain
headings and there were enough entries for the
work to make this worthwhile. The discussions
are generally arranged in chronological order,
and alphabetically by author within a given

year. However, in a number of cases it was natural to group together series of articles or exchanges prompted by a single work. C. Textual criticism. This section includes both proposed emendations and studies of manuscripts. The relation between textual criticism and philosophical interpretation being so close in the case of Plato, the choice between putting an article in section B or in this section was frequently difficult and it would be reasonable for a person to consult this section even if his primary interest is not philological.

a: COLLECTIONS OF PLATO'S COMPLETE WORKS

848* Plato, The Collected Dialogues, ed. by Hamilton E. & Cairns H. Bollingen Ser. LXXI, New York, Pantheon Books 1961 xxv&1743p.
Rev. BAGB 1962 126 Malve.
Personalist XLIII 1962 546-547 O'Neill.

849* The Dialogues of Plato, transl. with analyses & introds. by Jowett B. 4th edn. rev. Oxford, Clarendon Pr. 1964 4 vols. xxxi&696, 718, 804, & 657p.

850* Plato, Dialogues, transl. by Jowett B., ed. by Russell D.A. & Hare R.M. London, Sphere 1970 4 vols. 288, 304, 320 & 432p.

851* The Works of Plato, viz. his fifty-five Dialogues, and twelve Epistles, translated from the Greek; nine of the dialogues by... Floyer Sydenham, and the remainder by Thomas Taylor. New York, AMS Pr. 1972 5 vols. Reprint of 1804 edn.

852* Plato, Sämtliche Werke, I: Apologie, Kriton, Protagoras, Hippias 2, Charmides, Laches, Ion, Euthyphron, Gorgias, Briefe, in deutsche Übers. von Schleiermacher F., hrsg. von Otto W.F., Grassi E. & Plamboeck G. 4. Aufl. Rowohlts Klassiker d. Literatur u.d. Wissenschaft 1/1a, Reinbek b. Hamburg, Rowohlt 1960 338p.

853* Sämtliche Werke, II: Menon, Hippias I, Euthydemos, Menexenos, Kratylos, Lysis, Symposion; IV: Phaidros, Parmenides, Theaitetos, Sophistes,

115

nach der Übers. von Schleiermacher F. hrsg.
von Otto W.F., Grassi E. & Plamboeck G.
Rowohlts Klass. der Lit. u. d. Wiss. XIV,
XXXIX, Reinbek bei Hamburg, Rowohlt 1958 253 &
246p.

854* Platon, Sämtliche Werke, III: Phaidon, Politeia, in
der Übers. von Schleiermacher F. & Mueller H.
hrsg. von Otto W.F., Grassi E. & Plamboeck G.
Rowohlts Klass. der Lit. & der Wiss. XXVII,
Reinbek bei Hamburg, Rowohlt 1958 313p.
Rev. Helikon II 1962 745-746 Frenkian.

855* Platon, Sämtliche Werke, IV: Phaidros, Parmenides,
Theaitetos, Sophistes, nach der Übers. von
Schleiermacher F. & Mueller H. hrsg. von Otto
W.F., Grassi E. & Plamboeck G. Rowohlts Klass.
der Lit & der Wiss., Reinbek bei Hamburg,
Rowohlt 1958 248p.

856* Platon, Sämtliche Werke, V: Politikos, Philebos,
Timaios, Kritias, nach der Übers. von
Schleiermacher F. hrsg. von Otto W.F., Grassi
E. & Plamboeck G. Rowohlts Klass. der Lit.
u. d. Wiss., Reinbek bei Hamburg, Rowohlt 1959
233p.
Rev. JHPh I 1963 238-239 Merlan.

857* Platon, Sämtliche Werke, VI: Nomoi, nach der Übers.
von Schleiermacher F. & Mueller H. hrsg. von
Otto W.F., Grassi E. & Plamboeck G. Rowohlts
Klass. der Lit. u. der Wiss. LIV, Reinbek bei
Hamburg, Rowohlt 1959 327p.

858* Platon, Werke in 8 bänden, II: Des Sokrates
Apologie. Kriton. Euthydemos, Menexenos,
Gorgias, Menon, übers. von Schleiermacher F.,
bearb. von Hofmann H., Text von Croiset A.
Darmstadt, Wiss. Buchges. 1973 xiv&606p.

859* Platon, Werke in 8 Bänden, IV: Πολιτεία, bearb.
von Kurz D., Text von Chambry E., Übers. von
Schleiermacher F. Darmstadt, Wiss. Buchges.
1971 xiv&875p.
Rev. Platon XXIV 1972 336-338
Georgountzos.
Philosophia(Athens) II 1972 343-344
Skouteropoulos.
Hellenica XXVI 1973 129-130 Kakrides.
BO XXX 1973 484-486 Jonkers.

860* Platon, Werke in 8 Bänden. Bd. 6: Theaitetos, Der
Sophist, Der Staatsmann, hrsg. von Eigler G.,
bearb. von Staudacher P., griech. Text von
Dìes A., deut. Übers. von Schleiermacher F.
Darmstadt, Wiss. Buchges. 1970 xv&579p.

861* Platon, Werke in 8 Banden, VII: Timaios, Kritias,
Philebos, bearb. von Widdra K., griech. Text
von Rivaud A. & Dìes A., Übers. von Mueller H.
& Schleiermacher F. Darmstadt, Wiss. Buchges.
1972 xxvi&449p.

862* Platone, I dialoghi, l'apologia e le epistole, vers.
& interp. di Turolla E. 2a ed. riv. e
accresc. Milano, Rizzoli 1964 3 vols.

863* Platone, Opere, a cura di Giannantoni G. Bari,
Laterza 1967 2 vols. liv&1298, 1258p.
Rev. ArchPhilos XXXI 1968 305 Solignac.
CR XX 1970 310-312 Phillips.

864* Platone, Opere complete, Bari, Laterza 1971 9 vols.

865* Platón, Obras completas, trad. de Araújo M., García
Yagüe F., Gil L., Miguez J.A., Rico M. et al.,
pról. de Miguez J.A. Grandes Culturas, Madrid,
Aguilar 1966 1782p.
Rev. NG XVI 1969 118-120 Zamora.

866* Plato, Verzameld werk. Deel I: Kleine Hippias.
Euthydemus. Gorgias. Apologie. Crito.
Euthyphro. Io. Menexenus. Charmides. Laches.
Lysis. Meno. Protagoras. Alcibiades I. Grote
Hippias. Cratylus. Symposium. Phaedo, vert.
door Win X. de. Uitgeg. met medew. van de
Universitaire Stichting van België. Antwerpen,
De Nederlandsche Boekhandel 1965 xliii&1031p.
Rev. Hermeneus XXXVII 1966 260.

867* Plato, Verzameld werk, II: Staat, Phaedrus,
Theaetetus, Parmenides, Sofist, Staatsman,
Brieven, vert. door Win X. de. Haarlem,
Willink 1962 1021p.
Rev. DWB CVII 1962 742-747 Verbeke.
Mnemosyne XVI 1963 413 de Vries.
Hermeneus XXXV 1964 172 Pieters.

868* Plato, Verzameld werk. Deel III: Timaeus, Critias,
Philebus, De Wetten, Epinomis, Betwiste
geschriften, niet authentieke geschriften, vert.
door de Win X. Uitgeg. met medew. van de
Univ. stichting van België. Antwerpen, De

Nederlandsche Boekhandel 1963 996p.

869* Ἅπαντα Πλάτωνος. Athens, Hetaireia Hellenikon
Ekdoseon 1956-, 18 vols. vols. 1-14 Modern
Greek transl., introds. & notes by Kouchtsoglou
G.; vols. 15-18 Ancient Greek text.

870* Plato, Works, IV: Critias, Laws, Hebrew transl. by
Libes J.C. Tel-Aviv, Schocken 1964 424p.

871* Plato, Works Vol.V, Hebrew transl. by Libes J.G.
Tel-Aviv, Schocken 1966 469p.

872* Platon, Sochinenija [Works], red. Losev A.F. &
Asmus V.F. Moskva, Mysl 3 vols. T.1 1968
624p.; T.2 1970 612p.; T.3 1972 678p.
Rev. [of T.1] VF XXII 1968 169.
[of T.2] VF XXIV 1970 159.
[of T.3] VF XXVI 1972 46-56.

873* Plato, Complete Works, Korean transl. by Pak Y.W.
Chayu kyoyang ch'ongso [Freedom Culture Series],
Seoul, Kwangmyong Publ. 1966-. Vol. I
contains Apology, Protagoras and Crito.

874* The Collected Works of Plato, transl. by Okada S.
Tokyo, Zenkoku Shobo vol. I 1969 390p.; II 1969
380p.; III 1969 374p.; IV 1970 362p.; V 1971
378p.; VI 1972 417p.

875* Plato's Collected Works. Tokyo, Keiso Shobo. Vol.
I 1970 510p. (contains the essay "Socrates and
Plato" by Sakisaka and Japanese translations of
the Cratylus, Symposium, Parmenides and
Sophist); vol. II 1973 xxxiii&343p. (contains
Laws I-VI, transl. by Shikibu H.)

876* The Works of Plato, Japanese transl. Tokyo,
Kadokawa. vol. I (contains Euthyphro, Apology,
Crito, Phaedo, Cratylus) 1973 xxxv&525p.; vol.
III (contains Philebus, Symposium, Phaedrus,
Erastae) 1973 xxiii&465p.; vol. IV (contains
Alcibiades I, Laches, Lysis, Euthydemus,
Alcibiades II, Hipparchus, Theages, Charmides)
1973 xlvi&504p.; vol. VII (contains Laws
I-VII) 1973 451p.

See also 22.

III C b: ANTHOLOGIES

877* REEVES J.W., Body and mind in Western Thought.
London, Pelican Books 1958 403p. (p.34-37 and
188-213 contain translations of parts of the
Phaedo, Phaedrus, and Republic books 3, 7, 9.)

878* The Myths of Plato, original transl. & introd. by
Stewart J.A. Ed. and newly introd. by Levy
G.R. London, Centaur Pr. and Carbondale, Ill.,
Southern Illinois Univ. Pr. 1960 481p.
(Revised version of 1905 edn.) (Contains myths
of Phaedo, Gorgias, Republic III and X,
Politicus, Protagoras, Timaeus, Phaedrus,
Symposium.) Also New York, Barnes & Noble 1970.
Rev. HibJ LVIII 1959-1960 416-418
Tarrant.
ConR 1960 348 Banyard.
ModS L 1972-1973 83-86 Sweeney.

879* WILBUR J.B. & ALLEN H.J., The Worlds of Plato and
Aristotle. New York, American Book Co. 1962
xiii&172p.

880* VOGEL C.J. DE, Greek Philosophy. A Collection of
Texts, I: Thales to Plato. 3rd edn. Leiden,
Brill 1963 xi&334p. (ch.7, p.113-156 on
Socrates; ch.9, p.170-299 on Plato.)

881* HOFSTADTER A. & KUHNS R., Philosophies of Art and
Beauty. Selected Readings in Aesthetics from
Plato to Heidegger. New York, Modern Library
1964 701p.

882* SESONSKE A. ed., What is Art? Aesthetic Theory
from Plato to Tolstoy. New York, Oxford Univ.
Pr. 1965 428p.

883* CORNFORD F.M., Greek Religious Thought: From Homer
to the Age of Alexander. New York, Abrahams
Magazine Service 1969 xxxv&252p. Reprint of
1923 edn. (ch.15, p.188-225 contains excerpts
from Plato on religious subjects, in English
translation.)

884* DRAKE H.L., The People's Plato, New York, Philos.
Libr. 1958 xxiii&633p. Also appeared as
Plato's Complete Works, Abridged. Patterson,
N.J., Littlefield, Adams & co. 1959.
Rev. PhilosStud(Irel.) VIII 1958 216-217

Meany.
Personalist 1960 210 Searles.
CJ LVI 1960 45 MacClintock.

885* A Plato Reader, transl. by Jowett B., ed. by
Levinson R.B. Riverside Eds. C102, Boston,
Houghton Mifflin 1967 xlv&513p.

886* SEN N.B., Wit and Wisdom of Socrates, Plato and
Aristotle. New Delhi, New Book Society of India
1967 278p.

887* MATTHEWS G., Plato's Epistemology and related
Logical Problems. New York, Humanities Pr.
1973.

888* Platon, Logos, Eros, Mythos, hrsg. & eingel. von
Lehmann-Leander E.R. Denker d. Antike II,
Wiesbaden, Vollmer 1961 352p.

889* KRUEGER J., Aesthetik der Antike. Berlin,
Aufbau-Verl. 1964 600p.
Rev. RThPh XCIX 1966 131 Piguet.
StudClas X 1968 323 Ceaușescu.

890* KOCH K.D., Wer liest schon Platon! Eine durchaus
nicht zweckfreie, hemmungs- jedoch nicht
verantwortungslose Ausschlachtung e. alten
Autors f. neue Zeiten u. zeitlose Ziele.
Ausw. u. Übers., Vor- u. Nachw. von Koch
K.D. Bremen, Rover 1969 107p.

891 PATZIG G., "Texte zu Platons Ideenlehre neu
übersetzt". A&A XVI 1970 127-140.

892* SWOBODA H. ed., Der Traum vom besten Staat. Texte
aus Utopien von Platon bis Morris, hrsg. von
Swoboda H. München, Deutscher Taschenbuch-Verl.
1972 408p.

893* Les pages immortelles de Platon, choisies &
expliquées par Guitton J. Coll. Les pages
immortelles, Paris, Buchet-Chastel 1960 254p.
Also Spanish transl. El pensamiento vivo de
Platón. Coll. Biblioteca del pensamiento vivo,
Buenos Aires, Losada 1967 310p. (Contains
selections from Gorgias, Republic VII, VIII, X,
Timaeus, Phaedo, Symposium, Apology, Phaedrus,
Theaetetus, Laws, Meno, Seventh Letter.)

894* RODIS-LEWIS G., Platon et la chasse de l'Être,
présentation, choix de textes, bibliog.
Philosophes de tous les temps XIX, Paris,
Seghers 1965 191p. Also Italian transl.,
Platone, La vita, il pensiero, i testi
esemplari, trad. di Isella G. I memorabili
XXXVIII, Milano, Accademia 1972 268p.
Rev. REG LXXVIII 1965 692 Weil.

895* Platon, textes choisis [traduits] et presentées par
About P.J. Selection philos. Bordas, Paris,
Bordas 1967 192p.

896* ANGELINO G., Il dramma di Socrate dai dialoghi di
Platone. Crestomazia greca I, Torino, Loescher
s.d. [1958?] xvii&136p.

897* MARTANO G., Platone-Aristotele, Politeia. Antologia
degli scritti politici. 2a ed. Coll. class.
di filos., Napoli S. Viti s.d. [1958?] 138p.

898* Plato, Μῦθος. Antologia platonica, introd. e
commento di Sacerdoti N. Milano, Signorelli
1963 102p.

899* PLEBE A., Platone, Il pensiero estetico. Piccola
bibl. filos., Bari, Laterza 1964 159p.
Rev. GM 1964 834-835 Beschin.

900* VALGIMIGLI M., Poeti e filosofi di Grecia, I:
Traduzioni: Eschilo, Sofocle, Euripide,
Platone, Aristotele; II: Interpretazioni. 4a
ed. Bari, Laterza 1964 748 & 645 p.

901* PESCE D., Platone, La dottrina delle idee.
Antologia sistematica. Pensatori antichi e
moderni LXV, Firenze, La Nuova Italia 1964
xv&150p.

902* PLEBE A., Platone, Antologia di critica letteraria.
Traditio, Ser. greca IV, Milano, Dante
Alighieri 1965 150p.

903* MAGNINO D., Antologia platonica. Napoli, Morano
1967 149p.

904* Παιδεία. Il problema dell'educazione in Platone,
passi scelti e comm. da Ammendola G. Napoli,
Loffredo 1967 219p.

905* Eros, antologia dal Simposio e dal Fedro, introd. &
     note di Gallo I. Bibl. class. Ser. greca,
     Firenze, Sansoni 1968 187p.
          Rev. Vichiana V 1968 362 Pini.

906* Platone, Dialoghi socratici, antologia a cura di
     Casini N. Firenze, Le Monnier 1970 xii&375p.

907* CECCHI S., Antologia dai dialoghi politici di
     Platone. Napoli/Firenze, Il Tripode 1970 158p.

908* GALLINARI L., Saggezza antica. I sofisti, Platone,
     Aristotele, Lucrezio, Marco Aurelio. Filos. e
     scienze humane I, Cassino, Ciolfi [1971?] 639p.

909* Platone, Opere politiche, antologia a cura di Casini
     N. Firenze, Le Monnier 1972 xii&559p.

910* CASTAGNA L., Antologia di Platone. Il pensiero
     politico. Coll. di class. greci, Torino,
     Marietti 1973 234p.

911* HERNÁNDEZ RUIZ S., Antología pedagógica de Platón.
     Col. Ensayos pedagógicos, Mexico City,
     Fernández 1965 276p.

912* VRIES G.J. DE, Frustula platonica. Groningen,
     Wolters 1958 64p.
          Rev. MPh LXIV 1959 186 Broos.

913* MARTINKA J., Predsokratici a Platón [Presocratics
     and Plato], Zost. Martinka J., pred. Hrušovský
     I. Bratislava, Epocha 1970 541p.

See also 3275, 3410.

III C c: SELECTED DIALOGUES

914* The Republic and Other Works, transl. by Jowett B.
     Garden City, New York, Doubleday 552p.
     (Contains Republic, Symposium, Parmenides,
     Euthyphro, Apology, Crito, and Phaedo.)

915* Parmenides, Theaitetos, Sophist, Statesman, transl.
     with an introd. by Warrington J. Everyman's
     Libr., London, Dent and New York, Dutton 1961
     xii&294p.
          Rev. CR XII 1962 306 Bluck.

CW LVI 1962 49 Sprague.
CJ LVIII 1963 369 Hoerber.

916* The Sophist and the Statesman, transl. & introd.
by Taylor A.E., ed. by Klibansky R. & Anscombe
E. London, Nelson 1961 vii&344p. Also
Folkestone, Dawsons and New York, Barnes & Noble
1971.
Rev. AC XXX 1961 574-575 Janssens.
HeythropJ II 1961 285 T.G.
TLS 11 Aug. 1961 528.
ModS XXXIX 1961-1962 196 Sweeney.
RecSR L 1962 613 des Places.
JCS X 1962 136-141.
Athenaeum XL 1962 179-181 Untersteiner.
PhR LXXII 1963 122-124 Moravcsik.
AAHG XVI 1963 222 Braun.
CR XIV 1964 147-148 Allan.
Mnemosyne XVII 1964 408 Verdenius.

917* Symposium and other Dialogues, introd. & transl.
by Warrington J. London, Dent and New York,
Dutton 1964 xi&195p.

918* Lysis, or Friendship. The Symposium, Phaedrus,
transl. with introd. analyses by Jowett B.,
pref. by Oates W.J., ill. by Karlin E. New
York, Heritage Pr. 1969 208p.

919* Philebus and Epinomis, transl. & introd. by Taylor
A.E., ed. by Klibansky R., Calogero G. & Lloyd
A.C. Folkestone, Dawsons and New York, Barnes &
Noble 1972 vi&272p. Reprint of 1956 edn.

920* PLOCHMANN G.K., Plato. New York, Dell Publ. 1973
543p.
Rev. Thomist XXXVII 1973 793-799
Anagnostopoulos.

921* Laches and Charmides, transl. with an introd. and
notes by Sprague R.K. Indianapolis,
Bobbs-Merrill 1973 102p.
Rev. Dialogue XIII 1973 582 Mollenhauer.

922* Phaedrus and the Seventh and Eighth Letters, transl.
with introd. by Hamilton W. Harmondsworth,
Middx., Penguin 1973 160p.
Rev. TLS 30 Nov. 1973 1485.

923* The Sophistes and Politicus of Plato, with a revised
text and English notes by Campbell L. New York,
Arno Pr. 1973 xc&192p., lix&191p. [2 vols. in

1]. Reprint of 1867 edn.

924* Platon, Meisterdialoge, Phaidon, Symposion, Phaidros, Übertr. von Rufener R., eingel. von Gigon O. Zürich/Stuttgart, Artemis-Verl. 1958 lxxxvi&280p. Also in series Meisterwerk der Antike, Zürich, Buchclub Ex Libris 1970.
Rev. RBPh XXXVIII 1960 933 de Rijck.

925* Platon, Frühdialoge. Laches, Charmides, Lysis, Der grössere Hippias, Der kleinere Hippias, Protagoras, Euthydemos, Ion, Menexenos, eingel. von Gigon O., übertr. von Rufener R. Bibl. der Alten Welt, Zürich, Artemis-Verl. 1960 cv&392p.
Rev. PhilosRdschau X 1962 157-158.
RBPh XL 1962 243-244 Henry.
AAHG XV 1962 222 von Ivánka.
Gymnasium LXXI 1964 454-457 Voigtlaender.
SK LX 1960-1961 593-594 Husner.

926* Spätdialoge. Theaitetos, Der Sophist, Der Staatsmann, Kratylos, eingel. von Gigon O., übertr. von Rufener R. Bibl. der Alten Welt, Zürich, Artemis-Verl. 1965 li&426p.
Rev. RBPh XLIV 1966 186 des Places.
Universitas XXI 1966 538-539 M.L.
Du XXVI 1966 140 Mauch.

927* Platon, Spätdialoge. Philebos, Parmenides, Timaios, Kritias, eingel. von Gigon O., übertr. von Rufener R. Bibl. der Alten Welt, Zürich, Artemis-Verl. 1969 li&340p.
Rev. Sophia XL 1972 154-157.

928* Gastmahl, Phaidros, Phaidon, übertr. von Kassner R. 3. vom Übers. überarb. Aufl. Düsseldorf/Köln, Diederichs 1959 241p.

929* Gorgias-Protagoras, 2 sokratische Dialoge, übertr. von Feix J. München, Goldmann 1960 189p.

930* Über die Freundschaft, die Liebe und das Schöne. Lysis, Das Gastmahl, Phaidros, übers., erläut. und eingel. von Huebscher A. Bücher der Welt, München/Zürich, Droemer-Knaur 1960 287p.

931* Phaidros, Parmenides, Theaitetos, in der Übertr. von Schleiermacher F., eingel. von Endres H.M. München, Goldmann 1963 224p.

932* Menon, Euthydemos, Kratylos, übert. von
     Schleiermacher F., eingel. von Endres H.M.
     München, Goldmann 1964 171p.

933* Ion, Hippias I und II, Laches, Charmides, Lysis,
     Menexenos, eingel. von Endres H.M., übers. von
     Schleiermacher F. (Bd. 7 der Ausgewählten
     Werke Platons in 10 Bänden.) München, Goldmann
     1967 176p.

934* Philebos, Timaios, Kritias, übertr. von
     Schleiermacher F. & Susemihl F., eingel. von
     Endres H.M. München, Goldmann 1968 195p.

935* PIEPER J., Kümmert euch nicht um Sokrates! Drei
     Fernseh-Spiele. München, Koesel-Verl. 1968
     205p. (Dramatized versions of Plato's Gorgias,
     Symposium and Phaedo.)
            Rev. ZPhF XXIV 1970 639-640 Klamp.
            CW 1967 49 Etheridge.

936* Die Verteidigungsrede des Sokrates und Lobrede des
     Alkibiades auf Sokrates aus dem Gastmahl,
     übertr. von Schubring G. Drucke der
     Stefan-George-Stift, Düsseldorf, Kuepper 1973
     55p.

937* Le Banquet, Phèdre, Phédon, texte étab. et trad par
     Robin L. Club français du livre. Les Portiques
     LXX, Paris, Club français du livre 1961 714p.

938* Lachès et Lysis, éd., introd. & comm. de Vicaire
     P. Érasme, Coll. de textes grecs comm. VII,
     Paris, Presses Universitaires 1963 107p.
            Rev. REG LXXVII 1964 345 Dreyfus.
            RBPh XLII 1964 1094 Saunders.
            AC XXXIV 1965 229 Motte.
            JHS LXXXV 1965 207-208 Robinson.
            CR XV 1965 115 Luce.
            Mnemosyne XIX 1966 296 Begemann.

939* Le Banquet, Phèdre, trad., notices et notes reprises
     de l'édition Chambry É. Paris,
     Garnier-Flammarion 1964 187p.

940* Parménide, Théétète, Le Sophiste, texte étab. et
     trad. par Diès A. Club français du livre. Les
     Portiques LXXIX, Paris, Club francais du livre
     1965 526p.

941* Théétète, Parménide, trad., notices et notes par Chambry É. Garnier-Flammarion, Texte intégral CLXIII, Paris, Garnier-Flammarion 1967 319p.

942* Platon, Second Alcibiade. Hippias mineur. Premier Alcibiade. Euthyphron. Lachès. Charmide. Lysis. Hippias majeur. Ion, trad., notices et notes par Chambry É. Paris, Garnier-Flammarion 1967 445p.

943* Protagoras, Euthydème, Gorgias, Ménexène, Ménon, Cratyle, trad., notices et notes par Chambry É. Garnier-Flammarion, Texte intégral 146, Paris, Garnier-Flammarion 1967 508p.

944* Sophiste, Politique, Philèbe, Timée, Critias, trad., notices et notes par Chambry É. Garnier-Flammarion Texte intégral 203, Paris, Garnier-Flammarion 1969 512p.

945* Platone, Opere politiche, II: Politico, Leggi, a cura di Adorno F. Torino, Utet 1958 695p.
    Rev. A&R VI 1961 246 Savino.

946* Alcibiade, Alcibiade secondo, Ipparco, Rivali, introd., testo crit. e trad. a cura di Carlini A. Encicl. di autori class. LXXXII, Torino, Boringhieri 1964 405p.
    Rev. AC XXXIV 1965 228-229 des Places.
    Gnomon XXXVII 1965 754-757 Nicoll.
    REG LXXVIII 1965 422-423 Weil.
    GIF XVIII 1965 162 Grosso.
    AAHG XIX 1966 102-104 Doent.
    A&R XII 1967 58-60 Moreschini.
    RPh XLI 1967 314 Louis.
    Mnemosyne XX 1967 78-79 de Vries.
    RFIC XCV 1967 85-91 Alberti.
    JHS LXXXVIII 1968 158-160 Giorgetti.

947* Parmenides, Phaedrus, rec., adnot. crit. instr. Moreschini C. Bibl. Athena V, Roma, Ed. dell'Ateneo 1966 173p.
    Rev. AC XXXVI 1967 644 des Places.
    RPh XLII 1968 143-144 des Places.
    AAHG XXI 1968 278 Vretska.
    Mnemosyne XXII 1969 437-438 de Vries.
    REG LXXXII 1969 652-653 Vicaire.
    Gymnasium LXXVI 1969 95-97 Gaiser.
    Emerita XXXVII 1969 186-189 Lens.
    Ck XX 1970 312-313 Kidd.
    REA LXXII 1970 422-424 Thillet.
    GIF XXIII 1971 243-244 Vitali.

948* Platone, Dialoghi, nella versione di Acri F., a cura
     di Carena C., con un saggio introd. di Treves
     P. Torino, Einaudi 1970 xlvii&597p.
     Rev. RCCM XII 1970 221-225 Paratore.
     RRFC LXVI 1972 63-65.

949* Dialoghi filosofici, I, a cura di Cambiano G.
     Class. della filos., Torino, Utet 1970 662p.
     (Apologia di Socrate, Critone, Eutifrone, Ione,
     Carmide, Lachete, Liside, Ippia maggiore, Ippia
     minore, Protagora, Gorgia, Menone, Fedone,
     Eutidemo.)
     Rev. RIFD XLIX 1972 138-139.

950* Dialoghi politici e lettere, a cura di Adorno F. 2a
     ed. accresc. Class. della filos., Torino,
     Utet 1970 2 vols. (Vol. I: Repubblica, Timeo,
     Crizia, Politico; vol. II: Le Leggi,
     Epinomide, Minosse, Clitofonte, Menesseno,
     Lettere.)
     Rev. RIFD XLIX 1972 139.

951* Platón, Diálogos. Filebos, Timaios, Kritias,
     Apéndices: 1o Timaios de Lokres. Del alma del
     mundo. 2o Ploutarchos. Sobre la creación del
     alma en el Timaios de Platón, trad., noticias
     prelim., notas y estampa socrática de Bergua
     J.B. Bibl. de Bolsillo, Madrid, Ed. Ibéricas
     1960 480p.

952* Platón, Diálogos: Parmenides, Teaitetos, Sofista,
     Político, trad., noticias prelim., notas y
     estampa socrática de Bergua J.B. Bibl. de
     Bolsillo, Madrid, Ed. Ibéricas 1960 400p.

953* Diálogos. Menexenos, Menón, Kratilos, Faidros,
     trad. y notas de Bergua J.B. 4a ed., rev.,
     corr. & mejorad. Madrid, Ed. Ibéricas 1958
     409p.

954* El banquete o sobre el amor. Fedón o sobre el alma,
     trad., estudios prelim., notas y estampa
     socrática de Bergua J.B. Col. Tesoro Liter.,
     Madrid, Ed. Ibéricas 1963 430p.

955* Sobre la belleza y el amor (Fedro, Banquete,
     Hipias), trad. por Garcia Bácca J.D. Caracas,
     Edime and Madrid, Bravo 1963 164.

956* Diálogos. Hipias mayor, Ión, Fedro, introd. de
     García Bacca J.D. Mexico City, U.N.A.M. 1965
     xv&188p.

957* Platón, Diálogos, trad. de Ferrán de Mayoral J.
Barcelona, Plaza & Janés 1961 127p.

958* Diálogos: Eutifrón o de la santidad, Apología de
Socrates..., estudio prelim. de Larroyo F.
Mexico City, Ed. Porrua 1962 xxv&541p. Also 2a
ed. cor. y aument. 1964.

959* Diálogos socráticos. Apología, Critón, Eutifrón,
Fedón, Fedro, Banquete, Menón, estudio prelim.
de Vessalio A. Mexico City, Jackson 1963 411p.

960* Diálogos. Apología de Socrates, Fedón, Fedro, trad.
por Azcárate P. de. Montivideo, Min. de
Instruc. Públ. y Previs. Social 1963 224p.

961* Platon, Diálogos apócrifos y dudosos, I, trad.,
prólogos y notas de Tovar A. & Scandariali C.;
Vol.II, trad., prólogos y notas de Tovar A. &
Binda R.P. Buenos Aires, Ed. Universitaria
1966 136 & 112p.
Rev. Emerita XXXV 1967 165 Adrados.

962* Hipías Mayor, Fedro. Mexico City, U.N.A.M. 1967
384p.

963* El Banquete, Fedón, Fedro, trad. de Gil L. Madrid,
Ed. Guadarrama 1969 383p.
Rev. Helmantica XXI 1970 325 Ruiz.
EClas XIII 1969 123-124 Garcia Gual.
Emerita XLI 1973 227-228 Rico.

964* Platón, Diálogos. Fedón o De la inmortalidad del
alma. El Banquete o Del amor. Col. Clás.
univ. XXIV, Madrid, Ed. Susaeta 1969 235p.

965* Platón, Diálogos socráticos, ed., introd. & notas
de García Calvo A. Bibl. Gen. Salvat LVIII,
Barcelona, Ed. Salvat and Madrid, Alianza
Editorial 1972 143p.

966* Plato, Dialogen. Symposion. Apologie. Kritoon.
Phaidoon. Sokrates in leven en sterven, Ned.
van Schwartz M.A. Prisma-boeken 550, Utrecht,
Het Spectrum 1960 188p.

967* Vervoering en onsterfelijkheid van de ziel.
Phaidros. Phaidoon, vert. door Boutens P.C.,
Annot. van Radt S.L. Phoenix klassieke pockets
IV, Zeist, de Haan and Antwerpen,
Standaard-boekhandel 1964 178p.

III C c: SELECTED DIALOGUES

968* Charmides, Lysis, Menoon, vert. en toegelicht door
      Damste O. Phoenix klass. pockets VII, Zeist,
      W. de Haan and Antwerpen, Standaard-boekhandel
      1965 158p.

969* Sokrates in gesprek. Plato's Apologie, Krito, het
      slot van de Phaedo en Symposium, vert. door
      Loenen D., voorw. van Polak J.B.W. Athenaeum
      paperbacks, Amsterdam, Polak & Van Gennep 1966
      164p.

970* Sokrates spreekt met Phaidros, Protagoras, Ion,
      vert. door Schwartz M.A. Prisma-boeken 1345,
      Utrecht, Het Spectrum 1968 173p.

971* Platão, Diálogos, I: Menon, Banquete, Fedro. II:
      Fédon, Sofista, Político. III: A República,
      trad. de Paleikat J. e Vallandro L. Rio de
      Janeiro, Ed. de Ouro 1968 269, 351 & 267p.

972* Platão, Diálogos. O banquete, trad. de Cavalcante
      de Souza J., Fedon, Sofista e Politico, trad.
      de Paleikat J. e Cruz Costa J. São Paulo,
      Abril Cultural 1972 269p.

973* Platão, Diálogos. Teeteto, Crátilo, trad. de Nunes
      C.A. Belém, Univ. Federal do Pará 1973 194p.

974* Charmides, Lysis, przel. wstep. objaśn. illustr.
      Witwicki W., slowo od wyd Jesewska K. Warszawa,
      PWN 1959 175p.

975* Platon, Dialogi, przek., wstep. Joachimowicz L.
      Warszawa, Pax 1963 674p.

976* Pseudo-Platon. Alkibiades, I i inne dialogi oraz
      Definicje [Alcibiades I, other dialogues and the
      Definitions], Polish transl., introd. & comm.
      by Regner L. Warszawa, PWN 1973 207p.

977* Platon. Viisi tutkielmaa. Sokrateen puolustuspuhe.
      Kriton. Pidot. Faidros. Faidon [Five
      Dialogues. Apology of Socrates, Crito,
      Symposium, Phaedrus, Phaedo], intro. by
      Linkomies E., Finnish transl. by Oksala P. &
      Hollo J.A. Porvoo-Helsinki, Söderström 1961
      xvi&324p.

978* Dialoguri (Aparărea lui Socrate, Charmides, Menon,
      Gorgias, Banchetul, Fedon, Scrisaorea a VII-a)
      [Dialogues. (Apology of Socrates, Charmides,
      Meno, Gorgias, Symposium, Phaedo, Seventh

Letter)], după trad. lui Papacostea C. rev.
și întregite cu două trad. noi și cu "Viața lui
Platon" de Noica C. București, Ed. pentru Lit.
universală 1968 xxvii&444p. [Rumanian transl.]

979* POSESCU A., Platon. Filozofia dialogurilor.
București, Ed. stiințif. 1971 381p.

980* Platon. Izbrannye dialogi [Selected Dialogues],
Russian transl., introd. & comm. by Asmus V.F.
Moskva, Chudozhestv. Lit. 1965 442p.

981* Dialogai, Lithuanian transl. by Račkauskas M.
Vilnius, Vaga 1968 276p.

982* Sölen. Sevgi üstüne. Lysis. Dostluk üstüne
[Symposium. On Love. Lysis. On Friendship],
Turkish transl. by Erhat A. & Eyuboglu S. 2nd
edn. Istanbul, Remzi Kitabevi 1961 143p.

983* Küçük diyaloglar [short dialogues], Turkish transl.
Istanbul, Remzi Kitabevi 1960 426p.

984* Plato Selections, ed. by Tanaka M. Tokyo Sinchosha
1963 648p. (includes Charmides, Lysis, Ion,
Phaedrus, Symposium, Phaedo, Apology, Crito and
Gorgias in Greek, transliterated into Japanese
characters; Symposium in Japanese translation.)

985* FUJII Y., ed. The Philosophy of Life, covering the
entire World. Tokyo, Tsukuma Pr. 1963 451p.
(includes Xenophon, Symposium and Plato's Lysis
and Charmides in Japanese translation.)

986* Plato, vol. I . Collection of the World's
Classical Literature XIV, Tokyo Tsukuma Pr.
1964 524p. (contains Apology, Crito, Alcibiades
I, Theaetetus, Phaedo, Protagoras, Meno,
Symposium, Menexenus, Euthyphro, Laches and
Hippias Major in Japanese transl.)

987* Plato, II, transl. by Tanaka M. et al. Collection
of the World's Great Literature, Tokyo, Tsukuma
Shobo 1970 406p. (contains Republic, Letters,
Epinomis.)

988* Plato. Great Ideas of the World I, Tokyo, Kawade
Shobo 1965 446p. (includes Japanese translation
and commentary of Republic, Apology and Crito.)

III C c: SELECTED DIALOGUES

989* <u>Plato</u>, I. World's Great Literature VI, Tokyo, Chuokoronsha 1966 606p. (contains Japanese translation and commentary of Lysis, Symposium, Menexenus, Gorgias, Apology, Crito, Clitopho and Phaedo.)

990* <u>Plato</u>, <u>II</u>. World's Great Literature, Tokyo, Chuokoronsha 1969 506p. (contains Republic, Critias and Seventh Letter in Japanese transl.)

991* <u>Apology, Symposium</u>, transl. by Totsuka S. Tokyo, Obunsha 1969 262p.

992* <u>Plato</u>, <u>III</u>. World's Literature Series, Tokyo Tsukuma Shobo 1972 462p. (contains Japanese translations of Apology, Phaedo, Symposium, Protagoras, Meno, Laches, Alcibiades, and Theaetetus.)

III C d: INDIVIDUAL DIALOGUES

ALCIBIADES I
A. TEXTS AND TRANSLATIONS

993* <u>Alcíbiades; o de la naturaleza</u>, trad. Míguez J.A. 2a ed. Bibl. de iniciac. filos. XXIV, Buenos Aires, Aguilar 1959 138p. Also 3a ed. 1961 168p.

994* <u>Alcibiades</u> I, Turkish transl. by Şahinbaş I. 2nd edn. Yunan klâsikleri, XXV, Ankara, Millî Eğitim Basimevi 1963 88p.

For additional texts and translations see 942, 946, 948, 961, 976, 986, 992.

B. STUDIES OF THE ALCIBIADES I

995* PROCLUS, <u>Alcibiades I</u>, transl. & comm. by O'Neill W. Den Haag, Nijhoff 1965 ix&247p.
Rev. AJPh LXXXIX 1968 380-382 Westerink.
ArchPhilos XXX 1967 146-148 Solignac.
RM XIX 1965-1966 817 D.J.B.
MH XXIII 1966 252 Gelzer.
Mnemosyne XX 1967 492-493 Ferwerda.
CR XX 1970 32-34 Blumenthal.

III C d 1: ALCIBIADES I

996 MOTTE A., "Pour l'authenticité du Premier Alcibiade". AC XXX 1961 5-32.

997 ALLEN R.E., "Note on Alcibiades I 129b1". AJPh LXXXIII 1962 187-190.

998 CARLINI A., "Studi sul testo della quarta tetralogia platonica". SIFC XXXIV 1962-1963 169-189.

999* DOENT E., Untersuchungen zum pseudo-platonischen Grossen Alkibiades. Diss. Wien 1963 95p.

1000 DOENT E., "Vorneuplatonisches im Grossen Alkibiades". WS LXXVII 1964 37-51.

1001 WEIL R., "La place du Premier Alcibiade dans l'oeuvre de Platon". IL XVI 1964 75-84.

1002* KRATZSCH S., Platos grosser Alkibiades. Eine echtheitskritische Untersuchung. Diss. Jena 1965 186p.

1003* BOS C.A., Interpretatie, vaderschap en datering van de Alcibiades Maior. Diss. Amsterdam, Culemborg, Willink-Noordduijn 1970 120p. Rev. CR XXII 1972 271 Huby.

1004 BRUNSCHWIG J., "Sur quelques emplois d'ὄψις". p.24-39 in Zetesis (see 4579).

For additional discussions see 300, 762, 792, 2486, 2636, 3037, 3185, 3697.

C. TEXTUAL CRITICISM

For textual criticism see 810.

ALCIBIADES II
B. STUDIES OF ALCIBIADES II

For discussions of Alcibiades II see 998, 1104, 2636.

APOLOGY

A. TEXTS AND TRANSLATIONS

1005* The Last Days of Socrates. Euthyphro, The Apology,
       Crito, Phaedo, transl. & introd. by Tredennick
       H. Baltimore, Penguin 1959 199p.

1006* The Trial and Death of Socrates, being the
       Euthyphron, Apology, Crito, and Phaedo of Plato,
       transl. by Church F.J. 2nd edn. London,
       Macmillan 1959 lxxxix&213p. Also Freeport,
       N.Y., Books for Libraries 1972. Reprint of 1880
       edn.

1007* The Trial and Death of Socrates, transl. with
       introd. analyses by Jowett B., with a pref. by
       Cairns H., and ill. by Erni H. Printed for
       members of the Limited Editions Club at the
       Stamperia Valdonega 1962. Also New York,
       Heritage Pr. and Toronto, Reginald Saunders
       1963 274p. (Contains Euthyphro, Apology, Crito,
       Phaedo.)

1008* The Trial and Death of Socrates: Euthyphro,
       Apology, Crito, Phaedo, transl. with an introd.
       by Warrington J. Everyman's Libr. No.457,
       London, Dent 1963 xv&175p.
       Rev. CW LVII 1964 356 Hornsby.

1009* RICHARDS I.A., Why so, Socrates?, a dramatic version
       of Plato's Dialogues: Euthyphro, Apology,
       Crito, Phaedo. New York, Cambridge Univ. Pr.
       1964 58p.
       Rev. CW LVIII 1964 17 Parry.

1010* Plato, On the Trial and Death of Socrates.
       Euthyphro, Apology, Crito, Phaedo, transl. with
       an intr. and prefatory notes by Cooper L.
       Ithaca, N.Y., Cornell Univ. Pr. 1967 200p.

1011* The Trial and Execution of Socrates, transl. &
       introd. by George P., drawings by Ayrton M.
       London, Folio Society 1972 197p.

1012* RIDDELL J., The Apology of Plato. New York, Arno
       Pr. 1973 xlii&252p. Reprint of 1877 edn.

1013* The Martyrdom of Socrates: The Apologia and Crito
with selections from Phaedo, partly in the
original and partly in transl. Ed. by Doherty
F.C. London, Oxford Univ. Pr. 1973 112p.
Reprint of 1923 edn.

1014* Apologie des Sokrates und Kriton. Rahmenerzählung
des Phaidon, übers. von Kiefer O. & Kassner R.
Einl. & Anm. von Richter F. Schöninghs
deutsche Textausgaben, Paderborn, Schöningh 1958
91p.

1015* Apologie des Sokrates, griech. gesprochen von
Schadewaldt W. Die Stimme der Alten Welt,
Zürich, Artemis-Verl. 1956 1 Langspielplatte.
Rev. LEC XXVII 1959 331 van Ooteghem.
Gymnasium LXVII 1960 550-552 Sauter.

1016 SCHADEWALDT W., "Einleitung für die Schallplatte
'Apologie des Sokrates'". p.424-426 in
Schadewaldt W., Hellas und Hesperien.
Gesammelte Aufsätze zur Antike und zur neueren
Literatur, zum 60. Geburtstag, unter Mitarb.
von Bartels K. Zürich, Artemis-Verl. 1960.

1017* Die Verteidigung des Sokrates, mit. Vorw. von
Schleiermacher F. Freiburg i. Br.,
Hyperion-Verl. 1959 126p.

1018* Verteidigungsrede des Sokrates. Schlusswort nach
dem Todesurteil, nach Platon freie Gestaltung
von Wiemann M., gespr. von Krauss W. Hamburg,
Teldec 1959 Sprechplatte.

1019* Apologie, Kriton, Euthyphron, Phaidon, übers. von
Schleiermacher F., eingel. v. Endres H.M.
München, Goldmann 1962 176p.

1020* Apologie, Kriton, übers., eingel. & hrsg. von
Hildebrandt K. Nachdr. Reclams
Universal-Bibliothek 895, Stuttgart, Reclam 1962
80p.

1021* Apologie und Kriton nebst Abschnitten aus Phaidon,
Text hrsg. von Ronicke D. Neubearb. Aufl.
Aschendorffs Sammlung lat. & gr. Klass 27./29.
Münster, Aschendorff 1967 xv&95p.

1022* Apologie, Komm. von Weber F.J. Griech. Klass.,
Paderborn, Schoeningh 1969 101p.

1023* Apologie des Sokrates, mit einer Einführ.,
      textkritik. App. & Komm. von Weber F.J.
      Uni-Taschenbüch. LVII, Paderborn, Schoeningh
      1971 150p.
          Rev. Gymnasium LXXIX 1972 530-531 Nickel.
          CF XXV 1971 357-358 Cloeren.
          RPh XLVII 1973 133 Louis.
          REA LXXIV 1972 265 Moreau.

1024* Apologia di Socrate, trad., introd. e note di
      Stazzone V. Il pensiero, Brescia, La Scuola
      1959 xxxvi&79p.

1025* Apologie de Socrate, ed. Collin P. 5e éd. Coll.
      de Class. grecs, Liège, Dessain 1959 46p.

1026* Apologie de Socrate, prépar. annotée par Collin P.
      5e éd. Coll. de Prépar. d'auteurs grecs,
      Liège, Dessain 1960 98p.

1027* Apologie de Socrate, avec extraits du Criton, trad.
      par Guillon J. Paris, Hatier 64p.
          Rev. Hum(RES) XXXVI 1959-1960,9 38
      Cabanis.

1028* Apologie de Socrate. Criton. Phédon, trad. et
      notes par Chambry É. Paris, Garnier-Flammarion
      1966 192p.

1029* Apologie de Socrate, Criton, Phédon, trad. par
      Robin L. & Moreau J. Paris, Gallimard 1968
      256p.

1030* Plato, L'ultimo messaggio di Socrate. Antologia di
      dialoghi platonici. Apologia, Critone, Fedone,
      a cura di Izzo D'Accinni A. 2a ed. riv.
      Traditio, Serie greca XL, Milano, Soc. editrice
      Dante Alighieri 1961 191p.

1031* Apologia di Socrate, introd. e comm. di Costa V.
      Coll. di Classici Lat. e Greci, Palermo,
      Manfredi 1965 71p.
          Rev. RSC XIV 1966 299-300 Pimazzoni.

1032* Apologia di Socrate, a cura di Valgimigli M.
      Piccola bibl. filos. Laterza I, Bari, Laterza
      1966 124p.

1033* Apologia di Socrate, a cura di Cefali V.; Critone,
      a cura di Marchegiani L. trad. di Amodeo V. &
      Bergamin A.M. Class. per le scuole med. sup.
      VI, San Severino Marche, Varano 1968 146p.

1034* Apologia di Socrate, a cura di Cefali V., trad.   di
      Amodeo V. Class. del pensiero V, San Severino
      Marche, Varano 1968 94p.

1035* Interpretazione di Socrate (Dai Dialoghi), a cura di
      Pieri A. Milano, Mursia 1971 194p.

1036* L'Eutifrone, L'Apologia di Socrate, Il Critone,
      introd.,   trad.,   comm.   di Celotti T. Palermo,
      Andò 1971 114p.

1037* Apologia di Socrate, comm. di Masaracchia A. Testi
      e crestomazie, Torino, Loescher 1971 xx&93p.

1038* Defensa de Sócrates, trad., prólogo y notas de
      García Yagüe F. Madrid, Aguilar 1963 76p. Also
      2a ed. 1966 67p.

1039* Defensa de Sócrates, anotada por Fernández Galiano
      M. 2a ed. Clásicos Gredos. Textos Anotados,
      Madrid, Gredos 1964 100p.

1040* Eutifrón, Apología, Critón, trad., introds. & notas
      por García Bacca J.D.   Mexico City, U.N.A.M.
      1965 xxxiii&69&ci-civ p.

1041* Apología de Sócrates, trad. di Noussan-Lettry L.
      Col. Los fundamentales, Buenos Aires, Eudeba
      1968 152p.

1042* Apologia de Sócrates, Port. trad. e apêndice de
      Lacerda de Moura M., introd. de Amoroso Lima A.
      Rio de Janeiro, Ed. de Ouro 1969 138p.

1043* Apología de Sócrates, trad., est. prelim. y notas
      de Eggers Lan C. Buenos Aires, EULEBA 1971 188p.
      Rev.   CuadFilos XIII   1973   242-244
      Nesprías.

1044* Apología de Sócrates, trad., introd., notas y apénd.
      de Noussan-Lettry L. 3a ed. rev. y ampl.
      Filos. y Direcho I, Buenos Aires 1973 160p.

1045* Sokrates' försvarstal [Socrates' Defense Speech],
      utg. av Duering I. Lund, Gleerup 1960-1967 3
      vols. (Vol. I: Text; II: Ordförteckning
      [index] by Cavallin B.; III: Komm.)

1046* Eutyfron, Obrona Sokratesa [Socrates' Defense],
      Kriton, przel., wstep., objaśn., illustr.
      Witwicki W. Warszawa, PWN 1958 195p.

III C d 3: APOLOGY

1047* Obrana Sokratova [Socrates' Defense], Czech.
       transl. by Ludvikovský J. 2nd edn. Praha,
       Lyra Pragensis 1970 92p.

1048* Sokratin müdafaasi [Socrates' Defense]. Turkish
       transl. 2nd edn. Ankara, Yeni Matbaa 1962 40p.

1049* Szókratész védöbeszéde [Socrates' Defense Speech].
       Kriton, Hungarian transl. & afterword by Gábor
       D. Budapest, Magyar Helikon 1971 79p.

1050* Apology, Crito, Phaedo, transl. by Tanaka N. &
       Ikeda M. Tokyo, Shinchosha 1968 256p.

1051* Apology, Crito, Phaedo, Japanese transl. and comm.
       by Fukushima T. Tokyo Kodansha 1972 307p.

For additional texts and translations see 914, 920, 936,
       948, 949, 958, 959, 960, 966, 969, 977, 978,
       981, 984, 986, 988, 989, 991, 992.

B. STUDIES OF THE APOLOGY

1052 NUSSBAUM G., "Socrates' educational method in the
     Apology". Summary in PCA LV 1958 22.

1053 NUSSBAUM G., "Some Problems in Plato's Apology".
     Orpheus VIII 1961 53-64.

1054 PUCCI P., "Σοφία nell'Apologia platonica". Maia
     XIII 1961 317-329.

1055 FARIAS D., "Vigiliae platonicae. Il tema del sonno
     e del sogno nell'Apologia". RFNeo LIII 1961
     314-319.

1056 STRYCKER E. DE, "La structure littéraire de
     l'Apologie de Socrate". Summary in RBPh XXXIX
     1961 174.

1057* JAEKEL W. & ERASMUS S., Lehrerkommentar zu Platons
      Apologie. Stuttgart, Klett 1962 119p.
            Rev. Gnomon XXXV 1963 655-659
      Voigtlaender.
      AAHG XVI 1963 87 Vretska.
      Gymnasium LXXI 1964 119-122 Bayer.

137

III C d 3: APOLOGY

1058* MEYER T., <u>Platons Apologie</u>. Tübinger Beitr. zur
     Altertumswiss. XLII, Stuttgart, Kohlhammer 1962
     195p.
          <u>Rev</u>.   Gnomon   XXXV   1963   537-543
     Voigtlaender.
          CW LVI 1963 257 Costas.
          RThPh XIII 1963 85 Sulliger.
          PhilosRdschau XI 1963 310 Kuhn.
          GGA CCXVI 1964 130-141 Goergemanns.
          HTZ XIII 1962 305 Deku.
          Scholastik XXXIX 1964 456-457 Ennen.

1059 NOUSSAN-LETTRY L., "El redescubrimiento del texto de
     la Apologia platónica en la investigación
     contemporanea". CuadFilos IV 1963 47-59.

1060 ANASTAPLO G., "Human Being and Citizen: A Beginning
     to the Study of Plato's Apology of Socrates".
     p.16-49 in <u>Ancients and Moderns</u>. <u>Essays</u> <u>on</u> <u>the</u>
     <u>Tradition</u> <u>of</u> <u>Political</u> <u>Philosophy</u> <u>in</u> <u>honor</u> <u>of</u>
     <u>Leo</u> <u>Strauss</u>, ed. by Cropsey J. New
     York/London, Basic Books 1964.

1061 MASARACCHIA A., "Senso e problemi dell'Apologia
     platonica". Helikon IV 1964 111-152.

1062 NOUSSAN-LETTRY L., "El núcleo especulativo de la
     'Apología' platónica. Apología, 20c-23c".
     Philosophia(Argent) XXIX 1964 20-49.

1063 ARMLEDER P.J., "Death in Plato's Apologia". CB XLII
     1966 46.

1064 HOERBER R.G., "Note on Plato, Apologia XLII". CB
     XLII 1966 92.

1065 KRUEGER G., "Das Prooemium von Platons Apologie".
     AU R.9 Heft 5 1966 29-34.

1066 KEMPER H., "Platon Apologie in heutiger Sicht".
     Anregung XIII 1967 107-111.

1067 MUNDING H., "Sophia und Meinungsbildung zu Apol.
     21b-23b". AU XII 1969 51-61.

1068 RAUBITSCHEK A.E., "Prokrisis (Apologie 35a7-b2)".
     p.89-90 in <u>Politeia und Res Publica</u>. <u>Beiträge</u>
     <u>zum</u> <u>Verständnis</u> <u>von</u> <u>Politik,</u> <u>Recht</u> <u>und</u> <u>Staat</u> <u>in</u>
     <u>der</u> <u>Antike,</u> <u>dem</u> <u>Andenken</u> <u>Rudolf</u> <u>Starks</u> <u>gewidmet,</u>
     hrsg. von Steinmetz P. Palingenesia, Monogr.
     und Texte zur klass. Altertumswiss. IV,
     Wiesbaden, Steiner 1969.

III C d 3: APOLOGY

1069 ARGYLE A.W., "Χρησμολόγοι and μάντεις". CR XX 1970
      139.

1070 FERGUSON J., "An Athenian Remainder Sale". CPh LXV
      1970 173.

1071 HATHAWAY R.F., "Law and the Moral Paradox in Plato's
      Apology". JHPh VIII 1970 127-142.

1072 NOUSSAN-LETTRY L., "Νομίζειν θεούς. Platón, Apología
      35c4-d7". REC X 1966 26-36.

1073 NOUSSAN-LETTRY L., "El interrogatorio de Meleto.
      Inversión, hipérbole y parodia de la relación
      jurídico-positiva". EClas XIV 1970 297-310.

1074 CALDER W.M. III, "Plato's Apology of Socrates. A
      Speech for the Defense". BUJ XX 1972 42-47.

1075 CLAY D., "Socrates' Mulishness and Heroism".
      Phronesis XVII 1972 53-60.

1076 NOUSSAN-LETTRY L., "El segundo discurso de la
      Apología platónica. Incidencia textual de
      observaciones de Hegel". Philosophia(Argent)
      XXXVIII 1972 5-17.

1077 PIÉRART M., "Le second discours de Socrate à ses
      juges. Platon, Apologie, 35e-38b". LEC XL 1972
      288-293.

1078 SAKISAKA Y., "A certain Doubt in the Apology" [in
      Japanese]. Seishin Kagaku (Japan Univ.) XI
      1972.

For additional discussions see 40, 185, 221, 300, 423,
      874, 1177, 2016, 2673, 3159, 3181, 3631, 3632,
      3868, 4015, 4016, 4173, 4226, 4279, 4285, 4303,
      4318, 4332, 4422, 4458, 4463, 4503, 4504, 4505,
      4507, 4509, 4511, 4526.

C. TEXTUAL CRITICISM

1079 PUCCI P., "Notes critiques sur l'Apologie de
      Platon". RPh XXXVII 1963 255-257.

III C d 3: APOLOGY

1080 NICOLL W.S.M., "Some Manuscripts of Plato's Apologia
      Socratis". CQ XVI 1966 70-77.

1081 VOIGTLAENDER H.D., "Zu Platons Apologie 22a6/8".
      Hermes XCI 1963 120-123.

AXIOCHUS

A. TEXTS AND TRANSLATIONS

For texts and translations see 948, 961, 976.

B. STUDIES OF THE AXIOCHUS

1082 ISNARDI M., "Un discorso consolatorio del Corpus
      platonicum". RSF XVI 1961 33-47.

1083 KNIGHT W.F.J., "Axiochus". Pegasus no.1, juin 1964
      35-39.

1084 SECRET F., "La traduction de l'Axiochus par G.
      Postel". BHR XXVIII 1966 109-111.

For additional discussions see 568, 846.

CHARMIDES

A. TEXTS AND TRANSLATIONS

1085* Carmide, a cura di Diano C.   & Chiereghin F.
      Paideia II, Bologna, Ed. scolastiche Pàtron
      1969 95p.

1086* Charmides, Turkish transl. by Kösemihal N.S.   2nd
      edn.   Yunan klâsikleri XV, Ankara, Millî Eğitim
      Basimevi 1965 4,v&47p.

140

III C d 5: CHARMIDES

For additional texts and translations see 852, 866, 921, 925, 933, 942, 949, 968, 978, 984, 985.

B. STUDIES OF THE CHARMIDES

1087* PINILLA A., Sofrosine. Ciencia de la ciencia. Madrid, Consejo superior de investigaciones cientificas, Inst. "Luis Vives" de Filosofia 1959 200p.
Rev. VV XIX 1961 398-399 L. de M.
RPortFil XVIII 1962 324-325 A. de L.

1088 KANEMATSU, "A Study of σωφροσύνη based on Plato's Charmides" [in Japanese]. in A Collection of Essays published in honor of D.T. Suzuki 1960.

1089 WELLMAN R.R., "The Question Posed at Charmides 165a-166c". Phronesis IX 1964 107-113.

1090 UNTERSTEINER M., "Studi Platonici". Acme XVIII 1965 19-67.

1091 BONITZ H., "Bemerkungen zu dem Abschnitt des Dialogs Charmides p.165-172". p.243-253 in Bonitz H., Platonische Studien (see 4584).

1092 TIELSCH E., "Die Metastruktur- und -erkenntnistheorien des Charmenides [sic] und ihr Schicksal in Platons späterem Werk". Summary p.440-442 in Akten XIV. Intern. Kongr. Philos. Wien, 2.-9. September 1968. Vol. V. Wien, Herder 1968.

1093* TUCKEY T.G., Plato's Charmides. Amsterdam, Hakkert 1968 xiii&116p. Reprint of 1951 edn.

1094 ADAMIETZ J., "Zur Erklärung des Hauptteils von Platons Charmides (164a-175d)". Hermes XCVII 1969 37-57.

1095 HERTER H., "Selbsterkenntnis der Sophrosyne. Zu Platons Charmides". p.74-88 in Festschrift Karl Vretska zum 70. Geburtstag überreicht von seinem Freunden und Schülern, hrsg. von Ableitinger D. & Gugel H. Heidelberg, Winter 1970.

III C d 5: CHARMIDES

1096* WITTE B., Die Wissenschaft vom Guten und Bösen.
      Interpretationen zu Platons Charmides.
      Untersuch. zur antiken Lit. & Gesch. V,
      Berlin, de Gruyter 1970 x&166p.
         Rev. Perficit II 1970 446-450 Barcenilla.
         ArchPhilos XXXIII 1970 982-984
      Solignac.
         CR XXII 1970 196-198 Taylor.
         Angelicum   XLVII   1970   392-394
      Vansteenkiste.
         StudClas XIII 1971 314-315 Noica.
         CW LXIV 1971 159 Sparshott.
         AC XL 1971 241 des Places.
         Helmantica XXII 1971 189-190 Barcenilla.
         REA LXXIII 1971 452-453 Moreau.
         Pensamiento XXVII 1971 233-234 Igal.
         WJb V 1972 272-274 Heintel.
         Gymnasium LXXIX 1972 115-116 Effe.
         AGPh LV 1972 202-207 Ilting.
         Sophia XL 1972 154-157.

1097 EFFE B., "Platons Charmides und der Alkibiades des
      Aischines von Sphettos". Hermes XCIX 1971
      198-208.

1098 JULIA V., "El método Socrático". CuadFilos XII 1972
      63-67.

1099* BLOCH G., Platons Charmides. Die Erscheinung des
      Seins im Gespräch. Diss. Tübingen 1973 161p.

1100 ITO U., "The Knowledge of Knowledge in the
      Charmides" [in Japanese]. Studies in Philosophy
      (Kyushu Univ.) IX 1973

1101* MARTENS E., Das selbstbezügliche Wissen in Platons
      Charmides. München, Hanser 1973 127p.

1102 SANTAS G., "Socrates at work on Virtue and Knowledge
      in Plato's Charmides". p.105-132 in Exegesis
      and Argument, ed. by Lee E.N. et al. (see
      4608).

1103 SCHOFIELD M., "Socrates on conversing with Doctors".
      CR XXIII 1973 121-123.

For additional discussions see 40, 670, 2635, 2645, 2752,
      3037, 3471, 3631, 3632, 4449.

142

III C d 5: CHARMIDES

C. TEXTUAL CRITICISM

For textual criticism see 1360.

CLITOPHO

A. TEXTS AND TRANSLATIONS

For texts and translations see 871, 950, 961, 989.

B. STUDIES OF THE CLITOPHO

1104 CARLINI A., "Alcuni dialoghi pseudo-platonici e l'Accademia di Arcesilao". ASNP XXXI 1962 33-63.
For additional discussions see 517, 1950, 4018, 4186.

CRATYLUS

A. TEXTS AND TRANSLATIONS

1105* Cratilo, trad., introd, e note di Buccellato M. Coll. di Class. della Filos., Torino, Loescher 1958 192p.

1106* Cratilo, introd. e comm. a cura di Celentano L. Napoli, Ist. Ed. del Mezzogiorno 1969 144p.

1107* Crátilo, Port. vers., pref. e notas pelo Palmiera P.D. Col. de Clas. Sá da Costa, Lisboa 1963 160p.
Rev. RBF XV 1965 113-114 Vita.

III C d 7: CRATYLUS

For additional texts and translations see 866, 926, 932, 943, 953, 973.

B. STUDIES OF THE CRATYLUS

1108 BRUMBAUGH R., "Plato's "Cratylus". The Order of the Etymologies". RM XI 1957-1958 502-510.

1109 LEVINSON R.B., "Language and the Cratylus. Four Questions". RM XI 1957-1958 28-41.

1110 FUECK J.W., Criticism of an article by LeCerf J., "Remarque sur le Cratyle de Platon et la grammaire générale". Oriens XII 1959 285.

1111 GALLINI C., "Il Dio che scioglie". AFLC XXVIII 1960 529-558.

1112 LEROY M., "Du Cratyle de Platon à la linguistique moderne". Annales scientif. de l'Univ. A.I. Cuza de Iasi, 3e section VI,2 Suppl. 1960 41-45.

1113 DERBOLAV J., "Das Problem des Metasprachlichen in Platons Kratylos". p.181-210 in Lebendiger Realismus. Festschrift für Johannes Thyssen, hrsg. von Hartmann K. Bonn 1962.

1114 FERRANTE D., "Curiosità etimologiche nel Cratilo di Platone e nel De lingua latina di Varrone". GIF XV 1962 163-171.

1115 GIORDANO D., "Il Cratilo di Platone". Vichiana I 1964 390-406.

1116 LUCE J.V., "The Date of the Cratylus". AJPh LXXXV 1964 136-154.

1117 ROSE L.E., "On Hypothesis in the Cratylus as an Indication of the Place of the Dialogue in the Sequence of Dialogues". Phronesis IX 1964 114-116.

1118 IIO T., "On the Meaning of ὄνομα in Plato's Cratylus" [in Japanese]. HiroshimaUS XXIV 1965.

1119 LUCE J.V., "The Theory of Ideas in the Cratylus".
     Phronesis X 1965 21-36.

1120* SEASE V.W., The Cratylus. Plato and the Doctrine of
     the Academy. Diss. Univ. of California
     Berkeley 1966 174p. [microfilm]. Summary in DA
     XXVII 1967 4234A-4235A.

1121 LORENZ K. & MITTELSTRASS J., "On Rational
     Philosophy of Language. The Programme in
     Plato's Cratylus reconsidered". Mind LXXVI 1967
     1-20.

1122 GOULD J.B., "Plato, about Language. The Cratylus
     Reconsidered". Apeiron III,1 1969 19-31.

1123 LUCE J.V., "Plato on Truth and Falsity in Names".
     CQ XIX 1969 222-232.

1124 ROBINSON R., "A Criticism of Plato's Cratylus".
     p.118-138 in Robinson R., Essays in Greek
     Philosophy (see 4612). Reprinted from PhR 1956.

1125 ROBINSON R., "The Theory of Names in Plato's
     Cratylus". p.100-117 in Robinson R., Essays in
     Greek Philosophy (see 4612). Reprinted from
     RIPh 1955.

1126 TAKEMIYA A., "Nόμος-ness and φύσις-ness of   in
     Plato's Cratylus" [in Japanese]. Yamaguchi
     Univ. Literary Journal XIX 1968 and XX 1969.

1127 CALVERT B., "Forms and Flux in Plato's Cratylus".
     Phronesis XV 1970 26-47.

1128* ROTH M.D., An Examination of Plato's Cratylus.
     Diss. Univ. of Illinois 1969 111p.
     [microfilm]. Summary in DA XXXI 1970 804A.

1129 THORNTON M.T., "Knowledge and Flux in Plato's
     Cratylus (438-40)". Dialogue VIII 1970 581-591.

1130 WEINGARTNER R.H., "Making Sense of the Cratylus".
     Phronesis XV 1970 5-25.

1131 BERGER H., "Plato's Cratylus. Dialogue as
     Revision". PhilosForum II 1970-1971 213-233.

1132 HIROKAWA Y., "Word: principally on Plato's
     Cratylus" [in Japanese]. Bummei VI 1971.

1133 KRETZMANN N., "Plato on the Correctness of Names". APQ VIII 1971 126-138.

1134 SPRAGUE R.K., "Reply to Dr. Levinson". p.367-371 in Essays in ancient Greek Philosophy, ed. by Anton J.P. & Kustas G.L. (see 4581).

1135 ANAGNOSTOPOULOS G., "Plato's Cratylus. The two Theories of the Correctness of Names". RM XXV 1972 691-736.

1136 BOLLACK J., "L'en-deçà infini. L'aporie du Cratyle". Poétique III 1972 309-314.

1137 GENETTE G., "L'éponymie du nom ou le cratylisme du Cratyle". Critique XXVIII 1972 No.307 1019-1044.

1138 PFEIFFER W.M., "True and False Speech in Plato's Cratylus 385b-c". CanJPh II 1972 87-104.

1139* PFEIFFER W.M., The Cratylus. Plato's Investigation of Names. Diss. Univ. of Toronto 1971. [microfilm]. Summary in DA XXXII 1972 7047A.

1140 SÁNCHEZ MÁRQUEZ M.J., "El Cratilo. Arbitrariedad del signo lingüistico". p.267-278 in Actas del primer Simp. nac. de estud. clas., mayo 1970. Mendoza, Univ. nac. de Cuyo 1972.

1141 WOLF A., "Die Frage nach der Wahrheit in Platons Dialog Kratylos. Versuch einer Interpretation". SJP XV-XVI 1971-1972 27-37.

1142 ANAGNOSTOPOULOS G., "The Significance of Plato's Cratylus". RM XXVII 1973-1974 318-345.

1143* BOLTON R.H., Studies in Plato's Cratylus. Diss. Univ. of Michigan 1973 168p. [microfilm]. Summary in DA XXXIV 1974 7818A.

1144 KAHN C.H., "Language and Ontology in the Cratylus". p.152-176 in Exegesis and Argument, ed. Lee E.N. et al. (see 4608).

For additional discussions see 89, 256, 258, 268, 477, 570, 2596, 2598, 2599, 2633, 2668, 2821, 3559, 3693, 3703, 3704, 3965, 3977, 4026, 4028, 4030, 4031, 4032, 4035, 4037, 4038, 4041, 4043, 4049, 4053, 4057, 4058, 4059, 4060, 4105, 4161.

C. TEXTUAL CRITICISM

1145 SCHOFIELD M., "A Displacement in the Text of the Cratylus". CQ XXII 1972 246-253.

CRITIAS

A. TEXTS AND TRANSLATIONS

1146* Critias, o La Atlántida, trad., prol. y notas por Samaranch F. de P. Bibl. de Iniciac. Filos. LXXXIII, Buenos Aires, Aguilar 1963 62p.

1147* Crizia, a cura di Belli A. 2a ed. Traditio, Ser. greca XXI, Milano/Roma/Napoli, Soc. Ed. Dante Alighieri 1966 73p.

For additional texts and translations see 920, 927, 934, 944, 950, 951, 990, 2476, 2477, 2480.

B. STUDIES OF THE CRITIAS

1148 MANGANARO G., "Il mito dell'Atlantide e la logografia Ionica (La visione geopolitica di Platone)". GIF XII 1959 309-313.

1149 GALANOPOULOS A.G., "Ἔπι τοῦ μεγέθοῦς καὶ τῆς γεωγραφικῆς θέσεως τῆς Ἀτλαντίδος". PAA XXXV 1960 400-418.

1150 BRANT M., "'Vorsintflutlich'--mit der Atomuhr getestet. Platos Angaben über den Untergang von Atlantis im Spiegel der Vorgeschichtsforschung". SKZ LXV 1961 341.

1151 VIDAL-NAQUET P., "Athènes et l'Atlantide. Structure et signification d'un mythe platonicien". REG LXXVII 1964 420-444.

III C d 8: CRITIAS

1152 HERTER H., "Das Königsritual der Atlantis". RhM CIX
      1966 236-259.

1153 ANDREWS P.B.S., "Larger than Africa and Asia?". G&R
      XIV 1967 76-79.

1154 BALDI L., "Aspetti fantascientifici nel Crizia di
      Platone". p.91-94 in Diadosis. Voci di
      presenza classica. Rassegna ufficiosa a cura
      della cattedra di lett. class. del liceo C.
      Varese, Tortona 1967.

1155 GESSMAN A.M., "Plato's Critias: Literary Fiction or
      Historical Narrative?". LangQ VII 1968 17-31.

1156 BRISSON L., "De la philosophie politique à l'épopée.
      Le Critias de Platon". RMM LXXV 1970 402-438.

1157 MAVOR J.W., "Reise nach Atlantis". AW I 1970,4
      33-45.

1158 LUCE J.V., "Neues Licht auf Atlantis". AW II 1971,2
      13-21.

For additional discussions see 89, 1185, 3704.

CRITO

A. TEXTS AND TRANSLATIONS

1159* Critone, a cura di Casini N. Bibl. di Class.
      greci e lat., Firenze, Vallecchi 1959 95p.

1160* Il Critone, introd., trad. & note di Giovanni di
      Napoli. Roma, Paoline 1959 76p.
      Rev. FilosV 1961 89-90 Beschin.

1161* Critone, trad., introd. e comm. di Reale G.
      Brescia, La Scuola 1961 xliv&66p. Also 2a ed.
      1965 xlvi&66p.
      Rev. Aevum XXXVII 1963 358 Egi.

1162* Il Critone, testo con introd. e comm. per cura di
      Bosio G. Scritt. greci comm. per le scuole
      N.S., Torino, Soc. ed. internazionale 1961
      xix&48p. Also 1969 86p.

1163* Critone, trad., introd. e note di Calogero G. 2a
ed. riv. Col. scholastica di testi filos.,
Firenze, Sansoni 1961 xxxvi&31p. Also 3rd edn.
rev. 1968 xx&45p.

1164* Il Critone, costruzione diretta, versione lett. e
interlin., introd., argomento, bibliog. minima
e un piccolo lessico delle forme verbali, a cura
di Costa V. Coll. I Cirannini, Roma, Ciranna
1961 71p.
Rev. RSC X 1962 200 Fugaldi.

1165* Il Critone. Dialogo sul dovere del cittadino,
pref., trad. e note di Cella S. Roma, Ciranna
1962 38p.

1166* Il Critone, a cura di Valgimigli M. 10a ed.
Piccola bibl. filos., Bari, Laterza 1962 70p.

1167* Il Critone, trad. e comm. a cura di Composto R.
Coll. di filos. e pedag. ad uso delle scuole,
Firenze, Le Monnier 1966 51p.

1168* Critone, trad. di Acri F., introd. e note di
Laudenzi A. Class. della filos. e pedag.,
Napoli, Federico e Ardia 1966 72p.

1169* Critone, a cura di Marchegiani L. Coll. class.
del pensiero IV, San Severino Marche, Varano
1968 50p.

1170* Critone, trad., introd. e comm. di Lombardo G. 2a
ed. ricomposta. Pensatori antichi e moderni
XV, Firenze, La Nuova Italia 1968 xiii&33p.

1171* Il Critone, a cura di Musso O. Col. di class.
graeci, Torino, Marietti 1973 63p.

1172* Critón, trad., pról. y notas de García Yagüe F.
Bibl. de iniciac. filos., Buenos Aires,
Aguilar 1960 46p.
Rev. EClas VI 1961 200 Galiano.

1173* Critón, trad., introd., notas y apénd. de
Noussan-Lettry L. Col. Los Fundamentales,
Buenos Aires, Ed. Universitaria 1966 v&139p.
Also 2a ed. rev. y ampl. Filos. y Direcho
II, Buenos Aires 1973 147p.
Rev. Cultura VIII 1970 156 Sillitti.

III C d 9: CRITO

1174* <u>Kriton</u>, med inled. & anm. av Rudberg G. & Hölstad
R. 3. uppl. Lund, Gleerup 1963 x&55p.

For additional texts and translations see 852, 858, 866,
914, 948, 949, 959, 966, 969, 977, 981, 984,
986, 988, 989, 1005, 1006, 1007, 1008, 1009,
1010, 1011, 1013, 1014, 1019, 1020, 1021, 1027,
1028, 1029, 1030, 1033, 1035, 1036, 1040, 1046,
1049, 1050, 1051.

B. STUDIES OF THE CRITO

1175 GOMME A.W., "The Structure of Plato's Crito". G&R V
1958 45-51.

1176 HARDER R., "Platos Kriton". p.223-246 in Harder R.,
<u>Kleine Schriften</u> (see 4599). Reprinted from
<u>Platos Kriton. Text,</u> übers., <u>nachwort.</u> Berlin,
Weidmann 1934 42-73.

1177 GREENBERG N.A., "Socrates' Choice in the Crito".
HSPh LXX 1965 45-82.

1178 ROLLAND DE RENÉVILLE J.,"Criton ou de l'Obéissance".
RMM LXXI 1966 36-53.

1179 MILOBENSKI E., "Zur Interpretation des platonischen
Dialogs Kriton". Gymnasium LXXV 1968 371-390.

1180 DOENT E., "Pindar und Platon. Zur Interpretation
des Kriton". WS IV 1970 52-65.

1181 STRYCKER E. DE, "Le Criton de Platon, structure
littéraire et intention philosophique". LEC
XXXIX 1971 417-436.

1182 WEINHOLD H., "Zum fünften Kapitel von Platons
Kriton". Anregung 1963 35-36.

1183 NOUSSAN-LETTRY L., "Acercamiento al 'Criton' como
texto especulativo. Las introducciones:
43a1-46a8 y 50a6-c9". Philosophia(Argent) XXX
1965 41-82.

1184 NOUSSAN-LETTRY L., "Orden común facticidad y
libertad. El tercer estadió del Criton
(50c9-54e3)". Philosophia(Argent) XXXVII 1971
17-50.

III C d 9: CRITO

1185 PRESTIPINO V., "Sul contratto nel Critone".   AFLM
     III-IV 1970-1971 11-38.

1186 SEGL R., "Der unbefriedigende Kriton".   Gymnasium
     LXXVIII 1971 437-441.

1187 ALLEN R.E., "Law and Justice in Plato's Crito".   JPh
     LXIX 1972 557-567.

1188 NOUSSAN-LETTRY L., "Las sentencias del Critón".   REC
     XIV 1972 63-90.

1189 PLATIS E.N., "Ερμηνευτικὰ στὸν πλατωνικὸ Κρίτωνα. Τὸ
     φιλοσοφικὸ περιεχόμενο τοῦ διαλόγου" [in Greek
     with German summary]. Philosophia(Athens)   II
     1972 235-265.

1190 ROSEN F., "Obligation and Friendship in Plato's
     Crito". PolitTheor I 1973 307-316.

For additional discussions see 40, 185, 797, 1670, 2650,
     3159, 3631, 3632, 3737, 4116, 4318, 4332, 4334,
     4422, 4501, 4503, 4504, 4507, 4508, 4509.

C. TEXTUAL CRITICISM

1191 BERTI E., "Contributo allo studio dei manoscritti
     platonici del Critone". SCO XV 1966 210-220.

1192 BERTI E., "I manoscritti del Critone di Platone.
     Gli apografi del Venetus append. Cl. IV,1,
     coll. 542". Hermes XCVII 1969 412-431.

For additional textual discussion see 1360.

III C d 10: DEFINITIONES

DEFINITIONES

A. TEXTS AND TRANSLATIONS

For texts and translations see 961, 976.

B. STUDIES OF THE DEFINITIONES

1193* INGENKAMP H.G., Untersuchungen zu den
pseudoplatonischen Definitionen. Klass.-Philol.
Stud. XXXIV, Wiesbaden, Harrassowitz 1967 128p.
Rev. REG LXXXI 1968 295-296 des Places.
CR XIX 1969 375-376 Gulley.
RBPh XLVII 1969 647-648 de Strycker.
Gymnasium LXXVI 1969 543-546 Gaiser.
RFIC XCIX 1971 452-455 Sillitti.

C. TEXTUAL CRITICISM

1194 DOENT E., "Zwei Bemerkungen zu pseudoplatonischen
Schriften". RhM CX 1967 286.

DEMODOCUS

B. STUDIES OF THE DEMODOCUS

For discussion of the Demodocus see 811.

EPIGRAMS

B. STUDIES OF THE EPIGRAMS

1195 LUDWIG W., "Plato's Love Epigrams". GRBS IV 1963 59-82. Reprinted in German transl. as "Platons Liebesepigramme". p.56-84 in Das Epigramm. Zur Geschichte einer inschriftlichen und literarischen Gattung, hrsg. von Pfohl G. Darmstadt 1969.

1196 FOLLET S., "Deux épigrammes platoniciennes pour Phèdre". Summary in REG LXXVII 1964 p.xiii-xiv.

1197 MARIOTTI S., "Da Platone agli Epigrammi Bobbiesi. Appunti su due temi epigrammatici antichi". StudUrb XLI 1967 1071-1096.

1198 McKAY K.J., "Kallimachos Ep.60 Pf.". Mnemosyne XXV 1972 189-190.

EPINOMIS

A. TEXTS AND TRANSLATIONS

1199* Platonis Epinomis commentariis illustrata, par Novotný F. Textus breves Graeci & Latini, Praha, Čs. Akad. Věd 1960 246p.
Rev. SPFB X 1961 E6 298 Hošek.
AJPh LXXXIII 1962 313-317 Tarán.
RSC X 1962 194 d'Agostino.
GIF XV 1962 172-176 Specchia.
REG LXXVI 1963 476-478 des Places.
RecSR XLIX 1961 289-290 des Places.

1200* Epinomis, introd., testo crit. e comm. di Specchia O. Quaderni di cult. e scuola I, Firenze, Le Monnier 1967 139p.
Rev. AC XXXVI 1967 645 des Places.
BAGB 1968 143 Weil.
Helmantica XIX 1968 390 Jiménez Delgado.
REA LXX 1968 166-167 Moreau.

Aevum XLIII 1969 165 di Gregorio.
RPh XLIII 1969 132 Louis.
Gnomon XLI 1969 695-697 Goergemanns.
GM XXIV 1969 349-355 Sorge.
GIF XXII,1 1970 92-94 Berti.
BAGB 1973 508ff.

1201* Epinomis, introd., testo crit., trad. e comm. di
Castorina E. Firenze, Sansoni 1967 138p.

For additional texts and translations see 868, 871, 919,
946, 950, 987.

B. STUDIES OF THE EPINOMIS

1202 SPECCHIA O., "Introduzione all'Epinomis (XIII libro
delle Leggi di Platone)". GIF XII 1959 231-257.

1203* LIER H., Untersuchung zur Epinomis. Diss.
Phillipps-Univ. Marburg 1966 119p.
Rev. AAHG XXIII 1970 149-151 Doent.

1204 PLACES E. DES, "Vertu et bonheur (Platon, Epinomis,
977c3-d4)". MEFR LXXI 1959 135-144.

1205 PLACES E. DES, "Platon et le ciel de Syrie". MUB
XXXVII 1960-1961 201-205.

1206 PAVESE C., "Scienza e religiosità accademica
nell'Epinomide". PP XIX 1964 329-345.

1207 SPECCHIA O., "Platone, Epinomis 975e1-5; Democrito,
Framm. B157 D.K.". Vichiana II 1965 197-198.

1208 SORGE C., "Dottrine speusippee nell'Epinomide
pseudo-platonica". GM XXII 1967 30-57.

1209 ROVIGATTI F., "L'Epinomide e la crisi della polis".
AAP XIX 1969-1970 537-580.

1210 FESTUGIÈRE A.J., "L'Epinomis' et l'introduction des
cultes étrangers à Athènes". p.129-137 in
Festugière A.J., Études de Religion grecque et
hellenistique. Paris, Vrin 1972. Reprinted
from Coniectanea Neotestamentica 1947 66-74.

III C d 13: EPINOMIS

For additional discussions see 89, 342, 846, 1223, 1359, 3294, 3325, 3332.

C. TEXTUAL CRITICISM

1211 SOLMSEN F., "Epinomis 979e2". CPh LVI 1961 252-253. Reprinted p.1961 in Solmsen F., <u>Kleine</u> <u>Schriften</u> <u>II</u> (see 4615).

1212 SPECCHIA O., "Due note sulla tradizione indiretta dell'Epinomis di Platone". GIF XXI 1969 351-355.

ERASTAE

B. STUDIES OF THE ERASTAE

For discussions of the Erastae see 998, 1104.

ERYXIAS

A. TEXTS AND TRANSLATIONS

1213* <u>Pseudo</u> <u>Platone</u>, <u>Erissia</u>, a cura di Laurenti R. Piccola bibl. filos. Laterza N.S. XLVI, Bari, Laterza 1969 109p.
<u>Rev.</u> GM XXV 1970 129 Sorge.

For additional texts and translations see 946, 961, 976.

III C d 15: ERYXIAS

B. STUDIES OF THE ERYXIAS

1214 OŚWIĘCIMSKI S., "De artis criticae paradoxis quibusdam sive de dialogi socratici qui Eryxias inscribitur auctore" [in Polish]. Eos LVII 1967-1968 37-50.

1215* OŚWIĘCIMSKI S., The Economic Problems in the pseudo-Platonic Dialogue Eryxias [in Polish with English and Russian summaries]. Wrocław/Warszawa/Krakow/Gdansk, Editions de l'Acad. Pol. des Sciences 1971 155p.

1216 GIACCHERO M., "Raggionamenti socratici sulla ricchezza e sulla moneta nel dialogo pseudoplatonico Eryxias". RIN LXXV 1973 7-38.

For additional discussions see 476, 811, 1194.

EUTHYDEMUS

A. TEXTS AND TRANSLATIONS

1217* Euthydemus, with introd. & transl. by Sprague R.K. Libr. of Liberal Arts, Indianapolis, Bobbs-Merrill 1965 xv&70p.
Rev. CPh LXI 1966 290 Miller.
CW LIX 1966 313 Hornsby.
Mnemosyne XX 1967 466 de Vries.
CR XVIII 1968 236 Crombie.
ModS XLVI 1968-1969 179-180 Costelloe.
RPh 1972 39 Somville.

1218* The Euthydemus of Plato, ed. with revised text, introd., notes and indices by Gifford E.H. New York, Arno Pr. 1973 81p. Reprint of 1905 edn.

1219* Eutidemo, trad. di Zeppi Tutta A., introd., comm. e note di Zeppi S. Firenze, La Nuova Italia 1969 xci&97p.
Rev. RFNeo LXI 1969 795-796 Reale.

III C d 16: EUTHYDEMUS

For additional texts and translations see 853,   858,   866,
917, 925, 932, 943, 949.

B. STUDIES OF THE EUTHYDEMUS

1220 BONITZ H., "Euthydemos".   p.93-151   in   Bonitz H.,
Platonische Studien (see 4584).

1221 STRAUSS L., "On the Euthydemus".   Interpretation   I
1970 1-20.

1222* KEULEN H., Untersuchungen zu Platons   Euthydem.
Klass.-Philol.   Stud.   XXXVII,   Wiesbaden,
Harrassowitz 1971 ix&105p.
Rev. AC XLI 1972 660-661 de Ley.
RPh XLVII 1973 133 des Places.
Gnomon XLV 1973 493-494 de Vries.

1223* FESTUGIÈRE A.J., Les trois 'Protreptiques' de
Platon: Euthydème, Phédon, Epinomis. Bibl.
d'hist. de la philos., Paris, Vrin 1973 212p.

For additional discussions see 40, 240, 468,   2633,   2784,
2794, 2842, 2960, 4186, 4379.

C. TEXTUAL CRITICISM

1224 VRIES G.J. DE, "Notes on some Passages in the
Euthydemus". Mnemosyne XXV 1972 42-55.

EUTHYPHRO

A. TEXTS AND TRANSLATIONS

1225* ALLEN R.E., Plato's Euthyphro and the Earlier Theory
of Forms. Libr. of Philos. & Scientific
Method, London, Routledge & Kegan Paul, also New
York, Humanities Pr. 1970 xi&171p.

157

III C d 17: EUTHYPHRO

Rev. CW LXIV 1971 268 Hahm.
Philosophy XLVI 1971 170-172 Hamlyn.
ACR I 1971 72-73 Urdahl.
TLS LXX 1971 45.
AusJP XLIX 1971 331-334 Boyle.
Dialogue X 1971 565-568 Dybikowski.
PhilosStud(Irel.) XXI 1972 267-268
Tierney.
RM XXV 1971-1972 547-549 Sweeney.
NS XLVI 1972 275-278 Thomas.
PhilosForum XI 1972 207-208 Kiesau.
CPh LXVII 1972 153-154 Sprague.
PhilosQ XXII 1972 165-166 Sayre.
JHPh X 1972 354-358 Anagnostopoulos.
Mind LXXXI 1972 631-632 Robinson.
LEC XL 1972 441-442 Druet.
RIPh XXVI 1972 211 Somville.
Gnomon XLIV 1972 326-335 Ilting.
CR XXII 1972 330-332 Crombie.
JVI VII 1973 71-73 Mulhern.

1226* Euthyphron, Griechisch-Deutsch, übers. mit Einl.
und Anm. von Reich K. Philos. Bibl. Nr.269,
Hamburg, Meiner 1968 xviii&52p.
Rev. PLA XXIII 1970 82-84 Nickel.

1227* Eutifrone, a cura di Gazza V. Traditio, Nuova col.
di class. gr. e lat. con note. Ser. greca
XXVI, Milano, Soc. ed. Dante Alighieri 1958
109p.

1228* Eutifrone, costruzione diretta, versione litterale
interlin., introd., argomento, note e verbi a
cura di Costa V. Siracusa, Ciranna 1958 73p.
Rev. RSC VIII 1960 116 Lamia.

1229* Eutifrone, trad., introd. e comm. di Reale G.   Il
pensiero, Brescia, La Scuola [1964] xlv&95p.
Also 3a ed. accresc. 1970 xlv&100p.

1230* Eutifrón o de la piedad, pról., trad. y notas por
Miguez J.A. Bibl. de iniciac. filos.
LXXXVII, Buenos Aires, Aguilar 1963 88p.
Rev. Sapientia XIX 1964 72-73 Argerami.

For additional texts and translations see 852, 866, 914,
942, 948, 949, 958, 959, 986, 1005, 1006, 1007,
1008, 1009, 1010, 1019, 1035, 1036, 1040, 1046.

III C d 17: EUTHYPHRO

B. STUDIES OF THE EUTHYPHRO

1231 HOERBER R.G., "Plato's Euthyphro". Phronesis III
      1958 95-107.

1232 LLEDÓ IÑIGO E., "La estructura dialéctica del
      Eutifrón platónico". RFil(Madrid) XVII 1958
      363-393.

1233 REALE G., "L'Eutifrone, il concetto di santo e la
      prima teoria platonica delle idee". RFNeo LI
      1959 311-333.

1234 BEZZEL C., "Zur Struktur des Platonischen
      Frühdialogs (Euthyphron)". ZPhF XVII 1963
      42-65.

1235* MEYER R.S., Plato's Euthyphro: An Example of
      Philosophical Analysis. Communications of the
      Univ. of S. Africa, C45, Pretoria 1963 26p.

1236 PAGLIANO M., "Introduzione all'Eutifrone". Vichiana
      I 1964 376-389.

1237 GEACH P.T., "Plato's Euthyphro. An Analysis and
      Commentary". Monist L 1966 369-382.

1238* HOOPES J.B., An Interpretation of Plato's Euthyphro.
      Diss. Vanderbilt Univ. 1967 196p.
      [microfilm]. Summary in DA XXVIII 1968 4212A.

1239 BONITZ H., "Zur Erklärung des Dialogs Euthyphron".
      p.227-242 in Bonitz H., Platonische Studien (see
      4584).

1240 GIGON O., "Platons Euthyphron". p.188-224 in Gigon
      O., Studien zur antiken Philosophie (see 4597).
      Reprinted from Westöstliche Abhandlungen. R.
      Tschudi zum 70. Geburtstag. Basel 1952,
      p.6-38.

1241 DUNSHIRN A., "Platons Euthyphron". WJb VI 1973
      122-148.

1242 RABINOWITZ W.G., "Platonic Piety. An Essay toward
      the Solution of an Enigma". Phronesis III 1958
      108-120.

1243 MITSUI K., "A Study of Piety in Plato's Euthyphro. The metaphysical unity of Religion and Education" [in Japanese]. Jimbun Ronkyu XI,4 1961.

1244 RE M.C. DEL, "L'Eutifrone, difesa stragiudiziale di Socrate dall'accusa di empietà". RDPC 1961 963-969.

1245 MARTELLA A., "L'Eutifrone platonico, scritto apologetico". NRP 1964 55-63.

1246 NEUMANN H., "The Problem of Piety in Plato's Euthyphro". ModS XLIII 1966 265-272.

1247 WELCH C., "The Euthyphro and the Forms". GM XXII 1967 228-244.

1248 ROSEN F., "Piety and Justice. Plato's Euthyphro". Philosophy XLIII 1968 105-116.

1249 ANDERSON A., "Socratic Reasoning in the Euthyphro". RM XXII 1969 461-481.

1250 HADEN J., "On Platos Inconclusiveness". CJ LXIV 1969 219-224.

1251 HOOPES J.P., "Euthyphro's Case". CB XLVII 1970 1-6.

1252 MOUTAFAKIS N.J., "Plato's Emergence in the Euthyphro". JCritA II 1970 35-42. Also in Apeiron V 1971 23-31.

1253 MacKINNON D.M., "The Euthyphro Dilemma". PASS XLVI 1972 211-222.

1254 MEYNELL H., "The Euthyphro Dilemma". PASS XLVI 1972 223-234.

1255 PATZIG G., "Logic in the Euthyphro". p.293-305 in Islamic philosophy and the Classical tradition. Essays presented by his friends and pupils to Richard Walzer on his seventieth birthday, ed. by Stern S.M. et al. Oriental Studies V, Oxford, Cassirer and Columbia, S.C., Univ. of South Carolina Pr. 1972.

1256 ROHATYN D.A., "The Euthyphro as Tragedy: A brief Sketch". Dialogos IX 1973 147-151.

DISCUSSIONS OF EUTHYPHRO 10A-11B

1257 BROWN J.H., "The Logic of the Euthyphro 10a-11b". PhilosQ XIV 1964 1-14.

1258 ROSE L.E., "A Note on the Euthyphro, 10-11". Phronesis X 1965 149-150.

1259 HALL J.C., "Plato, Euthyphro 10a1-11a10". PhilosQ XVIlI 1968 1-11.

1260 COHEN S.M., "Socrates on the Definition of Piety. Euthyphro 10a-11b". JHPh IX 1971 1-13. Reprinted p.158-176 in The Philosophy of Socrates, ed. by Vlastos G. (see 4621).

1261 PAXSON T.D., "Plato's Euthyphro 10a to 11b". Phronesis XVII 1972 171-190.

1262 SHARVY R., "Euthyphro 9d-11b: Analysis and Definition in Plato and others". Nous VI 1972 119-137.

For additional discussions see 40, 830, 2016, 2842, 2995, 3631, 3632, 4173, 4318, 4422.

C. TEXTUAL CRITICISM

1263 FORDER M.P., "A Note on Plato Euthyphro 15d6-7". AClass V 1962 68-70.

1264 RADT S.L., "Platonica". Mnemosyne XXI 1968 287-289.

GORGIAS

A. TEXTS AND TRANSLATIONS

1265* Gorgias, a revised text with intro. & comm. by Dodds E.R. Oxford Univ. Pr. 1959 vi&406p. Rev. Athenaeum XXXVII 1959 334-335

Barigazzi.
CW LIII 1960 260 Hoerber.
GIF XIII 1960 268-270 Jannaccone.
RFIC XXXVIII 1960 293-296 Plebe.
REA LXII 1960 473-474 Moreau.
AC XXIX 1960 189-191 des Places.
REG LXXIII 1960 554-556 Weil.
TLS 4 March 1960 142.
Mnemosyne XIV 1961 154-157 van Gelder.
CPh LVI 1961 191-194 Levinson.
RPh XXXV 1961 141-142 de Romilly.
JHS LXXXI 1961 167-169 Bambrough.
JCS IX 1961 111-116 Kaku.
Emerita XXIX 1961 133 Adrados.
CR XI 1961 28-30 Bluck.
Phoenix XV 1961 234-239 Morrison.
A&R VI 1961 242 Ronconi.
PACA IV 1961 54-57 Longrigg.
Philosophy XXXVI 1961 379-380 Skemp.
Hermathena XCV 1961 86-91 Luce.
RBPh XXXIX 1961 1255-1259 de Strycker.
Euphrosyne III 1961 379-382 Rosado
Fernandez.
AAHG XIV 1961 174 Vretska.
PhilosQ XI 1961 79-86 Kidd.
AJPh LXXXIV 1963 110 Minar.
PP XVIII 1963 392-400 Moreschini.
Gymnasium LXX 1970 374-375 Voit.
Gnomon XXXVI 1964 120-136 Mueller.
Humanitas XV-XVI 1963-1964 541-543 da
Rocha Pereira.

1266 WEIL R., "Quelques nouveautés en philologie
classique. Autour de Platon et de Démosthene".
IL XIII 1961 104-108.

1267* Gorgias, transl. by Hamilton W. Harmondsworth,
Middx. and Baltimore, Penguin 1960 149p.
Rev. CW LIV 1960 96 Hoerber.
AUMLA 1960 No.14 60-61 Harris.
TLS 18 March 1960 182.
CR XI 1961 162 Bluck.
CJ LVIII 1962 128-130 Parry.

1268* The Gorgias of Plato, ed. with English notes,
introd. & appendix by Thompson W.H. New York,
Arno Pr. 1973 xx&201p. Reprint of 1871 edn.

1269* Gorgias oder Über die Beredsamkeit, übers. von
Schleiermacher F. neu hrsg. und eingel. von
Hildebrandt K. Reclams Universal-Bibl.
No.2046/7, Stuttgart, Reclam 1961 186p.

1270* Gorgias, bearb. von Frank A. 2 vols. (I: Text;
       II: Vorbereitungsheft). Aus dem Schatze des
       Altertums, Bamberg, Buchner 1963.

1271* Gorgias, extraits trad. par Millepierres F. Trad.
       Hatier. Grèce XL, Paris, Hatier 1962 64p.

1272* Gorgia, trad., introd. e note di Guarrella V.
       Roma, Signorelli 1958 116p.

1273* Gorgia, trad., introd. e comm. di Reale G. Il
       Pensiero, Brescia, La Scuola [1966] lviii&250p.

1274* Gorgia, a cura di Adorno F. Piccola bibl. filos.
       Laterza XXXIX, Bari, Laterza 1968 527p.

1275* Gorgia, trad., introd. & comm. a cura di
       Arangio-Ruiz V. Bibl. del Class. della
       Filos., Firenze, Vallecchi 1958 xxx&145p.

1276* Gorgias, trad., introd. y notas de García Yagüe F.
       Buenos Aires, Aguilar 1961 181p.
       Rev. EClas VII 1963 219 Adrados.

1277* Gorgias. Bibl. de Iniciac. filos. LXXIV, Buenos
       Aires, Aguilar 1964 192p.

1278* Gorgias. Col. Los fundamentales, Buenos Aires,
       Eudeba 1967 336p.

1279* Górgias ou a oratória, Port. trad., apresent. &
       notas de Bruna J. São Paulo, Difusão Européia
       do Livro 1970 194p.

1280* Gorgias en Sokrates. Een gesprek in Athene 2350
       jaar geleden, Nederlands van Gelder J. van.
       Ooievaars CXVI, 's Gravenhage, Daamen 1960 208p.

1281* Gorgias, przel., wstep., objaśn., illustr. Witwicki
       W. Warszawa, PWN 1958 228p.

1282* Chosaku-shu-Gorgias, Japanese transl. by Tanaka M.
       & Kaku A. Tokyo, Iwanami Shoten 1960 577p.

1283* Gorgias, Japanese translation. Tokyo, Iwanami
       Shoten 1967 326p.

For additional texts and translations see 852, 858, 866,
   893, 929, 935, 943, 949, 978, 984, 989.

B. STUDIES OF THE GORGIAS

1284* OLYMPIODORUS, In Platonis Gorgiam commentaria, ed.
Norvin W. Nachdr. d. Ausg. Leipzig 1936.
Hildesheim, Olms 1966 250p.

1285* OLYMPIODORUS, Olympiodori in Platonis Gorgiam
Commentaria, ed. Westerink L.G. Leipzig,
Teubner 1970 xxi&313p.
Rev. Humanitas XXI-XXII 1969-1970 479 de
Rocha Pereira.
LEC XXXIX 1971 371.
RPh XLV 1971 343 Louis.
ACR I 1971 86-87 Minar.
RSC XX 1972 446-447 d'Agostino.

1286 PIEPER J., "'Kümmert euch nicht um Sokrates...'
Schluss-Szene aus einem platonischen Lehrstück
für den Fernsehfunk". p.339-348 in
Interpretation der Welt. Festschrift für Romano
Guardini zum achtzigsten Geburtstag, hrsg. von
Kuhn H. et al. Würzburg 1965.

1287 BONITZ H., "Gorgias". p.1-46 in Bonitz H.,
Platonische Studien (see 4584).

1288 PAVAN M., "Il 'Gorgia' di Platone e i Memorabili di
Socrate di Senofonte". p.37-66 in Pavan M., La
grecità politica da Tucidide ad Aristotele.
Roma 1958.

1289 PARANDOWSKI J., "Dusza ze zlota i kamień probierczy.
Dotyczy Gorgiasza Platona [Soul in Flight and
Difficult Trials. On Plato's Gorgias]" [In
Polish]. Filomata(Krakow) 1959 no.133 162-171.

1290 KAKU A., "What is Plato's Motive in Gorgias?" [in
Japanese with English summary]. JCS VIII 1960
28-42.

1291 KUHN H., "Das Gute und die Ordnung. Ueber die
Grundlegung der Metaphysik in Platons Gorgias".
ZPhF XIV 1960 489-504.

1292 BLACKWOOD R., CROSSET J., & LONG H., "Gorgias 482b".
CJ LVII 1962 318-319.

1293 HARRISON E.L., "Plato, Gorgias 449d foll.". Eranos
LXI 1963 63-65.

III C d 18: GORGIAS

1294 TAKEMIYA A., "Twofold Qualification of τέχνη in
     Plato's Gorgias" [in Japanese with English
     summary]. JCS XI 1963 43-52.

1295 SÁNCHEZ LASSO DE LA VEGA J., "Notas al Gorgias".
     Emerita XXXV 1967 295-314.

1296 VLASTOS G., "Was Polus Refuted?". AJPh LXXXVIII
     1967 454-460.

1297 HENSCHEN-DAHLQUIST A.M., "Nagra reflexioner om
     insiktsdeterminism och psykologisk egoism i
     Platons Gorgias". p.128-139 in Sanning Dict
     Tro. Till Ingemar Hedenius, ed. by
     Henschen-Dahlquist A.M. et alii. Stockholm,
     Bonniers 1968.

1298 LAFRANCE Y., "La problématique morale de l'opinion
     dans le Gorgias de Platon". RPhL LXVII 1969
     5-29.

1299 ITO U., "On Pleasures in Plato's Gorgias. A
     Preliminary Stage in the study of the Good" [in
     Japanese]. Studies in Philosophy (Kyushu Univ.)
     VI 1970.

1300 KLAUK E., "Platon, Gorgias 521d6-522a7". DCG No.10
     1970 18-23.

1301 HALL R.W., "Techne and Morality in the Gorgias".
     p.202-218 in Essays in ancient Greek Philosophy,
     ed. by Anton J.P. & Kustas G.L. (see 4581).

1302 RIGOBELLO A., "Il Gorgia platonico in 'seconda
     lettura'". Proteus II 1971 145-159.

1303 NAITO S., "Τέχνη in the Gorgias" [in Japanese].
     Philosophy Miscellany (Tokyo Metropolitan Univ.)
     XVI 1973.

For additional discussions see 224, 225, 301, 318, 700,
     935, 1778, 2168, 2590, 2599, 2638, 3403, 3456,
     3477, 3631, 3632, 4014, 4478.

165

C. TEXTUAL CRITICISM

1304 BLUCK R.S., "Plato, Gorgias 493c1-3". CR XIII 1963 263-264.

1305 MERRY B., "Plato, Gorgias 467e-468a". CR XIV 1964 242.

1306 METZGER H., "Ein neues Gorgias-Fragment aus der Papyrussammlung Erzherzog Rainer in Wien (P. Graec. Vindob. 39880)". WS LXXVIII 1965 40-44.

1307 KOSTER W.J.W., "De locis Plat. Gorg. 461e sq. citatis". Mnemosyne XIX 1966 269.

1308 SÁNCHEZ LASSO DE LA VEGA J., "Notas al Gorgias". Emerita XXXVI 1968 97-119.

HIPPARCHUS

B. STUDIES OF THE HIPPARCHUS

For discussions of the Hipparchus see 998, 2636.

HIPPIAS MAJOR

A. TEXTS AND TRANSLATIONS

1309* Ippia maggiore, a cura di Zeppi S. Class. della
      filos., Padova, R.A.D.A.R. 1968 110p.

1310* Hippias Major, transl. into modern Greek by
      Karouzou C. & Kakrides I.T. Thessalonike,
      Inst. Neoell. Spoudon 1973.
           Rev. Platon XXV 1973 367-368
      Georgountzos.

For additional texts and translations see 853, 866, 871,
      925, 933, 942, 949, 955, 956, 962, 986.

B. STUDIES OF THE HIPPIAS MAJOR

1311 HOERBER R.G., "Plato's Greater Hippias". Phronesis
      IX 1964 143-155.

1312* HORN H.J., Hippias Maior. Untersuchungen zur
      Echtheitsfrage des Dialogs. Diss. Köln 1964
      100p.

1313 MALCOLM J., "On the Place of the Hippias Major in
      the Development of Plato's Thought". AGPh L
      1968 189-195.

1314* TELOH H.A., The Ontology of Plato's Hippias Major.
      Diss.   Univ. of Wisconsin 1972 144p.
      [microfilm]. Summary in DA XXXIII 1972 2432A.

III C d 20: HIPPIAS MAJOR

1315* HAAG A., Hippias Maior. Interpretation eines
      pseudo-platonischen Dialogs. Diss. Tübingen
      1973 258p.

For additional discussions see 3631, 3632, 3889, 4449.

C. TEXTUAL CRITICISM

For textual criticism see 1264.

HIPPIAS MINOR

A. TEXTS AND TRANSLATIONS

1316* Ippia minore, trad., introd. e note a cura di
      Lazzerini C. Firenze, La Nuova Italia 1962
      xxxv&46p.
      Rev. DeHomine I 1962 286-287 Giannantoni.

1317* Ippia minore, introd. e comm. di Traglia A. Testi
      e crestomazie, Torino, Loescher 1972 xxiv&45p.

For additional texts and translations see 852, 866, 925,
      933, 942, 949.

B. STUDIES OF THE HIPPIAS MINOR

1318 GUZZO A., "La parole et le divin Ulysse". EPh XIII
      1958 161-171.

1319 HOERBER R.G., "Plato's Lesser Hippias". Phronesis
      VII 1962 121-131.

1320 MARQUES M.L., "Hipias Menor de Platão". Itinerarium
      IX 1963 50-73.

III C d 21: HIPPIAS MINOR

1321 MULHERN J.J., "Τρόπος and πολυτροπία in Plato's
     Hippias Minor". Phoenix XXII 1968 283-288.

For additional discussions see 2633, 2711, 3116, 3631,
     3632.

                              ION

                A. TEXTS AND TRANSLATIONS

1322* Ion, griech. & dt. hrsg. von Flashar H.
      Tusculum-Bücherei, München, Heimeran 1963 72p.
      Rev. Gnomon XXXVI 1964 Koller.
      Gymnasium LXXII 1965 361-363 Baumgarten.
      AAHG XVIII 1965 87-88 Vretska.

1323* Ione, costruzione diretta, versione letterale
      interlin., introd., argomento, note e verbi a
      curi di Costa V. Siracusa, Ciranna 1958 54p.

1324* Ione, introd. e comm. di Borrelli F.L. Nuova ed.
      I class. greci, Roma, Signorelli 1965 71p.

1325* Ione, a cura di Battegazzore A.M. Civ. lett. di
      Gr. e di Roma. Autori. Serie greca V,
      Torino/Milano/Padova, Paravia 1969 xxvii&106p.
      Rev. Sophia XL 1972 154-157.

1326* Ione, a cura di Pratola V. Coll. Misc. selecta
      VI, L'Aquila, Japadre 1970 54p.

1327* Ione, a cura di Vita E. Class. lat. e gr.,
      Padova, R.A.D.A.R. 1972 66p.

1328* Ion, ed. & komm. door Verdenius W.J. Zwolle,
      Willink 1959 41p.
      Rev. RPhilos CL 1960 229-236 Schuhl.

1329* Ion, Norwegian transl. & comm. by Wyller E.A.
      Libr. of Classics ed. by the Norwegian Acad.
      of Lang. & Lit. II, Oslo, Aschehoug 1958 61p.
      Rev. Gnomon XXXI 1959 281 Föllesdal.

For additional texts and translations see 852, 866, 917,
     920, 925, 933, 942, 948, 949, 956, 970, 984.

                              169

b. STUDIES OF THE ION

1330* FLASHAR H., Der Dialog Ion als Zeugnis platonischer
       Philosophie. Deutsche Akad. der Wiss. zu
       Berlin, Schr. der Sekt. für Altertumswiss.
       XIV Berlin Akad.-Verl. 1958 vi&144p.
       Rev. Mnemosyne XII 1959 357-358 Verdenius.

1331 WYLLER E.A., "Platons Ion. Versuch einer
      Interpretation". SO XXXIV 1958 19-38.

1332 BERNARD P., "Note épidaurienne. La datation du
      temple d'Asclépios et l'Ion de Platon". BCH
      LXXXV 1961 400-402.

1333 HENNING R.B., "A Performing Musician looks at the
      Ion". CJ LIX 1964 241-247.

1334 GILBERT A.H., "Plato's Ion, comic and serious".
      p.259-284 in Studies in Honor of DeW.T.
      Starnes. Austin, Univ. of Texas 1967.

1335 RANTA J., "The Drama of Plato's Ion". JAAC XXVI
      1967 219-230.

1336 BLOOM A., "An Interpretation of Plato's Ion".
      Interpretation I 1970 43-62.

1337 HANCHER M., "The Science of Interpretation and the
      Art of Interpretation". ModLangNotes LXXXV 1970
      791-802.

1338 DILLER H., "Probleme der platonischen Ion".
      p.201-219 in Diller H., Kleine Schriften zur
      antiken Literatur, hrsg. von Newiger H.J. &
      Seyffert H. München, Beck 1971.

1339 SKIADAS A.D., "Über das Wesen des Dichters im
      platonischen Ion". SO XLVI 1971 80-89.

1340 DORTER K., "The Ion. Plato's Characterization of
      Art". JAAC XXXII 1973 65-78.

1341 MOORE J.D., "Limitation and Design in Plato's Ion".
      PCP VIII 1973 45-51.

For additional discussions see 40, 757, 778, 2168, 2752,
      2842, 3810, 3831, 3846, 3851, 3868, 3889, 3897,
      3899, 4149, 4173.

LACHES

A. TEXTS AND TRANSLATIONS

1342* Laches, ed. with introd. & notes by Tatham M.T.
London, Macmillan 1966 xxvi&99p. Reprint of
1888 edn.

1343* Laches, griech. & dt. neu übers. & hrsg. von
Schrastetter R. Philos. Bibl. Nr.270,
Hamburg, Meiner 1970 xxxix&101p.

1344* Laches, przel., wstep., objaśn., illustr. Witwicki
W. Warszawa, PWN 1958 95&5p.

1345* Laches, Turkish transl. by Kösemihal N.S. 3rd edn.
Yunan klâsikleri XXVIII, Ankara, Millî Eğitim
Basimevi 1967 42p.

For additional texts and translations see 852, 866, 917,
921, 925, 933, 938, 942, 949, 986, 992.

B. STUDIES OF THE LACHES

1346 KOHÁK E.V., "The Road to Wisdom: Lessons on
Education from Plato's Laches". CJ LVI 1960
123-132.

1347 GIL L., "La semblanza de Nicias en Plutarco". EClas
VI 1962 404-450.

1348 NAGEL W., "Zur Darstellungskunst Platons
insbesondere im Dialog Laches". p.119-142 in
Serta philol. Aenipontana, hrsg. von Muth R.
Innsbrucker Beitr. zur Kulturwiss. VII-VIII,
Innsbruck, Innrain 1962.

1349 O'BRIEN M.J., "The Unity of the Laches". YClS XVIII
1963 133-143. Also published as a monograph:
New Haven/London, Yale Univ. Pr. 1963.

1350 BUCCELLATO M., "Studi sul dialogo platonico, III:
La mimesis e la regia platonica dell'actio nel
Lachete". RSF XXII 1967 123-140.

III C d 23: LACHES

1351 INGENKAMP H.G., "Laches, Nikias und platonische Lehre". RhM CX 1967 234-247.

1352 BONITZ H., "Zur Erklärung des Dialogs Laches". p.210-226 in Bonitz H., Platonische Studien (see 4584).

1353* CATTANEI G., Civismo e valentia nel Lachete di Platone. Note sul disarmo dei polemarchi nell'utopia platonica. Genova, Fac. di Magistero Ist. di Scienze pedag. 1968 117p. Rev. Maia XXII 1970 387-389 Bertini. GM XXV 1970 771-772 Sorge.

1354 HINSKE N., "Zur Interpretation des platonischen Dialogs Laches". KantStud LIX 1968 62-79.

1355 HOERBER R.G., "Plato's Laches". CPh LXIII 1968 95-105.

1356 SANTAS G., "Socrates at Work on Virtue and Knowledge in Plato's Laches". RM XXII 1969 433-460. Reprinted p.177-208 in The Philosophy of Socrates, ed. by Vlastos G. (see 4621).

1357 SUEMORI S., "Some Comments on the Laches" [in Japanese]. Methodos II 1969.

1358 O'BRIEN M.J., "The Unity of the Laches". p.303-315 in Essays in ancient Greek Philosophy, ed. by Anton J.P. & Kustas G.L. (see 4581).

1359 VRIES G.J. DE, "Notes on four Passages in Plato". p.57-60 in Zetesis (see 4579).

For additional discussions see 40, 819, 1962, 2645, 3471, 3631, 3632, 4173, 4449.

C. TEXTUAL CRITICISM

1360 STARK R., "Bemerkungen zum Platontext". Philologus CVI 1962 283-290.

LAWS

A. TEXTS AND TRANSLATIONS

1361* The Laws, transl. by Taylor A.E. Everyman's
Library, London, Dent and New York, Dutton 1960
448p.
Rev. Hermathena 1963 129 Luce.

1362* The Laws, transl. with introd. by Saunders T.J.
Harmondsworth, Middx. Penguin 1970 550p.
Rev. DUJ XXXIII 1971 58-59 Skemp.
ACR I 1971 84 Farber.
JHS XCII 1972 200 Skemp.
CR XXIII 1973 88-89 Gulley.

1363* Las Leyes, ed., trad., notas y estudio prelim. por
Pabón J.M. & Fernández Galiano M. Clás.
Polít., Madrid, Inst. de Estud. Polít. 1960
lxxxvi&251, 279p.
Rev. Convivium 1961 203 Alsina.
AC XXXI 1962 336-337 des Places.
Humanidades XIV 1962 126-129 Solá.
Athenaeum XL 1962 425 Barigazzi.
REG LXXV 1962 579-580 Irigoin.
Helmantica XIII 1962 368-369 Rodríguez.
RPh XXXVII 1963 129 Weil.
CR XIII 1963 112 Gulley.
Mnemosyne XVI 1963 307-308 de Vries.
RFLL 1963 298-299 Antunes.
SicGymn XVI 1963 212-214 Cataudella.
RyF CLXVII 1963 548-549 Vives.
REA LXVI 1964 170-172 Carrière.
Augustinianum IV 1964 466 Méndez.

1364* Prawa [Laws], Polish transl. & discussion by
Maykowska M. Bibl. Klas. Filoz., Warszawa,
PWN 1960 xxviii&630p.

1365* Νόμοι, V-VI, text, introd. & notes by Philippa K.S.
Athens, Kollaros 1965, pp.225-320, 321-416.

For additional texts and translations see 868, 870, 893,
945, 950.

In the following section general works on the Laws are followed by specialized studies in the order of the passages
they treat.

B. STUDIES OF THE LAWS

1366* GABRIELI F. ed., Plato Arabus, vol.III: Alfarabius
      compendium legum Platonis, ed. et latine vertit
      Gabrieli F. Corpus Platonicum Medii Aevi,
      Nendeln, Liechtenstein, Kraus Reprint 1973
      xiv&37&46p. Reprint of 1952 London edn.

1367* GOERGEMANNS H., Beiträge zur Interpretation von
      Platons Nomoi. Diss. Würzburg 1959, Zetemata
      XXV, München, Beck 1960 xiv&231p.
           Rev. AC XXX 1961 218 des Places.
           LEC XXIX 1961 334 Moraux.
           MH XVIII 1961 239 Gigon.
           RFIC XXXIX 1961 413-415 Plebe.
           RecSR L 1962 614-615 des Places.
           REA LXIV 1962 433-434 Moreau.
           CPh LVII 1962 262-263 Hoerber.
           RBPh XL 1962 1407 Saunders.
           Gnomon XXXIV 1962 231-241 Ostwald.
           Gymnasium LXIX 1962 100-102 Gaiser.
           PhR LXXI 1962 543-544 Morrow.
           PhilosRdschau X 1962 277-282 Kullmann.
           AAHG XV 1962 162 Vretska.
           PP XVII 1962 73-79 Isnardi.
           Erasmus XV 1963 632-633 Koller.
           Scholastik XXXVIII 1963 99-101 Ennen.
           StimZ CLXXIV 1964 476-477 Klenk.
           EClas VIII 1964 40-41 Galiano.
           JCS XII 1964 162-165 Nagasaka.
           RBPh XLII 1964 601-604 de Strycker.
           JHS LXXXV 1965 208-209 Saunders.

1368* MORROW G.R., Plato's Cretan City. A Historical
      Interpretation of the Laws. Princeton,
      Princeton Univ. Pr. 1960 xxii&623p.
           Rev. AHR LXVI 1960-1961 708-709 Welles.
           REG LXXIV 1961 499-503 Weil.
           JHI XXII 1961 418-424 Kahn.
           REA LXIII 1961 480-483 Will.
           Lychnos 1960-1961 284-286 Duering.
           CW LIV 1961 185 North.
           RM XIV 1960-1961 570 J.A.B.
           LJ 1960 357 Stevens.
           Personalist LXII 1961 581-582 Miller.
           RM XV 1961-1962 67-80 Versenyi.
           CrossCurr 1961 145 Collins.
           PSQ 1961 439 Sinclair.
           UTQ 1962 394 Skemp.
           Ethics LXXII 1961-1962 216-217 Scarrow.

RecSR L 1962 614 des Places.
CPh LVII 1962 132-137 Levinson.
CR XII 1962 40-42 Russell.
JHS LXXXII 1962 181 Saunders.
JCS X 1962 141-146 Kawata.
Phoenix XVI 1962 281-283 Grube.
Mnemosyne XV 1962 57-60 Aalders.
ZRG LXXIX 1962 361-364 Berneker.
AJPh LXXXIII 1962 447-449 Oliver.
RPhL LXI 1963 144-146 Vanhoutte.
PhilosQ XIII 1963 171-172 Ewins.
Ph&PhenR   XXIV   1963-1964   278-280
Diamadopoulos.
Personalist XLV 1964 416-417 O'Neill.
AGPh XLVI 1964 118-121 Bormann.
PhR LXXV 1966 104-107 Crombie.

1369* MUELLER G., Studien zu den platonischen Nomoi. 2.
durchges. Aufl. mit einem Nachw. Zetemata
III, München, Beck 1968 214p. (1. Aufl.
1951.)
Rev. RBPh XLVIII 1970 119 des Places.

1370* HENTSCHKE A.B., Politik und Philosophie bei Plato
und Aristoteles. Die Stellung der Nomoi im
platonischen Gesamtwerk und die politische
Theorie des Aristoteles. Frankfurter wiss.
Beitr. Kulturwiss. Reihe XIII, Frankfurt,
Klostermann 1971 x&493p.
Rev. Gnomon XLV 1973 139-148 Ingenkamp.
PhilosRdschau XX 1973 140-141 Wyller.
PhJ LXXX 1973 188-191 Rupp.
BAGB 1973 508ff.

1371* SAUNDERS T.J., Notes on the Laws of Plato.   BICS
Suppl.   XXVIII, London Univ.   Pr.   1972
xvii&148p.
Rev. AC XLII 1973 237 de Ley.

1372 KATO H., "Plato's Nomos" [in Japanese]. Bulletin of
Akita Univ. Dept. of Liberal Arts X 1960.

1373* KNOCH W., Die Strafbestimmungen in Platons Nomoi.
Klass.-philol. Stud. XXIII, Wiesbaden,
Harrassowitz 1960 x&170p.
Rev. RBPh XL 1962 1408 Saunders.
LEC XXX 1962 126 Moraux.
Gnomon XXXIV 1962 541-543 Morrow.
CR XII 1962 306 Gulley.
Mnemosyne XV 1962 184-186 Aalders.
RHD XXX 1962 377-381 Pestman.
ZRG LXXIX 1962 365-368 Berneker.

AAHG XV 1962 164 Gerstinger.
MH XIX 1962 234 Wehrli.
RecSR L 1962 615-616 des Places.
Scholastik XXXVIII 1963 128-129 Ennen.
RPh XXXVII 1963 130 Weil.
JHS LXXXIII 1963 171 Saunders.

1374 KROYMANN J., "Betrachtungen zum platonischen und goethischen Alterswerk". p.133-150 in Aparchai. Gedenkschrift für G. Rohde IV 1961.

1375 STRÓZEWSKI W., "Plato's Last Dialogue" [in Polish]. Znak XIII 1961 1443-1447.

1376 KULLMANN W., "Die philosophische Bedeutung von Platons Nomoi". PhilosRdschau X 1962 277-282.

1377 SAUNDERS T.J., "The Structure of the Soul and the State in Plato's Laws". Eranos LX 1962 37-55.

1378 BORECKÝ B., "Platons Idealstaat in den Nomoi und die politische Theorie der Griechen". WZBer XII 1963 221-228.

1379 BORECKÝ B., "Die sozial-ökonomischen Grundlagen der griechischen Polis und Platons Gesetzesstaat". Eirene II 1963 81-95.

1380 SCHUCHMAN P., "Comments on the Criminal Code of Plato's Laws". JHI XXIV 1963 25-40.

1381 ZELLER E., "Ueber den Ursprung der Schrift von den Gesetzen". p.3-156 in Zeller E., Platonische Studien (see 4627).

STUDIES OF PARTICULAR ISSUES IN THE LAWS

1382* SANDVOSS E., Soteria. Philosophische Grundlagen der platonischen Gesetzgebung. Göttingen, Munsterschmidt 1971 381p.
Rev. WS VI 1972 254-255 Doent.
PhJ LXXX 1973 191-192 Rupp.

1383 GIGON O., "Das Einleitungsgespräch der Gesetze Platons". p.155-187 in Gigon O., Studien zur antiken Philosophie (see 4597). Reprinted from MH XI 1954 201-230.

1384 RANKIN H.D., "Toys and Education in Plato's Laws". Hermathena XCII 1958 62-65.

III C d 24: LAWS

1385* WEIL R., L'archéologie de Platon. Études &
Commentaires XXXII, Paris, Klincksieck 1959
171p.
        Rev. EPh XV 1960 565-566 Colnort-Bodet.
        GIF XIII 1960 270-271 Pepe.
        AAHG XIII 1960 150 von Ivánka.
        REA LXII 1960 474-476 Will.
        Lychnos 1960-1961 284-286 Duering.
        AC XXX 1961 218 des Places.
        Gnomon XXXIII 1961 344-349 Gaiser.
        CR XI 1961 30-31 Kerferd.
        RH CCXXV 1961 502-503 Cloché.
        Euphrosyne III 1961 415-417 Ureña Prieto.
        RecSR XLIX 1961 293-294 des Places.
        RPh XXXVI 1962 115-117 Defradas.
        Emerita XXX 1962 208-209 Lledó.
        Mnemosyne XV 1962 60-62 Aalders.
        RPhilos LXXXVII 1962 129-130 Schuhl.
        CPh LVII 1962 116-118 Kahn.
        EClas VII 1962-1963 392-396 Lasso de la
Vega.

1386 LOMBARDO M., "Le concezioni degli antichi sul ruolo
degli oracoli nella colonizzazione greca".
p.63-89 in Ricerche sulla colonizzazione greca,
a cura di Nenci G. ASNP Ser.3a II 1972 33-139.

1387 PLACES E. DES, "Des temples faits de main d'homme".
Biblica XLII 1961 217-223.

1388 SAUNDERS T.J., "The Property Classes and the Value
of the κλῆρος in Plato's Laws". Eranos LIX 1961
29-39.

1389 THOMPSON W.E., "The Demes in Plato's Laws". Eranos
LXIII 1965 134-136.

1390 SAUNDERS T.J., "The alleged Double Version of the
Sixth Book of Plato's Laws". CQ XX 1970
230-236.

1391 DAVIS M., "How many Agronomoi are there in Plato's
Laws?". CPh LX 1965 28-29.

1392 WILLETTS R.F., "A Note on Plato Lg. 773b". JHS
XCII 1972 184-185.

1393 SAUNDERS T.J., "Two Passages in Plato's Laws"
[794a-c & 848a]. CR XI 1961 101-102.

177

1394* PAPANIKOLAOU K.N., Ἡ ὀργάνωση τῆς παιδείας στοὺς Νόμους τοῦ Πλάτωνα. Μελέτη: Βασικὴ μορφωτικὴ Βιβλιοθηκή, Athens, Ed. Nikè 1962 37p.

1395 LACROIX L., "Les monnaies de Mantinée et les traditions arcadiennes". BAB LIII 1967 303-311.

1396 SALVIAT F. & VATIN C., "La répression des violences sexuelles dans la convention entre Delphes et Pellana, le droit d'Athènes et les Lois de Platon". p.63-75 in Inscriptions de Grèce centrale. Paris, de Boccard 1971.

1397* BISINGER J., Der Agrarstaat in Platons Gesetzen. Neudr. d. Ausg. 1925. Klio Beih. XVII, Aalen, Scientia Verl. 1963 viii&121p.

1398 JAULIN A., "Agriculture platonicienne". AUToul IX, No.6, Philosophie, II 1973 95-102.

1399 SAUNDERS T.J., "On Plato, Laws 850ab". Philologus CVI 1962 122-123.

1400 SAUNDERS T.J., "The Socratic Paradoxes in Plato's Laws. A Commentary on 859c-864b". Hermes XCVI 1968 421-434.

1401 McGIBBON D.D., "Plato's final Definition of Justice". PACA VII 1964 19-24.

1402 MAHIEU W. DE, "La doctrine des athées au Xe livre des Lois de Platon. Essai d'analyse". RBPh XLI 1963 5-24.

1403 MAHIEU W. DE, "La doctrine des athées au Xe livre des Lois de Platon. Étude des sources". RBPh XLII 1964 16-47.

1404 RAEDLE H., "Platons Freigelassenengesetze als Ausdruck attischer Standespolitik des 4. Jahrhunderts". Gymnasium LXXIX 1972 305-313.

1405 SILVERTHORNE M.J., "Militarism in the Laws? (Laws 942a5-943a3)". SO XLIX 1973 29-38.

1406 MORROW G.R., "The Nocturnal Council in Plato's Laws". AGPh XLII 1960 229-246.

1407 NAGASAKA K., "Self-caused Motion and induced Motion in the tenth Book of Plato's Laws" [in Japanese with English summary]. JCS XV 1967 37-51.

III C d 24: LAWS

For additional discussions see 89, 208, 229, 285, 318,
325, 335, 356, 362, 557, 793, 794, 1407, 2016,
2038, 2054, 2484, 2517, 2592, 2661, 3086, 3101,
3116, 3159, 3211, 3283, 3313, 3333, 3450, 3510,
3511, 3547, 3548, 3565, 3569, 3583, 3592, 3595,
3600, 3644, 3683, 3690, 3712, 3713, 3721, 3726,
3761, 3794, 3797, 3803, 3828, 3868, 3907, 3908,
3950, 3968, 4017, 4109, 4159.

C. TEXTUAL CRITICISM

1408 SOLMSEN F., "Textprobleme im zehnten Buch der
      platonischen Nomoi". p.265-278 in Studien zur
      Textgeschichte und Textkritik, G. Jachmann
      gewidmet, hrsg. von Dahlmann H. & Merkelbach
      R. Köln, Westdt. Verl. 1959. Reprinted
      p.59-71 in Solmsen F., Kleine Schriften II (see
      4615).

1409 BOUQUIAUX-SIMON O., "Bel âge ou fruit du moment
      (Platon, Lois VIII,837B-C)". AC XXX 1961
      349-360.

1410 PLACES E. DES, "La tradition indirecte des Lois de
      Platon (livres VII-XII)". p.473-479 in Studia
      Patristica, vol. V. Papers presented to the
      Third International Conference on Patristic
      Studies held at Christ Church, Oxford, 1959, ed.
      by Cross F.L. p.3: Liturgica, monastica et
      ascetica, philosophica. Texte u.
      Untersuchungen z. Geschichte d. altchristl.
      Literatur LXXX, Berlin, Akademie-Verl. 1962.

1411 KASSEL R., "Kritische und exegetische Kleinigkeiten,
      I". RhM CVI 1963 298-306.

For additional textual discussion see 1360, 2203.

LETTERS

A. TEXTS AND TRANSLATIONS

1412* <u>Plato's Epistles</u>, transl. with crit. essays &
notes by Morrow G. Libr. of Liberal Arts
CXXII, Indianapolis, Bobbs-Merrill 1962
viii&282p.
Rev. REG LXXV 1962 577 des Places.
RM 1962-1963 397 R.S.B.
Helicon II 1962 748-750 Frenkian.
EPh XVIII 1963 230-231 Moreau.
LEC XXXI 1963 95 Moreau.
CR XIII 1963 112 Bluck.
AC XXXII 1963 235 des Places.
RSF XIX 1964 108-109 Buccellato.
BA 1964 72 Hoerber.
Aevum XXXIX 1965 173 Musso.

1413* <u>Briefe</u>, übers. & eingel. von Irmscher J. Quellen
& Texte zur Gesch. der Philos., Berlin,
Akad.-Verl. 1960 122p.
Rev. CR XI 1961 291 Bluck.
DLZ LXXXIII 1962 117-119 Frenkian.
Helikon VII 1967 620 Pépin.

1414* Der <u>siebente Brief</u>, Übers. & Nachw. von Howald E.
Reclams Universal-Bibl. Nr.8892, Stuttgart,
Reclam 1964 72p.

1415* <u>Briefe</u>, griech.-dt. hrsg. von Neumann W., überarb.
von Kerschensteiner J. Tusculum-Bücherei,
München, Heimeran 1967 236p.
Rev. AAHG XXI 1968 278-279 Vretska.
Gymnasium LXXVI 1969 97-99 Reynen.

1416* <u>Lettere</u>, trad. di Carlini A. Encicl. di autori
class. XXXVII, Torino, Boringhieri 1960 120p.
Rev. REG LXXV 1962 577 Weil.

1417* Le <u>lettere di Platone</u>, a cura di Pasquali G. La
Civ. europ., Firenze, Sansoni 1967 xviii&262p.
Rev. NRS 1967 695-697 Treves.

1418 "Platão, Carta VII", trad. de Pinto de Carvalho A.
RBF XII, 1962 486-509.

III C d 25: LETTERS

1419* Epistolai, Turkish transl. by Şahinbaş I. 2nd edn.
Yunan klâsikleri XLIII, Ankara, Millî Eğitim
Basimevi 1962 91p.

1420* Plato's Letters, transl. by Yamamoto M. Tokyo,
Kadokawa 1970 x&235p.

For additional texts and translations see 852, 871, 893,
922, 950, 978, 987, 990.

B. STUDIES OF THE LETTERS (GENERAL)

1421 JAEGER W., Rev. of Howald E., Die Briefe Platons.
p.287-292 in Jaeger W., Scripta Minora I (see
4605). reprinted from DLZ 1924 Sp. 895-901.

1422 IRMSCHER J., "Die Platon-Briefe". Altertum VII 1961
137-146.

1423 MILLER T.A., "The Letters of Plato and Isocrates"
[in Russian]. p.26-57 in Antičnaja
epistolografija. Očerki, ed. by Grabar-Passek
M.E. Moscow, Nauka 1967. German summary in BCO
XIV 1969 85-86.

1424 AALDERS G.J.D., "Political Thought and Political
Programs in the Platonic Epistles". p.145-187
in Pseudepigrapha I, entretiens prép. &
présidés par Fritz K. von. Entretiens sur
l'antiquité class. XVIII, Vandoeuvres-Genève,
Fond. Hardt 1972.

1425 GULLEY N., "The Authenticity of the Platonic
Epistles". p.103-143 in Pseudepigrapha, I,
entretiens prép. & présidés par Fritz K. von.
Entretiens sur l'antiquité class. XVIII,
Vandoeuvres-Genève, Fond. Hardt 1972.

1426 MICHAELSON S. & MORTON A.Q., "The Authorship and
Integrity of the Platonic Epistles". RIPh XXVII
1973 3-9.

1427 SCHADEWALDT W., "Der Brife bei den Griechen. Ein
Instrument des Humanen". p.31-42 in Studia
Humanitatis. Ernesto Grassi zum 70.
Geburtstag, hrsg. von Hora E. & Kessler E.
Hum. Bibl. 1. Reihe XVI, München, Fink 1973.

III C d 25: LETTERS

1428* SCHIFF J., A Computerized Word-index to the Platonic
Epistles. Stud. Class. II, Univ. Park,
Pennsylvania State Univ. Dept. of Class. 1973
110p.

For further discussions see see 342, 348, 2912.

THE FIRST LETTER

For discussion of the First Letter see 1431.

THE SECOND LETTER

1429 STANNARD J., "Plato, Ep. II, 312a". Phronesis V
1960 53-55.

1430 BLUCK R.S., "The Second Platonic Epistle".
Phronesis V 1960 140-151.

1431 RIST J.M., "Neopythagoreanism and Plato's Second
Letter". Phronesis X 1965 78-81.

THE SEVENTH LETTER

1432* EDELSTEIN L., Plato's Seventh Letter. Philosophia
antiqua XIV, Leiden, Brill 1966 x&171p.
Rev. RecSR LIV 1966 600 des Places.
CW LX 1966 14 Hoerber.
REA LXIX 1967 132-133 Moreau.
REG LXXX 1967 632-633 Weil.
Phoenix XXI 1967 141-143 Robinson.
RSF XXII 1967 90-94 Isnardi Parente
(reprinted p.101-111 as "L'Epistola VII:
Un'Atetesi non convincente" in Isnardi Parente
M., Filosifia e politica nelle Lettere di
Platone (see 4603)).
Mnemosyne XXI 1968 88-89 Gulley.
RM XXI 1967-1968 549 R.D.
RPortFil XXIII 1967 504 Freire.
GGA CCXXI 1969 187-211 Mueller.

III C d 25: LETTERS

Gnomon XLI 1969 29-34 Solmsen.
RFIC XCVII 1969 190-197 Gismondi Grisoli.

1433 MORTON A.Q. & WINSPEAR A.D., "The Computer and Plato's Seventh Letter". CHum I 1966-1967 72-73.

1434 LEVISON M., MORTON A.Q., & WINSPEAR A.D., "The Seventh Letter of Plato". Mind LXXVII 1968 309-325.

1435 BRANDWOOD L., "Plato's Seventh Letter". RELO 1969,4 1-25.

1436 DEANE P., "Stylometrics do not exclude the Seventh Letter". Mind LXXXII 1973 113-117.

1437 MATSUI A., "A Note on the Authenticity of Plato's Seventh Letter" [in Japanese with English summary]. JCS XVIII 1970 64-74.

1438* BAER E., Die historischen Angaben der Platonbriefe VII und VIII im Urteil der modernen Forschung seit Ed. Meyer. Diss. Humboldt-Univ. Berlin [1958?] 213p.

1439 MATARASIS A.S., "Ερμηνεία και γλωσσικαι, συντακτικαι και φιλοσοφικαι παρατηρήσεις εἰς Πλάτωνος ἐπιστ. Ζ' 343Α-4Dᵃ. Platon X 1958 75-86.

1440 LLANOS A., "La septima carta de Platon". RevE IV 1959 290-295.

1441 BROECKER W., "Der philosophische Exkurs in Platons siebentem Brief". Hermes XCI 1963 416-425.

1442 BROECKER W., "Nachtrag zum philosophischen Exkurs in Platons siebentem Brief". Hermes XCIII 1965 132.

1443 GADAMER H.G., "Platons Traktat über Argumentation". p.417-430 in La théorie de l'argumentation, perspectives et applications. Mélanges publiés en hommage au Prof. Ch. Perelman. Louvain, Nauwelaerts/Paris, Béatrice-Nauwelaerts 1963 (= Logique et Analyse VI).

1444 ORTEGA A., "Observaciones a la Carta séptima de Platón". Helmantica XIV 1963 187-215.

1445 STEIN O., "Von der Schwachheit der Logoi. Einige
Gedanken zu Platons siebtem Brief". PaedProv
XVII 1963 225-231.

1446* GADAMER H.G., Dialektik und Sophistik im siebenten
platonischen Brief. SHAW 1964,2, Heidelberg,
Winter 1964 34p. Reprinted p.221-247 in Gadamer
H.G., Platos dialektische Ethik und andere
Studien zur platonischen Philosophie (see 4592).
Rev. ASSPh XXIV 1964 245-246 Wildermuth.
Gnomon XXXVII 1965 822-824 Ostwald.
Filosofia XVI 1965 185 Verra.
ArchPhilos. XXVIII 1965 259 Solignac.
RPortFil XXII 1966 208 Freire.

1447 ISNARDI PARENTE M., "Per l'interpretazione
dell'excursus filosofico della VII Epistola
platonica". PP XIX 1964 241-290. Reprinted
p.47-99 in Isnardi Parente M., Filosofia e
politica nelle Lettere di Platone (see 4603).

1448 JENZER H., "Das ärztliche Ethos im siebenten Brief
Platos". AGM XLVIII 1964 1-17.

1449 FRITZ K. VON, "Die philosophische Stelle im siebten
platonischen Brief und die Frage der
'esoterischen' Philosophie Platons". Phronesis
XI 1966 117-153.

1450 GUNDERT H., "Zum philosophischen Exkurs im 7.
Brief". p.85-105 in Idee und Zahl, hrsg. von
Gadamer H.G. & Schadewaldt W. (see 4594).

1451 KELESSIDOU-GALANOU A., "Le sense de l'amitié".
Platon XXII 1970 211-222.

1452 FRITZ K. VON, "The Philosophical Passage in the
Seventh Platonic Letter and the Problem of
Plato's 'esoteric' Philosophy". p.408-447 in
Essays in ancient Greek Philosophy, ed. by
Anton J.P. & Kustas G.L. (see 4581).

1453 FRITZ K. VON, "Der vermeintliche Augenarzt Lynkeus
in Platons siebtem Brief". AGPh LIII 1971
231-237.

1454 NAGASAKA K., "The 'Violence of Ignorance' and the
'Spark of Wisdom'. Plato's Seventh Letter" [in
Japanese]. Methodos IV 1971.

III C d 25: LETTERS

For further discussion of the Seventh Letter see 40, 199, 201, 846, 847, 2152, 2644, 2716, 2831, 3536, 3989, 4087.

Textual criticism of the Seventh Letter

1455 RENEHAN R., "Plato Epistle VII,337b". CPh LVII 1962 109.

1456 RENEHAN R., "Rectification". CPh LVIII 1963 170.

THE EIGHTH LETTER

1457 AALDERS G.J.D., "The Authenticity of the eighth Platonic Epistle reconsidered". Mnemosyne XXII 1969 233-257.

For additional discussion see 1438.

THE ELEVENTH LETTER

1458 SALVIAT F., "La Lettre XI de Platon. Léodamas de Thasos, Kallistratos d'Athènes et la fondation de Krénidès". AFLA XLIII 1967 43-56.

THE TWELFTH LETTER

For discussion see 1431.

THE THIRTEENTH LETTER

1459 YOUTIE H.C., "Σημεῖον in the Papyri and its
      Significance for Plato Epistle 13 (360a-b)".
      ZPE VI 1970 105-116.

LYSIS

A. TEXTS AND TRANSLATIONS

1460 Lysis, übertr. von Borchardt R. p.149-181 in
      Borchardt R., Gesammelte Werke, V:
      Uebertragungen, hrsg. von Borchardt M. unter
      Mitarb. von Zinn E. Stuttgart, Klett 1958
      548p. (Originally appeared in Borchardt R., Das
      Gespräch über Formen und Platons Lysis, Leipzig,
      Zeitler 1905.)

1461* Liside, introd. e comm. a cura di Bonaria M.   2a
      ed. corr. Nuova bibl. dei class. gr. e
      lat., Firenze, Le Monnier 1958 xv&82p.

1462* Il Liside, a cura di Laurenti R.   Roma, Signorelli
      1966 76p.
      Rev. GM XXII 1967 604-605 Sorge.
      Sophia XXXV 1967 133-134 Romano.

1463* Lysis, cu un eseu despre înţelesul grec al dragostei
      de oameni si lucruri de Noica C., postfaţa de
      Papadopol T. Bucureşti, Ed. pentru liter.
      universală 1969 144p.

For additional texts and translations see 853, 866, 918,
      925, 930, 933, 938, 942, 949, 968, 974, 982,
      984, 985, 989.

B. STUDIES ON THE LYSIS

1464 HOERBER R.G., "Plato's Lysis". Phronesis IV 1959 15-28.

1465* BEGEMANN A.W., Plato's Lysis. Onderzoek naar de plaats van den dialoog in het oeuvre. Diss. Amsterdam, Buijten & Schipperheyn 1960 541p. Rev. Mnemosyne XIX 1966 420-421 de Vries.

1466 NAKAMURA K., "On the ἀπορία in Plato's Lysis" [in Japanese]. Hokkaido Gakugei Univ. Bulletin XIV,2 1963; XV,2 1964.

1467 GÓMEZ MUNTÁN J.L., "La concepción platónica del amor, según el Lysis". Pensamiento XXII 1966 23-53.

1468 BUCCELLATO M., "Studi sul dialogo platonico, IV: Il tema della philia e il suo interesse civile nel Liside". RSF XXIII 1968 3-20.

1469* SCHOPLICK V., Der platonische Dialog Lysis. Diss. Freiburg. Augsburg Diss.-Dr. Blasaditsch 1969 90p.
Rev. CR XXII 1972 103 Huby.

1470 LEVIN D.N., "Some Observations concerning Plato's Lysis". p.236-258 in Essays in ancient Greek Philosophy, ed. by Anton J.P. & Kustas G.L. (see 4581).

1471 GADAMER H.G., "Logos und Ergon im platonischen Lysis". p.50-63 in Gadamer H.G., Kleine Schriften, III: Idee und Sprache. Platon, Husserl, Heidegger (see 4593).

For additional discussions see 40, 2635, 2752, 3214, 3464, 3478, 3631, 3632, 4173.

C. TEXTUAL CRITICISM

1472 MASARACCHIA A., "Platone, Lys. 204d5". Maia XII 1960 218-219.

MENEXENUS

A. TEXTS AND TRANSLATIONS

1473* Menesseno, a cura di Schiassi G. Firenze, Soc. ed.
Dante Alighieri 1961 122p.

1474* Menesseno, a cura di Adorno F. Class. lat. e gr.,
Padova, R.A.D.A.R. 1969 89p.

1475* Menexenos, Turkish transl. by Şahinbaş I. 2nd edn.
Yunan klâsikleri XXXI, Ankara, Millî Eğitim
Basimevi 31p.

For additional texts and translations see 853, 858, 866,
925, 933, 943, 950, 953, 986, 989.

B. STUDIES OF THE MENEXENUS

1476* SCHOLL N., Der platonische Menexenos. Temi e Testi
V, Roma, Ed. di Storia e Letteratura 1959 125p.
Rev. Gnomon XXXIII 1961 126-129
Rosenmeyer.
Gymnasium LXX 1963 443-445 Kullmann.
RecSR L 1962 610-611 des Places.

1477* LOEWENCLAU I. VON, Der platonische Menexenos.
Tübinger Beitr. zur Altertumswiss. XLI,
Stuttgart, Kohlhammer 1961 160p.
Rev. RecSR L 1962 610 des Places.
Scholastik XXXVII 1962 236-237 Ennen.
RBPh XL 1962 244-245 Henry.
Gymnasium LXX 1963 442-443 Kullmann.
Gnomon XXXVI 1964 244-253 Newiger.
Erasmus XVI 1964 418-425 Gottschalk.
Helikon VI 1966 778-779 Novotný.
PLA 1963 274-276 Vonessen.

1478 SCHIASSI G., "La questione del Menesseno platonico".
RIL XCVI 1962 37-58.

1479 KAHN C.H., "Plato's Funeral Oration. The Motive of
the Menexenus". CPh LVIII 1963 220-234.

III C d 27: MENEXENUS

1480* THUROW   R.,   Der   platonische   Epitaphios.
       Untersuchungen zur Stellung des Menexenos im
       platonischen Werk.   Diss.   Tübingen   1968,
       Stuttgart xix&195p.

1481 PENEDOS A. DOS, "O sentido polémico do Menexeno de
       Platão". RevFSF II 1972 43-51.

For additional discussions see 40, 4186.

                          MENO

                A. TEXTS AND TRANSLATIONS

1482* Meno, ed. with introd.   & comm.   by Bluck R.S.
       Cambridge Univ. Pr. 1961 viii&474p.
       Rev. AC XXX 1961 573-574 des Places.
       CF XVI 1962 56 Lynch.
       CW LV 1962 143 Hoerber.
       PhilosStud(Irel) XI   1961-1962   298-299
   Watson.
       PhilosBks Apr. 1962 3 Wasserstein.
       SciAmer Sept. 1962 279.
       RM XV 1961-1962 678 R.S.B.
       G&R 1962 91.
       Personalist XLIV 1963 249-250 O'Neill.
       Ethics LXXIII 1962-1963 228-229 Chappell.
       PhR LXXII 1963 530-531 Allen.
       Hermathena XCVII 1963 126-129 Luce.
       CPh LVIII 1963 120-121 Greene.
       JCS XI 1963 123-130 Kawata.
       RPh XXXVII 1963 129 Louis.
       Gnomon XXXV 1963 142-149 de Strycker.
       Phoenix XVII 1963 147-150 Rist.
       Emerita XXXI 1963 144-147 Ruiz de Elvira.
       CR XIII 1963 43-46 Kerferd.
       AAHG XVI 1963 36-39 Vretska.
       Gymnasium LXX 1963 440-442 Gaiser.
       AFC VIII 1961-1963 195-208 Eggers Lan.
       JHS LXXXIV 1964 190-191 Bambrough.
       AJPh LXXXV 1964 96-99 De Lacey.
       AGPh XLV 1963 292-299 & XLVI 1964 128
   Stokes.
       PhilosQ XIV 1964 73-74 Kemp.
       DUJ XXV 1963-1964 130 Skemp.
       RPortFil XXI 1965 206 Morão.

                          189

Maia XIX 1967 77-81 Carlini.
RPhL LXXI 1973 143-145 Brague.

1483* The Meno, ed. with introd., notes & excursuses by
Thompson E.S. Reprint of 1901 edn. Cambridge,
Heffer 1961 lxvi&319p.
Rev. TLS 2 Feb. 1962 26.
G&R 1962 91.
CR XIII 1963 46 Kerferd.

1484* Plato's Meno. Text and Criticism, ed. by Sesonske
A. & Fleming N. Belmont, Calif., Wadsworth
1965 vii&116p. (Jowetts transl. and essays by
various authors.)

1485* Plato's Meno, transl. by Guthrie W.K.C., with
essays ed. by Brown M. Bobbs text & comm.
ser. TC10, Indianapolis, Bobbs-Merrill 1971
xxxiv&314p.
Rev. Philosophy 1960 371 Lacey.
RM XXV 1971-1972 563-565 Sweeney.

1486* Menon, griech.-dt., auf der Grundlage der Übers.
von Apelt O. in Verbind. mit Zekl E. Neu
bearb. & hrsg. von Reich K. Philos. Bibl.
CCLXXVIII, Hamburg, Meiner 1972 xxi&128p.

1487* Menone, introd., trad. e note di Piemontese F. I
class. della filos. e della pegag., Torino,
S.E.I. 1960 118p.
Rev. FilosV 1961 86-88 Beschin.

1488* Menone, a cura di Reale G. Brescia, La Scuola 1962
xlii&114p.
Rev. Aevum XXXVII 1963 359 Egi.

1489* Menone, trad. di Acri F., introd. e note di
Sammartano N. I class. della Filos., Urbino,
Argalia 1964 128p.

1490* Menone, trad. D'Angelo G., introd. e note di Russo
S. Class. della filos., Messina/Firenze,
D'Anna 1965 70p.

1491* Menón, ed., trad., notas y estud. prelim. por Ruiz
de Elvira A. Clas. Polít., Madrid, Inst. de
Estud. Polít. 1958 lvii&68p.
Rev Xenium II 1958 57 Caturelli.
REA LX 1958 438 Moreau.
CR IX 1959 287 Kerferd.
Mnemosyne XII 1959 359 de Vries.
Paideia XIV 1959 276-277 Bonaria.

RPh XXXIV 1960 124 Louis.
EClas V 1960 385 Alsina.
JHS LXXX 1960 230 Tarrant.
REG LXXIII 1960 552-554 Weil.
AC XXX 1961 215-217 Meunier.
Helmantica XI 1960 532 Rodríguez.
A&R VII 1962 225-227 Carlini.

1492* Menón o sobre la virtud, trad. y notas de Criado A.
Bibl. de Clás. Universitarios, Madrid, Ed.
Escelicer 1964 131p.

1493* Menon, przel., wstep., objaśn., illustr. Witwicki
W. Warszawa, PWN 1959 95p.

1494* Meno, Hebrew transl. by Simon L. 3rd edn.
Jerusalem, The Magnes Press, The Hebrew Univ.
1966 xvi&96p.

For additional texts and translations see 853, 858, 866,
893, 917, 932, 943, 948, 949, 953, 959, 968,
971, 978, 986, 992.

B. STUDIES OF THE MENO

1495* KLEIN J., A Commentary on Plato's Meno. Chapel
Hill, Univ. of North Carolina Pr. 1965
viii&256p.
Rev. CW LIX 1965 54-55 Sprague.
YR 1965 xxvi.
RM XIX 1965-1966 155 R.J.W.
CJ LXII 1966 129-130 Etheridge.
PhR LXXVI 1967 523-525 Sesonske.
RM XX 1966-1967 650 Owens.
RSF XXIII 1968 104-105 Adorno.
CR XIX 1969 162-163 Gulley.
PhilosQ XX 1970 78-79 Crombie.
JCS XIX 1971 140-143 Soejima.
Hermathena CXI 1971 91 Luce.
Gnomon XLIV 1972 740-745 de Strycker.
RPhL LXXI 1973 145-151 Brague.

1496 HOERBER R.G., "Plato's Meno". Phronesis V 1960
78-102.

1497 BLUCK R.S., "Plato's Meno". Phronesis VI 1961
94-101.

1498 SESONSKE A., "Knowing and Saying. The Structure of
      Plato's Meno". ArchivPhilos XII 1963 3-13.
      Reprinted in Plato's Meno. Text and Criticism,
      ed. by Sesonske A. & Fleming N. (see 1484).

1499 ALEXANDRE M., "Introduction à la lecture du Ménon".
      REPh XV,1 1964 2-13.

1500 SCHWARZ B., "Bemerkungen zu Platons Menon".   SJP
      X-XI 1966-1967 361-380.

1501* ECKSTEIN J., The Platonic Method. An Interpretation
      of the dramatic-philosophic aspects of the Meno.
      New York, Greenwood 1968 133p.
           Rev. CW LXIII 1969 123 Sparshott.
           RUO XXXIX 1969 336 Paquet.
           JHPh VIII 1970 200-201 Schneider.
           CR XXI 1971 127 Gulley.

1502 HARE R.M., "Philosophical Discoveries".   Mind LXIX
      1960 145-162. Reprinted p.97-114 in Plato's
      Meno. Text and Criticism, ed. by Sesonske A.
      & Fleming N. (see 1484).

1503 BLUCK R.S., "On τραγυκή.   Plato,   Meno   76e".
      Mnemosyne XIV 1961 289-295.

1504* GRIMM L., Definition in Plato's Meno. An Inquiry in
      the Light of Logic and Semantics into the kind
      of Definition intended by Socrates when he asks
      'What is Virtue'?.   Skrifter utg. av Norske
      Videnskaps-Akad. i Oslo, Hist.-filos.   Kl.
      N.S. 1960,2, Oslo, Univ. Pr. 1962 53p.
           Rev.   Gnomon XXXV   1963   149-151   de
      Strycker.
           CR XIII 1963 113 Bluck.
           CJ LIX 1963 83-84 Etheridge.
           Philosophy XL 1965 177 Lacey.
           RPhilos CLV 1965 513-514 Brunschwig.
           CW 1964 277 Hoerber.

1505 KANEMATSU, "A Study of Plato's Meno: Anamnesis and
      Theia Moira" [in Japanese]. MOsaka no.9.

1506 PÉREZ PERAZZO E.E. DE, "Procedimiento del Menón en
      relación a la 'teoría de la ciencia' en
      Aristóteles". Episteme(Caracas) 1961-1963 5-39.

1507 GAISER K., "Platons Menon und die Akademie". AGPh
      XLVI 1964 241-292.   Reprinted p.329-393 (with
      Nachtrag) in Das Problem der ungeschriebene
      Lehre Platons, hrsg. von Wippern J. (see

III C d 28: MENO

4626).

1508 HALL R.W., "Ὁρθη δόξα and εὐδοξία in the Meno".
      Philologus CVIII 1964 66-71.

1509 VERDENIUS W.J., "Further Notes on Plato's Meno".
      Mnemosyne XVII 1964 261-280.

1510 PHILLIPS S., "The Significance of Meno's Paradox".
      p.77-83 in Plato's Meno. Text and Criticism,
      ed. by Sesonske A. & Fleming N. (see 1484).
      Reprinted from CW XLII 1948-1949 87-91.

1511 VLASTOS G., "Anamnesis in the Meno". Dialogue IV
      1965 143-167.

1512 BROWN M.S., "Plato Disapproves of the Slave-Boy's
      Answer". RM XXI 1967 57-93. Reprinted
      p.198-242 in Plato's Meno, transl. by Guthrie
      W.K.C. & essays ed. by Brown M. (see 1485).

1513 GUÉROULT M., "Note sur le Locus mathematicus du'
      Ménon (87a)". RPhilos CLIX 1969 129-146.

1514 KISSAVOU M.I., "Ψυχολογικὸν πείραμα τοῦ Σωκράτούς".
      EEAth XIX 1968-1969 339-350.

1515 MOLINE J., "Meno's Paradox?". Phronesis XIV 1969
      153-161.

1516 NARCY M., "Einseignement et dialectique dans le
      'Ménon'". RIPh XXIII 1969 474-494.

1517 TSUMURA K., "On Hypothesis in Plato's Meno" [in
      Japanese]. Nara University Bulletin VI 1969.

1518 MORAVCSIK J.M.E., "Learning as Recollection".
      p.53-69 in Plato I, ed. by Vlastos G. (see
      4619).

1519 ROSE L.E., "Plato's Meno, 86-89". JHPh VIII 1970
      1-8.

1520 THOMAS J.E., "A Re-examination of the Slave-boy
      Interview". LThPh XXVI 1970 17-27.

1521 TIGNER S.S., "On the Kinship of all Nature in
      Plato's Meno". Phronesis XV 1970 1-4.

1522 ANDERSON D.E., "The Theory of Recollection in
      Plato's Meno". SoJP IX 1971 225-235.

III C d 28: MENO

1523 ANDIC M., "Inquiry and Virtue in the Meno". p.262-314 in Plato's Meno, transl. by Guthrie W.K.C. & essays ed. by Brown M. (see 1485).

1524 EHRENFELS F. VON, "Bemerkungen zu Menon 82c bis 85e". AGPh LIII 1971 72-74.

1525 GOFF R., "The Language of Self-transformation in Plato and Augustine". ManWorld IV 1971 413-435.

1526 THOMAS J.E., "Plato's Methodological Device at 84a1". NS XLV 1971 478-486.

1527 MITIAS M.H., "Epistemological Explanation in the Meno". PakPJ XI 1972 16-27.

1528 COLBERT J.G. Jr., "El intelectualismo ético de Sócrates". AFUN VI 1973 11-28.

1529 EBERT T., "Plato's Theory of Recollection Reconsidered. An Interpretation of Meno 80a-86c". ManWorld VI 1973 163-181.

1530 PRANGE K., "Platos Lehre vom Lernen im Menon und das Problem des Allgemeinen". PaedagRdsch XXVII 1973 685-700.

For additional discussions see 40, 332, 435, 787, 2617, 2649, 2653, 2839, 3038, 3051, 3068, 3084, 3137, 3187, 3189, 3199, 3254, 3260, 3293, 3302, 3318, 3777, 3792, 3868, 3977, 3991, 4114, 4449, 4458, 4468.

MINOS

A. TEXTS AND TRANSLATIONS

For texts and translations see 871, 950, 961.

B. STUDIES OF THE MINOS

1531 CHROUST A.H., "A Note to the pseudo-platonic
Dialogue Minos". NLF XV 1970 171-174.

For additional discussions see 2636, 3682, 3758.

PARMENIDES

A. TEXTS AND TRANSLATIONS

1532* Plato and Parmenides. Parmenides' Way of Truth and
Plato's Parmenides, transl., introd. & comm.
by Cornford F.M. Library of Liberal Arts,
Indianapolis, Bobbs-Merrill n.d. xvii&251p.

1533* Parmenides, griech.-dt. übers. & hrsg. von Zekl
H.G. Philos. Bibl. CCLXXIX, Hamburg, Meiner
1972 xlii&195p.

1534* Parménide, dialogue de Platon, texte français de
Albert-Birot P., gravures orig. de Poliakoff S.
La Rose des vents IV, Paris, La Rose des vents
1964 89p.

1535* Parménide, texte français de Albert-Birot P. Paris,
Libr. Fischbacher 1966. 110 ex. sur vélin de
Rives à la forme, num. et signés, sous emboît.

1536* Parménides, trad., pról. y notas por Miguez J.A.
Bibl. de iniciac. filos. LXXXVIII, Buenos
Aires, Aguilar 1963 128p.
Rev. Sapientia XIX 1964 72-73 Argerami.

1537* Parmenides, przel., wstep., objaśn., illustr.
Witwicki W. Warszawa, PWN 1961 136p.

1538* Parmenid, transl. by Atanasijević K., pref. by
Korać V. Belgrade, Kultura 1959 xix&61p.

For additional texts and translations see 867, 914, 915,
927, 931, 940, 941, 947, 948, 952, 1550.

D. STUDIES OF THE PARMENIDES

The following list includes works on the
Parmenides not devoted to a single passage.
Studies of particular passages (e.g. the "Third
Man Argument") will be found in the subsequent
lists arranged according to the order of the
passages they treat.

1539* CORSINI E., Il trattato De divinis nominibus dello
Pseudo-Dionigi e i commenti neoplatonici al
Parmenide. Univ. di Torino, Pubbl. Fac. di
Lett. e Filos. XIII,4, Torino, Università 1963
177p.
Rev. RecSR LII 1964 140-142 Daniélou.
Aevum XL 1966 195-198 Scazzoso.
Bijdragen XXV 1964 641-642 Vanneste.

1540* DAMASCIUS, Damascii Successoris Dubitationes et
solutiones de primis principiis in Platonis
Parmenidem partim secundis curis recensuit,
partim nunc primum edidit Car. Aem. Ruelle.
Reprint of 1889 edn. 2 vols. Bruxelles,
Éditions Culture et Civilisation 1964 772p.

1541* DAMASCIUS, Dubitationes et solutiones de primis
principiis in Platonis Parmenidem, ed. Ruelle
C.A. 2 vols. Reprint of 1889 Paris edn.
Amsterdam, Hakkert 1966 xxi&324, 390p.

1542 HADOT P.H., "Fragments d'un commentaire de Porphyre
sur le Parménide". REG LXXIV 1961 410-438.

1543* PROCLUS, Procli Commentarius in Platonis Parmenidem,
hrsg. von Cousin V. Unveränd. Nachdr. von
Procli philosophi Platonici Opera inedita. Part.
3. (Paris 1864). Hildesheim, Olms 1961
p.604-1332. (pages numbered continuously with
parts 1 & 2).
Rev. RPortFil XIX 1963 327 Morão.

1544 BRUMBAUGH R.S., "A Latin Translation of Plato's
Parmenides [Plato Latinus, III: Parmenides.
ed. Klibansky R. & Labowsky C., London,
Warburg Inst. 1953.]". RM XIV 1960-1961
91-109.

1545* LYNCH W.F., An Approach to the Metaphysics of Plato
through the Parmenides. Washington D.C.,
Georgetown Univ. Pr. 1959 xiii&255p.

Rev. RM XIII 1959-1960 271-277 Brumbaugh.
NS XXXIV 1960 134-136 Owens.
Gregorianum XLI 1960 754 Caminero.
Personalist XLI 1960 370 P.M.
ModS XXXVII 1959-1960 326-327 Kaufmann.
CrossCurr X 1960 163-164 Collins.
Month XXIII 1960 59-60.
PhR LXX 1961 273-275 Robinson.
PhilosQ XI 1961 373 Cross.
JCS IX 1961 116-120 Takemiya.
CB XXXIX 1962 13 Barth.
Ph&PhenR XXIII 1962-1963 295 Rose.
Thought XXXVII 1962 144-146 Eslick.
CR XIII 1963 341 Kerferd.
JHS LXXXIII 1963 180 Gulley.
Inquiry VI 1963 200-206 Wyller.
Mind LXXII 1963 608-609 Taylor.
RSFil 1964 73-74 Riverso.
Pensamiento XXI 1965 201-202 Igal.
Scholastik XL 1965 450-451 Ivánka.
DT 1966 478-479 Visconti.

1546 RUNCIMAN W.G., "Plato's Parmenides". HSPh LXIV 1959
89-120. Reprinted p.149-184 in Studies in
Plato's Metaphysics ed. by Allen R.E. (see
4580).

1547* SPEISER A., Ein Parmenideskommentar. Studien zur
platonischen Dialektik. Neubearb. des Werkes
von 1937. Stuttgart, Koehler 1959 112p.

1548 BRUMBAUGH R.S., "Plato's Parmenides and positive
Metaphysics". RM XIII 1959-1960 271-277.

1549* WYLLER E.A., Platons Parmenides in seinem
Zusammenhang mit Symposion und Politeia.
Interpretationen zur platonischen Henologie.
Skrifter Norske Vidensk.-Akad., Hist.-fil. Kl.
II 1959,1, Oslo, Aschehoug 1960 220p.
Rev. Gnomon XXXIV 1962 308-310 Balme.
DLZ LXXXIV 1963 393-396 Szabó.
RPhilos CLVIII 1968 289-291 Vincent.
RecSR L 1962 612-613 des Places.
FZPT IX 1962 81-85 Morard.
PhilosRdschau X 1962 254-262 Perpeet.
PLA XV 1962 359-362 Niebergall.

1550* BRUMBAUGH R.S., Plato on the One. The Hypotheses in
the Parmenides. New Haven, Yale Univ. Pr.
1961 xv&364p. Also Port Washington, N.Y.,
Kennikat Pr. 1973; Folkestone (Kent), Bailey
Bros. & Swinfen 1973.

Rev. CW LV 1961 52 Hoerber.
RM XV 1961-1962 190 R.C.N.
RM XV 1961-1962 434-449 Ballard.
RecSR L 1962 611-612 des Places.
ModS XXXIX 1961-1962 166-169 Plochmann.
Thought 1962 146 Lynch.
Inquiry VI 1963 206-211 Wyller.
JCS XI 1963 130-136 Ono.
Gnomon XXXV 1963 304-306 Balme.
Mind LXXII 1963 606-608 Cross.
ArchPhilos XXVII 1964 121-124 Stokes.
Ph&PhenR XXIV 1963-1964 448-449 Rose.
AGPh XLVI 1964 121-124 Stokes.
AJPh LXXXVI 1965 296-301 Neumann.
Philosophy XL 1965 249-250 Lacey.

1551 VOLKMANN-SCHLUCK K.H., "Das Wesen der Idee in Platos
      Parmenides". PhJ LXIX 1961 34-45.

1552 PECK A.L., "Plato versus Parmenides?". PhR LXXI
      1962 159-184.

1553 RIST J.M., "The Parmenides Again". Phoenix XVI 1962
      1-14.

1554 WYLLER E.A., "Plato's Parmenides: Another
      Interpretation". RM XV 1962 621-640.

1555 ROSEN S., "Ideas". RM XVI 1963 407-441.

1556 WYLLER E.A., "Platons Parmenides. Form und Sinn".
      ZPhF XVII 1963 202-226.

1557 ALLEN R.E., "The Interpretation of Plato's
      Parmenides. Zeno's Paradox and the Theory of
      Forms". JHPh II 1964 143-155.

1558* FRIIS JOHANSEN K., Studier over Platons Parmenides i
      dens forhold til tidligere platoniske dialoger.
      Diss. København, Munksgaard 1964 471p.

1559 REAGAN J.T., "The Metaphysical Function of the
      Parmenides". ModS XLI 1964 262-272.

1560* KOUTSOYANNOPOULOS D.J., The Riddle of the Parmenides
      of Plato [in Greek]. Greek Soc. for hum.
      Stud. Publ. Ser. 1 XXIX, Athens 1965 26p.

1561 RYLE G., "Plato's Parmenides". p.97-147 in Studies
      in Plato's Metaphysics, ed. by Allen R.E. (see
      4580). Reprinted from Mind 1939. Also p.1-44
      in Ryle G., Collected Papers, I: Critical

Essays. New York, Barnes & Noble 1971.

1562 OWEN G.E.L., "Notes on Ryle's Plato". p.341-372 in Ryle, ed. by Wood O.P. & Pitcher G., intro. by Ryle G. Modern Studies in Philosophy, London, Macmillan and Garden City, N.Y., Doubleday Anchor 1971.

1563 KLEIN J., "A Note on Plato's Parmenides". p.431-432 in Orbis scriptus. Dmitrij Tschiżewskij zum 70. Geburtstag, hrsg. von Gerhardt D. et al. München 1966.

1564 KOUTSOYANNOPOULOS D.I., "Τίς ὁ Ἀριστοτέλης τοῦ Πλατωνικοῦ Παρμενίδου;"Platon XVIII 1966 206-211.

1565 TSUNODA Y., "A Study of Plato's Parmenides, especially on the Meaning of Part II" [in Japanese]. Philosophical Studies (Tokyo Kyoiku Univ.) XXIV 1966.

1566 WYLLER E.A., "The Architectonic of Plato's Later Dialogues". C&M XXVII 1966 101-115. Reprinted p.381-392 in Contemporary Philosophy in Scandinavia, ed. by Olson R.E. & Paul A.M. Baltimore/London, Johns Hopkins Univ. Pr. 1972.

1567 SCIACCA M.F., "La dialettica delle idee nel 'Parmenide'". p.364-396 in Sciacca M.F., Platone I (see 64). Reprinted from Logos n.2 1938.

1568 TROTIGNON P., "Introduction à la lecture du Parménide de Platon". REPh XVII 1966-1967, No.1 1-18, No.2 1-12.

1569* FORRESTER J.W., An Examination of the Second Part of Plato's Parmenides. Diss. Johns Hopkins Univ. 1968 498p. [microfilm]. Summary in DA XXIX 1968 1563A.

1570 NAITO S., "Aporia in Plato's Parmenides" [in Japanese]. Philosophy Miscellany (Tokyo Metropolitan Univ.) XI 1968.

1571 WYLLER E.A., "The Parmenides is the Philosopher". C&M XXIX 1968 27-39.

1572 PANAGIOTOU S., "The 'Parmenides' is the 'Philosopher': A Reply". C&M XXX 1969 187-210.

1573 PARAIN B., "Le Parménide de Platon". p.154-173 in
      Parain B., Petite métaphysique de la parole.
      Paris, Gallimard 1969.

1574* SUHR M., Platons Kritik an den Eleaten. Vorschläge
      z.   Interpretation d.   platon.   Dialogs
      Parmenides.   Schriften   der   Stiftung
      Europa-Kolleg Hamburg XII, Hamburg, Stiftung
      Europa-Kolleg; Hamburg, Fundament-Verlag Sasse
      1969 iv&147p.

1575 ZELLER E., "Ueber die Composition des Parmenides und
      seine Stellung in der Reihe der Platonischen
      Dialogen". p.157-196 in Zeller E., Platonische
      Studien (see 4627).

1576 RIST J.M., "Parmenides and Plato's Parmenides". CQ
      XX 1970 221-229.

1577* BARFORD R., The Criticisms of the Theory of Forms in
      the first Part of Plato's Parmenides. Diss.
      Indiana Univ. 1971 243p. [microfilm]. Summary
      in DA XXXI 1971 6655A-6656A.

1578 BERTI E., "Struttura e significato del Parmenide di
      Platone". GM XXVI 1971 497-527.

1579 HIRSCHBERGER J., "Ähnlichkeit und Seinsanalogie vom
      platonischen Parmenides bis Proklos". p.57-74
      in Philomathes. Studies and Essays in the
      Humanities in Memory of Philip Merlan, ed. by
      Palmer R.B. & Hamerton-Kelly R. Den Haag,
      Nijhoff 1971.

1580* KOUMAKIS G.C., Platons Parmenides. Zum Problem
      seiner Interpretation. Abh. zur Philos.,
      Psychol. & Paedag. LXXIV, Bonn, Bouvier 1971
      240p.
            Rev. Erasmus XXIV 1972 809-811 Lasserre.
            PhJ LXXIX 1972 410-415 Niewoehner.
            Platon XXIII 1971 380-382 Zoumpos.

1581* NIEWOEHNER F.W., Dialog und Dialektik in Platons
      Parmenides. Untersuchungen z. sogenannten
      Platon. Esoterik. Monogr. z. philos.
      Forsch. LXXVIII, Meisenheim, Hain 1971 iv&397p.
            Rev. TPh XXXV 1973 632-633 Steel.

1582 ROCHOL H., "The Dialogue Parmenides. An Insoluble
      Enigma in Platonism?". IPQ XI 1971 496-520.

1583 TOTSUKA S., "On the Criticism of the Theory of Division in the Parmenides" [in Japanese]. Proceedings of the Dept. of Humanities (Tokyo Metropolitan Univ.) LXXIX 1971.

1584* ZEKL H.G., Der Parmenides. Untersuchungen über innere Einheit, Zielsetzung und begriffliches Verfahren eines platonischen Dialogs. Diss. Marburg 1968. Marburg, Elwert 1971 iii&316p. Rev. PhJ LXXIX 1972 410-415 Niewoehner. ArchPhilos XXXVI 1973 158-159 Solignac.

1585 SCHOFIELD M., "The Dissection of Unity in Plato's Parmenides". CPh LXVII 1972 102-109.

1586 SINGEVIN C., "La pensee, le langage, l'écriture et l'être". RPhilos CLxII 1972 129-148, 243-288.

1587* VATER H., Die Dialektik von Idee und Teilhabe in Platons Parmenides. Hamburger Stud. zur Philos. II, Hamburg, Buske 1972 v&137p.

1588 BROWNSTEIN D., "Platonic Nominalism". SoJP IV 1973 37-48.

1589* COLEMAN C.C., Plato's Parmenides. An Analysis of the argumentative Devices and the relation of the Parts of the Dialogue. Diss. Univ. of Washington 1973 68p. [microfilm]. Summary in DA XXXIV 1973 2586A.

1590 SCHOFIELD M., "Eudoxus in the Parmenides". MH XXX 1973 1-19.

1591 SEIDL H., "Zum metaphysischen Gesichtspunkt im 2. Teil von Platons Parmenides". ZPhF XXVII 1973 24-37.

1592 TROUILLARD J., "Le Parménide de Platon et son interprétation néoplatonicienne". RThPh XXIII 1973 83-100.

STUDIES ON PARTICULAR PASSAGES IN PART I, INCLUDING THE 'THIRD MAN ARGUMENT'

The following list includes works on particular passages in the first part of the Parmenides (to 135). They are arranged according to the order of the passages they treat.

III C d 30: PARMENIDES

1593 ZADRO A., "Note al Parmenide". AIV CXIX 1960-1961
      675-690.

1594 MULHERN J.J., "Plato, Parmenides 130d3-4". Apeiron
      V 1971 17-22.

1595 BOOTH N.B., "Assumptions involved in the Third Man
      Argument". Phronesis III 1958 146-149.

1596 JUÁREZ-PAZ R., "Vlastos, Sellars y el 'tercer
      hombre' en el Parménides: notas sobre una
      polémica". RPGA XIV 1959 21-32.

1597 BUTLER R.J., "The Measure and Weight of the Third
      Man". Mind LXXII 1963 62-78.

1598 MORAVCSIK J.M.E., "The Third Man Argument and
      Plato's Theory of Forms". Phronesis VIII 1963
      50-62.

1599 STRANG C., "Plato and the Third Man". PASS XXXVII
      1963 147-164. Reprinted p.184-200 in Plato I,
      ed. by Vlastos G. (see 4619).

1600 REES D.A., "Plato and the Third Man". PASS XXXVII
      1963 165-176.

1601 VLASTOS G., "The Third Man Argument in the
      Parmenides". p.231-261 (with "addendum (1963)",
      p.261-263) in Studies in Plato's Metaphysics,
      ed. by Allen R.E. (see 4580). Reprinted from
      PhR LXIII 1954 319-349.

1602 GEACH P.T., "The Third Man Again". p.265-277 in
      Studies in Plato's Metaphysics, ed. by Allen
      R.E. (see 4580). Reprinted from PhR 1956.

1603 VLASTOS G., "Postscript to the Third Man: A Reply
      to Mr. Geach". p.279-291 in Studies in Plato's
      Metaphysics, ed. by Allen R.E. (see 4580).
      Reprinted from PhR LXV 1956 83-94.

1604 SELLARS W., "Vlastos and 'The Third Man': A
      Rejoinder". p.55-72 in Sellars W.,
      Philosophical Perspectives. Springfield, Ill.,
      Charles C. Thomas 1967.

1605 VOUDOURIS K.I., "Τὸ ἐπιχείρημα τοῦ Τρίτου Ἀνθρώπου
      εἰς τὸν τοῦ Πλάτωνος Παρμενίδην καὶ ἡ σημασία
      αὐτοῦ". Athena LXX 1968 203-222.

III C d 30: PARMENIDES

1606 RANKIN K.W., "The Duplicity of Plato's Third Man".
Mind LXXVIII 1969 178-197.

1607 SMITH T.G., "The Theory of Forms, Relations and
Infinite Regress". Dialogue VIII 1969 116-123.

1608 VLASTOS G., "Plato's 'Third Man' argument (Parm.
132a1-b2). Text and Logic". PhilosQ XIX 1969
289-301. Reprinted (with changes) p.342-365 in
Vlastos G., Platonic Studies (see 4622).

1609 YAMAKAWA T., "The third Man. An Interpretation of
Plato's Parmenides, I" [in Japanese]. Momoyama
Univ. Humanities Bulletin VI,2 1969.

1610 CENTORE F.F., "A Note on T.G. Smith's 'The Theory
of Forms, Relations and Infinite Regress'".
Dialogue VIII 1970 678-679.

1611 RANKIN K.W., "Is the Third Man Argument an
Inconsistent Triad?". PhilosQ XX 1970 378-380.

1612 SHINER R.A., "Self-predication and the Third Man
Argument". JHPh VIII 1970 371-386.

1613 COHEN S.M., "The Logic of the Third Man". PhR LXXX
1971 448-475.

1614 HARPER A.W.J., "On the Theory of Forms". Dialogue X
1971 558-560.

1615 PANAGIOTOU S., "Vlastos on Parmenides 132a1-b2.
Some of his Text and Logic". PhilosQ XXI 1971
255-259.

1616 DYBIKOWSKI J.Č., "Professor Owen, Aristotle and the
Third Man Argument". Mind LXXXI 1972 445-447.

1617 TELOH H.A. & LOUZECKY D.J., "Plato's Third Man
Argument". Phronesis XVII 1972 80-94.

1618 PETERSON S., "A Reasonable Self-predication Premise
for the Third Man Argument". PhR LXXXII 1973
451-470.

1619 MOREAU J., "Eidos y noema en Platón". p.331-335 in
Actas del II Congreso esp. de Estud. clás.
(Madrid-Barcelona, 4-10 de abril de 1961).
Publ. de la Soc. Esp. de Estud. clás. V,
Madrid 1964.

1620 HATHAWAY R.F., "The second 'Third Man'". p.78-100
     in Patterns in Plato's Thought, ed. by
     Moravcsik J.M.E. (see 4609).

1621 LEE E.N., "The second 'Third Man': An
     Interpretation". p.101-122 in Patterns in
     Plato's Thought, ed. by Moravcsik J.M.E. (see
     4609).

STUDIES ON PARTICULAR PASSAGES IN PART II

The following list includes works on particular
passages in the second part of the Parmenides
(from 135). They are arranged according to the
order of the passages they treat.

1623 ZADRO A., "Nota alla prima hypothesis del
     Parmenide". AIV CXX 1962 677-686.

1624 FORRESTER J.W., "Plato's Parmenides. The Structure
     of the First Hypothesis". JHPh X 1972 1-14.

1625 WHITTAKER J., "Neopythagoreanism and the
     Transcendent Absolute". SO XLVIII 1973 77-86.

1626 SCHOFIELD M., "A Neglected Regress Argument in the
     Parmenides". CQ XXIII 1973 29-44.

1627 ALLEN R.E., "The Generation of Numbers in Plato's
     Parmenides". CPh LXV 1970 30-34.

1628 CELARIER J.LeR., "Note on Plato's Parmenides 147c".
     Mind LXIX 1960 91.

1629 THYSSEN J., "Platons ἐξαίφνης und das Problem der
     historischen Krise". KantStud L 1958-1959
     391-394.

1630 WYLLER E.A., "Platons öyeblikksfilosofi eller
     dialogen Parmenides' 3. hypothese". p.7-26 in
     Tradisjon og fornyelse. Festskrift til A.H.
     Winsnes. Oslo, Aschehoug 1959.

III C d 30: PARMENIDES

1631 WYLLER E.A., "La philosophie de l'instant chez Platon ou la troisième hypothèse du Parménide". RS LXXXV,33-34 1964 9-29.

1632 BEIERWALTES W., "Έξαίφνης oder die Paradoxie des Augenblicks". PhJ LXXIV 1966-1967 271-283.

1633 PUDER M., "Die Synkopierung von έξαίφνης und νῦν in Platons Parmenides und am Schluss von Faust II. Notiz zum Aufsatz von Werner Beierwaltes über das έξαίφνης". PhJ LXXVI 1968-1969 420-422.

1634 BRISSON L., "L'instant, le temps, et l'éternité dans le Parménide (155e-157b) de Platon". Dialogue IX 1970-1971 389-396.

1635 SOULEZ-LUCCIONI A., "A propos de la huitième hypothèse de Parménide". RMM LXXV 1970 385-401.

For additional studies of the Parmenides see 280, 282, 299, 342, 358, 359, 368, 490, 497, 510, 514, 773, 786, 800, 1915, 2286, 2431, 2486, 2533, 2555, 2644, 2668, 2765, 2780, 2813, 2840, 2862, 2872, 2886, 2920, 2928, 2937, 2943, 2960, 2977, 3008, 3018, 3150, 3215, 3219, 3240, 3938, 3979, 4034, 4047, 4109, 4379.

C. TEXTUAL CRITICISM

1636 MORESCHINI C., "Note critiche al Parmenide di Platone". ASNP XXXIV 1965 415-421.

1637 MORESCHINI C., "Studi sulla tradizione manoscritta del Parmenide e del Fedro di Platone". ASNP XXXIV 1965 169-185.

1638 BRUMBAUGH R.S., "The Text of Plato's Parmenides". RM XXVI 1972 140-148.

For additional discussion of the text see 833, 834.

PHAEDO

A. TEXTS AND TRANSLATIONS

1639* Plato's Phaedo, transl. with intro., notes and
      appendices by Bluck R.S. Libr. of Liberal
      Arts, New York, Liberal Arts Pr. 1959 x&208p.
      Reprint of 1955 edn.
          Rev. CJ LV 1960 286 de Lacy.

1640* Plato's Phaedo, transl. with an introd. & comm.
      by Hackforth R. Libr. of Liberal Arts, New
      York, Liberal Arts Pr. 1960 xii&200p. Also
      Cambridge Univ. Pr. 1972. Reprint of 1955
      edn.
          Rev. [of 1960 edn.] Humanist 1961 187
      Wilbur.
          PhilosRdschau 1961 133-137 Manasse.
          EPh XVII 1962 129-130 Moreau.
          RPh XXXVI 1962 114 Louis.
          Gymnasium LXIX 1962 98-100 Bayer.
          [of 1972 edn.] AC xLII 1973 236 de Ley.
          MusAfr II 1973 91-93 Ferguson.
          Athenaeum LI 1973 454 Vegetti.

1641* The Phaedo of Plato, ed. by Archer-Hind R.D. New
      York, Arno Pr. 1973 169p. Reprint of 1894 edn.

1642* Phaidon [Ausz.] Hrsg. von Bayer K. [Nebst]
      Vorbereitungsh. Aus d. Schatze d. Altertums.
      A.32, Bamberg, Buchner 1958 61 & 54p.

1643* Phaidon oder Von der Unsterblichkeit der Seele, nach
      d. Übers. von Schleiermacher F. Neu durchges.
      Nachdr. Reclams Universal-Bibliothek 918-919,
      Stuttgart, Reclam 1959 127p.

1644* Phaedo, ed. Gigon O. 2. Aufl. Ed. Helveticae,
      Ser. Graeca II, Bern, Francke 1959 99p.
          Rev. A&R xII 1967 124-127 Carlini.

1645* Phaidon, hrsg. von Kloesel H. Schoeninghs griech.
      Klass. XXXV a, Paderborn, Schoeningh 1960 95p.

1646* Phaidon oder Von der Unsterblichkeit der Seele, nach
      der Übers. von Schleiermacher F. neu durchges.
      Reclams Universal-Bibl. 918-919, Stuttgart,
      Reclam 1966 144p.

1647* Phaidon, text & Komm. Hrsg. von Habrich E. &
       Leggewie O., neubearb. von Grimmelt B.
       Aschendorffs Samml. latein. & griech. Klass.,
       Münster, Aschendorff 1971 xv&90, 61p.

1648* Phédon, extraits trad. par Guillon J. Paris,
       Hatier 1960 64p.
              Rev. Hum(RES) XXXVI 1959-1960,9 38
       Cabanis.

1649* Phédon, extraits, texte grec annoté par Chabrol H.
       Les classiques pour tous. Coll. grecque,
       Paris, Hatier 1962 61p.

1650* Phaedo, Ed. Robin L. Coll. Calliope, Paris, Les
       Belles Lettres 1964 103p.

1651* Phédon, trad., introd. & notes de Vicaire P. Les
       grandes oeuvres de l'antiquité class. publ.
       par l'Assoc. G. Budé, Paris, Les Belles
       Lettres 1969 166p.
              Rev. RSC XVIII 1970 160-161 d'Agostino.
       AC XXXIX 1970 581 des Places.
       StudClas XIII 1971 263 Noica.
       RBPh XLIX 1971 667 Druet.
       RPh XLVI 1972 296 Chantraine.
       CR XXII 1972 103 Gulley.

1652* Le Phédon de Platon, I (57a-84b), comm. & trad. de
       Loriaux R. Bibl. Fac. de Philos. & Lettres
       de Namur XLV, Gembloux, Duculot 1969 232p.
              Rev. RBPh XLVIII 1970 119 des Places.
       AC XXXIx 1970 220-221 des Places.
       REA LXXII 1970 164-165 Moreau.
       ArchPhilos XXXIII 1970 984-985 Solignac.
       Gnomon XLIII 1971 545-551 Carlini.
       RPh XLV 1971 153 Louis.
       RSC XIX 1971 440-441 d'Agostino.
       NRTh XCIII 1971 665 Jacobs.
       AJPh XCII 1971 752-753 Brown.
       RPhilos CLxII 1972 38 Bernhardt.

1653* Il Fedone, con introd. e note di Casini N. Nuova
       Bibl. dei class. gr. e lat., Firenze, Le
       Monnier 1958 liii&205p. corrected edn. 1965.

1654* Il Fedone o dell'immortalità dell'anima, trad. di
       Acri F., introd. e note di Rotta P. Il
       pensiero, Brescia, La Scuola [1961?] 222p.

1655* Il Fedone, a cura di Goretti M. Coll. di filos. e
       pedag., Firenze, Le Monnier 1965 158p.

1656* Fedone, trad., introd. e comm. di Abbagnano N. 3a
       ed. Bibl. di filos. e pedag., Torino, Paravia
       1969 xxi&107p.

1657* Fedone, trad., introd. e comm. di Reale G. Il
       pensiero, Brescia, La Scuola 1970 lxxxii&258p.

1658* Fedón, trad., prol. y notas de Gil Fernandez L.
       Bibl. de Iniciac. Filos., Buenos Aires,
       Aguilar 1959 145p.

1659* El Fedón de Platón, ed. Eggers Lan C. Bibl. de
       Filos., Córdoba, Argent., Univ. Nac. de
       Córdoba 1967 290p.
               Rev. REG LXXXII 1969 653 Weil.
       CuadFilos IX 1969 327-328 Julia.

1660* El Fedón de Platón, ed. by Eggers Lan C. Buenos
       Aires, Eudeba 1972 234p.

1661* Fedón, introd., notas & comm. de Berenguer Amenós
       J. Col. Textos Clas. Griegos XVI, Barcelona,
       Bosch 1972 72p.

1662* Phaedo, vert. en ingeleid door Win X. de.
       Klassieke galerij XCIV, Antwerpen, De
       Nederlandsche Boekhandel 1970 144p.

1663* Fedon, Port. trad. de Dias Palmeira P., intro. by
       Carvalho J. de. Coimbra, Atlântida 1967
       ciii&112p.

1664* Diàlegs, VII: Fedó, text i [Catalan] trad. de
       Olives Canals J. Barcelona, Fund. Bernat Metge
       1962 150p.

1665* Fedon, przel., wstep., objaśn., illustr. Witwicki
       W. Warszawa, PWN 1958 202&6p.

1666* Phaedo, Turkish transl. by Yetkin S.K. & Atademir
       H.R. 3rd edn. Yunan klâsikleri XII, Ankara,
       Milli Eğitim Basimevi 1963 116p.

1667* Phaedo, Arabic transl. by Baladi N., Alnashar A.S.,
       & Alsharbini A. With essays "Phaedo in Western
       Christian Philosophy", "Phaedo in the Islam
       World", and "Phaedo in the Greek World".
       Alexandria, Mansha Alma'aref publ. 1961 322p.

III C d 31: PHAEDO

For additional texts and translations see 866, 878, 893,
        914, 920, 924, 928, 935, 937, 948, 949, 954,
        959, 960, 963, 964, 966, 967, 969, 971, 972,
        977, 978, 981, 984, 986, 989, 992, 1005, 1006,
        1007, 1008, 1009, 1010, 1011, 1013, 1014, 1019,
        1021, 1028, 1029, 1030, 1035, 1050, 1051.

B. STUDIES OF THE PHAEDO

The discussions of this dialogue are arranged as
follows: first those works dealing with the
dialogue generally and then those dealing with
various specific issues in the dialogue. The
latter are arranged following the order in which
the issues they treat occur in the dialogue.

1668* OLYMPIODORUS, In Platonis Phaedonem commentaria, ed.
        by Norvin W. Reprint of 1913 Leipzig edn.
        Hildesheim, Olms 1968 xi&272p.

1669 VERDENIUS W.J., "Notes on Plato's Phaedo".
        Mnemosyne XI 1958 193-243.

1670* KALOGERAS B.A., Ἀνάλυση Φαίδωνος καὶ Κρίτωνος.
        Thessalonike 1959 156p.
        Rev. Platon XII 1960 358 Manginas.

1671 JAEGER W., Rev. of Plato Latinus, ed. R.
        Klibansky, vol. II Phaedo interprete Henrico
        Aristippo. p.463-467 in Jaeger, W., Scripta
        Minora II (see 4605). Reprinted from Speculum
        XXIX 1954 155-159.

1672 GRIM G., "Auszug aus dem 'Phaidon' des Platon".
        Yana XIV 1961 171-177.

1673 SALMON A., "Le Socrate de David et le Phédon de
        Platon". RBPh XL 1962 90-111.

1674* PONI S., Il Fedone, i dialoghi socratici. Bologna,
        Cappelli 1963 176p.
        Rev. Vichiana II 1965 422 Citti.
        GM XXI 1966 757-758 Guazzoni Foà.

1675 SCHUHL P.M., "Répétition et composition dans le
        Phédon". Summary in REG LXXVI 3-4 1963
        p.xiv-xv.

III C d 31: PHAEDO

1676 WOLZ H.G., "The Phaedo. Plato and the Dramatic Approach to Philosophy". CrossCurr XIII 1963 163-186.

1677 LORIAUX R., "L'introduction du Phédon". LEC XXXIV 1966 209-230.

1678 THONHAUSER J., "Erzieherisches in Platons Phaidon". WS LXXIX 1966 178-186.

1679 ANTUNES M., "Nota sobre o carácter dramático do Fédon". Euphrosyne N.S. I 1967 161-168.

1680* CORONA G., Il Fedone. La Spezia, Tip. moderna 1967 11p.

1681 SCIACCA M.F., "Note al 'Fedone'". p.185-232 in Sciacca M.F., Platone I (see 64). Reprinted from an edn. of the Phaedo, 3a. ed. Milano, Principato 1965.

1682 SÁENZ-BADILLOS A., "El Fedón de Platón. Estudio filosófico". Perficit 2a Ser. II 1969 1-37.

1683 DORTER K., "The Dramatic Aspect of Plato's Phaedo". Dialogue VIII 1970 564-580.

1684 WEHRLI F., "Einführung zu Platons Phaidon". p.214-216 in Wehrli F., Theoria und Humanitas (see 4625). Reprinted from Platon, Phaidon oder Von der Unsterblichkeit der Seele, übers. von Georgii L., einführ. von Wehrli F. Zürich 1944.

1685 FERGUSON J., "Plato and Phaedo". MusAfr I 1972 9-17.

1686* PATTERSON R.L., Plato on Immortality. University Park, Pennsylvania State Univ. Pr. 1965 142p.
Rev. CW LIX 1965 131 Hoerber.
IPQ VI 1966 499-502 Hart.
JHPh V 1967 366-368 Stack.
RF LVIII 1967 91-92 Cambiano.
TLS 20 Jan. 1966 42.
IPS 1966 499 Hunt.

1687 TARÁN L., "Plato, Phaedo, 62a". AJPh LXXXVII 1966 326-336.

1688 BONITZ H., "Zur Erklärung von Platons Phädon p.62A". p.313-323 in Bonitz H., Platonische Studien (see 4584).

III C d 31: PHAEDO

1689 REYNEN H., "Phaidoninterpretationen". Hermes XCVI 1968 41-60.

1690 STRACHAN J.C.G., "Who aid forbid Suicide at Phaedo 62b?". CQ XX 1970 216-220.

1691 ROUX J. & G., "A propos de Platon. Réflexions en marge du Phédon 62b et du Banquet". RPh XXXV 1961 207-224.

1692 CHENE-WILLIAMS A., "Philosopher, c'est apprendre à mourir". Dialogue XI 1972 337-347.

1693 GADAMER H.G., "Die Unsterblichkeitsbeweise in Platons Phaidon". p.145-161 in Wirklichkeit und Reflexion. Walter Schulz zum 60. Geburtstag, hrsg. von Fahrenbach H. Pfullingen, Neske 1973.

1694 ZOUMPOS A.N., "Πλάτωνος Φαίδων 70e (ἐκ τῶν ἐναντίων τὰ ἐναντία)". Φιλοσοφικὰ σημειώματα IV, Athens 1961 1p.

1695 ZOUMPOS A.N., "Σύμμεικτα φιλοσοφικά". Platon XVI 1964 92-108.

1696 WOLFE J., "A Note on Plato's 'Cyclical Argument' in the Phaedo". Dialogue V 1966 237-238.

1697 LORIAUX R., "Phédon, 70c-d". LEC XXXV 1967 134-144.

1698 BONITZ H., "Die im Phädon enthaltenen Beweise für die Unsterblichkeit der menschlichen Seele". p.293-312 in Bonitz H., Platonische Studien (see 4584).

1699 GOOCH P.W., "Plato's Antapodosis Argument for the Soul's Immortality. Phaedo 70-72". p.239-244 in Seventh Inter-American Congress of Philosophy, 1967. Proceedings vol. 2. Quebec, Presses de l'Univ. de Laval 1968.

1700 WOLFE J., "Plato's 'Cyclical' Argument for Immortality". p.251-254 in Proceedings of the Seventh Inter-American Congress of Philosophy, vol. II. Quebec, Presses de l'Univ. de Laval 1968.

1701 ROBINSON T.M., "'Phaedo 70c': An Error and an Explanation". Dialogue VIII 124-125.

211

III C d 31: PHAEDO

1702 WiLLIAMS C.J.F., "On Dying". Philosophy XLIV 1969
217-230.

1703 KUCHARSKI P., "L'affinité entre les idées et l'âme
d'après le Phédon". ArchPhilos XXVI 1963
483-515.

1704 GRAU N.A., "La actividad del alma según el Fedón".
Nordeste 1965 39-64.

1705 RODIS-LEWIS G., "Limites de la simplicité de l'âme
dans le Phédon". RPhilos CLV 1965 441-454.

1706 GRAU N.A., "El clima religioso de lo espiritual en
el Fedón". Philosophia(Argent) 1966 no.31
20-28.

1707 RANKIN H.D., "An unresolved Doubt. Phaedo
76c14-d6". Apeiron I,2 1967 24-26.

1708 SCHILLER J., "Phaedo 104-105. Is the Soul a Form?".
Phronesis XII 1967 50-58.

1709 CAMPBELL M., "The Meaning of Immortality in the
Phaedo". Kinesis I 1968 29-36.

1710* DORTER K.N.M., The Doctrine of Recollection in
Plato's Phaedo. Diss. Pennsylvania State Univ.
1967 189p. [microfilm]. Summary in DA XXIX
1968 289A.

1711 EPP R.H., "Some Observations on the Platonic Concept
of Katharsis in the Phaedo". Kinesis I 1969
82-91.

1712 WIPPERN J., "Seele und Zahl in Platons Phaidon".
p.271-288 in Silvae. Festschrift für E. Zinn
zum 60. Geburtstag, hrsg. von Albrecht M. von
& Heck E. Tübingen, Niemeyer 1970.

1713 DORTER K., "Equality, Recollection, and
Purification". Phronesis XVII 1972 198-218.

1714 ACKRILL J.L., "Anamnesis in the Phaedo: Remarks on
73c-75c". p.177-195 in Exegesis and Argument,
ed. by Lee E.N. et al. (see 4608).

1715 MILLS K.W., "Plato's Phaedo 74b7-c6". Phronesis II
1957 128-147, III 1958 40-58.

1716 RANKIN H.D., "Immediate cognition of the Forms in the Phaedo?". Dialectica XII 1958 81-86.

1717 BLUCK R.S., "Plato's form of Equal". Phronesis IV 1959 5-11.

1718 GAUDRON E., "La théorie des idées dans le Phédon". LThPh XX 1964 50-73.

1719 HAYNES R.P., "The Form Equality, as a set of Equals. Phaedo 74b-c". Phronesis IX 1964 17-26.

1720 RIST J.M., "Equals and Intermediates in Plato". Phronesis IX 1964 27-37.

1721 GOSLING J., "Similarity in Phaedo 73b sq." Phronesis X 1965 151-161.

1722 WAGNER H., "Die Eigenart der Ideenlehre in Platons Phaedo". KantStud LVII 1966 5-16.

1723 LORIAUX R., "Phédon 74b-c". LEC XXXVII 1969 245-251.

1724 TAYLOR C.C.W., "Forms as Causes in the Phaedo". Mind LXXVIII 1969 45-59.

1725 VLASTOS G., "Reasons and Causes in the Phaedo". PhR LXXVIII 1969 291-325. Reprinted (with corrections) p.132-166 in Plato I, ed. by Vlastos G. (see 4619). Also reprinted (with corrections and new material in some footnotes) p.76-110 in Vlastos G., Platonic Studies (see 4622).

1726 WOLF E., "'Das Rechte selbst' (to dikaion auto) ist unvergänglich. Zur rechtsphilosophischen Interpretationen von Platons Phaidon". p.3-16 in Festschrift für Karl Engisch zum 70. Geburtstag, hrsg. von Bockelmann P. u.a. Frankfurt 1969.

1727 NAKAMURA K., "The Nature of the Theory of Ideas in Plato's Phaedo" [in Japanese]. Methodos III 1970.

1728 PIEPER A., "Vier Wege des Wissens. Interpretation der sokratischen Ursachenforschung nach Platons Dialog Phaidon". PhJ LXXVII 1970 378-397.

III C d 31: PHAEDO

1729 BURGE E.L., "The Ideas as Aitiai in the Phaedo".
     Phronesis XVI 1971 1-13.

1730 CASTAÑEDA H.N., "Plato's Phaedo Theory of
     Relations". JPh LXVIII 1971 617-618.

1731 CASTAÑEDA H.N., "Plato's Phaedo Theory of
     Relations". JPhilosLog I 1972 467-480.

1732 CASTAÑEDA H.N., "El análisis de Platón de las
     relaciones y de los hechos relacionales en el
     Fedón". RBF XXIII 1973 38-46.

1733 CRESSWELL M.J., "Plato's Theory of Causality.
     Phaedo 95-106". AusJP XLIX 1971 244-249.

1734* NEHAMAS A., Predication and the Theory of Forms in
      the Phaedo. Diss. Princeton Univ. 1971 199p.
      [microfilm]. Summary in DA XXXII 1972 6493A.

1735 BRENTLINGER J., "Incomplete Predicates and the
     two-world Theory of the Phaedo". Phronesis XVII
     1972 61-79.

1736 BROWN M., "The Idea of Equality in the Phaedo".
     AGPh LIV 1972 24-36.

1737 NEHAMAS A., "Predication and Forms of Opposites in
     the Phaedo". RM XXVI 1973 461-491.

1738 YAMAMOTO C., "The Theory of Ideas in the Phaedo" [in
     Japanese]. Methodos VI 1973.

1739 SHIKUBU H., "The δεύτερος πλοῦς in the Phaedo" [in
     Japanese with an English summary]. JCS VI 1958
     47-56.

1740 HUBY P.M., "Phaedo 99d-102a". Phronesis IV 1959
     12-14.

1741 PLASS P., "Socrates' Method of Hypothesis in the
     Phaedo". Phronesis V 1960 103-115.

1742 ROSE L.E., "The Deuteros Plous in Plato's Phaedo".
     Monist L 1966 464-473.

1743 ROSE L.E., "The deuteros plous in Plato's Phaedo".
     Summary in JPh LXII 1965 607-608.

1744 WAGNER H., "Platos Phaedo und der Beginn der
     Metaphysik als Wissenschaft [Phaedo 99d-107b]".
     p.363-382 in Kritik und Metaphysik. Studien.

214

III C d 31: PHAEDO

Heinz Heimsoeth zum achtzigsten Geburtstag,
hrsg. von Kaulbach F. & Ritter J. Berlin
1966.

1745 MATSUNAGA Y., "A Thought with a Beginning.
Commentary on Plato, Phaedo 95e-105c" [in
Japanese]. in Collection of Essays published in
commemoration of the fortieth anniversary of the
Department of Literature, Kyushu Univ. 1966.

1746 KAWADA S., "One aspect of the Idea of the Good, in
relation to the second-best in the Phaedo" [in
Japanese]. Christianity and Culture
(International Christian Univ. Report IV-B) III
1967.

1747 PREUS M. & FERGUSON J., "A Clue to the δεύτερος
πλοῦς". Arethusa II 1969 104-107.

1748 SPRAGUE R.K., "Socrates' Safest Answer. Phaedo
100d". Hermes XCVI 1968-1969 632-635.

1749 TSUMURA K., "The second voyage in the Phaedo" [in
Japanese]. Methodos III 1970.

1750 MAGATA T., "Δεύτερος πλοῦς. Phaedo 99d-107b" [in
Japanese with English summary]. JCS XX 1972
70-78.

1751 LORIAUX R., "Phédon 101d-e". p.98-107 in Zetesis
(see 4579).

1752 TELLE H., "Der Widerspruch der ὁρμηθέντα in Platons
Hypothesisverfahren". AClass XVI 1973 15-23.

1753 SCARROW D.S., "Phaedo, 106a-106e". PhR LXX 1961
245-253.

1754 KEYT D., "The Fallacies in Phaedo 102a-107b".
Phronesis VIII 1963 167-172.

1755 VOLKMANN-SCHLUCK K.H., "Seele und Idee. Der dritte
Unsterblichkeitsbeweis in Platos Phaidon".
p.253-264 in Dialektik und Dynamik der Person.
Festschrift für Robert Heiss zum 60. Geburtstag
am 22.1.1963. Köln 1963.

1756 O'BRIEN D., "The Last Argument of Plato's Phaedo,
I". CQ XVII 1967 198-231.

III C d 31: PHAEDO

1757 O'BRIEN D., "The last Argument of Plato's Phaedo, II". CQ XVIII 1968 95-106.

1758 ERBSE H., "Philologische Anmerkungen zu Platons Phaidon 102a-107a". Phronesis XIV 1969 97-106.

1759 HARTMAN E., "Predication and Immortality in Plato's Phaedo". AGPh LIV 1972 215-228.

1760 CALDER W.M. III, "The Spherical Earth in Plato's Phaedo". Phronesis III 1958 121-125.

1761 ROSENMEYER T.G., "The Shape of the Earth in the Phaedo. A Rejoinder". Phronesis IV 1959 71-72.

1762 MORRISON J.S., "The Shape of the Earth in Plato's Phaedo". Phronesis IV 1959 101-119.

1763 SALVIAT J., "Καλὸς γὰρ ὁ κύνδυνος, risque et mythe dans le Phédon". REG LXXVIII 1965 23-29.

1764 ANTON J.P., "The Ultimate Theme of the Phaedo". Arethusa I 1968 94-102. Summary p.423 in Akten XIV. Intern. Kongr. Philos. Wien, 2.-9. September 1968. Vol. V. Wien, Herder 1968.

1765 OZAWA K., "Eschatology in the Phaedo" [in Japanese]. Philosophy Miscellany (Tokyo Metropolitan Univ.) XIV 1971.

1766* GROSSO M.A., Death and the Myth of the true Earth in Plato's Phaedo. Diss. Columbia Univ. 1971 153p. [microfilm]. Summary in DA XXXIII 1972 357A.

1767 GOLDSCHMIDT V., "La vraisemblance en géométrie (Phéd. 92c-d)". p.427 in Akten XIV. Intern. Kongr. Philos. Wien, 2.-9. September 1968, Vol. V. Wien, Herder 1968. Reprinted p.49-50 in Goldschmidt V., Questions platoniciennes (see 4598).

1768 ABEL A., "Traces de religiosité vulgaire dans le Phédon". Summary in RBPh XLV 1967 1302.

For additional discussions see 40, 248, 250, 252, 293, 333, 355, 372, 374, 515, 615, 764, 777, 780, 803, 819, 823, 824, 935, 1223, 1686, 2173, 2486, 2574, 2575, 2577, 2587, 2594, 2596, 2597, 2598, 2600, 2612, 2614, 2615, 2707, 2786, 2812, 2863, 2869, 2973, 2996, 3038, 3039, 3068, 3097, 3129, 3137, 3138, 3159, 3187, 3199, 3254, 3318, 3404,

III C d 31: PHAEDO

3423, 3906, 3912, 3922, 3933, 3977, 4318, 4326,
4329, 4330, 4333, 4335, 4337, 4514.

C. TEXTUAL CRITICISM

1769 CURRIE H. MacL., "Phaedo 62a". Hermes LXXXVI 1958
124-125.

1770 LORIMER W.L., "Plato, Phaedo 84c". CR X 1960 7-8.

1771 SKARDASIS I.G., "Παρατηρήσεις εἰς Πλάτωνος Φαίδωνα".
Platon XIV 1962 138-142.

1772 CARLINI A., "Contributi allo studio dei manoscritti
platonici del Fedone". Maia XVII 1965 189-193.

1773 CARLINI A., "Su alcuni manoscritti platonici del
Fedone". SCO XV 1966 198-209.

1774 CARLINI A., "Testimonianze antiche al testo del
Fedone". SCO XVI 1967 286-307.

1775 UNTERSTEINER M., "Senocrate editore del Fedone?".
RFIC XCV 1967 397-411.

1776 CARLINI A., "Linee di una storia del testo del
Fedone". SCO XVII 1968 123-148.

1777 CARLINI A., "Note critiche al testo del Fedone".
BPEC XVI 1968 25-60.

1778 MUELLER G., "Unechte Zusätze im Platontext". MH
XXVI 1969 179-198.

1779 GRAESER A., "Kein unechter Zusatz in Phaidon
103c-105c". MH XXX 1973 20-24.

1780 CARLINI A., "Linee di una storia del testo del
Fedone dal I sec. a.C. all'età di Fozio e
Areta". ASNP XXXIX 1970 149-215.

1781 VRIES G.J. DE, "A Note on Plato, Phaedo 89b".
Mnemosyne XXIV 1971 386-387.

217

PHAEDRUS

A. TEXTS AND TRANSLATIONS

1782* Phaedrus, transl. with intro. & comm. by
Hackforth R. Libr. of Liberal Arts, New York,
The Liberal Arts Pr. 1960 vii&172p. Also
Cambridge Univ. Pr. 1972. Reprint of 1952
edn.
Rev [of 1972 Cambridge edn.]. REA LXXV
1973 142 Moreau.
Athenaeum LI 1973 454 Vegetti.

1783* The Phaedrus of Plato, with English notes &
dissertations by Thompson W.H. New York, Arno
Pr. 1973 xxviii&203p. Reprint of 1868 edn.

1784* Phaidros, dt. von Salin E. mit Erl. von Bollack
J. Exempla classica LXXXV, Frankfurt, Fischer
1963 164p.

1785* Phaidros, hrsg. & übers. von Buchwald W.
Tusculum-Bücherei, München, Heimeran 1964 189p.
Rev. RBPh XLIII 1965 1154 Schwartz.
Maia XVIII 1966 421-423 Valgiglio.

1786* Phaidros oder vom Schönen, übertr. & eingel. von
Hildebrandt K. Nachdr. Universal-Bibl.
5789-5790, Stuttgart, Reclam 1973 98p.

1787* Phèdre ou De la beauté des âmes, trad. intégr. &
nouvelle avec notes, suive du traité de Plotin
Sur le beau, par Meunier M. Nouv. éd. rev. &
corr. Paris, Albin Michel 1960 224p.
Rev. EPh XV 1960 413-414 Jagu.
REA LXIII 1961 147 Aubenque.

1788* Phaedrus, ed. Robin L. Coll. Calliope, Paris, Les
Belles Lettres 1964 96p.

1789* Phèdre, trad., introd. & notes de Vicaire P. Les
grandes oeuvres de l'antiquité class., Paris,
Les Belles Lettres 1972 168p.
Rev. RSC XX 1972 454-455 d'Agostino.

1790* Fedro, trad. a cura di Richelmy A. Torino, Einaudi
1959 xvi&185p.
Rev. Maia XII 1960 77-80 Lagorio.

III C d 32: PHAEDRUS

1791* Fedro, trad. de Galli G., introd. e note de Plebe
A. Pensatori antichi e mod. LXiV, Firenze, La
Nuova Italia 1964 xviii&109p.
Rev. Vichiana I 1964 455 Giordano.
SicGymn XIX 1966 282 Cataudella.

1792* Elskoven og sjelen, Faidros [Loves and Souls,
Phaedrus], Norwegian transl. with introd. &
afterword by Wyller E.A. Klassikerbibliotek IV,
Oslo, Aschehoug 1962 111p.

1793* Faidros (O lásce), přel. poznámkami opatřil a
doslov napsal Novotný F. Praha, Čs. Spisovatel
1958 81p.

1794* Fajdros, przel., wstep., objaśn., illustr. Witwicki
W., przedm. Jesewska K. Warszawa, PWN 1958
202p.

1795* Φαῖδρος, εἰσαγ., ἀρχαιο καὶ νέο κείμενο μὲ σχόλια,
ὑπὸ Theodorakopoulos J.N. 2nd edn. Athens 1968
475p.
Rev. Gymnasium LXXVII 1970 240-242 Bauer.

1796* Fayrdrūs aw 'an al-jamāl [Phaedrus, or On Beauty],
Arabic transl. & introd. by Maṭar A.H. Coll.
Maktabat al-dirāsāt al-falsafiyya XXIV, Cairo,
Dar al-Ma'aref 1969 135p.

1797* Phaedrus, transl. by Fujisawa N. Tokyo, Iwanami
Shoten 1967 210p.

For additional texts and translations see 855, 867, 878,
893, 918, 922, 924, 928, 930, 931, 937, 939,
947, 948, 953, 955, 956, 959, 960, 962, 963,
967, 970, 971, 977, 984.

B. STUDIES OF THE PHAEDRUS

1798* HERMEIAS OF ALEXANDRIA, In Platonis Phaedrum
scholia. Ad fidem codicis Parisini 1810 denuo
collati, ed. et apparatu critico ornavit
Couvreur P. Reprograf. Nachdr. d. Ausg.
Paris 1901. Novae huius libri impressioni
indicem verborum epilogumque addidit Zintzen C.
Hildesheim/New York, Olms 1971 xxiii&300p.

219

1799* THEMISTIUS, Plaidoyer d'un socratique contre le Phèdre de Platon, XXVIe discours de Themistius, Introd., texte ét. et trad. par Kesters H. Louvain, Nauwelaerts 1959 xvi&296p.
Rev. RecTh XXVI 1959 343-346 Petit.
Mnemosyne XIII 1960 357-358 Westerink.
RB LXX 1960 465-466.
RHE LV 1960 1169 Canart.
LEC XXVIII 1960 102-103 Loriaux.
RPh XXXV 1961 157 Louis.
FL II 1961 187-193 de Vogel.
AC XXX 1961 238-241 Henry.
MH XVIII 1961 239 Gigon.
CR XI 1961 163 Bambrough.
Mind LXX 1961 286-287 Hall.
RBPh XXXIX 1961 73-78 de Vries.
Gnomon XXXIV 1962 28-31 Regenbogen.
CPh LVII 1962 51 De Lacy.
Emerita XXX 1962 167-170 Millán.
ByzZ LV 1962 77-78 Imhof.
REG LXXV 1962 600-602 Harl.
RPhL LXI 1963 146-148 Motte.
NRTh LXXXV 1963 1090 de Give.
ASNP XXXI 1962 130-132 Carlini.

1800 LAFRANCE Y., "Socratismo contra Platonismo". RBF XIII 1963 551-565.

1801 LAFRANCE Y., "A propos d'une thèse de Kesters". Dialogue II 1963 83-95.

1802 MUELLER G.E., "The unity of the Phaidros". Sophia XXVI 1958 25-34.

1803 RAVASINI G.G., "Il Faidros come ganglio della coscienza". FilosUnic jan-mars 1961 no.34 38-40.

1804 REGENBOGEN O., "Bemerkungen zur Deutung des platonischen Phaidros". p.248-269 in Regenbogen O., Kleine Schriften, hrsg. von Dirlmeier F. München, Beck 1961. Reprinted from Academica Berolinensia II 1950 198-219.

1805 BEGEMANN A.W., "Opbouw en bedoeling van Plato's dialoog Phaidros". TPh XXIV 1962 652-667.

1806* PIEPER J., Begeisterung und göttlicher Wahnsinn. Ueber den platonischen Dialog Phaidros. München, Kösel 1962 175p. English trans. Enthusiasm and Divine Madness: The Platonic Dialogue Phaedrus, transl. by Winston R. & C.

New York, Harcourt, Brace & World 1964; publ.
in England under the title Love and Inspiration.
A Study of Plato's Phaedrus. London, Faber &
Faber 1965 xvi&109p. Also Spanish transl.:
Entusiasmo y delirio divino. Sobre el diálogo
platónico Fedro. Madrid, Rialp. 1965 159p.
Rev. [of German edn.] CW LVII 1964 255
Hoerber.
RecSR LII 1964 461 des Places.
PhJ LXXI 1963-1964 411-413 Esser.
JHPh I 1963 95-99 Merlan.
RFNeo 1963 429-432 Bonetti.
DT 1963 341-342 Mondin.
Bijdragen XXV 1964 323 Geurtsen.
EstFilos XIII 1964 404 García.
Scholastik XL 1965 250-251 Ennen.
[of English edn.]CR XVI 1966 235 Gulley.
NBFr XLVI 1965 649-650 O'Brien.
[of Spanish edn.] Studium VI 1966 396
García.
EstFilos XV 1966 433-434 J.L.A.
Stromata XXIII 1967 401-402.

1807 BONETTI A., "Intorno ad alcune interpretazioni del
      Fedro". RFNeo LV 1963 407-414.

1808 VRIES G.J. DE, "A New Indication for the Date of
      the Phaedrus?". Mnemosyne XVI 1963 286-287.

1809 WYCHERLEY R.E., "The Scene of Plato's Phaidros".
      Phoenix XVII 1963 88-98.

1810 LEVINSON R.B., "Plato's Phaedrus and the New
      Criticism". AGPh XLVI 1964 293-309.

1811 USENER H., "Abfassungszeit des Platonischen
      Phaidros". p.55-74 in Usener H., Kleine
      Schriften III (see 4618). Reprinted from RhM
      XXXV 1879 131-151.

1812* ARNIM H. VON, Platos Jugenddialoge und die
      Entstehungszeit des Phaidros. Nachdr. d.
      Ausg. Leipzig 1914. Amsteraam, Hakkert 1967
      viii&224p.

1813 BONITZ H., "Zur Erklärung des Dialogs Phädros".
      p.270-292 in Bonitz H., Platonische Studien (see
      4584).

1814 PLASS P., "The Unity of the Phaedrus". SO XLIII
      1968 7-38.

1815 RODIS-LEWIS G., "La fonction de la dialectique et la
     composition du Phèdre". p.48-52 in La
     Dialectique. Actes du XIVe Congrès des Sociétés
     de Philosophie de Langue française. Nice, 1-4
     sept. 1969. Paris, Presses Universitaires
     1969.

1816* VRIES G.J. DE, A Commentary on the Phaedrus of
     Plato. Amsterdam, Hakkert 1969 viii&274p.
     Rev. Mnemosyne XXIV 1971 94-95 Gulley.
     JCS XIX 1971 146-152 Kitajima.
     BAGB 1973 508ff.
     Gnomon XLV 1973 88-90 Easterling.

1817 CHEN C.H., "The Phaedrus as the Transition from the
     Platonism in the earlier Dialogues to the
     Dialectic and Theology in the later Dialogues".
     SIF IV 1972 77-90.

1818 BLUCK R.S., "The Phaedrus and Reincarnation". AJPh
     LXXIX 1958 156-164.

1819 EITREM S., "Götter und Daimonen. Einige Bemerkungen
     zu Platon, Phaidr. 246E". SO XXXIV 1958 39-42.

1820 GIL L., "De nuevo sobre el Fedro" (with resume in
     English). Emerita XXVI 1958 215-221.

1821 HOERBER R.G., "Love or Rhetoric in Plato's
     Phaedrus?". CB XXXIV 1958 33.

1822 MAGINAS S.C., "Ὁ Φαῖδρος τοῦ Πλάτωνος καὶ ὁ περὶ τοῦ
     ἔρωτος λόγος τοῦ Λυσίου". Athena LXIII 1959
     33-118.

1823 SÁNCHEZ LASSO DE LA VEGA J., "Notulae". Emerita
     XXVIII 1960 125-142.

1824 DAUMAS F., "Sous le signe du gattilier en fleurs".
     REG LXXIV 1961 61-68.

1825 MIELESI U. DE, "Musica e filosofia nel Fedone".
     p.9-30 in Scritti filosofici, I. Archivum
     Philosophicum Aloisianum. Serie IV,1, Milano,
     Marzorati 1961.

1826 PIEPER J., "Über den 'Göttlichen Wahnsinn'. Aus
     einer Interpretation des platonischen Dialogs
     'Phaidros'". Hochland LIV 1961-1962 508-522.

III C d 32: PHAEDRUS

1827 ROSENMEYER T.G., "Plato's Prayer to Pan (Phaedrus 279b8-c3)". Hermes XC 1962 34-44.

1828 VERDENIUS W.J., "Der Begriff der Mania in Platons Phaidros". AGPh XLIV 1962 132-150.

1829 ARMSTRONG A.H., "Platonic Love. A Reply to Professor Verdenius". DownsR LXXXII 1964 199-208.

1830 KESTERS H., "De ware redekunst volgens Platoons Phaidros" [in Dutch with French summary]. TPh XXV 1963 651-687.

1831 KESTERS H., "De ware redekunst volgens Platoons Phaidros" [with French summary]. TPh XXVI 1964 33-67, 405-441.

1832 MOTTE A., "Le pré sacré de Pan et des Nymphes dans le Phèdre de Platon". AC XXXII 1963 460-476.

1833 PIEPER J., "Sur la 'divine folie'. Réflexions à propos du Phèdre de Platon". TabR no.183 avr. 1963 77-94.

1834 SCHOTTLAENDER R., "Das Sibyllenbild der Philosophen". AAntHung XI 1963 37-48.

1835 SICKING C.M.J., "Organische Komposition und Verwandtes". Mnemosyne XVI 1963 225-242.

1836 BONETTI A., "Amore e filosofia nel 'Fedro'". RFNeo LVI 1964 561-580.

1837 McGIBBON D.D., "The Fall of the Soul in Plato's Phaedrus". CQ XIV 1964 56-63.

1838 BROWNSTEIN O.L., "Plato's Phaedrus: Dialectic as the genuine Art of Speaking". QJS LI 1965 392-398.

1839 GIL L., "Divagaciones en torno al mito de Theuth y de Thamus". EClas IX 1965 343-360.

1840 WOLZ H.G., "Plato's Discourse on Love in the Phaedrus". Personalist XLVI 1965 157-169.

1841 CAMBIANO G., "Dialettica, medicina, retorica nel Fedro platonico". RF LVII 1966 284-305.

III C d 32: PHAEDRUS

1842 FORTENBAUGH W.W., "Plato Phaedrus 235c3".   CPh LXI
      1966 108-109.

1843 SCHMALZRIEDT E., "Der Umfahrtsmythos des Phaidros".
      AU IX,5 1966 60-99.

1844 THESLEFF H., "Stimmungsmalerei oder Burleske? Der
      Stil von Plat. Phaidr. 230bc und seine
      Funktion". Arctos V 1967 141-155.

1845 ROBINSON T.M., "The Nature and Significance of the
      Argument for Immortality in the Phaedrus".
      Apeiron II,2 1968 12-18.

1846 ZUTHER G., "Plato's Phaedrus: Rhetoric as Example
      and Precept". UKBE XXII 1968 101-108.

1847 DUMORTIER J., "L'attelage ailé du Phèdre (246
      sqq.)". REG LXXXII 1969 346-348.

1848 FRIEDLAENDER P., "Plato Phaedrus 245a".   p.210-211
      in Friedlaender P., Studien zur antiken
      Literatur und Kunst (see 4589). Reprinted from
      CPh XXXVI 1941 51-52.

1849 MULHERN J.J., "Socrates on Knowledge and Information
      (Phaedrus 274b6-277a5)". C&M XXX 1969 175-186.

1850 ROSEN S., "The non-lover in Plato's Phaedrus".
      ManWorld II 1969 423-437.

1851 THOMPSON C.A., "Rhetorical Madness. An Ideal in the
      Phaedrus". QJS LV 1969 358-363.

1852 OSAWA K., "Insanity and God. Love, Beauty and the
      Human Question in the Phaedrus" [in Japanese].
      Philosophy Miscellany (Tokyo Metropolitan Univ.)
      XII 1970.

1853 BROWN M. & COULTER J., "The Middle Speech of
      Plato's Phaedrus". JHPh IX 1971 405-423.

1854 DORTER K., "Imagery and Philosophy in Plato's
      Phaedrus". JHPh IX 1971 279-281.

1855 OZAWA K., "The Fall of the Soul in the Phaedrus".
      [in Japanese] Philosophy Miscellany (Tokyo
      Metropolitan Univ.) XIII 1971.

1856 ROBINSON T.M., "The Argument for Immortality in
      Plato's Phaedrus". p.345-353 in Essays in
      ancient Greek Philosophy, ed. by Anton J.P. &

224

III C d 32: PHAEDRUS

Kustas G.L. (see 4581).

1857 LEBECK A., "The central myth in Plato's Phaedrus".
GRBS XIII 1972 267-290.

1858 NAWRATIL K., "Ein platonischer Kurzmythos". WJb V
1972 157-160.

1859 PAISSE J.M., "La métaphysique de l'âme humaine dans
le Phèdre de Platon". BAGB 1972 469-478.

1860 CALVO MARTINEZ J.L., "Sobre la manía y el
entusiasmo" [in Spanish with English summary].
Emerita XLI 1973 157-182.

1861 PINNOY M., "Phaedrus 227a-230e. Een kommentaar".
Kleio III 1973 2-8.

For additional discussions see 89, 275, 314, 315, 316,
384, 506, 615, 757, 774, 1359, 1691, 1857, 1860,
2305, 2354, 2355, 2486, 2565, 2580, 2581, 2602,
2608, 2609, 2610, 2611, 2644, 2649, 2693, 2701,
2712, 2714, 2715, 2717, 2735, 2768, 2909, 3001,
3039, 3060, 3068, 3120, 3189, 3199, 3405, 3478,
3697, 3803, 3831, 3851, 3868, 3889, 3899, 3900,
3901, 3950, 4014, 4015, 4109.

C. TEXTUAL CRITICISM

1863* VINZENT O., Textkritische Untersuchungen der
Phaidros-Papyri. Diss. Saarbrücken 1961 191p.

1864 MORESCHINI C., "Un nuovo manoscritto del Fedro
Platonico". ASNP XXXI 1962 247-251.

1865 BENDE G., "Eine übersehene Phaedruskonjektur
(Phaedr. I,22,2)". p.9-13 in Miscellanea
critica. Aus Anlass des 150jährigen Bestehens
der Verlagsgesellschaft und des graphischen
Betriebes B.G. Teubner, hrsg. von Irmscher J.
vol. II, Leipzig, Teubner 1965.

1866 MORESCHINI C., "Note critiche al Fedro di Platone".
ASNP XXXIV 1965 422-432.

225

1867 DECLEVA CAIZZI F., "Ἀειχύνητον ο αὐτοχύνητον? (Plat. Phaedr., 245c)". Acme XXIII 1970 91-97.

1868 SICKLE J. VAN, "Plat. Phaedr. 255d,3-6". MCr VIII-IX 1973-1974 198-199.

For additional studies of the text see 1360, 1637, 1845.

PHILEBUS

A. TEXTS AND TRANSLATIONS

1869* Plato's Examination of Pleasure. A Translation of
      the Philebus, with introd. & comm. by
      Hackforth R. Libr. of Liberal Arts, New York,
      The Liberal Arts Pr. 1960. Also Cambridge Univ.
      Pr. 1972 vi&144p. Reprint of 1945 edn.
      Rev [of 1972 edn.]. REA LXXV 1973 142
      Moreau.
      Athenaeum LI 1973 454 Vegetti.

1870* The Philebus of Plato, ed. with introd., notes &
      app. by Bury R.G. New York, Arno Pr. 1973
      lxxxvii&224p. Reprint of 1897 edn.

1871* Il Filebo e la questione del piacere nel IV secolo a.
      C., introd., trad. e note a cura di Repellini
      F.F. Collana filos., Milano, Principato 1971
      158p.

1872* Fileb, przel., wstep., objaśn., illustr. Witwicki
      W. Warszawa, PWN 1958 161p.

1873* Φίληβος (ἤ περὶ ἡδονῆς, ἠθικὸς), Β', introd., text,
      transl. & notes in modern Greek by Augerinos
      D.I. Athens 1961 p.89-168.

1874* Philebos, 2. bs. çev. Siyavuşgil S.E. Istanbul,
      Maarif Basimevi 1959 111p.

For additional texts and translations see 856, 861, 919,
      927, 934, 944, 951.

B. STUDIES OF THF PHILEBUS

1875* DAMASCIUS, Lectures on the Philebus, wrongly
      attributed to Olympiodorus. text, trans.,
      notes, and indices, ed. by Westerink L.G.
      Amsterdam, North-Holland Publ. 1959 xxii&149p.
      Rev. AGPh XLIII 1961 106-108 Wilpert.
      LEC XXVII 1959 456 Dorval.
      CW LIII 1959-1960 288-289 Rosenmeyer.

CPh LV 1960 268-270 Rich.
AC XXVIII 1959 360-361 Moraux.
RPh XXXIV 1960 299 Louis.
CR LXXIV 1960 212-213 Wasserstein.
REA LXIII 1961 163-164 Pépin.
RecSR XLIX 1961 301 des Places.
Gnomon XXXIII 1961 446-448 Beutler.
AAHG XIV 1961 101 Neuhauser.
PhilosRdschau X 1962 76-84 Beierwaltes.

1876* MARSILIO FICINO, Marsilio Ficino's Commentary on
the Philebus, ed. & transl. with an intro. by
Allen M.J.B. Diss. Univ. of Michigan 1970
492p. [microfilm]. Summary in DA XXXIII 1973
3571A.

1877 MacCLINTOCK S., "More on the Structure of the
Philebus". Phronesis VI 1961 46-52.

1878 GADAMER H.G., "Platos dialektische Ethik.
Phänomenologische Interpretationen zum
Philebos". p.xiii-xiv & 1-178 in Gadamer H.G.,
Platos dialektische Ethik und andere Studien
(see 4592). Reprint of 1931
Habilitationsschrift.

1879 GOLDSCHMIDT V., "Remarques sur le Philèbe". p.35-47
in Goldschmidt V., Questions platoniciennes (see
4598). Reprinted from L'information
philosophique 1951 45ff.

1880 YAMAUCHI T., "Interpretive essay on the Philebus of
Plato. Measure, World, and Man". MOsaka XX
1971 55-70.

1881 KLEIN J., "About Plato's Philebus". Interpretation
II 1971-1972 157-182.

1882 GOSLING J., "False Pleasures. Philebus 35c-41b".
Phronesis IV 1959 44-53.

1883 GALLOP D., "True and False Pleasures". PhilosQ X
1960 331-342.

1884 KENNY A., "False Pleasures in the Philebus. A Reply
to Mr. Gosling". Phronesis V 1960 45-52.

1885 GOSLING J., "Father Kenny on False Pleasures".
Phronesis VI 1961 41-45.

III C d 33: PHILEBUS

1886 THALBERG I., "False Pleasures". JPh LIX 1962 65-74.

1887 McLAUGHLIN A., "A Note on False Pleasures in the Philebus". PhilosQ XIX 1969 57-61.

1888 DYBIKOWSKI J.C., "False Pleasure and the Philebus". Phronesis XV 1970 147-165.

1889 DYBIKOWSKI J.C., "Mixed and False Pleasures in the Philebus. A Reply". PhilosQ XX 1970 244-247.

1890 PENNER T., "False Anticipatory Pleasures. Philebus 36a3-41a6". Phronesis XV 1970 166-178.

1891 MILLER F.D., "Can Pleasures be False?". SwJP II 1971 57-71.

1892 YAMAUCHI T., "Plato's Analysis of false Pleasure" [in Japanese]. Study of Ethics (Kansei Ethics Society) II 1972.

1893 TRAVASKIS J.R., "Classification in the Philebus". Phronesis V 1960 39-44.

1894 BOUSSOULAS N.I., "Recherches philosophiques". Analecta no.10 1961 27-144.

1895 BOUSSOULAS N.I., "Note sur la dernière doctrine platonicienne". BAGB 1963 404-436.

1896 BOUSSOULAS N.I., "Notes sur la pensée platonicienne". Platon XV 1963 87-125.

1897 BOUSSOULAS N.I., "Notes sur la pensée platonicienne". Sophia XXXI 1963 48-67.

1898 SCHUHL P.M., "Cosmos asômatos". REG LXXVI 1963 52-54.

1899 LEE J.M., "Philebus, 35a6-10". Phronesis XI 1966 31-34.

1900 SCHUHL P.M., "Sur le mélange dans le Philèbe". REG LXXX 1967 220-226.

1901 SCHUHL P.M., "Sulla mescolanza nel Filebo". DeHomine 1967 n.22-23 149-154.

1902 SCHUHL P.M., "Le mélange dans le Philèbe". BSPh LXII 1968 1-26. Followed by discussion p.27-31.

III C d 33: PHILEBUS

1903 SCHUHL P.M., "Γένεσις et répétition. Philèbe 23c
sqq.". RPhilos CLVII 1967 120-121.

1904 COOPER N., "Pleasure and Goodness in Plato's
Philebus". PhilosQ XVIII 1968 12-15.

1905 SCHUHL P.M., "Analyse de la composition de la
première partie du Philèbe (11a-31b)". RPhilos
CLVIII 1968 120-122.

1906 SCHUHL P.M., "Le Bien dans le Philèbe". p.419-422
in Akten XIV. Intern. Kongr. Philos. Wien,
2.-9. September 1968. Vol. V. Wien, Herder
1968.

1907 SCHUHL P.M., "Introduction à l'étude de Platon. Le
Bien dans le Philèbe". RPhilos CLIX 1969
243-246.

1908* STRIKER G., Peras und Apeiron. Das Problem der
Formen in Platons Philebos. Diss. Göttingen
1969. Hypomnemata XXX, Göttingen, Vandenhoeck &
Ruprecht 1970 84p.
        Rev. CW LXV 1971 132 Moore.
        AC XL 1971 721 des Places.
        CR XXII 1972 332-333 Huby.
        Gnomon XLV 1973 649-653 Ilting.

1909 KAMIOKA H., "Dialectic in the Philebus" [in
Japanese]. Philosophy Miscellany (Tokyo
Metropolitan Univ.) XIII 1971.

1910 MARACKI-GADJANSKI K., "On Plato's Philebus" [in
Serbo-Croatian with German summary]. ZAnt XXI
1971 123-129.

1911 SCHOFIELD M., "Who were οἱ δυσχερεῖς in Plato,
Philebus 44a ff.?". MH XXVIII 1971 2-20, 181.

1912 TALLON A., "The Criterion of Purity in Plato's
Philebus". NS XLVI 1972 439-445.

1913 WILPERT P., "Eine Elementenlehre im platonischen
Philebos". p.316-328 in Das Problem der
ungeschriebenen Lehre Platons, hrsg. von
Wippern J. (see 4626). Reprinted from Studies
presented to David Moore Robinson on his
seventieth birthday, II, ed. by Mylonas G.E. &
Raymond D. Washington Univ., St. Louis 1953,
p.573-582.

230

III C d 33: PHILEBUS

1914 SAKISAKA Y., "ἀληθεῖς ἡδοναί and καθαραὶ ἡδοναί. An
Interpretation of Orpheus' Remark (Philebus
66c)" [in Japanese with English summary]. JCS
XXI 1973 59-66.

1915 BOUSSOULAS N.I., "Μελέτες πάνω στὴν ἀρχαία
φιλοσοφία". EEThess XII 1973 227-299.

1916 SHIKIBU H., "The Division of Pleasure in the
Philebus of Plato" [in Japanese with English
summary]. JCS XXI 1973 50-58.

For additional discussions see 89, 351, 471, 509, 642,
699, 2299, 2486, 2797, 2888, 2937, 2973, 3008,
3240, 3979, 4026, 4159.

C. TEXTUAL CRITICISM

1917 LOGOTHETES K.I., "Κριτικὰ καὶ ἑρμηνευτικὰ εἰς χωρία
Πλατωνικά". Platon XI 1959 275-294.

1918 HARDING H.P. "Zum Text des platonischen Philebos".
Hermes LXXXVIII 1960 40-68.

PHILOSOPHUS

B. DISCUSSIONS OF THE PHILOSOPHUS

1919 SONTAG F., "Plato's Unwritten Dialogue: 'The
Philosopher'". p.159-167 in Atti XII Congresso
Internazionale di Filosofia. Venezia, 12-18
settembre 1958. Vol. XI: Storia della
Filosofia antica e medievale. Firenze, Sansoni
1960.

For additional discussions see 1571, 1572.

231

PROTAGORAS

A. TEXTS AND TRANSLATIONS

1920* Protagoras, vollständige Textausg. mit Komm.
besorgt von Dirlmeier F. & Scharold H.
München, Koesel 1959 149p.
Rev. Gymnasium LXIX 1962 568 Classen.
Scholastik XXXV 1960 449-450 Ivánka.

1921* Il Protagora, con introd. e comm. di Calogero G.
3a ed., riv. Bibl. scol. di class. lat. e
grec., Firenze, Sansoni 1958 xxx&165p.

1922* Protagora, trad., introd. & note a cura di Faggin
G. Class. della filos. e pedag., Torino, Soc.
Ed. Internazionale 1960 106p.

1923* Protagora, trad., introd. e comm. a cura di Reale
G. Il pensiero class. della filos. comm.,
Brescia, La Scuola 1969 lxviii&203p.

1924* Protagoras, przel., wstep., objaśn., illustr.
Witwicki W. Warszawa, PWN 1958 154p.

1925* Protagoras, Turkish transl. by Kösemihal N.S. 2nd
edn. Yunan klâsikleri XVIII, Ankara, Millî
Eğitim Basimevi 1965 6, xvii&79p.

1926* Protagoras, Hebrew transl. by Simon L. Jerusalem,
The Magnes Press, The Hebrew Univ. 1967
xvi&154p. Reprint of 1935 edn.

For additional texts and translations see 852, 866, 878,
920, 925, 929, 943, 949, 970, 986, 992.

b. STUDIES OF THE PROTAGORAS

1927* PAPANIKOLAOU K.N., Προβλήματα ἑρμηνείας τῶν
κλασσικῶν κειμένων: Σοφοκλέους Ἀντιγόνη. Πλάτωνος
Πρωταγόρας. Athens 1960 72p.

III C d 35: PROTAGORAS

1928* SLØK J., <u>Platons dialog</u> Protagoras. Filosofihist.
Monogr., København, Gyldendal 1963 121p.

1929 MOULINIER L., "Socrate devant Protagoras". AFLA
XXXIX 1965 101-125.

1930 BONITZ H., "Zur Erklärung des Dialogs Protagoras".
p.254-269 in Bonitz H., <u>Platonische Studien</u> (see
4584).

1931 GAGARIN M., "The Purpose of Plato's Protagoras".
TAPhA C 1969 133-164.

1932* GAGARIN M., <u>Plato</u> and <u>Protagoras</u>. Diss. Yale Univ.
1968 199p. [microfilm]. Summary in DA XXIX
1969 3988A.

1933 GIGON O., "Studien zu Platons Protagoras". p.98-154
in Gigon O., <u>Studien zur antiken Philosophie</u>
(see 4597). Reprinted from <u>Phyllobolia</u>.
<u>Festschrift für P. Vonder Muehll</u>. Basel 1948,
p.91-152.

1934 DUBOSE S., "The Argument laughs at Socrates and
Protagoras". <u>Dewey and his Influence</u>. Essays
<u>in honor of George Estes Barton</u> = TSPh XXII 1973
14-21.

1935 SICKING C.M.J., "Plato's Protagoras: confrontatie
of schijnconfrontatie?". Lampas VI 1973
200-229.

1936 GALLOP D., "Justice and Holiness in Protagoras
330-331". Phronesis VI 1961 86-93.

1937 O'BRIEN M.J., "The 'Fallacy' in Protagoras
349d-350c". TAPhA XCII 1961 408-417.

1938 SULLIVAN J.P., "The Hedonism in Plato's Protagoras".
Phronesis VI 1961 10-28.

1939 SESONSKE A., "Hedonism in the Protagoras". JHPh I
1963 73-79.

1940 WOLZ H.G., "The Protagoras Myth and the
Philosopher-Kings". RM XVII 1963 214-234.

1941 GALLOP D., "The Socratic Paradox in the Protagoras".
Phronesis IX 1964 117-129.

1942 SAVAN D., "Self-predication in Protagoras 330-331". Phronesis IX 1964 130-135.

1943 SAVAN D., "Socrates' Logic and the Unity of Wisdom and Temperance". p.20-26 in Analytical Philosophy, 2nd series, ed. by Butler R.J. New York, Barnes & Noble and Oxford, Blackwell 1965.

1944 GAUTHIER D.P., "The Unity of Wisdom and Temperance". JHPh VI 1968 157-159.

1945 TURNER E.G., "Athenians learn to Write. Plato, Protagoras 326d". BICS XII 1965 67-69.

1946 MOSER S. & KUSTAS G.L., "A Comment on the 'Relativism' of the Protagoras". Phoenix XX 1966 111-115.

1947 SALGUERO C.A., "Plato and the Law. Commentaries on the Protagoras". Athene(Chicago) XXVI,4 1966 3-7, 15.

1948 SANTAS G., "Plato's Protagoras and Explanations of Weakness". PhR LXXV 1966 3-33.

1949 MUELLER C.W., "Protagoras über die Götter". Hermes XCV 1967 140-158.

1950 NEUMANN H., "The Sophistry of Plato's Protagoras and Cleitophon". Sophia XXXV 1967 46-55.

1951 SAUPE W., "Neue Probleme der Platonforschung". Helikon VII 1967 537-545.

1952 SPRAGUE R.K., "An Unfinished Argument in Plato's Protagoras". Apeiron I,2 1967 1-4.

1953 WOLZ H.G., "Hedonism in the Protagoras". JHPh V 1967 205-217.

1954 PLACES E. DES, "Simonide et Socrate dans le Protagoras de Platon". LEC XXXVII 1969 236-244.

1955 SIMON E., "A Platóni Prótagorasz polisz-mitoszának egy újfajta ertelmezéséröl [A new kind of Interpretation of the Polis-Mythos in Plato's Protagoras]". MFS XIII 1969 549-551.

1956 VLASTOS G., "Socrates on Acrasia". Phoenix XXIII 1969 71-88.

1957 CAPIZZI A., "Il 'mito di Protagora' e la polemica
     sulla democrazia". Cultura VIII 1970 552-571.

1958 FESTUGIÈRE A.J., "Sur un passage difficile du
     Protagoras". p.315-322 in Festugière A.J.,
     Études de philosophie grecque (see 4587).
     Reprinted from BCH LXX 1946 179-186.

1959 GULLEY N., "Socrates' Thesis at Protagoras 358b-c".
     Phoenix XXV 1971 118-123.

1960 SCHUETRUMPF E., "Kosmopolitismus oder
     Panhellenismus? Zur Interpretation des
     Ausspruchs von Hippias in Platons Protagoras
     (337c ff.)". Hermes C 1972 5-29.

1961 SIMMONS G.C., "Protagoras on Education and Society".
     PaedHist XII 1972 518-537.

1962 VLASTOS G., "The Unity of Virtues in the
     Protagoras". RM XXV 1972 415-458. Reprinted
     with additions and corrections and appendix "The
     Argument in La. 197e ff.", p.221-269 in Vlastos
     G., Platonic Studies (see 4622).

1963 ADKINS A.W.H., "Ἀρετή, τέχνη, democracy, and
     sophists. Protagoras 316b-328d". JHS XCIII
     1973 3-12.

For additional discussions of the Protagoras see 40, 228,
     235, 262, 319, 320, 1691, 2173, 2661, 2668,
     2711, 2806, 3416, 3471, 3628, 3631, 3632, 3651,
     3742, 4032, 4468, 4478.

REPUBLIC

A. TEXTS AND TRANSLATIONS

1964* Republic. 2nd edn. Modern Student's Libr., New
      York, Scribner 1958 426p.

1965* Plato, Republic for Today, sel. and transl. with
      an educ. comm. by Boyd W. London, Heinemann
      1962 209p.

235

III C d 36: REPUBLIC

1966* The Republic, ed. with crit. notes, comm. &
append. by Adam J. 2nd edn. with an intro.
by Rees D.A. Cambridge Univ. Pr. 1963
lviii&364, 532p.
Rev. Hermathena XCVIII 1964 127 Luce.
CR XV 1965 167-168 Gulley.
TLS 26 March 1964 260.
Dialogue III 1964-1965 440-441 Reesor.
NS XXXIX 1965 404-405 Halton.

1967* Republic, ed. & transl. by Richards I.A.
Cambridge Paperback CAM359, Cambridge Univ. Pr.
1966 196p.
Rev. CW LX 1966 72 Reesor.
Hermathena CIII 1966 102-103 Luce.
AC XXXV 1966 626 des Places.
REG LXXIX 1966 545 Weil.
G&R XIV 1967 189 Sewter.
CB XLIII 1967 96 Stark.
LEC XXXV 1967 87 Delaunois.
DalR 1967 93 Page.
DUJ XXX 1969 157 Skemp.

1968* The Republic, transl. by Jowett B., notes by Masson
D. New York, Airmont 1968 413p.

1969* The Republic of Plato, transl. by Bloom A. with
notes & an interpretive essay. New York, Basic
Books 1968 xxi&487p.
Rev. CW LXIII 1970 270 Stewart.
PhilosQ XX 1970 269 Gulley.
NYRB XIII,8 1969 16-19 Ryle.
BW 20 Apr. 1969 14 Otis.
NYT 12 Jan. 1969 12 Warner.
PhilosForum X 1971 152-154 Edgar.
ModS XLVIII 1970-1971 280-284 Sweeney.

1970* Der Staat, eingel., übers. & erkl. von Vretska K.
Reclams Universal-Bibl. No. 8205/8212,
Stuttgart, Reclam 1958 656p.
Rev. AAHG XV 1962 87 Herter.

1971* Platons Staat in Auswahl, Text & Komm. hrsg. von
Gaehrken B. 2. Aufl. Münster, Aschendorff
1959 133 & 104p.
Rev. AAHG XIII 1960 43 Vretska.

1972* Der Staat, ausgew. & bearb. von Bretzigheimer F.
Aus dem Schatze des Altertums, Bamberg, Buchner
1960 69p.

1973* Der Staat, Über das Gerechte, übers. & erläut. von
Apelt O., durchges. von Bormann K., Einleit.
von Wilpert P. Hamburg, Meiner 1961 lx&486p.

1974* Der Staat, Übers. von Schleiermacher F., eingel.
von Endres H.M. München, Goldmann 1962 384p.
Rev. PhJ LXX 1962 201 Hommes.

1975* Der Weg zur philosophischen Bildung (Staat, 7.
Buch), übers. & erl. von Rufener R. Lebendige
Antike, Zürich, Artemis-Verl. 1962 64p.

1976* Plato, Ausgewählte Werke in acht Bänden. Der Staat,
Übers. von Schleiermacher F. München, Goldmann
1973 320p.

1977* Der Staat, eingel. von Gigon O., Übertr. von
Rufener R. 2. Aufl. Die Bibl. der Alten
Welt: Griech. Reihe, Zürich/München,
Artemis-Verl. 1973 653p.

1978* La République, livres VII et VIII, trad. par
Millepierres F. Traductions Hatier. Grèce.
XXIV, Paris, Hatier 1960 78p.

1979* La République, introd. de Diès A., trad. de
Chambry É. Bibl. Méditations I, Paris,
Gauthier 1963 366p.

1980* La République, introd., trad. et notes par Baccou
R. Garnier-Flammarion Texte intégral XC, Paris,
Garnier-Flammarion 1966 512p.

1981* La République, trad. par Chambry É., introd. par
Diès A. Nouv. éd. Club français du livre.
Portiques XXXIII, Club français du livre 1967
xlviii&520p.

1982* Republic, selected passages, introd. & comm. in
Hungarian by Sándor P., Hungarian transl. by
Jánosy I. 2nd edn. Budapest, Gondolat 1970
285p.

1983* La Repubblica, intro. di Gentile M., trad. e note
di Pozzo G.M. Il pensiero. Class. della filos
comm., Brescia, La Scuola 1959 xxvii&123p.

1984* La Repubblica, estratti a cura di Motzo Dentice di
Accadia C. Filos. e pedag., Napoli, Libr.
scient. editrice [1960?] 116p.

III C d 36: REPUBLIC

1985* La Repubblica, trad. a cura di Fraccaroli G.,
luoghi scelti & annot. a cura di Valgimigli M.
& Minio Paluello L. Firenze, La Nuova Italia
1961 280p.

1986* Trasimaco. Il primo libro della Repubblica,
introd., trad. e note di Lazzerini C.
Pensatori antichi e moderni LXVII, Firenze, La
Nuova Italia 1966 xxvi&70p.

1987* Repubblica X, studio intro., testo greco e comm. a
cura di Untersteiner M. Napoli, Loffredo 1966
355p.

1988* La giustizia (Dalla Repubblica), a cura di
Marchegiani L., trad. di Ferrai E. Univ.
degli studi di Camerino. Ist. giuridico.
Testi per esercitazioni, Sez. I,3, Milano,
Giuffrè 1967 70p.

1989* La Repubblica, libri VI e VII, trad. di Fraccaroli
G., comm. e note di Valgimigli M. & Minio
Paluello L. 4a ed. ricomposta. Pensatori
antichi e moderni IV, Firenze, La Nuova Italia
1968 xiii&104p.

1990* La Repubblica (libri V, VI, VII), a cura di Vegetti
M. Class. della filos., Padova, R.A.D.A.R.
1969 161p.

1991* Repubblica, introd., sommario, trad. a cura di
Sartori F. Coll. Universale Laterza, Bari,
Laterza 1970 lxxi&379p.

1992* La República, trad. del Míguez J.A. Madrid,
Aguilar 1959 680p.

1993* La República, trad., noticia prelim., notas y
estampa socrática de Bergua J.B. Madrid, Ed.
Ibéricas 1959 584p.

1994* República, trad. por Camarero A., introd. y notas
por Farré L. Buenos Aires, Eudeba 1963 543p.
Rev. RFil(La Plata) XIV 1964 103-105
Delucchi.

1995* La República. 2a ed. Col. Nuestros Clásicos XII,
Mexico City, U.N.A.M. 1963 368p.

1996* La república o el estado, vers., prol. & notas por
Palau E. 4a ed. Barcelona, Ed. Iberia 1966
384p.

III C d 36: REPUBLIC

1997* La República, trad., estudios prelim., notas y
     evocación ática de Bergua J.B. 3a ed. Madrid,
     Ed. Bergua 1966 644p.

1998* La República, ed. biling., notas & estudio prelim.
     por Pabón J.M. & Fernández Galiano M. T.I.
     Col. Clás. polít. 1a ed., 1a reimpr. Madrid,
     Inst. de Estudios polít. 1969 cxlii&104p.

1999* Πλάτωνος Πολιτεία. Platón, La República, versión,
     introd. & notas de Gómez Robledo A. Bibl.
     scriptorum graecorum et romanorum mexicana,
     Mexico City, U.N.A.M. 1971 cxxxviii&382,
     cxli-clxxxvi p.
          Rev. Dianoia XVIII 1972 328-331 Navarro.
     Dianoia XIX 1973 215-216 Aguayo Spencer.

2000* Platón, Diálogos. La República o El estado, trad.
     nuevamente rev. por Azcárate P. 4a ed. Col.
     Los Clásicos, Madrid, Edaf 1972 xxiv&1417p.

2001* La República. Col. Compendios Vosgos X, Barcelona,
     Ed. Vosgos 1972 93p.

2002* De staat, korte inhoud door Flam L. Problemen XV,
     Antwerpen, Uitg. Ontwikkeling 1961 48p.

2003* Staten, Swedish transl. by Dalsjö M., rev. and
     partly newly transl. by Tabachovitz D.
     Stockholm, Wahlström & Widstrand 1969 326p.

2004* A República, livros I, II, e III, Port. trad. de
     Espírito Santo L. do. Lisboa, Guimarães Ed.
     1965 188p.
          Rev. Humanitas XVII-XVIII 1965-1966
     259-260 da Costa Ramalho.

2005* A República (II) Livros IV, V, e VI, Port. trad.
     de Espírito Santo L. do. Lisboa, Guimarães
     1968 187p.

2006* A República, trad. de Menezes E. São Paulo, Hemus
     1970 301p.

2007* Państwo [Republic], z dodaniem siedmiu ksiag Praw,
     przekl., wstep., objaśn., illustr. Witwicki W.
     Warszawa, PWN 1958 462 & 591p.

2008* Πολιτεία, transl. into modern Greek by Gruparis
     I.N. Athens, Kollaros 1965 400p.

239

2009* Devlet [Republic], IV,2 dilim çev.   Tunga   T.
      Ankara, Maarif Basimevi 1960 63p.

2010* Devlet [Republic], çev. Eyüboğlu S. & Cimcoz A.
      Yunan ve Lâtin Klâs.   II, Istanbul, Remzi
      Kitabevi 1962 488p.

2011* Republic, Urdu transl. by Zakir H.   (taken from
      Jowett's English transl.) New Delhi, Sahitya
      Acad. 1967 xxiv&455p.

2012* Republic, Tamil transl. by Ramanujachari R.   New
      Delhi, Sahitya Akad. 1966 xx&493p.

2013* Republic, Japanese transl. and comm.   by Nagasawa
      N.   Tokai Univ. Pr.   Vol. I (books I-IV) 1970
      595p.;   vol.   II   (books   V-VIII)   1971
      pp.596-1196.

For additional texts and translations see 893, 914, 920,
      950, 971, 987, 988, 990.

B. STUDIES OF THE REPUBLIC

The large number of discussions dealing
primarily with the Republic made it imperative
to divide this section into a number of
categories.   Moreover, certain issues which are
prominent in the Republic have been placed
elsewhere. These are cross referenced below,
but the reader might wish to consult sections
V B (Metaphysics),   V C (Psychology),   V F
(Ethics), V G (Politics and Society),   V H
(Education) and V I (Aesthetics) [in this last,
cf. especially the special index on Plato's
Banishment of Poetry].

INTRODUCTIONS AND COMMENTARIES

2014* NETTLESHIP R.L., Lectures on the Republic of Plato.
      2nd edn. Papermacs XIV, New York, St. Martin's
      Pr. 1962 vii&364p.

III C d 36: REPUBLIC

2015* BOYD W., <u>An Introduction to the Republic of Plato</u>.
2nd edn. revised. London, Allen & Unwin 1962
115p. Also New York, Barnes & Noble 1963.
<u>Rev</u>. TLS 17 May 1963 362.
ModS XLII 1964-1965 332 Klubertanz.

2016* FEHL N.E., <u>A Guide to the Study of Plato's Republic</u>;
and <u>the Euthyphro, Apology and Laws X</u>. 2nd edn.
Philosophy of Life Ser. 1, Hong Kong, Chung Chi
College, Ma Liu Shui, N.T. 1962 102p.
<u>Rev</u>. Personalist XLIV 1963 391
Mollenhauer.

2017* FLAM L., <u>Plato, De Staat</u>. <u>Korte inhoud</u>. 2e,
aangevulde dr. Problemen XV, Antwerpen,
Ontwikkeling 1962 56p.

2018* CROSS R.C. & WOOZLEY A.D., <u>Plato's Republic</u>. A
<u>Philosophical Commentary</u>. London, Macmillan and
New York, St. Martin's Pr. 1964 xv&295p.
Chap. 5, "Knowledge, Belief and the Forms"
reprinted p.70-96 in <u>Plato I</u>, ed. by Vlastos G.
(see 4619).
<u>Rev</u>. PhilosQ XIV 1964 368-370 Crombie.
Mind LXXIV 1965 599-606 Mitchell.
CF XIX 1965 67-68 Anscombe.
Hermathena CI 1965 73-74 Luce.
CW LVIII 1965 221-222 Anton.
TLS 5 Nov. 1964 1004.
LJ 1964 1587 O'Brien.
PhilosBks Oct 1964 312 Hamlyn.
VQR 1965 xxvi.
AusJP 1965 261 Howes.
HeythropJ VI 1965 106-107 T.G.
Augustinus X 1965 122 Oroz Reta.
EPh XIX 1964 606-607 Moreau.
Dialogue III 1964 327-329 Malcolm.
PhilosRdschau XIII 1965-1966 80 Kuhn.
PhR LXXV 1966 405-407 Demos.
Phoenix XX 1966 251-253 Sparshott.
RF LVIII 1967 92-93 Cambiano.
GM XXII 1967 270-272 Deregibus.
Maia XX 1968 77-78 Moreschini.

2019* PROCLUS, <u>Procli Diadochi in Platonis Rem Publicam
Commentarii</u>, ed. Kroll G. 2 vols. Reprint of
Leipzig edn. 1899, 1901. Amsterdam, Hakkert
1965 vii&296, ix&476p.

2020* PROCLUS, <u>Commentaire sur la République</u>, trad. et
notes par Festugière A.J. 3 vols. Bibl. des
textes philosophiques, Paris, Vrin 1970 221, 195

241

III C d 36: REPUBLIC

    & 384p.

2021   GALLAVOTTI C., "Intorno ai commenti di Proclo alla Repubblica". BPEC XIX 1971 41-54.

2022* AVERROES, Averroes' Commentary on Plato's Republic, ed. with intro., transl., & notes by Rosenthal E.I.J. Repr. corr. & augm. Cambridge Univ. Oriental Publ. I, Cambridge, Univ. Pr. 1966 viii&339p.
        Rev. RecSR LIV 1966 616 des Places.

2023* HAGERTY T., Review notes and Study Guide to the Republic and the Dialogues of Plato. New York, Monarch Pr. 1966 112p.

WORKS ON THE REPUBLIC AS A WHOLE

2024   GREENE W.C., "The Paradoxes of the Republic". HSPh LXIII 1958 (Stud. Jaeger) 199-216.

2025   PLACES E. DES, "Los últimos temas de la República de Platón". transl. by Disandro C.A. RevE III 1958 23-29.

2026   HOERBER R.G., "Note on the Structure of the Republic". Phronesis VI 1961 37-40.

2027   MAZZANTINI C., "La Repubblica di Platone". p.1-63 in Esposizione critica di opere filosofiche, a cura di diversi autori. Orientamenti filosofici e pedagogici II, Milano, Marzorati 1962 vii&440p.

2028   RANKIN H.D., "Dream-vision as Philosophical Modifier in Plato's Republic". Eranos LXII 1964 75-83.

2029   GALLOP D., "Image and Reality in Plato's Republic". AGPh XLVII 1965 113-131.

2030   SCARCELLA A.M., Platone, Lo Stato. I class. greci, Roma, Signorelli [1966?] 93p.

2031   BRANN E., "The Music of the Republic". Agon I 1967 1-117.

2032 BRUMBAUGH R.S., "A new Interpretation of Plato's Republic". JPh LXIV 1967 661-670.

2033 IGAL ALFARO J., "El concepto physis en la República de Platón". Pensamiento XXIII 1967 407-436.

2034 SCIACCA M.F., "Sommario dei Libri II-V della 'Repubblica'"; "Note ai libri VI e VII della "Repubblica'"; "Sommario dei libri VIII-X della 'Repubblica'". p.323-331, 332-358, 359-363 in Sciacca M.F., Platone I (see 64). Reprinted from Sciacca M.F., Platone, Della Repubblica, Libri VI e VII. Napoli, Perrella 1935.

2035 CURCIO C., "Rileggendo la Repubblica di Platone". RIFD XLV 1968 498-523.

2036 RANKIN H.D., "A Modest Proposal about the Republic". Apeiron II,2 1968 20-22.

2037 UCHIYAMA K., "Through Politeia. An Essay on early Plato" [in Japanese]. Methodos II 1969.

2038 ADORNO F., "Uberti Decembris Prologus in Platone De Republica. Georgii Trapezuntii Praefatio in libros Platonis De Legibus". p.7-17 in Studi in onore di Antonio Corsano. Univ. di Bari Fac. di Lett. e Filos., Manduria, Lacaita ed. 1970.

2039* MILLS D.H., Image and Symbol in Plato's Republic. Diss. Univ. of Iowa 1971 384p. [microfilm]. Summary in DA XXXII 1971 1492A.

2040 WARTOFSKY M.W., "The Republic as Myth. The Dilemma of Philosophy and Politics". PhilosForum X 1971 249-266.

2041* Plato's Republic: the Greek Text. Vol. II: Essays, introd. with notes & essays by Jowett B. & Campbell L. New York, Arno Pr. 1973 xxxiv&356p. Reprint of 1894 edn.

REPUBLIC I

2042 VRETSKA K., "Platonica, III". WS LXXI 1958 30-54.

III C d 36: REPUBLIC

2043 MITSUI K., "Justice and Hope in Plato's early Philosophy. A Study of Politeia I" [in Japanese]. PhSJap I 1960.

2044 VASMANOLIS G.E., "Παρατηρήσεις εἰς τὰ δύο πρῶτα βιβλία τῆς Πλάτωνος Πολιτείας". Platon XVI 1964 175-204. Also reprinted separately: Athens, Sideri 1964.

2045 NACHMAN L.D., "A Prelude to the Republic". CW LIX 1966 301-304.

2046 SESONSKE A., "Plato's Apology, Republic I". Phronesis VI 1961 29-36. Reprinted p.40-47 in Plato's Republic, ed. by Sesonske A. (see 4614).

2047* SZE C.V.P., Plato's Republic I. Its Function in the Dialogue as a Whole. Diss. Yale Univ. 1971 255p. [microfilm]. Summary in DA XXXII 1972 6951A.

2048 KAYSER J.R., "Prologue to the Study of Justice: Republic 327a-328b". WPolQ XXIII 1970 256-265.

2049 SCIACCA M.F., "Il problema della giustizia nel libro I della 'Repubblica'". p.296-323 in Sciacca M.F., Platone I (see 64). Reprinted from Sciacca M.F., Studi sulla filos. antica. Napoli, Perella 1935.

2050 JOSEPH H.W.B., "The Argument with Polemarchus". p.6-16 in Plato's Republic, ed. by Sesonske A. (see 4614). Reprinted from Joseph H.W.B., Ancient and Modern Philosophy, Oxford 1935, p.1-14.

2051 HARRISON E.L., "A Red Herring in Plato's Republic". Eranos LX 1962 122-126.

2052 HOURANI G.F., "Thrasymachus' Definition of Justice in Plato's Republic". Phronesis VII 1962 110-120.

2053 KERFERD G.B., "Thrasymachus and Justice. A Reply". Phronesis IX 1964 12-16.

2054 KING-FARLOW J. & ROTHSTEIN J.M., "Paradigm Cases and the Injustice to Thrasymachus". PhilosQ XIV 1964 15-22.

2055 IKUSHIMA K., "An Analysis of the Dispute between Thrasymachus and Socrates in Book A of Plato's Republic" [in Japanese with English summary]. JCS XIII 1965 87-97.

2056 BARKER E., "Thrasymachus' Conception of Justice". p.17-20 in Plato's Republic, ed. by Sesonske A. (see 4614). Reprinted from Barker E., The Political Thought of Plato and Aristotle. New York 1906 p.94-99.

2057 SPARSHOTT F.E., "Socrates and Thrasymachus". Monist L 1966 421-459.

2058 HARRISON E.L., "Plato's Manipulation of Thrasymachus". Phoenix XXI 1967 27-39.

2059 DAVIS L.D., "The Arguments of Thrasymachus in the first Book of Plato's Republic". ModS XLVII 1970 423-432.

2060 HENDERSON T.Y., "In Defense of Thrasymachus". APQ VII 1970 218-228.

2061 KAHN C.H., "On the Interpretation of Thrasymachus in Republic I". Summary p.125-126 in Die Interpretation in der Altertumswiss. Ansprachen zur Eröffnung des 5. Kongr. der Fédération Internat. des Assoc. d'études clas. Bonn, 1.-6. Sept. 1969, hrsg. von Schmid W. Bonn, Bouvier 1971.

2062 MAGUIRE J.P., "Thrasymachus...or Plato?". Phronesis XVI 1971 142-163.

2063 HADGOPOULOS D.J., "Thrasymachus and Legalism". Phronesis XVIII 1973 204-208.

For further discussions see 262, 2448, 2767, 3508, 3509, 3514.

THE PROBLEM OF THE REPUBLIC

2064 KIRWAN C., "Glaucon's Challenge". Phronesis X 1965 162-173.

2065 NETTLESHIP R.L., "Statement of the Problem of the
       Republic". p.48-57 in Plato's Republic, ed.
       Sesonske A. (see 4614). Reprinted from
       Nettleship R.L., Lectures on the Republic of
       Plato. New York 1901 p.47-66.

                EDUCATION IN THE REPUBLIC

2066* NETTLESHIP R.L., La teoria dell'educazione nella
       Repubblica di Platone, trad. di Zampetti M.A.
       Educatori antichi e moderni No.249, Firenze, La
       Nuova Italia 1970 vi&136p.

2067 BROWN J., "Plato's Republic as an Early Study of
       Media Bias and a Charter for Prosaic Education".
       AmerAnthropol LXXIV 1972 672-675.

2068* BOSANQUET B., The Education of the Young in the
       Republic of Plato, transl. with notes and
       intro. by Bosanquet B. Folcroft Pa., Folcroft
       Lib. Eds. 1973. Reprint of 1917 edn.

2069 TOURLIDES G.A., "Ἡ παιδαγωγική ἀρχή περί τῆς ἐκλογῆς
       τῆς ὕλης κατά τήν Πολιτείαν τοῦ Πλάτωνος Β΄
       377-383". p.4-12 in Tourlides G.A., Φιλολογικά
       καί ἱστορικά μελετήματα. Athens 1973.

          THEORY OF THE SOUL AND HUMAN NATURE

2070 JAEGER W., "A new Greek Word in Plato's Republic.
       The Medical Origin of the Theory of the
       θυμοειδές". p.309-316 in Jaeger W., Scripta
       Minora II (see 4605). Reprinted from Eranos
       Rudbergianus XLIV, Gotoburgi 1946 123-130.

2071 ROBINSON T.M., "Soul and Immortality in Republic X".
       Phronesis XII 1967 147-151.

2072 KENNY A.J.P., "Mental Health in Plato's Republic".
       PBA LV 1969 229-253. Also printed as a
       monograph of the same title: London, Oxford
       Univ. Pr. 1969.

III C d 36: REPUBLIC

2073 YAMAUCHI T., "The Nature of the Soul in Plato's Republic. Harmonia and Phronesis" [in Japanese with German summary]. MOsaka XIX 1970 39-53.

2074 ROBINSON R., "Plato's Separation of Reason from Desire". Phronesis XVI 1971 38-48.

2075 SPARSHOTT F.E., "The Truth about Gods and Men". Dialogue X 1971 3-11.

2076* GILLESPIE A., The Just Man in the Just State. A Study of the Psychology of Plato's Republic in relation to its Political Philosophy. Diss. Univ. of Texas 1971 126p. [microfilm]. Summary in DA XXXII 1972 5759A.

2077 SHINER R.A., "Soul in Republic X,611". Apeiron VI,2 1972 23-30.

2078 STROLL A., "On a certain Tension in Plato's Republic". Dialogue XI 1972 499-508.

2079 HENIGAN D., "Plato's Theory of the Tripartite Soul: The Argument and its Implications". UJPhilos V 1973 10-21.

2080 WILLIAMS B., "The Analogy of City and Soul in Plato's Republic". p.196-206 in Exegesis and Argument, ed. by Lee E.N. et al. (see 4608).

For additional discussions see 3045, 3047, 3062, 3576, 3725, 4126.

ETHICS IN THE REPUBLIC

2081 MARGOLIS J., "Kafka vs. eudaimonia and duty". Ph&PhenR XIX 1958 27-42.

2082 DEMOS R., "A Note on Plato's Republic". RM XII 1958-1959 300-307.

2083 HALL R.W., "Justice and the Individual in the Republic". Phronesis IV 1959 149-158.

2084 HOERBER R.G., "More on the Justice in the Republic". Phronesis V 1960 32-34.

2085 SKEMP J.B., "Comment on Communal and Individual
      Justice in the Republic". Phronesis V 1960
      35-38.

2086 JOLY R., "La caractérologie antique jusqu'à
      Aristote". RBPh XL 1962 5-28.

2087 ÉTIENNE J., "Éléments pour une morale platonicienne
      fondamentale. Une lecture de la République".
      RPhL LXI 1963 537-560.

2088 SACHS D., "A Fallacy in Plato's Republic". PhR
      LXXII 1963 141-158. Reprinted p.66-81 in
      Plato's Republic, ed. by Sesonske A. (see
      4614); p.35-51 in Plato II, ed. by Vlastos G.,
      (see 4620).

2089 DEMOS R., "A Fallacy in Plato's Republic?" PhR
      LXXIII 1964 395-398. Reprinted p.52-56 in Plato
      II, ed. by Vlastos G. (see 4620).

2090 HASSEL D.J., "Επιτήδευμα or civic Vocation in
      Plato's Republic". ModS XLI 1964 145-157.

2091 SHIKIBU H., "Pleasure and Human Nature in the
      Republic. Plato's Argument concerning Pleasure,
      II" [in Japanese]. Annals of Ethics (Japanese
      Society of Ethics) XIII 1964.

2092 WEINGARTNER R.H., "Vulgar Justice and Platonic
      Justice". Ph&PhenR XXV 1964 248-252.

2093* COBB W.S., The Relationship between Internal and
      Social Justice in Plato's Republic. Diss.
      Vanderbilt Univ. 1966 192p. [microfilm].
      Summary in DA XXVII 1966 795a-796a.

2094 DUERING I., "Individual and Social Ethics in Plato
      and Aristotle" [in Swedish with English
      summary]. Ajatus XXVIII 1966 63-88.

2095 PRICHARD H.A., "Justice in the Republic". p.58-65
      in Plato's Republic, ed. by Sesonske A. (see
      4614). Reprinted from Prichard H.A., Moral
      Obligation. Oxford 1949, p.103-111.

2096 RANKIN H.D., "Plato, Republic 409a1-b2. An
      Intersection of Themes". AClass IX 1966
      143-147.

III C d 36: REPUBLIC

2097 HALL R.W., "Plato's Theory of Justice in the Republic". BR XV 1967 59-69.

2098* WILLIAMSON R.B., The Ambiguity of δικαιοσύνη in Plato's Republic. Diss. Univ. of Virginia 1967 269p. [microfilm]. Summary in DA XXVIII 1968 3721A.

2099 MORI S., "Injustice in books VIII-IX of Plato's Republic" [in Japanese]. Kansai Medical School Liberal Arts Dept. Bulletin 1968.

2100 HALL R.W., "Plato's Just Man: Thoughts on Strauss' Plato". NS XLII 1968 202-225.

2101 ANSBRO J.J., "Plato's Just Man: A Re-examination". NS XLIV 1970 278-285.

2102 HALL R.W., "Plato's Just Man: A Second Look". NS XLVI 1972 352-367.

2103 ANSBRO J.J., "Plato's just Man: A Rejoinder". NS XLVII 1973 490-500.

2104 MULGAN R.G., "Individual and Collective Virtues in the Republic". Phronesis XIII 1968 84-87.

2105 SCHILLER J., "Just Men and just Acts in Plato's Republic". JHPh VI 1968 1-14.

2106 VLASTOS G., "The Argument in the Republic that Justice Pays". JPh LXV 1968 665-674.

2107 SKEMP J.B., "Individual and Civic Virtue in the Republic". Phronesis XIV 1969 107-110.

2108 VLASTOS G., "Justice and Psychic Harmony in the Republic". JPh LXVI 1969 505-521.

2109 WRÓBLEWSKI W., "Z problemu arete w 'Politei' Platonskiej [The Problem of arete in Plato's Republic]". Polskie Towarzystwo Filozoficne, Krakow, 28.10.1967 Autorref. RuchFil XXVII 1969 152-153.

2110 CASSIN C.E., "Civic Sophrosyne and Dikaiosyne in the Republic". JCritA III 1971 56-66.

2111 MABBOTT J.B., "Is Plato's Republic Utilitarian?". p.57-66 in Plato II, ed. by Vlastos G. (see 4620). Revised version of a paper originally published in Mind 1937 386-393.

2112 HALL R.W., "The just and happy Man of the Republic.
      Fact or Fallacy?". JHPh IX 1971 147-158.

2113 VLASTOS G., "Justice and Happiness in the Republic".
      p.66-95 in Plato II, ed. by Vlastos G. (see
      4620). Reprinted p.111-139 in Vlastos G.,
      Platonic Studies (see 4622).

2114* BEATTY J., A Consideration of Plato's Argument for
      Justice in the Republic. Diss. Northwestern
      Univ. 1972 263p. [microfilm]. Summary in DA
      XXXIII 1972 2974A.

2115 HALL R.W., "Egalitarianism and Justice in the
      Republic". Apeiron VI,2 1972 7-19.

2116 KRAUT R., "Reason and Justice in Plato's Republic".
      p.207-224 in Exegesis and Argument, ed. by Lee
      E.N. et al. (see 4608).

2117 SARTORIUS R., "Fallacy and Political Radicalism in
      Plato's Republic". CanJPh III 1973-1974
      349-363.

2118 WATERLOW S., "The good of others in Plato's
      Republic". PAS LXXIII 1973 19-36.

For additional discussions see 670, 2091, 3456, 3474,
      3474, 3479, 3497, 3518, 3644, 3716, 4055.

THE IDEAL STATE IN THE REPUBLIC

2119 YAMANO K., "The ideal State in Plato's Republic.
      Its Interpretation through the Analogy of State
      and Individual" [in Japanese with English
      summary]. JCS VII 1959 73-90.

2120 CHROUST A.H., "Who is the Platonic Philosopher
      King?". NS XXXIV 1960 499-505.

2121 WELSKOPF E.C., "Zum Generationenproblem bei Hesiod
      und Platon". p.301-307 in Neue Beitr. zur
      Gesch. der alten Welt. Zweite Internaz.
      Tagung der Fachgruppe Alte Geschichte der
      Deutschen Historiker Gesellschaft vom 4. bis 8.
      September 1962 in Stralsund. I: Alter Orient
      und Griechenland, in Verb. mit Diesner H.J.,
      Guenther R., Mathwich J. & Schrot G. hrsg.

III C d 36: REPUBLIC

von Welskopf E.C. Berlin, Akad.-Verl. 1964.

2122 JANKE W., "Ἀληθεστάτη τραγῳδία. Eine Deutung der Metabole-Reihe im 8. Buch des Staates". AGPh XLVII 1965 251-260.

2123 RANKIN H.D., "Παράδειγμα and Realizability in Plato's Republic". Eranos LXIII 1965 120-133.

2124 RANKIN H.D., "Plato's eugenic εὐφημία and ἀπόθεσις in Republic, Book V". Hermes XCIII 1965 407-420.

2125 GOROSPE V.R., "Plato's Natural-law Theory in the Republic". ModS XLIII 1966 143-178.

2126 HAMMOND L.M., "Classes and Functions in Plato's Republic". SoJP IV 1966 242-247.

2127 NAKAMURA K., "Κατὰ φύσιν οἰκισθεῖσα πόλις. Plato's Republic 428e. On the φύσις of Man in Plato's Republic" [in Japanese]. Hokkaido Univ. Dept. of Literature Bulletin XV,1 1966.

2128 HALL R.W., "On the Myth of the Metals in the Republic". Apeiron I,2 1967 28-32.

2129 LEOTTA M., "L'autonomia dei distinti nella Repubblica di Platone". RivStCroc IV 1967 1733-185.

2130 NEUMANN H., "Plato's Republic: Utopia or Dystopia?". ModS XLIV 1967 319-330.

2131 RADEMACHER U., "Demokratie und Tyrannis in Platons 'Staat'". AU Reihe 11, Heft 5 1968 30-47.

2132 VLASTOS G., "Does Slavery exist in Plato's Republic?". CPh LXIII 1968 291-295. Reprinted p.140-146 in Vlastos G., Platonic Studies (see 4622).

2133 JÓZEFOWICZ M., "De fontibus quibus usus est Plato in compositione Politeiae" [in Polish with Latin summary]. Meander XXIV 1969 452-460.

2134 DESPOTOPOULOS C., "La cité parfaite de Platon et l'esclavage. Sur République 433d". REG LXXXIII 1970 26-37.

III C d 36: REPUBLIC

2135 OSTWALD M., "The two States in Plato's Republic".
p.316-327 in Essays in ancient Greek Philosophy,
ed. by Anton J.P. & Kustas G.L. (see 4581).

2136 GIGON O., "Timokratie und Oligarchie in Platons
Politeia". , p.75-95 in Τιμητικὸν ἀφιέρωμα
Κωνσταντίνῳ Ι. Μερεντίτη. Festschrift für K.J.
Merentitis. Athens 1972.

For additional discussions see 174, 442, 2878, 3522, 3542,
3547, 3548, 3550, 3579, 3587, 3600, 3615, 3625,
3662, 3680, 3681, 3687, 3698, 3712, 3717, 3734,
3759, 3760, 3763.

SUN, LINE AND CAVE

2137 BORMANN K., "Zu Platon, Politeia 514b8-515a3". AGPh
XLIII 1961 1-14.

2138 FERGUSON J., "Sun, Line and Cave Again". CQ XIII
1963 188-193.

2139 NITTA H., "The Problems of the three Analogies and
Philosophy in Republic VI-VII. Hypothesis and
Eidos" [in Japanese]. Methodos I 1968.

2140 IMASATO M., "The Three Analogies in the Republic"
[in Japanese]. Methodos II 1969.

2141 TANNER R.G., "Διάνοια and Plato's Cave". CQ XX 1970
81-91.

2142 FOGELIN R.J., "Three Platonic Analogies". PhR LXXX
1971 371-382.

2143* SCHMITZ-MOORMANN K., Die Ideenlehre Platons im
Lichte des Sonnengleichnisses des sechsten
Buches des Staates. Diss. München 1957.
Münster, Kramer 1959 104p.

2144 LUTHER W., "Wahrheit, Licht, Sehen und Erkennen im
Sonnengleichnis von Platons Politeia. Ein
Ausschnitt aus der Lichtmetaphysik der
Griechen". StudGen XVIII 1965 479-496.

2145 ROSS W.D., "The Sun and the Idea of Good". p.98-102
in Plato's Republic, ed. by Sesonske A. (see
4614). Reprinted from Ross W.D., Plato's Theory

of Ideas, 2nd edn. Oxford 1953 p.39-44.

2146 SAITO N., "Two kinds of ἀλήθεια. How shall we read the Passage called the Analogy of the Sun in Plato's Republic?" [in Japanese with English summary]. JCS XVI 1968 66-74.

2147 KUKUTSU K., "Analogies concerning the Idea of the Good. Plato's Republic 504a-519b" [in Japanese]. Methodos IV 1971.

2148 HAMLYN D.W., "Eikasia in Plato's Republic". PhilosQ VIII 1958 14-23.

2149 BRUMBAUGH R.S., "Plato and the History of Science". StudGen XIV 1961 520-527.

2150 SCHUHL P.M., "Carnet de notes". RPhilos LXXXVII 1962 371-382.

2151 MALCOLM J.F., "The Line and the Cave". Phronesis VII 1962 38-45.

2152 BRENTLINGER J.A., "The Divided Line and Plato's Theory of Intermediates". Phronesis VIII 1963 146-166.

2153 ROSE L.E., "Plato's Divided Line". RM XVII 1964 425-435.

2154 CORNFORD F.M., "Mathematics and Dialectic in the Republic VI-VII". p.61-95 in Studies in Plato's Metaphysics, ed. by Allen R.E. (see 4580). Reprinted from Mind 1932.

2155 HARE R.M., "Plato and the Mathematicians". p.21-38 in New Essays on Plato and Aristotle, ed. by Bambrough R. (see 4582).

2156 TAYLOR C.C.W., "Plato and the Mathematicians. An Examination of Professor Hare's Views". PhilosQ XVII 1967 193-203.

2157 NETTLESHIP R.L., "The Four Stages of Intelligence". p.103-115 in Plato's Republic, ed. Sesonske A. (see 4614). Reprinted from Nettleship R.L., Lectures on the Republic of Plato. New York 1901 238-258.

2158 DAVIES J.C., "Plato's Dialectic. Some Thoughts on the 'Line'". Orpheus XIV 1967 3-11.

2159* WEINER N.O., The Divided Line, the Convening Art and the Dramatic Structure of Plato's Republic. Diss. Univ. of Texas Austin 1969 330p. [microfilm]. Summary in DA XXX 1969 1604A.

2160 WU J.S., "A Note on the third Section of the Divided Line". NS XLIII 1969 269-275.

2161 GOLDSCHMIDT V., "La ligne de la République et la classification des sciences". p.203-219 in Goldschmidt V., Questions platoniciennes (see 4598). Reprinted from RIPh XXXII 1955 237ff.

2162 BRUMBAUGH R.S., "The Divided Line and the Direction of Inquiry". PhilosForum II 1970-1971 172-199.

2163 POMEROY S.B., "Optics and the Line in Plato's Republic". CQ XXI 1971 389-392.

2164 MACIEL J., "Sobra a theoria da relação, II". RBF XXII 1972 439-457.

2165* BALINSKY M.A., Plato's Divided Line. Diss. Univ. of Rochester, New York 1973 239p. [microfilm]. Summary in DA XXXIV 1973 2691A-2692A.

2166 BOYLE A.J., "Plato's Divided Line, essay I: The Problem of Dianoia". Apeiron VII 1973 1-11; "Essay II: Mathematics and Dialectic". Ibid. 11-18; "Appendix: The Function and Significance of the Line". Ibid. 19-21.

2167* MARTIN-DESLIAS N., Le mythe de la caverne. Coll. Pensées, Paris, Nagel 1959 87p.

2168 SCHUHL P.M., "Carnet de notes". RPhilos CL 1960 229-236.

2169 FAURE P., "Le mythe platonicien de la caverne et la Crète". Summary in REG LXXV 1962 p.xvi-xviii.

2170 WESTPHALEN K., "Platons Höhlengleichnis. Ein Beispiel für philosophische Propädeutik im Griechischunterricht". Anregung XII 1966 98-104.

2171 CHAUVOIS L., "Le 'cinéma populaire' en Grèce au temps de Platon et sa projection dans l'allégorie de la 'caverne aux idées'". RGSPA LXXIV 1967 193-196.

III C d 36: REPUBLIC

2172 DAVIES J., "A Note on the Philosopher's Descent into the Cave". Philologus CXII 1968 121-126.

2173 KLAER I., "Die Schatten im Höhlengleichnis und die Sophisten im homerischen Hades". AGPh LI 1969 225-259.

2174 FLEISCHER M., "Die zweifache Periagoge in Platons Höhlengleichnis". ZPhF XXIV 1970 489-498.

2175 NÉDONCELLE M., "Les données auditives et le problème du langage dans l'allégorie de la caverne". RSR XLIV 1970 165-178. Reprinted p.185-199 in Nédoncelle M., Explorations personnalistes (see 4610).

2176 LIER H., "Zur Struktur des platonischen Höhlengleichnisses". Hermes XCIX 1971 209-216.

For additional discussions see 209, 587, 2694, 2786, 2864, 3006, 3117, 3976.

OTHER WORKS ON THE EPISTEMOLOGY AND METAPHYSICS OF THE REPUBLIC

2177 BECKER O., "Erwiderung". RhM CII 1959 288.

2178 VRETSKA K., "Nochmals zu Platon, Pol. 514B". RhM CII 1959 286-287.

2179 GOSLING J., "Republic, Book V: Τὰ πολλὰ καλά, etc.". Phronesis V 1960 116-128.

2180 ALLEN R.E., "The Argument from opposites in Republic V". RM XV 1961-1962 325-335. Also p.165-175 in Essays in Ancient Greek Philosophy, ed. by Anton J.P. & Kustas G.L. (see 4581).

2181 BAUMGARTNER H.M., "Von der Möglichkeit, das Agathon als Prinzip zu denken. Versuch einer transzendentalen Interpretation zu Politeia 509b". p.89-101 in Parusia, hrsg. von Flasch K. (see 4588).

2182 COOPER N., "The Importance of διάνοια in Plato's Theory of Forms". CQ XVI 1966 65-69.

255

2183* UTERMOEHLEN O., Die Bedeutung der Ideenlehre für die platonische Politeia. Bibl. des klass. Altertumswiss. N.F. 2.R. XX, Heidelberg, Winter 1967 112p.
Rev. CW LXI 1968 183-184 Sparshott.
Gnomon XL 1968 828-829 Easterling.
REA LXX 1968 166 Moreau.
AC XXXVII 1968 286 Freund.
CR XIX 1969 108-109 Gulley.
Gymnasium LXXVI 1969 99-100 Schaefer.

2184 DUFF-FORBES D.R., "The Regress Argument in the Republic". Mind LXXVII 1968 406-410.

2185 CROMBIE I.M., "Duff-Forbes on Republic 10". Mind LXXX 1971 286-287.

2186 MILLS K.W., "Crombie on Republic 597c". Mind LXXXII 1973 602-603.

2187 ASANO N., "The Object of διάνοια in Plato's Politeia" [in Japanese]. Methodos I 1968.

2188 GOSLING J.C., "Δόξα and δύναμις in Plato's Republic". Phronesis XIII 1968 119-130.

2189 KUBO Y., "On the Object of διάνοια" [in Japanese]. Methodos I 1968.

2190 KRAEMER H.J., "Ἐπέκεινα τῆς οὐσίας. Zu Platon, Politeia 509b". AGPh LI 1969 1-30.

2191 MILLS K.W., "Plato's 'Non-Hypothetical Starting Point'". DUJ XXXI 1970 152-159.

2192* PHILLIPS A.M., The Theory of Intuition in Plato's Republic. Diss. Michigan State Univ. 1969 274p. [microfilm]. Summary in DA XXX 1970 3055A-3056A.

2193 ROBINSON R., "Hypothesis in the Republic". p.97-131 in Plato I, ed. by Vlastos G. (see 4619). Reprint of Robinson R., Plato's Earlier Dialectic 2nd edn. 1953, ch.10.

2194 STRYCKER E. DE, "L'idée du Bien dans la République de Platon". AC XXXIX 1970 450-467.

2195 VOGEL C.J. DE, "Encore une fois, le bien dans la République de Platon". p.40-56 in Zetesis (see 4579).

III C d 36: REPUBLIC

2196 KOUMAKIS G.C., "Τὸ πρόβλημα τῆς ἰδέας τοῦ ἀγαθοῦ εἰς τὴν Πολιτείαν τοῦ Πλάτωνος". Platon XXIII 1971 108-114.

2197 PHILIPPOUSSIS J., "La gnoséologie de Platon selon la République. Connaissance et dialectique". p.90-95 in La communication. Actes du XVe Congr. Assoc. Soc. Philos. de langue française. Pensée antique et communication. Montréal, Éditions Montmorency 1971.

2198 ROHATYN D.A. & RUDAITIS J.R., "A Paradox in Plato's Republic". Gymnasium LXXIX 1972 512-513.

For additional discussions see 2182, 2266, 2757, 2779, 2786, 2840, 2922, 2948, 3001, 3022, 3025, 3977, 4008.

REPUBLIC X

2199* ELSE G.F., The Structure and Date of Book 10 of Plato's Republic. AHAW 1972,3, Heidelberg, Winter 1972 74p.

2200 LIEB I.C., "Philosophy as Spiritual Formation: Plato's Myth of Er". IPQ III 1963 271-285.

For additional discussions of Book X see 549, 2184, 2185, 2186, 3225.

For discussions of the Republic which do not fall under the above categories see 27, 89, 173, 239, 265, 327, 373, 443, 486, 516, 522, 760, 829, 1359, 1549, 1739, 1778, 2183, 2484, 2586, 2589, 2590, 2603, 2605, 2616, 2617, 2618, 2644, 2661, 2675, 2692, 2695, 2702, 2721, 2725, 2728, 2733, 2797, 2804, 2912, 3073, 3090, 3094, 3116, 3254, 3259, 3300, 3301, 3307, 3318, 3323, 3334, 3335, 3336, 3340, 3354, 3404, 3447, 3536, 3539, 3560, 3572, 3586, 3639, 3673, 3688, 3697, 3784, 3792, 3794, 3797, 3799, 3803, 3817, 3886, 3897, 3935, 3961, 4107, 4125.

III C d 36: REPUBLIC

C. TEXTUAL CRITICISM

2201 BORMANN K., "Zu Platon, Politeia 461a5-b2". AGPh
XLII 1960 304.

2202 PASOLI E., "Varia philologica". Latinitas VIII 1960
29-36.

2203 KASSEL R., "Drei Platonemendationen". RhM CIV 1961
125-127.

2204 LACROIX M., "Remarques sur deux textes: Sophocle,
Antigone, 683 sq. et Platon, République VI,
492c". Summary in REG LXXIV 1961 p.xiii-xiv.

2205 SOLMSEN F., "Republic III, 389b2-d6. Plato's Draft
and the Editor's Mistake". Philologus CIX 1965
182-185. Reprinted p.55-58 in Solmsen F.,
Kleine Schriften II (see 4615).

2206 LOGOTHETOS K.I., "Κριτικα και ἑρμηνευτικα εἰς χωρία
Πλατωνικά".Platon XVIII 1966 3-18.

2207 MOULINIER L., "Platon, République 349b-350c". REG
LXXX 1967 227-233.

2208 HENRY A.S., "Plato Republic 328c". RhM CXI 1968
93-94.

2209 AMIT M., "Plato, Republic 566e". CR XIX 1969 4-6.

2210 DESJARDINS G., "A Gloss on Republic 487c". p.1-11
in Ancients and Moderns, ed. by Ryan J.K.
Studies in Philosophy and the History of
Philosophy V, Washington, The Catholic Univ. of
America Pr. 1970.

2211* SAUVANTIDIS G.P., Ἀπὸ τὴ χειρόγραφη παράδοση της
Πολιτείας τοῦ Πλάτωνος. Σχέση τοῦ κώδ. Τ
(Venetus App. Class. 4,1) μὲ τὸν κώδ. Α
(Parisinus 1807). Διόρθωση στὸ 509d τῆς
Πολιτείας. Ioannina 1970 43p.
Rev. Hellenica XXIV 1971 409-412 Atsalos.
Platon XXII 1970 Nos.43-44 358-359
Georgountzos.

2212 BASTA DONZELLI G., "Osservazioni al testo di
Platone, Repubblica X,601d". p.19-25 in Studi
classici in onore di Quintino Cataudella, II.
Catania, Fac. di Lett. e Filos. 1972.

III C d 36: REPUBLIC

2213 BERTI E., "Plato, Res publica 563d". RFIC CI 1973
     301-302.

For additional discussion of the text see 1360.

SOPHIST

A. TEXTS AND TRANSLATIONS

2214* Sophistes, griech.-dt. 3. neubearb. Aufl. von
       Wiehl R. Philos Bibl. Nr. 265, Hamburg,
       Meiner 1967 xlviii&215p.

2215* Sofista, trad., introd. e note di Riverso E.
       Class. di filos. e pedag., Torino, Ist.
       editoriale del Mezzogiorno 1964 127p.

2216* Il Sofista, trad. di Gentile M., a cura di Plebe A.
       Pensatori antichi e mod. LXVI, Firenze, La
       Nuova Italia 1965 xxiii&115p.

2217* Sofista, a cura di Arangio-Ruiz V. 2a ed. Piccola
       bibl. filos. Laterza XXX, Bari, Laterza 1968
       235p.

2218* El Sofista, ed. crít., trad., prólogo y notas por
       Tovar A. Clás. Polít., Madrid, Inst. de
       Estud. Polít. 1959 xxxv&102p.
       Rev. EClas V 1960 No.31 460 Rico.
       Arbor XLVIII 1961 373-374 Rodríguez
       Adrados.
       Helmantica XII 1961 145 Basabe.
       RyF CLXIII 1961 430 J.I.
       SicGymn XV 1962 258-259 Cataudella.

2219* Sophistes, Turkish transl. by Karasan M. 2nd edn.
       Yunan klâsikleri XVI, Ankara, Millî Eğitim
       Basimevi 1967 xl&121p.

For additional texts and translations see 855, 867, 915,
     916, 923, 926, 940, 944, 952, 971, 972.

B. STUDIES OF THE SOPHIST

The works in the present section are arranged in three categories. First, those few dealing with the dialogue as a whole. Second, the small number concerning the discussion at the beginning of the dialogue (to 231b). Third, those treating the remainder of the dialogue. The nature of this part of the dialogue made it impracticable to divide the entries further, despite their large number.

2220 GIORGIANTONIO M., "Sulla via delle teorie definitive di Platone". Sophia XXVII 1959 114-119.

2221 BONITZ H., "Sophistes". p.152-209 in Bonitz H., Platonische Studien (see 4584).

2222 LI CARRILLO V., "Las definiciones del Sofista". Episteme (Caracas) III 1959-1960 83-188.

2223 BENARDETE S., "Plato, Sophist 223b1-7". Phronesis V 1960 129-139.

2224 ALBURY W.R., "Hunting the Sophist". Apeiron V 1971 1-11.

2225 GOOCH P.W., "Vice is Ignorance. The Interpretation of Sophist 226a-231b". Phoenix XXV 1971 124-133.

2226 OSCANYAN F.S., "On six Definitions of the Sophist: Sophist 221c-231e". PhilosForum IV 1972-1973 241-259.

2227 MALVERNE L., "Remarques sur le Sophiste". RMM LXIII 1958 149-166.

2228 MORAVCSIK J.M.E., "Mr. Xenakis on truth and meaning". Mind LXVII 1958 533-537.

2229 MOUTSOPOULOS E., "Περὶ τῆς ὀντολογικῆς ὑποστάσεως τῆς τέχνης ἐν τῷ Σοφιστῇ τοῦ Πλάτωνος". Athena LXII 1958 369-379.

2230 LACEY A.R., "Plato's Sophist and the Forms". CQ IX 1959 43-52.

2231 WILLS G., "'Being' in the Sophist". ModS XXXVI 1959
197-205.

2232 ESLICK L.J., "Plato on Being: A Reply to Mr.
Wills". ModS XXXVI 1959 205-208.

2233 XENAKIS J., "Plato's Sophist. A defense of negative
Expressions and a Doctrine of Sense and of
Truth". Phronesis IV 1959 29-43.

2234 GAUDRON E., "Sur l'objet du Sophiste". LThPh XVI
1960 70-93.

2235 HAEZRAHI P., "The Interpretation of "pantelos on" in
Plato" [in Hebrew with English summary]. Iyyun
XI 1960 14-66.

2236 BEN-EZER E., "The 'Pantelos on' in Plato" [in Hebrew
with English summary]. Iyyun XI 1960 231-232.

2237 MORAVCSIK J.M.E., "Συμπλοκὴ εἰδῶν and the Genesis of
λόγος". AGPh XLII 1960 117-129.

2238 BEN-EZER E., "On the Problem of Error in Plato's
Sophist" [in Hebrew with English summary].
Iyyun XII 1961 185-189.

2239 RASCHINI M., "La dialettica del Sofista". GM XVI
1961 693-730.

2240 WOLTERSTORFF N., "Referring and Existing". PhilosQ
XI 1961 335-349.

2241* ZADRO A., Ricerche sul linguaggio e sulla logica del
Sofista. Proagones, Studi V, Padova, Ed.
Antenore 1961 163p.
Rev. Mnemosyne XVII 1964 408 Wiersma.

2242 MORAVCSIK J.M.E., "Being and Meaning in the
Sophist". APhFen XIV 1962 23-78.
Rev. PhilosQ XIV 1964 82 Bluck.

2243 PECK A.L., "Plato's Sophist. The συμπλοκὴ τῶν
εἰδῶν". Phronesis VII 1962 46-66.

2244* KAMLAH W., Platons Selbstkritik im Sophistes.
Zetemata XXXIII, München, Beck 1963 viii&64p.
Rev. AC XXXIII 1964 475-476 Joly.
CR XV 1965 357-358 Gulley.
CW LVIII 1965 139 Hoerber.
PhilosRdschau XIII 1965 39-42 Kuhn.
AAHG XVIII 1965 87 Vretska.

RecSR LIV 1966 600 des Places.
RF LVII 1966 104-105 Cambiano.
JHS LXXXVI 1966 225-226 Robinson.
RBPh XLIV 1966 1114-1116 de Strycker.
Gymnasium LXXIII 1967 301-302 de Vogel.
AJPh LXXXVIII 1967 232-236 Lee.
Paideia XXII 1967 185-186 Fabro.
ZPhF XXI 1967 629-631 Lumpe.

2245 KAMLAH W., "Zu Platons Selbstkritik im Sophistes".
Hermes XCIV 1966 243-245.

2246 SCHIPPER E.W., "The Meaning of Existence in Plato's
Sophist" [abstract]. JPh LX 1963 643.

2247 SCHIPPER E.W., "The Meaning of Existence in Plato's
Sophist". Phronesis IX 1964 38-44.

2248 TURNBULL R.G., "The Argument of the Sophist".
PhilosQ XIV 1964 23-34.

2249 SCHIPPER E.W., "Souls, Forms, and False Statements
in the Sophist". PhilosQ XV 1965 240-242.

2250 ACKRILL J.L., "Plato and the Copula: Sophist
251-9". p.207-218 in Studies in Plato's
Metaphysics, ed. by Allen R.E. (see 4580).
Also p.210-222 in Plato I, ed. by Vlastos G.
(see 4619). Reprinted from JHS LXXVII 1957 1-6.

2251 ACKRILL J.L., "Symploke Eidon". p.199-206 in
Studies in Plato's Metaphysics, ed. by Allen
R.E. (see 4580). Also p.201-209 in Plato I,
ed. by Vlastos G. (see 4619). Reprinted from
BICS II 1955 31-35.

2252 BERGER F.R., "Rest and Motion in the Sophist".
Phronesis X 1965 70-77.

2253 ITO U., "On δύναμις in Plato's Sophistes as the
Framework of Being" [in Japanese].
Philosophical Essays (Kyushu Univ.) I 1965.

2254* MARTEN R., Der Logos der Dialektik. Eine Theorie zu
Platons Sophistes. Berlin, de Gruyter 1965
viii&260p.
Rev. AC XXXIV 1965 586 des Places.
RSC XIII 1965 367-368 d'Agostino.
RThPh XCIX 1966 131-132 Schaerer.
Helmantica XVII 1966 147-149 Muñoz.
RF LVII 1966 104-105 Cambiano.
L&S I 1966 422 Pasquinelli.

CW LIX 1966 198 Philip.
CR XVII 1967 110-111 Lloyd.
Gnomon XXXIX 1967 332-341 Kuhn.
Pensiero XIII 1968 334-336 Guzzoni Foà.
Bijdragen XXX 1969 337 de Strycker.
Helmantica XX 1969 165 Barcenilla.

2255 REAGAN J.T., "Being and Nonbeing in Plato's Sophist". ModS XLII 1965 305-314.

2256 AUDOUARD X., "Le simulacre. Sur Platon: à propos du Sophiste". CahAnal 1966 n.3 57-72.

2257 LAUER Q., "The Being of Nonbeing in Plato's Sophist". p.141-156 in Wisdom in Depth. Essays in Honor of Henri Renard, ed. by Daues V.F. et al. Milwaukee, Bruce 1966.

2258 LORENZ K. & MITTELSTRASS J., "Theaitetos fliegt. Zur Theorie wahrer und falscher Sätze bei Platon (Soph. 251d-263d)". AGPh XLVIII 1966 113-152.

2259 MILNER J.C., "Le point du signifiant. Sur Platon: à propos du Sophiste". CahAnal 1966 n.3 73-82.

2260 TREVASKIS J.R., "The μέγιστα γένη and the Vowel Analogy of Plato, Sophist 253". Phronesis XI 1966 99-116.

2261* FREDE M., Prädikation und Existenzaussage. Platons Gebrauch von ist und ist nicht im Sophistes. Diss. Göttingen. Hypomnemata XVIII, Göttingen, Vandenhoeck & Ruprecht 1967 99p.
      Rev. CW LXII 1968 102 Reesor.
      AC XXXVII 1968 680 des Places.
      RPh XLIII 1969 309 des Places.
      Mnemosyne XXIII 1970 425-426 Ferwerda.
      CR XX 1970 28-30 Hamlyn.

2262 ITÔ U., "θάτερον in κοινωνία. Plato's Sophistes 251a-259b" [in Japanese with English summary]. JCS XV 1967 25-36.

2263 MALCOLM J., "Plato's Analysis of τὸ ὄν and τὸ μὴ ὄν in the Sophist". Phronesis XII 1967 130-146.

2264 SCIACCA M.F., "La dialettica delle idee nel 'Sofista'". p.397-446 in Sciacca M.F., Platone I (see 64). Reprinted from Logos n.3 1938.

2265 SHINKAI K., "The Theory of Truth and Falsity in Plato's Sophistes" [in Japanese]. Philosophy Miscellany (Tokyo Metropolitan Univ.) X 1967.

2266* MEINHARDT H., Teilhabe bei Platon. Ein Beitrag zum Verständnis platonischen Prinzipiendenkens unter besonderer Berücksichtigung des Sophistes. Symposion, Philos. Schriftenreihe, Freiburg/München, Alber 1968 116p.
Rev. ASSPh XXVIII 1968 196-197 Kunz.
Sophia XXXVII 1969 172-173 Romano.
ABG XIII 1969 99-100 Meinhardt.
TPh XXXI 1969 150-151 Berger.
SJP XIV 1970 329-331 Bauer.
Gnomon XLII 1970 726-727 Baerthlein.

2267 PHILIP J.A., "False Statement in the Sophistes". TAPhA XCIX 1968 315-327.

2268 LEE E.N., "Plato on Negation and Nonbeing in the Sophist". Abstract in JPh LXVI 1969 784.

2269 PHILIP J.A., "The megista gene of the Sophistes". Phoenix XXIII 1969 89-103.

2270 VAN FRAASSEN B.C., "Logical Structure in Plato's Sophist". RM XXII 1969 482-498.

2271 DEAÑO A., "El Sofista de Platón y la prehistoria de la lógica formal" [in Spanish with English summary]. Emerita XXXVIII 1970 131-147.

2272 GUARIGLIA O.N., "Platón, Sofista 244b6-245e2: La refutación de la tesis eleática". Dialogos VII 1970 73-82.

2273 MORI S., "Τὸ ὄν, ταὐτόν and θάτερον in the Sophist 251-259" [in Japanese with English summary]. JCS XVIII 1970 52-63.

2274 OWEN G.E.L., "Plato on Not-Being". p.223-267 in Plato I, ed. by Vlastos G. (see 4619).

2275 SAYRE K., "Falsehood, Forms and Participation in the Sophist". Nous IV 1970 81-91.

2276 WIGGINS D., "Sentence Meaning, Negation, and Plato's Problem of Non-Being". p.268-303 in Plato I, ed. by Vlastos G. (see 4619).

III C d 37: SOPHIST

2277* KETCHUM R.J., Truth and Being in Plato's Sophist.
     Diss. Univ. of Pennsylvania 1971 136p.
     [microfilm]. Summary in DA XXXII 1971 2135A.

2278 LOGOTHETES K.I., "Οἱ φίλοι τῶν εἰδῶν". Platon XXIII
     1971 354.

2279 LOGOTHETES K.I., "Καὶ πάλιν οἱ φίλσί τῶν εἰδῶν".
     Platon XXIV 1972 330-332.

2280* PESTER H.E., Platons bewegte Usia. Klass.-philol.
     Stud. XXXVIII, Wiesbaden, Harrassowitz 1971
     xi&179p.
     Rev. REA LXXIV 1972 266-267 Moreau.

2281 BONDESON W., "Plato's Sophist. Falsehoods and
     Images". Apeiron VI,2 1972 1-6.

2282* KRENTZ A.A., Being, not-being, appearing and the
     Nature of Sophistry. Some neglected Aspects of
     Plato's Sophist. Diss. Univ. of Waterloo,
     Ontario 1972 136p. [microfilm]. Summary in DA
     XXXIV 1973 361A.

2283 LEE E.N., "Plato on Negation and not-being in the
     Sophist". PhR LXXXI 1972 267-304.

2284 ANDIC M. & BROWN M., "False Statement in the
     Sophist and Theaetetus' Mathematics". Phoenix
     XXVII 1973 26-34.

2285* CASPER D.J., Being and Predication in Plato's
     Sophist. Diss. Univ. of Illionis, Urbana 1972
     742p. [microfilm]. Summary in DA XXXIV 1973
     818A.

2286 FLOROS A.T., "Προβλήματά τινα διερευνώμενα ὑπὸ τοῦ
     Πλάτωνος ἐν τῷ Παρμενίδῃ καὶ τῷ Σφφεστῇ" [in
     Greek with French summary]. Platon XXV 1973
     294-308.

2287 KEYT D., "Plato on Falsity: Sophist 263b".
     p.285-305 in Exegesis and Argument, ed. by Lee
     E.N. et al. (see 4608).

2288 KOSTMAN J.P., "False Logos and Not-Being in Plato's
     Sophist". p.192-212 in Patterns in Plato's
     Thought, ed. by Moravcsik J.M.E. (see 4609).

2289 LOGOTHETIS K.I., " Κριτικὰ καὶ ἑρμηνευτικὰ εἰς τὸν
     Πλατωνικὸν Σοφιστήν". Platon XXV 1973 234-251.

265

III C d 37: SOPHIST

2290 TSUMURA K., "Some Remarks on the Correspondence
between eidos and logos, Sophistes 259e5-6" [in
Japanese]. JCS XXI 1973 67-72.

2291 VLASTOS G., "An Ambiguity in the Sophist" (with
appendices "On the Interpretation of Sph.
248d4-e4" and "More on Pauline Predications in
Plato"). p.270-322 in Vlastos G., Platonic
Studies (see 4622).

For additional discussions see 89, 221, 242, 279, 354,
786, 1576, 1915, 2486, 2515, 2706, 2748, 2795,
2812, 2840, 2886, 2912, 2928, 2937, 2940, 2941,
2972, 2973, 3008, 3011, 3018, 3025, 3215, 3219,
3819, 3941, 3977, 3979, 4026, 4028, 4029, 4034,
4036, 4042, 4046, 4047, 4049, 4054, 4059.

C. TEXTUAL CRITICISM

2292 FREDE M., "Bemerkungen zum Text der Aporienpassage
in Platons Sophistes". Phronesis VII 1962
132-135.

2293 PHILIP J.A., "The Apographa of Plato's Sophistes".
Phoenix XXII 1968 289-298.

For additional discussion of the text see 2203.

STATESMAN

A. TEXTS AND TRANSLATIONS

2294* Platon, Oeuvres complètes, IX. 1er partie. Le
Politique, texte établi et trad. par Diès A.
3e éd. rev. & corr. Coll. des Universités de
France, Paris, Les Belles Lettres 1960 lxix&91p.

2295* Politico, trad., introd. e note di Riverso E.
Class. di filos. e pedag., Torino, Ist.
editoriale del Mezzogiorno 1964 115p.

III C d 38: STATESMAN

2296* <u>Devlet</u> <u>adami</u> [Statesman], Turkish transl. by Boran
      B. & Karasan M. Ankara, Millî Eğitim Basimevi
      1960 128p.

For additional texts and translations see 856, 860, 867,
      878, 915, 916, 923, 926, 944, 945, 950, 952,
      971, 972.

B. STUDIES OF THE STATESMAN

2297 HERTER H., "Gott und die Welt bei Platon. Eine
      Studie zum Mythos des Politikos". BJ CLVIII
      1958 106-117.

2298 SCHUHL P.M., "Sur le Politique 286b". REG LXXII
      1959 p.ix.

2299 KUCHARSKI P., "La conception de l'art de la mesure
      dans le Politique". BAGB XIX 1960 459-480.

2300 BENARDETE S., "Eidos and Diaeresis in Plato's
      Statesman". Philologus CVII 1963 193-226.

2301 GRIFFITHS J.G., "Plato on Priests and Kings in
      Egypt". CR XV 1965 156-157.

2302 VOLKMANN-SCHLUCK K.H., "Gedanken zu Platos
      Politikos". p.311-325 in <u>Die</u> <u>Frage</u> <u>nach</u> <u>dem</u>
      <u>Menchen.</u> <u>Aufriss</u> <u>e.</u> <u>philosoph.</u> <u>Anthropologie.</u>
      <u>Festschrift</u> <u>für</u> <u>Max</u> <u>Mueller</u> <u>zum</u> <u>60.</u> <u>Geburtstag,</u>
      hrsg. von Rombach H. Freiburg, Alber 1966.

2303 DAVIS M., "The Statesman as a Political Dialogue".
      AJPh LXXXVIII 1967 319-331.

2304 LAVELLE L., "Le Politique". p.55-64 in Lavelle L.,
      <u>Panorama</u> <u>des</u> <u>doctrines</u> <u>philosophiques</u> (see
      4607).

2305 ROBINSON T.M., "Demiurge and World Soul in Plato's
      Politicus". AJPh LXXXVIII 1967 57-66.

2306 SAKONJI S., "On the third Diairesis of Plato's
      Politicus" [in Japanese]. Philosophy (Tokyo)
      XVIII 1968.

267

2307 OWEN G.E.L., "Plato on the Undepictable". p.349-361
      in Exegesis and Argument, ed. by Lee E.N. et
      al. (see 4608).

For additional discussions see 89, 2149, 2571, 2572, 2573,
      3101, 3116, 3254, 3278, 3565, 3587, 3589, 3697,
      3757, 4026.

SYMPOSIUM

A. TEXTS AND TRANSLATIONS

2308* The Symposium, transl. by Hamilton W.   Baltimore,
      Penguin 1961 121p.
           Rev. Arion 1968 426 Gould.

2309* The Symposium of Plato, transl. by Jowett B.   with
      The Ananga ranga of Kalyana Malla, transl. by
      Burton R. & Arbuthnot F.F. London, Kimber 1963
      255p.

2310* The Symposium, a Dramatized Version, transl. by
      Kobler F. & Mueller E., introd. by Kobler F.,
      afterword by Mueller E., original music by
      Kauder H.   Milestones of Thought in the Hist.
      of Ideas M128, New York, Ungar 1966 v&101p.
           Rev. CW LX 1967 349 Etheridge.

2311* The Symposium of Plato, transl. by Groden S.Q., ed.
      by Brentlinger J.A., drawings by Baskin L.
      Amherst, The Univ. of Massachusetts Pr.   1970
      129p.
           Rev. QQ 1972 268 Duncan.

2312* Das Gastmahl (Symposion), übers. & erl.   von
      Eckstein F. München, Goldmann 1959 148p.

2313* Das Gastmahl, übers. & erl.   von Apelt O., mit
      griech.   Text neubearb.   von Capelle A., &
      ausführl. Literaturübersicht von Wilpert P. 2.
      Aufl.   Philos.   Bibl.   LXXXI, Hamburg, Meiner
      1960 xxxix&158p. Also Nachdr., mit Erg.   z.
      Literaturübers.   1973 xi&158p.
           Rev. Scholastik XXXVI 1961 445-446 Kern.
      PhJ LXX 1962 200-201 Hommes.

Helikon III 1963 704-705 Nádor.

2314* Das Gastmahl, Dt. Übers. Freiburg i. Br., Hyperion-Verl. 1961 172p.

2315* Ein Gastmahl, übertr. von Mueller E. Frankfurt a. M., Insel-Verl. 1961 79p.

2316* Symposion, für den Schulgebrauch hrsg. mit Komm. von Reynen H. Münster, Aschendorff 2 vols: I: Text 1961 106p.; II: Komm. 1962 188p. Rev. AAHG XVIII 1965 88 Hadamovsky.

2317* Das Gastmahl oder Von der Liebe, übertr. & eingel. von Hildebrandt K. Reclams Universal-Bibliothek 927/927a, Stuttgart, Reclam 1962 118p.

2318* Das Gastmahl oder Über die Liebe, übertr. von Kassner R. mit 9 Original-Radier. von Battke H. Ars librorum Druck. XII, Frankfurt, Ars libr.-Verl. 1965 68p.

2319* Symposion, hrsg. & übers. von Boll F., neu bearb. von Buchwald W. 6. verbesserte Aufl. Tusculum-Bücherei XXVI, München, Heimeran 1969 171p. Rev. RBPh LXIX 1971 668 de Strycker.

2320* Convivium, éd. par Robin L. Coll. Calliope, Paris, Les Belles Lettres 1963 vi&92p.

2321* Le banquet, trad. & notes de Robin L., introd. de Belaval Y. Le livre de poche No.2186, Paris, Le livre de poche 1967 191p.

2322* Le Banquet, nouv. trad. & comm. de Boutang P., 39 dessins de Silva V. da. Coll. L'esprit & la main, Paris, Hermann 1972 184p.

2323* Le banquet ou de l'amour, trad. par Robin L. & Moreau J., préf. de Châtelet F. Coll. Idées CCLXXXII Philosophie, Paris, Gallimard 1973 180p.

2324* Simposio, trad. di Colli G. Encicl. di autori class. XXXVI, Torino, Boringhieri 1960 112p.

2325* Il simposio, a cura di Baccini D. Class. latini e greci comm. per le scuole, Messina/Firenze, D'Anna 1964 174p.

2326* Banquete. 2a ed. Col. de Bolsillo edime IX,
Madrid, Mediterráneo 1969 168p.

2327* Symposium, een gesprek over de liefde, vert. door
Loenen D. Amsterdam, Polak & Van Gennep 1963
95p.
Rev. Hermeneus XXXV 1963 42-43 van
Lennep.

2328* O Banquete o do Amor, Port. trad. de Gomes P.
Coimbra, Atlântida 1968 113p.

2329* O banquete ou Do amor, Port. trad., introd. e
notas de Cavalcante de Souza J. São Paulo, Ed.
da Univ. de São Paulo 1966 201p. Also 2a ed.
São Paulo, Difusão Européia do Livro 1970 201p.

2330* Samdrykkjan [Symposium], Icelandic transl. by
Thorsteinsson S.B., ed. by Gíslason J.
Reykjavík, Bókaútgáfa Menningarsjóds 1959 134p.

2331* Al-ma'duba aw fī l-ḥubb [the Symposium or On Love],
Arabic transl. with an "Étude sur l'influence
du 'Banquet' sur la pensée philosophique", by
al-Nashshār S., Anawati G.C. & Sherbini A.A.
Alexandria, Dar al-kutub al-jami'iyya 1970 448p.

For additional texts and translations see 853, 878, 893,
905, 914, 917, 918, 920, 924, 928, 930, 935,
936, 937, 939, 948, 954, 955, 959, 963, 964,
966, 969, 971, 972, 977, 978, 981, 982, 984,
986, 989, 991, 992.

B. STUDIES OF THE SYMPOSIUM

2332* FICINO M., Comentario al 'Banquete' de Platón,
trad., estud. prelim. y notas de Díaz A.R.
Mendoza, Univ. Nac. de Cuyo Fac. de Filos. y
Letras (Anejo 1) 1968 160p.

2333 MARSILIO FICINO, Commentary on Love in Plato's
Symposium, Japanese transl. by Sato M. Ryutsu
Keizai Essays (Ryutsu Keizai Univ.) VI,2 1971;
VI,3 1971; VII,1 1972.

2334* FICINO M., Sopra lo amore o ver' Convito di Platone.
Comento di Marsilio Ficino fiorentino sopra il
Convito di Platone, a cura di Ottaviano G.

III C d 39: SYMPOSIUM

Scienze umane XIV, Milano, Celuc 1973 156p.

2335 ORTEGA Y GASSET J., "Commentario al Banquete de
Platon". Sur CCLXII 1960 2-18.

2336 ORTEGA Y GASSET J., "Commentaires au 'Banquet' de
Platón". RPhilos CLVII 1967 145-164. (Transl.
of unedited notes of Ortega y Gasset by Fabre G.
Foreword by Schuhl P.M.)

2337* ROSEN S., Plato's Symposium. New Haven, Yale Univ.
Pr. 1968 xxxix&346p.
Rev. RM XXII 1968-1969 387-388 W.D.T.
CW LXII 1969 224 Rist.
PhilosQ XIX 1969 354-355 Stewart.
TLS 27 Feb. 1969 218.
JHS XC 1970 209-210 Saunders.
Dialogue VIII 1969-1970 131-133 Gallop.
CR XXI 1971 362-364 Easterling.
Ph&PhenR XXXII 1971-1972 279-280 Rose.
AJPh XCIII 1972 612-616 More.
GM XXVIII 1973 408-409 Sorge.

2338 PLOCHMANN G.K., "Interpreting Plato's Symposium".
ModS XLVIII 1970 25-43.

2339* TANAKA M., Invitation to Plato's Symposium. Tokyo,
Tsukuma Shobo 1971 254p.

2340 BACON H.H., "Socrates Crowned". VQR XXXV 1959
415-430.

2341 VRETSKA K., "Zu Form und Aufbau von Platons
Symposion". p.143-156 in Serta Philologica
Aenipontana, hrsg. von Muth R. Innsbrucker
Beitr. zur Kulturwiss. VII-VIII, Innsbruck,
Innrain 1962.

2342* BUCHNER H., Eros und Sein. Erörterungen zu Platons
Symposion. Bonn, Bouvier 1965 167p.
Rev. ArchPhilos XXX 1967 136-137
Solignac.
Dialogos IV 1967 142-143 Kerkhoff.
RPhL LXXI 1973 151-159 Brague.

2343* HYLAND D.A., Eros and Philosophy. A Study of
Plato's Symposium. Diss. Pennsylvania State
Univ. 1965 321p. [microfilm]. Summary in DA
XXVII 1966 798A-799A.

271

2344 NEUMANN H., "On the Comedy of Plato's Aristophanes".
      AJPh LXXXVII 1966 420-426.

2345 QUITO E.S., "The Symposium of Plato".   PhilippSacra
      I 1966 477-495.

2346 REYNEN H., "Der vermittelte Bericht im platonischen
      Symposion". Gymnasium LXXIV 1967 405-422.

2347 MORI S., "Plato's Symposium" [in Japanese].   Izuni
      1968.

2348 DORTER K., "The Significance of the Speeches in
      Plato's Symposium". Ph&Rh II 1969 215-234.

2349* MOORE J.D., The Symposium and Plato's Development.
      Diss. Stanford Univ. 1969 257p. [microfilm].
      Summary in DA XXX 1969 1156A-1157A.

2350 RODRÍGUEZ ADRADOS F., "El banquete platónico y la
      teoría del teatro" [in Spanish with English
      summary]. Emerita XXXVII 1969 1-28.

2351 GIERSE G., "Zur Komposition des platonischen
      Symposion". Gymnasium LXXVII 1970 518-520.

2352 WOLZ H.G., "Philosophy as Drama. An Approach to
      Plato's Symposium". Ph&PhenR XXX 1970 323-353.

2353 KISLOVA M.M., "Comic Types in Plato's Symposium" [in
      Russian]. VKF V 1973 158-169.

2354 MOORE J.D., "The Relation between Plato's Symposium
      and Phaedrus".   p.52-71 in Patterns in Plato's
      Thought, ed. by Moravcsik J.M.E. (see 4609).

2355 DILLON J., "Comments on John Moore's Paper".
      p.72-77 in Patterns in Plato's Thought, ed. by
      Moravcsik J.M.E. (see 4609).

2356 MATTINGLY H.B., "The date of Plato's Symposium".
      Phronesis III 1958 31-39.

2357 DOVER K.J., "The Date of Plato's Symposium".
      Phronesis X 1965 2-20.

2358 HERTER H., "Platons Symposion in Sykutris' Sicht".
      GriechischesBull 1958,1 1-2.

2359 KRANZ W., "Platonica". Philologus CII 1958 74-83.

III C d 39: SYMPOSIUM

2360 BOLLACK J., "Le mythe d'Aristophane dans le Banquet de Platon". Summary in REG LXXV 1962 p.ix-x.

2361 VRETSKA K., "Zu Platon, Symposion 183a". WS LXXV 1962 22-27.

2362 REYNEN H., "Noch einmal Plat. Sympos. 183a". WS LXXX 1967 74-78.

2363 REYNEN H., "Philosophie und Knabenliebe. Zu Plat. Symp. 183a". Hermes XCV 1967 308-316.

2364 PLOCHMANN G., "Hiccups and Hangovers in the Symposium". BR XI,3 1963 1-18.

2365 BAYONAS A.M., Παρατηρήσεις ἐπὶ τοῦ νοήματος τῆς νομοθεσίας εἰς τὸ Συμπόσιον τοῦ Πλάτωνος. p.251-271 in Χάρις K.I. Vourveris. ἀφιέρωμα τῶν μαθητῶν τοῦ ἐπὶ τῇ ἑξηκονταπενταετηρίδι βίου αὐτοῦ, ed. by Anastassiou A., Kambylis A., & Skiadas A. Athens 1964.

2366 DOVER K.J., "Eros and Nomos (Plato, Symposium 182a-185c)". BICS XI 1964 31-42.

2367 MORRISON J.S., "Four Notes on Plato's Symposium". CQ XIV 1964 42-55.

2368 NEUMANN H., "On the Sophistry of Plato's Pausanias". TAPhA XCV 1964 261-267.

2369 NEUMANN H., "On the Madness of Plato's Apollodorus". TAPhA XCVI 1965 283-289.

2370 NEUMANN H., "Diotima's Concept of Love". AJPh LXXXVI 1965 33-59.

2371 WIPPERN J., "Eros und Unsterblichkeit in der Diotima-Rede des Symposions". p.123-129 in Synusia. Festgabe für Wolfgang Schadewaldt zum 15. März 1965, hrsg. von Flashar H. & Gaiser K. Pfullingen, Neske 1965.

2372 ALLEN R.E., "A Note on the Elenchus of Agathon. Symposium 199c-201c". Monist L 1966 460-463.

2373 DOVER K.J., "Aristophanes' Speech in Plato's Symposium". JHS LXXXVI 1966 41-50.

2374 LURKER M., "Der Kreis als symbolischer Ausdruck der kosmischen Harmonie". StudGen XIX 1966 523-533.

273

2375 WIPPERN J., "Zur unterrichtlichen Lektüre der Diotima-Rede in Platons Symposion". AU R.9 1966 35-59.

2376 EDELSTEIN L., "The Role of Eryximachus in Plato's Symposium". p.153-171 in Ancient Medicine. Selected Papers of L. Edelstein, ed. by Temkin O. & C.L. Baltimore, Johns Hopkins Pr. 1967. Reprinted from TAPhA LXXVI 1945 85-103.

2377 SCIACCA M.F., "L'idea del bello". p.233-276 in Sciacca M.F., Platone I (see 64). Reprinted from "Il discorso di Socrate nel 'Convito' platonico". Humanitas n.2 1952.

2378 SCIACCA M.F., "L'idea del bello nel 'Convito' di Platone". CultScuola XXII 1967 99-109.

2379 STÉGEN G., "Platon, Banquet 189b". Latomus XXVI 1967 195.

2380 KOUTROUMBOUSSIS G.L., "Interpretation der Aristophanesrede im Symposion Platons" [in German with Greek summary]. Platon XX 1968 194-211.

2381 PELTZ R., "The True, the Good, and the Humanities". JAE II 1968 9-20.

2382 THEILER W., "Diotima neuplatonisch". AGPh L 1968 29-47.

2383 MARTIN H., "Amatorius 756E-F. Plutarch's Citation of Parmenides and Hesiod". AJPh XC 1969 183-200.

2384 WELLMAN R.R., "Eros and Education in Plato's Symposium". PaedHist IX 1969 129-158.

2385* POINLÂNE E., Le désir d'agapè dans le Banquet de Platon. Thèse Lettres, Paris, 1970 xi&334p.

2386* SIMMONDS K.C., Philosophical Comments on Symposium 201d-7a. Diss. Ohio State Univ. 1969 397p. [microfilm]. Summary in DA XXX 1970 4503A.

2387 CORNFORD F.M., "The Doctrine of Eros in Plato's Symposium". p.119-131 in Plato II, ed. by Vlastos G. (see 4621). Reprinted from Cornford F.M., The Unwritten Philosophy and Other Essays, Cambridge 1950.

2388 MARKUS R.A., "The Dialectic of Eros in Plato's Symposium". p.132-143 in Plato II, ed. by Vlastos G. (see 4620). Reprinted from DownsR LXXIII 1955 219-230.

2389 MORAVCSIK J.M.E., "Reason and Eros in the 'ascent' passage of the Symposium". p.285-302 in Essays in ancient Greek Philosophy, ed. by Anton J.P. & Kustas G.L. (see 4581).

2390 PLOCHMANN G.K., "Supporting Themes in the Symposium". p.328-344 in Essays in ancient Greek Philosophy, ed. by Anton J.P. & Kustas G.L. (see 4581).

2391 SOLMSEN F., "Parmenides and the Description of Perfect Beauty in Plato's Symposium". AJPh XCII 1971 62-70.

2392 SPRAGUE R.K., "Symposium 211a and Parmenides Frag.8". CPh LXVI 1971 261.

2393 BOSSOULAS N.I., "Démon socratique et Éros créateur dans le Banquet de Platon". Hellenica XXV 1972 56-77.

2394 GORISSEN P., "Plato, Symposium 205d en 207d". p.342-344 in Zetesis (see 4579).

2395 MARTIN FERRERO F., "El puesto de Aristodemo entre los comensales y su desaparición de la serie de oradores en el Banquete de Platón". CFC V 1973 193-206.

For additional discussions see 227, 328, 502, 573, 767, 935, 1549, 1691, 2382, 2471, 2553, 2579, 2580, 2595, 2638, 2673, 2691, 2693, 3039, 3060, 3097, 3169, 3403, 3478, 3697, 3889, 3916, 3933, 3977, 4173, 4305, 4574.

C. TEXTUAL CRITICISM

2396 ROBERTSON D.S., "Symposium 195D,E". CR VIII 1958 221.

2397 REYNEN H., "Platon, Symposion 183a". Hermes LXXXIX 1961 495-498.

2398 VRIES G.J. DE, "A Note on Symp. 173d". Mnemosyne
    XIX 1966 147.

2399 MOORE J.D., "The Philosopher's Frenzy". Mnemosyne
    XXII 1969 225-230.

2400 RENEHAN R., "Plato, Symposium 219a2-4". CR XIX 1969
    270.

2401 VRIES G.J. DE, "The Philosophaster's Softness".
    Mnemosyne XXII 1969 230-232.

2402 SKEMP J.B., "The Philosopher's Frenzy". Mnemosyne
    XXIII 1970 302-304.

2403 REEVE M.D., "Eleven Notes". CR XXI 1971 324-329.

For additional studies of the text see 2361, 2362, 2363.

THEAETETUS

A. TEXTS AND TRANSLATIONS

2404* Theaetetus, transl. by Cornford F.M., ed. by Piest
    O. The Library of Liberal Arts, New York,
    Liberal Arts Pr. 1959 x&163p.

2405* Theaetetus, transl. by Lewis T., ed. by Somers W.,
    with an introd. "On Looking into Lewis'
    Theaetetus" by Peterson S. Idol XXXIV,4,
    Schenectady, N.Y., Union Coll. 1963 61p.
    Rev. CW LVII 1964 322 Sprague.
    AC XXXIII 1964 165 Joly.
    REA LXVI 1964 412 Brun.
    Mnemosyne XVIII 1965 423 de Vries.

2406* Theaetetus, transl. with notes and a comm. by
    McDowell J. Clarendon Plato Series, Oxford,
    Clarendon Pr. 1973 264p.

2407* The Theaetetus of Plato, with a revised text and
    English notes by Campbell L. New York, Arno Pr.
    1973 227p. Reprint of 1861 edn.

III C d 40: THEAETETUS

2408* <u>Teeteto</u>, introd. e comm. di Zeppi S., trad. di
       Zeppi Tutta A. Pensatori antichi e moderni,
       Firenze, La Nuova Italia 1966 xx&224p.

2409* <u>Teeteto o della conoscenza</u>, trad. di Bonghi R., a
       cura di Sammartano N. Class. della filos. e
       pedag., Urbino, Argalia 1966 196p.

2410* <u>Teeteto</u>, trad., introd. e note stor.-eseg. a cura
       di Russo A. & Santaniello M. Messina, Minerva
       Italica 1967 192p.

2411* <u>Teeteto o de la ciencia</u>, vers. de Míguez J.A.
       Bibl. Iniciac. filos., Buenos Aires, Ed.
       Aguilar 1960. 2a ed. 1963 238p.
       Rev. Sapientia XV 1960 297 Bolzán.

2412* <u>Teajtet</u>, przel., wstep., objaśn., illustr. Witwicki
       W. Warszawa, PWN 1959 208p.

2413* <u>Theaetetus</u>, Hebrew transl. by Simon A., ed. by
       Ruth C. 3rd edn. Hebrew Univ., Jerusalem,
       Magnes Pr. 1968 xv&225p.

2414* <u>Theaetetus</u>, Arabic transl. by Barbara F.G.
       Damascus, Ministry of Information 1971 262p.

2415* <u>Theaetetus</u>, transl. by Tanaka M. Tokyo, Iwanami
       Shoten 1966 317p.

For additional texts and translations see 855, 860, 867,
       893, 915, 926, 931, 940, 952, 973, 986, 992.

B. STUDIES OF THE THEAETETUS

The studies of this dialogue are classified
under four headings. First, treatments of the
dialogue as a whole or of general questions
concerning the dialogue. Afterwards come those
works dealing specifically with each of the
three main sections of the dialogue.

2416 CAPELLE A., "Protagoreer oder Politiker? (Platon,
       Theaetet 172b-177c)". RhM CIV 1961 191-192.

III C d 40: THEAETETUS

2417 MOUTSOPOULOS E., "Ἐπιστημολογία καὶ ὀντολαγία ἐν τῷ
Πλατωνικῷ Θεαιτήτῳ". Athena LXV 1961 230-238.

2418 BLUCK R.S., "Knowledge by Acquaintance in Plato's
Theaetetus". Mind LXXII 1963 259-263.

2419 HICKEN W.F., "Knowledge and Forms in Plato's
Theaetetus". p.185-198 in Studies in Plato's
Metaphysics, ed. by Allen R.E. (see 4580).
Reprinted from JHS 1957.

2420 GRECA C., "Il Teeteto". ALGP III-IV 1966-1967
281-298.

2421 VLĂDUŢESCU G., "The Problem of Science in Plato's
Theaetetus" [in Rumanian with Russian and French
summaries]. AUBuc XVI 1967 63-70.

2422 BONITZ H., "Theätetos". p.47-92 in Bonitz H.,
Platonische Studien (see 4584).

2423* BURDICK J.M., Knowledge, Simplicity and Discourse in
Plato's Theaetetus. Diss. Univ. of Wisconsin
1968 160p. [microfilm]. Summary in DA XXIX
1968 630A.

2424 BROWN M.S., "Theatetus, Knowledge as Continued
Learning". JHPh VII 1969 359-379.

2425* SIDER D., A Literary Study of Plato's Theaetetus.
Diss. Columbia Univ. 1969 117p. [microfilm].
Summary in DA XXX 1970 4433A.

2426 O'TOOLE E.J., "Forms and Knowledge in the
Theaetetus". PhilosStud(Irel) XIX 1970 102-118.

2427 VOROS F., "Εἶναι δυνατὸς ὁ ὁρισμὸς τῆς γνώσεως; Τὸ
πρόβλημα τοῦ Πλατωνικοῦ Θεαιτήτου" [with English
summary]. Philsophia(Athens) I 1971 250-263.

2428* CADY D.L., Knowledge in Plato's Theaetetus. Diss.
Brown Univ. 1971 97p. [microfilm]. Summary in
DA XXXII 1972 5279A-5280A.

2429 RORTY A.O., "A Speculative Note on some Dramatic
Elements in the Theaetetus". Phronesis XVII
1972 227-238.

2430* FLOWER R.J., The Mathematical Ontological Conditions
Kinematic μάθησις. A Study of Plato's
Theaetetus. Diss. Syracuse Univ. 1973 413p.
[microfilm]. Summary in DA XXXIV 1974 6698A.

STUDIES OF PART I (TO 187A)

2431 ALRIVIE J.J., "Les prologues du Théétète et du Parménide". RMM LXXVI 1971 6-23.

2432 CAPELLE A., "Bemerkungen zu Platons Theaetet". Hermes LXXXVIII 1960 265-280.

2433 BLUCK R.S., "The Puzzles of Size and Number in Plato's Theaetetus". PCPhS N.S. VII 1961 7-9.

2434 ZOUMPOS A.N., "Εἰς Πλάτωνος Θεαύτητον 152d". Φιλοσοφικὰ σημειώματα, IV, Athens 1961 3p.

2435 CAPELLE A., "Zur Frage nach den κομψότεροι in Platons Theaetet 156a". Hermes XC 1962 288-294.

2436 ZOUMPOS A.N., "Ποικίλα φιλολογικὰ καὶ φιλοσοφικά". Platon XV 1963 141-153.

2437 COLE A.T., "The Apology of Protagoras". YClS XIX 1966 101-118.

2438 MEJER J., "Plato, Protagoras and the Heracliteans. Some Suggestions concerning Theaetetus 151D-186E". C&M XXIX 1968 40-60.

2439 BONDESON W.B., "Perception, true Opinion and Knowledge in Plato's Theaetetus". Phronesis XIV 1969 111-122.

2440 COOPER J.M., "Plato on Sense-perception and Knowledge (Theaetetus 184-186)". Phronesis XV 1970 123-146.

2441 MIZUSAKI H., "On part I of the Theaetetus: the μυστηρία in 156a-157c and sensation and the theory of Knowledge in 158e-160e" [in Japanese]. Studies in Philosophy (Kyushu Univ.) VI 1970.

2442 BIERMAN A.K., "Socratic Humor. Understanding the most Important Philosophical Argument". Apeiron V,2 1971 23-42.

2443 JORDAN J.E., "Protagoras and Relativism. Criticisms bad and good". SwJP II 1971 7-29.

2444 TIGNER S.S., "The exquisite Argument at Tht. 171a". Mnemosyne XXIV 1971 366-369.

2445   MANSFELD J., "Man the Measure and Sense-perception (Plato, Tht., 151e-187a)". Th-P I 1972 128-139.

2446   HOLLAND A.J., "An Argument in Plato's Theaetetus, 184-186". PhilosQ XXIII 1973 97-116.

2447   LEE E.N., "'Hoist with his own Petard': Ironic and Comic Elements in Plato's Critique of Protagoras (Tht. 161-171)". p.225-261 in Exegesis and Argument, ed. by Lee E.N. et al. (see 4608).

2448   MAGUIRE J.P., "Protagoras, or Plato?". Phronesis XVIII 1973 115-138.

2449   MANSFELD J., "Notes on some Passages in Plato's Theaetetus and in the Anonymous Commentary". p.108-114 in Zetesis (see 4579).

STUDIES OF PART II (187A-201C)

2450   RIST J.M., "The Aviary Model in the Theaetetus". Dialogue I 1962-1963 406-409.

2451   DEICKE W., "Platon, Theaetet 192c10". Phronesis IX 1964 136-142.

2452   ACKRILL J., "Plato on false Belief. Theaetetus 187-200". Monist L 1966 383-402.

2453   ROBINSON R., "Forms and Error in Plato's Theaetetus". p.39-73 in Robinson R., Essays in Greek Philosophy (see 4612). Reprinted from PhR 1950.

2454   McDOWELL J., "Identity Mistakes: Plato and the Logical Atomists". PAS LXX 1969-1970 181-195.

2455   WILLIAMS C.J.F., "Referential Opacity and false Belief in the Theaetetus". PhilosQ XXII 1972 289-302.

2456   LEWIS F.A., "Foul Play in Plato's Aviary: Theaetetus 195b ff.". p.262-284 in Exegesis and Argument, ed. by Lee E.N. et al. (see 4608).

2457   LEWIS F.A., "Two Paradoxes in the Theaetetus". p.123-149 in Patterns in Plato's Thought, ed. by Moravcsik J.M.E. (see 4609).

2458 BOGEN J., "Comments on Lewis". p.150-157 in
     Patterns in Plato's Thought, ed. by Moravcsik
     J.M.E. (see 4609).

STUDIES OF THE THIRD PART (FROM 201C)

2459 HICKEN W., "The Character and Provenance of
     Socrates' "dream" in the Theaetetus". Phronesis
     III 1958 126-145.

2460 MEYERHOFF H., "Socrates' Dream in the Theaetetus".
     CQ LII 1958 131-138.

2461 DRUART T.A., "La notion de stoicheïon (élément) dans
     le Théétète de Platon". RPhL LXVI 1968 420-434.

2462 BONDESON W.B., "The Dream of Socrates and the
     Conclusion of the Theaetetus". Apeiron III,2
     1969 1-13.

2463 LESHER J.H., "Γνῶσις and ἐπιστήμη in Socrates' Dream
     in the Theaetetus". JHS LXXXIX 1969 72-78.

2464 BURNYEAT M.F., "The Material and Sources of Plato's
     Dream". Phronesis XV 1970 101-122.

2465 MORROW G.R., "Plato and the Mathematicians. An
     Interpretation of Socrates' Dream in the
     Theaetetus (201e-206c)". PhR LXXIX 1970
     309-333.

For additional discussions of the Theaetetus see 89, 273,
     274, 353, 422, 1695, 2633, 2797, 2812, 2861,
     2886, 2940, 3011, 3022, 3033, 3134, 3219, 3289,
     3304, 3316, 3324, 3335, 3977, 3979, 3993, 3999,
     4000, 4026, 4046, 4047, 4054, 4058, 4449.

C. TEXTUAL CRITICISM

2466 HICKEN W.F., "The Y Tradition of the Theaetetus".
     CQ XVII 1967 98-102.

III C d 40: THEAETETUS

2467   IGAL J., "Observaciones al Teeteto platónico
       (152d-157c)". Helmantica XIX 1968 247-275.

2468   CAMERER R., "Zu Plato Theaetet 183a2-b5".   Hermes
       XCVI 1968-1969 635-637.

2469   WESTERINK L.G., "A Variant on Plato Theaetetus
       186c9". CPh LXV 1970 48-49.

2470   WHITE F.C., "Ὡς ἐπιστήμη οὖσα. A Passage of some
       Elegance in the Theaetetus". Phronesis XVII
       1972 219-226.

THEAGES

A. TEXTS AND TRANSLATIONS

For texts and translations see 871, 961.

B. STUDIES OF THE THEAGES

2471   TARRANT D., "The Touch of Socrates".   CQ LII 1958
       95-98.

2472   MUELLER C.W., "Weltherrschaft und Unsterblichkeit im
       pseudoplatonischen Theages und in der
       eudemischen Ethik". p.135-147 in Politeia und
       Res Publica. Beiträge zum Verständnis von
       Politik, Recht und Staat in der Antike, dem
       Andenken Rudolf Starks gewidmet, hrsg. von
       Steinmetz P. Palingenesia Monogr. & Texte zur
       klass. Altertumswiss. IV, Wiesbaden, Steiner
       1969.

For additional discussion see 1104.

TIMAEUS

A. TEXTS AND TRANSLATIONS

2473* Timaeus, transl. by Cornford F.M. Libr. of
Liberal Arts, New York, Liberal Arts Pr. 1959
xxvi&117p.

2474* Timaeus, transl. & introd. by Lee H.D.P.
Harmondsworth, Middx./Baltimore, Penguin Books
1965 124p.
Rev. CW LIX 1966 314 Etheridge.
RPortFil XXIII 1967 503 Freire.
Arion 1968 426 Gould.

2475* Timaeus, transl. & introd. by Warrington J.
Everyman's Libr. No.493, London, Dent 1965
xv&138p.
Rev. CW LX 1966 16 Etheridge.

2476* The Timaeus and the Critias or Atlanticus, transl.
by Taylor T. Oxford Univ. Pr. 1969 250p.
Reprint of 1944 edn.

2477* The Timaeus and Critias, transl. with introd. &
appendix by Lee H.D.P. Harmondsworth, Middx.,
Penguin 1971 167p.
Rev. MLJ 1973 382 Sider.

2478* The Timaeus of Plato, ed. & transl. with introd.
and notes by Archer-Hind R.D. New York, Arno
Pr. 1973 358p. Reprint of 1888 edn.

2479* Timeo, trad., pról. y notas por Samaranch F. de P.
Bibl. Iniciac. filos. LXXXIV, Buenos Aires,
Aguilar 1963 215p.

2480* Timaios i Kritias, przel., wstep., objaśn., illustr.
Witwicki W. Warszawa, PWN 1960 203p.

For additional texts and translations see 856, 861, 868,
878, 893, 920, 927, 934, 944, 948, 950, 951,
2476, 2477, 2480.

B. STUDIES OF THE TIMAEUS

Many treatments of subjects raised in the Timaeus will be found in sections V D and V E. They are cross referenced at the end of the present section, but the reader might wish to examine those sections in toto.

2481* CALCIDIUS, Timaeus a Calcidio translatus commentarioque instructus in societatem operis coniuncto Jensen P.J. edidit Waszink J.H. Corpus Platonicum Medii Aevi, Plato Latinus, ed. Klibansky R. Vol. IV, London, Warburg Inst.; Leiden, Brill 1962 clxxxiii&436P.
Rev. CW LVI 1963 258 Hoerber.
REL XL 1962 349-351 Langlois.
RPhL LXII 1964 164-170 Mansion.
AC XXXIII 1964 165 Joly.
RecSR LII 1964 476 des Places.
Mnemosyne XVII 1964 441-443 Westerink.
BTh IX 1963 220-222 Petit.
GIF XVI 1963 339-349 Sodano.
DLZ LXXXV 1964 405-407 Boese.
Scholastik XXXIX 1964 114-116 Kutsch.
JPhilos LXII 1965 14-17 Kristeller.
RFIC XCIII 1965 102-105 Franceschini.
Aevum XXXIX 1965 191 Franceschini.
Gnomon XXXVII 1965 26-32 Mensching.
JPh LXII 1965 14-17 Kristeller.
RecSR LIV 1966 300-302 Daniélou.

2482* CALCIDIUS, Plato, Timaeus. Interprete Chalcidio cum eiusdem comm.. (Unveränd. Nachdr. d. Ausg. Leipzig, Teubner 1876.) Frankfurt a.M., Minerva-Verl. 1963 xxiv&398p.

2483 WASZINK J.H., "Calcidius' Erklärung von Tim. 41e2-42a4". MH XXVI 1969 271-280.

2484* KRAUS P. & WALZER R., Plato Arabus, vol.I: Galeni compendium Timaei Platonis aliorumque dialogorum synopsis quae extant fragmenta, ed. Kraus P. & Walzer R. Nendeln, Liechtenstein, Kraus Reprint 1973 xii&118&67p. Reprint of 1951 London edn.

2485* DILLON J.M., Iamblichus' Commentary on the Timaeus. Diss. Univ. of California, Berkeley 1969 476p. Summary in DA XXX 1970 4431A-4432A.

III C d 42: TIMAEUS

2486* IAMBLICHUS, Iamblichi Chalcidensis in Platonis
dialogos commentariorum fragmenta, ed. with
transl. & comm. by Dillon J.M. Philos.
antiqua XXIII, Leiden, Brill 1973 viii&450p.
Rev. Durius I 1973 395-396 Cuodrado.

2487* PORPHYRY, Porphyrii In Platonis Timaeum
Commentariorum Fragmenta, coll. & disposiut
Sodano A.R. Napoli, Ist. della Stampa 1964
xxiv&140p.
Rev. Aegyptus XLIII 1963 415 Daris.
LEC XXXII 1964 300 Dumont.
GIF XVII 1964 177 Scivoletto.
Latomus XXIII 1964 837-839 Courcelle.
REA LXVII 1965 214-215 Pépin.
Vichiana II 1965 216 del Grande.
RPh XXXIX 1965 320 Louis.
CR XV 1965 168-169 Armstrong.
AAHG XVIII 1965 90 von Ivánka.
RecSR LIV 1966 611 des Places.
REAug XII 1966 183 Madec.
A&R XII 1967 87 Moreschini.
RBPh XLVII 1969 605 Hadot.

2488* HADOŢ P., Porphyre et Victorinus. 2 vols. Paris,
Études augustiniennes 1968 504 & 175p. (vol.
II contains fragments of Porphyry's commentary
on Plato's Parmenides.)
Rev. REG LXXXII 1969 242-244 Trouillard.
JThS XX 1969 637-639 Armstrong.
Erasmus XXI 1969 621-626 Beierwaltes.
RThPh 1970 346-347 Brunner.
RHE LXV 1970 126-131 Camelot.
IPQ X 1970 322-324 Clark.
JHPh VIII 1970 340-341 Lloyd.
Gregorianum LI 1970 752-754 Orbe.
Augustinus XV 1970 216-217 Oroz Reta.
Latomus XXIX 1970 547-550 de Ley.
ArchPhilos XXXIII 1970 645-650 Solignac.
VChr XXIV 1970 71-75 van Winden.
JHS XC 1970 242 Rist.
BTh XI 1971 207-208 Hissette.
RPhL LXX 1972 428-430 Hissette.

2489 SODANO A.R., "I frammenti dei commentari di Porfirio
al Timeo di Platone nel De aeternitate mundi di
Giovanni Filopono". RAAN XXXVII 1962 97-125.

2490* PROCLUS, Procli Diadochi in Platonis Timaeum
Commentaria, ed. Diehl E. 3 vols. Reprint of
Leipzig edn. 1903, 1904, 1906. Amsterdam,
Hakkert 1965 liv&476, vi&334, xiv&504p.

2491* PROCLUS, Commentaire sur le Timée, trad. & notes
par Festugière A.J. 2 vols. Paris, Vrin vol.
I: 1966 264p.; vol. II: 1967 341p.
Rev. Gnomon XLl 1969 127-134 Beierwaltes.
CRAI 1969 118 Festugière.

2492* PROCLUS, Commentaire sur le Timée, trad. et notes
par Festugière A.J. Tome III: Livre 3. Tome
IV: Livre 4. Tome V: Livre 5, Index général.
Bibl. des textes philosophiques, Paris, Vrin
1967-1968 362, 204, & 279p.

2493* FACKELDEY H., Zur Einheit des platonischen Timaios.
Diss. Köln 1958 113p.

2494 HACKFORTH R., "Plato's Cosmogony (Timaeus 27d ff.)".
CQ IX 1959 17-22.

2495 KYTZLER B., "Die Weltseele und der musikalische
Raum". Hermes LXXXVII 1959 393-414.

2496* ARNOUX G., Musique platonicienne, âme du monde.
Paris, Dervy-Livres 1960 296p.

2497 GULLEY N., "The Interpretation of Plato, Timaeus
49d-e". AJPh LXXXI 1960 53-64.

2498 SKEMP J.B., "Ὕλη and ὑποδοχή". p.201-212 in
Aristotle and Plato in the mid-fourth Century
(see 4586).

2499 DOHERTY K.F., "The Demiurge and the Good in Plato".
NS XXXV 1961 510-524.

2500 ARMLEDER P.J., "Some Observations on Plato's
Timaeus". CB XXXIX 1962 9-10.

2501 HOFFMANN E., "Platons Lehre von der Weltseele".
p.9-28 In Hoffmann E., Drei Schriften zur
griechischen Philosophie (see 4602). Reprinted
from Jahresbericht des philologischen Vereins zu
Berlin XLI 1915 187-211.

2502 KUSAYAMA K., "On the Disorderly Motion in the
Timaeus" [in Japanese with English summary].
JCS XII 1964 56-73.

2503* DISERTORI B., Il messaggio del Timeo. Padova, Cedam
1965 xiv&344p.
Rev. GIF XVIII 1965 358-361 Turolla.
Gregorianum XLVII 1966 418-419 Díaz de
Cerio.

Vichiana V 1968 149-152 Pini.
Sophia 1966 127-128 Romano.
Humanitas XX 1965 1188-1189 Demarchi.
Sophia XXXV 1967 397-401 Pavese.

2504 PAVESE R., "Il messagio del Timeo". Sophia XXXV 1967 396-401.

2505 GAISER K., "Platons Farbenlehre". p.173-222 in Synusia. Festgabe für Wolfgang Schadewaldt zum 15. März 1965, hrsg. von Flashar H. & Gaiser K. Pfullingen, Neske 1965.

2506* MOREAU J., L'âme du monde de Platon aux Stoïciens. Reprogr. Nachdr. der Ausg. Paris 1939. Hildesheim, Olms 1965 200p.

2507 MORROW G.R., "Necessity and Persuasion in Plato's Timaeus". p.421-437 in Studies in Plato's Metaphysics, ed. by Allen R.E. (see 4580). Reprinted from PhR 1950.

2508 OWEN G.E.L., "The Place of the Timaeus in Plato's Dialogues". p.313-338 in Studies in Plato's Metaphysics, ed. by Allen R.E. (see 4580). Reprinted from CQ 1953.

2509 CHERNISS H.F., "The Relation of the Timaeus to Plato's Later Dialogues". p.339-378 in Studies in Plato's Metaphysics, ed. by Allen R.E. (see 4580). Reprinted from AJPh 1957.

2510 VLASTOS G., "The Disorderly Motion in the Timaeus". p.379-399 in Studies in Plato's Metaphysics, ed. by Allen R.E. (see 4580). Reprinted from CQ 1939.

2511 VLASTOS G., "Creation in the Timaeus: Is it a Fiction?". p.401-419 in Studies in Plato's Metaphysics, ed. by Allen R.E. (see 4580).

2512 KUCHARSKI P., "Eschatologie et connaissance dans le Timée". ArchPhilos XXIX 1966 5-36.

2513 KUSAYAMA K., "On the Cosmogony of the Timaeus, I" [in Japanese]. Shoin Jr. College Bulletin VII 1966.

2514 LEE E.N., "On the Metaphysics of the Image in Plato's Timaeus". Monist L 1966 341-368.

2515 OWEN G.E.L., "Plato and Parmenides on the Timeless Present". Monist L 1966 317-340.

2516 CHERRY R.S., "Timaeus 49c7-50b5". Apeiron II 1967 1-11.

2517 EASTERLING H.J., "Causation in the Timaeus and Laws X". Eranos LXV 1967 25-38.

2518 LEE E.N., "On Plato's Timaeus 49d4-e7". AJPh LXXXVIII 1967 1-28.

2519 RAITH O., "ὁ Νεῖλος λυόμενος". Philologus CXI 1967 27-33.

2520 MILLS K.W., "Some Aspects of Plato's Theory of Forms. Timaeus 49c ff.". Phronesis XIII 1968 145-170.

2521 MORROW G.R., "Plato's Theory of the Primary Bodies in the Timaeus and the Later Doctrine of Forms". AGPh L 1968 12-28.

2522 OSTENFELD E., "Disorderly Motion in the Timaeus". C&M XXIX 1968 22-26.

2523 WOOD R.J., "The Demiurge and his Model". CJ LXIII 1968 255-258.

2524 KUSAYAMA K., "Notes on the problems of Interpretation. Timaeus Interpretation and Timaeus Natural Interpretation" [in Japanese]. Methodos II 1969.

2525 MAULA E., "Plato's Agalma of the Eternal Gods". Ajatus XXXI 1969 7-36.

2526 MORTLEY R.J., "The Bond of the Cosmos. A Significant Metaphor (Tim. 31c ff.)". Hermes XCVII 1969 372-373.

2527* POHLE W.B., Studies in the Physical Theory of Plato's Timaeus. Diss. Princeton Univ. 1969 172p. [microfilm]. Summary in DA XXX 1969 1204A.

2528 ROBINSON T.M., "Deux problèmes de la psychologie cosmique platonicienne". RPhilos CLIX 1969 247-253.

III C d 42: TIMAEUS

2529 SCHUHL P.M., "La pathologie mentale selon Platon dans le Timée". AThPsy IV 1969 246-250.

2530 MAULA E., "Plato's 'Mirror of Soul' in the Timaeus". Ajatus XXXII 1970 160-184.

2531* MAULA E., Studies in Plato's Theory of Forms in the Timaeus. AASF CLXIX 1970 31p.

2532 BENARDETE S., "On Plato's Timaeus and Timaeus' Science Fiction". Interpretation II 1971 21-63.

2533 KEYT D., "The mad Craftsman of the Timaeus". PhR LXXX 1971 230-235.

2534* KREBBS N.A.,Plato's errant Cause. Diss. Univ. of Washington 1971 85p. [microfilm]. Summary in DA XXXII 1971 2744A.

2535 LEE E.N., "On the 'gold-example' in Plato's Timaeus (50a5-b5)". p.219-235 in Essays in ancient Greek Philosophy, ed. by Anton J.P. & Kustas G.L. (see 4581).

2536 TARÁN L., "The Creation Myth in Plato's Timaeus". p.372-407 in Essays in ancient Greek Philosophy, ed. by Anton J.P. & Kustas G.L. (see 4581).

2537* BRENNAN W.T., Cosmogenesis as Myth. A Philosophical Analysis and Comparison of the Timaios of Plato and the Babylonian Enuma elish. Diss. De Paul Univ., Chicago 1970 243p. [microfilm]. Summary in DA XXXII 1972 4655A.

2538 MOVIA G., "Creazione e destino umano nel Timeo di Platone". p.287-291 in Mondo storico ed Escatologia. Atti del XXVI Convegno del Centro di Studi Filosofici tra Professori Universitari, Gallarate, 1971. Brescia, Morcelliana 1972.

2539* BRISSON L., Le même et l'autre dans la structure ontologique du Timée de Platon. Un commentaire systématique du Timée de Platon. Publ. de l'Univ. de Paris X-Nanterre, Ser.A, Thèses et travaux XXIII, Paris, Klincksieck 1973 589p.

2540 DOUDA E., "Platons Weltbaumeister". Altertum XIX 1973 147-156.

2541 SUZUKI T., "Again on Plato's Demiurgos" [in Japanese]. Osaka City Univ. Dept. of Literature, Studies XXV 1973 suppl. 4.

289

For additional discussions see 89, 251, 263, 266, 267,
        276, 367, 382, 400, 404, 418, 481, 492, 510,
        520, 523, 525, 615, 744, 755, 756, 772, 775,
        784, 790, 799, 1108, 1151, 1895, 1915, 2149,
        2269, 2305, 2519, 2584, 2591, 2698, 2704, 2825,
        2943, 3047, 3062, 3086, 3094, 3129, 3159, 3211,
        3215, 3218, 3219, 3222, 3223, 3225, 3226, 3231,
        3232, 3236, 3238, 3239, 3241, 3242, 3243, 3267,
        3298, 3300, 3306, 3307, 3315, 3330, 3346, 3347,
        3348, 3349, 3350, 3351, 3352, 3353, 3354, 3356,
        3357, 3360, 3365, 3366, 3367, 3368, 3369, 3370,
        3371, 3372, 3373, 3375, 3376, 3377, 3379, 3380,
        3382, 3383, 3384, 3389, 3393, 3396, 3399, 3400,
        3407, 3409, 3410, 3412, 3419, 3693, 3917, 3918,
        3921, 3932, 3940, 3944, 3977, 3989, 4058, 4064,
        4109.

C. TEXTUAL CRITICISM

2542 PINI F., "Varianti del Codice Vossiano Latino Q 10
     al testo del Timeo". Ciceroniana 1960,1-2
     161-163.

2543 JEAUNEAU E., "Gloses sur le Timée et commentaire du
     Timée dans deux manuscrits du Vatican". REAug
     VIII 1962 365-373.

2544 JEAUNEAU E., "Gloses sur le Timée, du manuscrit
     Digby 217 de la Bodléienne, à Oxford". SEJG
     XVII 1966 365-400.

2545 JEAUNEAU E., "Gloses marginales sur le Timée de
     Platon, du manuscrit 226 de la Bibliothèque
     municipale d'Avranches". SEJG XVII 1966 71-89.

2546 WHITTAKER J., "Timaeus 27d5 ff.". Phronesis XXIII
     1969 181-185. Reprinted ch.8, p.212-223 in
     Whittaker J., God, Time, Being. Studies in the
     Transcendental Tradition in Greek Philosophy.
     Bergen 1970.

2547 BERTI E., "Plato, Timaeus 52a1". RFIC CI 1973 194.

2548 WHITTAKER J., "Textual Comments on Timaeus 27c-d".
     Phoenix XXVII 1973 387-391.

For additional discussion of the text see 1360.

IV: PLATO AS WRITER

A: LANGUAGE, PROSE STYLE AND FIGURES OF SPEECH

2549 TARRANT D., "More Colloquialisms, Semi-proverbs, and
      Word-play in Plato". CQ LII 1958 158-160.

2550* CLASSEN C.J., Sprachliche Deutung als Triebkraft
      platonischen und sokratischen Philosophierens.
      Zetemata XXII, München, Beck 1959 xii&187p.
           Rev. PhilosRdschau VII 1959 195-198
      Beierwaltes.
           PACA III 1960 29-30 Skemp.
           Mnemosyne XIII 1960 352-353 de Vries.
           AAHG XIII 1960 234 Vretska.
           RecSR XLIX 1961 291 des Places.
           CPh LVI 1961 68-69 Hoerber.
           RPh XXXV 1961 142-143 Humbert.
           JHS LXXXI 1961 187 Adkins.
           AC XXX 1961 220 Duchesne-Guillemin.
           Gnomon XXXIII 1961 87 Kuhn.
           MH XVIII 1961 239 Wehrli.
           CR XI 1961 217-219 Baldry.
           REA LXIII 1961 147-148 Goldschmidt.
           Euphrosyne III 1961 419-420 Galiano.
           Gymnasium LXX 1963 182 Oehler.
           ArchPhilos XXV 1962 611-612 Braun.
           Erasmus XV 1963 628-632 Koller.

2551* PLASS P.C., Plato's Symbolism. Diss. Univ. of
      Wisconsin 1959 229p. [microfilm]. Summary in
      DA XX 1959 1019-1020.

2552* REZZANI M., Note e ricerche intorno al linguaggio di
      Platone. Padova, Cedam 1959 58p.
           Rev. RSF XIV 1959 355 Buccellato.
           RRFC LIII 1959 159 Pignoloni.
           RPhL LIX 1961 124-125 Canart.
           Sapienza XIII 1960 462-463 Passeri
      Pignoni.

2553* BUCHHEIT V., Untersuchungen zur Theories des Genos
      epideiktikon von Gorgias bis Aristoteles.
      München, Hueber 1960 260p.
           Rev. CR LXXVI 1962 37-38 Douglas.
           AAHG XV 1962 156-160 Quadlbauer.
           AJPh LXXXIII 1962 326-329 Kennedy.
           DLZ LXXXIV 1963 24-26 Augustyniak.

IV A: LANGUAGE, PROSE STYLE AND FIGURES OF SPEECH

Gymnasium LXX 1963 371-372 Voit.

2554* ROETTGER J., Das Zitat bei Platon. Diss. Tübingen
1960 202p.
Rev. Helikon V 1965 688-698 Kövendi.

2555 KLEVE K., "The Unum Venerabilissimum and Plato's
Mystical Style (Parm. 142a)". SO XXXVII 1961
88-95.

2556 PLACES E. DES, "Constructions grecques de mots à
fonction double (ἀπὸ κοινοῦ)". REG LXXV 1962
1-12.

2557 BENARDETE S., "The Right, the True, and the
Beautiful". Glotta XLI 1963 54-62.

2558 KELLS J.H., "Assimilation of Predicate-material to
the Object in Plato Rep. VII 518c and other
Passages". Philologus CVIII 1964 72-79.

2559 PLACES E. DES, "Platon et la langue des mystères".
AFLA XXXVIII 1964 9-23.

2560* BENKENDORF K.A., Untersuchungen zu den platonischen
Gleichnissen, Vergleichen und Metaphern aus dem
Bereich der Gymnastik und Agonistik. Diss.
Tübingen 1966 211p.

2561 OGUSE A., "Sur des emplois peu connus de l'infinitif
précédé de l'article". RPhL XL 1966 59-69.

2562* THESLEFF H., Studies in the Styles of Plato. Acta
Philosophica Fennica XX, Helsinki, Soc. Philos.
Fennica 1967 192p.
Rev. RPh XLII 1968 332 des Places.
AC XXXVII 1968 677-678 Schwartz.
REG LXXXI 1968 291-292 Weil.
REA LXX 1968 460-461 Vicaire.
CW LXII 1968 29 Hoerber.
JHS LXXXVIII 1968 160-161 Brandwood.
Gnomon XLI 1969 636-639 Dover.
CR XIX 1969 41-42 Gulley.
CPh LXIV 1969 128-129 Sprague.
PhilosRdschau XVI 1969 312.
CJ LXV 1969 31-34 Robinson.
JHPh VII 1969 202-206 Hathaway.
Erasmus XXII 1970 683-684 Clavaud.
BIEH IV 1970 59-61 Conejero.
Mnemosyne XXIII 1970 420-422 de Vries.
AAHG XXIII 1970 151-153 Vretska.
RBPh XLIX 1971 171 de Strycker.

IV A: LANGUAGE, PROSE STYLE AND FIGURES OF SPEECH

2563 THESLEFF H., "Genitive Absolute and Platonic Style". Arctos VI 1969 121-131.

2564 WITTWER M., "Über die kontrastierende Funktion des griechischen Suffixes -τερος". Glotta XLVII 1969 54-110.

2565 WISHART D. & LEACH S.V., "A Multivariate Analysis of Platonic Prose Rhythm". CompSt III 1970 90-99.

2566 THESLEFF H., "Colloquial Style and its use in Plato's Later Works". Arctos VII 1972 219-227.

2567 GUNDERT H., "'Perspektivische Täuschung' bei Platon und die Prinzipienlehre". p.80-97 in Zetesis (see 4579).

2568 VRIES G.J. DE, "Mystery Terminology in Aristophanes and Plato". Mnemosyne XXVI 1973 1-8.

For further discussions of this topic see 213, 1903, 2207, 4551.

STUDIES OF PARTICULAR IMAGES AND EXPRESSIONS, INCLUDING THEIR LATER HISTORY

2569 CADIOU R., "Atomes et éléments graphiques". BAGB 1958,3 54-64.

2570 CAPELLE W., "Farbenbezeichnungen bei Throphrast". RhM CI 1958 1-41.

2571 COURCELLE P., "Problème de transmission du platonisme à l'Occident patristique et médiéval, à propos de l'expression du Politique 273d: τόπος ἀνομοιότητος". EHE 1957-1958, 61.

2572 COURCELLE P., "Témoins nouveaux de la 'région de dissemblance' (Platon, Politique 273d)". BECh CXVIII 1960 20-36.

2573 COURCELLE P., "Treize textes nouveaux sur la région de dissemblance (Platon, Politique, 273d)". REAug XVI 1970 271-281.

2574 COURCELLE P., "La colle et le clou de l'âme dans la tradition néo-platonicienne et chrétienne (Phédon 82e; 83d)". RBPh XXXVI 1958 72-95.

2575 COURCELLE P., "Variations sur le clou de l'âme (Platon, Phédon, 83d)". p.38-40 in Mélanges offerts à Chr. Mohrmann, éd. par Engels L.J., Hoppenbrouwers H.W.F.M. & Vermeulin A.J. Utrecht, Spectrum Ed. 1963.

2576 AUBINEAU M., "Le thème du bourbier dans la littérature grecque profane et chrétienne". RecSR XLVII 1959 185-214.

2577 COURCELLE P., "Trames veritatis. La fortune patristique d'une métaphore platonicienne (Phédon 66b)". p.203-210 in Mélanges offerts à Étienne Gilson. Toronto, Pontifical Inst. of Medieval Studies and Paris, Vrin 1959.

2578 LUCCIONI J., "Platon et la mer". REA LXI 1959 15-47.

2579 NOVOTNÝ F., "Poros, father of Eros" [in Czech with French summary]. LF VII 1959 39-49.

2580 ORCIBAL J., "Une formule de l'amour extatique de Platon à saint Jean de la Croix et au cardinal de Bérulle". p.447-463 in Mélanges offerts à Étienne Gilson. Toronto, Pontifical Inst. of Medieval Studies and Paris, Vrin 1959.

2581 SCHOENBERGER O., "Zikaden. Ein platonisches Motiv im modernen Hörspiel". A&A VIII 1959 119-124.

2582* AICHROTH R., Schauspiel und Schauspiel-Vergleich bei Platon. Diss. Tübingen 1960 151p.

2583* CLASSEN C.J., Untersuchungen zu Platons Jagdbildern. Dt. Akad. der Wiss. zu Berlin, Schriften der Sektion für Altertumswiss. XXV, Berlin, Akad.-Verl. 1960 viii&64p.
    Rev. Gnomon XXXIV 1962 241-245 Goergemanns.
    Helikon II 1962 367-368 Alsina.
    CR XXI 1961 217 Baldry.
    RecSR L 1962 610 des Places.

2584 COURCELLE P., "Escae malorum (Timée 69d)". p.244-252 in Hommages à L. Herrmann. Coll. Latomus XLIV, Berchem-Bruxelles 1960.

IV A: LANGUAGE, PROSE STYLE AND FIGURES OF SPEECH

2585 ELIADE M., "Mythes et symboles de la corde".
Eranos-Jb XXIX 1960 109-137.

2586 HOMMEL H., "Der Weg nach oben. Betrachtungen zu
lateinischen Spruchgut". StudGen XIII 1960
296-299.

2587 JONG M. DE, "Een Portugees sentiment bij Plato".
Hermeneus XXXII 1960 4-7.

2588 TARRANT D., "Greek Metaphors of Light". CQ X 1960
181-187.

2589 VERNANT J.P., "Le fleuve Amélès et la Mélétè
Thanatou". RPhilos CL 1960 163-179.

2590 BRUNSCHWIG J., "Correspondance. Sur Amélès et
Mélétè". RPhilos CLIII 1963 267-268.

2591 TABACHOVITZ D., "Πολλὰ πολλῶν ". Eranos LIX 1961
5-48.

2592 HOŠEK R., "Zur Geschichte einer Redewendung (τους
νόμους καταπατεῖν)". p.93-99 in Charisteria F.
Novotný octogenario oblata, cur. Stiebitz F. &
Hošek R. Opera Univ. Purkynianae Brunensis,
Fac. Philos. XC, Praha, Státni Pedag. Naklad.
1962.

2593 RANKIN H.D., "Plato and Man the Puppet". Eranos LX
1962 127-131.

2594 BOYANCÉ P., "Note sur la φρουρά platonicienne". RPh
XXXVII 1963 7-11.

2595 COLACLIDES P., "Variations sur une métaphore de
Platon". C&M XXVII 1966 116-117.

2596 COURCELLE P., "Tradition platonicienne et traditions
chrétiennes du corps-prison (Phédon 62b;
Cratyle 400c)". Summary in CRAI 1965 341-343.

2597 COURCELLE P., "L'âme en cage". p.103-116 in
Parusia, hrsg. von Flasch K. (see 4588).

2598 COURCELLE P., "Tradition platonicienne et traditions
chrétiennes du corps-prison (Phédon 62b, Cratyle
400c)". REL XLIII 1965 406-443.

IV A: LANGUAGE, PROSE STYLE AND FIGURES OF SPEECH

2599 COURCELLE P., "Le corps-tombeau. Platon, Gorgias
493a, Cratyle 400c, Phèdre 250c". REA LXVIII
1966 101-122.

2600 LORIAUX R., "Note sur la φρουρά platonicienne
(Phédon 62b-c)". LEC XXXVI 1968 28-36.

2601 HOERBER R.G., "The Socratic Oath 'By the Dog'". CJ
LVIII 1963 268-269.

2602 BUCCA S., "La imagen del carro en el Fedro de Platón
y en la Katha-Upaniṣad". AFC VIII 1964 5-28.

2603 REYNEN H., "Ewiger Frühling und goldene Zeit. Zum
Mythos des goldenen Zeitalters bei Ovid und
Vergil". Gymnasium LXXII 1965 415-433.

2604 RINGBOM S., "Plato on Images". Theoria XXXI 1965
86-109.

2605 PLACES E. DES, "Un thème platonicien dans la
tradition patristique, le juste crucifié
(Platon, République, 361e4-362a2). p.30-40 in
Studia Patristica IX. Papers presented to the
Fourth International Conference on Patristic
Studies held at Christ Church, Oxford, 1963, 3:
Classica. Philosophica et Ethica. Theologica.
Augustiniana. Postpatristica. Untersuchungen
zur Geschichte der altchristlichen Literatur CI,
Berlin, Akad.-Verl. 1966.

2606* DRIESCH R., Platons Wegbilder. Untersuchungen zur
Funktion der Wegbilder und -metaphern im Aufbau
der Dialoge Platons. Diss. Köln 1967 115p.

2607 TOMADAKIS N.V., "Λήθης βυθού, Λήθης πέδον, Λήθης
πεδίον". EHBS XXXV 1966-1967 68.

2608 COURCELLE P., "Le visage de Philosophie". REA LXX
1968 110-120.

2609 COURCELLE P., "Le personnage de Philosophie dans la
littérature latine". JS 1970 209-252.

2610 COURCELLE P., "La plaine de vérité. Platon, Phèdre
248b". MH XXVI 1969 199-203.

2611 MADEC G., "'In planissimo campo veritatis'
(Augustin, 'Epistula' 37,2)". REAug XVI 1970
289-290.

IV A: LANGUAGE, PROSE STYLE AND FIGURES OF SPEECH

2612 FRIEDLAENDER P., "Δὶς καὶ τρὶς τὸ καλόν". p.206-209 in Friedlaender P., Studien zur antiken Literatur und Kunst (see 4589). Reprinted from TAPhA LXIX 1938 375-380.

2613 KOHNKE F.W., "Das Bild der echten Münze bei Philon von Alexandria". Hermes XCVI 1968-1969 583-590.

2614 WILLETTS R.F., "More on the Black Hunter". PCPhS XV 1969 106-107.

2615 CARACCIOLO A., "Sul significato dell'antitesi φιλοσώματος-φιλόσοφος nel Fedone platonico". Proteus I 1970 77-107.

2616 NICKEL R., "Der diomedische Zwang (Platon, Politeia 493d)". AU XIII 1970 93-100.

2617 TIGNER S.S., "Plato's Philosophical Uses of the Dream Metaphor". AJPh XCI 1970 204-212.

2618 GALLOP D., "Dreaming and Waking in Plato". p.187-201 in Essays in ancient Greek Philosophy, ed. by Anton J.P. & Kustas G.L. (see 4581).

2619 GEWEHR W., "Der Topos 'Augen des Herzens'. Versuch einer Deutung durch die scholastische Erkenntnistheorie". DVLG XLVI 1972 626-649.

2620 WEHRLI F., "Der Arztvergleich bei Platon". p.206-214 in Wehrli F., Theoria und Humanitas (see 4625). Reprinted from MH VIII 1951 177-184.

2621 SCHAEFER E., "Das Staatsschiff. Zur Präzision eines Topos". p.259-292 in Toposforschung, hrsg. von Baeumer M.L. Wege der Forsch. CXCV, Darmstadt, Wiss. Buchges. 1973.

For further discussions see 579, 1055, 1075, 1311, 1405, 1427, 1464, 1675, 1844, 1847, 2028, 2029, 2039, 2364, 2526, 2717, 4026, 4272.

IV B: DIALOGUE: STRUCTURE, TECHNIQUE,
CHARACTERIZATION AND INTENTION

2622 LOEWENCLAU I. VON, "Mythos und Logos bei Platon".
      StudGen XI 1958 731-741.

2623* GAISER K., Protreptik und Paränese bei Platon.
      Untersuchungen zur Form des platonischen
      Dialogs. Tübinger Beitr. zur Altertumswiss.
      XL, Stuttgart, Kohlhammer 1959 232p.
            Rev. RBPh XXXIX 1961 197-199 Janssens.
            DLZ LXXXII 1961 134-136 Frenkian.
            RThPh XI 1961 96-97 Lasserre.
            PLA XIV 1961 65-67 Lumpe.
            RecSR XLIX 1961 291-292 des Places.
            Scholastik XXXVII 1962 119-120 Ennen.
            Gnomon XXXIV 1962 13-21 de Strycker.
            ArchPhilos XXV 1962 610-611 Valentin.
            Erasmus XVI 1964 418-422 Gottschalk.
            AGPh XLV 1963 68-75 Voigtlaender.

2624 DESMONDE W., "The Ritual Origin of Plato's
      Dialogues". AmIm XVII 1960 389-406.

2625 GUNDERT H., "Ὁ Πλατωνικὸς διάλογος". EEThess VIII
      1960 191-210.

2626 LABORDERIE J., "La forme du dialogue platonicien de
      la maturité". IL XII 1960 64-70.

2627 WITLOX A., "Plato, de dramaturg". Streven XIII
      1959-1960 1068-1072.

2628* MUTHMANN F., Untersuchungen zur Einkleidung einiger
      platonischer Dialoge. Diss. Bonn
      Friedrich-Wilhelms-Univ. 1961 139p.
            Rev. CR XIII 1963 113 Gulley.
            AAHG XVI 1963 87 Thummer.
            Mnemosyne XVI 1963 73 de Vries.
            RPh XXXVIII 1964 138 Louis.
            Gymnasium LXXII 1965 256-257 Merlan.
            Helikon VII 1967 660-667 Koevendi.

2629 STENZEL J., "Forma letteraria e contenuto filosofico
      dei dialoghi". p.226-251 in Antologia della
      critica filosofica, ed. Rossi P. (see 4613).
      Reprinted in Ital. transl. from Stenzel J.,
      Kleine Schriften zur griechischen Philosophie.
      Darmstadt, Wissenschaftl. Buchges. 1956 32-47.

2630 WYCHERLEY R.E., "Peripatos. The Athenian
      Philosophical Scene". G&R VIII 1961 152-163, IX
      1962 2-21.

2631 EDELSTEIN L., "Platonic Anonymity". AJPh LXXXIII
1962 1-22.

2632 PLASS P., "Philosophic Anonymity and Irony in the
Platonic Dialogues". AJPh LXXXV 1964 254-278.

2633* SPRAGUE R.K., Plato's Use of Fallacy. A Study of
the Euthydemus and Some other Dialogues.
London, Routledge & Kegan Paul 1962 xvi&106p.
Rev. TLS 12 Dec. 1963 1036.
PhilosBks May 1963 27 Lemmon.
CR XIII 1963 284-285 Crombie.
CW LVI 1963 183 Hoerber.
CJ LIX 1963 130-132 Hoerber.
JHS LXXXIV 1964 189-190 Robinson.
Mind LXXIII 1964 142-144 Moravcsik.
Gnomon XXXVI 1964 335-340 Gehler.
PhilosQ XIV 1964 78-80 Robinson.
JCS XIII 1965 175-177 Takemiya.
RPhilos CLVIII 1968 291-294 Vincent.

2634 BUCCELLATO M., "Studi sul dialogo platonico". RSF
XVIII 1963 527-560.

2635* COHEN M.H., Plato's Use of Ambiguity and Deliberate
Fallacy. An Interpretation of the Implicit
Doctrines of the Charmides and Lysis. Diss.
Columbia Univ. New York 1963 287p.
[microfilm]. Summary in DA XXIV 1964 3785.

2636 DOENT E., "Die Stellung der Exkurse in den
pseudoplatonischen Dialogen". WS LXXVI 1963
27-51.

2637* GOLDSCHMIDT V., Les Dialogues de Platon. Structure
et méthode dialectique. 2e ed. Bibl. de phil.
contemp., Paris, Presses Universitaires 1963
xxviii&376p.

2638 PIEPER J., "Platonische Figuren". p.256-283 in
Pieper J., Tradition als Herausforderung.
Aufsätze und Reden. München, Kösel 1963.
Reprinted from NDH 1954 & 1955.

2639 WOLZ H.G., "Philosophy as Drama. An Approach to the
Dialogues of Plato". IPQ III 1963 236-270.

2641 LLEDÓ E., "El fundamento de la anámnesis platónica". p.326-331 in Actas del II Congreso Esp. de Estud. clás. (Madrid-Barcelona, 4-10 de abril de 1961). Publ. de la Soc. Esp. de Estud. clás. V, Madrid 1964.

2642 DERBOLAV J., "Was Plato 'sagte' und was er 'gemeint hat'. Erörterung einer hermeneutisch bedeutsamen Differenz". p.161-187 in Beispiele. Festschrift für Eugen Fink zum 60. Geburtstag, hrsg. von Landgrebe L. Den Haag, Nijhoff 1965.

2643 OKADA S., "What Encouraged Plato to write the Dialogues?" [in Japanese with English summary]. JCS XIII 1965 1-14.

2644* SINAIKO H.L., Love, Knowledge, and Discourse in Plato. Dialogue and Dialectic in Phaedrus, Republic, Parmenides. Chicago, Univ. of Chicago Pr. 1965 xii&314p.
Rev. CPh LXI 1966 265-266 Sprague.
CJ LXII 1966 130-132 Rist.
CW LIX 1966 313 Stewart.
RSF XXI 1966 455-457 Buccellato.
PhilosStud(Irel.) XV 1966 323-324 Watson.
ModS XLIII 1965-1966 429-432 Neumann.
ASM 1966 124-126 González Pazos.
Phoenix XXI 1967 64-65 Timothy.
CR XVII 1967 28-30 Gulley.
EPh XXII 1967 112 Pépin.
NS XLI 1967 529-530 Kreilkamp.
Dialogue V 1966-1967 102-103 Reesor.
RM XX 1966-1967 732 D.J.B.
RMM LXXIII 1968 367-369 Brunschwig.
RBPh XLVII 1969 524-526 de Strycker.
ArchPhilos XXXIII 1970 141-142 Moreau.

2645* DIETERLE R., Platons Laches und Charmides. Untersuchungen zur elenktisch-aporetischen Struktur der platonischen Frühdialoge. Diss. Freiburg 1966 323p.
Rev. REG LXXXI 1968 615-616 Vicaire.
CR XVIII 1968 326-327 Easterling.
Gymnasium LXXVI 1969 93-95 Mansfeld.

2646 SERRES M., "Le troisième homme ou le tiers exclu". EPh XXI 1966 463-469.

2647 MOULINIER L., "Dans quel sens et dans quelle mesure les dialogues de Platon sont-ils des pièces de théâtre?". Dioniso XLI 1967 186-193.

2648 GUNDERT H., "Dialog und Dialektik. Zur Struktur des
platonischen Dialogs". StudGen XXI 1968
295-379,387-449.

2649* GUNDERT H., Der platonische Dialog. Bibl. der
klass. Altertumswiss. N.F. 2.R. XXVI,
Heidelberg, Winter 1968 59p.
Rev. Dialogos VI 1969 126-128 Gómez Lobo.
CW LXII 1969 280 Costas.
REA LXXI 1969 145-146 Moreau.
AC XXXVIII 1969 230 Lasserre.
Gymnasium LXXVII 1970 242-244
Voigtlaender.
CR XX 1970 248 Gulley.

2650 HYLAND D.A., "Why Plato wrote Dialogues". Ph&Rh I
1968 38-50.

2651 SÁNCHEZ LASSO DE LA VEGA J., "El diálogo y la
filosofía platónica del arte". EClas XII 1968
311-374.

2652 BERNHARDT J., "Dialogue et dialectique dans les
dialogues de Platon". p.20-22 in La
Dialectique. Actes du XIVe Congrès des Sociétés
de Philosophie de Langue française. Nice, 1-4
sept. 1969. Paris, Presses Universitaires
1969.

2653 GOULD J.B., "Klein on Ethological Mimes, for
example, the Meno". JPh LXVI 1969 253-265.

2654 HERMANN K.F., "Über Platos schriftstellerische
Motive". p.33-57 in Das Platonbild, hrsg. von
Gaiser K. (see 4595). Reprinted from Hermann
K.F., Gesammelte Abhandlungen und Beiträge zur
klassischen Literatur und Altertumskunde.
Göttingen 1849, p.281-305.

2655 KUHN H., "Die wahre Tragödie--Platon als Nachfolger
der Tragiker". p.231-323 in Das Platonbild,
hrsg. von Gaiser K. (see 4595). Reprinted as
Sonderausdruck. Hildesheim/New York, Olms 1970.
Originally appeared in HSPh LII 1941 1-40 & LIII
1942 37-88 as "The True Tragedy--On the
Relationship between Greek Tragedy and Plato".

2656 ROBINSON R., "Plato's Consciousness of Fallacy".
p.16-38 in Robinson R., Essays in Greek
Philosophy (see 4612). Reprinted from Mind
1942.

2657* SCHAERER R., La question platonicienne, étude sur
      les rapports de la pensée et de l'expression
      dans les Dialogues. 2e éd. rev. & augm.
      d'une postface: "À la recherche de Platon".
      Mém. de l'Univ. de Neuchâtel X, Neuchâtel
      Univ. & Paris, Vrin 1969 343p.
      Rev. ASSPh XXIX 1969 224 Christoff.

2658 ANDERSON J.M., "On the Platonic Dialogue". p.5-17
      in Essays in Metaphysics by the Members of the
      Philosophy Department of The Pennsylvania State
      University, ed. by Vaught C.G. University
      Park, Penn./London, The Penn. State Univ. Pr.
      1970.

2659* GILL C.J., Plato's Use of Characters in his
      Dialogues. Diss. Yale Univ. 1970 305p.
      [microfilm]. Summary in DA XXXI 1970 6574A.

2660 LATTRE A. DE, "La liberté socratique et le dialogue
      platonicien". KantStud LXI 1970 467-495.

2661* RANDALL J.H., Plato, Dramatist of the Life of
      Reason. New York, Columbia Univ. Pr. 1970
      xiv&274p.
      Rev. CW LXIV 1970 86-87 Sprague.
      HeythrJ XI 1970 430-432 Copleston.
      PhilosStud(Irel.) XX 283-284 Ardley.
      Dialogue X 1971 568-572 Shiner.
      PhilosForum IX 1971 357-359 Bondeson.
      DalR 1971 121 Page.
      RM XXIV 1970-1971 753 L.G.
      Gymnasium LXXVIII 1971 254-255 Nickel.
      LEC XL 1972 442 Druet.
      Gnomon XLIV 1972 716-717 Hentschke.
      CR XXII 1972 270 Charlton.
      IPQ XII 1972 142-145 Neville.
      JHPh X 1972 459-472 Machle.
      Thought XLVII 1972 313-315 Gilligan.
      CJ LXVIII 1972 183-185 Robinson.
      AJPh XCIV 1973 202-204 Neumann.
      NS XLVII 1973 414-418 Sweeney.
      Mittelstrass J., "Philosophy as Artistic
      Achievement?", JHI XXXII 1971 459-470.

2662 BURRELL D.B., "What the Dialogues show about
      Inquiry". PhilosForum III 1971 104-125.

2663* GEDDES J., An Essay on the Composition and Manner of
      Writing of the Ancients, Particularly Plato.
      New York, Garland Publ. 1971 362p. Reprint of
      1748 edn.

IV B: DIALOGUE

2664 JERPHAGNON L., "Platon et les 'Ηλίθιοι".   RMM LXXVI
      1971 24-31.

2665 HASLAM M.W., "Plato, Sophron, and the Dramatic
      Dialogue". BICS XIX 1972 17-38.

2666 TREVASKIS J.R., "Form and Content in Plato's
      Dialogues". Summary p.77 in AULLA XIV.
      Proceedings and Papers of the fourteenth
      Congress of the Australasian Universities
      Language and Literature Assoc., held 19-26 Jan.
      1972 at the Univ. of Otago, Dunedin, New
      Zealand, ed. by Maslen K.I.D. Dunedin, N.Z.,
      University of Otago 1972.

2667 LANG B., "Presentation and Representation in Plato's
      Dialogues". PhilosForum IV 1972-1973 224-240.

2668* WEINGARTNER R.A., The Unity of the Platonic
      Dialogue. The Cratylus, the Protagoras, the
      Parmenides. Libr. of Liberal Arts CCXXIV,
      Indianapolis, Indiana, Bobbs-Merrill 1973
      x&205p.
      Rev.   Ph&PhenR   XXIV   1973   132-133
      Harrington.
      Thomist   XXXVII   1973   793-805
      Anagnostopoulos.
      RM XXVII 1973-1974 626-627 Rudoff.

For further discussions of this topic see 25, 1056, 1181,
      1231, 1234, 1334, 1335, 1348, 1349, 1350, 1351,
      1355, 1464, 1468, 1496, 1497, 1556, 1581, 1584,
      1676, 1677, 1679, 1683, 1685, 1854, 2340, 2341,
      2346, 2352, 2364, 2368, 2369, 2380, 2429, 2562,
      2752, 2760, 2794, 2824, 3662, 4438.

IV C: MYTH AND ALLEGORY

2669* HILDEBRANDT K., Platon. Logos und Mythos. 2.
      durchgesehene und durch ein Nachwort ergänzte
      Aufl. Berlin, de Gruyter 1959 viii&396p.
      Rev. RUB XII 1959-1960 257-258 Janssens.
      ASSPh XX 1960 162-163 Schaerer.
      StudUrb XXXIV 1960 190.
      RSF 1960 261-262 Hildebrandt.
      ModS XXXVII 1959-1960 338.
      RSFil XIII 1960 261-262 N.P.
      WWeish XXIV 1961 72-73 Calama.

NG IX 1962 194-195 Ventosa.
Pensamiento XVII 1961 364-365 Gerardo.

2670 MATHIEU V., "Convergenza verso il bene e mito schematico in Platone". RAL XV 1960 102-122.

2671 REINHARDT K., "Platons Mythen". p.219-295, 414 in Reinhardt K., Vermächtnis der Antike. Gesammelte Essays zur Philosophie und Geschichtsschreibung. Göttingen 1960.

2672 PIEPER J., "Ueber die Wahrheit der platonischen Mythen". p.289-296 in Einsichten. G. Krueger zum 60. Geburtstag, hrsg. von Oehler K. & Schaeffer R. Frankfurt, Klostermann 1962.

2673 COULTER J.A., "Plato and Sophistic Myth. Studies in Plato's Apology and Symposium". HSPh LXVII 1963 307-308.

2674 MUELLER G., "Die Mythen der platonischen Dialoge". Antrittsvorles. Giessen 1963. Nachr. der Giessener Hochschulges. XXXII 1963 77-92.

2675 ANTON J.P., "Plato's Philosophical Use of Myth". GOh IX 1963-1964 161-180.

2676 BRUNET C., "Mythes et croyances". RMM LXIX 1964 276-288.

2677 GARCÍA CALVO A., "Dialectica y mito". p.300-317 in Actas del II Congr. esp. de Est. clás. (Madrid-Barcelona, 4-10 de abril de 1961). Publ. de la Soc. Esp. de Estud. Clás. V, Madrid 1964.

2678 PIEPER J., "Platons eschatologische Mythen". NDH CII 1964 54-60.

2679* PIEPER J., Über die platonischen Mythen. München, Kösel 1965 96p.
Rev. GGA CCXIX 1967 12-20 Mueller.
Pensamiento 1967 218-219 Gómez Muntán.
PLA XIX 1966 209-210 Klamp.
RBPh XLIV 1966 186 des Places.
FolHum III 1965 747 Arasa.
Streven XVIII 1964-1965 931 den Ottolander.
PhilosStud(Irel.) XIV 1965 258 Watson.
CISymb VIII 1965 103 Witte.
Stromata XXI 1965 529-530.
NG XIII 1966 372 Rivera de Ventosa.

IV C: MYTH AND ALLEGORY

RPortFil XXII 1966 208-209 Freire.

2680 DOERRIE H., "Der Mythos im Verständnis der Antike, II: Von Euripides bis Seneca". Gymnasium LXXIII 1966 44-62.

2681 MACH D., "Die Wahrheit des Mythos. Zu drei Büchern von W.F. Otto und Josef Pieper". Kairos VIII 1966 246-257.

2682 GIANNINI A., "Mito e utopia nella letteratura greca prima di Platone". RIL CI 1967 101-132.

2683 LAVELLE L., "Les mythes platoniciens". p.45-54 in Lavelle L., Panorama des doctrines philosophiques (see 4607).

2684 ESCUDERO C., "Mito y filosofia. El mito platónico y su significado". Perficit I.11-14 janv.-avr. 1968 243-302, 307-345.

2685 GREGORY M.J., "Myth and Transcendence in Plato". Thought XLIII 1968 273-296.

2686* SCHUHL P.M., La fabulation platonicienne. 2e éd. rév. & mise à jour. Bibl. d'hist. de la philos., Paris, Vrin 1968 140p.
Rev. IL XX 1968 233 Weil.
REA LXXI 1969 146 Moreau.
CRAI 1968 559-560 Courcelle.
RSR XLV 1971 185 Nedoncelle.
JPNP LXVII 1970 227 Meyerson.

2687 THEODORAKOPOULOS J.N., "El mito platónico". FolHum VII 1969 243-249.

2688 GAFFNEY S.K., "Dialectic, the Myths of Plato, Metaphor and the Transcendent in the World". PACPhA XLV 1971 77-85.

2689* HIRSCH W., Platons Weg zum Mythos. Habil.-Schr. Köln. Berlin, de Gruyter 1971 xx&399p.
Rev. Platon XXIII 1971 395-396 Zoumpos.
Angelicum XLIX 1972 289-291 Vansteenkiste.
AC XLI 1972 658-660 de Ley.
CW LXV 1972 112 Robinson.
ArchPhilos XXXV 1972 329-330 Solignac.
RPh XLVI 1972 123 des Places.
PLA XXV 1972 226-228 Thurnher.
JCS XXI 1973 124-127 Sakonii.

IV C: MYTH AND ALLEGORY

2690* DOERRIE H., Der Mythos und seine Funktion in der
       antiken Philosophie. Innsbrucker Beitr. zur
       Kulturwiss. Diss. philol. Aenipont. II,
       Innsbruck, Inst. für vergl. Sprachwiss. 1972
       20p. (for Plato see p.6ff.)
       Rev. Platon XXV 1973 323-326
       Georgountzos.

2691* FLAHAULT F., L'extrême existence. Essai sur des
       représentations mythiques de l'intériorité.
       Paris, Maspero 1972 190p.

                    PARTICULAR MYTHS

2692 HANFMANN G.M.A., "Lydiaka". HSPh LXIII 1958 (Stud.
      Jaeger) 65-88.

2693 CHATTE REME C., "Los mitos en el Fedro y el
      Banquete". RevE IV 1960 1-22.

2694 SCHUHL P.M., "I temi della caverna". p.252-264 in
      Antologia della critica filosofica, ed. Rossi
      P. (see 4613). Reprinted from Schuhl P.M., La
      fabulation platonicienne. Paris, P.U.F. 1947,
      p.45-53, 57-64.

2695 BIANCHI U., "Razza aurea, mito delle cinque razze ed
      Elisio. Un' analisi storico religiosa". SMSR
      XXXIX 1963 143-210.

2696 CZARNECKI Z., "The Social Origin of Plato's
      Eschatology" [in Polish]. Euhemer VIII 1964
      17-30. German summary in BCO XII 1967 243-245.

2697 DURIĆ M.N., "Vier Fassungen über Gyges" [in Serbian
      with German summary]. ZAnt XIII 1963-1964
      67-72.

2698 STEWART D.J., "Man and Myth in Plato's Universe".
      BR XIII,1 1965 72-90.

2699 WATTENBERG F., "Saltés, la isla de la Atlántida y
      Tartessos". BSEAA XXXII 1966 125-205.

2700 GLADIGOW B., "Pneumatik und Kosmologie". Philologus
      CXI 1967 1-20.

IV C: MYTH AND ALLEGORY

2701 FLUSSER V., "Breve relato de um encontro em Platão".
RBF XIX 1969 444-446.

2702 FAUTH W., "Zum Motivbestand der platonischen
Gygeslegende". RhM CXII 1970 1-42.

2703 HERTER H., "Eine altgeübte Mordmethode". RhM CXIII
1970 96.

2704 ROUSSEAUX M., "Une Atlantide en Méditerranée
occidentale". BAGB 1970 337-358.

2705 SEASE V.W., "The Myth in Plato's Theory of Ideas".
SwJP I 1970 186-197.

2706 REICHE H., "Myth and Magic in Cosmological Polemics.
Plato, Aristotle, Lucretius". RhM CXIV 1971
296-329.

2707 SCARAMELLA D.G., "El mito tradicional y el mundo del
más allá en el mito del Fedón". p.279-289 in
Actas del primer Simp. nac. de estud. clás.,
mayo 1970. Mendoza, Univ. nac. de Cuyo 1972.

2708 ALFONSI L., "Varia". Euphrosyne VI 1973-1974
125-127.

For further discussions relevant to this topic see 502,
584, 602, 666, 1148, 1149, 1150, 1151, 1152,
1153, 1154, 1155, 1156, 1157, 1158, 1763, 1766,
1832, 1839, 1843, 1847, 1858, 1940, 1955, 1957,
1961, 2039, 2123, 2128, 2173, 2200, 2297, 2300,
2360, 2380, 2536, 2537, 2589, 2590, 2622, 2728,
3076, 3153, 3183, 4107.

IV D: HUMOR AND IRONY

2709 RANKIN H.D., "Laughter, Humour and Related Topics in
Plato". C&M XXVIII 1967 186-213.

2710 BEHLER E., "Der Ursprung des Begriffs der tragischen
Ironie". Arcadia V 1970 113-142.

2711* NEUMANN F., Über das Lachen und Studien über den
platonischen Sokrates. Den Haag, Nijhoff 1971
viii&169p.
Rev. TPh XXXIV 1972 825-827 De Klerck.
JThS XXIV 1973 332 Halliburton.

IV D: HUMOR AND IRONY

For further discussions relevant to this topic see 1073,
1334, 1335, 1951, 2344, 2353, 2442, 2447, 2632,
4457.

IV E: PLATO'S ESTIMATE OF WRITING

2712 GIL L., "El logos vivo y la letra muerta. En torno
a la valoración de la obra escrita en la
antigüedad" [with English summary]. Emerita
XXVII 1959 239-268.

2713 ROIG A.A., "La escritura, el escritor y el libro en
Platón". REC VII 1960 109-161.

2714 LUTHER W., "Die Schwäche des geschriebenen Logos.
Ein Beispiel humanistischer Interpretation,
versucht am sogenannten Schriftmythos in Platons
Phaidros (274b6 sqq.)". Gymnasium LXVIII 1961
526-548.

2715 ERBSE H., "Platon und die Schriftlichkeit". A&A XI
1962 7-20.

2716 PIEPER J., "Das Gesprach als Ort der Wahrheit".
p.283-285 in Pieper J., Tradition als
Herausforderung. Aufsätze und Reden. München,
Kösel 1963. Reprinted from Der Brief
(Mitteilungsblatt der Pädagogischen Akad.
Essen), Weihnachten 1955.

2717 FISHER J., "Plato on Writing and Doing Philosophy".
JHI XXVII 1966 163-172.

2718 MUTH R., "Randbemerkungen zur griechischen
Literaturgeschichte. Zur Bedeutung von
Mündlichkeit und Schriftlichkeit der Wortkunst".
WS LXXIX 1966 246-260.

2719 DIRLMEIER F., "Mündlichkeit und Schriftlichkeit bei
Platon und Aristoteles". Summary of a
conference. p.37-39 in Acta Philologica
Aenipontana, Bd. II, hrsg. von Muth R.
Innsbruck, Wagner 1967.

2720 SCHWARZ F.F., "De philosophia litteris mandata".
Jahrbuch des Stiftsgymnasiums Wilhering-Linz
LVIII 1968 30-38.

IV E: PLATO'S ESTIMATE OF WRITING

For further discussions relevant to this subject see 1445,
1449, 1835, 1839, 1849, 4022, 4070, 4081, 4089.

V: PLATO'S THOUGHT

This section contains treatments of topics in Plato's philosophy which are not limited to or primarily concerned with a single dialogue. Cross references are provided to discussions of these topics which are grouped under individual works. The nature of Plato's style and thought resists categorization even of the general type I have attempted here. It was obvious that a certain amount of organization was necessary, but equally obvious that attempts to subdivide finely would misrepresent the nature of Plato's thought and of Platonic scholarship, and would thus be counterproductive. The compromize which I have reached is to leave the number of categories quite small and to provide indices which list the numbers of entries relevant to certain topics within the larger categories. In this way it is possible to refer conveniently to works on these topics which are located under individual works of Plato. In the categories where these special indices are provided (sections V A (Dialectic), V C (Psychology), V F (Ethics), V G (Politics and Society), and V I (Aesthetics)), the entries included in the list of cross references for the section as a whole are concerned with other areas of those categories than the ones covered by the special indices.

A: DIALECTIC, LOGIC, AND PLATO'S CONCEPTION OF PHILOSOPHY

For convenience of reference I have prepared special indices referring to works both in this section and elsewhere which deal significantly with the subjects of Plato's Conception of Philosophy, Plato and Logic, Hypothesis and the Hypothetical Method, Plato's Method of Division, and Argument by Analogy and Other Forms of Argument in the Dialogues. These appear at the end of the present section.

V A: DIALECTIC

2721 AXELOS C., "Das Phaenomen des Scheines und der
     Gedanke der Wahrscheinlichkeit im griechischen
     Denken". Platon X 1958 209-225.

2722* CUSHMAN R.E., Therapeia. Plato's Conception of
     Philosophy. Chapel Hill, Univ. of North
     Carolina Pr. 1958 xxii&322p.
          Rev. ThS XIX 1958 643-646 Conway.
          JHI XIX 1958 574-577 Boas.
          CJ LV 1959 40 DeLacy.
          CPh LIV 1959 267-268 Sprague.
          HibJ LVII 1958-1959 195 Tarrant.
          RSF XV 1960 101-102 Giannantoni.
          Mind LXIX 1960 114-115 Diamadopoulos.
          JPh LVII 1960 455-460 Anton.
          CR X 1960 115-116 Bambrough.
          JCS IX 1961 105-111 Kawada.
          REAug VII 1961 265 A.d.V.
          Gnomon XXXIV 1962 7-13 Sandvoss.
          PhilosQ XI 1961 186-187 Cross.
          PhilosRdschau 1961 236-241 Manasse.

2723* GUZZONI G., Untersuchung des Phanomens der σκέψις
     mit Beschränkung auf ihr σκοπούμενον in den
     Dialogen Platos. Diss. Freiburg 1958 175p.

2724 LACHIÈZE-REY P., "Reflexiones sobre un procedimiento
     de Platón". RevE III 1958 218-226.

2725 LÁSCARIS COMNENO C., "Los perros filósofos de
     Platón". Actas primer Congr. Español de Estud.
     clásicos (Madrid 15-19 Abril 1956), Madrid 1958
     p.338-342.

2726 PACI E., "La dialettica in Platone". RF XLIX 1958
     134-153. Reprinted p.18-37 in Studi sulla
     dialettica, per Abbagnano N., Paci E., et alii.
     Documenti e ricerche. Biblioteca di cultura
     contemporanea. 2a ed. Torino, Taylor 1969.
     (1a ed. = RF XLIX 1958 123-354.)

2727 PAGLIARO A., "La dottrina dell'analogia e i suoi
     precedenti". RicLing IV 1958 1-18.

2728 AIMO M.A., "Contributi all'interpretazione del
     pensiero di Platone. L'esigenza dell'assoluto".
     RSC VII 1959 111-117.

2729 CALLOT E., "La découverte de l'instrument
     philosophique: la dialectique chez Socrate et
     chez Platon". p. 105-126 in Callot E.,
     Questions de doctrine et d'histoire de la

philosophie. T.1: Histoire. Annecy, Gardet
1959.

2730* PÉREZ RUIZ F., El concepto de filosofía en los
escritos de Platón. Filosofía y sabiduria.
Comillas, Miscelánea Comillas 1959 152p.
Rev. Gregorianum XLI 1960 753 Caminero.
RPhL LX 1962 273 Rutten.
CiFe XVI 1960 473-475 Simian.
Pensamiento XVI 1960 246-247 Domínguez.
RecSR XLIX 1961 292 des Places.
RPortFil XVII 1961 220-221 Matos.

2731 STANNARD J., "Socratic Eros and Platonic Dialectic".
Phronesis IV 1959 120-134.

2732 BEIN E., "Einführung in Platons 'Lehre' von der
Wirklichkeit". PaedProv XIV 1960 90-96.

2733 BLUCK R.S., "Dialectic in Plato's Republic".
p.49-54 in Atti del XII Congresso Internazionale
di Filosofia. Venezia, 12-18 settembre 1958.
Vol. XI: Storia della Filosofia antica e
medievale. Firenze, Sansoni 1960.

2734 DIONYSOS I., "Platon et le symbolisme". Atlantis
(nov.-dec. 1960) No. 204, 88-91.

2735 KOLLER H., "Die dihäretische Methode". Glotta XXXIX
1960 6-24.

2736 NERLICH G.C., "Regress Arguments in Plato". Mind
LXIX 1960 88-90.

2737 PFLAUMER R., "Zum Wesen von Wahrheit und Täuschung
bei Platon". p.189-223 in Die Gegenwart der
Griechen im neueren Denken. Festschrift für
H.G. Gadamer zum 60. Geburtstag. Tübingen,
Mohr 1960.

2738 ROSENMEYER T.G., "Plato's Hypothesis and the Upward
Path". AJPh LXXXI 1960 393-407. Reprinted
p.354-367 in Essays in Ancient Greek Philosophy,
ed. by Anton J.P. & Kustas G.L. (see 4581).

2739 ROBINSON R., "Up and Down in Plato's Logic". AJPh
LXXXIV 1963 300-303.

2740 SCHULZ W., "Das Problem der Aporie in den
Tugenddialogen Platos". p.261-275 in Die
Gegenwart der Griechen im neueren Denken.
Festschrift für H.G. Gadamer zum 60.

Geburtstag. Tübingen, Mohr 1960.

2741 STAHL H.P., "Ansätze zur Satzlogik bei Platon. Methode und Ontologie". Hermes LXXXVIII 1960 409-451. Reprinted in shortened form as "Beginnings of propositional logic in Plato", p.180-197 in Plato's Meno (see 1485).

2742* FRANCHINI R., Le origini della dialettica. Coll. Storia e Pensiero VIII, Napoli, Giannini 1961 368p.; 2nd edn. 1965. (Ch. 2 "Da Pitagora a Socrate"; ch. 3 "La doppia dialettica di Platone".)
Rev. Orpheus VIII 1961 177-180 Sciuto.
Crisis XI 1964 472-473 Vásquez.
Personalist XLVII 1966 453-454 DeGennaro.

2743* GRIEDER H., Die Bedeutung der Sophistik für die platonisch-aristotelische Aussagelogik. Diss. Basel 1961 94p.

2744* ROSE L.E., Hypothesis and Deduction in Plato's Methodology. Diss. Univ. of Pennsylvania 1961 226p. [microfilm]. Summary in DA XXII 1961 1214.

2745 SICHIROLLO L., "Figure e problemi della dialettica platonica". Pensiero VI 1961 300-319.

2746 SICHIROLLO L., "Διαλέγεσθαι, dialettica". A&R VI 1961 1-14.

2747* STENZEL J., Studien zur Entwicklung der platonischen Dialektik von Sokrates zu Aristoteles. 3. Aufl. Unveränd. Nachdr. d. 2. Aufl. 1931. Darmstadt, Wissenschaftl. Buchges. 1961 xi&208p. Also English transl.: Plato's Method of Dialectic, trans. and ed. by Allen D.J. New York, Russell & Russell 1964 xliii&170p.

2748 TESKE R.J., "Plato's Later Dialectic". ModS XXXVIII 1961 171 sq.

2749 VACCARINO G., "L'origine della logica". Scientia LV 1961 103-109.

2750* WALDENFELS R., Das Sokratische Fragen. Aporie, Elenchos, Anamnesis. Monogr. zur Philos. Forsch. XXVI, Meisenheim, Hain 1961 156p.
Rev. AC XXX 1961 576 Janssens.
Gnomon XXXIV 1962 122-126 Sandvoss.
RFil(La Plata) XI 1962 119-122 Fortuny.

Gregorianum XLIII 1962 844 Caminero.
Gymnasium LXX 1963 67-68 Classen.
JCS XII 1964 151-155 Ito.

2751* ARNOLD U., Das Voraussetzungsproblem im Begriff der Möglichkeit bei Platon und Aristoteles. Diss. Wien 1962 164p.

2752 COHEN M.H., "The aporias in Plato's early Dialogues". JHI XXIII 1962 163-174.

2753* GIANNANTONI G., Dialogo e dialettica nei dialoghi giovanili di Platone. Univ. degli studi di Roma, Fac. di Lett. e Filos., Roma, Ediz. dell'Ateneo 1963 312p.

2754* KNEALE W. & M., The Development of Logic. Oxford, Clarendon Pr. 1962 770p. (For Plato see p.7-22.)

2755 NÁDOR G., "Il metodo analogico di Platone". Helikon II 1962 465-484.

2756* NUÑO MONTES J.A., La dialéctica platónica, su desarrollo en relación con la teoría de las formas. Caracas, Univ. Central de Venezuela Inst. de Filos. 1962 208p.
Rev. Mnemosyne XVI 1963 218.
CR XIII 1963 282-284 Gulley.
RM XVI 1962-1963 397 A.T.
GM XX 1965 205-206 Guazzoni Foà.
RPhL LXIV 1966 308 Mansion.
RM 1962 397 A.T.
RPortFil XXI 1965 219-220 Morão.

2757 JOHNSON J.P., "The Ontological Argument in Plato". Personalist XLIV 1963 24-34.

2758* MATOS V.R. DA C., O acesso à filosofia platónica, I: Problema metodológico. Fac. de Letras da Univ. de Coimbra, Publ. do Inst. de Est. Filos., Serie de Filosofia, Coimbra, Univ. de Coimbra 1963 234p.
Rev. RPortFil XX 1964 254-255 Freire.

2759 PIEPER J., "Über den Philosophie-Begriff Platons". p.216-240, 340-341 in Pieper J., Tradition als Herausforderung. Aufsätze und Reden. München, Kösel 1963. Reprinted from the publ. of Arbeitsgemeinschaft für Forschung des Landes Mordsheim-Westfalen, Köln, Opladen 1955.

2760 VERBEKE G., "De zin van het filosofisch gesprek bij Plato" [in Dutch with French summary]. TPh XXV 1963 439-475.

2761 BERKA K., "The Evolution of Dialectic from Socrates and Plato to Aristotle" [in Czech]. Acta Univ. Carolinae Philos. & Hist. 1964,1 97-105. (German summary in BCO X 1965 250-251.)

2762 DEMAN A., "Sur l'expression des facteurs logiques dans les langues anciennes". LogAn VII 1964 164-167.

2763 DILLER H., "Ausdrucksformen des methodischen Bewusstseins in den hippokratischen Epidemien". ABG IX 1964 133-150.

2764 FUJISAWA N., "The Logic of Argument in Plato. The Foundation of Western Philosophy" [in Japanese]. Shiso April 1964.

2765 HOFFMANN E., "Der historisches Ursprung des Satzes vom Widerspruch". p.53-64 In Hoffmann E., Drei Schriften zur griechischen Philosophie (see 4602). Reprinted from Jahresbericht des philologischen Vereins zu Berlin XLIX 1923 1-13.

2766 SORABJI R., "Function". PhilosQ XIV 1964 289-302.

2767 THAYER H.S., "Plato. The Theory and Language of Function". PhilosQ XIV 1964 303-318. Reprinted p.21-39 in Plato's Republic, ed. by Sesonske A. (see 4614).

2768 THEODORAKOPOULOS I.N., "Πίστις καὶ λογική". EEAth XV 1964-1965 339-345.

2769 TAKEMIYA A., "On Plato's Method: concerning the two questions τί ἐστιν and ὁποῖόν ἐστιν" [in Japanese]. Philosophy Annual (Kyushu Univ.) XXV 1964.

2770 TSUMURA K., "Concerning τί ἐστιν in Plato and Aristotle" [in Japanese]. Philosophy (Tokyo) XIV 1964.

2771 KUCHARSKI P., "Sur l'évolution des méthodes du savoir dans la philosophie de Platon". RPhilos CLV 1965 427-440.

V A: DIALECTIC

2772 LLOYD A.C., "Plato's Description of Division".
p.219-230 in Studies in Plato's Metaphysics, ed.
by Allen R.E. (see 4580). Reprinted from CQ
1954.

2773 MANNSPERGER D., "Zur Sprache der Dialektik bei
Platon". p.161-171 in Synusia. Festgabe für
Wolfgang Schadewaldt zum 15. März 1965, hrsg.
von Flashar H. & Gaiser K. Pfullingen, Neske
1965.

2774* MUELLER G.E., Plato, the Founder of Philosophy as
Dialectic. New York, Philosophical Libr. 1965
xx&331p.
Rev. AusJP 1965 416 Rankin.
CJ LXI 1965 131 Hoerber.
CW LIX 1965 12 Hornsby.
JHPh IV 1966 169-170 Christensen.
RM XIX 1965-1966 156 R.J.W.
RSF XXII 1967 331-332 Buccellato.
ModS XLIV 1966-1967 378-379 Sweeney.

2775 SAINATI V., "Tra Parmenide e Protagora. Le premesse
storiche della logica greca". Filosofia XVI
1965 49-83.

2776* SICHIROLLO L., Storicità della dialettica antica.
Platone, Aristotele, Hegel. Padova, Marsilio
1965 356p. Also new edn. Firenze, La Nuova
Italia 1969.
Rev. CS V 1966 820-822 Timpanaro.
RF LVIII 1967 93-95 Cambiano.
RPhilos CLIX 1969 271 Somville.

2777* VIVES-SOLÉ J., Analogía y ética en los diálogos de
Platón. Barcelona Univ. 1965 16p.

2778 GIANNANTONI G., "Il problema della genesi della
dialettica platonica". Cultura IV 1966 12-41.

2779 KRAEMER H.J., "Über aen Zusammenhang von
Prinzipienlehre und Dialektik bei Platon. Zur
Definition des Dialektikers Politeia 534b-c".
Philologus CX 1966 35-70. Reprinted (with
Nachtr.) p.394-448 in Das Problem der
ungeschriebenen Lehre Platons, hrsg. von
Wippern J. (see 4626).

2780* LEINFELLNER W., Die Entstehung der Theorie. Eine
Analyse des kritischen Denkens in der Antike.
Freiburg, Alber 1966 207p. (ch.6 "Der
sophistische Konzeption der sophistische

Rationalismus und Skeptizismus der Erkenntnis
und dessen Überwindung durch Platon", p.51-78;
ch.7 "'Parmenides' oder der Versuch einer
theoretisch-logischen Weltkonstitution",
p.79-119.)
Rev. Th&Ph XLII 1967 453 de Vries.
RBPh XLV 1967 973.
Gnomon XXXVIII 1966 832-834 Seeck.
Ph&PhenR XXIX 1968 317 Hart.

2781 LUCAS J.R., "Not 'therefore' but 'but'". PhilosQ
XVI 1966 289-307.

2782 McKEON R., "Philosophy and the Development of
Scientific Methods". JHI XXVII 1966 3-22.

2783* MIRRI E., Il concetto della filosofia in Platone.
Bologna, Ed. Alfa 1966 163p.
Rev. GM XXIII 1968 363-365 Pieretti.
Ethica VI 1967 79.

2784 OEHLER K., "Der geschichtliche Ort der Entstehung
der formalen Logik". StudGen XIX 1966 453-461.

2785 PHILIP J.A., "Platonic Diairesis". TAPhA XCVII 1966
335-358.

2786 ROSE L.E., "Plato's Unhypothetical Principle". JHPh
IV 1966 189-198.

2787* SICHIROLLO L., Διαλέγεσθαι. Dialektik von Homer bis
Aristoteles. Hildesheim, Olms 1966 vii&214p.
(ch.3 "Rhetorik, Sophistik und Dialektik",
p.34-60, partly on Socrates; ch.4 "Gestalten
und Probleme der platonischen Dialektik",
p.61-84; Anh. I "Wie Hegel Platon las",
p.171-183.)
Rev. Ph&Rh I 1968 174-181 Janssens.
Gnomon XLIII 1971 330-335 Sprute.
RPhL LXV 1967 550-551 Dhondt.
PLA XXI 1968 275-277 Huebner.

2788 ARDLEY G., "The Role of Play in the Philosophy of
Plato". Philosophy XLII 1967 226-244.

2789 ARMLEDER P.J., "Plato on Philosophy versus
Theology". CB XLIV 1967 1-3.

2790 BUBNER R., "Zur platonischen Problematik von Logos
und Schein". p.129-139 in Das Problem der
Sprache. Achter Deutscher Kongress für
Philosophie. Heidelberg 1966, hrsg. von

Gadamer H.G. München, Fink 1967.

2791 KOEVENDI D., "Gedanken zu Stenzels Platonbild". Helikon VII 1967 511-532.

2792 LAVELLE L., "La dialectique platonicienne". p.65-73 in Lavelle L., Panorama des doctrines philosophiques (see 4607).

2793 MONDIN B., "Il problema dei rapporti tra fede e ragione in Platone e in Filone Alessandrino". P&I IX 1967 9-16.

2794 SPRAGUE R.K., "Logic and Literary Form in Plato". Personalist XLVIII 1967 560-572.

2795 TREVASKIS J.R., "Division and its Relation to Dialectic and Ontology in Plato". Phronesis XII 1967 118-129.

2796* BIANCO C., Critica alla dialettica di Platone. Ancora più oltre VI, [s.l.], Edizioni di Studi e Ricerche 1968 86p.

2797 DUBOSE S., "Sophistic Measures". TSPh XVII 1968 13-20.

2798 ELIAS J.A., "'Socratic' vs. 'Platonic' Dialectic". JHPh VI 1968 205-216.

2799 GUNDERT H., "Juego y verdad entre los griegos". Helmantica XIX 1968 5-30.

2800 KUHN H., "Platon und die Grenze philosophischer Mitteilung". p.151-173 in Idee und Zahl, hrsg. von Gadamer H.G. & Schadewaldt W. (see 4594).

2801* KUEMMEL F., Platon und Hegel. Zur ontologischen Begründung des Zirkels in der Erkenntnis. Tübingen, Niemeyer 1968 xv&336p.

2802 MARTEN R., "Die Methodologie der platonischen Dialektik". StudGen XXI 1968 218-249.

2803 MAYR F.K., "Der Gott Hermes und die Hermeneutik". TPh XXX 1968 535-625.

2804 BANU I., "Le République dans l'évolution da la dialectique platonicienne". RRSS XIII,1 1969 39-57.

2805 COHEN M., "The logical Background of Plato's Writing". JHPh VII 1969 111-141.

2806* DALLERY R.C., Philosophy as Integrative Speech. Studies in Plato and Merleau-Ponty, with an Appendix, a Translation of Maurice Merleau-Ponty's L'oeil et l'esprit. Diss. Yale Univ. 1968 328p. [microfilm]. Summary in DA XXX 1969 1596A-1597A.

2807 DELEUZE G., "Platon et le simulacre". p.292-306 in Deleuze G., Logique du sens, Coll. Critique, Paris, Ed. de Minuit 1969.

2808 FRIEDLAENDER P., Review of Robinson R., Plato's Earlier Dialectic. p.193-202 in Friedlaender P., Studien zur antiken Literatur und Kunst (see 4589). Reprinted from CPh XL 1945 253-259.

2809 GUNDERT H., "Enthusiasmos und Logos bei Platon". p.176-197 in Das Platonbild, hrsg. von Gaiser K. (see 4595). Reprinted from Lexis II 1949 25-46.

2810 NATORP P., "Genesis der platonischen Philosophie" and "Platons Logik". p.58-95 in Das Platonbild, hrsg. von Gaiser K. (see 4595). Excerpts from the chap. "Platon" in Grosse Denker, hrsg. von Aster E. von. Leipzig 1911 99-136.

2811 PAISSE J.M., "Le platonisme, une philosophie problématique". RMM LXXIV 1969 146-160.

2812* SAYRE K.M., Plato's Analytical Method. Univ. of Chicago Pr. 1969 xi&250p.
            Rev. NYRB XIII,8 1969 16-19 Ryle.
            NS XLIV 1970 620-624 Thomas.
            PhilosBks Oct. 1970 30 Gulley.
            CW LXIII 1970 269-270 Thomas.
            Philosophy XLV 1970 250-251 Lacey.
            Ph&PhenR XXXII 1971-1972 280-281 Rose.
            PhilosQ XXI 1971 261-262 Cross.
            Metaphilosophy II 1971 267-275 Gould.

2813 FÁJ A., "Anticipazioni della logica stoica in Platone". GM XXV 1970 675-691.

2815 GOLDSCHMIDT V., "Sur le problème du 'système de Platon'". p.23-33 in Goldschmidt V., Questions Platoniciennes (see 4598). Reprinted from RSF 1950 169ff.

2816 KAMIOKA H., "Plato's Divisions" [in Japanese]. Philosophy Miscellany (Tokyo Metropolitan Univ.) XII 1970.

2817* KURZ D., ἀκρίβεία. Das Ideal der Exaktheit bei den Griechen bis Aristoteles. Göppinger Akad. Beitr. VIII, Göppingen, Kümmerle 1970 vi&173p. (ch.5 "Das Ideal der Exaktheit in der Philosophie Platons", p.88-123.)

2818 PREUS A., "The Continuous Analogy. The Uses of Continuous Proportions in Plato and Aristotle". Agora I,2 1970 21-42.

2819 SURDU A., "Judecata ca principiu formal [Antisthenes, Plato, Aristotle]" [in Rumanian]. Probleme de logică (Bucureşti Acad.) II 1970 269-301.

2820 ACKRILL J.L., "In Defense of Platonic Division". p.373-392 in Ryle, ed. by Wood O.P. & Pitcher G., intro. by Ryle G. Modern Studies in Philosophy, London, Macmillan and Garden City, N.Y., Doubleday Anchor 1971.

2821* ANAGNOSTOPOULOS G., Some Philosophical Problems in Plato's Early Dialogues and the Search for a Method. Diss. Brandeis Univ. 1971 223p. [microfilm]. Summary in DA XXXII 1971 1007A.

2822 DUMITRIU A., "Histoire de la logique. Les étapes de son évolution". Scientia LXV 1971 571-584.

2823 FÁJ A., "Platonic Anticipation of Stoic Logic". Apeiron V,2 1971 1-19; VI,1 1972 1-24.

2824* GUNDERT H., Dialog und Dialektik. Zur Struktur des Platonischen Dialogs. Stud. zur antiken Philos. I, Amsterdam, Grüner 1971 viii&166p.
Rev. ACR II 1972 220 Stewart.
JHPh XI 1973 540-541 Schneider.
BAGB 1973 508ff.
PLA XXV 1972 16-20 Niewoehner.
RM XXVII 1973-1974 387-388 Sweeney.

2825 HENAO ZAPATA L., "San Justino y Las Anteriores
      Dialécticas Platónicas". Franciscanum XIII 1971
      91-124.

2826* LLOYD G.E.R., Polarity and Analogy. Two Types of
      Argumentation in Early Greek Thought. Cambridge
      Univ. Pr. 1971 503p. (for Plato see
      especially p.127-155, 275-285, 389-403.)

2827 NAKHNIKIAN G., "Plato's Theory of Definitions".
      p.440 in Abstracts IVe Congr. Intern. Log.,
      Méthod. et Philos. Sci.. Bucarest, Centre
      d'Information et de Document. des Sciences
      Politiques et Sociales 1971.

2828 NAKHNIKIAN G., "Elenctic Definitions". p.125-157 in
      The Philosophy of Socrates, ed. by Vlastos G.
      (see 4621).

2829 OGILVY J.A., "Socratic Method, Platonic Method and
      Authority". ET XXI 1971 3-16.

2830 TANAKA M., "Plato and Method" [in Japanese]. Riso
      no.455 1971.

2831* THEILL-WUNDER H., Die archaische Verborgenheit. Die
      philosophischen Wurzeln der negativen Theologie.
      Humanist. Bibl. I,8, München, Fink 1971 204p.
      (Part A.1: "Die platonische Lehre über die
      Unmöglichkeit der logischen Vermittlung der
      höchsten Erkenntnis", p.28-64.)
          Rev. Th&Ph XLVIII 1973 264-265 Brugger.

2832* BANU I., Platon heracliticul. Contribuţie la
      istoria dialecticii [Plato the Heraclitean.
      Contributions to the History of Dialectic].
      Bucureşti, Ed. Acad. Republ. Soc. România
      1972 241p.
          Rev. StudClas XV 1973 285-288 Noica.

2833 BANU I., "En repensant Platon". RRSS XVI 1972
      369-381.

2834 DIONÍSIO S.A., "Noção de filosofo (Platão)". RBF
      XXII 1972 202-204.

2835 DUMONT J.P., "Trophos ou la gouvernante de Platon".
      p.9-29 in Les signes et leur interprétation.
      Centre de Recherches de l'U.E.R. de
      Philosophie, Lille, Univ. de Lille III, Paris,
      Édit. Universitaires 1972.

V A: DIALECTIC

2836* DYNNIK M.A. et al., Istorija antichnoj dialektiki
[History of ancient Dialectic] [in Russian].
Moskva, Mysl 1972 334p. (ch.10 on Socrates by
Asmus V.F., p.142-166; ch.11 on Plato by Dynnik
M.A., p.178-200.)

2837 LASALA M.E., "El método dialéctico en Platón".
CuadFilos XII 1972 69-92.

2838 MUTHMANN F., "Anmut und Milde. Das sanfle Gesetz
Platonischer Dialektik". AU XV 1972,2 5-11.

2839 PAPOULIA B., "Προβλήματα πλατωνικῆς παρουσίας, I: Ἡ
ὑστορικότητα τῆς μεθόδου" [in Greek with German
summary]. Philosophia(Athens) II 1972 201-221.

2840* ROIG A.A., Platón o la filosofía como libertad y
expectativa. Coll. de estud. filos. V,
Mendoza, Univ. Nac. de Cuyo, Fac. de Filos.,
Inst. de Filos. 1972 200p.
Rev. Philosophia(Argent) 1973 154-157
Padrón.

2841 ROIG A.A., "Sobre el asombro en los diálogos
platónicos". p.241-256 in Actas del primer
Simp. nac. de estud. clás., mayo 1970.
Mendoza, Univ. nac. de Cuyo 1972.

2842 ALDERMAN H., "Dialectic as philosophical Care".
ManWorld VI 1973 206-220.

2843* BURRELL D., Analogy and Philosophical Language. New
Haven, Conn./London, Yale Univ. Pr. 1973
xi&278p. (ch.3 "Plato: Inquiry as Dialectic",
p.37-67.)

2844 DETEL W., "Zur Argumentationsstruktur im ersten
Hauptteil von Platons Aretedialogen". AGPh LV
1973 1-29.

2845 GROZEV G., "Plato's Idealistic Dialectic" [in
Bulgarian]. FilosMis'l XXIX 1973 78-87.

2846 HIROKAWA Y., "The nature of logic. Λόγον διδόναι
and δι' εἰκόνος λέγειν in Plato" [in Japanese].
in An Attempt at a Theory of Civilization.
Tokai Univ. Pr. 1973.

2847 HIROKAWA Y., "The Technique of Image-Making and
Philosophy. The Meaning of δι' εἰκόνος λέγειν"
[in Japanese]. Methodos VI 1973.

2848 LAFRANCE Y., "Amour et violence dans la dialectique platonicienne". Dialogue XII 1973 288-308.

2849 MORAVCSIK J.M.E., "Plato's Method of Division". p.158-180 in Patterns in Plato's Thought, ed. by Moravcsik J.M.E. (see 4609).

2850 COHEN S.M., "Plato's Method of Division". p.181-191 in Patterns in Plato's Thought, ed. by Moravcsik J.M.E. (see 4609).

2851 MORAVCSIK J.M.E., "The Anatomy of Plato's Divisions". p.324-348 in Exegesis and Argument, ed. by Lee E.N. et al. (see 4608).

2852 NOUSSAN-LETTRY L., "Sobre diferencia hermeneutica y lenguaje". CuadFilos XIII 1973 11-22.

2853* SCHENK G., Zur Geschichte der logischen Form, I: Einige Entwicklungstendenzen von der Antike bis zum Ausgang des Mittelalters. Berlin, Deutsche Verl. der Wiss. 1973 377p. (sec. 2.1 on Plato and on the Socratic method, p.47-102.)

2854* SCHMITT A., Die Bedeutung der sophistischen Logik für die mittlere Dialektik Platons. Diss. Würzburg 1973 2&303p.

2855 SCOLNICOV S., "Plato on A and not-A" [in Hebrew]. Iyyun XXIV 1973 217-226.

2856 VEGETTI M., "Nascita dello scienzato". Belfagor XXVIII 1973 641-663.

2857 WEIZSAECKER C.F. VON, "Die Aktualität der Tradition. Platons Logik". PhJ LXXX 1973 221-241.

For other works relevant to this subject see 25, 56, 242, 345, 378, 399, 423, 426, 431, 432, 451, 461, 483, 504, 519, 662, 676, 1053, 1090, 1131, 1255, 1262, 1443, 1446, 1468, 1504, 1516, 1526, 1547, 1561, 1567, 1568, 1576, 1578, 1581, 1583, 1587, 1716, 1725, 1728, 1739, 1740, 1741, 1742, 1743, 1747, 1748, 1749, 1749, 1750, 1751, 1752, 1759, 1763, 1817, 1828, 1838, 1841, 1878, 1879, 1893, 1895, 1896, 1909, 1915, 2029, 2154, 2155, 2156, 2158, 2162, 2164, 2166, 2191, 2193, 2197, 2225, 2233, 2234, 2238, 2239, 2242, 2254, 2264, 2299, 2454, 2461, 2465, 2515, 2648, 2652, 2662, 2669, 2677, 2685, 2688, 2885, 2887, 2918, 2936, 2963, 2990, 3011, 3119, 3183, 3191, 3264, 3279, 3550,

V A: DIALECTIC

3727, 3825, 3830, 3989, 4004, 4026, 4027, 4097, 4128, 4424, 4430, 4458, 4469.

SPECIAL INDICES

PLATO'S CONCEPTION OF PHILOSOPHY

This subject is treated in the following studies:
463, 1692, 2225, 2722, 2725, 2730, 2759, 2783,
2789, 2799, 2834, 2838, 2840, 2842, 2848.

PLATO AND LOGIC

Plato's contributions to and views on this subject are
treated in the following studies:
350, 452, 1254, 2241, 2270, 2271, 2721, 2732,
2736, 2737, 2741, 2743, 2749, 2751, 2754, 2762,
2765, 2775, 2781, 2784, 2790, 2794, 2805, 2810,
2813, 2814, 2819, 2822, 2823, 2852, 2853, 2854,
2855, 2857, 4141.

HYPOTHESIS AND THE HYPOTHETICAL METHOD

This subject is treated in the following studies:
1117, 1517, 1519, 2738, 2739, 2744, 2756, 2757,
2786, 3006, 3318.

THE METHOD OF DIVISION

This subject is treated in the following studies:
413, 418, 1583, 1916, 2300, 2735, 2748, 2772, 2785, 2795, 2816, 2820, 2849, 2850, 2851.

ARGUMENT BY ANALOGY AND OTHER FORMS OF ARGUMENT

These subjects are treated in the following studies:
1589, 2054, 2724, 2727, 2734, 2736, 2740, 2752, 2755, 2766, 2767, 2777, 2781, 2797, 2818, 2826, 2828, 2844, 3272.

V B: METAPHYSICS

The present section contains studies devoted to the Theory of Ideas and other areas of Plato's metaphysical thought. Treatments of metaphysical issues in particular dialogues will be found listed under those dialogues, and are cross referenced at the end of this section. Although the section is large, the various areas of the subject are so intimately related that any attempt to subdivide it would have been arbitrary and artificial.

2858 BERGENTHAL F., "Das Wesen der Platonischen Idee. Eine Besinnung auf den Grund jeder abendländischen Bildung". VWP XXXIV 1958 260-273.

2859 MIZUNO H., "A Remark on Plato's Theory of ideal Numbers" [in Japanese with English summary]. JCS VI 1958 57-67.

2860 WICHMANN O., "Idee und Idealismus in der Platondeutung". KantStud XLIX 1957-1958 401-422.

2861 XENAKIS J., "Essence, being and fact in Plato. An Analysis of one of Theaetetus' 'koina'". KantStud XLIX 1957-1958 167-181.

2862 XENAKIS J., "Plato's Theory of Forms". C&M XIX 1958 1-6.

2863 ALLEN R.E., "Forms and Standards". PhilosQ IX 1959 164-167.

2864 BOUSSOULAS N.I., "La créativité du bien et la métaphysique de la mixis platonicienne". Sophia XXVII 1959 209-219.

2865 BROECKER W., "Platons ontologischer Komparativ". Hermes LXXXVII 1959 415-425.

2866* MAINBERGER G., Die Seinsstufung als Methode und Metaphysik. Untersuchungen über Mehr und Weniger als Grundlage zu einem möglichen Gottesbeweis bei Platon und Aristoteles. Studia Friburgensia N.S. XXIV, Freiburg i. d.

Schweiz., Univ.-Verl. 1959 xxxii&248p.
Rev. Gnomon XXXI 1959 739 Kuhn.
FZPT VI 1959 320-321 Negro.
ZKTh LXXXI 1959 373-374 Coreth.
Scholastik XXXV 1960 112-113 de Vries.
Gregorianum XLI 1960 321-322 Kořínek.
RSPh XLIV 1960 371-372 Montagnes.
RecSR XLIX 1961 292-293 des Places.
BThom XI 1960-1962 406-407 Guérard des
Lauriers.
RThPh XCVIII 1965 118 Brunner.

2867* MUELLER M., Idées et archétypes, de Platon à Élie
Cartan. Coll. Être & Penser XLIX, Neûchatel,
Ed. de la Baconnière 1959 110p.
Rev. ASSPh XX 1960 163-164 Gex.
TPh XXII 1960 687 van Peursen.
RS LXXXII 1961 Nos.22-24 152-153
Bernard-Maître.

2868* STENZEL J., Zahl und Gestalt bei Platon und
Aristoteles. 3. durchges. Aufl. Darmstadt,
Wissenschaftl. Buchgesellschaft 1959 xi&191p.

2869 ALLEN R.E., "Participation and Predication in
Plato's Middle Dialogues". PhR LXIX 1960
147-164. Reprinted p.43-60 in Studies in
Plato's Metaphysics (see 4580); p.167-183 in
Plato. A Collection of Critical Essays, I:
Metaphysics and Epistemology (see 4619).

2870 BRUMBAUGH R.S., "'Aphilosophical first Philosophy".
p.55-58 in Atti del XII Congresso Internazionale
di Filosofia. Venezia, 12-18 settembre 1958.
Vol. XI: Storia della Filosofia antica e
medievale. Firenze, Sansoni 1960.

2871 DOHERTY K.F., "Location of the Platonic Ideas". RM
XIV 1960 57-72.

2872 INOUE T., "The Secret of 'One'. The Challenge to
Plato, III" [in Japanese]. Tokyo Univ.
Proceedings of the Dept. of Humanities.
Philosophy Series XXVII.

2873 INOUE T., "The Mystery of the Ideal Numbers. The
Challenge to Plato", II, I" [in Japanese].
Tokyo Univ. Proceedings of the Dept. of
Humanities. Philosophy Series XXII 1960.

2874 JAEGER W., Rev. of Stenzel J., Zahl und Gestalt bei
      Platon und Aristoteles. p.293-301 in Jaeger W.,
      Scripta Minora I (see 4605). Reprinted from DLZ
      1924 Sp. 2046-2055.

2875* RICOEUR P., Être, essence et substance chez Platon
      et Aristote. Cours professé à l'Université de
      Strasbourg en 1953-1954. Les Cours de Sorbonne,
      Paris, Centre de documentation universitaire
      1960 149p.

2876 THEODORAKOPOULOS I., "Ἡ θεωρία τῶν ἰδεῶν τοῦ
      Πλάτωνος". PAA XXXV 1960 207-228.

2877 BOSQUE M.S. DEL, "Vaciedad de los seres y
      escepticismo en Platon". UnivAnt 1961 47-60.

2878* BRUN J., Les conquêtes de l'homme et la séparation
      ontologique. Paris, Presses Universitaires 1961
      298p. (ch. 2 "Platon: La séparation et la
      cité, p.22-43.)

2879 MARTIN G., "Platons Lehre von der Zahl und ihre
      Darstellung durch Aristoteles". p.7-18 in
      Martin G., Gesammelte Abhandlungen Bd. I
      (Kantstudien, Ergänzungsh. LXXXI). Köln,
      Kölner Universitäts-Verl. 1961. Reprinted from
      ZPhF VII 1953.

2880 MARTIN G., "Das metaphysische Problem der Ideenlehre
      Platons". KantStud LIII 1961-1962 411-440.
      Rev. Platon XV 1963 393-395 Georgoulis.

2881* NATORP P., Platos Ideenlehre. Eine Einführung in d.
      Idealismus. 3. Aufl. Unveränd. Nachdr. d.
      2. Aufl. von 1922. Darmstadt, Wissenschaftl.
      Buchges. 1961 xii&571p.

2882 SCHIPPER E.W., "Perceptual Judgments and Particulars
      in Plato's Later Philosophy". Phronesis VI 1961
      102-109.

2883 BINDEL E., "Die Zahlen in platonischer und
      aristotelischer Auffassung". Antaios IV 1962
      238-250.

2884 BOUSSOULAS N.J., "Ἡ δημιουργικότης τοῦ ἀγαθοῦ καὶ ἡ
      μεταφυσικὴ τῆς πλατωνικῆς μείξεως". Platon XIV
      1962 177-226. Also appeared in Analecta no.11
      1962 99-162. Also in French as "La causalité du
      Bien et la métaphysique du Mélange platonicien".
      RMM LXVII 1962 65-109.

2885 BRUNET C., "L'être univoque et l'analogie esthétique chez Platon". RMM LXVII 1962 344-361.

2886* ROLLAND DE RENÉVILLE J., Essai sur le problème de l'un-multiple et de l'attribution chez Platon et les Sophistes. Bibl. d'Hist. de la Philos., Paris, Vrin 1962 282p. Summary in AUP XXXII 1962 397-398.
      Rev. LEC 1963 376 Pépin.
      RecSR LII 1964 462 des Places.
      RThPh XCVIII 1965 322-323 Schaerer.
      RPhilos CLVII 1967 105-107 Moreau.

2887* AMADO LÉVY-VALENSI E., Les niveaux de l'être, la connaissance et le mal. Paris, Presses Universitaires 1963 674p. (Ch.1 "Les niveaux de l'Être dans la philosophie platonicienne. Le chemin de la dialectique" p.15-72.)

2888 BECKER O., "Versuch einer neuen Interpretation der platonischen Ideenzahlen". AGPh XLV 1963 119-124.

2889* CHIEREGHIN F., Storicità e originarietà nell'idea platonica. Univ. di Padova, Pubbl. Fac. di Lett. e Filos. XL, Padova, CEDAM 1963 144p.
      Rev. Paideia XIX 1964 206-209 Fabro.
      RSF XIX 1964 458-459 Buccellato.
      CR XV 1965 116 Easterling.
      Filosofia XVI 1965 187 Berti.
      GM XXIII 1968 534-535 Guazzoni Foà.

2890* FRITZ K. VON, Philosophie und sprachlicher Ausdruck bei Demokrit, Plato und Aristoteles. (Unveränd. Nachdr. d. Ausg. 1938) Darmstadt, Wissenschaftl. Buchges. 1963 92p.

2891 GUZZONI G., "Considerazioni provvisorie sulla domanda dell'essere in Platone ed Aristotele". Pensiero VIII 1963 352-386.

2892 HAAG K.H., "Das Unwiederholbare". p.152-161 in Zeugnisse. Theodor W. Adorno zum 60. Geburtstag, hrsg. von Horkheimer M. Frankfurt a.M., Europäische Verl. 1963.

2893 MENDE G., "Bemerkungen zur Entstehungsgeschichte des objektiven Idealismus". WZLeip 1963 101-109.

2894* PAPAY J.L., Metaphysics in Process. A Selected History of Ancient Philosophy as an Introduction to the Philosophy of Being. Madison, N.J.,

Florham Park Pr. 1963 xv&347p. (ch.5 "Socrates and the Lesser Socratics", p.107-117; ch.6 "Platonic Metaphysics", p.118-205; ch.7 "The Platonic Tradition: A Second Look", p.206-246.) Rev. CW LVII 1964 353 Hoerber.

2895* ROBIN L., La Théorie platonicienne des idées et des nombres d'après Aristote. Étude historique et critique. Reprint of 1908 edn. Hildesheim, Olms 1963 xvii&702p. Rev. GM XVIII 1963 505 École.

2896 RUSSELL B., "Plato's Theory of Ideas". p.171-184 in Plato, Totalitarian or Democrat? ed. by Thorson T.L. (see 4617). Reprinted from Russell B., A History of Western Philosophy, ch. XV.

2897 BIGGER C., "The Theory of Participation in Plato's Later Dialogues". p.261-268 in XIII Congreso Internacional de Filosofía. Mexico, D.F., 7-14 de Setiembre de 1963. Comunicaciones Libres, sección XI: Historia de la Filosofía: Vol. IX. Mexico City, Univ. Nac. Aut. de México 1964.

2898 BLOCK I., "Plato, Parmenides, Ryle and Exemplification". Mind LXXIII 1964 417-422.

2899 PECK A.L., "Plato, Parmenides, Block and Exemplification". Mind LXXVI 1967 595.

2900* BROUSSARD J.D., Eternity in Greek and Scholastic Philosophy. Diss. Catholic Univ. of America 1963. Philos. Stud. CCVIII 244p. [microfilm]. Summary in DA XXIV 1964 3784-3785.

2901* HAEZRAHI P., On the Perfect Being. Studies in Plato and his Predecessors [in Hebrew]. Mif'al Haschichpul, the Publishing House of the Student's Organisation, Jerusalem, Faculty of Humanities, Hebrew Univ. 1964 399p.

2902 HARE R.M., "A Question about Plato's Theory of Ideas". p.61-81 in The Critical Approach to Science and Philosophy. In Honor of Karl R. Popper, ed. by Bunge M. London, Collier-Macmillan 1964.

2903 HOFFMANN E., "Methexis und Metaxy bei Platon". p.29-51 In Hoffmann E., Drei Schriften zur griechischen Philosophie (see 4602). Reprinted from Jahresbericht des philologischen Vereins zu Berlin XLV 1919 48-70.

2904 IMAMICHI T., "Idea and general Concept in Plato" [in Japanese with English summary]. JCS XII 1964 40-55.

2905 ISNARDI PARENTE M., "Platone e la prima Accademia di fronte al problema delle idee degli artefacta". RSF XIX 1964 123-158.

2906* LEDIGO LOPEZ M., Bien, Dios, hombre. Estudios sobre el pensamiento griego. ASal XVIII 1964 136p. (A collection of three studies, of which the first is on the metaphysics of the Good in Plato, p.13-55.)
Rev. RFil(Madrid) XXIV 1965 396 R.F. Augustinus XI 1966 87-88 Ruiz Pascual.

2907* LEIDER K., Platon und seine Ideenlehre. Vortragsreihe der Philosophischen Akademie zu Lübeck. Grosse Philosophen, Lübeck, Selbstverlag 1964 66p.

2908 RIST J.M., "The Immanence and Transcendance of the Platonic Form". Philologus CVIII 1964 217-232.

2909 RÚBERT CANDAU L., "El eidos en Platón". p.335-338 in Actas del II Congr. esp. de Estud. clás. (Madrid-Barcelona, 4-10 de abril de 1961). Publ. de la Soc. Esp. de Estud. Clás. V, Madrid 1964.

2910* STEWART J.A., Plato's Doctrine of Ideas. New York, Russell & Russell 1964 206p. (Reprint from 1909 Oxford edn.)

2911 THEILER W., "Einheit und unbegrenzte Zweiheit von Plato bis Plotin". p.89-104 in Isonomia. Studien zur Gleichheitsvorstellung im griechischen Denken, hrsg. von Mau J. & Schmidt E.G. Dt. Akad. der Wiss. Arbeitsgr. für hell.-röm. Philos. IX, Berlin, Akad.-Verl. 1964. Also verbess. Nachdr., Amsterdam, Hakkert 1971. Reprinted p.460-483 in Theiler W., Untersuchungen zur antiken Literatur. Berlin, de Gruyter 1970.

2912* ARNOLD U., Die Entelechie. Systematik bei Platon und Aristoteles. Überlieferung und Aufgabe II, München, Oldenbourg 1965 285p.
Rev. ArchPhilos XXX 1967 138-139

V B: METAPHYSICS

Solignac.
CW LXIII 1969 88-89 Byrne.

2913 CHERNISS H.F., "The Philosophical Economy of the
      Theory of Ideas". p.1-12 in Studies in Plato's
      Metaphysics, ed. by Allen R.E. (see 4580).
      Also p.16-27 in Plato I, ed. by Vlastos G.
      (see 4619). Reprinted from AJPh LVII 1936
      445-456.

2914 CROSS R. C., "Logos and Forms in Plato". p.13-31 in
      Studies in Plato's Metaphysics, ed. by Allen
      R.E. (see 4580). Reprinted from Mind 1954.

2915 BLUCK R.S., "Logos and Forms in Plato: A Reply to
      Prof. Cross". p.33-41 in Studies in Plato's
      Metaphysics, ed. by Allen R.E. (see 4580).
      Reprinted from Mind 1956.

2916* FATTORE V., L'Essere e il Non-essere: valore e
      limiti della loro conciliazione in Platone e
      Aristotele. Roma, Pontif. Univ. S. Tommaso
      1965 79p.
      Rev. Sophia 1967 383-384 Manno.

2917 GIOÈ S., "Trascendenza dell'idea in Platone e
      trascendentalità della forma in Aristotele".
      ALGP II 1965 466-470.

2918* HARTMANN N., Platos Logik des Seins. 2. Aufl.
      [Unveränd. Nachdr. d. 1. Aufl. 1909.]
      Berlin, de Gruyter 1965 x&512p.

2919* HARTMANN N., Aristóteles y el problema del concepto,
      sobre la doctrina del eidos en Platón y
      Aristóteles. Mexico City, U.N.A.M., Centro de
      Estudios filosóficos 1965.

2920 KOPPER J., "Über die Negation als Prinzip der
      Reflexion. Ein Beitrag zum Problem der Teilhabe
      des Vielen am Einen". p.45-70 in Parusia, hrsg.
      von Flasch K. (see 4588).

2921 MARKOVIĆ Z., "Platons Theorie über das Eine und die
      unbestimmte Zweiheit und ihre Spuren in der
      griechischen Mathematik". p.308-318 in Zur
      Geschichte der griechischen Mathematik, hrsg.
      von Becker O. Wege der Forschung XXXIII,
      Darmstadt, Wissens. Buchges. 1965.

2922 RINTELEN F.J. VON, "Die Frage nach dem Guten bei
      Plato". p.71-88 in Parusia, hrsg. von Flasch
      K. (see 4588).

2923 SCHAAF J., "Beziehung und Idee. Eine platonische
      Besinnung". p.3-20 in Parusia, hrsg. von
      Flasch K. (see 4588).

2924* SCHIPPER E.W., Forms in Plato's Later Dialogues.
      Den Haag, Nijhoff 1965 viii&78p.
            Rev. EtFr XV 1965 98-101 Person.
            PhilosQ XVI 1966 361 Cross.
            CR XVI 1966 312-314 Easterling.
            AusJP 1966 124-125 Blaney.
            JCS XV 1967 145-147 Shinkai.
            RM XXI 1967-1968 378 S.A.S.
            RMM LXXIII 1968 369-370 Brunschwig.
            RPortFil XXIV 1968 443-444 Freire.

2925 TOEPLITZ O., "Das Verhältnis von Mathematik und
      Ideenlehre bei Plato". p.45-75 in Zur
      Geschichte der griechischen Mathematik, hrsg.
      von Becker O. Wege der Forschung XXXIII,
      Darmstadt, Wissensch. Buchges. 1965.
      Reprinted from Quellen u. Studien z. Gesch.
      d. Math., Astron., und Phys. Abt. B, Bd. I
      1929-1931 3-33.

2926 VLASTOS G., "Degrees of Reality in Plato". p.1-19
      in New Essays on Plato and Aristotle, ed. by
      Bambrough R. (see 4582). Reprinted p.58-75 in
      Vlastos G., Platonic Studies (see 4622).

2927 WARNER D.H.J., "Form and Concept". JHPh III 1965
      159-166.

2928 ANSCOMBE G.E.M., "The new Theory of Forms". Monist
      L 1966 403-420.

2929 BAERTHLEIN K., "Zur platonischen Vorgeschichte der
      alten Transzendentalphilosophie". KantStud LVII
      1966 72-89.

2930* BARTH H., Philosophie der Erscheinung, I: Altertum
      und Mittelalter. 2. Aufl. Basel, Schwabe 1966
      xv&404p. (part 2 "Idee und Erscheinung in der
      Philosophie Platos", p.53-123.)
            Rev. ThZ XXIII 1967 453 Vályi-Nagy.
            RLT I 1966 77-80.

V B: METAPHYSICS

2931 BIERI P., "Zur Geschichte des Begriffsproblems". StudGen XIX 1966 462-476.

2932 BRUEHL K.A., "Hinweise zur Interpretation der platonischen Ideenlehre". AU R.9 1966 5-18.

2933 DELEUZE G., "Renverser le platonisme (Les simulacres)". RMM LXXI 1966 426-438.

2934 INOUE T., "Ideai. Plato" [in Japanese]. Philosophy (Tokyo) XVI 1966.

2935 JOJA A., "La théorie de l'universel, I: Platon". ALBuc IX 1966 33-94.

2936* JOJA A., Studii de logica. vol. II. Bucureşti, Ed. Academiei RPR 1966 526p. ("Doctrina universalului la Platon", p.309-370.)

2937 PAISSE J.M., "Une métaphysique de la relation". RMM LXXI 1966 439-462.

2938 PERPEET W., "Das Gute als Einheit. Zur Agathonspekulation Platons". KantStud LVII 1966 17-31.

2939 PHILIP J.A., "The 'Pythagorean' Theory of the Derivation of Magnitudes". Phoenix XX 1966 32-50.

2940* PRAUSS G., Platon und der logische Eleatismus. Berlin, de Gruyter 1966 226p.
        Rev. RPortFil XXIII 1967 503-504 Freire.
        Pensamiento 1967 341-342 Martínez Gómez.
        Angelicum 1967 384-385 Vansteenkiste.
        Dialogos IV 1967 139-142 Kerkhoff.
        RSC XV 1967 278-279 d'Agostino.
        LEC XXXV 1967 293-294 Moraux.
        AC XXXVI 1967 272 des Places.
        JCS XVI 1968 147-149 Amagasaki.
        CR XVIII 1968 38-40 Hamlyn.
        CW LXII 1968 138-139 Lee.
        Gnomon XLI 1969 460-463 Marten.
        RThPh 1969 58 Schaerer.
        DLZ LXXXIX 1968 579-581 Doent.
        ModS XLVII 1969-1970 227-229 Sweeney.

2941 SHINKAI K., "On ὄν and μὴ ὄν in Plato" [in Japanese]. Philosophy Miscellany (Tokyo Metropolitan Univ.) VIII 1966.

2942 VLASTOS G., "A Metaphysical Paradox". PAAPA XXXIX
      1966 5-19. Reprinted p.43-57 in Vlastos G.,
      Platonic Studies (see 4622).

2943* YOSHIOKA K., Plato and Metaphysics [in Japanese].
      Tokyo, Sakaishoten 1966 214p.

2944 AZAR L., "The Elusive One. Some historical
      Explorations". PhilosStud(Irel) XVI 1967
      104-115.

2946* FRAZER J.G., The Growth of Plato's Ideal Theory.
      New York, Russell & Russell 1967. Reprint.

2947 GROZEV G., "Ucenieto na Platon za ideite [Plato's
      Doctrine of Ideas]" [in Bulgarian]. FilosMis'l
      XXIII 1967 67-76. English abstract in Bulgarian
      Academy of Sciences, Abstracts of Bulgarian
      Scientific Literature. Philosophie & Pedagogics
      1967 p.10-11.

2948 LODETTI M., "L'idée du lit et l'idée du bien". REPh
      XVII,3 1967 1-4.

2949 MARTEN R., "Denkbarkeit und Mitteilbarkeit des
      ineffabile. Ein Problem der Platonauslegung".
      p.145-162 in Die Philosophie und die
      Wissenschaften. Simon Moser zum 65.
      Geburtstag, hrsg. von Oldemeyer E. Meisenheim
      am Glan, Hain 1967.

2950 MARTEN R., "'Selbstprädikation' bei Platon".
      KantStud LVIII 1967 209-226.

2951 MATSUNAGA Y., "On grasping Being in the Theory of
      Ideas" [in Japanese]. Riso no.409 1967.

2952 MAULA E., "On Plato and Plenitude". Ajatus XXIX
      1967 12-50.

2953* MOREAU J., La Construction de l'idéalisme
      platonicien. Reprint of 1st edn., Paris 1939.
      Hildesheim, Olms 1967 viii&516p.

V B: METAPHYSICS

2954* MOREAU J., Le sens du platonisme. Paris, Les Belles
       Lettres 1967 vi&395p.
            Rev. RPortFil XXIV 1968 442-443 Freire.
            REG LXXXI 1968 613-614 Trouillard.
            AC XXXVII 1968 678 des Places.
            EPh XXIV 1969 251-252 Duméry.
            ArchPhilos XXXIII 1970 138-141 Agaesse.
            GM XXV 1970 105-106 Sorge.
            Mnemosyne XXIII 1970 422-424 Sprute.
            CR XX 1970 27-28 Gulley.
            RPh XLIV 1970 321-322 Louis.
            RPhL LXIX 1971 590 Druart.
            JCS XIX 1971 143-146 Imabayashi.
            RThPh 1971 379 Brunner.
            Gymnasium LXXIX 1972 254 Mansfeld.

2955 MOREAU J., "Spiegazione semplice". GM XXV 1970
       693-694.

2956 NOICA C., "The Significance of Categories in European
       Culture. The Categories of Plato" [in
       Rumanian]. RevFiloz XIV 1967 1411-1420.

2957 RAVIS G., "L'idée de relation chez Platon". REPh
       XVIII,5 1967 11-34.

2958 RIST J.M., "Knowledge and Value in Plato". Phoenix
       XXI 1967 283-295.

2959 SCHEIBE E., "Über Relativbegriffe in der Philosophie
       Platons". Phronesis XII 1967 28-49.

2960 SPRAGUE R.K., "Parmenides' sail and Dionysodorus'
       ox". Phronesis XII 1967 91-98.

2961* WEDDLE P.D., On Plato's Doctrine of Ideas. Diss.
       Univ. of Nebraska 1967 172p. [microfilm].
       Summary in DA XXVIII 1968 2740A.

2962* BIGGER C.P., Participation. A Platonic Inquiry.
       Baton Rouge, Louisiana State Univ. Pr. 1968
       xv&223p.
            Rev. CW LXIII 1970 270 Jones.
            ModS XLVII 1969-1970 232-237 Sweeney.
            JVI IV 1970 158-160 Brumbaugh.
            RM XXII 1968-1969 747 M.M.H.

2963 ERBSE H., "Über Platons Methode in den sogenannten
       Jugenddialogen". Hermes XCVI 1968 21-40.

2964* GIACON C., I primi concetti metafisici. Platone,
       Aristotele, Plotino, Avicenna, Tommaso.
       Bologna, Zanichelli 1968 362p.
       Rev. RLT III 1968 146-149.
       P&I X 1968 338-339 Pozzo.
       Salesianum XXXI 1969 349 Composta.
       Filosofia XX 1969 366-369 Movia.
       EPh XXIV 1969 237 Duméry.
       RFNeo LXI 1969 320-325 Reale.
       CivCatt CXX 1969 405 Bortolaso.
       Pensiero XIV 1969 309-310 Pozzo.
       Sapientia XXIV 1969 157-158 Derisi.
       GM XXV 1970 341-343 Piemontese.
       DT LXXIII 1970 248-251 Mondin.
       Aquinas XIII 1970 514-517 Beschin.
       RRFC LXV 1971 124-129 Terzi.

2965 GRIMALDI N., "Le platonisme, ontologie de l'échec".
       RMM LXXIII 1968 261-279.

2966 HUENERMANN P., "Das göttliche Gute Platons. Eine
       Besinnung auf den Weg seines Denkens in den
       früheren Schriften". PhJ LXXV 1967-1968
       264-278.

2967 JOJA A., "La théorie de l'universel, I: Platon".
       RRSS XII 1968 99-157.

2968 KAPP E., "The Theory of Ideas in Plato's Earlier
       Dialogues". p.55-150 in Kapp E., Ausgewählte
       Schriften (see 4606).

2969* MAZIARZ E.A. & GREENWOOD T., Greek Mathematical
       Philosophy. New York, Ungar 1968 xii&271p.
       (Part II "The Mathematical Ontology of Plato",
       p.83-152.)
       Rev. Isis LX 1969 406 Gericke.
       CW LXIV 1970 59-60 Eisele.
       PhR LXXIX 1970 427-428 Mueller.

2970 WHITTAKER J., "The Eternity of the Platonic Forms".
       Phronesis XIII 1968 131-144. Reprinted ch.2,
       p.44-72 in Whittaker J., God, Time, Being.
       Studies in the Transcendental Tradition in Greek
       Philosophy. Bergen 1970.

2971 HARTMANN N., "Zur Lehre von Eidos bei Platon und
       Aristoteles". p.140-175 in Das Platonbild,
       hrsg. von Gaiser K. (see 4595). Reprinted
       from Abhandl. d. Preuss. Akad. d.
       Wissensch., phil.-hist. Kl., Berlin 1941, Nr.8.
       Also in Hartmann N., Kleinere Schriften, Bd.

II. Berlin 1957 129-164.

2972 KEYT D., "Plato's Paradox that the Immutable is Unknowable". PhilosQ XIX 1969 1-14.

2973 KUCHARSKI P., "La théorie des Idées selon le Phédon se maintient-elle dans les derniers dialogues?". RPhilos CLIX 1969 211-229.

2974 MANSION S., "L'objet aes mathématiques et l'objet de la aialectique selon Platon". RPhL LXVII 1969 365-388.

2975 MOREAU J., "The Platonic Idea and its threefold Function. A Synthesis". IPQ IX 1969 477-517.

2976 SCOLNICOV S., "The Epistemological Significance of Plato's Theory of Ideal Numbers" [in Hebrew with English summary p.301-300]. Iyyun XX 1969 186-211. Also in English: MH XXVIII 1971 72-97.

2977 VLASTOS G., "Self-predication in Plato's Later Period". PhR LXXVIII 1969 74-78. Reprinted as "Self-predication and Self-participation in Plato's Later Period", p.335-341 in Vlastos G., Platonic Studies (see 4622).

2978 ASANO N., "The question of Universality. A comparison of Plato's and Aristotle's views and the views of the modern analytical Philosophers" [in Japanese]. PhSJap XLIV,9 no.515 1970 and XLIV,10 no.516 1970.

2979* BOWLES G.M., Did Plato Believe in Immanent Universals? Diss. Stanford Univ. 1970 227p. Summary in DA XXXI 1970 6106A.

2980* BRENTLINGER J.A., The Theory of Forms in Plato's Later Dialogues. Diss. Yale Univ. 1962 324p. [microfilm]. Summary in DA XXXI 1970 1318A-1319A.

2981* BURGE E.L., Plato's Concept of Aitia. Diss. Princeton Univ. 1969 358p. [microfilm]. Summary in DA XXXI 1970 796A.

2982* HAGER F.P., Der Geist und das Eine. Untersuchungen zum Problem der Wesenbestimmung des höchsten Prinzips als Geist oder als Eines in der griechischen Philosophie. Noctes Romanae XII, Bern, Haupt 1970 ix&451p. ("Der Begriff des

V B: METAPHYSICS

göttlichen Geistes als Ursache der Welt und der
Begriff des Einen selbst als höchstes Prinzip
bei Platon", p.5-156.)
Rev. ACR II 1972 80 Dillon.
CR XXIII 1973 209-212 Herford.

2983 IKEDA Y., "On Plato's Degrees of Reality and related
Problems" [in Japanese]. Methodos III 1970.

2984 KELESSIDOU-GALANOU A., "Ἡ προβληματικὴ τῆς ἐννοίας
τοῦ ἑνὸς ἐν τῇ ἀρχαίᾳ ἑλληνικῇ φιλοσοφίᾳ". EEAth
XX 1969-1970 212-224.

2985 LOSEV A.F., "Elemente des körperlichen
Verständnisses der Wirklichkeit in der
Ideenlehre Platons". Philologus CXIV 1970 9-27.

2986 MOUTSOPOULOS E., "Ὀντολογικὴ αὐτοτέλεια". EEAth XX
1969-1970 187-192.

2987 PAISSE J.M., "L'idéalisme platonicien". RPhilos CLX
1970 25-65.

2988 PATZIG G., "Platons Ideenlehre, kritisch
betrachtet". A&A XVI 1970 113-126.

2989 TROTIGNON P., "Que signifie l'idée du bien?". AIP
1970 7-24.

2990 TSOUYOPOULOS N., "Die Entdeckung der Struktur
komparitiver Begriffe in der Antike. Zur
Begriffsbildung bei Aristoteles und Proklos".
ABG XIV 1970 152-171.

2991 VOGEL C.J. DE, "Some Controversial Points of Plato
Interpretation Reconsidered". p.183-209 in
Vogel C.J. de, Philosophia I (see 4624).

2992 VOGEL C.J. DE, "Platon a-t-il ou n'a-t-il pas
introduit le mouvement dans son monde
intelligible?". p.176-182 in Vogel C.J. de,
Philosophia I (see 4624). Reprinted from Actes
du XIe Congr. Intern. de Philos., Bruxelles
1953, T.12 61-67.

2993 WEDBERG A., "The Theory of Ideas". p.28-52 in Plato
I, ed. by Vlastos G. (see 4619). Reprinted
from Wedberg A., Plato's Philosophy of
Mathematics, 1955 ch.3.

341

V B: METAPHYSICS

2994* WEIER W., Sinn und Teilhabe. Das Grundthema der
abendländischen Geistesentwicklung. Salzburg.
Stud. zur Philos., München, Pustet 1970 636p.
(for Plato see esp. p.70-104.)
Rev. REAug XVII 1971 378 Madec.

2995 ALLEN R.E., "Plato's Earlier Theory of Forms".
p.319-334 in The Philosophy of Socrates, ed. by
Vlastos G. (see 4621).

2996 CASTAÑEDA H.N., "El análisis de Platón de las
relaciones y de los hechos relacionales en el
Fédon" [in Spanish with English summary].
Critica V 1971 No.14 3-18.

2997 CRESSWELL M.J., "Essence and Existence in Plato and
Aristotle". Theoria XXXVII 1971 91-113.

2998* DESCOMBES V., Le platonisme. Coll. SUP Le
philosophe XCIX, Paris, Colin 1971 128p.
Rev. RIPh XXVII 1973 541 Somville.

2999 KAMIOKA H., "Plato's Theory of Being" [in Japanese].
Philosophy Miscellany (Tokyo Metropolitan Univ.)
XIV 1971

3000 LOSEV O.F., "The Problem of the Somatic Significance
of Plato's Ideas" [in Ukranian with Russian
summary]. FilDum No.6 1971 57-68.

3001 MUÑOZ M.J., "El mundo real de Platón". Franciscanum
XIII 1971 125-151.

3002 SCHIPPER E.W., "Is Plato an Idealist?". StudGen
XXIV 1971 583-597.

3003 VOGEL C.J. DE, "À propos de quelques aspects dits
néoplatonisants du platonisme de Platon".
p.7-16 in Le néoplatonisme (see 4578).

3004 BAMBROUGH R., "The Disunity of Plato's Thought, or
What Plato did not say". Philosophy XLVII 1972
295-307.

3005 BIANCHI U., "Ο σύμπας αἰών". p.277-286 in Ex orbe
religionum. Studia G. Widengren. Numen Suppl.
XXI, Leiden, Brill 1972.

3006 BORMANN K., "Platon. Die Idee". p.44-83 in
Grundprobleme der grossen Philosophen, hrsg.
von Speck. J. (see 4616).

342

3007 BRENTLINGER J.A., "Particulars in Plato's Middle Dialogues". AGPh LIV 1972 116-152.

3008 CRESSWELL M.J., "Is there one or are there many one and many Problems in Plato?". PhilosQ XXII 1972 149-154.

3009 DERBOLAV J., "The philosophical Origins of Plato's Theory of Ideas". AGPh LIV 1972 1-23.

3010 FINDLAY J.N., "Plato's Reduction of the Forms to Numbers". Abstract in JPh LXIX 1972 674.

3011 GAJENDRAGADKAR V., "Two Modes of Predication in Plato and Aristotle". JUBA XL 1972 162-177.

3012* GOHLKE P.E., Die Lehre von der Abstraktion bei Plato und Aristoteles. Hildesheim/New York, Olms 1972 118p. Reprint of 1914 edn.

3013 IMPARA P., "Γένεσις εἰς οὐσίαν in Platone". Proteus III 1972 81-92.

3014 KELESSIDOU-GALANOS A., "À la recherche de la valeur suprême. Platon et l'Un absolu" [in French with Greek summary]. Philosophia(Athens) II 1972 152-200.

3015* PEIPERS D., Ontologia Platonica. Ad notionum terminorumque historiam symbola. Osnabrück, Zeller 1972 xiv&606p. Reprint of 1883 edn.

3016* RINTELEN F.J. VON, Values in European Thought, I. Pamplona, Ed. Univ. de Navarra 1972 565p. (ch.3B on Socrates and Plato.)
        Rev. Philosophia(Athens) III 1973 472-479 Dragona-Monachou.
        Gregorianum LIV 1973 785-787 de Finance.

3017 VOGEL C.J. DE, "Was Plato a Dualist?". Th-P I 1972 4-60.

3018 BONDESON W., "Non-Being and the One: Some Connections between Plato's Sophist and Parmenides". Apeiron VII,2 1973 13-22.

3019 BREMER D., "Hinweise zum griechischen Ursprung und zur europäischen Geschichte der Lichtmetaphysik". ABG XVII 1973 7-35. (for Plato see esp. sec.2, p.22-33.)

3020 CLEGG J.S., "Self-Predication and Linguistic Reference in Plato's Theory of the Forms". Phronesis XVIII 1973 26-43.

3021 FOTINIS A.P., "A Critical Evaluation of Universals in Nominalism" [in English with Greek summary]. Philosophia(Athens) III 1973 382-404.

3022 IRWIN T.H., "Plato's Heracliteanism". Abstract in JPh LXX 1973 580-581.

3023 KOZY J. Jr., "The Self-destruction of Metaphysics: A Justification of Living under the Influence of Ideals". IdealStud III 1973 72-79.

3024 LEGOWICZ J., "Problem der Zahl als Zwischenideeweltbegriff in der Sprache bei Plato". DYP X 1973 7-20.

3025* MARTIN G., Platons Ideenlehre. Berlin/New York, de Gruyter 1973 iii&296p.

3026 STROLL A., "Linguistic Clusters and the Problem of Universals". Dialectica XXVII 1973 219-259.

3027 TELOH H., "Self-predication or Anaxagorean Causation in Plato". Abstract in JPh LXX 1973 581.

3028* UPHUES K., Sprachtheorie und Metaphysik bei Platon, Aristoteles und in der Scholastik, hrsg. von Plach K. Opuscula philosophica II, Frankfurt, Minerva-Verl. 1973 xiii&465p. Reprint of a collection of the author's works published between 1869 and 1882.

For further studies relevant to various aspects of Plato's metaphysical thought see 57, 165, 259, 285, 286, 342, 343, 370, 374, 377, 380, 392, 398, 415, 420, 421, 424, 427, 429, 430, 434, 445, 449, 453, 464, 465, 470, 484, 489, 500, 507, 514, 643, 687, 688, 720, 759, 770, 891, 1089, 1119, 1127, 1134, 1144, 1225, 1232, 1233, 1247, 1252, 1291, 1443, 1446, 1545, 1546, 1548, 1549, 1550, 1551, 1552, 1553, 1554, 1555, 1556, 1557, 1558, 1559, 1561, 1563, 1566, 1567, 1576, 1577, 1579, 1582, 1585, 1587, 1588, 1591, 1593, 1594, 1595, 1596, 1597, 1598, 1599, 1600, 1601, 1602, 1603, 1604, 1605, 1606, 1607, 1608, 1609, 1610, 1611, 1612, 1613, 1614, 1615, 1616, 1617, 1618, 1619, 1620, 1621, 1627, 1703, 1716, 1717, 1718, 1719, 1720, 1721, 1722, 1723, 1724, 1725, 1726, 1727, 1728, 1729, 1730, 1731, 1732, 1733, 1734, 1735,

1736, 1737, 1738, 1744, 1746, 1748, 1894, 1895,
1896, 1897, 1900, 1901, 1902, 1903, 1906, 1907,
1913, 1942, 2139, 2143, 2144, 2145, 2146, 2147,
2152, 2153, 2154, 2158, 2163, 2164, 2179, 2180,
2181, 2182, 2183, 2184, 2185, 2186, 2190, 2191,
2194, 2195, 2196, 2220, 2227, 2229, 2230, 2231,
2232, 2234, 2235, 2236, 2237, 2239, 2242, 2243,
2244, 2245, 2246, 2247, 2249, 2251, 2253, 2255,
2257, 2263, 2264, 2266, 2268, 2270, 2272, 2273,
2274, 2275, 2277, 2278, 2280, 2282, 2285, 2288,
2297, 2307, 2342, 2377, 2378, 2417, 2419, 2426,
2453, 2461, 2499, 2500, 2514, 2515, 2516, 2520,
2521, 2523, 2528, 2531, 2533, 2539, 2540, 2604,
2688, 2705, 2748, 2779, 2800, 2840, 2861, 2882,
2901, 3033, 3058, 3086, 3143, 3183, 3215, 3231,
3264, 3278, 3314, 3520, 3750, 3883, 3902, 3940,
3974, 4001, 4004, 4006, 4042, 4045, 4048, 4055,
4068, 4082, 4091, 4092, 4093, 4097, 4100, 4110,
4144, 4145.

V C: PSYCHOLOGY, HUMAN NATURE
AND THE HUMAN CONDITION

The close interconnections among the branches of
this subject made subdivision unworkable, but to
facilitate access to certain major topics I have
prepared a number of special indices referring
to works (both in this section and elsewhere) on
Immortality of the Soul, Metempsychosis, and
Eschatology, Mental Illness, Anamnesis,
Sense-Perception, The Forms and Ways of Human
Intelligence and Reasoning, and The Human
Condition, Human Life and Death. The indices
are located at the end of the present section.

3029 BLUCK R.S., "Plato, Pindar and Metempsychosis".
AJPh LXXIX 1958 405-414.

3030* LAÍN ENTRALGO P., La curación por la palabra en la
antigüedad clásica. Madrid, Revista de
Occidente 1958 356p. English transl. by Rather
L.J. & Sharp J.M. The Therapy of the Word in
Classical Antiquity. New Haven, Yale Univ. Pr.
1970 xxii&254p.
Rev. [of Spanish edn.] Emerita XXVII 1959
183-185 Adrados.
EClas V 1960 380-381 Galiano.
Helmantica XI 1960 373-375 Panyagua.
[of English edn.]YR 1970 592 Wimsatt.
LEC XXXIX 1971 118-119 Delaunois.
BHM XLV 1971 188-190 Boas.
CM VI 1971 251-252 López Piñero.
IJPsy LII 1971 325-327 Padel.
ACR II 1972 81-82 Scarborough.
CR XXIII 1973 95-96 Phillips.
Gnomon XLV 1973 410-412 Kudlien.

3031 LAÍN ENTRALGO P., "La racionalización platónica del
ensalmo y la invención de la psicoterapia
verbal". AIHM X 1958 133-160. Also in German:
"Die Platonische Rationalisierung der
Besprechung (ἐπῳδή) und die Erfindung der
Psychotherapie durch das Wort". Hermes LXXXVI
1958 298-323.

3032* MONDOLFO R., La comprehensione del soggetto umano
nell'antichità classica, trad da Bassi L. Il
pensiero classico VI, Firenze, La Nuova Italia

1958 xii&758p.
Rev. Athenaeum XXXVII 1959 348-353
Alfieri.
P&I I 1959 232 Berti.
RF L 1959 247-248 Viano.
RFil(Madrid) XVIII 1959 511 Aróstegui.
PhilosRdschau VII 1959 74-75 Gadamer.
Aquinas II 1959 400-410 Giannini.
CivCatt CX 1959 298.
Filosofia X 1959 323-324 Guzzo.
RSFil XII 1959 84-86 Petruzzellis.
RFIC XXXVIII 1960 292-293 Lana.
Maia XII 1960 157-162 Grassi.
FilosV I 1960 75-77 Beschin.
RSPh XLIV 1960 103 Saffrey.
RFNeo LII 1960 687-689 Bonetti.
Orpheus VIII 1961 79-80 Rapisarda.
RecSR XLIX 1961 136-137 des Places.
KantStud LIII 1961-1962 376-383 Oedingen.
RPhL LX 1962 433-434 Thiry.
NRTh LXXXVI 1964 1003 Thiry.

3033 NUÑO J.A., "Ser y conocer en la filosofía platónica.
      Fundamentos e implicaciones ontológicas de la
      teoría crítica del conocimiento del Teetetos".
      Episteme (Caracas) II 1958 217-276.

3034 OEDINGEN K., "Der Ursprung des europäischen
      Rationalismus". ZPhF XII 1958 218-240.

3035* RIGOBELLO A., L'intellettualismo in Platone.
      Padova, Liviana 1958 vii&121p.
      Rev. Teoresi XIV 1959 106-109 Anastasio.
      StudPat VI 1959 174-176 Berti.

3036 VERBEKE G., "De spiritualistische visie op de mens.
      Het mensenbeeld van Plato". DWB 1958 409-420.

3037 ZANTORP H., "Das Problem der Selbsterkenntnis bei
      Platon, Kant und Schopenhauer". p.67-90 in Im
      Dienste der Wahrheit. Paul Häberlin zum 80.
      Geburtstag. Bern, Franke 1958.

3038 ALLEN R.E., "Anamnesis in Plato's Meno and Phaedo".
      RM XIII 1959-1960 165-174.

3039 FRAISSE J.C., "Ascétisme et valeur de la vie chez
      Platon". RPhilos CXLIX 1959 104-108.

3040 JAEGER W., "The Greek Ideas of Immortality". HThR
      LII 1959 135-147.

V C: PSYCHOLOGY

3041 SÁNCHEZ LASSO DE LA VEGA J., "El Eros pedagógico de
Platón". p.101-148 in Fernández Galiano M.,
Sánchez Lasso de la Vega J., Rodríguez Adrados
F., El descubrimiento del amor en Gracia, Seis
Conferencias. Madrid, Fac. de Filos. y Letras
1959.

3042 MITSUI H., "Love, Life and Death in Plato" [in
Japanese]. in Kwansei Univ. seventieth
anniversary publication. Kwansei Univ. Dept.
of Letters 1959.

3043* REY ALTUNA L., La inmortalidad del alma a la luz de
los filósofos. Bibl. Hisp. de Filos. XVIII,
Madrid, Ed. Gredos 1959 506p. (For Socrates
and Plato see p.9-19.)
        Rev. RFil(Madrid) XX 1961 91-92 Carreras
Artau.

3044* TOPITSCH E., Die platonisch-aristotelischen
Seelenlehren in weltanschauungskritischer
Beleuchtung. SAWW CCXXXIII,4, Wien, Rohrer 1959
32p.
        Rev. DLZ LXXXII 1961 503-504 van Boekel.
AAHG XV 1962 36-38 Schwabl.

3045 WILFORD F.A., "The Status of Reason in Plato's
Psychology". Phronesis IV 1959 54-58.

3046 DIRLMEIER F., "Vom Monolog der Dichtung zum inneren
Logos bei Platon und Aristoteles". Gymnasium
LXVII 1960 26-41. Reprinted p.142-154 in
Dirmleier F., Ausgewählte Schriften zu Dichtung
und Philosophie der Griechen, hrsg. von
Goergemanns H. Heidelberg, Winter 1970.

3047 MOUTSOPOULOS E., "Μουσικὴ κίνησις καὶ ψυχολογία ἐν
τοῖς ἐσχάτοις πλατωνικοῖς διαλόγοις". Athena
LXIV 1960 194-208.

3048* MUELLER F.L., Histoire de la psychologie de
l'antiquité à nos jours. Paris, Payot 1960
444p. (For Socrates and Plato see pp.49-63.)

3049* COREA P.V., The Will and its Freedom in the Thought
of Plato, Aristotle, Augustine and Kant. Diss.
Boston Univ. 1961 364p. Summary in DA XXII
1961 884-885.

3050* HAMLYN D.W., Sensation and Perception. A History of
the Philosophy of Perception. New York,
Humanities Pr. 1961 xii&210p. (p.10-16 on

Plato.)

3051 LLEDÓ IÑIGO E., "La anámnesis dialéctica en Platón"
[in Spanish with German summary]. Emerita XXIX
1961 219-239.

3052* MASON M.E., Active Life and Contemplative Life. A
Study of the Concepts from Plato to the Present.
Milwaukee, Marquette Univ. Pr. 1961 xi&127p.
Rev. ThS XXIII 1962 164 Sponga.

3053 MIFSUD J., "À propos de la notion de perversion chez
Platon: les irrécupérables". p.302-306 in La
nature humaine. Actes du XI Congrès des
Sociétés de Philosophie de langue française,
Montpellier, 4-6 sept. 1961. Paris, Presses
Universitaires 1961.

3054 VOGEL C.J. DE, "Aristotele e l'ideale della vita
contemplativa". GM XVI 1961 450-466. Reprinted
as "Plato, Aristoteles en het ideaal van het
beschouwende leven". p.154-171 in Vogel C.J.
de, Theoria (see 4623).

3055* OEHLER K., Die Lehre vom noetischen und
dianoetischen Denken bei Platon und Aristoteles.
Ein Beitrag zur Erforschung der Geschichte des
Bewusstseinsproblems in der Antike. Zetemata
XXIX, München, Beck 1962 x&294p.
Rev. Bijdragen XXIV 1963 338 Robbers.
CR XIII 1963 285-287 Gulley.
AC XXXII 1963 238 des Places.
REA LXV 1963 428-430 Moreau.
RBPh XLI 1963 647 Joly.
Paideia XVIII 1963 68-70 Fabro.
Gymnasium LXXI 1964 541-543 Stark.
RecSR LII 1964 464 des Places.
CW LVIII 1964 53 Costas.
Salesianum 1964 380-382 Composta.
AAHG XVIII 1965 37-41 Braun.
SJP IX 1965 315-318 Beierwaltes.
Gnomon XXXVIII 1966 752-760 Tugendhat.
Mnemosyne 1968 86-88 Verdenius.

3056* RODRÍGUEZ ADRADOS F., El heroe tragico y el filosofo
platonico. Cuad. de la Fund. Pastor VI,
Madrid, Ed. Taurus 1962 75p.
Rev. Humanidades XV 1963 225 Mayor.
REG LXXVI 1963 258-259 Weil.
Arbor LV 1963 138-140 González Laso.
RPh XXXVIII 1964 302 Louis.
Helmantica XV 1964 417 Oroz Reta.

CR XV 1965 225-226 Garton.

3057 VERSENYI L. "Eros, Irony and Ecstasy". Thought
XXXVII 1962 598-614.

3058 ARDLEY G., "Plato as Tragedian". PhilosStud(Irel)
XII 1963 7-24.

3059 GONZALEZ DE LA FUENTE A., "El connubio platónico
entre la contemplación y la acción". Studium
III 1963 287-299.

3060* GOULD T., Platonic Love. London, Routledge & Kegan
Paul/New York, Free Press of Glencoe 1963
viii&216p.
Rev. TLS 5 Nov. 1964 1004.
PhilosBks May 1964 18 Cloud.
CR XIV 1964 262-264 Gulley.
CW LVII 1964 256 Rosenmeyer.
Athene(Chicago) XXV,4 1964-1965 41 Rexine.
RBPh XLII 1964 1095-1096 Saunders.
Ethics LXXIV 1964 229.
AJPh LXXXVI 1965 333-334 Rist.
CPh LX 1965 124-126 Greene.
CJ LX 1965 282-285 Etheridge.
JHS LXXXV 1965 202-204 Rankin.
PhilosQ XIV 1964 91 Crombie.
PhR LXXIV 1965 534-537 Moravcsik.

3061* HALL R.W., Plato and the Individual. Den Haag,
Nijhoff 1963 and New York, Humanities Pr. 1965
224p.
Rev. PhilosBks Oct. 1964 12 Hamlyn.
IPQ V 1965 327-329 Nemetz.
RPortFil XXI 1965 216 Morão.
REG LXXVIII 1965 416-417 Salviat.
JHS LXXXV 1965 205-206 Baldry.
RSF XXI 1966 339-340 Isnardi Parente.
EPh XX 1965 362 Pépin.
CR XVI 1966 28-31 Adkins.
PhilosQ 1966 72 Cross.
JHPh III 1965 260-261 Anton.
Gnomon XXXIX 1967 6-13 Kuhn.
RMM LXXII 1967 379-382 Brunschwig.
DLZ LXXXIX 1968 5-7 Schottlaender.
Eos LVII 1967-1968 409-413 Wróblewski.

3062 HALL R.W., "Ψυχή as Differentiated Unity in the
Philosophy of Plato". Phronesis VIII 1963
63-82.

3063* PFEIL H., Das platonische Menschenbild. Aschaffenburg, Pattloch 1963 113p.
Rev. Augustinianum IV 1964 467 Pold.
ZKTh LXXXVII 1965 133 Pechhacker.
Arbor LXI 1965 237-238 Blarer.
Salmanticensis 1966 212 Rivera de Ventosa.
SJP VIII 1964 276 Beck.

3064 SPANNEUT M., "L'amour, de l'hellénisme au christianisme". MSR XX 1963 5-19.

3065 BRUN J., "Les avatars d'Erôs". BSPh LVIII 1964 97-126.

3066 DIEGO RIVERO A., "Amor y filosofía en Platón". Humanidades XVI 1964 33-44.

3068* HUBER C.E., Anamnesis bei Plato. Pullacher Philos. Forsch. VI, München, Hueber 1964 xxxii&665p.
Rev. PhilosStud(Irel.) XIV 1965 262-263 Watson.
Stromata XXI 1965 530.
REG LXXVIII 1965 418-421 Moreau.
Angelicum XLIII 1966 109-111 Vansteenkiste.
ModS XLIII 1965-1966 421-423 Kornmueller.
RecSR LIV 1966 598 des Places.
ZKTh LXXXVIII 1966 91 Muck.
NRTh LXXXVIII 1966 320 de Give.
RPhL LXIV 1966 309 Semeese.
Th&Ph XLI 1966 270-276 Ennen.
CR XVI 1966 166-168 Easterling.
Gnomon XXXIX 1967 829-831 Skemp.
PhJ LXXIV 1966-1967 415-417 Beierwaltes.
Studium VII 1967 239-240 Manzanedo.
GM XXIV 1969 104-105 Guazzoni Foà.

3069 JOLY R., "Les origines de l'ΟΜΟΙΩΣΙΣ ΘΕΩ". RBPh XLI 1964 91-95.

3070 LE DÉAUT R., "Φιλανθρωπία dans la littérature grecque jusqu'au Nouveau Testament (Tite III,4)". p.255-294 in Mélanges E. Tisserant I: Écriture sainte. Ancien Orient. Studi e Testi CCXXXI, Città del Vaticano, Bibl. Apostol. Vaticana 1964.

3071* MORGAN D.N., Love. Plato, the Bible and Freud. A
Spectrum Book S82, Englewood Cliffs, N.J.,
Prentice-Hall 1964 xiii&174p. (Part I:
"Platonic Love", p.5-46.)
Rev. CW LVIII 1964 85 Hoerber.

3072* PLACES E. DES, Syngeneia. La parenté de l'homme
avec Dieu, d'Homère à la patristique. Études &
Commentaires LI, Paris, Klincksieck 1964 223p.
(Platon, p.63-102.)
Rev. AC XXXIV 1965 312 Crahay.
Gnomon XXXVII 1965 730-731 Wehrli.
CW LIX 1965 50-51 Segal.
JHS LXXXV 1965 213-214 Pollard.
RecSR LIII 1965 165-168 Daniélou.
REA LXVII 1965 275-277 Courcelle.
GIF XVIII 1965 78-80 Rossi.
RBPh XLIII 1965 295 Joly.
RFIC XCIII 1965 450-452 Lugarini.
CRAI 1965 87 Chantraine.
Gregorianum XLVII 1966 558 Orbe.
BIEH II,1 1968 76 Alsina.
CR XXI 1971 148-149 Adkins.

3073* RANKIN H.D., Plato and the Individual. London,
Methuen/New York, Barnes & Noble 1964 156p.
Paperback edn. University Paperbacks, London,
Methuen 1969.
Rev. Philosophy XL 1965 362 Guthrie.
CW LIX 1965 84 Gould.
PhilosQ XVI 1966 271 Ralls.
Crisis XII 1965 129 Oroz Reta.
ModS XLIII 1965-1966 89-91 Neumann.
Augustinus X 1965 261 Oroz Reta.
RPortFil XXII 1966 208 Freire.
PhilosBks May 1965 22 Hamlyn.
AusJP 1965 269 Blaney.

3074* RIST J.M., Eros and Psyche. Studies in Plato,
Plotinus and Origen. Phoenix Suppl. VI, Univ.
of Toronto Pr. 1964 xi&238p.
Rev. RSC XII 1964 345-346 d'Agostino.
AC XXXIV 1965 674-675 Rutten.
CJ LXI 1965 32-34 Morgan.
Hermathena CI 1965 72 Charlton.
CW LVIII 1965 285-286 Sullivan.
Salesianum XXVII 1965 482 Composta.
PhilosStud(Irel.) XIV 1965 260-262 Watson.
Dialogue III 1964-1965 438-440 Merlan.
DownsR   LXXXIII   1965   311-326
Sheldon-Williams.
Tablet 1965 326 Markus.

UTQ 1965 403 Armstrong.
PhilosBks Oct. 1965 24 Lloyd.
HeythropJ VII 1966 108-109 T.G.
R.M. XIX 1965-1966 383 E.A.R.
RecSR LIV 1966 599 des Places.
NRTh LXXXVIII 1966 321 de Give.
Gnomon XXXVIII 1966 659-662 Theiler.
CPh LXI 1966 276-278 Hoerber.
CR XVI 1966 84-86 Gulley.
Gregorianum XLVII 1966 126-127 Orbe.
LEC XXXV 1967 202 Moraux.
JCS XVI 1968 154-156 Kakuta.
JHS LXXXVIII 1968 202-204 Rankin.

3075* ROBIN L., La théorie platonicienne de l'amour.
nouv. éd., préf. de Schuhl P.M. Bibl. de
Philos. contemp., Paris, Presses Universitaires
1964 viii&191p. Also Italian transl. La teoria
platonica dell'amore, pref. di Reale G., trad.
di Gavazzi Porta D. Scienze umane XII, Milano,
Celuc 1973 255p.

3076* ROMANO F., Logos e Mythos nella psicologia di
Platone. Pubbl. dell'Ist. Univ. di Magistero
di Catania, Ser. filos., Saggi e Monogr.
XLVIII, Padova, Cedam 1964 viii&248p.
Rev. REG LXXVII 1964 609-610 Moreau.
BAGB 1965 414 Trouillard.
AC XXXIV 1965 227 Joly.
Vichiana II 1965 98-100 Pagliano.
LEC XXXIII 1965 440 Loriaux.
RMM LXXI 1966 253-254 Brunschwig.
GM XXI 1966 494-498 Sorge.
JHS LXXXVII 1967 167 Saunders.

3077 SCHUHL P.M., "Remarques sur quelques doctrines
platoniciennes envisagées comme réponses à
certaines questions fondamentales". p.11-13 in
Études sur l'histoire de la philosophie en
hommage à Martial Guéroult. Paris, Fischbacher
1964.

3078* WILD J.D., Plato's Theory of Man. An Introduction
to the Realistic Philosophy of Culture. New
York, Octagon Books 1964 320p.

3079 BACIGALUPO M.V., "Teriomorfismo e trasmigrazione".
Filosofia XVI 1965 267-290.

3080* BALDRY H.C., The Unity of Mankind in Greek Thought.
Cambridge Univ. Pr. 1965 viii&223p. (ch.3
"Socrates and the fourth Century" [includes

Plato], p.52-112.)

3081* BALLARD E.G., Socratic Ignorance. An Essay on
Platonic Self-Knowledge. Den Haag, Nijhoff 1965
ix&189p.
    Rev. EPh XXI 1966 401-402 Wencelius.
    CJ LXII 1966 133-134 Hoerber.
    PhilosBks Oct. 1966 2 Gulley.
    JHPh V 1967 365-366 Neumann.
    CR XVII 1967 26-28 Easterling.
    IPQ VII 1967 340-356 Neville.
    RM XX 1966-1967 145-146 Willer.
    RPortFil XXIII 1967 514 Peixoto.
    PhilosRdschau XV 1968 157 H.K.
    RPhilos   CLVIII   1968   294-296
    Vincent-Viguier.
    Erasmus XXI 1969 94-96 Lasserre.
    Gnomon XLII 1970 614-615 Ilting.

3082* BANCHETTI S., La persona umana nella morale dei
Greci. Milano, Marzorati 1965 290p. (ch.3
"Motivi di impersonalismo nella speculazione
socratica", p.149-196; ch.4 "Motivi di
impersonalismo nei grandi sistemi della
classicità. A. Platone", p.197-220.)
    Rev. GM XXIII 1968 372-373 Sorge.
    Sophia XXXV 1967 382-383 Manno.
    Sapienza XX 1967 547-549 Manno.
    Dialogo V 1968 322-323 Armetta.
    Filosofia XXIII 1972 321-322 Zambelloni.

3083 CARBONARA NADDEI M., "L'immortalità dell'anima nel
pensiero dei greci". Sophia XXXIII 1965
272-300.

3084* CORNFORD F.M., Principium Sapientiae. New York,
Harper & Row 1965 viii&270p. Reprint of 1952
edn. (ch.4 "Anamnesis"; ch.5 "The Quarrel of
the Seer and the Philosopher".) (ch.4 also
reprinted p.108-127 in Plato's Meno, transl. by
Guthrie W.K.C., essays ed. by Brown M. (see
1485).)

3085 CUBELLS F., "Evolución y sentido de la vida personal
en Platón y Aristóteles". Asclepio XVII 1965
3-68.

3086 DOENT E., "Bemerkungen zu Platons Spätphilosophie
und zu Philipp von Opus". WS LXXVIII 1965
45-57.

3087* GONZÁLEZ DE LA FUENTE A., Acción y contemplación
según Platón. Jalones para una filosofía de la
vida activa y un connubio entre teoría y
práctica. Madrid, Inst. Luis Vives de Filos.
1965 210p.
Rev. Crisis XII 1965 133-134 Oroz Reta.
RFNeo LIX 1967 150-151 A.G.
EstFilos XV 1966 431-432 J.L.A.
Stromata XXII 1966 159-160.
RPortFil XXII 1966 327 Freire.
RPhL LXIV 1966 626 Decloux.
RThPh XCIX 1966 339 Borel.
Pensamiento 1967 91-92 Gómez Muntán.
Angelicum 1967 382-383 Huerga.
Franciscanum IX 1967 82 Herrera.
CiTom XCV 1968 197-199 Cudeiro.
Erasmus XX 1968 421-422 Clavaud.
Helmantica XIX 1968 161 Oroz.
Aquinas 1966 132-133 Sales.

3088 HART R.L., "The imagination in Plato". IPQ V 1965
436-461.

3089 HODGSON L., "Life after Death. II: The
Philosophers Plato and Kant". ExposT LXXVI 1965
107-109.

3090 HYPPOLITE J., "Le mythe et l'origine. À propos d'un
texte de Platon". Demitizzazione e morale,
ArchFilos 1965 No.1-2 21-24. Also p.21-24 in
Démythisation et morale. Actes du Colloque.
Rome, 7-12 janvier 1965. Paris, Aubier 1965.
Also p.1-6 in Hyppolite J., Figures de la pensée
philosophique. Écrits (1931-1968). Paris,
Presses Universitaires 1971, T.1.

3091 PAISSE J.M., "La thème de la réminiscence dans les
dialogues de Platon". LEC XXXIII 1965 225-252 &
376-400.

3092* RALFS G., Stufen des Bewusstseins. Vorlesungen zur
Erkenntnistheorie. KantStud Erg.-Heft XCI,
Köln, Kölner Univ.-Verl. 1965 283p.

3093 RODIS-LEWIS G., "Limites de la simplicité de l'âme
dans le Phédon". RPhilos CLV 1965 441-454.

3094 ROSEN S., "The Role of Eros in Plato's Republic".
RM XVIII 1965 452-475.

3095* SCHIAVONE M., Il problema dell'amore nel mondo
       greco, I: Platone. Pubbl. dell'Ist. di
       Filos. dell'Univ. di Genova XXXV, Milano,
       Marzorati 1965 392p.
       Rev. Augustinus 1966 323 Alesanco.
       RMM LXXI 1966 484-486 Brunschwig.
       CD CLXXIX 1966 369-370 Alvarez Turienzo.
       ModS XLIV 1966-1967 379-381 Sweeney.
       Antonianum XLII 1967 152 Lasić.
       JPh LXV 1968 379 Randall.

3096 TOPITSCH E., "Mythische Modelle in der
       Erkenntnislehre". StudGen XVIII 1965 400-418.

3097 TSIRPANLIS E.C., "The Immortality of the Soul in
       Phaedo and Symposium" [in English with Greek
       summary]. Platon XVII 1965 224-234.

3098 WELCH C., "Plato and Aporia". GM XX 1965 82-90.

3099* CHAIGNET A.E., Psychologie de Platon. Repr. of
       1862 edn. Bruxelles, Éditions Culture et
       Civilisation 1966 484p.

3100 CILENTO V., "Esperienza religiosa di un filosofo
       greco". RSLR II 1966 405-426.

3101* HOFFMANN G., Unmittelbarkeit und Bewusstheit.
       Kritische Interpretationen zu Platons Nomoi, zum
       Politikos und zu dem sokratischen Paradox:
       Arete ist Episteme. Diss. Hamburg 1966 162p.

3102 IWASAKI T., "On the 'Seeing the Truth' of Plato" [in
       Japanese with English summary]. JCS XIV 1966
       15-25.

3103 KUHN H., "Plato über den Menschen". p.284-310 in
       Die Frage nach dem Menschen. Aufriss e.
       philosoph. Anthropologie. Festschrift für Max
       Mueller zum 60. Geburtstag, hrsg. von Rombach
       H. Freiburg, Alber 1966.

3104* REDLOW G., Theoria, Theoretische und praktische
       Lebensauffassung im philosophischen Denken der
       Antike. Berlin, VEB Deutscher Verlag der
       Wissenschaften 1966 166p.
       Rev. DLZ LXXXVIII 1967 4-7 Albrecht.
       PLA XX 1967 145-147 Brandt.
       DZP XV 1967 578-581 Warnke.

V C: PSYCHOLOGY

3105* SCHRASTETTER R., Der Weg des Menschen bei Plato.
      Diss. München 1966 180p.

3106* SINGER I., The Nature of Love. Plato to Luther.
      New York, Random House 1966 xiii&395p. (ch.4
      "Platonic Eros", p.49-90.)
      Rev. JHI 1968 141-151 Moore.
      PhR 1968 519-521 Waingrow.

3107 WELLMAN R.R., "A Note on Platonic 'Anamnesis'". ET
      XVI 1966 169-175.

3108* BIELER L., Theios anēr. Das Bild des göttlichen
      Menschen in Spätantike und Frühchristentum.
      Unveränd. Nachdr. d. Ausg. Wien 1935-1936,
      Band 1/2. Darmstadt, Wissens. Buchges. 1967
      xvi&130p.

3109 BUECHELE M., "Problemgeschichtliche Überlegungen zum
      Begriff des Lernens". VWP XLIII 1967 177-192.

3110* EDELSTEIN L. The Idea of Progress in Classical
      Antiquity. Baltimore, Johns Hopkins Pr. 1967
      xxxiii&211p. (for Plato, see esp. ch.3.)

3111 GUENZLER C., "Platons Begriff des Lernens und das
      Problem der Sachlichkeit". PaedagRdsch XXI 1967
      887-904.

3112* HAZO R., The Idea of Love. Concepts in Western
      Thought Ser. Inst. for Philos. Research, New
      York, Praeger 1967 xvii&488p. (for Plato see
      esp. p.183-197.)

3113* KREEFT P.J., A Study of Wonder in Plato and
      Augustine. Diss. Fordham Univ. 1966 233p.
      [microfilm]. Summary in DA XXVII 1967 3083A.

3114 LAVELLE L., "La contemplation et l'action dans le
      platonisme". p.74-83 in Lavelle L., Panorama
      des doctrines philosophiques (see 4607).

3115 LÓPEZ-DÓRIGA E., "Inmortalidad y personalidad en
      Platón". Pensamiento XXIII 1967 167-176.

3116* NEUHAUSEN K.A., De voluntarii notione Platonica et
      Aristotelica. Klass.-philol. Stud. XXXIV,
      Wiesbaden, Harrassowitz 1967 ix&201p.
      Rev. REG LXXXI 1968 612 des Places.
      REA LXX 1968 468-470 Moreau.
      Gnomon XLII 1970 194-196 Skemp.

V C: PSYCHOLOGY

3117 NEVILLE R.C., "Intuition". IPQ VII 1967 556-590.

3118 PAISSE J.M., "Les rapports de Platon et de la philosophie présocratique. Les sources du thème platonicien de la réminiscence". LEC XXXV 1967 15-33.

3119 PAISSE J.M., "Réminiscence et dialectique platoniciennes". LEC XXXV 1967 225-248.

3120 PLASS P., "Play and Philosophic Detachment in Plato". TAPhA XCVIII 1967 343-364.

3121 SCIACCA M.F., "Il problema dell'immortalità e la metempsicosi prima di Platone". p.97-165 in Sciacca M.F., Platone I (see 64). Reprinted from Sciacca M.F., Studi sulla filos. antica. Napoli, Perrella 1935.

3122 VOGEL C.J. DE, "Plato, Aristotle and the Ideal of the Contemplative Life". PhilippSacra II 1967 672-692.

3123 WISSER R., "Tod und Unsterblichkeit in der Sicht Platons". Begegnung XXII 1967 119-122. Also "Muerte e inmortalidad en el sentir de Platón". FolHum V 1967 533-544.

3124* BRÈS Y., La psychologie de Platon. Publ. de la Fac. des Lett. & Sci. hum. de Paris-Sorbonne Sér. Recherches XLI, Paris, Presses Universitaires 1968 438p.
     Rev. EPh XXIII 1968 447 Quoniam.
     REA LXXI 1969 146-150 Moreau.
     CR XX 1970 156-157 Gulley.
     RFIC XCVIII 1970 446-451 Vegetti.
     RThPh 1970 201-203 Schaerer.
     JPNP LXVIII 1971 104-106 Vernant.
     ArchPhilos XXXV 1972 512-515 Narcy.
     BAGB 1973 508ff.

     CuadFilos XIII 1973 239-241 Lasala.
     RSF XXVIII 1973 457-461 Buccellato.
     LaFrance Y., "La psychologie de Platon selon Yvon Brès", Dialogue X 1971 134-145.

3125 BRISSON L., "Platon psychoanalysé". REG LXXXVI 1973 224-232.

3126 BRÈS Y., "La psychologie de Platon". RPhilos CLVIII 1968 201-218.

358

V C: PSYCHOLOGY

3127 BRÈS Y., "Amour et philosophie dans l'oeuvre de Platon". p.424-426 in Akten XIV. Intern Kongr. Philos. Wien, 2.-9. September 1968. Vol. V. Wien, Herder 1968.

3128 DEMOS R., "Plato's Doctrine of the Psyche as a self-moving Motion". JHPh VI 1968 133-145.

3129* GRAU N.A., Notas sobre la antropología platónica. Cuad. de Humanitas XXX, Tucumán, Univ. Nac. 1968 120p. Rev. REA LXXI 1969 484 Moreau. CuadFilos XIII 1973 248-249 La Croce.

3130 GRAU N.A., "Le rôle du corps dans l'anthropologie platonicienne". Summary p.428-430 in Akten XIV. Intern. Kongr. Philos. Wien, 2.-9. September 1968. Vol. V. Wien, Herder 1968.

3131 HYLAND D.A., "Ἔρως, ἐπιθυμία and φιλία in Plato". Phronesis XIII 1968 32-46.

3132 KAPP E., "Theorie und Praxis bei Aristoteles und Platon". p.167-179 in Kapp E., Ausgewählte Schriften (see 4606). · Reprinted from Mnemosyne III 1938 179-194.

3133 MANZANEDO M.F., "La imagen del hombre en la filosofía antigua". RFil(Madrid) XXVII 1968 27-89. (p.33-34 on Socrates; p.34-37 on Plato.)

3134* MORTON J., The Development of Plato's Theory of Sense Perception. Diss. Johns Hopkins Univ. 1968 168p. [microfilm]. Summary in DA XXIX 1968 1570A.

3135 PATZIG G., "Platon und das Problem des Irrtums". NSam VIII 1968 44-56.

3136 ROSEN G., "Some Notes on Greek and Roman Attitudes toward the Mentally Ill". p.17-23 in Medicine, Science and Culture. Historical Essays in Honor of Owsei Temkin, ed. by Stevenson L.G. & Multhauf R.P. Baltimore, Johns Hopkins Pr. 1968.

3137* TIGNER S.S., The Nature of Plato's Theory of Anamnesis. Diss. Univ. of Michigan 1968 183p. [microfilm]. Summary in DA XXX 1969 768A-769A.

V C: PSYCHOLOGY

3138* WORTHEN T.D.V., Death in Plato. Diss. Univ. of
      Washington 1968 180p. [microfilm]. Summary in
      DA XXIX 1969 2238A.

3139 ZEMKO M., "The Problem of the perfect Man in the
      Philosophy of Plato" [in Slovak with Russian and
      English summaries]. Filozofia XXIII 1968
      389-403.

3140 ZWOLSKI E., "On the Threshold of Greek
      Eschatological Thought" [in Polish with French
      summary]. ZNUL XI 1968 45-57.

3141* ARMETTA F., La libertà del volere da Omero a
      Platone. Palermo, Ed. Dialogo 1969 148p.

3142* BOBONIS G.J., Memory in Plato, Aristotle, and
      Plotinus. Diss. Claremont Graduate School and
      Univ. Center 1969 175p. [microfilm]. Summary
      in DA XXX 1969 1201A-1202A.

3143 CATAN J., "Plato on noetic Intermediaries". Apeiron
      III,2 1969 14-19.

3144 COCAGNAC A.M., "Platon: entre l'âme et le corps il
      n'y a que la musique". ArtS 1969 23-29.

3145 DELGADO VARELA J.M., "Los elementos en Amor. Ruibal
      y Platón". Crisis XVI 1969 437-451.

3146 DUBSKÝ I., "On the Path" [in Czech]. FilosCas 1969
      703-713.

3147* GRAESER A., Probleme der platonischen
      Seelenteilungslehre. Überlegungen zur Frage der
      Kontinuität im Denken Platons. Zetemata XLVII,
      München, Beck 1969 x&117p.
      Rev. CW LXIV 1970 21-22 Rist.
      Erasmus XXIII 1971 374-376 Lasserre.
      Helmantica XXII 1971 342 Orosio.
      CR XXI 1971 451-452 Gulley.
      RPh XLV 1971 342 Louis.
      RBPh XLIX 1971 670 des Places.
      Mnemosyne XXVI 1973 190 de Vries.

3148* GROETHUYSEN B., Antropologia filosofica, trad. di
      Doriano P. Bibl. di saggistica I, Napoli,
      Guida 1969 330p. Italian transl. of
      Anthropologie philosophique, Paris 1952
      (Contains a chapter on Plato.)

3149 HEITSCH E., "Erscheinung und Meinung. Platons Kritik an Protagoras als Selbstkritik". PhJ LXXVI 1968-1969 23-36. Also p.101-117 in Heitsch E., Neue Einsichten. Beiträge zum altsprachlichen Unterricht. Dialog Schule-Wiss., Klass. Sprachen & Lit. V, München, Bayer. Schulbuch-Verl. 1970.

3150 KNOX T.M., "Thought and its Objects". PhilosQ XIX 1969 193-203.

3151 LOENEN J.H.M.M., "Ware werkelijkheid en ware menselijkheid in Plato's filosofie". WPMW IX 1968-1969 82-97.

3152 MATOS V., "Conceito platónico da pessoa humana". Summary in Actas da Assemblia internacional de Estudios filosóficos, Braga 29 a 31 de Outubro de 1967 = RPortFil XXV 1969 37.

3153 PAISSE J.M., "Réminiscence et mythe platoniciens". LEC XXXVII 1969 19-43.

3154 PARTEE C., "The Soul in Plato, Platonism, and Calvin". SJTh XXII 1969 278-295.

3155 PLASS P., "Eros, Play and Death in Plato". AmIm XXVI 1969 37-55.

3156* REICH E., Plato as an Introduction to Modern Criticism of Life. Port Washington, N.Y., Kennikat Pr. 1969 335p. Reprint of 1906 edn.

3157 ROIG A.A., "La experiencía en la filosofía de Platón". Philosophia(Argent) XXXV 1969 5-42.

3159* WEBER M.F., An Immanent Interpretation of five Platonic Dialogues. Apology, Crito, Phaedo, Timaeus, and Laws X. Diss. Catholic Univ. of America 1968 214p. [microfilm]. Summary in DA XXIX 1969 4527A-4528A.

3160* ADKINS A.W.H., From the Many to the One. A Study of Personality and Views of Human Nature in the Context of Ancient Greek Society, Values and Beliefs. Stud. in the Humanities, Ithaca, N.Y., Cornell Univ. Pr. and Ideas of Nature Ser., London, Constable 1970 xv&312p. (ch.6 "Plato", p.127-169.)

V C: PSYCHOLOGY

3161 GOLDSCHMIDT V., "Le paradigme dans la théorie
platonicienne de l'action". p.79-102 in
Goldschmidt V., Questions platoniciennes (see
4598). Reprinted from REG LVIII 1945 118ff.

3162* KLEIN D.B., A History of Scientific Psychology. Its
Origins and Philosophical Backgrounds. New
York, Basic Books 1970 xii&907p. (ch.3 "From
Plato to Freud", p.47-70.)

3163* KNIGHT W.F.J., Elysion: On Ancient Greek and Roman
Beliefs Concerning a Life after Death, with an
intro. by Knight G.W. London, Rider 1970 208p.
(ch.10 "Plato and Aristotle", p.91-96.)

3164 KUHN H., "Praxis und Theorie im platonischen
Denken". p.27-43 in Zur Theorie der Praxis.
Interpretationen und Aspekte, hrsg. von
Engelhardt P. Walberberger Studien der
Albertus-Magnus Akademie. Philosophische Reihe,
Bd.4, Mainz 1970. Also Spanish transl. "Teoría
y praxis en Platón", trad. de Kerkhoff M.
Dialogos VII 1970 89-112.

3165 LLOYD A.C., "Non-discursive Thought. An Enigma of
Greek Philosophy". PAS LXX 1969-1970 261-274.

3166 PAISSE J.M., "Le thème platonicien de la
réminiscence et la purification morale". LEC
XXXVIII 1970 274-284.

3167* ROBINSON T.M., Plato's Psychology. Phoenix Suppl.
VIII, Toronto, Univ. of Toronto Pr. 1970
xii&202p.
Rev. REG LXXXIII 1970 260-262 Brès.
Emerita XXXVIII 1970 484-486 García Gual.
REA LXXII 1970 424-425 Moreau.
Dialogue X 1971 347-349 Philip.
PhilosBks XII Feb. 1971 25-26 Hamlyn.
Gnomon XLIII 1971 342-346 Graeser.
RPh XLV 1971 152 Louis.
CW LXIV 1971 158 Hoerber.
PhilosQ XXI 1971 172-173 Stewart.
Hermathena CXI 1971 91-92 Luce.
PhR LXXXI 1972 244-246 Santas.
CPh LXVII 1972 63-64 Sprague.
JHPh X 1972 217-221 Anagnostopoulos.
CanJPh III 1973 131-142 Dybikowski.
CR XXII 1972 335-339 Skemp.
JCS XXI 1973 121-124 Mori.
BAGB 1973 508ff.
Crisis XX 1973 425-426 Ortall.

3168* ROLOFF D., Gottähnlichkeit, Vergöttlichung und
      Erhöhung zum seligen Leben. Untersuchungen zur
      Herkunft der platonischen Angleichung an Gott.
      Diss. Münster 1967. Untersuch. zur antiken
      Lit. & Gesch. IV, Berlin, de Gruyter 1970
      243p.
            Rev. Platon XXII 1970 332-335 Skiadas.
            Helmantica XXII 1971 194-195 Barcenilla.
            ArchPhilos XXXIV 1971 510-512 Solignac.
            LF XCIV 1971 300 Vidman.
            Gnomon XLIV 1972 307-308 Suhr.
            CuadFilos XII 1972 181-184 Lisi.
            CR XXIII 1973 49-50 Wallis.

3169 SOMIGLIANA A., "Divinazione e filosofia
     nell'antichità". Sophia XXXVIII 1970 235-243.

3170 SOULEZ P., "L''involutionnisme' de Platon". CISoc
     XLIX 1970 151-162.

3171* VAN DER WEY A., Grote filosofen over de mens. Van
      Plato tot Teilhard (Labyrint). Utrecht,
      Bijleveld 1970 156p.

3172 VICAIRE P., "Platon et la divination". REG LXXXIII
     1970 333-350.

3173* BLANKENSHIP J.D., The Theory of the Soul in Plato's
      Metaphysics. Diss. Johns Hopkins Univ. 1971
      436p. [microfilm]. Summary in DA XXXII 1971
      2738A.

3174 DODDS E.R., "Plato and the Irrational Soul".
     p.206-229 in Plato II, ed. by Vlastos G. (see
     4620). Reprinted from Dodds E.R., The Greeks
     and the Irrational. Berkeley, Univ. of
     California Pr. 1951, ch.7.

3175 GUTHRIE W.K.C., "Plato's Views on the Nature of the
     Soul". p.230-243 in Plato II, ed. by Vlastos
     G. (see 4620). Reprinted from Recherches sur
     la tradition platonicienne. Entretiens III,
     Genève, Fond. Hardt 1957 2-19.

3176 IMAMICHI T., "Subject of Thinking. An Essay on
     Plato's Epistemology" [in Japanese with English
     summary]. JCS XIX 1971 1-5.

3177 JOHNSON J.P., "The Idea of Human Dignity in
     Classical and Christian Thought". JThought VI
     1971 23-37.

V C: PSYCHOLOGY

3178 JUNG E., "Directions de recherche sur l'inconscient chez Platon". BAGB XXX 1971 581-645.

3179 KELESSIDOU-GALANOS A., "Ὁ Πλάτων καὶ τὸ 'παρά-λογο'" [with French summary]. Philosophia(Athens) I 1971 264-273.

3180 KOLLER H., "Die Jenseitsreise, ein pythagoreischer Ritus". Symbolon VII 1971 33-52.

3181 LUKIG M., "Socrates and Indifference towards Death". SoJP IX 1971 393-398.

3182* MANSFELD J., The pseudo-Hippocratic Tract περὶ ἑβδομάδων, ch.1-2 and Greek Philosophy. Assen, van Gorcum 1971 271p. (p.66ff. on Self-motion in Plato.)

3183* MASI G., Il potere della ragione (Eraclito, Platone, Hegel). Collana di studi filos. XXI, Padova, Gregoriana 1971 145p. (chs.2-5, p.37-121 on Plato.)
     Rev. RFNeo LXIII 1971 725-726 Babolin.

3184 PENNER T., "Thought and Desire in Plato". p.96-118 in Plato II, ed. by Vlastos G. (see 4620).

3185* PÉPIN J., Idées grecques sur l'homme et sur Dieu. Coll. d'Études anciennes, Paris, Les Belles Lettres 1971 402p. (for Plato see especially part I chs.3-6.)
     Rev. AC XLI 1972 722-724 Bodson.
     ArchPhilos XXXVI 1973 505-507 Solignac.
     JThS XXIV 1973 573-574 Armstrong.
     VChr XXVII 1973 230-232 van Winden.
     RHR 1973 No.183 200-202 Turcan.
     GIF XXV 1973 71-74 Negri.
     StudClas XV 1973 282-285 Noica.
     NRTh XCV 1973 87 Gilbert.
     RSLR IX 1973 150-152 Simonetti.
     StudMon XV 1973 553 Pifarré.
     REA LXXV 1973 144-146 Boyancé.

3186* VALENTIN P., L'idée des limites du savoir humain chez Héraclite, Parménide et Platon. Thèse doctorat ès lettres, Paris, 7 Mars 1970. Lille, Thèse. ronéot. (Service de reprod. de l'Univ. de Lille) 1971 406p.

3187 EGGERS LAN C., "Anámnesis en el Menón y en el Fedón". p.137-147 in Actas del primer Simp. nac. de est. clás., mayo 1970. Mendoza, Univ.

nac. de Cuyo 1972.

3188 FRANCO R. DE, "Morte e alienazione". GCFI LI 1972
263-272.

3189 HOAGLUND J., "Anamnesis from Meno to Phaedrus".
Abstract in JPh LXIX 1972 674.

3190 MASI G., "L'escatologia platonica". p.260-276 in
Mondo storico ed Escatologia. Atti del XXVI
Convegno del Centro di Studi Filosofici tra
Professori Universitari, Gallarate, 1971.
Brescia, Morcelliana 1972.

3191 MOREAU J., "Doxa et logos. Apparence, jugement,
fondement". p.3-15 in Scritti in onore di Carlo
Giacon. Miscellanea erudita XXI, Padova, Ed.
Antenore 1972.

3192 MUELLER R., "Der Humanismus in der griechischen
Klassik". WZJena XXI 1972 839-859.

3193 NAVARRO B., "Sobre la función y el objeto de los
sentidos en la gnoseología platónica". Dianoia
XVIII 1972 15-39.

3194 SOMMER R., "The Platonic Concept of Intellectual
Beauty and its modern Value" [in Rumanian].
RevFiloz XIX 1972 795-803.

3195* WOLFRAM F., Zum Begriff der pistis in der
griechischen Philosophie (Parmenides, Plato,
Aristoteles). Diss. Wien 1972 vi&195p.

3196 BETZ H.D., "Humanisierung des Menschen. Delphi,
Plato, Paulus". p.41-55 in Neues Testament und
christliche Existenz. Festschrift für Herbert
Braun zum 70. Geburtstag am 4. mai 1973, hrsg.
von Betz H.D. & Schottroff L. Tübingen, Mohr
1973.

3197 BLANCHÉ L., "L'âme humaine chez Platon". REPh XXIII
1973 1-6.

3198 CACOULLOS A.R., "The Doctrine of Eros in Plato" [in
English with Greek summary]. Diotima I 1973
81-99.

3199 COBB W.S., "Anamnesis. Platonic Doctrine or
Sophistic Absurdity?". Dialogue XII 1973
604-628.

V C: PSYCHOLOGY

3200   COLLINS A., "The Objects of Perceptual Consciousness
       in Philosophical Thought". SocRes XL 1973
       153-176.

3201   DODDS E.R., "Plato and the Irrational".   p.106-125
       in Dodds E.R., The Ancient Concept of Progress
       and other Essays in Greek Literature and Belief.
       Oxford, Clarendon Pr. 1973. Reprinted from JHS
       LXV 1945 16-25.

3202   GIGON O., "Theorie und Praxis bei Platon   und
       Aristoteles". MH XXX 1973 65-87, 144-165.

3203   GRAU N.A., "Platón y Freud. Las anticipaciones
       'psicoanalíticas' del filósofo ateniense".
       CuadFilos XIII 1973 125-138.

3204   HINTIKKA J., "Remarks on Praxis, Poiesis, and   Ergon
       in Plato and Aristotle". Studia philosophica in
       honorem Sven Krohn = AUT CXXVI 1973 53-62.

3205   IMPARA P., "θεία μοῖρα e ἐνθουσιασμός in Platone".
       Proteus IV 1973 41-56.

3206   KOLLER H., "Jenseitsreise des   Philosophen".
       AsiatStud XXVII,1 1973 35-57.

3207* KREMEN A.F., Platons metaphysische . Psychologie.
       Diss. Köln 1973 92p.

3208   LEFEVRE C., "La personne comme être en relation chez
       Platon et Aristote". MSR XXX 1973 161-183.

3209   OZAWA K., "The Eternal Cycle and   Eschatology:
       Plato's Case" [in Japanese]. Proceedings of the
       Dept. of Humanities (Tokyo Metropolitan   Univ.)
       XCIV 1973.

3210   OZAWA K., "The Question of Judgment in Plato's
       Eschatology" [in Japanese]. Philosophy
       Miscellany (Tokyo Metropolitan Univ.) XVI 1973.

3211   SAUNDERS T.J., "Penology and Eschatology in Plato's
       Timaeus and Laws". CQ XXIII 1973 232-244.

3212   SIMON B., "Models of Mind and mental Illness in
       ancient Greece, II: The Platonic Model". JHBS
       IX 1973 5-17.

3213   TROTIGNON P., "Retour à Platon". RDCC No.78 1973
       61-80.

3214   VLASTOS G., "The Individual as Object of Love in
        Plato" (with appendices "Is the Lysis a Vehicle
        of Platonic Doctrine?" and "Sex in Platonic
        Love").   p.3-42 in Vlastos G., Platonic Studies
        (see 4622).

For further discussions of these topics see 356, 369, 389,
        391, 658, 1465, 1467, 1514, 1716, 1764, 2075,
        2080, 2157, 2174, 2188, 2269, 2393, 2445, 2507,
        2559, 2593, 2940, 2949, 3006, 3016, 3016, 3069,
        3087, 3429, 3579, 3619, 3723, 3725, 3916, 4510.

INDICES

IMMORTALITY OF THE SOUL, METEMPSYCHOSIS
AND REINCARNATION

These subjects are treated in the following studies:
515, 597, 607, 722, 755, 1686, 1693, 1694, 1695,
1696, 1697, 1698, 1699, 1700, 1705, 1709, 1713,
1755, 1756, 1757, 1759, 1765, 1766, 1818, 1837,
1845, 1855, 1856, 2071, 2077, 2371, 2471, 2472,
2512, 2678, 2958, 3029, 3040, 3043, 3077, 3079,
3083, 3089, 3097, 3100, 3115, 3121, 3123, 3138,
3140, 3163, 3180, 3190, 3206, 3209, 3210, 3211,
3211, 3924.

STRUCTURE OF THE HUMAN SOUL
INCLUDING ITS AUTOKINETIC NATURE

This subject is treated in the following studies:
293, 293, 405, 406, 437, 440, 513, 1377, 1407,
1703, 1705, 1706, 1708, 1712, 1845, 1859, 1898,
1902, 2070, 2073, 2074, 2076, 2077, 2079, 2086,
2220, 2269, 2305, 2494, 2502, 2510, 2511, 2517,
2522, 3044, 3045, 3047, 3048, 3061, 3062, 3128,
3147, 3154, 3160, 3162, 3173, 3175, 3182, 3184,
3197, 3203, 3207, 3412, 4126, 4133, 4134, 4134.

MENTAL ILLNESS

This subject is treated in the following studies:
        1711, 2072, 2225, 2529, 2722, 3030, 3031, 3136,
        3212.

ANAMNESIS

This subject is treated in the following studies:
        155, 1505, 1511, 1518, 1520, 1522, 1523, 1529,
        1710, 1713, 1714, 2641, 2750, 3038, 3051, 3068,
        3084, 3091, 3107, 3118, 3119, 3137, 3153, 3166,
        3187, 3189, 3199, 3977, 3978, 3987, 3988.

SENSE PERCEPTION

This subject is treated in the following studies:
        389, 444, 2439, 2440, 2445, 2882, 3134, 3193,
        3200, 3977, 4058.

THE FORMS AND WAYS OF HUMAN INTELLIGENCE
AND REASONING

These subjects are treated in the following studies:
276, 670, 1094, 1095, 1204, 1297, 1521, 1524,
1704, 1910, 2144, 2148, 2160, 2166, 2182, 2192,
2389, 2440, 2512, 2644, 2909, 3033, 3034, 3045,
3046, 3055, 3059, 3076, 3086, 3087, 3088, 3092,
3096, 3098, 3101, 3102, 3109, 3111, 3113, 3114,
3117, 3142, 3143, 3149, 3150, 3165, 3172, 3173,
3176, 3183, 3184, 3186, 3191, 3195, 3213, 3445,
3515, 3641, 3851, 3977, 3986, 3991, 3997, 4059,
4139, 4150, 4151, 4159.

LOVE AND MADNESS

These subjects are treated in the following studies:
35, 438, 766, 1806, 1814, 1821, 1822, 1828,
1829, 1833, 1836, 1840, 1843, 1850, 1852, 1852,
1853, 1860, 2342, 2343, 2366, 2366, 2369, 2370,
2371, 2372, 2383, 2384, 2385, 2387, 2388, 2389,
2399, 2580, 2922, 3041, 3042, 3057, 3057, 3060,
3064, 3066, 3071, 3074, 3075, 3094, 3095, 3106,
3112, 3120, 3127, 3131, 3145, 3155, 3183, 3198,
3214, 3961, 4025, 4454.

HUMAN NATURE, THE HUMAN CONDITION,
HUMAN LIFE, AND DEATH

These subjects are treated in the following studies:
410, 467, 555, 597, 652, 658, 771, 1063, 1064,
1687, 1764, 1858, 2078, 2086, 2538, 2593, 2661,
3032, 3035, 3036, 3037, 3039, 3042, 3049, 3052,
3053, 3054, 3056, 3058, 3061, 3063, 3069, 3070,
3072, 3073, 3078, 3080, 3081, 3082, 3085, 3087,
3090, 3103, 3104, 3105, 3108, 3110, 3115, 3116,
3122, 3129, 3130, 3133, 3138, 3139, 3141, 3144,
3146, 3148, 3151, 3152, 3155, 3156, 3157, 3159,
3160, 3161, 3164, 3166, 3168, 3170, 3171, 3174,
3177, 3178, 3179, 3181, 3185, 3188, 3192, 3194,
3196, 3201, 3202, 3204, 3205, 3402, 3418, 3489,
3619, 3744, 3916, 4146, 4510.

V D: THE PHYSICAL WORLD (GENERAL)

3215 BOUSSOULAS N.I., "Essai sur la structure de la mixis
      platonicienne. Être et non-être chez Platon".
      RSF XIII 1958 131-147.

3216* JANNARAS A., Zufall und Bewegung bei Platon. Diss.
      Freiburg 1960 202p.

3217 MUGLER C., "Pluralisme matériel et pluralisme
      dynamique dans la physique grecque d'Anaximandre
      à Épicure". RPh XXXV 1961 67-86.

3218 JANNARAS A., "Zufall und Bewegung bei Platon".
      Platon XIV 1962 20-131.

3219* REAGAN J.T., The Material Substrates in the Platonic
      Dialogues. Diss. St. Louis Univ. 1960 225p.
      [microfilm]. Summary in DA XXI 1961 3123.

3220 VIDAL-NAQUET P., "Temps des dieux et temps des
      hommes. Essai sur quelques aspects de
      l'expérience temporelle chez les Grecs". RHR
      CLVII 1960 55-80.

3221 HERTER H., "Arete adespoton". RhM CV 1962 1-9.

3222 ESLICK L.J., "The Material Substrate in Plato".
      p.59-74 (with discussion p.75-78) in McMullin E.
      ed., The Concept of Matter. Notre Dame, Ind.,
      Univ. of Notre Dame Pr. 1963.

3223* GIOSCIA V.J., Plato's Image of Time. An Essay in
      Philosophical Sociology. Diss. Fordham Univ.
      1963 286p. [microfilm]. Summary in DA XXIV
      1963 775-776.

3224 SOLMSEN F., "Nature as Craftsman in Greek Thought".
      JHI XXIV 1963 473-496. Reprinted p.332-355 in
      Solmsen F., Kleine Schriften I (see 4615).

3225* WOOLEY A.D., Cosmic and divine Ananke from its
      origin through Plato. Diss. Princeton Univ.
      1962 249p. [microfilm]. Summary in DA XXIII
      1963 4347-4348.

3226 BRUNNER F., "La notion d'espace depuis les origines
      grecques jusqu'au XVIIIe siècle". ASSPh XXIV
      1964 42-65.

3227* BUFORD T.O., The Idea of Creation in Plato,
       Augustine and Emil Brunner. Diss. Boston Univ.
       Graduate School 1963 380p. [microfilm].
       Summary in DA XXIV 1964 4231.

3228 LEYDEN W. VON, "Time, Number, and Eternity in Plato
       and Aristotle". PhilosQ XIV 1964 35-52.

3229 RUST E.C., "History and Time". p.167-188 in The
       Teacher's Yoke. Studies in Memory of H.
       Trantham, ed. by Vardaman E.J. & Garrett J.L.
       Waco, Texas, Baylor Univ. Pr. 1964.

3230 FLASCH K., "Ars imitatur naturam. Platonischer
       Naturbegriff und mittelalterliche Philosophie
       der Kunst". p.265-306 in Parusia, hrsg. von
       Flasch K. (see 4588).

3231 KOEVENDI D., "Zum Problem der Platonischen
       Ideenlehre". Altertum XI 1965 24-36.

3232* SCHULZ D.J., Das Problem der Materie in Platons
       Timaios. Abhandlungen zur Philosophie,
       Psychologie und Pädagogik XXXI, Bonn, Bouvier
       1966 131p.

3233* ZIMMERMANN A., Tyche bei Platon. Diss. Bonn 1966
       171p.
                 Rev. Gymnasium LXXIV 1967 461-463 Bayer.
       Gymnasium LXXIV 1967 463-465 de Vogel.
       REG LXXX 1967 629 des Places.
       CR XVIII 1968 237 Gulley.
       CPh LXIII 1968 323-324 Hoerber.
       Mnemosyne XXIII 1970 86-88 Wiersma Buriks.

3234 JOHNSON H.J., "Three ancient Meanings of Matter.
       Democritus, Plato, and Aristotle". JHI XXVIII
       1967 3-16.

3235 SKEMP J.B., The Theory of Motion in Plato's Later
       Dialogues. 2nd enlarged edn. of Cambridge
       Class. Stud. 1942. Amsterdam, Hakkert 1967
       xv&197p.
                 Rev. DUJ XXX 1968-1969 51-52
       Bargrave-Weaver.
       CR XIX 1969 163-164 Gulley.

3236* SINNIGE T.G., Matter and Infinity in the Presocratic
       Schools and Plato. Wijsger. teksten & stud.
       XVII, Assen, van Gorcum 1968 252p.
                 Rev. RecSR LVI 1968 615 des Places.
       EPh XXIII 1968 489 Marietti.

RM XXII 1968-1969 388 J.J.R.
Sapientia XXIV 1969 306-307 Bolzán.
PhilosQ XIX 1969 280 Hamlyn.
BJPS XX 1969 163-167 O'Brien.
ModS XLVII 1969-1970 229-232 Sweeney.
CR XX 1970 26-27 Gulley.
JHPh VIII 1970 92-95 Scolnicov.
JHS XC 1970 240-241 Bicknell.
ABG XIV 1970 127-129 Sinnige.
Lychnos 1969-1970 400-402 Regnell.
Gnomon XLIII 1971 82-84 Mourelatos.
ACR II 1972 54-55 Minar.
Helmantica XXIII 1972 159-160 Oroz.
Mnemosyne XXVI 1973 69 Mansfeld.

3237* MANNSPERGER D., <u>Physis bei Platon</u>. Diss. Tübingen
1963. Berlin, de Gruyter 1969 vii&336p.
<u>Rev</u>. CW LXIII 1969 52 DeLacy.
Salesianum XXXI 1969 532 Composta.
AC XXXVIII 1969 547 des Places.
Pensamiento XXVI 1970 97-98 Martínez
Gómez.
Crisis XVII 1970 423-424 Oroz.
Angelicum XLVII 1970 522-524
Vansteenkiste.
WJb III 1970 274-276 Heintel.
Gnomon XLIII 1971 130-138 Noerenberg.
Sophia XXXIX 1971 130-131 Hoefer.
Helmantica XXI 1970 497-498 Oroz.
RSC XIX 1971 422-423 d'Agostino.
AGPh LIII 1971 112-116 Sprute.
Gymnasium LXXIX 1972 113-114 Goergemanns.
MH XXX 1973 237-238 Graeser.

3238 MAULA E., "Is Time a Child or a Grandchild of
Eternity? (Tm. 37d, 50d)". Ajatus XXXI 1969
37-61.

3239 VOLLRATH E., "Platons Lehre von der Zeit im
Timaeus". PhJ LXXVI 1969 257-263.

3240 DIANO C., "Il problema della materia in Platone dal
Parmenide al Filebo". GCFI XLIX 1970 12-36.

3241 DIANO C., "Il problema della materia in Platone. La
chora del Timeo". GCFI XLIX 1970 321-335.

3242* MAULA E., <u>On the Semantics of Time in Plato's
Timaeus</u>. Acta Acad. Aboensis Ser. A Humaniora
<u>XXXVIII</u>,3, Åbo 1970 37p.
<u>Rev</u>. Theoria XXXVIII 1971 156-162 Fowler.

V D: THE PHYSICAL WORLD (GENERAL)

3243 REAGAN J.T., "Plato's Material Principle". ModS
        XLVII 1970 177-193.

3244 PATRICIOS N.N., "The Spatial Concepts of the Ancient
        Greeks". AClass XIV 1971 17-36.

For further discussions see 106, 251, 263, 379, 382, 395,
        441, 460, 501, 524, 1402, 1630, 1631, 1634,
        1895, 1898, 1915, 2495, 2498, 2502, 2507, 2511,
        2516, 2864, 2865, 2982, 3016, 3047, 3077, 3361,
        3439, 3445, 3619, 4101, 4134, 4135.

V E: MATHEMATICS AND SCIENCE

a: SCIENCE AND TECHNOLOGY (GENERAL) INCLUDING τέχνη

3245 SAINT-ÉDOUARD [Mère], "La division aristotélicienne
      des sciences selon le professeur A. Mansion".
      LThPh XV 1959 215-235.

3246* MUGLER C., La physique de Platon. Études &
      Commentaires XXXV, Paris, Klincksieck 1960 263p.
      Rev. AC XXX 1961 219-220 des Places.
      RecSR L 1962 608-609 des Places.
      CPh LVII 1962 138 Hoerber.
      REG LXXV 1962 580-581 Weil.
      RPh XXXVI 1962 113 Louis.
      LEC XXX 1962 127 Ghislain.
      JHS LXXXII 1962 188 Gulley.
      Emerita XXX 1962 205-206 Lledó.
      AAHG XV 1962 226 von Ivánka.
      RH CCXXVIII 1962 463-464 Cloché.
      REA LXIV 1962 434-436 Moreau.
      RBPh XLI 1963 509-514 de Strycker.
      GIF XVI 1963 74-76 Jacobelli.

3247 SIWECKI J., "On the Classification of Sciences in
      Plato and Aristotle" [in Polish]. p.239-250 in
      Charisteria. Philosophical Dissertations offered
      to W. Tatarkiewicz [in Polish]. Warszawa, PWN
      1960.

3248* DESANTILLANA G., The Origins of Scientific Thought
      from Anaximander to Proclus. Chicago, Univ. of
      Chicago Pr. 1961 320p. (Socrates, esp. ch.
      11 "The Care of the Soul"; Plato, esp. ch. 12
      "The Flight to the Trans-Uranian".)

3249 FRITZ   K.   VON,   "Der   Beginn
      universalwissenschaftlicher Bestrebungen und der
      Primat der Griechen". StudGen XIV 1961 546-583,
      601-636.

3250* GRUENENFELDER J.B., Plato's Theory of Scientific
      Knowledge in the Later Dialogues. Diss. Univ.
      of Notre Dame 1961 308p. [microfilm]. Summary
      in DA XXII 1961 1211.

3251 HORNE R.A., "Plato and the Rise of the Anti-scientific Sentiment". Physis III 1961 336-343.

3252 SANTILLANA G. DE, "A proposito di reazione antiscientifica". Physis IV 1962 97-100.

3253 CHIEREGHIN F., "Problematicità scientifica e problematicità filosofica secondo Platone". p.241-251 in La filosofia di fronte alle scienze: XIX Congresso naz. di filos., Bari, 1961. Bari, Ed. Adriatica 1962, Vol. II.

3254* MITTELSTRASS J., Die Rettung der Phänomene. Ursprung und Geschichte eines antiken Forschungsprinzips. Berlin, de Gruyter 1962 281p.
     Rev. PLA XVII 1964 7-9 Barwirsch.
     IPQ IV 1964 492-493 de Strycker.
     PhilosQ XIV 1964 89-90 Wightman.
     Philosophy XXXIX 1964 80 Heinemann.
     CPh LX 1965 282-283 Hoerber.
     DCI II 1965 697-707 de Anquin.
     PhilosRdschau XIV 1966-1967 60-62 Beierwaltes.
     Mnemosyne XX 1967 189-191 Verdenius.
     WJb IV 1971 280-289 Oeser.

3255* PAZZINI A., La quiddità della scienze nel pensiero greco-italiota. Roma, Istituto di Storia della Medicina dell'Università 1962 vii&141p.

3256* ROBIN L., La pensée grecque et les origines de l'esprit scientifique. New edn. with bibl. by Schuhl P.M. Coll. L'évolution de l'humanité, Paris, Albin Michel 1963 xxi&517p. (Livre 3, ch.2 "Socrate", p.178-193; ch.4 "Platon", p.210-284.)
     Rev. RHE LIX 1964 701 Mallet.
     EPh XVIII 1963 375 École.
     GM XVIII 1963 505-506 École.

3257 TATARKIEWICZ W., "Classification of Arts in Antiquity". JHI XXIV 1963 231-240.

3258 KRAFFT F., "Der Mathematikos und der Physikos. Bemerkungen zu der angeblichen platonischen Aufgabe, die Phänomene zu retten". Alte Probleme, neue Ansätze, Beitr. zur Gesch. der Wiss. & der Technik V, Wiesbaden, Steiner 1965 5-24.

3259 MITTELSTRASS J., "Die Entdeckung der Möglichkeit von Wissenschaft". AHES II,5 1965 410-435.

3260 POPPER K.R., "The Nature of Philosophical Problems and their Roots in Science". ch.2 in Conjectures and Refutations. 2nd edn. London, Routledge & Kegan Paul 1965. Reprinted from BJPS III 1952. Also reprinted p.128-179 in Plato's Meno, trans. by Guthrie W.K.C. with essays ed. by Brown M. (see 1485)

3261 TANAKA M., "On gijutsu". PhSJap VI 1965 59-94.

3262* THEILER W., Zur Geschichte der teleologischen Naturbetrachtung bis auf Aristoteles. 2. Aufl. Berlin, de Gruyter 1965 ix&109p.
     Rev. Emerita XXXV 1967 206 Alsina.
     CR XVII 1967 111-112 Stokes.
     AC XXXIV 1965 587 des Places.
     Angelicum XLIII 1966 108-109 Vansteenkiste.
     Salesianum XXVIII 1966 432 Composta.
     Pensamiento XXIV 1968 129-130 Igal.
     CR LXXXII 1968 295-297 Lloyd.
     REAug XIII 1967 341-342 Madec.
     RThPh CI 1968 203-204 Schaerer.
     Irenikon XL 1967 609-610 M.v.P.

3263 DeLACY P., "Plato and the Method of the Arts". p.123-132 in The Classical Tradition. Literary and Historical Studies in Honor of H. Caplan, ed. by Wallace L. Ithaca, Cornell Univ. Pr. 1966.

3264 FRITZ K. VON, "Platons Stellung zur Wissenschaft. Ideenlehre und platonische Dialektik". p.250-278 in Fritz K. von, Grundprobleme der Geschichte der antiken Wissenschaft (see 4591).

3265* ISNARDI PARENTE M., Techne. Momenti del pensiero greco da Platone a Epicuro. Bibl. di cultura LXXVI, Firenze, La Nuova Italia 1966 425p.
     Rev. DeHomine 1967 214-216 M.I.P.
     Humanidades XIX 1967 114 Mayor.
     RecSR LVI 1968 611 des Places.
     RPh XLII 1968 332 Louis.
     Gnomon XL 1968 415-416 DeLacy.
     RBPh XLVII 1969 646-647 de Strycker.
     GM XXIV 1969 110-112 Beraldi.
     Mnemosyne XXII 1969 306-307 Ferwerda.
     RFNeo LXII 1970 731-734 Baldassari.

3266 RADKAU H., "Platon ist der Begründer geistwissenschaftlicher Überheblichkeit gegenüber Technik und Naturwissenschaften". Klepzigs LXXIV 1966 W5-W6.

3267 LLOYD G.E.R., "Plato as a Natural Scientist". JHS LXXXVIII 1968 78-92.

3268 SOLMSEN F., "Plato and the Unity of Science". p.326-331 in Solmsen F., Kleine Schriften I (see 4615). Reprinted from PhR XLIX 1940 566-571.

3269 SOLMSEN F., "Die Entstehung der Wissenschaften". p.316-325 in Solmsen F., Kleine Schriften I (see 4615). Reprinted from Das Humanistische Gymnasium XLII 1931 65-74.

3270 KUSAYAMA K., "Natural Science and Teleology. Εἰκὼς λόγος (3), I" [in Japanese]. Shoin Women's College Bulletin XI 1969.

3271 MONDOLFO R., "Ciencia y technica en la Grecia antigua". RevUNC 1969 no.3-4 367-380.

3272 BORTOLOTTI A., "Le arti nel pensiero di Platone". RSF XXV 1970 355-386.

3273 KUSAYAMA K., "Rational View of Nature. Εἰκὼς λόγος (3), II" [in Japanese]. Shoin Women's College Bulletin XII 1970.

3274* LLOYD G.E.R., Early Greek Science: Thales to Aristotle. Ancient Culture and Society VII, New York, Norton and London, Chatto & Windus 1970 xvi&156p. (ch.6 "Plato", p.66-79.)
        Rev. Hermathena CXII 1971 101 Luce.
        ACR I 1971 245-246 Natunewicz.
        TLS LXX 1971 376.
        StudClas XIV 1972 317-319 Petre.
        AHR LXXVII 1972 1421 Jameson.
        RPh XLVI 1972 292 Mugler.
        REA LXXIV 1972 263-264 Mugler.
        AC XLII 1973 676 Donnay.

3275* VIRIEUX-REYMOND A., Platon, ou la géometrisation de l'univers, présentation avec choix de textes & bibliogr. Savants du Monde entier XLIII, Paris, Seghers 1970 180p.
        Rev. ASSPh XXXII 1972 209-210 Voelke.
        RPhilos CLXII 1972 52 Schuhl.
        Espiritu XXII 1973 171-172 Guy.

V E a: SCIENCE AND TECHNOLOGY (GENERAL)

3276* CAMBIANO G., Platone e le techniche. Piccola Bibl.
Einaudi CLXX, Torino, Einaudi 1971 269p.
Rev. RSI LXXXV 1973 785-788 Isnardi
Parente.
Maia XXV 1973 177-178 Battegazzore.
BollFil VI 1972 81-82 Cararero Porccedu.
Filosofia XXIV 1973 75-78 Ravera.

3277 FIDIO P. DE, "Il demiurgo e il ruolo delle technai
in Platone". PP XXVI 1971 233-263.

3279* REIDEMEISTER K., Das exakte Denken der Griechen.
Beitr. z. Deutung von Euklid, Plato,
Aristoteles. Darmstadt, Wiss. Buchges. 1972
108p. Unveränd. reprograf. Nachdr. d. 1.
Aufl., Hamburg 1949.

3280 BORTOLOTTI A., "Nuove prospettive degli studi
platonici". RSF XXVIII 1973 28-33.

3281 LALUMIA J., "la 'conservation' des phénomènes et
l'évolution de la théorie scientifique".
Diogene LXXXIII 1973 119-137.

3282 MEYER-ABICH K.M., "Eikos Logos. Platons Theorie der
Naturwissenschaft". p.20-44 in Einheit und
Vielheit. Festschrift für Carl Friedrich von
Weizsaecker zum 60. Geburtstag, hrsg. von
Scheibe E. & Suessmann G. Göttingen,
Vandenhoeck & Ruprecht 1973.

For additional discussions see 157 230, 291, 494, 687. 747,
1294, 1301, 1303. 1331. 1337. 1339, 1402. 2092.
2161, 2229, 2421, 2782, 2856. 3387, 3428. 3444,
3897, 4014, 4467.

V E b: MATHEMATICS (INCLUDING MATHEMATICAL OPTICS AND MUSIC)

3283 BRUINS E.M., "Platon et la table égyptienne 2/n". Janus XLVII 1958 253-263.

3284 JUNGE G., "Von Hippasus bis Philolaus. Das Irrationale und die geometrischen Grundbegriffe". C&M XIX 1958 41-72.

3285 MOUTSOPOULOS E., "La musique dans l'oeuvre de Platon". Thesis summarized in AUP XXVIII 1958 635-636.

3286* MUGLER C., Dictionnaire historique de la terminologie géometrique des Grecs I. Introduction, A-K; II. Λ-Ω. Études et Commentaires XXVIII, Paris, Klincksiek 1958 272&184p.

3287 STAMATIS E., "Παρατηρήσεις τινὲς ἐπὶ τῶν δι' ἐπαναλήψεως διαδοχικῶν προσεγγύσεων παρὰ τοῖς ἀρχαίοις ". Platon X 1958 321-327.

3288 SZABÓ A., "Die Grundlagen in der frühgriechischen Mathematik". SIFC XXX 1958 1-51.

3289 WASSERSTEIN A., "Theaetetus and the History of the Theory of Numbers". CQ LII 1958 165-179.

3290 BECKER O., "Die Archai in der griechischen Mathematik. Einige ergänzende Bemerkungen zum Aufsatz von K. von Fritz". ABG IV 1959 210-226.

3291 MARTIN R., "Proportions et rapports mathématiques dans l'architecture grecque". BAClLg VII,1 1959 1-8.

3292* MOUTSOPOULOS E., La musique dans l'oeuvre de Platon. Coll. Bibl. de Philos. contemporaine, Paris, Presses Universitaires 1959 428p.
      Rev. REG LXXIII 1960 548-549 Weil.
      AC XXIX 1960 454 des Places.
      RPhL LIX 1961 537-540 Motte.
      RyF CLXI 1960 319 de Castro y Delgado.
      EPh XV 1960 294 Colnort-Bodet.
      RecSR XLIX 1961 291 des Places.
      RHR CLIX 1961 103-104 Daumas.
      RThPh XI 1961 98 Lasserre. ·
      DLZ LXXXII 1961 625-630 Wille.
      REA LXIX 1962 437-438 Aubenque.
      Ph&PhenR XXIII 1962-1963 465 Block.

V E b: MATHEMATICS

3293 HAUSER G., "Das Problem vierten Grades im 'Menon'".
PraxMath II 1960 264-266.

3294 WAERDEN B.L. VAN DER, "Grosse Terz, Oktave und
Harmonie". MH XVII 1960 111-114.

3295* WORTMANN E., Ariston oder Die platonischen
Zahlenrätsel. Das grosse Finale zu Platons
göttlicher Harmonie. Bad Godesberg,
Selbstverlag (Sedanstr. 12) 1959 78p.

3296 ETTELT W., "Mathematische Beispiele bei Platon".
Gymnasium LXVIII 1961 124-145.

3297 MARCOVIĆ Z., "Les mathématiques chez Platon et
Aristote". Scientia LV 1961 37-41.

3298 WEDEPOHL E., "Massgrund und Grundmass der Propyläen
von Athen". BJ CLXI 1961 252-262.

3299* RICHTER L., Zur Wissenschaftslehre von der Musik bei
Platon und Aristoteles. Deutsche Akad. der
Wiss. zu Berlin Schriften der Sektion für
Altertumswiss. XXIII, Berlin, Akad-Verl. 1961
xii&202p.
Rev. Gnomon XXXV 1963 513-515 Duering.
CR XIII 1963 160-161 Borthwick.
Sophia XXXII 1964 163 Romano.
DLZ LXXXVI 1965 153-154 Witkowski.
Eos LIV 1964 385-388 Witkowski.

3300* WORTMANN E., Die platonischen Zahlenrätsel.
Politeia, Timaios. Schwerste, schönste u.
bedeutungsvollste Rätsel d.
Menschheitsgeschichte erneut gelöst. Bad
Godesberg, Selbstverlag 1961 137p. (See 3354.)

3301 EHRENFELS F. VON, "Zur Deutung der platonischen
Hochzeitszahl". AGPh XLIV 1962 240-244.

3302 STAMATIS E.S., "A Contribution to the Intepretation
of a Geometric Passage of the Dialogue Menon
86e-87b". Platon XIV 1962 315-320.

3303* FRAJESE A., Platone e la matematica nel mondo
antico. Testi e Documenti IV, Roma, Ed.
Studium 1963 224p.
Rev. Humanitas XIX 1964 287-288 Valetti.

3304 SZABÓ A., "Der mathematische Begriff δύναμις und das
sog. geometrische Mittel". Maia XV 1963
219-256.

3305* LASSERRE F., The Birth of Mathematics in the Age of
      Plato. London, Hutchinson 1964, New York,
      Meridian 1966 191p.
         Rev. RPh XXXIX 1965 318-319 Mugler.
         RFIC XCIII 1965 464-472 Barbieri.
         RF 1966 497-499 Viano.
         PhilosQ XVI 1966 270-271 Bulmer.
         AC XXXIV 1965 314-315 Donnay.
         Gnomon XXXVII 1965 457-460 von Fritz.
         ASSPh XXVI 1966 300-302 Grize.
         Mnemosyne XIX 1966 432 vander Wielen.
         RThPh XCIX 1966 132-133 Virieux-Reymond.
         Isis LVII 1966 137-138 Crowe.
         CW LIX 1966 264 Boyer.
         RecSR LIV 1966 605 des Places.

3306 CAVEING M., "Quelques remarques sur le Timée et les
      mathématiques". REPh XV,6 1965 1-10.

3307 CHEVALIER J.M., "Les passages mathématiques du Timée
      et de la République". REPh XV,2 1965 1-9.

3308* HARVEY F.D., "Two Kinds of Equality". C&M XXVI 1965
      101-146. Also "Corrigenda". C&M XXVII 1966
      99-100.

3309* ANDERSON W.D., Ethos and Education in Greek Music.
      Cambridge, Mass., Harvard Univ. Pr. 1966 306p.
      (ch.3 "Plato", p.64-110.)

3310 FRITZ K. VON, "Die APXAI in der griechischen
      Mathematik". p.335-429 in Fritz K. von,
      Grundprobleme der Geschichte der antiken
      Wissenschaft (see 4591).

3311 FRITZ K. VON, "Gleichheit, Kongruenz und
      Ähnlichkeit in der antiken Mathematik bis auf
      Euklid". p.430-508 in Fritz K. von,
      Grundprobleme der Geschichte der antiken
      Wissenschaft (see 4591).

3312 GIGON O., "Zum antiken Begriff der Harmonie".
      StudGen XIX 1966 539-547.

3313 GOERGEMANNS H. & NEUBECKER A.J., "Heterophonie bei
      Platon". ArchivMusik XXIII 1966 151-169.

3314 ORSI C., "Matematica e filosofia nel pensiero
      platonico". RSFil XIX 1966 183-205.

V E b: MATHEMATICS

3315 STAMATIS E.S., "Συμβολὴ εἰς τὴν ἑρμηνείαν μουσικοῦ χωρίου τοῦ διαλόγου τοῦ Πλάτωνος Τίμαιος" Platon XVIII 1966 257-276.

3316 SZABÓ A., "Theaitetos und das Problem der Irrationalität in der griechischen Mathematikgeschichte". AAntHung XIV 1966 303-358.

3317 VIRIEUX-REYMOND A., "Le progrès des théories de l'Optique des Présocratiques à Platon". ASHSN CXLVI 1966 171-172.

3318 CAMBIANO G., "Il metodo ipotetico e le origini della sistemazione euclidea della geometria". RF LVIII 1967 115-149.

3319 FRAJESE A., "Platone fonte per la storia della matematica". DeHomine 1967 n.22-23 83-102.

3320 ISNARDI PARENTE M., "Platone e i metodi matematici". Cultura V 1967 19-39.

3321* BRUMBAUGH R.S., Plato's Mathematical Imagination. The Mathematical Passages in the Dialogues and their Interpretation. Reprint of 1954 edn. New York, Kraus Reprint 1968 302p.

3322 STAMATIS E.S., "Περὶ τοῦ ἀξιώματος τοῦ συνεχείας". Platon XX 1968 144-147.

3323 FRIES J.F., "Platons Zahl, De Republica L.8 p.546 Steph. Eine Vermutung". p.355-384 in Fries J.F., Sämtliche Schriften, Bd. 20. Aalen, Scientia-Verl. 1969. Originally published in 1823.

3324* FRITZ K. VON, Platon, Theaetet und die antike Mathematik, mit einem Nachtr. zum Neudr. Libelli Nr.257, Darmstadt, Wissensch. Buchges. 1969 103p. (originally appeared in Philologus N.F. XLI 1932 40-62, 136-178.)
Rev. AGM LIII 1969 446-447 Hofmann.
AIHS XXIII 1970 268-270 Itard.
OLME No.335 16 May 1970 Stamatis.

3325 HAASE R., "Ein Beitrag Platons zur Tetraktys". Antaios XI 1969 85-91.

3326* MARCZEWSKI E. & ŁANOWSKI J., On the degradation of Contemplation [in Polish with French summary]. Wrocław, Towarzystow Naukowe 1969 67p.

384

V E b: MATHEMATICS

3327* MUGLER C., Platon et la recherche mathématique de son époque. Reprint of 1948 Straatsburg edn. Naarden, van Bekhoven 1969 xxviii&427p.

3328 SOLMSEN F., "Platos Einfluss auf die Bildung der mathematischen Methode". p.125-139 in Das Platonbild, hrsg. von Gaiser K. (see 4595). Reprinted from Quellen und Studien zur Geschichte der Mathematik, Abt.B,1 1931 93-107.

3329* SZABÓ A., Anfänge der griechischen Mathematik. München, Oldenbourg 1969 494p.
Rev. Lychnos 1969-1970 444-445 Hagstroem.
Philosophia(Athens) I 1971 445-450 Vasiliou.
Physis XIII 1971 333-335 Timpanaro Cardini.
Erasmus XXIII 1971 102-105 Burkert.
Proteus I 1970 129-142 Barnocchi.
BSMB XXII 1970 201-204 Hirsch.
BJPS XXI 1970 305-307 Mahoney.
CW LXIII 1970 23 Boyer.
RHS XXIV 1971 263-266 Itard.
RPhilos XCVIII 1973 375-378 Sinaceur.
RHS XXVI 1973 262-264 Sinaceur.

3330 POPPER K.R., "Plato, Timaeus 54e-55a". CR XX 1970 4-5.

3331 STAMATIS E.S., "Ἡ θεωρία τῶν συνδυασμῶν κατὰ τὴν ἀρχαιότητα" [with English summary]. DEME N.S. XI,2 1970 1-10.

3332 SZABÓ A., "Ein Lob auf die altpythagoreische Geometrie (Epinomis 990d1-6)". Hermes XCVIII 1970 405-421.

3333 BRUN V., "À quelle époque a-t-on pour la première fois observé l'incommensurabilité?". p.29 in Résumés Communic. XIIe Congr. Intern. Hist. Sci., Paris 1968; p.27-30 in Actes du XIIe Congr. Intern. Hist. Sci., T.IV Paris, Blanchard 1971.

3334 MOUTSOPOULOS E., "Science harmonique et empiricisme musical chez Platon". p.158 in Résumés Communic. XIIe Congr. Intern. Hist. Sci., Paris 1968; p.109-112 in Actes du XIIe Congr. Intern. Hist. Sci., T.IIIA. Paris, Blanchard 1971.

3335 PAEV M.E., "Two Mathematical Passages in Plato" [in Russian]. Résumés Communic. XIIIe Congr. Intern. Hist. Sci., Moscow 1971; p.34-36 in Actes du Congr. Intern. Hist. Sci., Moscow 1971, sect. III-IV. Moscow, Nauka 1974.

3336 PAIOW M., "Die mathematische Staatstelle, I". AHES VIII 1971 1-8.

3337 SERRES M., "La diagonale chez Platon. Sur la méthode des dichotomies". p.205-206 in Résumés Communic. XIIe Congr. Intern. Hist. Sci., Paris 1968; p.147 in Actes du XIIe Congr. Intern. Hist. Sci., T.IV. Paris, Blanchard 1971.

3338 WASCHKIES H.J., "Eine neue Hypothese zur Entwicklung der inkommensurabeln Grössen durch die Griechen". AHES VII 1971 325-353.

3339 FUJISAWA N., "Plato and Mathematics" [in Japanese]. Modern Mathematics suppl. vol. Oct. 1972.

3340 KAYAS G.J., "Le nombre géometrique de Platon. Essai d'interprétation". BAGB 1972 431-468.

3341 MARACCHIA S., "Aspetti apollinei e faustiani della matematica greca". Scientia LXVI 1972 495-499.

3342 MAROS DELL'ORO A., "Note sulla realtà matematica nei Presocratici". RSF XXVII 1972 3-18.

3343 ROBIN L., "Untersuchungen über die Bedeutung und Stellung der Physik in der Philosophie Platons". p.261-298 in Das Problem der ungeschriebenen Lehre Platons, hrsg. von Wippern J. (see 4626). Originally publ. as "Études sur la signification et la place de la physique dans la philosophie de Platon". RPhilos XLIII 1918 177-220, 370-415.

3344 WATERHOUSE W.C., "The Discovery of the regular Solids". AHES IX 1972 212-221.

3345 SATOH K., "Comparison of views on the Doctrine of Proportions among the Greeks" [in Japanese]. KagakushiKenkyu XII 1973 122-127.

For further discussions see 353 782 1507 1512 1513 1524. 1526, 1590, 1627. 1767. 1825, 1895, 2154, 2155, 2163, 2284. 2465, 2495, 2521, 2921, 2925, 2939, 2969, 2974, 3354, 3996, 4113.

V E c: COSMOLOGY AND ASTRONOMY

3346 BRIGNOLI F.M., "Problemi di fisica celeste nel Timeo
      di Platone". GIF XI 1958 97-110.

3347 BRIGNOLI F.M., "La dinamica immobilità della terra
      nella concezione platonica dell'universo". GIF
      XI 1958 246-260.

3348 DONNAY G., "Le système astronomique de Platon".
      RBPh XXXVIII 1960 5-29.

3349 LIBES J.G., "The Five Worlds in the Timaeus of
      Plato" [in Hebrew with English summary]. Iyyun
      XI 1960 177-187.

3350* PERLS H., Platon. Sa conception du kosmos. New
      York, Ed. de la Maison française 1945 & Paris,
      Flammarion 1960 310 & 226p.
              Rev. Gnomon XXXIII 1961 722-723 Balme.
              PLA XIV 1961 310-313 Stockhammer.

3351 KUSAYAMA K., "Plato's View of the Cosmos, especially
      in relation to the Theme of the ψυχή" [in
      Japanese]. Shoin Jr. College Bulletin VI 1965.

3352 MERKELBACH   R.,   "Die   Kosmogonie   der
      Mithrasmysterien".   Eranos-Jb   XXXIV   1965
      219-257.

3353* SOEJIMA T., Plato, On his Cosmology [in Japanese].
      Tokyo, Risosha 1965 207p.

3354* WORTMANN E., Das Gesetz des Kosmos. Die göttliche
      Harmonie nach Platons Politeia-Timaios. Die
      platonische Zahlenrätsel erneut gelöst und
      dargestellt. Remagen, Reichel 1965 102p.

3355 FRITZ K. VON, "Die Entwicklung der antiken
      Astronomie".   p.132-197 in Fritz K. von,
      Grundprobleme der Geschichte der antiken
      Wissenschaft (see 4591).

3356 BOYANCÉ P., "Note sur l'éther chez les
      Pythagoriciens, Platon et Aristote". REG LXXX
      1967 202-209.

3357 SCIACCA M.F., "Il problema cosmologico e il
      demiurgo". p.65-262 in Sciacca M.F., Platone II
      (see 64). Reprinted from Sciacca M.F., II

387

metafisica di Platone, vol. I: Il problema
cosmologico. Roma, Perrella 1938.

3358 BLANCHÉ L., "Les précurseurs de la cosmogonie et de
la théogonie platoniciennes". REPh XIX
1967-1968,5 1-8.

3359* HEATH T.L., Greek Astronomy. New York, AMS Press
1969. lvii&192p. Reprint of 1932 U.S. edn.
(p.xxxix-xliv, 40-65 on Plato.)

3360 MORTLEY R.J., "Plato's Choice of the Sphere". REG
LXXXII 1969 342-345.

3361 MUGLER C., "Kosmologische Formeln". Hermes XCVI
1968-1969 515-526.

3362 SINNIGE T.G., "Plato's leer der fundamentele
gestalten in het verband van zijn kosmologie".
WPMW IX 1968-1969 109-123.

3363 BLANCHÉ L., "L'hypothèse astronomique de Platon".
REPh XX 1969-1970 No.4 22-55.

3364* DICKS D.R., Early Greek Astronomy to Aristotle. New
York, Cornell Univ. Pr. 1970 272p. (ch.5
"Plato", p.92-150.)

3365 DUBOSE S., "Poiesis and Cosmos". TSPh XIX 1970
21-26.

3366 MAULA E., "Plato's 'Cosmic Computer' (Tm.
35a-39e)". Ajatus XXXII 1970 185-244.

3367 SALTZER W., "Zum Problem der inneren Planeten in der
vorptolemäischen Theorie". ZWG LIX 1970
141-172.

3368 FERGUSON J., "Δῖνος". Phronesis XVI 1971 97-115.

3369 MAULA E., "Eudoxus Encircled". Ajatus XXXIII 1971
201-253.

3370 STAMATIS E.S., "The Heliocentric System of the
ancient Greeks" [in Greek with German summary].
PAA XLVI 1971 65-84.

3371 FIERZ M., "Vorlesungen zur Entwicklungsgeschichte
der Mechanik". LecNPhys XV 1972 1-97.

V E c: COSMOLOGY AND ASTRONOMY

3372* HANSON H.R., Constellations and Conjectures.
Dordrecht, Reidel 1973 282p. ("Plato's
Astronomical Speculation", p.33-39.)

3373 McCLAIN E., "Plato's Musical Cosmology".
MainCurrents XXX 1973 34-41.

3374 WAERDEN B.L. VANDER, "Die Vorgänger des Copernicus
im Altertum". PhilosNat XIV 1973 407-415.

For further discussion see 43. 263 404, 448, 723, 755,
756, 1205, 1206, 1760, 1761, 1762, 1766, 2269,
2305. 2359, 2510, 2511, 2513, 2533, 2534, 2536,
2537, 2538, 2686, 2706, 3254, 3267, 3277, 3292,
3341, 3412, 3825, 4109, 4133.

V E d: PHYSICS AND CHEMISTRY

3375 MORTLEY R.J., "Primary Particles and Secondary
Qualities in Plato's Timaeus". Apeiron II,1
1967 15-17.

3376 VLASTOS G., "Plato's Supposed Theory of Irregular
Atomic Figures". Isis LVIII 1967 204-209.
Reprinted p.366-373 in Vlastos G., Platonic
Studies (see 4622).

3377 WOOD R.J., "Plato's Atomism". IPQ VIII 1968
427-441.

3378 MUGLER C., "À propos de quelques survivances
animistes dans la terminologie physique de
Platon et d'Aristote". EtClass III 1968-1970
205-215.

3379 DORFMAN J.A.G., "Molecular Physics in Plato" [in
Russian]. Summary in Résumés Communic. XIIIe
Congr. Intern. Hist. Sci., Moscow 1971;
p.30-33 in Actes du XIIIe Congr. Intern. Hist.
Sci., Moscow 1971, section III-IV. Moscow,
Nauka 1974.

3380 POHLE W., "The Mathematical Foundation of Plato's
Atomic Physics". Isis LXII 1971 36-46.

3381* GOLTZ D., Studien zur Geschichte der Mineralnamen in
Pharmazie, Chemie und Medezin von den Anfängen
bis Paracelsus. AGM Beiheft XIV 1972 455p.

V E d: PHYSICS AND CHEMISTRY

3382 POHLE W., "Dimensional Concepts and the Interpretation of Plato's Physics". p.306-323 in Exegesis and Argument, ed. by Lee E.N. et al. (see 4608).

For further discussion see 2521, 2527, 3267, 3362.

V E e: BIOLOGY AND MEDICINE

3383 MUGLER C., "Alcméon et les cycles physiologiques de Platon". REG LXXI 1958 42-50.

3384 ELAUT L., "Hart en bloedvaten in Platoons Timaios". SH I 1959 128-133.

3385 KAESTNER H., "Ärztliches bei Platon in moderner Sicht". ArzPraxis XII 1960 398-399.

3386 SCHUHL P.M., "Platon et la médecine". REG LXXIII 1960 73-79.

3387 WICHMANN O., "Platons Verhältnis zur Medezin seiner Zeit. Ein Beispiel für das Zusammenwirken der Wissenschaften in der Akademie". F&F XXXIV 1960 14-18.

3388 JOLY R., "Platon et la médecine". BAGB 1961 435-451.

3389 MITROPOULOS K., "Πλάτωνος ἰατρικά". Platon XIII 1961 16-58.

3390 SOLMSEN F., "Greek Philosophy and the Discovery of the Nerves". MH XVIII 1961 150-167, 169-197. Reprinted p.536-582 in Solmsen F., Kleine Schriften I (see 4615).

3391 LAÍN ENTRALGO P., "Die ärztliche Hilfe im Werk Platons". AGM XLVI 1962 193-210.

3392 LAÍN ENTRALGO P., "La asistencia médica en la Atenas de Platón y en las ciudades del siglo XX". Summary in EClas VI 1962 552-553.

3393 MILLER H.W., "The Aetiology of Disease in Plato's Timaeus". TAPhA XCIII 1962 175-187.

3394 HERTER H., "Die Treffkunst des Arztes in hippokratischer und platonischer Sicht". AGM XLVII 1963 247-290.

3395 MODRZEWSKI T., "Medycyna w pismach Platona [Medicine in the Writings of Plato]". ArchHistMed XXVI 1963 1-22.

3396 RANKIN H.D., "On ἀδιάπλαστα ζῷα (Plato, Timaeus 91d3)". Philologus CVII 1963 138-145.

3397* TRACY T.J., Physiological Theory and the Doctrine of the Mean in Plato and Aristotle. Diss. Princeton Univ. 1962 436p. [microfilm]. Summary in DA XXIV 1963 291.

3398 RAMIREZ CORRIA F., "Platón y la historia del zoospermo". Finlay III 1964 19-24.

3399 HALL T.S., "The Biology of the Timaeus in historical Perspective". Arion IV,1 1965 109-122.

3400* MORIN H., Der Begriff des Lebens im Timaios Platons unter Berücksichtigung seiner früheren Philosophie. Studia philos. Upsaliensia I, Stockholm, Almqvist & Wiksell 1965 150p.
     Rev. Sophia XXXIV 1966 138-139 Romano.
     Th&Ph XLIII 1968 457 Ennen.

3401 VEGETTI M., "La medicina in Platone". RSF XXI 1966 3-39.

3402* REGNELL H., Ancient Views on the Nature of Life. Three Studies in the Philosophy of the Atomists, Plato, and Aristotle. Libr. of Theoria X, Lund, Gleerup 1967 267p.
     Rev. CW LXII 1968 101 Tarán.
     RF LIX 1968 102-103 Cambiano.
     RPh XLIII 1969 130 Mugler.
     Dialogue VII 1968-1969 502-504 Dybikowski.
     BJPS XIX 1968-1969 265-267 Evans.
     RSF XXIV 1969 90-91 Vegetti.
     Lychnos 1969-1970 402 Alexanderson.
     Sapientia XXV 1970 144 Bolzán.
     CR XXI 1971 403-405 Adkins.

3403 VEGETTI M., "La medicina in Platone, II: Dal Gorgia al Simposio". RSF XXII 1967 251-270.

3404 VEGETTI M., "La medicina in Platone, III: Fedone e Repubblica". RSF XXIII 1968 251-267.

3405   VEGETTI M., "La medicine in Platone, IV: Il Fedro".
        RSF XXIV 1969 3-22.

3406   VIRIEUX-REYMOND A., "Les préoccupations médicales et
        biologiques dans l'oeuvre de Platon".   p.195-202
        in Comptes Rendus du XIXe Congr.   internat.
        Histoire de la Médicine, Bâle 1964. Basel,
        Karger 1966.

3407   DABASIS I.N., "Η ἰατρικὴ τοῦ Πλάτωνος παρὰ Μένωνι"
        [with English summary].   Platon XX 1968 87-105.

3408   EGERTON F.N.   III, "Ancient Sources for Animal
        Demography".   Isis LIX 1968 175-189.

3409   SOLMSEN F., "On Plato's Account of Respiration".
        p.583-587 in Solmsen F., Kleine Schriften I (see
        4615).   Reprinted from SIFC XXVII-XXVIII 1956
        544-548.

3410   SOLMSEN F., "Tissues and the Soul.   Philosophical
        Contributions   to   Physiology".   p.502-535   in
        Solmsen F.,   Kleine   Schriften I   (see   4615).
        Reprinted from PhR LIX 1960 435-468.

3411   FISCHER-HOMBERGER G., "Hysterie und Misogynie.   Ein
        Aspekt   der   Hysteriegeschichte".   Gesnerus XXVI
        1969 117-127.

3412*   TRACY T.J., Physiological Theory and the Doctrine of
        the Mean in Plato and Aristotle. Stud. in
        Philosophy XVII, Chicago, Loyola Univ.   Pr.   and
        Den   Haag,   Mouton   1969   396p.   (Ch.3
        "Physiological Theory and 'The Mean' in   Plato",
        p.77-156.)
                Rev.   Bijdragen XXXI 1970 459-460 Nota.
                IJPR I 1970 258-260 Harrison.
                CPh LXVI 1971 292-293 Sprague.
                Phoenix XXV 1971 171-174 Sparshott.
                ACR I 1971 140-141 Christiansen.
                SIF II 1970 181-184 Preus.
                CW LXV 1972 171 Hoerber.
                Mind LXXXI 1972 148-149 Charlton.
                CR XXII 1972 419-420 Phillips.

3413   GHIRARDI   D.A.,   "Escalas   y   sistemas   de   la
        naturaleza".   Sapientia(Argentina)   XXV   1970
        89-104.

3414   HEST F. VAN, "Over de heiligheid van de heilige
        ziekte. Enkele opvattingen omtrent de epilepsie
        bij Hippokrates en Plato".   Hermeneus XLI 1970

227-230.

3415* KORNEXL E., Begriff und Einschätzung der Gesundheit des Körpers in der griechischen Literatur von der Anfängen bis zum Hellenismus. Commentationes Aenipontanae XXI, Innsbruck, Wagner 1970 153p.

3416 EGERTON F.N., "The Concept of Competition in Nature before Darwin". p.41-46 in Actes du XIIe Congr. Intern. Hist. Sci, Paris 1968 T.8. Paris, Blanchard 1971.

3417 SOBOL S.L. & ROŽANSKIJ I.D., "Biology in ancient Greece to the Hellenistic Age in ancient Rome" [in Russian]. p.20-35 in Istorija biologii. S drevnejših vremen du načala XXe veka. Moscow 1972.

3418 DICKASON A., "Anatomy and Destiny: The Role of Biology in Plato's View of Women". PhilosForum V 1973 45-53.

3419* HARRIS C.R.S., The Heart and the Vascular System in ancient Greek Medicine. From Alcmaeon to Galen. Oxford, Clarendon Pr. 1973 xii&474p. (for Plato see esp. p.117-121.)

For further discussions see 267, 275, 357, 400, 523, 1448, 1831, 1841, 2070, 2072, 2529, 2686, 3073, 3129, 3267, 3381, 3694, 3944.

V F: ETHICS

3420 BRINK C.O., "Plato on the natural Character of Goodness". HSPh LXIII 1958 (Stud. Jaeger) 193-198.

3421* FERGUSON J., Moral Values in the Ancient World. London, Methuen 1958 256p. (See esp. ch. 3 "The cardinal Virtues", ch. 5 "Eros".)
Rev.ThS XX 1959 318 Bodnar.
CJ LV 1959 92 Rexine.
CW LII 1959 253 Hoerber.
CR X 1960 50-52 Adkins.
JHS LXXX 1960 232 Kerferd.
PACA III 1960 32-34 Carney.
JR XXXIX 1959 197-198 McCasland.
RSF XV 1960 320-321 Untersteiner.
JPh LVI 1959 687-688 Hadas.
HibJ LVII 1958-1959 297 Armstrong.
DUJ XXI 1959-1960 41-43 Badian.
Philosophy 1960 76 Kolnai.
Personalist 1960 75 Miller.
JRH I 1961 250-252 Harris.
RecSR XLIX 1961 138 des Places.
NS XXXV 1961 130-132 Oates.

3422 FUNKE G., "Die wahlbestimmende Kraft der "ethischen" Lebensgewohnheiten (Platon)". p.32-45 in Funke G., Gewohnheit = ABG III 1958.

3423 KOBAYASHI I., "'Politikè aretè' and 'anthropinè aretè'. Considerations on the development of the ethical thought of Plato" [in Japanese with English summary]. Bunka XXII 1958 134-155.

3424 O'BRIEN M., "Modern Philosophy and Platonic Ethics". JHI XIX 1958 451-472.

3425 CAZENEUVE J., "Un panorama des commentaires sur la morale de Platon". RPhilos LXXXVI 1961 69-72.

3426 PLACES E. DES, "L'éducation des tendances chez Platon et Aristote". ArchPhilos XXI 1958 410-422.

3427 RAUBITSCHEK A.E., "Ein neues Pittakeion". WS LXXI 1958 170-172.

3428 CALLOT E., "La naissance de la réflexion morale:
les rapports de la science et de la morale chez
Platon". p.127-145 in Callot E., Questions de
doctrine et d'histoire de la philosophie. T.1:
Histoire. Annecy, Gardet 1959.

3429* LIEBERG G., Geist und Lust. Untersuchungen zu
Demokrit, Plato, Xenokrates und Herakleides
Pontikus. Tübingen, Selbstverl. Philol.
Seminar 1959 43p.

3430 LIEBERG G., "Die Stellung der griechischen
Philosophie zur Lust von den Pythagoreern bis
auf Aristoteles". Gymnasium LXVI 1959 128-137.

3431* OPSTELTEN J.C., Beschouwingen naar aanleiding van
het outbreken van ons ethisch wilsbegrip in de
oud-griekse ethiek. Meded. Nederl. Akad, van
Wet., Afd. Letterk. N.R. XXII,1, Amsterdam,
Noord-Holl. Uitg. Maats. 1959 66p.
Rev. Hermeneus XXXI 1959 62-63 Bakker.
Mnemosyne XIII 1960 246-247 van Straaten.
CR X 1960 258 Rose.
AAHG XIV 1961 227 Ivánka.
REG LXXVI 1963 476-478 des Places.

3432* ADKINS A.W.H., Merit and Responsibility. Oxford,
Clarendon Pr. 1960 xv&380p. (Ch. 13, Plato:
Logic and Elenchus; ch. 14, Plato: Ideal
States.) Italian transl. La morale dei Greci.
Da Omero ad Aristotele, trad. di Ambrosini R.,
a cura di Plebe A. Bibl. di Cultura Moderna,
Bari, Laterza 1964 515p.
Rev. HibJ LVIII 1959-1960 410-411 Lunt.
TLS 15 Apr. 1960 246.
RSF XV 1960 319-320 Giannantoni.
CW LIII 1960 260 Burrows.
JRH I 1961 252-253 Harris.
RecSR XLIX 1961 138-139 des Places.
JHS LXXXI 1961 186-187 Kerferd.
CR LXXV 1961 127-128 Bluck.
PhR LXX 1961 421-423 Ackrill.
Ethics LXXII 1961-1962 144-146 Scarrow.
AJPh LXXXIII 1962 209-211 Will.
Phoenix XVI 1962 205-207 Sparshott.
PhilosQ XII 1962 366-367 Bambrough.
Philosophy XXXVII 1962 277-279 Robinson.
Hermathena XCVII 1963 137-139 Luce.
CPh LVI 1961 194-197 Levinson.
JHS LXXXI 1961 186-187 Kerferd.
Mind LXX 1961 568-569 Ralls.
TC 1963 122 MacIntyre.

JCS XII 1964 149-151 Shikibu.
Gnomon XXXVIII 1966 724-725 Oehler.
[of Italian edn.] RMM LXX 1965 116-117
Brunschwig.
RF LVIII 1967 471-482 Viano.

3433 MUELLER G., "Probleme der aristotelischen
Eudaimonielehre". MH XVII 1960 121-143.

3434* VOIGTLAENDER H.D., Die Lust und das Gute bei Platon.
Würzburg, Triltsch 1960 218p.
Rev. AAHG XIV 1961 99 Vretska.
RBPh XL 1962 571-572 Mommaers.
CR XII 1962 38-40 Gulley.
RPh XXXVI 1962 309 Louis.
Emerita XXX 1962 206-208 Adrados.
Mnemosyne XV 1962 182-184 de Vries.
REA LXIV 1962 436-437 Moreau.
CPh LVII 1962 194-196 Hoerber.
Gnomon XXXV 1963 423-425 Oehler.
MH XX 1963 243 Gigon.
Athenaeum XLI 1963 171-175 Alfieri.
Gymnasium LXX 1963 65-66 Flashar.

3435 KREILCAMP H., "Plato's Word for Today". NS XXXV
1961 202-209.

3436* MALCOLM J.F., Plato's Conception of Moral Knowledge.
Diss. Princeton Univ. 1961 164p. [microfilm].
Summary in DA XXII 1962 4371-4372.

3437 VIVES J., "Episteme y doxa en la ética platónica".
Convivium(Barcelona) XI-XII 1961 99-136.

3438* CANOSA CAPDEVILLE Y., En torno a la axiología de
Platón en su tensión perenne ético-religiosa.
Montevideo, Tall. Gráf. Barreiro y Ramos 1962
69p.

3439 HAGER F.P., "Die Materie und das böse im antiken
Platonismus". MH XIX 1962 73-103.

3440 HERTER H., "Gut und Böse bei Platon". Summary
p.51-52 in Acta Philologica Aenipontana I, hrsg.
von Muth R. Innsbruck, Wagner 1962.

3441 HINTIKKA J., "Miksi hyve oli kreikkalaisten mielestä
tietoa? [Why was Virtue Knowledge for the
ancient Greeks?]". Suomalainen Suomi VI 1962
341-349. Reprinted p.59-74 in Hintikka J.,
Tieto on Valtaa (see 4600).

V F: ETHICS

3442* PEARSON L., Popular Ethics in Ancient Greece.
Stanford Univ. Pr. 1962 262p. (esp. ch. 1,
"Greek Popular Ethics--A Sketch").
Rev. CW LV 1962 256 Halporn.
SatR 23 June 1962 48 Grene M.
LJ 1962 563 Stevens.
G&R 1963 90.
RM XVI 1962-1963 585 W.G.E.
Gnomon XXXV 1963 742-746 Westman.
PACA VI 1963 62-64 Kyriakidou-Nestoros.
CJ LVIII 1963 323-324 O'Brian.
JHS LXXXIII 1963 179 Kerferd.
RF LIV 1963 107-108.
REG LXXVI 1963 459-460 de Romilly.
RBPh XLI 1963 256-257 Flacelière.
RBPh XLI 1963 663-664 van den Bruwaene.
TG LXXVI 1963 333-334 Loenen.
RPh XXXVIII 1964 303 Louis.
JCS XII 1964 159-161 Matsui.
CR XIV 1964 70-72 Adkins.
RFIC XCII 1964 196-198 Carena.
AJPh LXXXVI 1965 93-94 Ehrenberg.
REA LXVII 1965 256-258 Defradas.

3443 PIATKOWSKI A., "Εκων αμαρτανειν" [in Rumanian with
Russian and French summaries]. StudClas IV 1962
79-93.

3444 HALL R.W., "Plato--A Minority Report". SoJP II 1964
168-173.

3445* HAGER F.P., Die Vernunft und das Problem des Bösen
im Rahmen der platonischen Ethik und Metaphysik.
Noctes Romanae X, Bern, Haupt 1963 xii&261p.
Also 2. erw. Aufl. 1970 xii&295p.
Rev.CR XIV 1964 261-262 Easterling.
CW LVII 1964 379 Hoerber.
MH XXI 1964 244 Wehrli.
AC XXXIII 1964 164 des Places.
Gnomon XXXVII 1965 460-465 Voigtlaender.
CPh LX 1965 139-140 Hoerber.
RThPh XIV 1964 248 de Muralt.
JCS XIV 1966 149-150 Shikibu.
JHS LXXXVI 1966 226-227 Kerferd.
REL XLV 1967 552 Langlois.
RMM LXXII 1967 126-128 Brunschwig.
PLA XVIII 1965 77-79 Stockhammer.
RM 1966-1967 549 M.J.V.
Maia XXII 1970 188-189 Guazzoni Foà.
[of 2nd edn.] CR XXIII 1973 89 Easterling.

3446* WEHRLI F., Hauptrichtungen des griechischen Denkens.
Erasmus-Bibl., Zürich, Artemis-Verl. 1964 235p.
(II. Die Philosophische Ethik. B. Die
Sokratik. a. Sokrates p.136-144; b. Platon
p.144-158.)
Rev. Gnomon XXXVII 1965 529-532 Adkins.
CW LIX 1965 10-11 Long.
Gymnasium LXXII 1965 542-543 Oehler.
RecSR LIV 1966 576 des Places.
DLZ LXXXVII 1966 867-869 Saupe.
ANQ 1965 28 Thompson.

3447 KOUTSOYANNOPOULOS D.J., "Ἡ ἔννοια τῆς τρυφῆς παρὰ
Πλάτονι". Platon XVII 1965 3-10.

3448 LOVINFOSSE J.M., "La morale de Platon". AC XXXIV
1965 484-505.

3449 LUKES S., "Moral Weakness". PhilosQ XV 1965
104-114.

3450 MOUTSOPOULOS E., "The fourfold Root of Practical
Wisdom in Plato" [in Greek with French summary].
Athena LXVIII 1965 12-16.

3451 PARRY A., "A Note on the Origins of Teleology". JHI
XXVI 1965 259-262.

3452 SCHMIDT J., "Μέτρον ἄριστον. Mass und Harmonie".
EEAth XV 1964-1965 514-563.

3453 SCHOTTLAENDER R., "Platon und das Prinzip des
Bösen". Helikon V 1965 173-176.

3454* STEIN R., Megaloprepeia bei Platon. Diss. Bonn
1965 189p.
Rev. REG LXXVIII 1965 692 Gauthier.
AAHG XIX 1966 253-255 Vretska.
RPh XL 1966 314 des Places.
Gymnasium LXXIV 1967 367 Flashar.
CPh LXII 1967 137 Hoerber.
RBPh XLVI 1968 623 Strachan.
CR XXI 1971 290 Adkins.

3455 TROTIGNON P., "Fondement et fondation de la
moralité. Réflexions sur Platon". REPh XV,5
1965 1-13.

3456* MacINTYRE A., A Short History of Ethics. New York,
Macmillan 1966 viii&280p. (ch.3 "The Sophists
and Socrates"; ch.4 "Plato: The Gorgias";
ch.5 "Plato: The Republic"; ch.6 "Postscript

to Plato".)

3457 ROMILLY J. DE, "La condamnation du plaisir dans l'oeuvre de Thucydide". WS LXXIX 1966 142-148.

3458 BOSCO N., "Né Themis né Dike". Filosofia XVIII 1967 469-510.

3459 DEMOS R., "Plato on Moral Principles". Mind LXXVI 1967 125-126.

3460 GRAHAM F.B., "A Note on Mr. Demos' Note on Plato on Moral Principles". Mind LXXVIII 1969 596-597.

3461* HUBY P., Greek Ethics. London, Macmillan and New York, St. Martin's Pr. 1967 vi&76p. (Ch.3 "Socrates", p.15-25; ch.4 "Plato", p.26-40.)
        Rev. VF XXII 1968 170-171.
        CW LXII 1968 27 O'Brien.
        PhilosQ XVIII 1968 180-181 Atkinson.
        PhilosBks Jan. 1968 15 Adkins.

3462* JONES L.C., The Problem of Justice in Plato and Aristophanes. Diss. The American Univ. 1967 95p. [microfilm]. Summary in MAb V,4 1967 15.

3463 PROSCH H., "Toward an Ethics of Civil Disobedience". Ethics LXXVII 1967 176-192.

3464 BASHOR P.S., "Plato and Aristotle on Friendship". JVI II 1968 269-280.

3465* BLUMENFELD W., Vom sittlichen Bewusstsein. Kritische und Konstruktive Beiträge zu den Problemen der Ethik. Conscientia. Studien zur Bewusstseinsphilosophie Bd.2, Bonn, Bouvier 1968 141p.

3466* BOSCO N., Idea e concezioni della giustizia nelle civiltà occidentali, I: L'antichità. Torino, Ed. di Filosofia 1968 xxxii&220p.
        Rev. GM XXV 1970 364-366.

3467 KLEVER W.N.A., "Integrale zelfverwerkelijking. Beschouwingen over een ethisch kernbegrip in Plato's dialogen. Een tekststudie". Dialoog VIII 1967-1968 113-200.

3468* LODGE R.C., Plato's Theory of Ethics. The Moral Criterion and the Highest Good. Hamden, Conn., The Shoe String Pr. 1968 558p. Reprint of 1928 London edn.

3469* MONTONERI L., Il problema del male nella filosofia
      di Platone. Pubbl. dell'Ist. Univ. di
      Magistero di Catania, Serie filosofica. Saggi e
      monografie LXII, Padova, Cedam 1968 475p.
      Rev. Sophia XXXVIII 1970 95-99 Turolla.
      Filosofia XXI 1970 441 Dollo.
      REG LXXXIV 1971 575-576 Vicaire.
      CR XXI 1971 128 Charlton.
      GM XXVI 1971 276 Sorge.

3470 MONTONERI L., "Il problema del male nella filosofia
      di Platone". Sophia XXXVII 1969 339-349.

3471 COOLEY K.W., "Unity and Diversity of the Virtues in
      the Charmides, Laches, and Protagoras". Kinesis
      I 1969 100-106.

3472* CURRAN T.J., The teachability of Virtue according to
      Plato. Diss. Univ. of Southern California
      1969 359p. [microfilm]. Summary in DA XXX 1969
      2072A.

3473* REINICKE H., Das Verhängnis der Übel im Weltbild
      griechischer Denker. Berlin, Heenemann 1969
      54p.
      Rev. ZRGG XXV 1973 88 Strohm.

3474 THAYER H.S., "Models of moral Concepts and Plato's
      Republic". JHPh VII 1969 247-262.

3475* WATERFALL D.E., Plato and Aristotle on Akrasia.
      Diss. Princeton Univ. 1969 234p. [microfilm].
      Summary in DA XXXI 1970 805A-806A.

3476 CHI-LU CHUNG A., "The Principle of Rectification of
      Confucius, Plato, and Aristotle". ChinCult XI
      1970 69-76.

3477 DAVIES J.C., "Some Thoughts on Plato's View of
      Pleasure". Euphrosyne IV 1970 173-181.

3478* DUNCAN R.B., The Role of the Concept of Philia in
      Plato's Dialogues. Diss. Yale Univ. 1969
      348p. [microfilm]. Summary in DA XXX 1970
      3499A-3500A.

3479* KRAUT R., Two Studies in Classical Greek Moral
      Philosophy. Diss. Princeton Univ. 1969 213p.
      [microfilm]. Summary in DA XXXI 1970 800A-801A.

3480 RORTY A., "Plato and Aristotle on Belief, Habit and Akrasia". APQ VII 1970 50-61.

3481 SELLARS W., "On Knowing the Better and Doing the Worse". IPQ X 1970 5-19.

3482 SPARSHOTT F.E., "Five Virtues in Plato and Aristotle". Monist LIV 1970 40-65.

3483* VIVES J., Génesis y evolución de la ética platónica. Estudios de las analogías en que se expresa la ética de Platón. Bibl. hispánica de Filos. LXIV, Madrid, Ed. Gredos 1970 329p.
      Rev. Espiritu XIX 1970 91-92 C.V.M.
      Perficit II 1970 446-450 Barcenilla.
      Helmantica XXI 1970 333-334 Ruiz.
      RSC XVIII 1970 294-295 d'Agostino.
      BIEH V,2 1971 63-64 Alsina.
      RS XCII 1971 311 Margolin.
      Sophia XL 1972 154-157.
      AC XLII 1973 232-234 de Strycker.

3484* WATERFALL D.E., Plato and Aristotle on Akrasia. Diss. Princeton Univ. 1969 234p.. [microfilm]. Summary in DA XXXI 1970 805A-806A.

3485 BURNYEAT M.F., "Virtues in Action". p.209-234 in The Philosophy of Socrates, ed. by Vlastos G. (see 4621).

3486 CHERNISS H.F., "The Sources of Evil according to Plato". p.244-258 in Plato II, ed. by Vlastos G. (see 4620). Reprinted from PAPhS XCVIII 1954 23-30.

3487 ELBRECHT J., "The Grand Tradition of Platonism and its Implicit Dominant Ethics". StudGen XXIV 1971 757-772.

3488 FESTUGIÈRE A.J., "Réflexions sur le problème du mal chez Eschyle et Platon". p.8-37 in Festugière A.J., Études de philosophie grecque (see 4587). Reprinted from RPh XXII 1948 147-177.

3489 FESTUGIÈRE A.J., "Les trois vies". p.117-156 in Festugière A.J., Études de philosophie grecque (see 4587). Reprinted from Acta Congressus Madvigiani, II 131-174.

3490 FESTUGIÈRE A.J., "La doctrine du plaisir des premiers sages à Épicure". p.81-116 in Festugière A.J., Études de philosophie grecque

V F: ETHICS

(see 4587). Reprinted from RSPh 1936 233-268.

3491 FRESCO M.F., "Agathon en Hedone". Dialoog XI 1970-1971 90-100.

3492 GEELS D., "Plato and the Pay-Off of Justice". Personalist LII 1971 449-458.

3493 HARTMAN R.S., "El origen de la axiometría en La República de Platón". Dianoia XVII 1971 103-128.

3494* NOVAK D., Suicide and Morality in Plato, Aquinas, and Kant. Diss. Georgetown Univ. 1971 302p. [microfilm]. Summary in DA XXXII 1971 2748A.

3495 SCHIPPER E.W., "Motives and Virtues in the Platonic Ethics". Ratio XIII 1971 67-75. Also "Beweggrund und Tugend in der platonischen Ethik". Ratio(Hamburg) XIII 1971 58-65.

3496 SHOREY P., "Plato's Ethics". p.7-34 in Plato II, ed. by Vlastos G. (see 4620). Reprint of Shorey P., The Unity of Plato's Thought. Chicago 1903, ch.1.

3497 ARONSON S.H., "The Happy Philosopher. A Counterexample to Plato's Proof". JHPh X 1972 383-398.

3498 EPP R.H., "Plato's Quest for Purification". Platon XXIV 1972 38-50.

3499 GAUSS H., "Das philosophische Ethos des Platonikers". p.401-421 in Gauss H., Opuscula Philosophica (see 4596).

3500 GAUSS H., "Die Willensfreiheit bei Plato". p.457-482 in Gauss H., Opuscula Philosophica (see 4596).

3501* GOOCH P.W., Socratic Paradoxes in Plato. A Study in Virtue, Knowledge, and related Concepts in Plato's Dialogues. Diss. Univ. of Toronto 1971. [microfilm]. Summary in DA XXXII 1972 5284A.

3502* GOULD J., The Development of Plato's Ethics. New York, Russell & Russell 1972 xiii&240p. Reprint of 1955 edn.

3503* HERMANN A., Untersuchungen zu Platons Auffassung von
       der Hedoné. Ein Beitrag zum Verständnis des
       platonischen Tugendbegriffes. Hypomnemata XXXV,
       Göttingen, Vandenhoeck & Ruprecht 1972 80p.
       Rev. AC XLII 1973 621-623 de Ley.

3504* HUBY P., Plato and Modern Morality. New Stud. in
       Practical Philos., London, Macmillan 1972 80p.
       Rev. PhilosBks XIV 1973,2 10-11 Cross.

3505* LÓPEZ LÓPEZ J.L., El mal en el pensamiento
       platónico. Anales de la Univ. Hispalense.
       Ser. Filos. y Letras X, Sevilla, Universidad
       1972 173p.

3506 REES D.A., "The Classification of Goods in Plato and
       Aristotle". p.327-336 in Islamic Philosophy and
       the Classical Tradition. Essays presented by
       his friends and pupils to Richard Walzer on his
       seventieth birthday, ed. by Stern S.M. et al.
       Oriental Studies V, Oxford, Cassirer and
       Columbia, S.C., Univ. of South Carolina Pr.
       1972.

3508 VERSENYI L., "Virtue as a self-directed Art
       (Republic 338-347)". Personalist LIII 1972
       274-289.

3509 HILL R., "Virtue as a Self-directed Art".
       Personalist LIII 1972 290-300.

3510 WOOZLEY A.D., "Plato on Killing in Anger". PhilosQ
       XXII 1972 303-317.

3511 SAUNDERS T.J., "Plato on Killing in anger. A Reply
       to Professor Woozley". PhilosQ XXIII 1973
       350-356.

3512 BONANNO M.G., "Osservazioni sul tema della giusta
       reciprocità amorosa da Saffo ai comici". QUCC
       1973 No.16 110-120.

3513 BUBNER R., "Action and Reason". Ethics LXXXIII 1973
       224-236.

3514 FLEW A., "Must Morality pay? or, What Socrates
      should have said to Thrasymachus". p.109-133 in
      Skepticism and Moral Principles. Modern ethics
      in Review, ed. with intro. by Carter C.L.
      Evanston, Ill., New Univ. Pr. 1973.

3515* IRWIN T.H., Theories of Virtue and Knowledge in
      Plato's Early and Middle Dialogues. Diss.
      Princeton Univ. 1973 842p. [microfilm],
      Summary in DA XXXIV 1973 821A.

3516 JANDA J., "The Platonic Quest for Justice" [in
      Czech]. ZJKF XV,3 1973 9-28.

3517 KRAUT R., "Egoism, Love, and Political Office in
      Plato". PhR LXXXII 1973 330-344.

3518 NAKHNIKIAN G., "Salvation in Plato and St. Paul:
      An Essay in Normative Ethics". CanJPh II 1973
      325-344.

3519 VLASTOS G., "Socratic Knowledge and Platonic
      'Pessimism'". p.204-217 in Vlastos G., Platonic
      Studies (see 4622). (Review of Gould J., The
      Development of Plato's Ethics.) Reprinted from
      PhR LXVI 1957 226-238.

3520 WILSON F.E., "Some Reflections on 'Action and
      Reason'". Ethics LXXXIII 1973 237-247.

For additional discussions of Plato's Ethics see 381, 439,
      464, 474, 753, 1071, 1087, 1096, 1102, 1190,
      1204, 1248, 1253, 1254, 1297, 1298, 1301, 1356,
      1400, 1470, 1523, 1878, 1936, 2072, 2087, 2094,
      2109, 2111, 2118, 2151, 2183, 2225, 2613, 2620,
      2711, 2777, 2988, 3006, 3016, 3061, 3116, 3160,
      3309, 3641, 3701, 3770, 3776, 4119, 4128, 4154,
      4155, 4478, 4486.

INDICES

JUSTICE

This subject is discussed in the following studies:
1401, 1468, 2043, 2048, 2049, 2052, 2053, 2055,
2056, 2062, 2063, 2076, 2082, 2083, 2084, 2085,
2088, 2089, 2090, 2092, 2093, 2095, 2097, 2098,
2099, 2100, 2101, 2102, 2103, 2104, 2105, 2106,
2107, 2108, 2110, 2112, 2113, 2114, 2115, 2116,
2117, 2365, 3458, 3462, 3466, 3479, 3492, 3497,
3512, 3516, 4055.

PLEASURE AND HEDONISM

These subjects are discussed in the following studies:
1299, 1882, 1883, 1884, 1885, 1886, 1887, 1888,
1889, 1890, 1891, 1892, 1894, 1896, 1897, 1904,
1914, 1938, 1939, 1953, 2091, 3429, 3430, 3434,
3457, 3477, 3490, 3491, 3503, 3507.

MORAL KNOWLEDGE

This subject is discussed in the following studies:
1528, 1941, 3428, 3436, 3437, 3441, 3450, 3472,
3501, 3515.

HAPPINESS (ΕΥΔΑΙΜΟΝΙΑ)

This subject is discussed in the following studies:
447, 2965, 3433, 3479, 3492, 3497.

MORAL WEAKNESS (AKRASIA)

This subject is discussed in the following studies:
1948, 3443, 3449, 3475, 3480, 3481, 3484.

THE PROBLEM OF EVIL

This subject is discussed in the following studies:
3439, 3440, 3445, 3453, 3469, 3470, 3473, 3486,
3488, 3505.

V G: POLITICS AND SOCIETY

Again, in order to make access to this large
section more feasible I have prepared special
indices for a number of topics. These indices
appear at the end of the present section and
contain references to entries both in this
section and elsewhere. They cover Books and
Articles on Plato's Political Philosophy in
General, The Utopian Character of Plato's States
and the Question of their Realizability, Plato
on the Nature of Political Authority, Plato and
Freedom, Democracy, and Totalitarianism, Plato's
Political Views and their Contemporary
Relevance, Man and State, Political Ethics,
Philosophy of Law, Particular Issues in the
Organization and Legislation of Plato's States,
Plato and Slavery, Plato as Social Philosopher,
Plato as Economic Thinker, and Plato's Use of
History.

3521 DURIĆ M., "Was Plato a Machiavellian?". ARSPh XLIV
     1958 79-93.

3522 FALKE R., "Utopies d'hier et d'aujourd'hui".
     Diogene No. 23 1958 18-28.

3523 HERTER H., "Macht und Idee. Zur Interpretation von
     Thukydides und Platon". Summary in WHB 1958 no.
     1 26-32.

3524 HODGES D.C., "Judicial Supremacy". JPh LV 1958
     101-111.

3525 KELSEN H., "Plato und die Naturrechtslehre". OEZOR
     N.F. VIII 1957-1958 1-43.

3526 LANG H., "Gossekärlek och platonism" [Pederasty and
     Platonism]. Värld och Vetande VIII 1958, no.4
     107-110.

3527* LUCCIONI J., La pensée politique de Platon. Publ.
     Fac. des Lettres d'Alger XXX, Paris, Presses
     Universitaires 1958 345p.
          Rev. EPh XIII 1958 554-555 Jagu.
          Gnomon XXXI 1959 373-374 Kerferd.
          REA LXI 1959 172-173 Moreau.
          Erasmus XII 1959 693-694 Kassel.
          RH CCXXII 1959 159-161 Cloché.

RPhL LVII 1959 447-451 Vanhoutte.
AC XXVIII 1959 356-360 Gorteman.
RPh XXXIV 1960 285-286 Louis.
RThPh X 1960 256 Schaerer.
REG LXXIII 1960 292-293 Weil.
Paideia XIX 1964 47-52 Sartori.
RPhilos CLXII 1972 41-42 Aubenque.

3528* MOEBUS G., Die politischen Theorien von den Anfängen
bis zu Machiavelli. Politische Theorien, I.
Köln, Westdt. Verl. 1958 217p. (For Plato,
see especially p.39-54, 95-127.)
Rev. HJ LXXVIII 1959 157-158 Brack.

3529 MORRISON J.S., "The Origins of Plato's
Philosopher-Statesman". CQ LII 1958 198-218.

3530 TRAUGOTT E., "Plato in uns selbst. Platons
Staatslehre und der moderne Totalitarismus".
Christ und Welt XI 1958 no.37 p.16.

3531* VERDROSS A., Abendländische Rechtsphilosophie. Ihre
Grundlagen und Hauptprobleme in geschichtlicher
Schau. Wien, Springer 1958 X&270p. Spanish
translation: La Filosofía del Derecho del Mundo
Occidental, trad. de M. de la Cueva. Mexico
City, Centro de Estudios Filosóficos 1962 433p.
(See ch. 5, part 1 Socrates; part 2 Plato.)
Rev. RF L 1959 484-489 Bobbio.
AGPh XLII 1960 312-316 Waider.
Erasmus XVI 1964 134-140 Friedrich.
Scholastik XXXIV 1959 440-442 Hartmann.
ARSPh XLV 1959 312-314 Topitsch.
StimZ CLXVII 1960 234-235 Soder.
BTh IX 1962 16-17 Lottin.

3532 VOIGT A., "Die Rechtswissenschaft an Platons
Akademie. Ein Kapitel Geschichte der
Rechtswissenschaft". ErlU XI 1958 2-3.

3533 WEINSTOCK H., "Die Freiheit bei Platon und
Aristoteles". p.49-60 in Weinstock H., Realer
Humanismus, 2. Aufl. Heidelberg 1958.

3534* BARKER E., The Political Thought of Plato and
Aristotle. New York, Russell & Russell 1959
581p.; New York, Dover 1960 xxii&559p.;
Gloucester, P. Smith 1961.
Rev. AC XXX 1961 222 Moraux.
Gnomon XXXIV 1962 91 Morrow.
EPh XV 1960 526-527 Deledalle.

3535 BARKER E., "Communism in Plato's Republic". p.82-97 in Plato's Republic, ed. by Sesonske A. (see 4614). Reprinted from Barker E., The Political Thought of Plato and Aristotle. New York 1906 p.137-162.

3536 BEIERWALTES W., "Platon. Zu Ep. VII 325c sqq. und Rep. 520c sqq.". Anregung 1959 325-337.

3537 BLUCK R.S., "Plato's Ideal State". CQ IX 1959 166-168.

3538* CROSSMAN R.H.S., Plato Today. New York, Oxford Univ. Pr. 1959 215p. Reprint of 1937 edn. with minor revisions. Excerpt reprinted as "Plato and the perfect State" p.15-40 in Plato, Totalitarian or Democrat? (see 4617).
    Rev. NewSt LVIII 1959 224-225 Hampshire.
    Humanidades XIII 1960 261 Mayor.
    CR XI 1961 81 Bambrough.
    CB XXXVII 1961 46 Rexine.

3539* EHRHARDT A.A.T., Politische Metaphysik von Solon bis Augustin, I: Die Gottesstadt der Griechen und Römer. Tübingen, Mohr 1959 x&323p. (Numerous references to Plato.)
    Rev. RSPh XLIV 1960 562-563 Camelot.
    JThS XI 1960 401-404 Frend.
    RHPhR XL 1960 58-64 Freund.
    TG LXXIV 1961 235-237 Aalders.
    HZ CXCII 1961 369-375 Langerbeck.
    RHD XXIX 1961 357-358 von Schmid.
    RHE LVI 1961 984.
    Erasmus XIV 1961 165-170 Pédech.
    PhilosRdschau IX 1961 47-64 Wilckens.
    ZRG LXXIX 1962 369-374 Ehrenberg.
    Gnomon XXXV 1963 529-533 von Fritz.
    NRTh LXXXV 1963 98 Martin.

3540* McILWAIN C.H., Il pensiero politico occidentale dai Greci al tardo medioevo, a cura di Ferrara G. Venezia, Pozza 1959 482p. Transl. of 1932 edn. (ch.2 on Plato.)
    Rev. RIFD XXXVI 1959 341.
    RIFD XXXVII 1960 513-517 Capurso.
    Convivium(Barcelona) XXXV 1967 231-236 Telmon.

3541* PRELOT M., Histoire des idées politiques. Coll. Précis, Paris, Dalloz 1959 648p. (ch.5 "L'utopisme philosophique: Platon", p.51-72.)

V G: POLITICS AND SOCIETY

3542 ROMILLY J. DE, "Le classement des constitutions
d'Hérodote à Aristote". REG LXXII 1959 81-99.

3543* TOUCHARD J. [et alii], Histoire des idées
politiques, I: Des origines au XVIIIe siècle.
Coll. Thémis, Paris, Presses Universitaires
1959 XII, 382&vip. (Plato, p.28-36.)
Rev. RH CCXXIII 1960 135-136 Droz.
SZG IX 1959 586-587 von Albertini.
REA LXI 1959 517-521 Labrousse.
TG LXXIII 1960 266-268 Schaper.
EPh XV 1960 127-128 Arbousse-Bastide.

3544 VILJOEN G. VAN N., "Plato and Aristotle on the
exposure of infants at Athens". AClass II 1959
58-69.

3545 WEISS T., "Consideraţii asupra evoluţiei concepţilor
utopice în Antichitatea Greacă [Considerations
on the Evolution of the Concept of Utopia in
Greek Antiquity]" [in Rumanian with Russian &
French summaries]. SUCPh IV,2 1959 139-161.

3546* BARKER E., Greek Political Theory. Plato and his
Predecessors. Univ. Paperbacks, New York,
Barnes & Noble and London, Methuen 1960 468p.

3547 COLEMAN W.R., "Knowledge and Freedom in the
Political Philosophy of Plato". Ethics LXXI
1960 41-45.

3548 DAVIS M., "The Place of Law in projected Platonic
Cities". SO XXXVI 1960 72-85.

3549* LABROUSSE R., Introduction à la philosophie
politique, trad. de l'espagnol par Labrousse E.
Bibl. des Sciences polit. & soc., Paris,
Rivière 1960 294p.

3550 LLEDÓ IÑIGO E., "Philosophos basleus (Platón,
República 473d-e)". RFil(Madrid) XIX 1960
37-55.

3551 MASSIMI A., "Introduzione all'ellenismo, II: La
fine delle polis e la nuova società". GIF XIII
1960 114-133.

3552* MAYR F., Das Freiheitsproblem in Platons
Staatschriften. Diss. Wien 1960 289p.

3553 MONDOLFO R., "Platón y el concepto unitario de la cultura humano". p.109-120 in Mondolfo R., En los orígenes de la filosofía de la cultura. Buenos Aires, Hachette 1960.

3554 RANFT H., "Platons Grundsätze der Auslese". Altertum VI 1960 149-152.

3555 ARNOLD K.H., "Zu Platons Grundsätzen und seinem Staat". Altertum VII 1961 19-24.

3556* SAUER R., Untersuchung zum platonischen Freiheitsbegriff. Diss. Frankfurt 1960 145p.
Rev. RPhL LXVIII 1970 263 Jordens.

3557 KOEVENDI D., "Die kosmische Freiheit bei Platon". Helikon VI 1966 696-704.

3558* WAŚKIEWICZ H., History of the Philosophy of Law. The Philosophy of Law in Antiquity, I: Greece. Pre-Attic and Attic Philosophy of Law [in Polish]. Rozprawy Wydz. Nauk Spol. Towarz. Nauk. Katol. Uniw. Lubelskiego XIII, Lublin 1960 109p. (ch.3 "Sokrates", p.67-75; ch.4 "Platon", p.76-87.)
Rev. Eos LI 1961 384-386 Chodorowski.
BCO X 1965 47-50 [German summary].

3559 BUCCELLATO M., "Linguaggio e società alle origini del pensiero filosofico greco". [article in 4 parts.] RSF XV 1960 339-353, XVI 1961 3-32, 259-277, 363-384.

3560 DIAMOND S., "Plato and the Definition of the Primitive". p.118-141 in Culture in History. Essays in Honor of P. Radin, ed. by Diamond S. New York, Columbia Univ. Pr. 1961.

3561* FOSTER M.B., Plato to Machiavelli. Boston, Houghton Mifflin 1961 ix&302p.

3562* GAISER K., Platon und die Geschichte. Tübingen Antrittsvorles. 1960, Stuttgart, Frommann-Holzboog 1961 42p.
Rev. RecSR L 1962 608 des Places.
Gregorianum XLIII 1962 627 Díaz de Cerio.
Gnomon XXXV 1963 211 Waldenfels.
Platon XV 1963 389-392 Georgoulis.
Gymnasium LXXI 1964 397 de Vogel.
AGPh XLV 1963 75-79 Voigtlaender.
RThPh XIV 1964 58 Rivier.
GM XX 1965 371-373 Chiereghin.

3563* MANELI M., Historia doktryn polityczno-prawnych, I: Starożytność [History of Political and Juridical Doctrines, I: Antiquity] [in Polish]. Warszawa, Uniw. Warsz. Dzial Wydawnictw. 1961 327p.

3564 MEYERHOFF H., "Plato among Friends and Enemies". Encounter, Dec. 1961 45-50. Reprinted as p.187-198 in Plato, Popper and Politics, ed. by Bambrough R. (see 4583).

3565* PERNICE G., Delineazioni informative per uno studio del pensiero politico di Platone. Stasimon, Periodico del Liceo-Gynn. Carlo Varese di Tortona 1961 10p.

3566* SINCLAIR T.A., Il pensiero politico classico a cura di Firpo L., trad. da Giorgi A.S. & Zallone E. Coll. storica, Bari, Laterza 1961 xvi&529p. Also in English, A History of Greek Political Thought. Cleveland/New York, Meridian Books 1968 x&345p. (ch. 5 on Socrates; chs. 7-10 on Plato.)
Rev. PP XVI 1961 233-240 Lepore.
GIF XIV 1961 277-278 Marmorale.
RFIC XL 1962 80-83 Lana.
RCCM IV 1962 265-281 Pavan.

3567 STOCKHAMMER M., "Reine Rechtsphilosophie. Eine Platon-Studie". ARSPh XLVII 1961 333-354.

3568* TOZZI G., Economisti greci e romani. Milano, Feltrinelli 1961 514p. (ch.3 "Presupposti politici in Platone", p.49-122.)

3569 VOURVERIS K.I., "Τὸ νόημα τοῦ πολιτικοῦ φαινομένου τῆς ζωῆς (Αἰσχύλος-Πλάτων)". EEAth XI 1960-1961 249-265.

3570 WILD J., "Plato and Natural Law". OEZOR 1961 177-200.

3571 BAMBROUGH J.R., "Plato's Modern Friends and Enemies". Philosophy XXXVII 1962 97-113. Reprinted p.3-19 in Plato, Popper and Politics, ed. by Bambrough R. (see 4583).

3572 BAXTER J.F.G., "Plato and Modern Justice". GM XVII 1962 135-156.

412

V G: POLITICS AND SOCIETY

3573 CHROUST A.H., "A Second (and Closer) Look at Plato's
Political Philosophy". ARSPh XLVIII 1962
449-486.

3574* DI LEONARDO G., Il problema dello stato presso i
Sofisti, Platone, Aristotele. Sistemazione
organica. Palermo, U. Manfredi 1962 72p.

3575 FOY E., "The Value of Idealism for Political
Philosophy". PhilosStud(Irel) XI 1961-1962
147-157.

3576 GIGON O., "Platon und die politische Wirklichkeit".
Gymnasium LXIX 1962 205-219. Reprinted
p.225-241 in Gigon O., Studien zur antiken
Philosophie (see 4597).

3577 HERTER H., "Platons Staatsideal in zweierlei
Gestalt". p.177-195 in Der Mench und die
Künste, Festschrift H. Lützler. Düsseldorf,
Schwann 1962.

3578 KODRĘBSKI J., "Plato and the Problem of Slavery" [in
Polish]. LodskiZN 1962 3-18.

3579 MAYR F., "Freiheit und Bindung in Platons Politeia".
WS LXXV 1962 28-50.

3580* POPPER K.R., The Open Society and its Enemies. Vol.
I: The Spell of Plato. 4th edn. revised.
London, Routledge & Kegan Paul 1962/New York,
Harper & Row 1963 xi&351p. Also 5th edn.
revised: London, Routledge & Kegan Paul 1966
xi&361p.
Rev. Personalist XLVI 1965 399-401
O'Neill.

3581 POPPER K.R., "Plato as Enemy of the Open Society".
p.41-102 in Plato, Totalitarian or Democrat?,
ed. by Thorson T.L. (see 4617). Major
portions of chs.6-8 of Popper K.R., The Open
Society and its Enemies.

3582 POPPER K.R., "Reply to a Critic (1961)". Addendum
to The Open Society and its Enemies, vol. I.
Reprinted p.199-219 in Plato, Popper and
Politics, ed. by Bambrough R. (see 4583).

3583 REVERDIN O., "Crise spirituelle et évasion".
p.83-120 in Grecs et Barbares. Entretiens sur
l'antiquité classique VIII, Genève-Vandoeuvres,
Fondation Hardt 1962.

413

3584 SANTONASTASO G., "Il pensiero politico de Platone ed
      Aristotele". p.77-123 in Momenti di storia
      della filosofia, a cura di diversi autori.
      Orientamenti filosofici e pedagogici I, Milano,
      Marzorati 1962.

3585* TSATSOS C.I., 'Η κοινωνικὴ φιλοσοφία τῶν ἀρχαίων
      'Ελλήνων. Athens, Diphros 1962. 2nd edn.
      Athens, Hestia 1970 328p. French transl. La
      philosophie sociale des anciens Grecs, trad.
      Duisit F., avant-propos de Merlier O. Coll.
      Pensées, Paris, Nagel 1971 343p. (ch.6 on
      Socrates; ch.8-11 on Plato.)
            Reviews of French transl. Philosophia I
      1971 454-457 Bayonas.
            RS XCIII 1972 314-315 Mortley.
            NRTh XCIV 1972 741 Jacobs.

3586 WALSH W.H., "Plato and the Philosophy of History:
      History and Theory in the Republic". HistTheor
      II 1962 3-16.

3587 BRAUNERT H., "Theorie, Ideologie und Utopie im
      griechisch-hellenistischen Staatsdenken". GWU
      XIV 1963 145-158.

3588 CROSSMAN R.H.S., "Plato and the Perfect State".
      p.15-40 in Plato, Totalitarian or Democrat?, ed.
      by Thorson T.L. (see 4617). (excerpt from
      Crossman, R.H.S., Plato Today. 2nd edn. 1959.)

3589 CROSSON F.J., "Plato's Statesman: Unity and
      'Pluralism". NS XXXVII 1963 28-43.

3590 FARIAS D., "Alle radici della concezione platonica
      del bene comune". RFNeo LV 1963 577-594.

3591 HALLOWELL J.H., "Plato and the Moral Foundation of
      Democracy". p.129-150 in Plato, Totalitarian or
      Democrat? ed. by Thorson T.L. (see 4617).
      Excerpt from Hallowell J.H., The Moral
      Foundation of Democracy. Chicago, Univ. of
      Chicago Pr. 1954.

3592 SAUNDERS T.J., "Two Points in Plato's Penal Code".
      CQ XIII 1963 194-199.

3593 STRAUSS L., "On Classical Political Philosophy".
      p.153-170 in Plato, Totalitarian or Democrat?,
      ed. by Thorson T.L. (see 4617). Reprinted
      from SocRes XII 1945 98-117.

V G: POLITICS AND SOCIETY

3594 STRAUSS L., "Plato". p.7-63 in A History of
Political Philosophy, ed. by Strauss L. &
Cropsey J. Chicago, Rand McNalley 1963. (2nd
edn. 1971).

3595 TRIANTAPHYLLOPOULOS J., "Τὰ κένα τοῦ νόμου ἐν τῷ
ἀρχαίῳ Ἑλληνικῷ δικαίῳ (θεωρία Ἀριστοτέλους καὶ
μεθοδολογία Θουκυδίδου)". EEN XXX 1963 753-758.

3596* UCHTENHAGEN A., Zur Lehre von der Macht. Platon,
Aristoteles, Machiavelli. Zürich, Juris-Verl.
1963 196p.

3597 WELSKOPF E.C., "Zur Entstehung der Utopie bei
Platon". WZBer XII 1963 229-235.

3598 WILD J., "Plato as an Enemy of Democracy: A
Rejoinder". p.105-128 in Plato, Totalitarian or
Democrat?, ed. by Thorson T.L. (see 4617).
Excerpt from Wild J., Plato's Modern Enemies and
the Theory of Natural Law. Chicago, Univ. of
Chicago Pr. 1953.

3599* ANDERSON W., Man's Quest for Political Knowledge.
The Study and Teaching of Politics in Ancient
Times. Minneapolis, Univ. of Minnesota Pr.
1964 ix&381p. (Ch.7 "Socrates and Political
Education" p.203-213; ch.8 "Plato and
anti-politics", p.214-239.)
        Rev. CW LVII 1964 15 Frost.
        LJ 1964 3011 Heimanson.
        CJ LX 1964 133 Samuel.
        AAAPSS 1965 172 Jones.
        Latomus XXIV 1965 987 Liebmann-Frankfort.
        RSC XIII 1965 240 Verdière.
        CPh LX 1965 196-198 Oost.
        AHR LXX 1964-1965 505-506 Brown.
        CR XV 1965 340-341 Murray.
        JHPh IV 1966 250 Doyle.
        Thought 1966 318 Constanzo.
        JHS LXXXVIII 1967 170-171 Caven.

3600 DAVIS M., "On the Imputed Possibilities of
Callipolis and Magnesia". AJPh LXXXV 1964
394-411.

3601 DERBOLAV J., "Ursprungsmotive und Prinzipien des
Platonischen Staatsdenkens". KantStud LV 1964
260-305.

3602 DÍEZ DEL CORRAL L., "La actualidad del pensamiento politico de Platón y su doctrina del regimen mixto". p.283-300 in Actas II Congr. esp. de Estud. clás. (Madrid-Barcelona, 4-10 de abril de 1961). Publ. de la Soc. Esp. de Estud. Clás. V, Madrid 1964.

3603* HARMON M.J., Political Thought. From Plato to the Present. New York, McGraw-Hill 1964 469p. (ch.3: "Plato", p.29-52.)

3604 VLACHOS G., "Le principe de légalité et l'idée de l'"homme royal" dans la pensée de Platon". p.193-213 in Le droit subjectif en question. Archives de philosophie du droit IX, Paris, Éd. Sirey 1964.

3605* OPRIŞAN M., Economic Thought in Ancient Greece. Xenophon, Plato, Aristotle [in Rumanian]. Bucureşti Ed. Acad. RPR 1964 299p. German summary in BCO X 1965 304-309.

3606* PAPANIKOLAOU K.N., Ἡ πλατωνικὴ φιλοσοφία τῆς ἱστορίας. Συμβολή: Ἐπιστημ. Ἔκδοσις Ἰωνιδείου Πρότυπου Σχολῆς Πειραιῶς, Athens 1964 65p.

3607* ROEHRIG P., Politische Bildung. Herkunft und Aufgabe. Stuttgart, Klett 1964 280p.
        Rev. PaedagRdsch XXI 1967 531-532 Poeggeler.

3608 SCHOTTLAENDER R., "Der Streit um Platon". Altertum X 1964 142-154.

3609 MENDE G., "Zum 'Streit um Platon'". Altertum X 1964 230-234.

3610 SCHWARZKOPF E., "Kritische Anmerkung zum Streit um Platon". Altertum XI 1965 137-143.

3611 KOEVENDI D., "Reflexionen zum Streit um Platon". Altertum XII 1966 15-17. Also in Hungarian: "Egy Platón-vitáról". MFS X 1966 323-327.

3612 VLASTOS G., "ΙΣΟΝΟΜΙΑ ΠΟΛΙΤΙΚΗ". p.1-35 in Isonomia. Studien zur Gleichheitsvorstellung im griechischen Denken, hrsg. von Mau J. & Schmidt E.G. Dt. Akad. der Wiss. Arbeitsgr. für hell.-röm. Philos. IX, Berlin, Akad.-Verl. 1964. Also verbess. Nachdr., Amsterdam, Hakkert 1971. Reprinted p.164-203 in Vlastos G., Platonic Studies (see 4622).

3613* VOURVERIS K.I., Zum Begriff der Gemeinschaft bei
      Platon. ῾Ελλην. ᾽Ανθρωπ. ῾Εταιρεια, Σειρά 1:
      ᾽Αρχαιότης καὶ σύγχρονα προβλήματα XXV, Athens
      1964 14p.

3614 VOURVERIS K.I., "Zum Begriff der Gemeinschaft bei
      Platon". EEAth XV 1964-1965 47-58.

3615 WROBLEWSKI W., "Utopijny charakter Panstwa Platona
      [The utopian Character of Plato's State]" [in
      Polish]. Filomata(Krakow) no.182 1964 114-124.

3616* AGARD W., What Democracy meant to the Greeks.
      Madison/Milwaukee/London, Univ. of Wisconsin
      Pr. 1965 x&278p. (ch.15, "Plato's Appraisal"
      p.206-220.)

3617* FOSTER M.B., The Political Philosophies of Plato and
      Hegel. New York, Russell & Russell 1965
      xiii&207p. Also New York, Oxford Univ. Pr.
      1968. Reprint of 1935 edn. (Plato, p.1-71;
      Hegel's Criticism of Plato, p.72-109.)

3618* GOULDNER A.W., Enter Plato. Classical Greece and
      the Origins of Social Theory. New York, Basic
      Books 1965 and London, Routledge & Kegan Paul
      1967 xiv&407p.
            Rev. CJ LXII 1966 132-133 Berry.
            CW LX 1966 14 Bacon.
            AmSocR XXXI 1966 548-549 Vlastos.
            CrossCurr XVI 1966 168 Collins.
            NYRB 18 Aug. 1966 27 Finley.
            Phoenix XXI 1967 149-150 Gallop.
            CPh LXII 1967 155-156 Oost.
            BJSoc 1967 198-199 Hopkins.
            CCHist XV 1967 210-219 Nová & Sláma.
            TLS 26 Oct. 1967 1012.
            Economist 17 June 1967 1246.
            Eirene VII 1968 119-124 Oliva.
            PhilosQ XVIII 1968 360-361 Adkins.
            RPortFil XXIV 1968 440-441 Freire.
            CR XIX 1969 43-44 Baldry.
            Dialogue VII 1968-1969 315-318 Dybikowski.
            cf. Gouldner, "On Hopkins' Review of my
      Enter Plato", BJSoc 1967 451-453.

3619* GRENE D., Greek Political Theory. The Image of Man
      in Thucydides and Plato. Originally publ. in
      1950 as Man in his Pride. Chicago, Univ. of
      Chicago Pr. 1965 229p. (Part II, p.95-204 on
      Plato.)

3620* JOSHI N., Political Ideals of Plato. Bombay, Manaktalas 1965 127p.

3621* KAGAN D., The Great Dialogue. History of Greek Political Thought from Homer to Polybius. Hist. of Western Thought & Sources of Western Polit. Thought I, New York, Free Pr. 1965 xiii&274p. (ch.7 "Politics and Morality: The Sophists and Socrates" p.113-132; ch.9 "Plato" p.155-194.)
Rev. TLS 26 Aug. 1965 738.
CW LIX 1965-1966 81 Stewart.
CPh LXI 1966 113-114 Oost.
AHR LXXI 1966 522-523 Finley.
CJ LXI 1966 378-379 McGregor.
Athenaeum XLIV 1966 172-175 Perlman.
PP XX 1965 261-274 Levi.

3622 LEYS W.A.R., "Was Plato Non-political?". Ethics LXXV 1965 272-276. Reprinted (with "An Afterthought". p.184-186) p.166-173 in Plato II, ed. by Vlastos G. (see 4620).

3623 SPARSHOTT F.E., "Plato as Anti-Political Thinker". Ethics LXXVII 1967 214-219. Reprinted p.174-183 in Plato II, ed. by Vlastos G. (see 4620).

3624* LIBRIZZI C., Platone o la ricerca della libertà. 2a ed. Padova, Cedam 1965 viii&211p. Also Pubbl. dell'Ist. univ. di Magistero di Catania. Serie filosofica: Saggi e monografie LI, Padova, Cedam 1968 212p.
Rev. Sophia XXXIV 1966 123-125 d'Orsi.
Helmantica XXII 1971 340 Reta.

3625 MAGUIRE J.P., "The Individual and the Class in Plato's Republic". CJ LX 1965 145-150.

3626 PÉTREMENT S., "Platon et l'esclavage". RMM LXX 1965 213-225.

3627* ROMUALDI A., Platone (La critica alla democrazia). Roma, Volpe 1965 135p.

3628 THEILER W., "Νόμος ὁ πάντων βασιλεύς". MH XXII 1965 69-80.

3629 TOVAR A., "Sobre la teoría política de Sócrates y Platón". EClas IX 1965 No.44 65-75. (Followed by discussion, p.77-103.)

3630 VOURVERIS K.I., Η ἑλληνικη συνείδησις τοῦ Πλάτωνος". EEAth XV 1964-1965 498-513.

3631* BAYONAS A.C., The Idea of Legislation in the Earlier Platonic Dialogues. Athens 1966 189p. Rev. RPhilos 1968 287-288 Somville.

3632 BAYONAS A.C., "The Idea of Legislation in the earler Platonic Dialogues" [in English with Greek summary]. Platon XVII 1965 26-116, XVIII 1966 103-177.

3633 BORECKÝ B., "Platon und Isonomia". LF LXXXIX 1966 245-251.

3634 CUFFEL V., "The Classical Greek Concept of Slavery". JHI XXVII 1966 323-342.

3635* FASSO G., Storia della filosofia del diritto, I: Antichità e medioevo. Bologna, Ed. Il Mulino 1966 368p. (ch.3 "Socrate e i Socratici minori", p.53-64; ch.4 "Platone", p.65-80.)

3636 FERGUSON J., "Plato and Politics". N&C IX 1966 12-27.

3637 HINTIKKA J., "Yksilö ja valtion päämäärät". Ajatus XXVIII 1966 23-37. Reprinted p.75-87 in Hintikka J., Tieto on Valtaa (see 4600); also in English "Some Conceptual Presuppositions of Greek Political Theory", Scandinavian Political Studies II 1967 11-25.

3638* IMAI N., Study on Plato's Doctrine of Ideal State. Kyoto, Horitsu-bunkasha 1966 360p.

3639 JOHNSON V.L., "Plato in America". CB XLIII 1966 1-6, 19-23.

3640 KLINZ A., "Platon und die Politik". PaedProv XX 1966 215-227.

3641* NORTH H., Sophrosyne. Self-knowledge and Self-restraint in Greek Literature. Ithaca, Cornell Univ. Pr. 1966 xx&391p. (ch.4 Plato, p.150-196.)

3642* PATZER H., Die Entstehung der wissenschaftlichen Politik bei den Griechen. Sitz.-Ber. Wiss. Ges. Frankfurt IV,2, Wiesbaden, Steiner 1966 22p.

V G: POLITICS AND SOCIETY

3643* RODRÍGUEZ ADRADOS F., Ilustración y Política en la
Grecia Clásica. Madrid, Revista de Occidente
1966 588p. (part 3 "Sócrates y Platón y su
nuevo planteamiento", ch.1 "El moralismo
socrático", p.489-524; ch.2 "La alternativa
platónica", p.525-554.)

3644 TSATSOS K., "Πλάτωνος Πολιτικά, I: Οἱ σκόποι τῆς
Πολιτείας; II: Οἱ ἄρχοντες καὶ οἱ Νόμοι". PAA
XLI 1966 1-53.

3645 VERDROSS A., "Die Begründung der antiken
Rechtsphilosophie durch Hesiod". AAWW CIII 1966
23-32.

3646* VOURVERIS K.I., Die Geschichte als ancilla
philosophiae bei Platon [in German and Greek].
Ἑλλην. Ἀνθρωπ. Ἑταιρ. Σειρά 1: Ἀρχαιότης καὶ
σύγχρονα προβλήματα XXXII, Athens 1966 18p.
Also see EEAth XVI 1965-1966 141-147. Also
p.67-72 in Vourveris K.I., Studien zur
Geschichte und Philosophie des Altertums.
Budapest, Akad. Kiadó 1968.

3647* VOURVERIS K.I., Ἱστορικαὶ γνώσεις τοῦ Πλάτωνος,
Α': Βαρβαρικά, α': Πλάτων καὶ Βάρβαροι.
2nd edn.; Β': Ἑλληνικὰ, β': Πλάτων καὶ Ἀθῆναι.
2nd edn. Ἑλλην. Ἀνθρωπ. Ἑταιρ. Σειρά 2, Μελέται
καὶ Ἔρευναι X & XI, Athens 1966 181 & 243p.
Rev. CR XVIII 1968 352 Thomson.

3648* VOURVERIS K.I., Ἱστορικαὶ γνώσεις τοῦ Πλάτωνος, Β':
Ἑλληνικά II, Τόμος Γ': Πλάτων καὶ Ἕλληνες πλὴν
Ἀθηναίων, μέρος 1. Κείμενον: Δημοσιεύμ. τῆς
Ἑλλην. ἀνθρωπ. Ἑταιρ. Σειρά 2, Μελέται καὶ
Ερευναι XXV, Athens 1973 61p.

3649 ACTON H.B., "The alleged Fascism of Plato". p.38-48
in Plato, Popper and Politics, ed. by Bambrough
R. (see 4583). Reprinted from Philosophy XIII
1938 302-312.

3650 BAMBROUGH R., "Plato's Political Analogies".
p.152-169 in Plato, Popper and Politics, ed. by
Bambrough R. (see 4583). Also p.187-205 in
Plato II, ed. by Vlastos G. (see 4620).
Reprinted from Philosophy, Politics, and
Society, ed. by Laslett P. Oxford, Blackwell
1956 98-115.

3651 BAYONAS A., "L'art politique d'après Protagoras". RPhilos CLVII 1967 43-58.

3652* CAIRNS H., Legal Philosophy from Plato to Hegel. Baltimore, Johns Hopkins Pr. 1967 583p. Reprint of 1949 edn. (ch.2 "Plato", p.29-76.)

3653 FIELD G.C., "On Misunderstanding Plato". p.71-84 in Plato, Popper and Politics, ed. by Bambrough R. (see 4583). Reprinted from Philosophy XIX 1944 49-62.

3654 GOMBRICH E.H., "The Open Society--A Comment". p.146-148 in Plato, Popper and Politics, ed. by Bambrough R. (see 4583). Reprinted from BJSoc III 1952 358-360.

3655 HOERNLÉ R.F.A., "Would Plato have approved of the National-Socialist State?". p.20-36 in Plato, Popper and Politics, ed. by Bambrough R. (see 4583). Reprinted from Philosophy XIII 1938 166-182.

3656 KAKU A., "Plato's Politics" [in Japanese]. Riso no.409 1967.

3657 KRAEMER H.J., "Das Problem der Philosophenherrschaft bei Platon". PhJ LXXIV 1967 254-270.

3658* MORRIS C., Western Political Thought, I: Plato to Augustine. New York, Basic Books 1967 xi&282p. (ch.2 "Plato", p.35-79.)

3659* O'DAY J.J., Plato's Theory of Political Justice. Thesis, The American Univ. 1967 147p. [microfilm]. Summary in MAb V,3 1967 18.

3660 PLAMENATZ J., "The Open Society--A Rejoinder". p.149-151 in Plato, Popper and Politics, ed. by Bambrough R. (see 4583). Reprinted from BJSoc IV 1953 76-77.

3661 PLAMENATZ J., "The Open Society and its Enemies". p.136-145 in Plato, Popper and Politics, ed. by Bambrough R. (see 4583). Reprinted from BJSoc III 1952 264-273.

3662 RANDALL J.H., "Plato's Treatment of the Theme of the good Life and his Criticism of the Spartan Ideal". JHI XXVIII 1967 307-324.

3663 RUESS H., "Rechtskunde und Heilkunde in Platons Staat". p.95-104 in Μελήματα. Festschrift für Werner Liebbrand zum 70. Geburtstag, hrsg. von Schumacher J. Mannheim, Boehringer 1967.

3664 RUSSELL B., "Philosophy and Politics". p.109-134 in Plato, Popper and Politics, ed. by Bambrough R. (see 4583). Reprinted from Russell B., Unpopular Essays. London, Allen & Unwin 1950, p.9-34.

3665 RYLE G., Review of K.R. Popper, The Open Society and its Enemies. p.85-90 in Plato, Popper and Politics, ed. by Bambrough R. (see 4583). Reprinted from Mind 1948 167-172.

3666 SOLOMON J.H.M., "Exousia in Plato". Platon XIX 1967 189-197.

3667 UNGER E., "Contemporary Anti-Platonism". p.91-107 in Plato, Popper and Politics, ed. by Bambrough R. (see 4583). Reprinted from The Cambridge Journal 1949 643-659.

3668* CHANCE R., Until Philosophers are Kings. A Study of the Political Theory of Plato and Aristotle in Relation to the Modern State, with a foreword by Laski H.J. Port Washington, New York, Kennikat Pr. 1968 293p. Reprint of 1928 edn.

3669 CHATELET F., "Remarques sur le concept de violence". EPh XXIII 1968 31-38.

3670 FINLEY M.I., "Plato and Practical Politics". p.73-88 in Finley M.I., Aspects of Antiquity. London, Chatto & Windus/New York, Viking 1968. Reprinted from The Listener.

3671 FREIRE A., "A Pólis ideal secundo Platão". RPortFil XXIV 1968 389-411.

3672 GUNNELL J.G., Political Philosophy and Time. Middletown, Conn., Wesleyan Univ. Pr. 1968 x&314p. (chs. 5-6 on Plato.)

3673 HALL R.W., "The Individual and the State in Plato's Republic". p.430-436 in Akten XIV. Intern. Kongr. Philos. Wien, 2.-9. September 1968. Vol. V. Wien, Herder 1968.

3674 HINSKE N., "Zwischen Demoskopie und Experten. Über die Aktualität Platons und die gegenwärtige Lage der Bundesrepublik". NDH CXIX 1968 113-121.

3675 KUHN H., "Plato". p.1-35 in Klassiker des politischen Denkens, I: von Plato bis Hobbes, hrsg. von Maier H. et alii. München, Beck 1968.

3676 KUYPERS K., "Het cultuurbegrip der Grieken en het cultuurideaal van Plato". p.112-132 in Kuypers K., Verspreide geschriften, I: Mens en geschiedenis. Assen, van Gorcum 1968.

3677* LESKY A., Der Kampf um die Rechtsidee im griechischen Denken [with Greek summary]. Ἕλλην. Ἄνθρωπ. Ἑταιρεία Σειρά 2 XVIII, Athens 1968 30p.

3678 MINDÁN M., "Verdad y libertad". RFil(Madrid) XXVII 1968 5-26.

3679 MOGGI M., "La tradizione sulle guerre persiane in Platone". SCO XVII 1968 213-226.

3680 PONS A., "Tyrannie, politique et philosophie". EPh XXIII 1968 169-184.

3681 SANDVOSS E., "Asebie und Atheismus im klassischen Zeitalter der griechischen Polis". Saeculum XIX 1968 312-329.

3682* STRAUSS L., Liberalism Ancient and Modern. New York/London, Basic Books 1968 xi&276p. (ch.4 "On the Minos", p.65-75.) Also Italian transl. Liberalismo antico e moderno, trad. di Antonelli S. & Geraci C. Milano, Giuffrè 1973 339p.

3683 TRIANTAPHYLLOPOULOS I., "Τὰ πραγματικὰ ἐλαττώματα τοῦ πωληθέντος κατὰ τὰ ἀρχαῖα Ἑλληνικὰ δίκαια ἐξαιρέσει τῶν παπύρων". EEN XXXV 1968 1-11.

3684* VIDALIN J., Pouvoir et dialectique, I: La pensée politique de la Grèce. Fac. de Droit et des Sciences Economiques de Rennes 1968 217p.
    Rev. RESE IX 1971 325-326 Piatkowski.

3685* WOLF E., Griechisches Rechtsdenken, IV,1: Platon. Frühdialoge und Politeia. Frankfurt, Klostermann 1968 437p.
    Rev. Erasmus XX 1968 361-366 Lasserre.

V G: POLITICS AND SOCIETY

RecSR LVI 1968 620 des Places.
DLZ XC 1969 683-684 Doent.
Gymnasium LXXVI 1969 541-543 Poláček.
PhilosRdschau XVII 1970 274-280 Sandvoss.

3686* WOLF E., Griechisches Rechtsdenken, IV: Platon, 2: Dialoge der mittleren und späteren Zeit. Briefe. Frankfurt, Klostermann 1970 480p. Rev. Erasmus XXIII 1971 246-248 Lasserre.

3687 ARDLEY G.W.R., "The Meaning of Plato's Marital Communism". PhilosStud(Irel) XVIII 1969 36-47.

3688 BIEN G., "Das Theorie-Praxis-Problem und die politische Philosophie bei Platon und Aristoteles". PhJ LXXVI 1968-1969 264-314.

3689* BYKER D., Plato's Philosophy of Natural Law as a Key to his View of Persuasion. Diss. Univ. of Michigan 1969 132p. [microfilm]. Summary in DA XXXI 1970 847A-848A.

3690 DAVIS M., "Monetary Fines and Limitations in Plato's Magnesia". CPh LXIV 1969 98-101.

3691 GUNDERT H., "θεῖος im politischen Denken Platos". p.91-107 in Politeia und Res Publica. Beiträge zum Verständnis von Politik, Recht und Staat in der Antike, dem Andenken Rudolf Starks gewidmet, hrsg. von Steinmetz P. Palingenesia, Monogr. & Texte zur klass. Altertumswiss. IV, Wiesbaden, Steiner 1969.

3692 HAHM D.E., "Platos 'noble lie' and political Brotherhood". C&M XXX 1969 211-227.

3693 HERTER H., "Urathen der Idealstaat". p.108-134 in Politeia und Res Publica. Beiträge zum Verständnis von Politik, Recht und Staat in der Antike, dem Andenken Rudolf Starks gewidmet, hrsg. von Steinmetz P. Palingenesia, Monogr. & Texte zur klass. Altertumswiss. IV, Wiesbaden, Steiner 1969.

3694 JOLY R., "Esclaves et médecins dans la Grèce antique". AGM LIII 1969 1-14.

3695 LEITZ A., "Gerechtigkeit und Gesetz bei Plato und Xenophon". AU XII 1969,2 104-121.

3696* MOSSÉ C., Histoire des doctrines politiques en
Grèce. Coll. Que sais-je? No.1340, Paris,
Presses Universitaires 1969 128p. (for Plato
see especially ch.3 "Le développement de la
pensée politique au IVe siècle", p.44-93.)
Rev. RBPh XLVII 1969 1078-1079 Verdin.
RD XLVII 1969 735-736 Imbert.
G&R XVI 1969 226 Sewter.
REG LXXXIII 1970 214 Weil.
CPh LXV 1970 141-142 Larsen.
RH XCV 1971 No.246 99 Will.
History LVI 1971 78-79 Rodewald.

3697* MOULAKIS A., Homonoia. Untersuchungen zum
politischen Denken der Griechen. Diss. Bochum
1969. (ch.5 on Plato.)
Rev. ABG XIII 1969 101 Moulakis.

3698 NEUMANN H., "The Philosophy of Individualism. An
Interpretation of Thucydides". JHPh VII 1969
237-246.

3699 ROBINSON R., "Dr. Popper's Defence of Democracy".
p.74-99 in Robinson R., Essays in Greek
Philosophy (see 4612). Reprinted from PhR 1951.

3700 ROHRMOSER G., "Platons politische Philosophie".
StudGen XXII 1969 1094-1134.

3701 STARK R., "Die Einheit von Ethik und Politik im
griechischen Staatsdenken bis Aristoteles". A&A
XV 1969 24-28.

3702 STENZEL J., "Wissenschaft und Staatsgesinnung bei
Platon". p.96-108 in Das Platonbild, hrsg. von
Gaiser K. (see 4595). Reprinted from Rede zur
Reichgründungsfeier der
Christian-Albrechts-Universität, Kiel 1927.

3703 TENEKIDES G., "Platón, théoricien de l'organisation
internationale". ACUM XXII 1968-1969 63-78.

3704 TENEKIDES G., "Une ébauche d'organisation
internationale dans le Critias de Platon. Mythe
et réalité". Summary in REG LXXXII 1969,2
p.xxiv-xxv & REL XLVII 1969 9-10.

3705* XIROTYRIS I.N., Ἡ κοινωνιολογικὴ σκέψη καὶ ὁ
Πλάτων. Thessalonike 1969 90p.
Rev. Platon XXI 1969 386 Georgountzos.

3706* WAGNER F., Das Bild der frühen ökonomik. Salzburg/München, Stifterbibliothek 1969 222p. (p.87-115, 148-178, 189-199 on οἰκονόμος, οἰκονομικη in Plato.)
Rev. PLA XXIII 1970 76-79 Lumpe. PhilosRdschau XVII 1970 301-302 Goergemanns. PhJ LXXVIII 1971 228-229 Kuhn.

3707 WEBER-SCHAEFER P., "Platons Politeia". p.65-94 in Das politische Denken der Griechen. Klassische Politik von der Tragödie bis zu Polybios, hrsg. von Weber-Schaefer P. List Hochschulreihe. Gesch. des polit. Denkens Nr.1507, München, List 1969.

3708 WHEELER A.M., "Creativity in Plato's States". ET XIX 1969 249-255.

3709 SICHEL B.A., "Comments on Arthur M. Wheeler's 'Creativity in Plato's States'". ET XXI 1971 208-218.

3710 WHEELER A.M., "Creativity: A Rejoinder to Professor Sichel". ET XXII 1972 208-211.

3711 FEINBERG B.S., "Creativity and the Political Community: The Role of the Lawgiver in the Thought of Plato, Machiavelli and Rousseau". WPolQ XXIII 1970 471-484.

3712 GOLDBACH J., "Plato, Aristotle, and the new Metropolitics". WPolQ XXIII 1970 197-209.

3713 GOLDSCHMIDT V., "La théorie platonicienne de la dénonciation". p.173-201 in Goldschmidt V., Questions platoniciennes (see 4598). Reprinted from RMM 1953 352ff.

3714* HELLO G., La guerre chez Platon. Rennes, Inst. Armoricain de Rech. Hist. 1970.
Rev. ABret LXXIX 1972 482.

3715* LEVINSON R.B., In Defense of Plato. New York, Russell & Russell 1970 674p. Reprint of 1953 edn.

3716* MAURER R., Platons Staat und die Demokratie. Historisch-systematische Überlegungen zur politischen Ethik. Berlin, de Gruyter 1970 xvi&349p.
Rev. RIFD XLIX 1972 666-667.

DLZ XCII 1971 301-303 Schottlaender.
WJb V 1972 268-272 Heintel.

3717 MICHEL A., "De Socrate à Maxime de Tyr. Les problèmes sociaux de l'armée dans l'idéologie romaine". REL XLVIII bis. (Mélanges Durry) 1970 237-251.

3718 PIPERNEA E., "Plato's Theories and Aristotle's Conception of Sovereignty" [in Rumanian]. AUIJ XVI 1970 95-101.

3719 SINNIGE T.G., "Authority and Relations in Plato" [in Dutch with English summary]. TPh XXXII 1970 455-470.

3720 SPREY K., "Plato nu. De ideale staat". Hermeneus XLI 1970 275-288.

3721 TANDOI V., "Le donne ateniensi che non devono piangere". SIFC XLII 1970 154-178.

3722 TREU M., "Einwände gegen die Demokratie in der Literatur des 5.-4. Jh.". StudClas XII 1970 17-31.

3723* VOUDOURIS C., Soul and State, An Investigation on Plato's Conception of Politics [in Greek]. Athens, Univ. of Athens 1970 298p.

3724 VOUDOURIS C., "Ἡ εἰς τοὺς πρωίμους Πλατωνικοὺς διαλόγους περὶ ὑπάρξεως ἀντίληψις καὶ αἱ πολιτικαὶ αὐτῆς ὑποδηλώσεις". Platon XXII 1970 57-77.

3725* ANDERSSON T.J., Polis and Psyche. A Motif in Plato's Republic. Acta Univ. Gothoburg. Studia Graeca & Latina Gothoburg. XXX, Stockholm, Almqvist & Wiksell 1971 263p.
Rev. AC XLI 1972 662 Piérart.
Athenaeum LI 1973 453-454 Vegetti.
REA LXXV 1973 365-366 Vicaire.

3726 BARDIS P.D., "Overpopulation, the Ideal City, and Plato's Mathematics". Platon XXIII 1971 129-131.

3727 BAYONAS A., "Législation et dialectique d'après la République de Platón" [in French with Greek summary]. Philosophia(Athens) I 1971 274-295.

3728 BORECKÝ B., "Die politische Isonomie". Eirene IX 1971 5-24.

3729* CECI G., L'ideale politico di Platone. San Benedetto del Tronto, Tip. Ficcadendi 1971 24p.

3730 GRAESER A., "Bemerkungen zu Platons Versuch über den Rechtsstaat". A&A XVII 1971 91-95.

3731 ISRAEL R., "Plato versus Popper". Kinesis III 1971 103-110.

3732 MORROW G.R., "Plato and the Rule of Law". p.49-70 in Plato, Popper and Politics, ed. by Bambrough R. (see 4583). Also p.144-165 in Plato II, ed. by Vlastos G. (see 4620). Reprinted from PhR L 1941 105-126.

3733* MUELLER A., Autonome Theorien und Interessedenken. Studien zur politischen Philosophie bei Platon, Aristoteles und Cicero. Wiesbaden, Steiner 1971 150p.
     Rev. Latomus XXXII 1973 658-659 Boyancé.

3734 NEU J., "Plato's Analogy of State and Individual. The Republic and the Organic Theory of the State". Philosophy XLVI 1971 238-254.

3735 PIATKOWSKA A., "L'apparition du despotisme de type oriental dans la vision des penseurs grecs (Ve et IVe siècles av. n. ère)". p.391-397 in Acta Conventus XI Eirene, 21-25 oct. 1968. Warszawa, Ossolineum 1971.

3736 PINES S., "The Societies Providing for the bare Necessities of life according to Ibn Khaldūn and to the Philosophers". SIsl XXXIV 1971 125-138.

3737* ROMILLY J. DE, La loi dans la pensée grecque des origines à Aristote. Paris, Les Belles Lettres 1971 270p. (ch.6 "La Défense de Socrate: Le Contrat Sociale", p.115-138; ch.9 "Loi et Justice chez Platon", p.179-201.)
     Rev. CRAI 1971 657 Chantraine.
     MSR XXIX 1972 109 Dumortier.
     AC XLI 1972 718 de Ley.
     LEC XL 1972 443 Jacobs.
     ACR II 1972 227-228 Starr.
     ASNP II 1972 927-932 Lombardo.
     Emerita XL 1972 520-523 Roura.
     RFIC CI 1973 225-231 Battegazzore.
     GIF XXV 1973 74-75 Negri.

RD LI 1973 279-281 Houlou.
CW LXVI 1973 431-434 Ostwald.
JHS XCIII 1973 243-244 Lloyd-Jones.
Euphrosyne   VI   1973-1974   259-268
Nascimento.

3738 THOMAS Y., "Politique et droit chez Platon. La
nature du juste". ArchPD XVI 1971 119-130.

3739 VERSENYI L.G., "Plato and his liberal Opponents".
Philosophy XLVI 1971 222-237.

3740 VOGT J., "Die Sklaverei im utopischen Denken der
Griechen". RSA I 1971 19-32.

3741 BALL T., "Theory and Practice. An Examination of
the Platonic and Aristotelian Conceptions of
Political Theory". WPolQ XXV 1972 534-545.

3742 DESPOTOPOULOS C.I., " Σχόλια στὴν Πολιτειολογία τοῦ
Πλάτωνος" [in Greek with French summary].
Philosophia(Athens) II 1972 222-234.

3743 EIJK T.H.C. VAN, "Marriage and Virginity, Death and
Immortality". p.209-235 in Epektasis. Mélanges
patristiques offerts à Jean Daniélou, publ. par
Fontaine J. & Kannengiesser C. Paris,
Beauchesne 1972.

3744 ESTÉBANEZ E.G., "La índole social del hombre en una
muestra de autores antiguos y modernos".
EstFilos XXI 1972 111-139.

3745* ETEROVICH F.H., Approaches to Natural Law, from
Plato to Kant. Jericho, N.Y., Exposition Pr.
1972 194p. (For Socrates see p.27-28; for
Plato, p.28-30.)

3746 GOLDSCHMIDT V., "Les renversements du concept
d'égalité, des Anciens aux Modernes".
ArchPhilos XVII 1972 299-318.

3747* LINARES F., Der Philosoph und die Politik. Monogr.
z. philos. Forsch. XCI, Meisenheim, Hain 1972
127p.

3748* MILANI P.A., La schiavità nel pensiero politico dai
Greci al basso Medio Evo. Milano, Giuffrè 1972
402p. (for Plato see p.82-104.)

3749 OOSTHUIZEN D.C.S., "Popper, Plato and Plans". PhilPapers I 1972 67-81.

3750 VOLKMANN-SCHLUCK K.H., "Wie die Idee zur Utopie wurde". Praxis VIII 1972 39-46.

3751* WRÓBLEWSKI W., The Aristocratism of Plato [in Polish]. Warszawa, PWN 1972 120p.

3752 CUMMING A., "Pauline Christianity and Greek Philosophy. A Study of the Status of Women". JHI XXXIV 1973 517-528.

3753 DEMOS R. & TSATSOS K., "Plato's Political Philosophy" [in Greek with English summary]. Includes comments by Tsatsos on Demos' paper. Philosophia(Athens) III 1973 187-207.

3754 GIANNARAS A., "Platon und K.R. Popper. Zur Kritik der politischen Philosophie Platons" [in German with Greek summary]. Philosophia(Athens) III 1973 208-225.

3755 LAMB R., "The Paradox of System Builders: Plato and Hobbes". SocRes XL 1973 708-727.

3756 McCOY C.N.R., "On the Revival of Classical Political Philosophy". RevPol XXXV 1973 161-179.

3757 MERCIER-JOSA S., "Autorité, anarchisme". Referate des Antwerpener Hegel-Kongresses = Hegel-Jb 1973 27-58.

3758 OPOCHER E., "Legge e verità: riflessioni su di un passo platonico". RIFD L 1973 754-764.

3759 PIERCE C., "Equality. Republic V". Monist LVII 1973 1-11.

3760 PLENIO W., "Der Mensch als utopisches Wesen. Utopie-Modelle von Homer bis Marcuse". Gymnasium LXXX 1973 152-171.

3761* RAMEIL A., Die Wirtschaftsstabilität und ihre Problematik in Platons Gesetzesstaat. Diss. München. Fotodr. Frank 1973 88p.

3762 RIJK L.M. DE, "Plato, Popper en het fundament der samenleving" [in Dutch with English summary]. Lampas VI 1973 267-280.

3763   VILLERS R., "Sujets et citoyens   dans   l'antiquité".
       RIDA XX 1973 255-271.

3764   VLASTOS G., "Slavery in Plato's Thought".   p.147-163
       in Vlastos G., Platonic Studies (see 4622).
       Reprinted from PhR L 1941 289-303.   Also
       reprinted p.133-149 in Slavery in Classical
       Antiquity, ed. by Finley M.I.   Cambridge,
       Heffer 1960.

For additional studies related to these areas of Plato's
       thought see 239, 335, 439, 446, 631, 695, 1061,
       1071, 1156, 1184, 1288, 1377, 1385, 1424,   2026,
       2063, 2122, 2136, 2303, 2578, 3080, 3277, 3444,
       3765, 3907, 3924, 3951, 4122, 4124.

BOOKS AND ARTICLES ON PLATO'S POLITICAL
PHILOSOPHY IN GENERAL, INCLUDING
CHAPTERS ON THIS SUBJECT IN HISTORIES
OF POLITICAL PHILOSOPHY

For general treatments of these kinds, see the following
studies:
3527, 3528, 3534, 3539, 3540, 3541, 3543, 3546,
3549, 3561, 3563, 3565, 3566, 3573, 3574, 3584,
3594, 3599, 3603, 3617, 3621, 3629, 3640, 3642,
3643, 3656, 3658, 3668, 3672, 3675, 3684, 3696,
3700, 3702, 3707, 3733, 3741, 3747, 3753.

THE UTOPIAN CHARACTER OF PLATO'S STATES
AND THE QUESTION OF THEIR REALIZABILITY

These subjects are discussed in the following studies:
1378, 2028, 2119, 2123, 2130, 2135, 2878, 3522,
3537, 3545, 3575, 3577, 3587, 3589, 3597, 3600,
3601, 3615, 3638, 3662, 3670, 3671, 3688, 3693,
3729, 3742, 3750, 3755, 3760.

PLATO ON THE NATURE OF POLITICAL AUTHORITY
INCLUDING THE PHILOSOPHER KINGS

These subjects are treated in the following stueies:
199, 419, 1940, 2120, 2135, 2172, 3521, 3523,
3529, 3536, 3550, 3596, 3657, 3692, 3698, 3718,
3719, 3730, 3757, 3763.

PLATO AND FREEDOM, DEMOCRACY
AND TOTALITARIANISM

These subjects are discussed in the following studies:
446, 710, 1185, 1957, 2130, 2131, 3530, 3533,
3535, 3538, 3547, 3552, 3554, 3556, 3564, 3571,
3575, 3579, 3580, 3581, 3582, 3588, 3591, 3593,
3598, 3616, 3620, 3624, 3627, 3649, 3650, 3653,
3654, 3655, 3657, 3660, 3661, 3664, 3665, 3666,
3667, 3678, 3699, 3708, 3709, 3710, 3715, 3716,
3719, 3722, 3731, 3739, 3749, 3754, 3762, 3957.

PLATO'S POLITICAL VIEWS AND THEIR
CONTEMPORARY RELEVANCE

This subject is discussed in the following studies:
3538, 3572, 3636, 3639, 3655, 3668, 3674, 3720,
3771.

THE RELATION BETWEEN MAN AND STATE

This subject is discussed in the following studies:
1353, 2076, 2100, 2101, 2102, 2878, 3061, 3073,
3569, 3576, 3613, 3614, 3625, 3650, 3673, 3674,
3698, 3723, 3724, 3725, 3734, 3751.

POLITICAL ETHICS

This subject is discussed in the following studies:
1187, 2076, 2100, 2101, 2102, 2103, 2957, 3466,
3476, 3601, 3612, 3633, 3641, 3644, 3659, 3701,
3716, 3728, 3738, 3746, 3751, 3759.

PHILOSOPHY OF LAW AND NATURAL RIGHTS

This subject is discussed in the following studies:
1180, 1186, 1187, 1191, 1380, 1726, 1947, 2125,
2365, 3466, 3524, 3525, 3531, 3532, 3548, 3558,
3563, 3567, 3570, 3604, 3628, 3631, 3632, 3635,
3645, 3652, 3663, 3677, 3685, 3686, 3689, 3695,
3711, 3727, 3732, 3737, 3738, 3745, 3756, 3758.

PARTICULAR ISSUES IN THE ORGANIZATION AND
LEGISLATION OF PLATO'S STATES

These subjects are discussed in the following studies:
557, 1353, 1373, 1380, 1388, 1389, 1391, 1396,
1396, 1397, 1404, 1405, 1406, 2090, 2124, 2126,
2127, 2129, 2172, 3510, 3511, 3526, 3544, 3554,
3555, 3592, 3595, 3681, 3683, 3687, 3690, 3703,
3704, 3708, 3709, 3710, 3712, 3713, 3714, 3717,
3721, 3726, 3752, 3759, 3849, 3927.

SLAVERY

This subject is discussed in the following studies:
455, 2132, 2134, 3578, 3626, 3634, 3694, 3740,
3748, 3764.

PLATO AS SOCIAL PHILOSOPHER

This subject is discussed in the following studies:
721, 1379, 1955, 2128, 3160, 3223, 3553, 3559,
3560, 3583, 3585, 3590, 3618, 3630, 3676, 3705,
3736, 3743, 3744, 3948.

PLATO AS ECONOMIC THINKER

This subject is discussed in the following studies:
761, 1215, 1216, 1379, 3568, 3605, 3706, 3761.

PLATO'S VIEW AND USE OF HISTORY

These subjects are discussed in the following studies:
3562, 3586, 3606, 3646, 3647, 3648, 3679.

V H: EDUCATION

3765 MURAI M., "Plato's Way of Thinking concerning State and Education" [in Japanese with English summary]. Philosophy (Tokyo) 1958 n.34.

3766 MARION A.A., "Platón: sus ideales morales y políticos; crítica de la educación contemporánea". El monitor de la Educación Commun (Buenos Aires) LXIX 1959 65-70.

3767 SMITH J.M., "A Critical Estimate of Plato's & Dewey's Educational Philosophies". ET IX 1959 109-115.

3768 JAEGER W., "Die platonische Philosophie als Paideia". p.142-157 in Jaeger W., Humanistische Reden und Vorträge (see 4604). Also p.109-124 in Das Platonbild, hrsg. von Gaiser K. (see 4595). Reprinted from Die Antike IV, 1928 161-176.

3769 MOECKELMANN J., "Die Leibeserziehung in Platons Staatsschriften". Leibeserziehung 1960 364-368.

3770 BOULAY J., "Le rôle de la musique dans l'éducation". LThPh XVII 1961 262-274.

3771 DURIĆ M.N., "Lebendiges und Totes in Platons Philosophie" [in Serbian with German summary]. ZAnt XI 1961 43-56.

3772 HARWAS E., "The Pedagogy of Plato in its Contradictions with the Materialist Theory of Education" [in Polish]. SprawPTPN 1961 268-269.

3773* STENZEL J., Platon der Erzieher. Unveränd. Neudr. der Ausg. Leipzig 1928 mit einer Einführ. von Gaiser K. Hamburg, Meiner 1961 xxx&337p.
Rev. REG LXXV 1962 576 Weil.
AAHG XV 1962 225 Vretska.
Gnomon XXXV 1963 422-423 Schudoma.
CR XIII 1963 342 Gulley.
JHPh I 1963 239-246 Manasse.
PLA XVII 1964 43-44 Niebergall.

3774 GERDES O., "Ritmische gymnastiek in pedagogisch perspectief". PaedStud XL 1963 432-453.

V H: EDUCATION

3775 PAPAS C., "Die pädagogische Grundlage bei Plato im Verhältnis zur heutigen Problematik". Platon XV 1963 226-242.

3776* HARTH H., Dichtung und Arete. Untersuchungen zur Bedeutung der musischen Erziehung bei Plato. Diss. Frankfurt 1965 219p.

3777 WOODBRIDGE F.J.E., "Education". p.38-48 in Plato's Meno. Text and Criticism, ed. by Sesonske A. & Fleming N. (see 1484). Reprinted from Woodbridge F.J.E., The Son of Apollo, 1929, p.127-147.

3778 ALBERT K., "Platons philosophische Pädagogik". PaedProv J.20 1966 205-214.

3779* GUENTHER H.F.K., Platon als Hüter des Lebens. Platons Zucht und Erziehungsgedanken und deren Bedeutung für die Gegenwart. 3. Aufl. Pähl, v. Bebenburg 1966 84p.

3780 MARTANO G., "Platone educatore". RIFPS 1966 243-251.

3781 NEUMANN H.,"Goethe's Faust and Plato's Glaucon. The Political Necessity for Philosophy". StudGen XIX 1966 627-632.

3782* STENZEL J., Platone educatore, tr. da Gabrieli F. 2a ed. Bari, Laterza 1966 326p. (Originally Platon der Erzieher. Leipzig 1928.) Rev. RSF XXI 1966 454-455 Adorno.

3783 WISSMUELLER K.H., "Platon als Erzieher". AU R.9 1966 19-28.

3784 NEUMANN H., "Kierkegaard and Socrates on the Dignity of Man". Personalist XLVIII 1967 453-460.

3785 SCIACCA M.F., "Il παῖς di Cebete". p.166-184 in Sciacca M.F., Platone I (see 64). Reprinted from GM 1946 & 1947 (where it appeared under the pseudonym of Williger C.F.).

3786 GADAMER H.G., "Platos Staat der Erziehung". p.205-220 in Gadamer H.G., Platos dialektische Ethik und andere Studien (see 4592).

3787* MEMMERT W., Die Geschichte des Wortes 'Anschauung' in pädagogischer Hinsicht von Platon bis Pestalozzi. Diss. Erlangen, Hogl 1968 v&246p.

3788 RITZEL W., "Die Vielheit pädagogischer Theorien und
      die Einheit der Pädagogik". VWP XLIV 1968
      237-281.

3789* DEBESSE M. & MIALARET G., Traité des sciences
      pédagogiques. Paris, Presses Universitaires
      1969 204p.

3790 IMAI N., "Plato's Philosophy of Education" [in
     Japanese]. Studies in Philosophy (Kyushu Univ.)
     V 1969.

3791* TOURLIDES G.A., Ἀνάλεκτα φιλολογικὰ καὶ ἱστορικά.
      Athens 1969 32p.

3792 BRUMBAUGH R.S., "Plato's Philosophy of Education.
     The Meno Experiment and the Republic
     Curriculum". ET XX 1970 207-228.

3793* DOMMANGET M., Les grands socialistes et l'éducation:
      de Platon à Lénine. Paris, Colin 1970 471p.
      (Ch.1: "Platon", p.7-31.)

3794* FINK E., Metaphysik der Erziehung im Weltverhältnis
      von Plato und Aristoteles. Frankfurt,
      Klostermann 1970 327p. (Sec.II, "Platon:
      Politeia und Nomoi", p.43-185.)
         Rev. PaedagRdsch XXV 1971 376-380 Menze.
         PHist IV 1971 143-144 Brann.
         CD CLXXXIV 1971 165-166 Uña.
         RP II 1972 173-176 Capuzzi.

3795* LICHTENSTEIN E., Der Ursprung der Pädagogik im
      griechischen Denken. Das Bildungsproblem in der
      Gesch. des europäischen Erziehungsdenkens I,1,
      Hannover, Schroedel 1970 202p.
         Rev. Gnomon XLIV 1972 71-73 Haag.
         PLA XXV 1972 20-23 Nickel.

3796* LODGE R.C., Plato's Theory of Education. New York,
      Russell & Russell 1970 viii&322p. Reprint of
      1947 edn. with an appendix "The Education of
      Women according to Plato", by Frank S.

3797* MASTANDREA D., Il concetto di educazione nelle opere
      platoniche della Repubblica e delle Leggi.
      Mercato S. Severino, Linotip. B. Moriniello
      1970 32p.

3798 SADDINGTON D.B., "The Education of an Ideal Man.
     The Views of Plato, Cicero, Augustine".
     Akroterion XV 1970 5-16.

V H: EDUCATION

3799   GRAVEL P., "Philosophie et pédagogie".   Dialogue XII
         1973 465-476.

For further discussions of Plato and   education   see   198,
         209,   223, 235, 356, 673, 728, 1354, 1384, 1394,
         1530, 1678, 1929, 1961, 2066, 2067, 2068,   2069,
         2075,   2170, 2384, 3041, 3292, 3309, 3472, 3825,
         3995.

V I: AESTHETICS

There were enough treatments of the following topics in this section to make special indices worthwhile: General Treatments of Plato's Aesthetics, Mimesis, Plato's Banishment of Poetry, and Plato's View of Poetic Inspiration. These indices are located at the end of the section.

3800 EKMAN R., "Platons estetik". Insikt och Handling II 1958 22-32.

3801 LLEDÓ IÑIGO E., "Poiesis Mimesis". p.321-327 in Actas primer Congr. Español de Estud. clásicas (Madrid 15-19 Abril 1956). Madrid, 1958.

3802 PHILIPSON M.H., "Some Reflections on Tragedy". JPh LV 1958 197-203.

3803 VICAIRE P., "Platon et Dionysos". BAGB 1958,3 15-26.

3804 GOLA W., "Música e filosofia". RBF IX 1959 380-387.

3805 PLEBE A., "Origini e problemi dell'estetica antica". p.1-80 in Momenti e problemi di storia dell'estetica, I: Dall'antichità al Barocco. Milano, Marzorati 1959.

3806 ROSEN S.H., "Collingwood and Greek Aesthetics". Phronesis IV 1959 135-148.

3807* SACK E., Platons Musikaesthetik. Stuttgart, Dt. Apotheker-Verl. 1959 41p.

3808 VELA R., "Il concetto di arte in Platone". Sapienza XII 1959 162-171.

3809* DEMARCHI S., Il Pensiero estetico di Platone. Bolzano, Tip. Moderna 1960 xix&108p. Rev. Humanitas 1962 169-170 Gilmozzi.

3810 NAHM M.C., "Plato's Poet as 'A Light and Winged and Sacred Thing' and as a Problem for Aesthetic Criticism". p.156-161 in Actes IV Congrès internat. Esth.. Athens 1960.

3811 PLEBE A., "Le formulazioni platoniche dei concetti di inganno poetico e di mimesi artistica". p.759-788 in Studi in onore di L. Castiglioni. Firenze, Sansoni 1960 2 vols.

3812 STANNARD J., "Platonism and Art". GM XV 1960 576-593.

3813* TATARKIEWICZ W., History of Aesthetics, I: Ancient Aesthetics [in Polish]. Wroclaw, Ossolineum 1960 410p. English trans. Den Haag, Mouton 1970 352p. (part II.9: The Aesthetics of Plato.)
    Rev. BCO VI 1961 316-320.
    PrzegladHuman V 1961 177-183 Galecki.
    Nowe Ksiazki 1961 47-48 Najder.
    KultSpol V 1961 185-199 Morawski.
    RivE VII 1962 279-288 Rzepinska.
    EPh XXI 1966 97-98 Guy.
    BA 1963 466 Giergielewicz.
    AusJP 1963 135 Gibson & Srzednicki.
    RPhL LXV 1967 140-142 Kalinowski.
    [of English edn.] JAAC XXXI 1972 129-130 Rieser.

3814* VICAIRE P., Platon critique littéraire. Études & Commentaires XXXIV, Paris, Klincksieck 1960 viii&448p.
    Rev. LEC XXVIII 1960 461.
    REG LXXIII 1960 545-546 des Places.
    REA LXIII 1961 148-149 Luccioni.
    Helmantica XI 1960 552-553 Rodriguez.
    CR XI 1961 214-217 Sinclair.
    Euphrosyne III 1961 411-413 Antunes.
    IL XIII 1961 76 Weil.
    AUP XXXI 1961 235-237.
    REAug VI 1960 401-402 Thonnard.
    RPh XXXVI 1962 117-120 Defradas.
    JHS LXXXII 1962 180 Baldry.
    CPh LVII 1962 52-57 Greene.
    AAHG XV 1962 38-40 Vretska.
    A&R VII 1962 102-104 Masaracchia.
    RBPh XL 1962 246-247 Mason.
    GIF XV 1962 77-78 Pepe.
    Emerita XXXI 1963 328-330 Pericay.
    Orpheus X 1963 77-78 Rapisarda.
    RFil(La Plata) XII-XIII 1963 93-95 Delucchi.
    AFC VIII 1961-1963 248-250 Delucchi.
    RSF XVII 1962 337-340 Tagliasacchi.
    Mnemosyne XVII 1964 192-193 Verdenius.

V I: AESTHETICS

3815 AOKI S., "On Plato's View of Art" [in Japanese].
Hoko I 1961.

3816 LOSEV A.F., "Plato's Aesthetic Terminology" [in Russian]. Summary in BCO XI 1966 276-277.

3817 MORAES M.J. DE, "Platão e a poesia (Livros II e III da República)". Anuário da Faculdade de Filosofia "Sedes Sapientiae" (Univ. catól. de São Paulo) XVIII 1960-1961 81-92.

3818* PERPEET W., Antike Aesthetik. München, Karl Alber 1961 114p. (ch. 3, "Platons Dialektik des Schönen".)
Rev. PhilosRdschau X 1962 291-293 Lledó.
Mnemosyne XVI 1963 429 de Vries.
Helikon VII 1967 654-656 Krueger.
PhJ LXX 1962 236-237 A.H.

3819 PHILIP J.A., "Mimesis in the Sophistes of Plato".
TAPhA XCII 1961 453-468.

3820 STÉPHAN L., "Symmetria". RevEsth XIV 1961 319-337.

3821* GRASSI E., Die Theorie des Schönen in der Antike.
Geschichte der Ästhetik I, Antike, Köln, DuMont Schauberg 1962 287p. Italian trans. Arte come antiarte. Torino, Paravia 1972 xii&242p. (ch. 3 "Die Verurteilung der Kunst. Platon".)
Rev. [of German edn.] CW LVII 1964 375 Lazenby.
Streven XVII 1963-1964 1125 Bekaert.
PhilosRdschau XIII 1965-1966 42-54 Perpeet.
Gnomon XXXVIII 1966 98-100 Flashar.
[of Ital. edn.] RivStCroc 1973 360-362 Bonelli.

3822 MOUTSOPOULOS E., "Euripide et la philosophie de la musique". REG LXXV 1962 396-452.

3823 STADELMANN L.I.J., "Objeto da estética de Platão".
Estudos XXII 1962 70-76.

3824* WARRY J.G., Greek Aesthetic Theory. A Study of Callistic and Aesthetic Concepts in the Works of Plato and Aristotle. London, Methuen 1962 viii&168p.
Rev. REG LXXV 1962 579 des Places.
RSC X 1962 273 d'Agostino.
Tablet 1962 751 Gorner.
TLS 31 August 1962 662.

V I: AESTHETICS

AusJP 1963 130 Williamson.
G&R 1963 86.
EPh XVIII 1963 121-122 Boudet.
LEC XXXI 1963 340 Moraux.
Gnomon XXXV 1963 515 Meyerhoff.
CW LVI 1963 135 Anton.
RF LIV 1963 108.
RPh XXXVIII 1964 303 Louis.
CR XIV 1964 33-34 Hudson-Williams.
Mind LXXIII 1964 147-148 Taylor.
PhilosQ XIV 1964 87 Fowlie.
AC XXXIV 1965 309 Minguet.
CPh LX 1965 45-46 Harris.
PACA VIII 1965 49 Skemp.
Mnemosyne XVIII 1965 414-415 Sicking.

3825 MOUTSOPOULOS E., "Dialectique musicale et
dialectique philosophique chez Platon". AFLA
XXXVII 1963 159-167.

3826 PAWLOW T., "Die mystisch-idealistische Ästhetik
Platons". p.21-35 in Beiträge zur Geschichte
der Ästhetik. Berlin, Aufbau-Verl 1963.

3827 RONNET G., "Le sentiment du tragique chez les
Grecs". REG LXXVI 1963 327-336.

3828 SCHIPPER E.W., "Mimesis in the Arts in Plato's
Laws". JAAC XXII 1963 199-203.

3829 SIMONDON M., "L'unité primitive de la fonction
poétique". RevEsth XVI 1963 337-349.

3830 VERENE D.P., "Plato's Conception of Philosophy and
Poetry". Personalist XLIV 1963 528-538.

3831 VICAIRE P., "Les Grecs et le mystère de
l'inspiration poétique". BAGB IV 1963 68-85.

3832 WEBSTER T.B.L., "Platon et la tragédie". BFS XLII
1963-1964 179-188.

3833 DAVYDOV I., "Oedipus Rex, Plato, and Aristotle.
Ancient Tragedy as Aesthetic Phenomenon" [in
Russian]. VL 1964 150-176.

3834* DEUGD C. DE, From Religion to Criticism. Notes on
the Growth of the Aesthetic Consciousness in
Greece. Utrechtse Publ. voor alg.
Literatuurwet. VI, Utrecht, Inst. voor alg.
Literatuurwet. 1964 83p. (Ch. 3 "Plato",
p.52-61.)

V I: AESTHETICS

Rev. RSC XIII 1965 238-239 d'Agostino.
Gymnasium LXXIII 1966 273 ter Vrugt-Lentz.
CR XVI 1966 239 Lucas.
Mnemosyne XXI 1968 94-96 Sicking.

3835 GOULD T., "Plato's Hostility to Art". Arion III,1
1964 70-91.

3836 IMAMICHI T., "On Plato's Philosophy of Art" [in
Japanese]. Riso no.376 Sept. 1964.

3837 MAGUIRE J.P., "The Differentiation of Art in Plato's
Aesthetics". HSPh LXVIII 1964 389-410.

3838 MAGUIRE J.P., "Beauty and the fine arts in Plato.
Some Aporiai". HSPh LXX 1965 171-193.

3839 MOUTSOPOULOS E., "La philosophie de la musique et la
théâtre d'Aristophane". p.201-237 in Χάρις K.I.
Vourveris ἀφιέρωμα τῶν μαθητῶν τοῦ ἐπὶ τῇ
ἑξακονταπεντατηρίδι τοῦ βίου αὐτοῦ, ed. by
Anastassiou A., Kambylis A., Skiadas A. Athens
1964.

3840 NIČEV A., "Plato and Aristoteles über die Wirkung
der Tragödie". Helikon IV 1964 229-252.

3841 OMORI S., "Plato's Philosophy of Art" [in Japanese].
Bigaku LIX 1964.

3842* RUGE A., Die platonische Aesthetik. Reprint of 1832
edn. Osnabrück, Zeller 1965 xiv&232p.

3843 YAMANO K., "Ἐνθουσιασμός;and μίμησις. On Plato's View
of the Poet" [in Japanese]. Osaka Furitsu Univ.
Bulletin. Ser. C, Humanities & Social Sciences
VI 1965.

3844 ADORNO F., "Platone e le arti del suo tempo".
p.3-42 in Adorno F., Studi sul pensiero greco.
Firenze, Sansoni 1966.

3845* BEARDSLEY M.C., Aesthetics from Classical Greece to
the present. A Short History. New York,
Macmillan 1966 414p. (ch.2 "Plato", p.30-53.)
Rev. Athene(Chicago) XXVI,4 1966 22.
Philosophy XLIII 1968 63-65 Eshleman.
PhR LXXVIII 1969 270-273 Kennik.
JAAC XXV 1966-1967 213-215 Pepper.
RM XX 1966-1967 362 W.B.K.

3846* BRUNIUS T., Inspiration and Katharsis. The Interpretation of Aristotle's 'The Poetics VI, 1449b26'. Laokoon, Swedish Studies in Aesthetics III, Acta Univ. Uppsaliensis, Uppsala, Univ. of Uppsala 1966 88p.

3847 DEMOS R., "Word versus Deed in Plato". p.168-173 in Philosophy, Religion, and the Coming World Civilization. Essays in Honor of William Ernest Hocking, ed. by Rouner L.S. Den Haag, Nijhoff 1966.

3848 LOGROSCINO G., "Processo all'estetica platonica". Sophia XXXIV 1966 86-100.

3849 RUCKER D., "Plato and the Poets". JAAC XXV 1966 167-170.

3850* SÖRBOM G., Mimesis and Art. Studies in the Origin and early Development of an Aesthetic Vocabulary. Stockholm, Svenska Bokförl. 1966 218p.
Rev. AC XXXVI 1967 321 Minguet.
PhilosQ XVII 1967 377-378 Matthews.
RPh XLII 1968 333 Louis.
CJ LXIII 1968 179-180 Golden.
CR XVIII 1968 190-192 Lucas.
JAAC 1968 106-108 Shields.
BJAes 1967 396 Osborne.
ArchClass XX 1968 400-404 Moreno.
Gnomon XLI 1969 225-228 Landfester.
PhR LXXVIII 1969 273-276 Gosling.
AJPh XCI 1970 253-255 Podlecki.
Etc. 1970 467 Berleant.

3851 CARTER R.E., "Plato and Inspiration". JHPh V 1967 111-121.

3852 HOLWERDA D., "De artis metricae vocabulis quae sunt δάκτυλος et ένόπλυος ". p.51-58 in Κωμψδοτραγήματα. Studia Aristophanea W.J.W. Koster in Honorem, ed. Westendorp Boerma R.E.H. Amsterdam, Hakkert 1967.

3853 MacKINNON D.M., "Theology and Tragedy". RelStud II 1967 163-169.

3854* RICHTER P.E. ed., Perspectives in Aesthetics. Plato to Camus. New York, Odyssey Pr. 1967 xv&472p. (ch.1 "Art under Scrutiny. Plato", p.24-53.)

3855 ROGGIANO A.A., "El problema de la creación poética en Platón". AUQuito XCV 1967 293-309.

3856 BIANCHI BANDINELLI R., "Plato und die Malerei seiner Zeit". p.426-427 in Antiquitas Graeco-Romana ac tempora nostra. Acta Congressus internationalis habiti Bruni diebus 12-16 mensis Aprilis MCMLXVI, ed. cur. Burian J. & Vidman L. Praha, Českoslov Akad. Věd 1968.

3857 CASTILLO C., "Numerus, qui Graece ῥυθμός dicitur" [in Spanish with English summary]. Emerita XXXVI 1968 279-308.

3858* DAVYDOV J.N., Iskusstvo kak sociologicheskij fenomen. K charakteristike estet-polit. vzgljadov Platona i Aristotelja [Art as sociological Phenomenon. Towards the characteristic aesthetic-political View of Plato and Aristotle] [in Russian]. Moskva, Izd. Nauka 1968 284p. Also Polish transl. Sztuka jako zjawisko socjologiczne. Przyczynek do charakterystyki pogladów estetyczno-politycznych Platona i Arystotelesa, transl. by Pomian K. Warszawa, Państwowy Inst. Wyd. 1971 419p.

3859 GADAMER H.G., "Plato und die Dichter". p.179-204 in Gadamer H.G., Platos dialektische Ethik und andere Studien (see 4592).

3860 GILBERT A.H., "Did Plato Banish the Poets?". M&RS II 1968 35-55.

3861 RANDALL J.H., "Plato as the Philosopher of Artistic Experience". ASchol XXXVII 1968 502-511.

3862* SCHAPER E., Prelude to Aesthetics. London, Allen & Unwin 1968 179p. (p.20-55 on Plato.)
Rev. Philosophy XLIV 1969 351-352 Jones.

3863* SCHUHL P.M., Platón y el arte de su tiempo. Buenos Aires, Ed. Paidós 1968 198p.
Rev. BIEH IV 1970 77 Soler.

3864 GOLDEN L., "Mimesis and Katharsis". CPh LXIV 1969 145-153.

3865 LANGEN G., "De houding van Plato en Plotinus ten aanzien van de beeldende kunst". Hermeneus XL 1969 340-342.

V I: AESTHETICS

3866* LOSEV A.F., Istorija antičnoj éstetiki. Sofisty,
Sokrat, Platon. Moskva, Iskousstvo 1969 714p.
(p.51-142 on Socrates; p.143-end on Plato.)
Rev. VF XXIII 1969 170.

3867 SMOLDERS D., "Via Plato van de esthetica naar de
mystiek". WPMW IX 1968-1969 98-108.

3868* TIGERSTEDT E.N., Plato's Idea of Poetical
Inspiration. Commentationes Hum. Litt. Soc.
Scient. Fennicae XLIV,2, Helsinki 1969 77p.
Rev. BAGB 1970 431-432 Lachenaud.
REA LXXII 1970 165-166 Moreau.
RBPh XLIX 1971 669 Druet.
RSC XIX 1971 266-267 d'Agostino.
Gnomon XLIV 1972 641-645 Maehler.
CPh LXVII 1972 145-146 Combellack.
BIEH VI 1972 145-146 Corominas.
Mnemosyne XXVI 1973 427-429 Schenkeveld.

3869 VILLANUEVA B.M., "El concepto de mimesis en Platón".
Perficit 2a Ser. II 1969 181-246.
Rev. RPh XLV 1971 152 Louis.

3870* VRIES G.J. DE, De zang der Sirenen. Groningen,
Wolters-Noordhoff 1969 vii&169p.
Rev. Hermeneus XLI 1970 143-149
Hoeppener.

3871 WAGNER H.R., "Idealität und Allgemeinheit. Zwei
Aspekte der antiken Mimesistheorie" [in German
with Greek summary]. Platon XXI 1969 234-250.

3872 GOLDSCHMIDT V., "Le problème de la tragédie d'après
Platon". p.103-140 in Goldschmidt V., Questions
platoniciennes (see 4598). Reprinted from REG
LXI 1948 19ff.

3873 ORTEGA A., "Poesía y verdad en Píndaro". Helmantica
XXI 1970 353-372.

3874 PARTEE M.H., "Plato's Banishment of Poetry". JAAC
XXVIII 1970 209-222.

3875 TIGERSTEDT E.N., "Furor poeticus. Poetic
Inspiration in Greek Literature before
Democritus and Plato". JHI XXXI 1970 163-178.

3876 CAVARNOS C., "Plato's Critique of the Fine Arts" [in
English with Greek summary].
Philosophia(Athens) I 1971 296-314.

3877 PARTEE M.H., "Inspiration in the Aesthetics of Plato". JAAC XXX 1971 87-95.

3878 ROSALES C., "La concepción platónica de la poesia". RevHum VIII 1971 125-147.

3879 TRIMPI W., "The ancient Hypothesis of Fiction. An Essay on the Origins of Literary Theory". Traditio XXVII 1971 1-78.

3880 VERDENIUS W.J., "Plato's Doctrine of artistic Imitation". p.259-273 in Plato II, ed. by Vlastos G. (see 4620). Reprinted from Verdenius W.J., Mimesis. Leiden 1949, ch.1.

3881 VERSENYI L., "The Quarrel between Philosophy and Poetry". PhilosForum II 1970-1971 200-212.

3882 VIRCILLO D., "L'estetica di Platone (in metafisica dialettica e critica)". Teoresi XXVI 1971 63-150.

3883* CALLICOTT J.B., Plato's Aesthetics and Introduction to the Theory of Forms. Diss. Syracuse Univ. 1972 556p. [microfilm]. Summary in DA XXXIII 1972 356A-357A.

3884 CLAVIE D., "Histoires de masques. La Mimesis platonicienne". AUToul VIII 1972 No.3, Philosophie 1,21-41.

3885 FUJITA K., "On the Principle of Poiesis in the Philosophy of Plato and Aristotle" [in Japanese]. Bigaku XXIII 1972 44.

3886 GONZÁLEZ ROLÁN T., "Breve introducción a la problemática de los géneros literarios. Su clasificación en la antigüedad clásica". CFC IV 1972 213-237.

3887 IOANNIDES K., "Le rhythme de l'harmonie. La place de la musique et de la danse dans la philosophie de Platon". Summary. AEHE Ve Sect. LXXIX 1971-1972 449-450.

3888* MUIR D.G., Plato's Aesthetics, his positive Theory of the Arts. Diss. Syracuse Univ. 1971 261p. [microfilm]. Summary in DA XXXII 1972 4661A.

3889* OATES W.J., Plato's View of Art. New York, Scribners 1972 81p.
      Rev. YR 1972 127 Moulton.

V I: AESTHETICS

VQR 1972 clvi.

3890 PIPPIDI D.M., "Platon şi problema poezici". p.53-76
in Pippidi D.M., Formarea ideilor literare in
antichitate. Enciclopedia de Buzunar,
Bucureşti, Ed. encicl. română 1972.

3891 ROBINSON D., "The Ethical Critique of Art in the
Republic". Dianoia 1972 25-39.

3892 WEHRLI F., "Der erhabene und der schlichte Stil in
der poetisch-rhetorischen Theorie der Antike".
p.97-120 in Wehrli F., Theoria und Humanitas
(see 4625). Reprinted from Phyllobolia P. Von
der Muehll, Basel. 1946, p.9-34.

3893 ANTON J.P., "Tragic Vision and Philosophic θεωρία in
classical Greece" [in English with Greek
summary]. Diotima I 1973 11-31, 225-226.

3894* CAVARNOS C., Plato's Theory of Fine Art. Athens,
Astir 1973 98p.

3895 FUKADA Y., "Plato's Aesthetics" [in Japanese]. in
Fukada Y., Collected Works, II. Tokyo, Tamagawa
Univ. Pr. 1973.

3896 JELLESEN L., "Platon og de to digtere: Om Staffeldt
og Platon [Plato and the two Poets: On
Staffeldt and Plato]" [in Danish]. Kritik VII
1973 46-59.

3897* MENZA V.G., Poetry and the τέχνη Theory. An
Analysis of the Ion and Republic, books III and
X. Diss. The Johns Hopkins Univ. 1972 387p.
[microfilm]. Summary in DA XXXIII 1973 6402A.

3898 MURRAY M., "The Crisis of Greek Poetics. A
Re-interpretation". JVI VII 1973 173-187.

3899 PARTEE M.H., "Plato on the Criticism of Poetry".
PhQ LII 1973 629-642.

3900 STANFORD W.B., "Onomatopoetic Mimesis in Plato,
Republic 396b-397c". JHS XCIII 1973 185-191.

3901 VRIES G.J. DE, "The Extent of the Literary Corpus
among the Greeks and in modern Theory" [in
Dutch]. MKNA XXXVI 1973 3-14.

V I: AESTHETICS

For additional discussions of Plato's aesthetics   see   27,
        376, 396, 407, 707, 795, 1330, 1333, 1334, 1335,
        1339, 1340, 1341, 1848, 1851, 2029, 2350, 2655,
        3084, 3144, 3212, 3292, 3313, 3774, 3825, 4056,
        4136, 4149.

INDICES

GENERAL TREATMENTS OF PLATO'S AESTHETICS

For general discussions see the following studies:
        889, 3805, 3809, 3818, 3821, 3824,   3834,   3842,
        3845, 3854, 3862, 3866, 3889, 3894.

MIMESIS

This subject is discussed in the following studies:
        486, 3801, 3806, 3808, 3811, 3819,   3828,   3850,
        3864, 3869, 3871, 3880, 3884, 3900)

PLATO'S BANISHMENT OF POETRY

This subject is discussed in the following studies:
        373, 443, 457, 3821, 3829, 3830, 3835,   3840,
        3848, 3849, 3859, 3860, 3874, 3876, 3881, 3889,
        3891, 3898.

PLATO AND POETIC INSPIRATION

This subject is discussed in the following studies:
757, 3810, 3831, 3846, 3851, 3868, 3875, 3877.

V J: RELIGION AND THEOLOGY

3902* MANNO A., Sul rapporto tra le idee e Dio in Platone.
Risposta a un critico del Teismo di Platone.
Napoli, Ist. sup. di Scienze e Lett. S.
Chiara 1958 128p.
Rev. GM XIV 1959 739-742 Cavaciuti.
RPhL LVII 1959 446-447 Rutten.
Helmantica XIV 1963 524-525 Alesanco.
RRFC LIII 1959 310-311 Scarlata.
Pensamiento XVI 1960 127 Valverde.

3903 SOLERI G., "Le dottrine teologiche di Platone".
RSFI XI 1-30, 133-160.

3904 TRUSSO F.E., "Los dos humanismos". Sapientia
(Argentina) XIII 1958 138-141.

3905* FEIBLEMAN J.K., Religious Platonism. The Influence
of Religion on Plato and the Influence of Plato
on Religion. London, Allen & Unwin; New York,
Barnes & Noble 1959 236p.
Rev. Sophia XXIX 1961 484-485 Torraca.
CW LVI 1963 184 North.
GM XVIII 1963 684-687 Deregibus.
CR XLV 1960 371-372 E.A.S.
PhilosStud(Irel.) IX 1959 222-223 Finan.
EPh XV 1960 278-279 Deledalle.
CQR CLXI 1960 363-365 Fox.
BThom XI 1960-1962 90 Saffrey.
Personalist XLII 1961 125-126 D.H.R.

3906 McLENDON H.J., "Plato without God". JR XXXIX 1959
88-102.

3907* REXINE J.E., Religion in Plato and Cicero. New
York, Philos. Libr. 1959 72p. Reprinted New
York, Greenwood Pr. 1968.
Rev. CW LIII 1960 163 Cavarnos.
Personalist XLI 1960 539-540 P.M.
CPh LVI 1961 131-133 Levine.
CB XXXIX 1962 14 Cavarnos.

3908 SIEGMUND G., "Platon über Unglauben". ThG XLIX 1959
374-379.

3909 SOLERI G., "Il preteso teismo di Platone". RSFI XII
234-254.

3910 STRUGLIA G., "Razionalità e dogmatismo nell'evoluzione dell'idea della tolleranza religiosa. Nell'antichità e nel medioevo (Nota preliminare)". AFLC XXVII 1959 345-413.

3911 VIDAL M., "La 'theophilia' dans la pensée religieuse des Grecs". RecSR XLVII 1959 161-184.

3912 McMINN J.B., "Plato as a philosophical theologian". Phronesis V 1960 23-31.

3913* PROCLUS, Procli In theologiam Platonis libri VI, edidit Aemilius Portus (Hamburg 1618). Nachdr. Frankfurt, Minerva-Verl. 1960 560p.
     Rev. Bijdragen XXII 1961 227-228 Verhaak.

3914 SOLERI G., "Politeismo e monoteismo nel vocabolario teologico della letteratura greca da Omero a Platone". RSC VIII 1960 24-56.

3915 ChEN C.H., "Plato's Theistic Teleology". AngThR XLIII 1961 71-87. Summary in CJ LVII 1962 179.

3916 ANTON J.P., "Some Dionysian References in the Platonic Dialogues". CJ LVIII 1962 49-55.

3917 CLASSEN C.J., "The Creator in Greek Thought from Homer to Plato". C&M XXIII 1962 1-22.

3918 LUCE J.V., "Plato's Religious Experience". Hermathena XCVI 1962 73-91.

3919 PLACES E. DES, "Platone e il politeismo". Summary in SMSR XXXIII 1962 196-198.

3920* GOLDSCHMIDT V., A religião de Platão, trad. de Porchat Periera I. & O. São Paulo, Difusão Européia do Livro 1963 151p.
     Rev. Kriterion XV 1962 746-748 Barata Vianna.

3921* LEDIGO LÓPEZ M., El problema de Dios en Platón. La teología del demiurgo. Theses et Studia philol. Salmanticensia XI, Salamanca, Consejo Sup. de Investig. Cientif. 1963 242p.
     Rev. Arbor 1963 no.56 309-311 Bravo Lozano.
     Helmantica XV 1964 419-420 Roca Meliá.
     Emerita XXXIV 1966 201 Ozaeta.
     EstFilos XIII 1964 168-169 García.
     DCI II 1965 95-98 Cerezo.

3922 MERLAN P., "Religion and Philosophy from Plato's Phaedo to the Chaldaean Oracles". JHPh I 1963 163-176, II 1964 15-21.

3923 SOUILHÉ J., "La philosophie religieuse de Platon". ArchPhilos XXVI 1963 227-275, 379-441.

3924* MARSILIO FICINO Théologie platonicienne de l'immortalité des âmes, texte crit. établi & trad. par Marcel R. Coll. Les classiques de l'humanisme, Paris, Les Belles Lettres 1964 638 & 596p.

3925* PÉPIN J., Théologie cosmique et théologie chrétienne (Ambroise, Exam. I,1,1-4). Bibl. de philos. contemp., Paris, Presses Universitaires 1964 597p.
  Rev. AC XXXIII 1964 517 Masai.
  VChr XVIII 1964 249-251 van Winden.
  RThPh XIV 1964 375-376 Brunner.
  REG LXXVII 1964 558-567 Boyancé.
  RSPh XLVIII 1964 750-751 Camelot.
  RecSR LIII 1965 151-157 Daniélou.
  AGPh XLVII 1965 319-320 Stelzenberger.
  ArchPhilos XXVIII 1965 295-300 Solignac.
  RMM LXX 1965 114-116 Solignac.
  REA LXVII 1965 271-275 Moreau.
  REAug XII 1966 282-284 Madec.
  GM XX 1965 305-316 Berti.
  Critique XXII 1966 259-269 Fontaine.
  RSR XL 1966 158-177 Giet.
  Dialogue IV 1965-1966 557-558 Leroux.
  Salesianum XXVIII 1966 420-422 Composta.
  JHS LXXXVI 1966 237 Armstrong.
  BTh X 1967 259-260 Botte.
  RPhL LXVIII 1970 81-84 Lefèvre.

3926 VOGEL C.J. DE, "Plato's gedachten over God" [in Dutch with English summary]. AClass VII 1964 32-43. Reprinted p.126-138 in Vogel C.J. de, Theoria (see 4623).

3927 CZARNECKI Z., "Filozoficzna religia Platona a religia w jego utopiach [Plato's Philosophical Religion and the Religion of his Utopias]". Euhemer IX,1 1965 23-40. German summary in BCO XII 1967 245-247.

3928 HACKFORTH R., "Plato's Theism". p.439-447 in Studies in Plato's Metaphysics, ed. by Allen R.E. (see 4580). Reprinted from CQ 1936.

3929 McDONALD H.D., "Monopolar Theism and the Ontological Argument". HThR LVIII 1965 387-416.

3930 MORROW G.R., "Plato's Gods". RiceUS LI 1965 121-134.

3931* THOMAS G.F., Religious Philosophies of the West. A Critical Analysis of the Major Figures from Plato to Tillich. New York, Scribners 1965 xx&454p. (ch.1 "Theistic Idealism: Plato", p.1-25.)

3932 VOGEL C.J. DE, "Het godsbegrip bij Plato, II". AClass VIII 1965 38-52. Reprinted in Japanese in Greek Philosophy and Religion. Tokyo 1969; also in English transl. as "What was God for Plato?", p.210-242 in Vogel C.J. de, Philosophia (see 4624), also as "Platos gedachten over God (2)", p.139-158 in Vogel C.J. de, Theoria (see 4623).

3933 MUEHL M., "Die Traditionsgeschichtlichen Grundlagen in Platons Lehre von den Dämonen (Phaidon 107d, Symposion 202e)". ABG X 1966 242-270.

3934 NOMACHI A., "Telos and God. Theaetetus 176a-b and Timaeus 29e" [in Japanese]. Review of Literature (Hirosaki Univ.) II,4 1966.

3935* SKOVGAARD JENSEN S., Dualism and Demonology. The Function of Demonology in Pythagorean and Platonic Thought, with an Introduction on some Aspects of the General Theory of Metaphysics and Religious Dualism and an Appendix on the Interpretation and Pythagorean Background of Plato's Republic 524d-526c. Diss. Copenhagen, Munksgaard 1966 132p.
Rev. REG LXXXI 1968 612 des Places.
AC XXXVIII 1969 307 des Places.
Gnomon XLI 1969 501-503 Merlan.
CR XIX 1969 374-375 Skemp.

3936 ADRIANI M., "Deus ludens". SMSR XXXVIII 1967 8-23.

3937 ALBERT K., "Metaphysik des Festes". ZRGG XIX 1967 140-152.

3938 CAPPS W.H., "Plurality of Theologies: A Paradigmatic Sketch". RelStud III 1967 355-367.

3939 CORVEZ M., "Le Dieu de Platon". RPhL LXV 1967 5-35.

3940 FREIRE A., "Aspectos da ideia de Deus em Platão".
RPortFil XXIII 1967 135-160.

3941 GADAMER H.G., "Gott und Sein im Denken der
Griechen". Summary in JHAW 1966-1967 131.

3942 HERTER H., "Allverwandtschaft bei Plato". p.64-73
in Religion und Religionen. Festschrift für G.
Mensching. Bonn, Roehrscheid 1967.

3943 McKOWN D.B., "Deception and Development of Plato's
Theology". SoJP V 1967 173-179.

3944 MUGLER C., "Les corps des dieux et l'organisme des
hommes". AFLNice 1967 No.2 7-13.

3945 SCIACCA M.F., "La riforma religiosa". p.9-62 in
Sciacca M.F., Platone II (see 64). Reprinted
from Sciacca M.F., Plato, Eutifrone. Milano,
Principato 1942.

3946 SKEMP J.B., "Plato's Account of Divinity". DUJ XXIX
1967 26-33.

3947 WEINGARTNER P., "Platons Beweis der
Unveränderlichkeit Gottes". SJP X-XI 1966-1967
455-457.

3948* CZARNECKI Z.J., Religia i społeczenstwo w poglądach
Platona [Religion and Society in Plato's
Thought]. Warszawa, Ksiązka i Wiedza 1968 215p.

3949 WRÓBLEWSKI W., "Platon, ale jaki? [Plato, but
Why?]" [in Polish]. StudFiloz 1970 201-214.

3950 DOENT E., "Bemerkungen zu Phaidros 249 und Nomoi
897". Hermes XCVI 1968 369-371.

3951* PROCLUS, Théologie platonicienne, livre I, texte
établi et trad. par Saffrey H.D. & Westerink
L.G. Paris, Les Belles Lettres 1968 cxcv&173p.
Rev. AAHG XXII 1969 214-215 Klein.
CRAI 1969 129 Festugière.
RThPh 1970 201 Brunner.
Sophia XXXVIII 1970 277-278 Giorgiantonio.
RPh XLIV 1970 139-140 des Places.
JHS XC 1970 241-242 Dodds.
CR XX 1970 324-326 Wallis.
CW 1969 20 Rist.
AC XXXIX 1970 228-229 Lasserre.

Gnomon XLIII 1971 9-16 Graeser.
Byzantion XLI 1971 554-556 Aubineau.
Scriptorium   XXV   1971   370-372
Lagarde-Lamberts.
REG LXXXIV 1971 144-150 Charles.
Mnemosyne XXVI 1973 196-198 Beierwaltes.
CPh 1973 230 O'Neill.

3952* RAHE H., Göttliche Epimeleia.   Studien   zu   Inhalt,
Bedeutung und Funktion eines Motivs in den
Dialogen Platons. Diss. Münster 1968 163p.

3953 SKEMP J.B., "Plato's Account of Divinity". DUJ XXIX
1967-1968 26-33.

3954* SOLMSEN F., Plato's Theology.   Reprint of 1942
Cornell edn. New York, Johnson Reprint 1968
201p.

3955 FRIEDLAENDER P., Review of Solmsen F., Plato's
Theology. p.203-205 in Friedlaender P., Studien
zur antiken Literatur und Kunst (see 4589).
Reprinted from PhR LII 1942 507-509.

3956 GADAMER H.G., "Über das Göttliche im frühen Denken
der Griechen". p.397ff. in Das Altertum und
jedes neue Gute. Festschrift für Wolfgang
Schadewaldt   zum 15.3.1970. Stuttgart 1970.
Reprinted p.64-79 in Gadamer H.G., Kleine
Schriften III (see 4593).

3957* GOLDSCHMIDT V., Platonisme et pensée contemporaine.
Coll.   Présence   &   Pensée,   Paris,
Aubier-Montaigne 1970 272p.
Rev.   ArchPD   XVI   1971   416-420
Despotopoulos.
EPh 1971 372-373 École.
RPhilos CLXII 1972 43-44 Poirier.
RIPh XXVI 1972 209-210 Somville.
ArchPhilos XXXV 1972 327-328 Agaësse.
RPhL LXX 1972 479 Deschepper.
RS XCIII 1972 88-90 Bernhardt.

3958* STARK C.L., The Idea of God in the late Dialogues of
Plato.   Diss.   Princeton Univ.   1970 242p.
[microfilm]. Summary in DA XXXI 1970 2981A.

3959* WA SAÏD D., Theosophies of Plato, Aristotle and
Plotinus. New York, Philosophical Libr. 1970
xv&205p.
Rev. ACR I 1971 251 Epp.

3960 WATSON G., "The Theology of Plato and Aristotle". IThQ XXXVII 1970 56-64.

3961 BLUM W., "Kleists Marionettentheater und das Draht-puppengleichnis bei Platon". ZRGG XXIII 1971 40-49.

3962 CARMODY J., "Plato's Religious Horizon". PhilosToday XV 1971 52-68.

3963 FREIRE A., "As provas da existência de Deus em Platão". RPortFil XXVII 1971 225-256.

3964 HERTER H., "θεῖα σώματα". p.12-24 in Philomathes. Studies and Essays in the Humanities in Memory of Philip Merlan, ed. by Palmer R.B. & Hamerton-Kelly R. Den Haag, Nijhoff 1971.

3965 KATSIMANIS K.S., "Religion et métaphysique chez Platon. À propos de l'Apollon du Cratyle 405a-e". Platon XXIII 1971 278-295.

3966* MONDIN B., Il problema del linguaggio teologico dalle origini ad oggi. Bibl. di teol. contemp. VIII, Brescia, Queriniana 1971 508p.

3967* WEISCHEDEL W., Der Gott der Philosophen. Grundlegung einer Philosophischen Theologie im Zeitalter des Nihilismus. Darmstadt, Wissens. Buchges. 1971 xxii&516p. (p.47-48 on Socrates; p.48-54 on Plato.)

3968* AMAR M.A., Collective Religion in Plato's Laws. Diss. Princeton Univ. 1972 310p. [microfilm]. Summary in DA XXXIII 1972 291A.

3969 WEHRLI F., "Antike Gedanken über Voraussagung der Zukunft". p.32-39 in Wehrli F., Theoria und Humanitas (see 4625). Reprinted from Schweizerisches Archiv für Volkskunde XLVII 1951 225-232.

3970* BOYANCÉ P., Le Culte des muses chez les philosophes grecs. Bibl. des Écoles françaises d'Athènes et de Rome, fasc. CXLI, Paris, de Boccard 1973 397p. Reprint of 1937 edn. (Part II, chs.1-2, p.155-184: "Les Incantations platoniciennes", "Platon et la théorie des fêtes religieuses".)

3971 CHIRASSI COLOMBO I., "La salvezza nel aldilà nella cultura greca arcaica". StudClas XV 1973 23-29.

3972   MORI S., "Alienation of Man and God. From the Words
       of Heraclitus to Plato" [in Japanese]. Japan
       and the Japanese 1973.

3973   SKEMP J.B., "Plato's Concept of Deity".   p.115-121
       in Zetesis (see 4579).

For additional discussions of this subject see 284,   514,
       613,   776, 1206, 1231, 1233, 1242, 1243, 1246,
       1248, 1253, 1254, 1386, 1387, 1402, 1403, 1407,
       1706, 1768, 1817, 1819, 1832, 2087, 2141, 2297,
       2499, 2655, 2722, 2789, 2825, 2866, 2982, 3072,
       3086, 3100, 3185, 3220, 3358, 3438, 3539, 4128,
       4561.

V K: EPISTEMOLOGY

3974 CRISTALDI M., "Oggettivismo antico e filosofia".
Teoresi XIII 1958 31-69. (Section 3 on Plato.)

3975 LASSERRE F., "Nombre et connaissance dans la
préhistoire du platonisme". MH XV 1958 11-26.

3976 BROECKER W., "Das Höhlenfeuer und die Erscheinung
von der Erscheinung". p.31-42 in Die Gegenwart
der Griechen im neueren Denken. Festschrift für
H.G. Gadamer zum 60. Geburtstag. Tübingen,
Mohr 1960.

3977* GULLEY N., Plato's Theory of Knowledge. London,
Methuen 1962 viii&203p.
　　　　　　Rev. RSC X 1962 274 d'Agostino.
　　　　　　PACA V 1962 57-60 Peck.
　　　　　　REG LXXV 1962 578 des Places.
　　　　　　TLS 31 Aug. 1962 659.
　　　　　　Tablet 1962 751 Gorner.
　　　　　　PhilosBks Oct. 1962 12 Mitchell.
　　　　　　EPh XVIII 1963 94-95 Moreau.
　　　　　　Bijdragen XXIV 1963 228 Robbers.
　　　　　　PhilosStud(Irel.) XII 1963 264-265 Watson.
　　　　　　AusJP 1963 133 Sykes.
　　　　　　RPh XXXVII 1963 301 Louis.
　　　　　　CR XIII 1963 281-282 Bluck.
　　　　　　GW LVI 1963 185 Rosenmeyer.
　　　　　　Athenaeum XLI 1963 408-410 Arrighetti.
　　　　　　AC XXXII 1963 236-237 Janssens.
　　　　　　RBPh XLI 1963 930 des Places.
　　　　　　RF LIV 1963 242-243 Viano.
　　　　　　JCS XII 1964 171-174 Tsumura.
　　　　　　PhilosRdschau XII 1964 140-141 Kuhn.
　　　　　　JPh LX 1963 348-354 Diamadopoulos.
　　　　　　REA LXVII 1965 195-198 Salviat.
　　　　　　AESocCiv XIX 1964 1028 Vidal-Naquet.
　　　　　　DUJ XXV 1963-1964 33-35 Mills.
　　　　　　JHS LXXXV 1965 204-205 Skemp.
　　　　　　PhilosQ XIV 1964 76-78 Robinson.
　　　　　　Mind LXXIV 1965 451-454 Kirwan.
　　　　　　Mnemosyne XX 1967 79-81 Verdenius.
　　　　　　JHPh III 1965 113-116 Rein'l.

3978* KLEVER W.N.A., Ἀνάμνησις en ἀναγωγή. Gesprek met
Plato en Aristoteles over het menselijk kennen.
Wijsgerige Teksten en Stud. VII, Assen, van
Gorcum 1962 175p.
　　　　　　Rev. AGPh XLIX 1967 324-326 Mansfeld.

V K: EPISTEMOLOGY

3979* KUNCIMAN   W.G.,   Plato's   Later   Epistemology.
       Cambridge, Cambridge Univ. Pr. 1962 vii&138p.
       Rev. RM XV 1961-1962 678 D.P.B.
       PhilosBks Oct. 1962 18 Wasserstein.
       Dialogue I 1962-1963 334-337 Malcolm.
       A&R VII 1962 120-121 Lamacchia.
       CW LV 1962 202 Rist.
       PhilStud XII 1963 265-266.
       HeythropJ IV 1963 76-77 Copleston.
       CPh LVIII 1963 183-184 Sprague.
       JCS XI 1963 119-123 Tsumura.
       RPh XXXVII 1963 300 Louis.
       Phoenix XVII 1963 68-69 Bluck.
       CR XIII 1963 36-39 Bluck.
       JHS LXXXIII 1963 180 Rankin.
       LF XI 1963 159-161 Machovec.
       AAHG XVI 1963 85 Vretska.
       RFIC XLI 1963 348-349 des Places.
       Hermathena XCVII 1963 124-126 Luce.
       RThPh XIII 1963 85 Schaerer.
       RBPh XLI 1963 646 Saunders.
       PhR LXXII 1963 532-534 Santas.
       Mnemosyne XVI 1963 414-416 de Vries.
       Gnomon XXXVI 1964 721 Allen.
       Gymnasium LXXI 1964 457-460 de Vogel.
       Emerita XXXII 1964 137 Adrados.
       REG LXXVII 1964 347 Weil.
       Philosophy XXXIX 1964 185 Lacey.
       PhilosQ XIV 1964 81-82 Cross.
       JHPh II 1964 255-256 Saunders.
       RSF XX 1965 82-84 Giannantoni.
       ArchPhilos XXVIII 1965 293-295 Kucharski.
       Athenaeum XLIII 1965 220-221 Arrighetti.
       PhilosRdschau 1968 241-267 Wiehl.

3980 WIEHL R., "Erkenntnistheorie, Ontologie und Logik in
       Plato's späten Dialogen". PhilosRdschau XV 1968
       241-267.

3981* SPRUTE J., Der Begriff der δόξα in der platonischen
       Philosophie. Diss. Göttingen 1961 190p.
       Hypomnemata II, Göttingen, Vandenhoeck &
       Ruprecht 1962 130p.
               Rev.AC XXXII 1963 632 des Places.
               PLA 1963 285-287 Lumpe.
               RecSR LII 1964 461 des Places.
               Mnemosyne XVII 1964 407-408 de Vries.
               JHS LXXXIV 1964 191 Gulley.
               CW LVII 1964 277 Hoerber.
               Gymnasium LXXII 1965 465-467 Voigtlaender.
               REG LXXVIII 1965 421 Weil.
               AAHG XVIII 1965 86 Vretska.

CR XXI 1971 127 Huby.

3982 EBERT T., "Der Begriff der Doxa in der platonischen
Philosophie". PhilosRdschau XIV 1966-1967
40-47.

3983 SPRUTE J., "Zur Problematik der Doxa bei Platon".
AGPh LI 1969 188-194.

3984 EBERT T., "Zu Doxa und Wahrnehmung bei Platon".
AGPh LII 1970 302-306.

3985* UBINK J.B., Plato's Paradox en Bohr's Idee. Rede,
uitgesproken bij de aanvaarding van het ambt van
buitengewoon hoogleraar in de wijsbegeerte der
exacte   natuurwetenschappen   aan   de
Rijksuniversiteit te Utrecht op 14 Mei 1962.
Arnheim, Van Loghum Slaterus 1962 22p.

3986 AGOGLIA R.M., "Conocimiento y valoración en Platón".
RFil(La Plata) XII-XIII 1963 39-52.

3987 HEITSCH E., "Wahrheit als Erinnerung". Hermes XCI
1963 36-52.

3988 ODEGARD D., "Essences and Discovery. Plato, Locke,
and Leibniz". Dialogue III 1964 219-234.

3989 WITTE B., "Der εἰκως λόγος in Platos Timaios.
Beitrag   zur   Wissenschaftsmethode   und
Erkenntnistheorie des späten Plato". AGPh XLVI
1964 1-16.

3990 GALLAGHER P., "Knowledge as Duality. Plato to
Avicenna". PhilosStud(Irel) XV 1966 176-198.

3991* GRENE M., The Knower and the Known. London, Faber &
Faber 1966 283p. (ch.1 "The Legacy of the
Meno", p.17-35.)

3992 GROZEV G., "Kritika na Platonovata gnoseologija
[Criticism of Plato's Epistemology]" [in
Bulgarian]. FilosMis'l XXIII 1967 87-99.

3993* LESHER J.H., Gnosis and episteme in Plato's
Theaetetus. A Study in Plato's later
Epistemology. Diss. Univ. of Rochester 1967
182p. [microfilm]. Summary in DA XXVIII 1967
261A.

3994 MIZUSAKI H., "The Development of Plato's Epistemology. The Meaning of ή τῶν ὀνομάτων ὀρθότης" [in Japanese]. Studies in Philosophy (Kyushu Univ.) III 1967.

3995 NAKURA S., "Education and the Essence of Knowledge in Plato's Dialogues" [in Japanese]. Nagoya Jr. College Bulletin VIII 1967.

3996* BROWN M.S., Plato's Theory of Knowledge and its Mathematical Background. Diss. Columbia 1966 233p. [microfilm]. Summary in DA XXIX 1968 928A.

3997 KUCHARSKI P., "La place de la notion de 'vue d'ensemble' (synopsis) dans l'épistémologie platonicienne". p.436-440 in Akten XIV. Intern. Kongr. Philos. Wien, 2.-9. September 1968. Vol. V. Wien, Herder 1968.

3998 LAFRANCE Y., "La notion de doxa chez Platon". Summary of dissertation. RPhL LXVI 1968 761.

3999 SPRUTE J., "Über den Erkenntnisbegriff in Platons Theaitet". Phronesis XIII 1968 47-67.

4000* ANNIS D.B., Knowledge and Belief. The Relation of the two Concepts. Diss. Univ. of Illinois 1969 211p. [microfilm]. Summmary in DA XXX 1970 3049A.

4001* LEVI A., Il problema dell'errore nella metafisica e nella gnoseologia di Platone, opera postuma a cura di Reale G. Coll. di testi e saggi II, Padova, Liviana Ed. 1970 xxviii&219p.
Rev. BollFil IV 1970 177-178 Chiereghin.
DT LXXIV 1971 510-511 Visconti.
RSC XIX 1971 106-107 d'Agostino.
RFIC XCIX 1971 303-306 Berti.
Antonianum XLVI 1971 193 Manzano.
Crisis XIX 1972 440-441 Oroz.
CR XXII 1972 334-335 Huby.
JHPh X 1972 474-475 Tejera.
EPh 1972 93-94 Moreau.
LEC XL 1972 441 Druet.
RSF XXVII 1972 96-98 Isnardi Parente.

4002 REALE G., "Un libro inedito di Adolfo Levi su Platone". RFNeo LXII 1970 321-333.

4003* TIELSCH E., Die platonische Versionen der griechischen Doxalehre. Ein philosophisches Lexikon mit Kommentaren. Monogr. zur philos. Forsch. LVIII, Meisenheim, Hain 1970 xvi&486p. Rev. Erasmus XXIII 1971 434-436 Lasserre. REA LXXIII 1971 454 des Places. PHist IV 1971 48-50 Brann. Mnemosyne XXV 1972 438-439 Verdenius.

4004 HINTIKKA J., "Knowledge and its Objects in Plato". Ajatus XXXIII 1971 168-200. Also p.1-30 in Patterns in Plato's Thought, ed. by Moravcsik J.M.E. (see 4609). Also appeared in Finnish: "Tieto ja tiedon kohteet Platonilla". p.135-165 in Hintikka J., Tieto on Valtaa (see 4600).

4005 SANTAS G., "Hintikka on Knowledge and its Objects in Plato". p.31-51 in Patterns in Plato's Thought, ed. by Moravcsik J.M.E. (see 4609).

4006 KELESSIDOU-GALANOS A., "Le platonisme sub specie aeternitatis. Réflexions critiques sur la théorie platonicienne et plotinienne de l'absolu". Platon XXIII 1971 167-185.

4007* LARMI O.J., Plato on the Unknowability of Sensibles. Diss. Univ. of Pennsylvania 1971 163p. [microfilm]. Summary in DA XXXII 1971 2137A-2138A.

4008 TANAKA K., "Γνῶσις and δόξα as the Criterion distinguishing between φιλόσοφος and φιλοδόξος" [in Japanese]. Methodos IV 1971 and VI 1973.

4009 GIGON O., "Der Begriff der Wissenschaft bei Platon und Aristoteles (Stichworte)". Summary p.27-30 in Second Intern. human. Sympos. (Athens-Delphi, Sept.24-Oct.2, 1972). Summaries. Hell. Soc. for hum. Stud. Internat. Centre for hum. Research, 2nd Ser.: Studies & Researches XXIII, Athens 1972.

4010 KAISER N., "Plato on Knowledge". Apeiron VI,2 1972 36-43.

4011* KRC M.P., Plato's Distinction between Knowledge and Opinion. Diss. Univ. of Wisconsin 1973 82p. [microfilm]. Summary in DA XXXIV 1973 821A.

For additional discussions of this subject see 243, 709, 1092, 1094, 1101, 1102, 1129, 1298, 1498, 1505, 1508, 1510, 1515, 1516, 1520, 1521, 1523, 1525,

4012 BLACK E., "Plato's View of Rhetoric". QJS XLIV 1958
      361-374.

4013 STRYCKER E. DE, "Plato's opvatting over de
      filosofische retoriek". p.125-126 in Hand.
      XXIIIe Vlaams Filologencongres. Brussel 1-3
      april 1959. Geldenaakse Vest 20, Leuven, De
      Vlaamsche Philologencongressen 1959.

4014 KUCHARSKI P., "La rhétorique dans le Gorgias et le
      Phèdre". REG LXXIV 1961 371-406.

4015* KENNEDY G., The Art of Persuasion in Greece.
      Princeton, Princeton Univ. Pr. 1963 xi&350p.
      (Frequent references to Plato, esp. p.74-79
      "Plato's Phaedrus", p.149-152 "The Trial of
      Socrates".)

4016 COULTER J.A., "The Relation of the Apology of
      Socrates to Gorgias' Defense of Palamedes and
      Plato's Critique of Gorgianic Rhetoric". HSPh
      LXVIII 1964 269-303.

4017 VIANO C.A., "Retorica, magia e natura in Platone".
      RF LVI 1965 411-453.

4018 CARLINI A., "Osservazioni sui tre εἴδη τοῦ λόγου in
      Ps. Demetrio, De eloc. 296 sq.". RFIC XCVI
      1968 38-46.

4019 HIROKAWA Y., "Rhetoric and Philosophy. A Study of
      Plato and Cicero" [in Japanese]. Tokai Univ.
      Dept. of Literature Bulletin XVI 1971.

4020 MURPHY J.J., "The Metarhetorics of Plato, Augustine,
      and McLuhan. A Pointing Essay". Ph&Rh IV 1971
      201-214.

4021 PETRUZZELLIS N., "La diagnosi platonica della
      demagogia". RSFil XXIV 1971 379-381.

4022* ENGEL E.S., Plato on Rhetoric and Writing. Diss.
      Yale Univ. 1973 176p. [microfilm]. Summary in
      DA XXXIV 1973 2696A.

4023 HELLWIG A., Untersuchungen zur Theorie der Rhetorik
      bei Platon und Aristoteles. Hypomnemata
      XXXVIII, Göttingen, Vandenhoeck & Ruprecht 1973

374p.

4024   IJSSELING S., "Philosophy and Rhetoric" [in Dutch].
       DWB CXVIII 1973 333-343.

4025   KELLEY W.G., "Rhetoric as Seduction".   Ph&Rh VI 1973
       69-80.

For additional discussions of this subject see   220,   384,
       390,   1298,   1302, 1318, 1805, 1814, 1821, 1827,
       1830, 1831, 1833, 1838, 1841, 1846, 1851, 1853.

V M: LINGUISTICS AND PHILOSOPHY OF LANGUAGE

4026 RYLE G., "Letters and Syllables in Plato". PhR LXIX
      1960 431-451. Reprinted p.54-71 in Ryle G.,
      Collected Papers, I: Critical Essays, New York,
      Barnes & Noble 1971.

4027 GALLOP D., "Plato and the Alphabet". PhR LXXII 1963
      364-376.

4028* STEINTHAL H., Geschichte der Sprachwissenschaft bei
      den Griechen und Römern, mit besonderer
      Rücksicht auf die Logik. 2. erw. & verb.
      Aufl. [Berlin, Dümmler 1890-1891], Nachdr.
      Bonn, Dümmler 1961 xvi&374; xii&368p. (For
      Plato see esp. vol. I p.41-168.)
      Rev. Kratylos VII 1962 207 Deroy.
      QIG VI 1961 135-138 Calboli.

4029 TREPANIER E., "Philosophes et grammairiens sur la
      définition du verbe". LThPh XVII 1961 87-99.

4030 DEMOS R., "Plato's Philosophy of Language". Also
      comments by ACKRILL J.L. JPh LXI 1964 595-613.

4031 FERRANTE D., "Le etimologie nei Dialoghi di
      Platone". RIL XCVIII 1964 162-170.

4032 FEHLING D., "Zwei Untersuchungen zur griechischen
      Sprachphilosophie". RhM CVIII 1965 212-229.

4033 KACZMARKOWSKI M., "Z Platonem u kolebki mowy
      ludzkiej". Filomata(Krakow) 1965 No.189
      465-473.

4034 MAYR F.K., "Philosophie der Sprache seit ihrem
      griechischen Anfang". PhJ LXXII 1964-1965
      290-321.

4035* STEWART M.A., Plato's Investigations into Language,
      with special Reference to Cratylus. Diss.
      Univ. of Pennsylvania 1965 464p. [microfilm].
      Summary in DA XXVI 1966 7370-7371.

4036 SCHULTZ J.C., "An Anachronism in Cornford's Plato's
      Theory of Knowledge". ModS XLIII 1965-1966
      397-406.

4037   ECHTERNACH H., "Wort und Sinn. Ein platonischer
       Dialog heute". K&D XIII 1967 27-53.

4038* LEKY M., Plato als Sprachphilosoph. Würdigung d.
       platon.   Kratylos.   Nachdr.   d.   Ausg.
       Paderborn, Schoeningh 1919. Studien zur Gesch.
       und   Kultur   des   Altertums,   Bd.10,   H.3,   New
       York/London, Johnson 1967 87p.

4039   RIVERSO E., "Filosofia ed analisi della proposizione
       da Platone a Wittgenstein". GCFI XLVI 1967
       466-483.

4040   ANTON J.P., "The Aristotelian Doctrine of Homonyma
       in the Categories and its Platonic Antecedents".
       JHPh VI 1968 315-326. Cf. Platon XX 1968
       318-333.

4041   LEROY M., "Etymologie et linguistique chez Platon".
       BAB LIV 1968 121-152.

4042   TILGHMAN B.R., "Parmenides, Plato, and Logical
       Atomism". SoJP VII 1969 151-160.

4043* COSERIU E., Die Gechichte der Sprachphilosophie von
       der Antike bis zur Gegenwart. Eine Übersicht,
       I: Von der Antike bis Leibnitz Nachschr. einer
       Vorles.   besorgt von Narr G.   & Windisch R.
       Tübinger Beitr. zur Linguistik XI, Tübingen
       1970 vi&162p. (secs.4-8, p.27-58 on Plato.)

4044   GOULD J.B., "Palabras y cosas en la filosofía de
       Platón", trad. de Canales Azpeita O. Dialogos
       VII 1970 105-124.

4045* KACHI Y., Language and Reality in Plato's Theory of
       Characters. Diss. Princeton Univ. 1970 264p.
       [microfilm]. Summary in DA XXXI 1970
       1841A-1842A.

4046* LEWIS F.A., Two Essays on Plato's Philosophy of
       Language. Diss. Princeton Univ. 1970 214p.
       [microfilm]. Summary in DA XXXI 1970 6575A.

4047* MULHERN J.J., Problems of the Theory of Predication
       in Plato's Parmenides, Theaetetus and Sophista.
       Diss. State Univ. of New York, Buffalo 1970
       203p. [microfilm]. Summary in DA XXXI 1971
       4841A-4842A.

4048 ADRADOS F.R., "Lengua, ontología y lógica en los sofistas y Platón". ROcc No.96 1971 340-365; No.99 1971 285-309.

4049 LEVINSON R.B., "Language, Plato, and Logic". p.259-284 in Essays in ancient Greek Philosophy, ed. by Anton J.P. & Kustas G.L. (see 4581). Reprinted from RM XI 1957 28-41.

4050 SPRAGUE R.K., "Reply to Dr. Levinson". p.367-371 in Essays in ancient Greek Philosophy, ed. by Anton J.P. & Kustas G.L. (see 4581).

4051 ADAMATSU H., "Plato's Theory of Language" [in Japanese]. Ideal no.464 1972.

4052* BODUNRIN P.O., Plato and his Contemporaries on the Possibility of Falsehood. Diss. Univ. of Minnesota 1971 248p. [microfilm]. Summary in DA XXXII 1972 6484A.

4053* DERBOLAV J., Platons Sprachphilosophie im Kratylos und in den späteren Schriften. Impulse der Forsch. X, Darmstadt, Wiss. Buchges. 1972 333p.
         Rev. AC XLII 1973 625-627 de Ley.

4054* DETEL W., Platons Beschreibung des falschen Satzes im Theätet und Sophistes. Hypomnemata XXXVI, Göttingen, Vandenhoeck & Ruprecht 1972 114p.
         Rev. MH XXX 1973 238-239 Graeser.
         AC XLII 1973 619-621 de Ley.

4055 KAHN C.H., "The Meaning of Justice and the Theory of Forms". JPh LXIX 1972 567-579.

4056 PAGLIARO A., "Linguistica e critica letteraria". Helicon XI-XII 1971-1972 3-19.

4057 PARTEE M.H., "Plato's Theory of Language". FoundLang VIII 1972 113-132.

4058 REED N.H., "Plato on Flux, Perception, and Language". PCPhS XVIII 1972 65-77.

4059 JOJA C., "Le sens moderne de la διάνοια, ou l'univers du discours chez Platon". RRSS XVII 1973 359-370.

4060 LEROY M., "Théories linguistiques dans l'antiquité". LEC XLI 1973 385-401.

4061* NUCHELMANS G., Theories of the Proposition. Ancient and Medieval Conceptions of the Bearers of Truth and Falsity. North-Holland Linguistic Ser. VIII, Amsterdam, North-Holland Publ. 1973 ix&309p.

4062* RIVERSO E., Il linguaggio nel pensiero filosofico e pedagogico del mondo antico. Filos. e problemi d'oggi XXVIII, Roma, Armando 1973 262p.

For additional discussions of these subjects see 477, 1109, 1110, 1112, 1113, 1121, 1122, 1123, 1125, 1126, 1130, 1132, 1133, 1135, 1136, 1138, 1139, 1140, 1141, 1142, 1144, 1552, 1557, 1734, 2175, 2228, 2233, 2237, 2238, 2240, 2241, 2242, 2247, 2248, 2249, 2250, 2251, 2252, 2258, 2259, 2260, 2261, 2262, 2265, 2267, 2268, 2274, 2275, 2276, 2277, 2281, 2283, 2284, 2285, 2287, 2288, 2290, 2291, 2454, 2604, 2861, 3009, 3020, 3028, 4039.

4063* KRAEMER H.J., Arete bei Platon und Aristoteles. Zum
Wesen und zur Geschichte der platonischen
Ontologie. Diss. Tübingen 1958. AHAW 1959,6,
Heidelberg, Winter 1959 600p. 2nd ed.
Amsterdam 1967.
    Rev. CW LIV 1960 96 Hoerber.
    CJ LVII 1961 131 Hoerber.
    MH XIX 1962 135-136 Koller.
    Scholastik XVI 1961 251-253 Ennen.
    Gymnasium LXIX 1962 102-106 Flashar.
    Mnemosyne XVII 1964 311 Verdenius.
    AGPh XLV 1963 194-211 Voigtlaender.
    AAHG XVIII 1965 33-37 Vretska.
    CR XVI 1966 31-34 Adkins.
    ArchPhilos XXVIII 1965 251-265 Aubenque.
    PhilosRdschau X 1962 253-271 Perpeet.
    RecSR L 1962 616-617 des Places.

4064 VLASTOS G., "On Plato's Oral Doctrine". Gnomon XLI
1963 641-655. (review of Kraemer H.J., Arete
bei Platon und Aristoteles. Heidelberg 1959.
Reprinted with appendix "Does Ti. 53c8-d7 give
Support to the Esotericist Thesis?", p.379-403
in Vlastos G., Platonic Studies (see 4622).

4065* GAISER K., Platons ungeschriebene Lehre. Studien
zur systematischen und geschichtlichen
Begründung der Wissenschaften in der
platonischen Schule. Stuttgart, Klett 1963
xii&574p.
    Rev. RThPh XIV 1964 57-58 Lasserre.
    CW LVII 1964 380 Hornsby.
    RFIC XCII 1964 337-341 Berti.
    AC XXXIII 1964 163-164 Joly.
    REG LXXVII 1964 608-609 Mugler.
    RecSR LII 1964 463 des Places.
    DLZ LXXXV 1964 868-871 Flashar.
    CPh LX 1965 136-139 Hoerber.
    AJPh LXXXVI 1965 439-444 Manasse.
    Gnomon XXXVII 1965 131-144 Ilting.
    Centaurus XI 1965 67-68 Gericke.
    Platon XVI 1964 346-348 Georgoulis.
    Gymnasium LXXII 1965 543-547 Merlan.
    AGM XLVIII 1964 188-190 Krafft.
    Helikon IV 1964 471-500 Koevendi.
    ArchPhilos XXVIII 1965 251-265 Solignac.
    RF LVII 1966 87-90 Cambiano.
    AAHG XIX 1966 39-43 Vretska.

PhR LXXV 1966 531-534 Morrow.
AIHS XX 1967 117-120 Hoffmann.
Lychnos 1965-1966 419-421 Duering.
Antonianum XLII 1967 326-329 Platzeck.
Bijdragen XXVIII 1967 102 Nota.
RBPh 1967 116-123 de Strycker.
JPh LXV 1968 379 Randall.
Dialogos V 1968 165-172 Kerkhoff.

4066 BERTI E., "Una nuova ricostruzione delle dottrine non scritte di Platone". GM XIX 1964 546-557. Reprinted as "Eine neue Rekonstruktion der ungeschriebenen Lehre Platons". p.240-258 in Das Problem der ungeschriebenen Lehre Platons (see 4626).

4067 HAGER F.P., "Zur philosophischen Problematik der sogenannten ungeschriebenen Lehre Platos". ASSPh XXIV 1964 90-117.

4068 KOEVENDI D., "Platons wahre Lehre von den Ideen". Helikon IV 1964 471-500.

4069 KRAEMER H.J., "Die platonische Akademie und das Problem einer systematischen Interpretation der Philosophie Platons". KantStud LV 1964 69-101. Reprinted p.198-230 in Das Platonbild, hrsg. von Gaiser K. (see 4595).

4070 KRAEMER H.J., "Retraktionen zum Problem des esoterischen Platon". MH XXI 1964 137-167.

4071 VRIES G.J. DE, "Marginalia bij een esoterische Plato" [in Dutch with French summary]. TPh XXVI 1964 704-719.

4072 BERTI E., Comment on Kraemer H.J., "Retraktionen zum Problem des esoterischen Platon". RSF XX 1965 231-235. Reprinted in German transl. as "Über das Verhältnis von literarischem Werk und ungeschriebener Lehre bei Platon in der Sicht der neueren Forschung". p.88-94 in Das Problem der ungeschriebenen Lehre Platons, hrsg. von Wippern J. (see 4626).

4073 MACH D., "Die platonische Lehre". ZGF IX 1965 194-217.

4074 OEHLER K., "Neue Fragmente zum esoterischen Platon". Hermes XCIII 1965 397-407. Reprinted p.222-233 in Oehler K., Antike Philosophie und byzantinisches Mittelalter. Aufsätze zur

Geschichte des griechischen Denkens. München, Beck 1969.

4075 OEHLER K., "Der entmythologisierte Platon. Zur Lage der Platonforschung". ZPhF XIX 1965 393-420. Reprinted p.66-94 in Oehler K., Antike Philosophie und byzantinisches Mittelalter. Aufsätze zur Geschichte des griechischen Denkens. München, Beck 1969; also p.95-129 in Das Problem der ungeschriebenen Lehre Platons, hrsg. von Wippern J. (see 4626).

4076 SOLIGNAC A. & AUBENQUE P., "Une nouvelle dimension du platonisme. La doctrine non écrite de Platon". ArchPhilos XXVIII 1965 251-265.

4077 BROECKER W., "Platos Vorlesungen". F&F XL 1966 89-92.

4078 KRAEMER H.J., "Aristoxenos über Platons ΠΕΡΙ ΤΑΓΑΘΟΥ". Hermes XCIV 1966 111-112.

4079 FRITZ K. VON, "Zur Frage der esoterischen Philosophie Platons". AGPh XLIX 1967 255-268.

4080 MITTELSTRASS J., "Ontologia more geometrica demonstrata". PhilosRdschau XIV 1966-1967 27-40.

4081 STRYCKER E. DE, "L'enseignement oral et l'oeuvre écrite de Platon". RBPh XLV 1967 116-123.

4082 GADAMER H.G., "Platons ungeschriebene Dialektik". p.9-30 in Idee und Zahl, hrsg. von Gadamer H.G. & Schadewaldt W. (see 4594). Reprinted p.27-49 in Gadamer H.G., Kleine Schriften III (see 4593).

4083 ILTING K.H., "Platons 'ungeschriebene Lehren'. Der Vortrag über das Gute". Phronesis XIII 1968 1-31.

4084 PÉPIN J., "Redécouverte de Platon". Preuves 1968 No.206 76-84.

4085 SCHWARZ F.F., "Platon-Esoterik und Akademie. Zum derzeitigen Stand der Forschung". Die allgemeinbildende höhere Schule XVII 1968 149-153.

V N: ESOTERIC DOCTRINES

4086   VRIES G.J. DE, "Aristoxenos über Περὶ τἀγαθοῦ ".
       Hermes XCVI 1968 124-126.

4087   ISNARDI PARENTE   M.,   "La   VII Epistola   e   Platone
       esoterico".   RSF XXIV 1969 416-431.   Reprinted
       p.147-167 in Isnardi Parente M., Filosofia e
       politica nelle lettere di Platone (see 4603).

4088   MERLAN P., "War   Platons   Vorlesung   Das   Gute
       einmalig?". Hermes XCVI 1968-1969 705-709.

4089   MERLAN P., "Bemerkungen zum neuen Platobild".   AGPh
       LI 1969 111-126.

4090   ROUTILA L., "'Agrapha Dogmata'.   Katsaus Platonin
       esoteeriseen   oppiin   ja   sen   tutkimuksen
       nykyvaiheeseen". Ajatus XXXI 1969 62-90.
       English summary "'Agrapha Dogmata'. A Review of
       Plato's Esoteric Doctrine and its Current
       Research" p.90-92.

4091* SCHMALZRIEDT E., Platon. Der Schriftsteller und die
       Wahrheit. München, Piper 1969 398p.
              Rev. Erasmus XXII 1970 104-105 Marietti.
       RFil(La Plata) XXII 1970 126-128 Maliandi.
       EPh 1970 104-105 Kremer-Marietti.
       CR XXI 1971 364-367 Long.
       PhilosRdschau XIX 1972 273-276 Marten.
       Mnemosyne XXVI 1973 72-73 de Vries.
       MH XXX 1973 237 Graeser.
       PHist VI 1973 165-167 Brann.

4092   VOGEL C.J. DE, "La dernière phase de la philosophie
       de Platon et l'interprétation de Léon Robin".
       p.243-255 in Vogel C.J. de, Philosophia I (see
       4624). Reprinted with changes from Studia varia
       C.W. Vollgraff 1948, p.165-178.   Also   in
       German: "Die Spätphase der Philosophie Platons
       und ihre Interpretation durch Léon Robin".
       p.201-216 in Das Problem der ungeschriebenen
       Lehre Platons, hrsg. von Wippern J. (see
       4626).

4093   VOGEL C.J. DE, "Problems concerning Plato's Later
       Doctrine".   p.256-292 in Vogel C.J. de,
       Philosophia I (see 4624).   Reprinted with
       revisions from Mnemosyne 4a Ser. II 1949
       197-216, 299-318. Also in German: "Probleme
       der späteren Philosophie Platons". p.41-87 in
       Das Problem der ungeschriebenen Lehre Platons,
       hrsg. von Wippern J. (see 4626).

V N: ESOTERIC DOCTRINES

4094 BRUNSCHWIG J., "E.E. I8, 1218a15-32 et le Περὶ
τἀγαθοῦ". p.197-222 in Akten des 5. Symposium
Aristotelicum (Oosterbeck, Niederlande, 21.-29.
August 1969), hrsg. von Moraux P. & Harlfinger
D. Peripatoi. Philologisch-historische Studien
zum Aristotelismus, Bd. I, Berlin, de Gruyter
1971.

4095 GOMPERZ H., "Platons philosophisches System".
p.159-165 in Das Problem der ungeschriebenen
Lehre Platons, hrsg. von Wippern J. (see
4626). Reprinted from Proc. seventh Internat.
Congr. of Philos., ed. by Ryle G. Oxford
1931, p.426-431.

4096 LEISEGANG H., "Platons Diairesis der Ideen und
Zahlen in der Deutung von Julius Stenzel".
p.133-158 in Das Problem der ungeschriebenen
Lehre Platons, hrsg. von Wippern J. (see
4626). Originally published in Die
Platondeutung der Gegenwart, Karlsruhe, Braun
1929, p.90-117.

4097 STENZEL J., "Die Dialektik des platonischen
Seinsbegriffs". p.299-315 in Das Problem der
ungeschriebenen Lehre Platons hrsg. von Wippern
J. (see 4626). Reprinted from Stenzel J.,
Metaphysik des Altertums, München/Berlin,
Oldenbourg 1929/1931, p.128-139.

4098 WILPERT P., "Neue Fragmente aus ΠΕΡΙ ΤΑΓΑΘΟΥ".
p.166-200 in Das Problem der ungeschriebenen
Lehre Platons, hrsg. von Wippern J. (see
4626). Reprinted from Hermes LXXVI 1941
225-250.

4099 FRANCO-REPELLINI F., "Gli agrapha dogmata di
Platone. La loro recente ricostruzione e i suoi
presupposti storico-filosofici". Acme XXVI 1973
51-84.

For further discussions of this subject see 342, 459, 460,
826, 827, 1449, 1452, 1507, 1581, 1951, 2190,
2784, 2873, 2895, 3314, 3325, 4063, 4564.

VI. PLATO'S TERMINOLOGY

The present section contains only studies
devoted primarily to Plato's use of certain
words. It was not feasible to include all works
which treat his use of particular words in
passing. The reader might also wish to consult
section IV A for certain phrases used by Plato.
In addition, see section XIII for general items
such as des Places' Lexique.

In general see 4551.

αἰτία

4100 DRUART T.A., "Le vocabulaire de la causalité chez
      Platon". RPhL LXXI 1973 844.

αἰών

4101* DEGANI E., Αἰών, da Omero ad Aristotele. Univ. di
      Padova, Pubbl. della Fac. di Lett. e Filos.
      XXXVII, Padova, Cedam 1961 163p.
            Rev. Athenaeum XXXIX 1961 364-368
      Untersteiner.
            Gnomon XXXIV 1962 366-370 Classen.
            RPh XXXVI 1962 290-292 Chantraine.
            RSC X 1962 187-188 d'Agostino.
            RCCM IV 1962 117-119 Dazzi.
            Maia XIV 1962 162-165 Masaracchia.
            SMSR XXXIII 1962 171-172.
            Gymnasium LXX 1963 432-433 Schwabl.
            AJPh LXXXIV 1963 329-332 Solmsen.
            CPh LVIII 1963 52-53 Sprague.
            Emerita XXXII 1964 121-128 Lasso de la
      Vega.
            Mnemosyne XVII 1964 328-329 Degani.
            REG LXXVIII 1965 386-388 Détienne.

479

4102 DEGANI E., "Epilegomena su αἰών". RFIC XLI 1963
      104-110.

ἀλήθεια

4103 HEITSCH E., "Die nicht-philosophische ἀλήθεια".
      Hermes XC 1962 24-33.

4105 RANKIN H.D., "Ἀ-λήθεια in Plato". Glotta XLI 1963
      51-54.

4106 HIRSCH W., "Platon und das Problem der Wahrheit".
      p.207-234 in Durchblicke. Martin Heidegger z.
      80. Geburtstag, hrsg. von Klostermann V.
      Frankfurt, Klostermann 1970

For additional discussions of the word see 678, 3149,
      4123.

ἀνάγκη

4107* SCHRECKENBERG H., Ananke. Untersuchungen zur
      Geschichte des Wortgebrauches. Zetemata XXXVI,
      München, Beck 1964 vii&188p. (P.81-105 "Platon:
      Der Ananke-Mythos der Politeia.)

For additional discussion of the word see 3225.

ἄνω καὶ κάτω

4108 VERDENIUS W.J., "ἄνω καὶ κάτω". Mnemosyne XVII 1964
      387.

VI: TERMINOLOGY

ἀρετή

For discussion of the word see 4154.

ἁρμονία

For discussion of the word see 3312.

ἀρχή

4109* EHRHARDT A., The Beginning. A Study in the Greek
Philosophical Approach to the Concept of
Creation from Anaximander to St. John.
Manchester Univ. Pr. 1968 xvi&212p. (ch.6
"Plato", p.87-106.)
For additional discussion of the word see 4100.

αὐτός

4110 PUNTA F. DEL, "Sulla traduzione del termine αὐτός
in Platone". RSF XV 1960 292-294.

4111 PLACES E. DES, " αὐτός et ὁ αὐτός chez Platon".
p.127-130 in Charisteria. F. Novotný
octogenario oblata, cur. Stiebitz F. & Hošek
R. Opera Univ. Purkynianae Brunensis, Fac.
Philos XC, Praha, Státni Pedag. Naklad. 1962.

βλέπειν

4112* PAQUET L., Platon. La médiation du regard. Essai
d'interprétation. Leiden, Brill 1973 viii&484p.
Rev. LEC XLI 1973 462 Druet.

481

VI: TERMINOLOGY

γένεσις

For discussion of the word see 1903, 3237.

γνῶσις

For discussion of the word see 2463, 4123.

δεῖ

For discussion of the word see 4162.

δείκνυμι

4113 SZABÓ A., "Δείκνυμι als mathematischer Terminus für Beweisen". Maia X 1958 106-131.

4114 SZABÓ A., Summary of a paper on the use of δεῖξις in Plato's Meno, given at the Twelfth Colloquium on the History of Mathematics, Mathematical Research Inst. of Oberwolfach, Germany. Janus LIV 1967 146-149.

διαλεκτική, διαλέγεσθαι

For discussion of the words see 2746.

διώκω

4115 KONIARIS G., "On Sappho, fr. 1 (lobel-Page)". Philologus CIX 1965 30-38.

VI: TERMINOLOGY

δόξα

For discussion of the word see 3981, 4003.

δοῦλος, δουλεύειν

4116 NOUSSAN-LETTRY L., "Das Bedeutete und das Gesagte.
Zu δοῦλος, δουλεύειν in Platons Kriton".
WissWelt XXVI 1973 147-150.

δύναμις

For discussion of the word see 3304, 3306, 3329.

εἶδος

For discussion of the word see 2890, 2909, 2985.

εἰκών

For discussion of the word see 595.

εἶναι

4117 PLACES E. DES, "La langue philosophique de Platon.
Le vocabulaire de l'être". CRAI 1961 88-94.

εἴρων, εἰρώνεια

4118 BERGSON L., "Eiron und Eironeia". Hermes XCIX 1971
      409-422.

ἐνθουσιασμός

For discussion of the word see 3205.

ἐνύπνιον

For discussion of the word see 2028.

ἐξαίφνης

For discussion of the word see 1633.

ἐξουσία

For discussion of the word see 3666.

ἐπιείκεια

4119* AGOSTINO F. D', Epieicheia. Il tema dell'equità
      nell'antichità greca. Pubbl. Ist. di Filos.
      del dir. Univ. di Roma III,8, Milano, Giuffrè
      1973 xii&204p.

VI: TERMINOLOGY

ἐπιθυμία

For discussion of the word see 3131.

ἐπιρρυθμίζειν

4120 LEY H. DE, "Δόξις ἐπιρυσμίη. A critical Note on Democritus, fr.7". Hermes XCVII 1969 497-498.

ἐπιστήμη

For discussion of the word see 996, 2463, 4123, 4153.

ἑρμήνεια

For discussion of the word see 1331.

ἔρως

4121 BRANGLIDOR S., "Étude du vocabulaire de l'amour et de l'amitié chez Platon et Aristote". in Répertoire raisonné des doctorats d'État Lettres et Sciences Humaines, inscrit d'oct. 1971 à mars 1973. Univ. de Paris X-Nanterre, CDSH-CNRS 1973.

For additional discussion of the word see 3131.

VI: TERMINOLOGY

ἑταῖρος, ἑταιρία

4122 SARTORI F., "Platone e le eterie". Historia VII
      1958 157-171.

ἑτεροφωνία

For discussion of the word see 3313.

εὑρίσκειν

For discussion of the word see 4123.

ζητεῖν

4123 PLACES E. DES, "La langue philosophique de Platon.
      Le vocabulaire de l'accès au savoir et de la
      science". SicGymn XIV 1961 71-83.

θαυμάζειν

For discussion of the word see 2841.

θεία μοῖρα

For discussion of the expression see 3205.

VI: TERMINOLOGY

θεῖος

4124 BATTEGAZZORE A.M., "Il termine 'divino' nel pensiero
      etico-politico di Platone". PPol III 1970
      409-417.

For additional discussion of the word see 3108, 3691.

θεολογία

4125 GOLDSCHMIDT V., "Theologia". p.141-172 in
      Goldschmidt V., Questions platoniciennes (see
      4598). Reprinted (with additions) from REG
      LXIlI 1950 20ff.

θεοφιλία

For discussion of the word see 3911.

θυμοειδές

4126 OPSTELTEN J.C., "How to Translate the Idea of the
      'Thumoeides' in Plato" [in Dutch]. ANTP LXI
      1969 209-211.

For additional discussion of the word see 2070.

ἰδέα

For discussion of the word see 2890, 2985, 3237.

VI : TERMINOLOGY

ἰσονομία

For discussion of the word see 3612, 3633.

κάθαρσις

4127 LAÍN ENTRALGO P., "Reflexiones sobra lo puro y la
pureza a la luz de Platón". CHisp XXXIV 1958
12-22.

4128* EPP R.H., <u>Katharsis in the Early Platonic Dialogues
and its Cultural Antecedents</u>. Diss. State
Univ. of New York, Buffalo 1971 185p.
[microfilm]. Summary in DA XXXII 1971 1564A.

καί

4129 McARTHUR H.K., "Καί Frequency in Greek Letters".
NTS XV 1969 339-349.

καιρός

4130 KERKHOFF M., "Zum antiken Begriff des Kairos". ZPhF
XXVII 1973 256-274.

καλός

4131 LAURENTANO B., "ΚΑΛΟΣ nel lèssico platonico".
p.477-490 in <u>Actes du IV Congrès intern. Esth.</u>
Athens 1960.

VI: TERMINOLOGY

κοινωνία

For discussion of the word see 4142.

κόρη

4132 DAVISON J.A., "Meanings of the word κόρη".   CR   XVI
      1966 138-141.

κυεῖν

For discussion of the word see 2367.

λῆθη

For discussion of the word see 2607.

λόγος

For discussion of the word see 2909.

μανθάνειν

For discussion of the word see 4123.

VI: TERMINOLOGY

μανία

For discussion of the word see 1828.

μάντις

For discussion of the word see 1069.

μετεωρολογία

4133 GAUDIN C., "Remarques sur la 'météorologie' chez
       Platon". REA LXXII 1970 332-343.

μίμησις

For discussion of the word see 3850.

μίξις

4134 BOUSSOULAS N.I., "Étude sur l'esthétique de la
       composition platonicienne des mixtes". RMM LXV
       1960 422-448; LXVI 1961 142-158.

4135 BOUSSOULAS N.I., "La structure du mélange dans la
       pensée antique". BAGB 1960 481-498.

VI: TERMINOLOGY

μοῦσα, μουσική, μουσικός

4136* VICAIRE P., Recherches sur les mots désignant la
    poésie et le poète dans l'oeuvre de Platon.
    Publ. Fac. des Lettres Montpellier XXII,
    Paris, Presses Universitaires 1964 179p.
        Rev. REG LXXVII 1964 610 des Places.
        AC XXXIV 1965 229 des Places.
        LEC XXXIII 1965 326 Demblon.
        RPh XL 1966 128-129 Louis.
        BSL LXI 1966,2 40-41 Humbert.

νόησις

For discussion of the word see 2909.

νόμος

4137 CASTELLANO A.M., "Vicende semantiche del gr.
    νόμος". AGlI No.55 1970 68-86.

νοῦς

4138 NAGASAKA K., "A Brief Analysis of Nous. A Study of
    a term used by Plato in the Later Days of his
    Life" [in Japanese]. Philosophical Studies
    (Kyoto Univ.) no.476 1961.

4139* JAEGER G., Nus in Platons Dialogen. Hypomnemata
    XVII, Göttingen, Vandenhoeck & Ruprecht 1967
    183p.
        Rev. RecSR LVI 1968 620 des Places.
        AC XXXVII 1968 679 des Places.
        CW LXII 1968 102 Sparshott.
        ABG XII 1968 127-133 Jaeger.
        RPh XLIII 1969 309 des Places.
        CJ LXIV 1969 283-284 Robinson.
        Gnomon XLII 1970 446-449 Skemp.
        Mnemosyne XXIII 1970 424-425 Ferwerda.

VI: TERMINOLOGY

PhilosRdschau XVII 1970 266-274 Ebert.
CR XXI 1971 184-186 Long.
Th&Ph XLV 1970 142 de Vries.

νῦν

For discussion of the word see 1633.

οἰκονομικῄ, οἰκονόμος

For discussion of the words see 3706.

ὁμοιοπαθής

4140   VERDENIUS W.J., "Plato, Rep. 409ab and the Meaning
       of ὁμοιοπαθής". Mnemosyne XX 1967 294-296.

ὁμολογία

4141   ADORNO F., "Appunti su ὁμολογεῖν e ὁμολογία nel
       vocabolario di Platone". DArch II 1968 152-172.

ὁμόνοια

4142   ROMILLY J. DE, "Les différents aspects de la
       concorde dans l'oeuvre de Platon". RPh XLVI
       1972 7-20.

492

VI: TERMINOLOGY

ὄν

For discussion of the word see 4117.

ὄναρ

For discussion of the word see 2028.

ὄνομα

For discussion of the word see 1118.

ὀρείχαλκος

4143 HALLEUX R., "L'orichalque et le laiton". AC XLII 1973 64-81.

οὐσία

4144* BERGER H.H., Ousia in de dialogen van Plato. Een terminologisch onderzoek [with English and German summaries]. Diss. inaug. Batavae ad res antiquas pertinentes VI, Leiden, Brill 1961 x&326p.
    Rev. Gnomon XXXVI 1964 253-258 Widdra.
    Mnemosyne XVII 1964 90-91 Muskens.
    RPhL LXII 1964 665-667 Dhondt.
    RecSR L 1962 609-610 des Places.

4145* MARTEN R., Οὐσία im Denken Platons. Monogr. zur philos. Forsch. XXIX, Meisenheim am Glan, Hain 1962 84p.
    Rev. Gnomon XXXV 1963 829-830 Ilting.
    FR LV 1964 236-237 Cambiano.

VI: TERMINOLOGY

Scholastik XXXVIII 1963 587-588 Ivánka.
Gnomon XXXIX 1967 332-341 Kuhn.
Pensamiento XX 1964 102 Colomer.

For additional discussions of the word see 3237, 4117.

ὄψις

For discussion of the word see 1004.

παίζειν

4146 GUNDERT H., "Wahrheit und Spiel bei den Griechen".
p.13-34 in Das Spiel, Wirklichkeit und Methode.
Freiburger Dies Universitatis XIII 1966.
Freiburg, Schulz 1966.

παράδειγμα

For discussion of the word see 2123.

πλάνη

4147 LOEWENCLAU J. VON, "Die Wortgruppe πλάνη in den
platonischen Schriften". p.111-122 in Synusia.
Festgabe für Wolfgang Schadewaldt zum 15. März
1965, hrsg. von Flashar H. & Gaiser K.
Pfullingen, Neske 1965.

ποίημα, ποιητής, ποιητικός

For discussion of the words see 4136.

ποίησις

4148* LLEDÓ IÑIGO E., El concepto poiesis en la filosofía
griega. Heráclito, Sofistas, Platón. Madrid,
Inst. Luis Vives, Consejo Sup. de Investig.
Cientif. 1961 158p.
Rev. REG LXXIV 1961 490-493 Vicaire.
GIF XIV 1961 359-360 Jannaccone.
PhilosRdschau X 1962 272-277 von Albrecht.
EClas VI 1962 617-619 Adrados.
Athenaeum XL 1962 195-196 Marenghi..
Helmantica XIII 1962 133-134 Rodriguez.
RPh XXXVII 1963 300-301 Louis.
CR XIII 1963 116 Kerferd.
AGPh XLV 1963 98-100 Colomer.

πολύτροπος

For discussion of the word see 1321.

ῥάψῳδός

4149 TARDITI G., "Sull'origine e sul significato della
parola rapsodo". Maia XX 1968 137-145.

σοφία

4150 LOSEV A., "Uber die Bedeutung des Terminus σοφία
bei Plato". Meander XXII 1967 340-347.

For additional discussion of the word see 1054, 4153.

VI: TERMINOLOGY

συμμετρία

For discussion of the word see 4100.

στοιχεῖον

For discussion of the word see 3820.

συμφωνία

For discussion of the word see 4142.

συνείδησις

4151* CANCRINI A., Syneidesis. Il tema semantico della con-scientia nella Grecia antica. Lessico intellettuale europeo VI, Roma, Ed. dell'Ateneo 1970 170p. (for Plato see esp. p.87-103.)
       Rev. BAGB 1971 433-434 Levet.
       RPh XLVI 1972 108 des Places.

σύνεσις

4152 RODGERS V.A., "Σύνεσις and the Expression of Conscience". GRBS X 1969 241-254.

VI: TERMINOLOGY

τέχνη

4153* LYONS J., Structural Semantics. An Analysis of Part
of the Vocabulary of Plato. Publ. of the
Philol. Soc. XX, Oxford, Blackwell 1963 237p.
Rev. REG LXXVII 1964 345 des Places.
ALing XVII 1965 53-55 Collinge.
Emerita XXXIII 1965 159-161 Adrados.
RPh XXXIX 1965 321 des Places.
JHS LXXXV 1965 206-207 Brandwood.
CR XV 1965 311-314 Robinson.
Language XLI 1965 504-512 Wyatt.
CPh LXI 1966 280-282 Rist.
AAHG   XIX   1966   242-244   von
Lochner-Huettenbach.
Mnemosyne XIX 1966 416-420 Gonda.

4154* KUBE J., Τέχνη und ἀρετή. Sophistisches und
platonisches Tugendwissen. Quellen & Stud. zur
Gesch. der Philos. XII, Berlin, de Gruyter
1969 x&255p.
Rev. AC XXXVIII 1969 546 des Places.
REA LXXI 1969 479-481 Moreau.
Salesianum XXXII 1970 730.
DLZ XCI 1970 393-394 Schottlaender.
Angelicum   XLVII   1970   524-525
Vansteenkiste.
WJb III 1970 269-271 Heintel.
Bijdragen XXXII 1971 446-447 Berghs.
StudClas XIII 1971 315-317 Noica.
Gnomon XLIII 1971 235-239 Jaeger.
CR XXI 1971 28-30 Skemp.
RPh XLV 1971 341 Louis.
ACR I 1971 245 O'Brien.
RFIC C 1972 489-492 Isnardi Parente.
RSC XX 1972 443-445 d'Agostino.
Mnemosyne XXVI 1973 189-190 Ferwerda.

4155 BATTEGAZZORE A.M., "Il termine techne in Platone
nella   sua   connotazione   teoreca   ed
etico-pratica". PPol V 1972 493-504.

For additional discussions of the word see 996, 3261,
3276.

τραγικός, τραγῳδεῖν

4156 DALFEN J., "Übertragener Gebrauch von τραγικός und
τραγῳδεῖν bei Platon und anderen Autoren des 5.
und 4. Jahrhunderts". Philologus CXVI 1972
76-92. For additional discussion of the word
see 1503.

τρόπος

For discussion of the word see 1321.

ὕπαρ

For discussion of the word see 2028.

ὑπόθεσις

For discussion of the word see 3288, 3290.

ὑπομένειν

4157 FESTUGIÈRE A.J., "῾Υπομονή dans la tradition
grecque". p.273-282 in Festugière A.J., Études
de philosophie grecque (see 4587). Reprinted
from RSR XXI 1931 477-486.

φιλία

For discussion of the word see 3131, 4121.

φιλοσοφία

4158 BURKERT W., "Platon oder Pythagoras? Zum Ursprung
      des Wortes Philosophie". Hermes LXXXVIII 1960
      159-177.

φρόνησις

4159* BUFF E.N., Phronesis in the Works of Plato's Last
      Period. Diss. Cornell 1962 116p. [microfilm].
      Summary in DA XXIII 1963 2907-2908.

φύσις

4160* BEERETZ F.L., Die Bedeutung des Wortes φύσις in den
      Spätdialogen Platons. Diss. Köln 1963 128p.
      Rev. RPhL LXIV 1966 310 Roelants.

For additional discussion of the word see 2033, 3237.

φωνή

4161 LEROY M., "Sur un emploi de φωνή chez Platon". REG
      LXXX 1967 234-241.

χρή

4162   BENARDETE   S., "Χρή and δεῖ in   Plato   and   Others".
           Glotta XLIII 1965 285-298.

For discussion of the word see 1069.

SOCRATES

VII: GENERAL STUDIES ON SOCRATES

A: BOOKS ON SOCRATES

4163* ADORNO F., Introduzione a Socrate. Bari, Laterza
      1970 214p.
          Rev. RF LXI 1970 432-434 Federici
      Vescovini.
          Filosofia XXII 1971 117-118 Ravera.
          A&R XVII 1972 30-34 Beraldi.
          Maia XXIV 1972 191-192 Ouesta.

4164* BANFI A., Socrate. Bibl. Mod. Mondadori 767-768,
      Milano, Mondadori 1963 332p.
          Rev. CW LVIII 1965 221 Urdahl.

4165* BIRNBAUM W., Sokrates. Urbild abendländischen
      Denkens. Persönlichkeit & Gesch. LXXXI,
      Göttingen, Munsterschmidt 1973 85p.

4166* BRUN J., Socrate. Coll. Que sais-je? No.899,
      Paris, Presses Universitaires 1960 128p. Also
      in English: Socrates, transl. by Scott D. New
      York, Walker 1963 xix&120p. Also in Japanese:
      Sokuratesu, transl. by Arita J. Tokyo,
      Hakusuisha 1962 136p.
          Rev. RSF XVI 1961 113-114 del Punta.
          RThPh XI 1961 96 Piguet.
          BAGB 1961 300 Malye.
          AC XXX 1961 577 Loreau.
          RPhL LIX 1961 521-522 Lefèvre.
          ME X 1961 56 Loreau.
          REA LXIV 1962 166 Aubenque.
          Sophia XXX 1962 371 Montoneri.
          Pensamiento XIX 1963 247-248 Martínez
      Gómez.
          LJ 1963 1530 Lazenby.
          [of English edn.] CW LVII 1964 277 Anton.

4167* CALLOT E., La doctrine de Socrate. Bibl. philos.,
      Paris, Rivière 1970 178p.
          Rev. RS XCIII 1972 85-88 Bernhardt.

VII A: BOOKS ON SOCRATES

4168* CARBONARA C., La filosofia greca. Socrate, i
socratici minori. 2a ed. Filosofia e
pedagogia, Napoli, Libreria scientifica editrice
1965 86p.

4169* CROSS R.N., Socrates, the man and his Mission.
Freeport, New York, Books for Libraries 1970
344p. Reprint of 1914 edn.

4170* CRESSON A., Socrate. Sa vie, son oeuvre, avec un
exposé de sa philosophie. 3e éd. Coll.
Philosophes, Paris, Presses Universitaires 1962
132p.

4171* FESTUGIÈRE A.J., Socrate. Coll. Les chemins du
réel XIX, Paris, Éd. du Fuseau 1966 160p.
Rev. BAGB 1967 147 Wartelle.
RS LXXXVIII 1967 254 Bernard-Maître.

4172* FISCHER J.L., Sokrates nelegendární [Socrates the
non-legendary]. Acta Univ. Palackiana.
Olomucensis Fac. Philosophica XXXV, Praha,
Státni Pedagogické Nakl. 1965 137p.
Rev. OMF 1965 664-665 I.H.
FilosCas 1966 133-135 Bartoš.
LitNov XV 1966 7 Zumr.

4173* GALLI G., Socrate ed alcuni dialoghi platonici
(Apologie, Convito, Lachete, Eutifrone, Liside,
Ione). Univ. di Torino, Pubbl. della Fac. di
Magistero XII Torino, Giapichelli 1958 250p.
Rev. RPhL LVII 1959 445-446 Rutten.
ASSPh XVIII 1958 190 Reymond.
PLA XIII 1960 357-360 Niebergall.
RFil(Madrid) XIX 1960 516 Díaz.
RPhilos LXXXVII 1962 127-128 Namer.
Pensamiento XVII 1961 236 Martínez.
GM XVII 1962 712-716 Schiavone.

4174* GIANNANTONI G., Che cosa ha veramente detto Socrate.
Che cosa hanno veramente detto XXXIV, Roma,
Ubaldini 1971 210p. Also Spanish transl. Qué
ha dicho verdaderamente Sócrates, trad. por
Fernández F. Col. Qué ha dicho verdaderamente
XV, Madrid, Ed. Doncel 1972 218p.

4175* GÓMEZ ROBLEDO A., Sócrates y el socratismo. Mexico
City, Fondo de Cultura económica 1966 205p.
Rev. Gregorianum 1968 575-584 Gonzáles
Caminero.
CuadFilos 1968 154-156 LaCroce.
Dianoia XIV 1968 267-272 Navarro.

4176* GULLEY N., The Philosophy of Socrates. London,
Macmillan 1968 ix&222p.
Rev. PhilosBks May 1969 10 Hamlyn.
TLS LXVIII 1969 862.
CW LXII 1969 325-326 Etheridge.
JHPh VIII 1970 335-338 Neumann.
Mind LXXXIX 1970 149-150 Charlton.
PhilosQ XX 1970 77-78 Telfer.
PhR LXXIX 1970 565-568 Robinson.
CR XX 1970 355-357 Crombie.
Dialogue VIII 1969-1970 346-349 Seligman.
GCFI XLIX 1970 89-93 Montuori.
JVI V 1970-1971 73-75 Howie.
JCS XIX 1971 137-140 Mori.

4177* GUTHRIE W.K.C., A History of Greek Philosophy, III:
The Fifth-Century Enlightenment. Cambridge
Univ. Pr. 1969 xvi&544p.
Rev. Sapientia XXV 1970 152 Bolzán.
Hermathena CX 1970 104 Luce.
Studium IX 1969 549-550 Manzanedo.
Erasmus XXII 1970 426-430 Nickel.
AHR LXXV 1969-1970 1705-1706 Thayer.
NG XVII 1970 437-438 Zamora.
Phoenix 1970 348 Woodbury.
DalR 1970 262 Treash.
Tablet 1970 129 Armstrong.
TLS 30 Apr. 1970 476.
Lychnos 1969-1970 394-396 Regnell.
DLZ XCI 1970 693-695 Schottlaender.
Logos I 1970 350-353 Montuori.
CPh LXVI 1971 117-118 Sprague.
JHPh IX 1971 376-382 Robinson.
JHS XCI 1971 178-186 Skemp.
AusJP XLIX 1971 219-223 Rankin.
BO XXVIII 1971 231-233 de Vogel.
Mnemosyne XXIV 1971 306-307 Verdenius.
TPh XXXIII 1971 783-787 Smets.
RPh XLV 1971 151 Mugler.
SIF III 1971 219-221 Preus.
RPortFil XXVII 1971 214-216 Martins.
NS XLV 1971 625-628 Cleve.
PhilosBks Oct. 1971 9 Wasserstein.
PhilosQ XXII 1972 357-358 Adkins.
Gymnasium LXXIX 1972 108-110 de Vogel.
ArchPhilos XXXV 1972 678-680 Solignac.
Philosophia(Athens) III 1973 443-454
Bayonas.
PhilosRdschau XX 1973 136 Gadamer.
CF XXVII 1973 92-97 Cloeren.
CJ LXIX 1973 168-169 Allen.
CR XXII 1972 52-56 Kerferd.

Kriterion XX 1973-1974 326-328 Barata
Vianna.

4178* GUTHRIE W.K.C., Socrates. Cambridge Univ. Pr.
1971 vii&200p. (Taken from Guthrie W.K.C., A
History of Greek Philosophy, vol. III.)
Rev. AC XLI 1972 719 Janssens.
EPh 1973 86-88 Moreau.
DUJ XXXIV 1973 318-320 Mills.
RHR 1973 No.184 79-80 Turcan.
DT LXXVI 1973 405-406 Rohatyn.

4179* HUMBERT J., Socrate et les petits socratiques.
Coll. Les grands penseurs, Paris, Presses
Universitaires 1967 293p.
Rev. MSR XXIV 1967 49-51 Dumortier.
AC XXXVI 1967 722 Joly.
RPhL LXV 1967 549 Druart.
REA LXIX 1967 386-388 Moreau.
RS LXXXVIII 1967 254-255 Bernard-Maître
BAGB 1967 352 Malye.
RMM LXXIII 1968 366-367 Brunschwig.
LEC XXXVI 1968 277-278 Loriaux.
REG LXXXI 1968 288-291 Vicaire.
ArchPhilos XXXI 1968 487-488 Chatelard.
CR XVIII 1968 290-292 Gulley.
RPh XLII 1968 326 Louis.
Gnomon XLI 1969 335-338 Wehrli.
Helmantica XX 1969 404-405 Ortall.

4180* JASPERS K., Die massgebenden Menschen. Sokrates,
Buddha, Konfuzius, Jesus. Piper Paperback,
München, Piper 1964 210p. Also Berlin, Dt.
Buch-Gemeinschaft 1967 239p. Taken from Die
grossen Philosophen, Bd.I, 1957.
Rev. FolHum III 1965 86 Guardiet.

4181* JASPERS K., Socrates, Buddha, Confucius, Jesus. The
Paradigmatic Individuals, ed. by Arendt H.,
transl. by Manheim R. New York, Harcourt Brace
& World 1962 104p.

4182* JASPERS K., Les grands philosophes, I: Ceux qui ont
donné la mesure de l'humain, Socrate, Boudha,
Confucius, Jésus. Coll. Le mond en 10/18
Nos.349-350, Paris, Union général d'éd. 1966
320p.
Rev. RevNouv XLI 1965 180-184
VanderGucht.
ASSPh XXVI 1966 307-308 Christoff.
JSS 1965 268 Friedman.

4183* JASPERS K., Los grandes filósofos. Vol. I: Los
      hombres decisivos. Sócrates, Buda, Confucio,
      Jesús, Version castellana de Simon P. Buenos
      Aires, Ed. Sudamericana 1966 256p.

4184* JASPERS K., Socrates, Boeddha, Confucius, Jezus.
      (Die Massgebenden Menschen. Eerste gedeelte
      uit: Die grosse Philosophen, I, vert. en
      ingeleid door Sperna Weiland J. Wetenschap en
      Bezinning. Utrecht, Erven J. Bijleveld 1960
      174p.
            Rev. Streven XIV 1960-1961 614-615 Nota.

4185* JENSEN P.J., Sokrates [in Danish]. København, Gad
      1969 95p.

4186* KESTERS H., Kérygmes de Socrate. Essai sur la
      formation du message socratique. Louvain,
      Nauwelaerts 1965 174p.
            Rev. LEC XXXIV 1966 183-184 Delaunois.
            EPh XXI 1966 415 Jagu.
            Gnomon XXXIX 1967 624 Kuhn.
            RPh XLI 1967 160 des Places.
            Mnemosyne XX 1967 467 de Vries.
            Antonianum XLII 1967 576 Ferreira.
            NRTh LXXXIX 1967 98 de Give.
            RBPh XLV 1967 974-975 Henry.
            PhilosQ XVII 1967 358 Huby.
            AC XXXVII 1968 743 Joly.
            RPhL LXVII 1969 492 Jordens.
            CR XXI 1971 292 Charlton.

4187* KROKIEWICZ A., Sokrates. Warszawa, Inst. Wydawn.
      Pax 1958 187p.
            Rev. Kultura(Paris) CXXXIX 1959 142-146
      Jordan.
            A&R VI 1961 41-43 Wiśniewski.

4188* KRONSKA I., Sokrates. Warszawa, Wiedza Powszechna
      1964 239p. Also 2nd edn. 1968 255p.
            Rev. StudFiloz 1965 167-169 Kotarbiński.
            VF XXIII 1969 172.

4189* KUHN H., Sokrates. Versuch über den Ursprung der
      Metaphysik. München, Koesel 1959 223p. Also
      Italian transl. Socrate. Indagini sull'origine
      della metafisica, a cura di Rigobello A.
      Milano, Fabbri 1969 230p.
            Rev. [of German edn.] ZKTh LXXXI 1959 373
      Koreth.
            FZPT VI 1959 316-317 Morard.
            ThQ CXXXIX 1959 481-482 Schmuecker.

Gnomon XXXII 1960 275-276 Kerferd.
PhilosRdschau VIII 1960 160-170 Gaiser.
BA 1960 158 Hertal.
PLA XIV 1961 3-9 Poeggeler.
NkTh LXXXIII 1961 973 Hayen.
RBPh XI 1962 1417 de Strycker.
Paideia XVII 1962 73 Beschin.
Bijdragen XXV 1964 326-327 Geurtsen.
[of Ital. edn.] RIFD XLIX 1972 132-133
d'Agostino.

4190 RIEZU J., "Vigencia y actualidad de Sócrates" [on
Kuhn's book]. EstFilos XX 1971 113-130.

4191* LASAULX E. VON, Des Sokrates Leben, Lehre und Tod.
Nachwort von Mattke G. Denken, Schauen, Sinnen
VI, Stuttgart, Verl. Freies Geistesleben 1958
75p. Kurzausg. Orig. Ausg. 1857.
Rev. ZRGG XI 1959 392.

4192* LEIDER K., Sokrates. Vortragsreihe der Philos.
Akad. zu Lübeck, Hamburg, Matthies 1970 28p.

4193* MAIER H., Sokrates. Sein Werk und seine
geschichtliche Stellung. Aalen, Scientia-Verl.
1964 xii&638p. Reprint of 1913 edn.

4194 JAEGER W., Rev. of H. Maier's Sokratesbuch.
p.187-200 in Jaeger, W., Scripta Minora I (see
4605). Reprinted from DLZ 1915 Sp. 333-340,
381-384.

4195* MONDOLFO R., Sócrates. 3a ed. Col. Cuadernos
VIII, Buenos Aires, Eudeba 1959 63p. 6a ed.
1969 152p. Also Portuguese transl. Sócrates,
trad. de Licurgo Gomes da Motta. São Paulo,
Mestre Jou 1963 113p.

4196* MONTUORI M., Socrate dal mito alla storia. Quad.
dell'Ist. ital. di cultura I, Atene 1967 68p.
Rev. Cultura VI 1968 433-437 Capizzi &
Sillitti.
ArchPhilos XXXII 1969 346-347 Solignac.
GM XXIV 1969 340-341 Sorge.

4197* NEBEL G., Sokrates. Stuttgart, Klett 1969 208p.
Rev. RBPh XLVIII 1970 117-118 Druet.
Helmantica XXI 1970 326 Orosio.
CW LXIII 1970 237 Fortenbaugh.
RH XCIV 1970 441-448 Will.
ArchPhilos XXXIII 1970 979-981 Solignac.
Bijdragen XXXI 1970 459 Poncelet.

PHist V 1972 40-41 Frede D.

4198* PETANDER K., Sokrates, personlighetstankens förkunnare [Socrates. The Prophet of the Idea of Personality]. Stockholm, Natur och Kultur 1959 202p.

4199* PONI S., Il Fedone, I dialoghi socratici. Saggio filosofico. Rocca San Casciano, Cappelli 1963 173p.
Rev. GM XXI 1966 Guazzoni Foà.

4200* RUSCITTI R., Socrate. Vicenza, R.A.D.A.R. 1969 62p.

4201* SAUVAGE M., Sokrates, Dutch transl. by Brommer P. Pictura Pocket VII, Utrecht, Spectrum 1959 192p. Spanish transl. by Ramales I.G. de, Sócrates y la conciencia del hombre. Madrid, Ed. Aguilar 1959 219p. Italian transl. by Piaggi A., Socrate. Milano, Mondadori 1960 192p. English transl. by Hepburne-Scott P., Socrates and the human Conscience. New York, Harper & Row and London, Longmans 1960 191p. French edn. Socrate e la conscience de l'homme. Maîtres spirituels IX, Paris 1960.
Rev. [of Dutch transl.] Hermeneus XXXI 1960 142 van Straaten.
[of Spanish transl.] RFil(LaPlata) XI 1962 118-119 Garat.
[of Italian transl.] RSF XVI 1961 113-114 del Punta.
PedVit 1961 Bellanti.
[of English transl.] CW LIV 1961 226 Hoerber.
CJ LVII 1962 232 Furley.
Personalist XLII 1961 285 P.J.W.M.
ChQR LVII 1962 232 Furley.

4202* SILVERBERG R., Sócrates. Col. Moderna XCVIII, Mexico City, Diana 1967 156p.

4203* SPRANGER E., Das Rätsel Sokrates, translated from the German into modern Greek with an intro. by Koniditsiotis B.A. Athens 1971 54p. Originally appeared in German in 1954.

4204* TATAKIS V.N., Ὁ Σωκράτης. Ἡ ζωή του, ἡ διδασκαλία του. Athens, Astir 1970 147p.
Rev. Philosophia(Athens) I 1971 450-453 Bayonas.

ACR I 1971 215-216 Karavites.
JHS XC 1970 243 Kustas.

4205* TAYLOR A.E., El pensiamento de Sócrates, trad. de
hernández Barroso M., rev. de Frost E.C.
Mexico City/Buenos Aires, Fondo de Cultura
Económica 1961 160p.
Rev. RbF XII 1962 258-260 Vita.
Humanitas IV 1963 724-727 Rangel Guerra.
RPortFil XIX 1963 328 Alves.
Convivium 1963 236-237 Espinosa.

4206* TURLINGTON B., Socrates, the Father of Western
Philosophy. Immortals of Philos. & Relig., New
York, Watts 1970 x&245p.
Rev. CR XXI 1971 458 Charlton.

4207* VERSÉNYI L., Socratic Humanism, with a forward by
Brumbaugh R.S. New Haven, Yale Univ. Pr. 1963
xiii&187p.
Rev. Arion III 1964 112-115 Gould.
CW LVII 1964 355 Anton.
JPh LXI 1964 343-347 West.
CJ LXI 1965 30-32 Best.
CB XV 1965 356-357 Crombie.
CPh LXI 1966 200-201 Sprague.
Hermathena CII 1966 118-120 Luce.
JHS LXXXVI 1966 224-225 Goodman.
EPh XXII 1967 112 Pépin.
ModS XLVI 1968-1969 183-184 Costelloe.
JHPh VII 1969 79-81 Palmer.
PhilForum IX 1971 114-119 Plochmann.
PhilForum IX 1971 119-122 Wild.
PhilForum IX 1971 122-129 Versényi (reply
to Plochmann & Wild.)

4208* VLOEMANS A., Sokrates. Helden van de geest XXIII,
s'Gravenhage, Kruseman 1963 160p.

4209* WINSPEAR A.D. & SILVERBERG T., Who was Socrates?
New York, Russell & Russell 1960 96p. Reprint
of 1936 edn. Also Ital. transl., Realtà di
Socrate, trad. di Bertondini A. Studi filos.,
Urbino, Argalia 1965 148p.
Rev [of Italian edn.]. StudUrb XXXIX 1965
500-502.
DeHomine 1966 341-342 Giannantoni G.
RF LVIII 1967 203-204 Cambiano.

4210* VALASTRO F., La tesi politica su Socrate di A.
Winspear e T. Silverberg. Siracusa, Società
tipograf. di Siracusa 1970 93p.

VII A: BOOKS ON SOCRATES

4211* ZELLER E., Socrates and the Socratic Schools, transl. by Reichel O. 3rd edn. reissue. New York, Russell & Russell 1962 410p.

VII B: CHAPTERS ON SOCRATES IN HISTORIES OF ANCIENT PHILOSOPHY

For these works the reader should consult section I B above.

VII C: SECTIONS ON SOCRATES IN OTHER WORKS

4212 LANDMANN M., "Sokrates". p.65-69 in Landmann M. u.a. De Homine. Der Mensch im Spiegel seines Gedankens. Freiburg, Alber 1962.

4213* PANNWITZ R., Gilgamesch-Sokrates. Titanentum und Humanismus. Stuttgart, Klett 1966 xx&344p.
Rev. Erasmus XIX 1967 737-740 Lasserre.
OLZ LXIII 1968 560 Jaritz.
RBPh XLVI 1968 163 Limet.
CW LXI 1968 406 Best.

4214 KIDD I.G., "Socrates". Encyclopedia of Philosophy, ed. by Edwards P. vol. III, 480-486. New York/London, Collier-Macmillan 1967.

4215* DETTELBACH H. VON, Von Sokrates bis Sartre. Gestalten der europäischen Geistesgeschichte. Graz/Wien/Köln, Verl. Styria 1968 295p. (p.23-30 "Die Grösse des Sokrates".)

4216* EHRENBERG V., From Solon to Socrates. Greek History and Civilisation during the sixth and fifth centuries B.C. London, Methuen 1968 xv&493p. (for Socrates see esp. p.362-375.)

4217 BELAVAL Y., "Socrate". p.451-463 in Histoire de la Philosophie, I, sous la direction de Parain B. Encyclopédie de la Pléiade XXVI, Paris, Gallimard 1969.

VII C: SECTIONS ON SOCRATES IN OTHER WORKS

4218* TANAKA M., Collected Works, III: The Sophists, Socrates and Others. Tokyo, Tsukuma Shobo 1969.

4219 GOLDSCHMIDT V., "Socrate". p.53-62 in Goldschmidt V., Questions platoniciennes (see 4598). Reprinted from Les philosophes célèbres, éd. par Mazenod L. 1956 p.58ff.

4220 SCHMALZRIEDT E., "Sokrates". p.542-553 in Enzykl. Die Grossen der Weltgesch. Bd.I. Zürich, Kindler 1971.

4221* SCIACCA M.F., Studi sulla filosofia antica. Milano, Marzorati 1971 449p. ("Socrate", p.207-224 [reprinted from Orientamenti filosofici e didattici, I, 2a ed. Milano, Marzorati 1969 57-76]; "Il significato e i limiti dell'ironia di Socrate", p.225-234 [reprinted from Logos 1937].)

VII D: ARTICLES TREATING SOCRATES AND HIS PLACE IN PHILOSOPHY IN GENERAL

4222 BUCKE R.M., "Sokrates". MenschS XII 1958 Nr.7 11-12.

4223 KUHN H., "Sokrates. Versuch über den Ursprung der Metaphysik". NRdschau LXX 1959 328-351.

4224 BANU I., "Critical Appreciation of the Socratic Moment in the History of Greek Philosophy" [in Rumanian with Russian and French summaries]. StudClas II 1960 99-125.

4225 BRANÇA MIRANDA M. DE, "O mensagem de Sócrates aos nossos dias". Vozes LV 1961 81-87.

4226 DREXLER H., "Gedanken über den Sokrates der Platonischen Apologie". Emerita XXIX 1961 177-201.

4227 METZGER A., "Die sokratische Todessehnsucht". Merkur XV 1961 301-328.

4228 HAHN L.C.G., "Het denkmoment 'Sokrates'". Dialoog II 1961-1962 114-124.

VII D:GENERAL ARTICLES ON SOCRATES

4229 BRUNT N., "De Socratische vergissing". ANTP LV
      1962-1963 189-199.

4230 ENGLER F., "Sokrates". ELeb XII 1963 25-26.

4231 CALOGERO G., "Il messaggio di Socrate". Cultura IV
      1966 289-301.

4232 BRUNNER C., "Sokrates--der erste freie Mann". Zeit
      XXII 1967 10.

4233 HARTMANN O.J., "Sokrates, Vater des Abendlandes,
      Revolutionär des Geistes und Martyrer seines
      Auftrags". Kommenden XXI 1967 16-18.

4234 VOGEL C.J. DE, "Was Socrates een humanist?".
      p.85-105 in Vogel C.J. de, Theoria (see 4623).

4235 WINDELBAND W., "Socrate", a cura di Cristaldi R.V.
      & Mueller H.O. Teoresi XXII 1967 3-13.

4236 AUBENQUE P., "La conversion socratique". EPh 1970
      159-166.

4237 DAVIES C., "Socrates". HT XX 1970 799-805.

4238 SHIKANO H., "A portrait of Socrates" [in Japanese].
      Humanity Studies (Osaka Medical School) III
      1972.

For further discussion see 4482.

VIII: THE SOURCES FOR OUR KNOWLEDGE OF SOCRATES

A: COLLECTIONS OF SOURCES

4239* CORNFORD F.M., Greek Religious Thought. From Homer
to the Age of Alexander. New York, Abrahams
Magazine Service 1969 xxxv&252p. Reprint of
1923 edn. (ch.14, p.158-187 contains excerpts
from Aristophanes, Plato, and Xenophon on
Socrates' religious views.)

4240* FERGUSON J., Socrates. A Source Book, compiled and
in part transl. by Ferguson J. Open Univ. Set
Book Arts Found. Course, London, Macmillan 1970
xii&335p.
Rev. DUJ XXXIII 1971 57-58 Skemp.
G&R XVIII 1971 106-107 Sewter.
TLS LXX 1971 376.
Athenaeum XLIX 1971 224-225 Franco
Repellini.
AC XL 1971 778 Bastaits.
CR XXII 1972 280-281 Charlton.
JHS XCII 1972 212-214 Robinson.
LEC XL 1972 439 Druet.
Phoenix 1972 413 Schroeder.

4241* LEHMANN-LEANDER E.R., Sokrates und die
Vorsokratiker, hrsg. & eingel. von
Lehmann-Leander E.R. Wiesbaden, Vollmer 1959
279p.

4242* MARTIN G., Sokrates in Selbstzeugnissen und
Bilddokumenten, die Zeittafel u. d. Bibliog.
besorgte Vollmer G. Rowohlts Monographien
CXXVIII, Hamburg, Rowohlt 1967 158p. 2. Aufl.
1968.
Rev. RUB XX 1967-1968 162 Janssens.

4243* FRAISSE A. & FRAISSE J.C., Socrate, Portraits et
enseignements, textes choisis & trad. par
Fraisse A. & J.C. Coll. Les grands textes,
Paris, Presses Universitaires 1972 238p.

4244* RIGOBELLO A., Il messagio di Socrate, a cura di
Rigobello A. Antologia di scritti di Platone,
Senofonte, Aristotele. Il pensiero, Brescia, La
Scuola 1958 xxxi&109p.

4245* BARCHI M., Socrate. La vita e il pensiero. Testi scelti e illustrati di Platone, Senofone e Aristotele. Spoleto, Accademia spoletina 1959 109p.

4246* ADORNO F., I sofisti e Socrate. Una antologia dai frammenti e dalle testimonianze. Torino 1961 lvii&223p. (For Socrates see esp. part III, p.109-218.)

4247* LABRIOLA A., La dottrina di Socrate secondo Senofonte, Platone ed Aristotele, a cura di Pane L. dal. Milano, Feltrinelli 1961 294p. Reprint of 1871 edn.
Rev. RSI LXXIII 1961 560-567 Isnardi.
IRSH VI 463.
NRS XLV 1961 627-631 Capanna.
GCFI XLI 1962 132-133 Plebe.

4248 BERTONDINI A., "Intorno al Socrate di Labriola e Spaventa". StudUrb XXXV 1961 236-248.

4249* CAMBIANO G. ed., Socrate nella letteratura socratica antica, trad., introd. e note a cura di Cambiano G. Milano, Principato 1970 99p.

4250* GIANNANTONI G. et al., Socrate. Tutte le testimonianze da Aristofane e Senofonte ai Padri Cristiani, introd. e indici di Giannantoni G., trad. di Giannantoni G., Gigante M., Laurenti R., Marzullo B., Celluprica E., Felice M.C. de, Joppolo A.M. & Panvini A. Bari, Laterza 1971 xx&594p.
Rev. Sophia XLI 1973 115 Ottaviano.

4251* PIERI A., Interpretazione di Socrate, a cura di Pieri A. Bibl. di class. greci, Milano, Mursia 1971 194p.

4252* CAPIZZI A., Socrate, Antologia di testi, a cura di Capizzi A. Pensatori antichi e moderni XCII, Firenze, La Nuova Italia 1973 xxii&121p.

4253* SOCRATES: Sources, Platão, Defesa de Sócrates, trad. de Bruna J., Aristófanes, As nuvens, trad. de Reale Starzynski G.M., Xenofonte, Feitos memoráveis de Sócrates; Apologia de Sócrates, trad. de Rangel L. São Paulo, Abril Cultural 1972 230p.

4254* Xenophon, Spomienky nu Sokrata [Reminiscences on Socrates]; Platon, Sokratova obrana [Socrates' Defense], Czech. transl. & comm. by Šimkovič E. & Špaňár J. Bratislava, Tatran 1970 232p. Rev. SlovPohl 1971 138-139 D.H.

For additional collections see 985, 4273.

VIII B: DISCUSSION OF THE SOURCES

4255* RODRÍGUEZ BRASA S., En torno a la Apología de Sócrates de Jenofonte. Salamanca, Col. de San Estanislao 1958 120p.
Rev. Helmantica IX 1958 345 Jiménez Delgado.

4256 GIGON O., "Die Sokratesdoxographie bei Aristoteles". MH XVI 1959 174-212.

4257* LONGO V., Άνηρ ώφέλιμος. Il problema della composizione dei 'Memorabili di Socrate' attraverso lo scritto di difesa. Univ. di Genova Fac. di Lett. Pubbl. dell'Istituto di filologia class. XIV, Genova, Ist. di filol. class. 1959 93p.

4258 ERBSE H., "Die Architektonik im Aufbau von Xenophons Memorabilien". Hermes LXXXIX 1961 257-287.

4259 FLACELIÈRE R., "A propos du Banquet de Xénophon". REG LXXIV 1961 93-118.

4260 MAIER H., "Il problema delle fonti socratiche". p.180-190 in Rossi P. ed., Antologia della critica filosofica (see 4613). Reprinted from Maier H., Socrate, la suo opera e il suo posto nella storia, trad. di Sanna G. Firenze, La Nuova Italia 1943, vol.I, p.7-16.

4261 VOGEL C.J. DE, "Il Socrate di Olof Gigon". p.191-202 in Rossi P. ed., Antologia della critica filosofica (see 4613). Italian transl. of "Une nouvelle interprétation du problème socratique", Mnemosyne I 1951 30-39.

4262 HALPERN S., "Free Association in 423 B.C. Socrates in 'The Clouds' of Aristophanes". PsychR L 1963 69-86.

VIII B: SOURCES FOR SOCRATES: DISCUSSION

4263 VOGEL C.J. DE, "Who was Socrates?". JHPh I 1963
143-161. Revised version p.109-130 in Vogel
C.J. de, Philosophia (see 4624).

4264 VRIES G.J. DE, "Novellistic Traits in Socratic
Literature". Mnemosyne XVI 1963 35-42.

4265 FRITZ K. VON, "Das erste Kapitel des zweiten Buches
von Xenophons Memorabilien und die Philosophie
des Aristipp von Kyrene". Hermes XCIII 1965
257-279.

4266 OKAL M., "L'attitude d'Aristophane envers Socrate".
SFBP XVII 1965 107-124.

4267* MONTUORI M., Socrate tra Nuvole prime e Nuvole
seconde. Atti Accad. di Sc. mor. e polit.
della Soc. naz. di Sc., Let. ed Arti in
Napoli LXXVII 1966 57p.
Rev. Vichiana IV 1967 438.
REG LXXX 1967 603-604 Humbert.

4268* STRAUSS L., Socrates and Aristophanes. New York,
Basic Books 1966 321p.
Rev. CW LX 1966 119 Stewart.
JHPh V 1967 287-288 Fox.
Phoenix XXI 1967 231-232 O'Brien.
CJ LXIII 1967 128-129 Murphy.
Thought 1967 477 Schwandt.
QJS 1967 78 Arnott.
MassR 1968 399 Klein.
Commentary 1967 102 Momigliano.
NR 1967 423 Parry.

4269 BARZIN M., "Sur les Nuées d'Aristophane". BAB LIV
1968 378-388.

4270* DOVER K.J., Aristophanes' Clouds, ed. with intro.
& comm. Oxford, Clarendon Pr. 1968
cxxviii&285p. (for Socrates see Intro. sec.V,
p.xxxii-lvii.)

4271 NEUMANN H., "Socrates in Plato and Aristophanes".
AJPh XC 1969 201-214.

4272 ADKINS A.W.H., "Clouds, Mysteries, Socrates and
Plato". Antichthon IV 1970 13-24.

4273* STRAUSS L. & LORD C., Xenophon's Socratic
Discourse. An Interpretation of the
Oeconomicus, with a transl. by Lord C. Ithaca,
Cornell Univ. Pr. 1970 viii&211p.

Rev. JHPh X 1971 239-243 Neumann.
Thought XLVI 1971 315-317 Schwandt.
CW LXV 1972 240 Anderson.
ACR I 1971 215 Raubitschek.
REA LXXIV 1972 264-265 Will.

4274 DOVER K.J., "Socrates in the Clouds". p.50-77 in The Philosophy of Socrates, ed. by Vlastos G. (see 4621).

4275 LACEY A.R., "Our Knowledge of Socrates". p.22-49 in The Philosophy of Socrates, ed. by Vlastos G. (see 4621).

4276* ROGERS A.K., The Socratic Problem. New York, Russell & Russell 1971 200p. Reprint of 1933 edn.

4277 ROSSETTI L., "Recenti sviluppi della questione socratica". Proteus II 1971 161-187.

4278 BRUMBAUGH R.S., "Scientific Approaches Onstage in 423 B.C.". YClS XXII 1972 215-221.

4279 HAVELOCK E.A., "The Socratic Self as it is parodied in Aristophanes' Clouds". YClS XXII 1972 1-18.

4280* STRAUSS L., Xenophon's Socrates. Ithaca, Cornell Univ. Pr. 1972 181p.
Rev. G&R XX 1973 87 Rees.
CW LXVI 1973 470-471 Rosen.
YR 1972 127 Moulton.

4281 KARAVITES P., "Socrates in the Clouds". CB L 1973-1974 65-69.

4282 SARRI F., "Rilettura delle Nuovole di Aristofane come fonte per la conoscenza di Socrate". RFNeo LXV 1973 532-550.

For further discussion see 3795, 4199, 4249, 4293.

IX: SOCRATES' LIFE AND HIS RELATIONS
WITH OTHERS

For this subject see also section VIII B and for
Socrates' relationship with Plato see section II
C a.

A: SOCRATES' LIFE (INCLUDING HIS DAIMON)

4283 CALDER W.M., "Socrates at Amphipolis (Ap.   28e)".
      Phronesis VI 1961 83-85.

4284 GUÉRY   L.,   "Un   soldat   nommé   Socrate".
      RevFacCathOuest II 1961 16-26.

4285 PARKE H.W., "Chaerephon's Inquiry about Socrates".
      CPh LVI 1961 249-250.

4286 SCIACCA M.F., "El demonio de Sócrates".   Nación,   9
      jul. 1961, 4a secc.

4287 GIANNANTONI G., "La pritania di Socrate nel 406
      a.C.". RSF XVII 1962 3-25.

4288* MONTUORI M., Socrate du mythe à l'histoire.
      Beyrouth 1963 43p.

4289 RIST J.M., "Plotinus and the Daimonion of Socrates".
      Phoenix XVII 1963 13-24.

4290 CRANAKI M., "Note sur les 'Memorables'".   p.88-93 in
      L'aventure de l'esprit Mélanges Alexandre
      Koyré, publiés à l'occasion de son 70e
      anniversaire. T.2. Paris, Hermann 1964.

4291 FERGUSON J., "On the Date of Socrates' Conversion".
      Eranos LXII 1964 70-73.

4292* MEUNIER M., La légende de Socrate.   Paris, Albin
      Michel 1965 187p.

4293 ERBSE H., "Sokrates und die Frauen".   Gymnasium
      LXXIII 1966 201-220.

4294 ROBBERECHTS L., "Périclès et Socrate". RevNouv XLIV 1966 270-285.

4295* TOVAR A., Vida de Sócrates. 3a ed. Madrid, Ed. Rev. de Occidente 1966 498p.
Rev. REC X 1966 158 Granero.

4296 VIDMANOVÁ A., "Socrates Alexandri magister" [in Czech with Latin summary]. ZJKF VIII 1966 77-80.

4297 DOERRIE H., "Xanthippe, die Gattin des Sokrates". RE IX A2 1335-1342.

4298 FINLEY M.I., "Socrates and Athens". p.58-72 in Finley M.I., Aspects of Antiquity. London, Chatto & Windus and New York, Viking 1968.

4299 NEUMANN H., "Socrates and the Tragedy of Athens". SocRes XXXV 1968 426-444.

4300 FITTON J.W., "'That was no Lady, that was...'". CQ XX 1970 56-66.

4301 TERAOKA H., "Daimon in Socrates" [in Japanese]. Misaka Women's College Bulletin III (Misaka Jr. College Bulletin XV) 1970.

4302* GIANNINI H., Sócrates o el oráculo de Delfos. Libros para el estudiante, Santiago, Ed. Universitaria 1971 66p.

4303 MORICHÈRE B., "Sur la méconnaissance de Socrate". RMM LXXVI 1971 441-447.

4304 CHROUST A.h., "A Comment on Aristotle's On Noble Birth". WS VI 1972 19-32.

4305 KRELL D.F., "Socrates' Body". SoJP X 1972 443-451.

4306 WOODBURY L., "Socrates and the Daughter of Aristides". Phoenix XXVII 1973 7-25.

For additional discussions see 185, 1061, 1951, 3452.

4307 BURNOUF D., "Le crime politique de Socrate: l'opposition à l'idéologie nationale". RPP XIII 1958 355-358.

4308 KENDALL W., "The People versus Socrates Revisited". ModA III 1958-1959 98-111.

4309 REINACH J., "A proposito di Il processo di Socrate di N. Casini". Iura IX 1958 121-122.

4310 CASINI N., "In margine al processo di Socrate". Iura X 1959 114-117.

4311 BICKEL E., "Seneca und Seneca-Mythus". Altertum V 1959 90-100.

4312 DIONISIO S.A., "A morte de Sócrates". RBF X 1960 173-178.

4314 LANGAN J., "Socrates and Cicero. Two Approaches to the Role of Philosophy". CB XXXVII 1960 17-19, 25.

4315 SAMSON B., "Der Prozess Sokrates". p.354-388 in Aktuelle Probleme aus dem Gesellschaftsrecht und anderen Rechtsgebieten. Festschrift für Walter Schmidt zum 70. Geburtstag am 18. Dezember 1959, hrsg. von Samson B. Berlin, de Gruyter 1960.

4316 RE M.C. DEL, "Il processo di Socrate e la sua problematica nella critica moderna". A&R VI 1961 83-94.

4317 SALVADOR DE LIMA P.H., "O julgamento de Sócrates". Verbum XVIII 1961 149-168.

4318* GUARDINI R., The Death of Socrates. An Interpretation of the Platonic Dialogues Euthyphro, Apology, Crito and Phaedo, transl. by Wrighton B. Cleveland, World 1962 xiii&177p. Reprint of 1948 U.S. edn. Also Spanish transl. La muerte de Sócrates, trad. de Eggers Lan C. Buenos Aires, Emece 1960 269p.

IX b: THE TRIAL AND DEATH OF SOCRATES

4319 VANDIEST J., "Proces van Sokrates". Dialoog III
1962-1963 46-66, 115-138.

4320 ERASMUS S., "Richterzahl und Stimmenverhältnisse im
Sokratesprozess". Gymnasium LXXI 1964 40-42.

4321 SALGUERO C.A., "An Inquiry concerning Socrates'
Trial". Athene(Chicago) XXV,2 1964 13-14 & 17.

4322 RAOSS M., "Alla ricerca del κατήγορος di Socrate nei
Memorabili di Senofonte". p.53-176 in
Miscellanea greca e romana. Studi pubbl. dall'
Ist. ital. per la storia ant. XVI, Roma 1965.

4323 SEIBERT C., "Der Prozess des Sokrates". MDR XX 1966
295.

4324* ELIOT A., Socrates. A fresh Appraisal of the most
celebrated case in History. New York, Crown
1967 143p.
Rev. CW LXII 1969 192-193 Stewart.

4325 RAOSS M., "Ai margini del processo di Socrate".
p.47-291 in Seconda miscellanea greca e romana.
Studi pubbl. dall'Ist. ital. per la storia
antica XIX, Roma 1968.

4326 CAPUDER A., "Note complémentaire au dernier mot de
Socrate". ZAnt XIX 1969 21-23.

4327* FISCHER J.L., The Case of Socrates, transl. from
the Czech by, Lewitowa I. Rozpravy Ceskoslov.
Akad. Ved, Rada Spolecensk. Ved LXXIX,8,
Praha, Academia 1969 91p.
Rev. CW LXIV 1971 316 Heilbrunn.
ACR 1 1971 50 Rist.
ZPhF XXV 1971 630-631 Nickel.
Mind LXXXI 1972 149-150 Kirwan.
CR XXII 1972 118-119 Gulley.
PLA XXV 1972 47-48 Titze.
StudFiloz 1971 204-206 Paulo de Silva.

4328 JACCARD R., "Socrate et le kamikaze". Critique XXVI
1970 457-461.

4329 CARAFIDES J.L., "The last Words of Socrates".
Platon XXIII 1971 229-232.

4330 MINADEO R., "Socrates' Debt to Asclepius". CJ LXVI
1971 294-297.

4331* ALARCO L.F., Sócrates y Jesus ante la muerte, I: Socrates. Lima, Universidad nac. major de San Marcos 1972 496p.

4332 ANDERSON A., "Was Socrates unwise to take the Hemlock?". HThR LXV 1972 437-452.

4333 GILL C., "The Death of Socrates". Summary in PCA LXIX 1972 29.

4334 SPECHT E.K., "Der Traum des Sokrates". Psyche XXVI 1972 656-688.

4335 STEWART J.D., "Socrates' Last Bath". JHPh X 1972 253-259.

4336 BLUMENTHAL H., "Meletus the Accuser of Andocides and Meletus the Accuser of Socrates: One Man or Two?". Philologus CXVII 1973 169-178.

4337 GILL C., "The Death of Socrates". CQ XXIII 1973 25-28.

For additional discussions see 1016, 1061, 1074, 1077, 1177, 1677, 2568, 2612, 4362.

IX C: SOCRATES AND HIS PREDECESSORS
AND CONTEMPORARIES

ALCIBIADES

4338 LITTMAN R.J., "The Loves of Alcibiades". TAPhA CI 1970 263-276.

ARCHELAUS

4339 CAPPELLETTI A.S., "Arquelao, maestro de Sócrates". RFil(La Plata) IX 1960 79-96.

4340 WOODBURY L., "Socrates and Archelaus". Phoenix XXV 1971 299-309.

ARISTIPPUS

4341   CLASSEN C.J., "Aristippos". Hermes LXXXVI 1958
        182-192.

DEMOCRITUS

For discussion of Socrates and Democritus see 265.

GORGIAS

4342   CALOGERO G., "Gorgias and the Socratic Principle
        Nemo sua sponte peccat". p.176-186 in Essays in
        Ancient Greek Philosophy, ed. by Anton J.P. &
        Kustas G.L. (see 4581).

PRODICUS

4343   ROSATI P., "Intorno a Prodico di Ceo". Logos III
        1972 389-414.

PYTHAGORAS AND THE PYTHAGOREANS

4344   CAVAIGNAC E., "Pythagore et Socrate". RPh XXXIII
        1959 246-248.

SOPHISTS

4345 DURIĆ M.N., "The Greek Skeptics" [in Serbian with French summary]. ZAnt VIII 1958 3-20.

4346 SCHUHL P.M., "Socrate et le travail rétribué". RPhilos CLI 1961 91-92.

4347 OŚWIECIMSKI S., "Socrates fueritne sophistes?" [in Polish with Latin summary]. Eos LVI 1966 242-255.

4348 OJOADE J.O., "Socrates. Was he really a Sophist?". Phrontisterion V 1967 48-61.

4349 MUÑOZ VALLE I., "El racionalismo griego. Los sofistas. Su concepto del hombre y la sociedad". RFil(Madrid) XXVII 1968 201-212.

4350 MUÑOZ VALLE I., "El racionalismo griego". BIEH VI 1972 47-55.

For additional discussions of Socrates and the Sophists see 1929, 1931, 2806, 4436, 4439.

SOPHISTIC WRITINGS

4351 RAMAGE E.S., "An early Trace of Socratic Dialogue". AJPh LXXXII 1961 418-424.

XENOPHON

4352* SCHAERER R., L'homme antique et la structure du monde intérieur d'Homère à Socrate. Bibl. hist., Paris, Payot 1958 416p. (ch.11 "Xénophon et la sagesse Socratique", p.343-353.)

ZOROASTER

4353* AFNAN R.M., Zoroaster's Influence on Anaxagoras, the Greek Tragedians and Socrates. New York, Philos. Libr. 1969 161p. (Ch.5: "Socrates",

IX C: PREDECESSORS AND CONTEMPORARIES

p.129-154.)
Rev. IPQ 1968 640 Cleve.
TPh XXXI 1969 378-379 Smets.
JHPh VIII 1970 469-470 Cleve.
RPhilos CLXI 1971 225 Poirier.
ArchPhilos XXXIII 1970 977-978.
ACR I 1971 72 Edinger.
PhilosReform XXXVI 1971 81-87 K.J.P.
RS XCII 1971 109.

For additional discussion see 754.

IX D: SOCRATES AND LATER CLASSICAL LITERATURE

4354 WILKINSON L.P., "Cicero and Socrates. The
      Significance of the De Oratore". Summary in PCA
      LXI 1964 33.

4355 BRITO O.T. DE, "A vocação filosófica de Cícero".
      Romanitas 1965 Nos.6,7 90-101.

4356 HATHAWAY R.F., "Cicero De re publica II, and his
      Socratic view of History". JHI XXIX 1968 3-12.

4357 REITZENSTEIN E., "Die Cornelia-Elegie des Properz
      (IV,11). Eine Formuntersuchung und ihre
      Erbegnisse für die Textkritik". RhM CXII 1969
      126-145.

4358 KILLEEN J.F., "Horace, Odes I,29,14ff.". Orpheus XX
      1973 163-164.

For additional discussion see 4314.

IX E: SOCRATES AND CHRISTIANITY

4359 CARTER R.E., "St. John Chrysostom's use of the
      Socratic distinction between kingship and
      Tyranny". Traditio XIV 1958 367-371.

4360* FASCHER E., Sokrates und Christus. Beiträge zur
      Religionsgeschichte. Leipzig, Koehler & Amelang
      1959 463p.

4361* LEIST F., Moses, Sokrates, Jesus. Um die Begegnung
      mit dem biblischen und antiken Welt. Frankfurt,
      Knecht 1959 488p. Also Dutch transl. Mozes,
      Sokrates, Jezus. Ontmoetingen met de bijbelse
      en antieke wereld, vert. door Wagemans H.
      Hilversum, Brand 1961 460p.
              Rev. [of German edn.] Gregorianum XLI
      1960 754 Caminero.
      Augustinianum II 1962 358 San Luigi.
      ThRev LIX 1963 9 Schedl.
      Kairos II 1960 121 Berbuin.
      Scholastik XXXVI 1961 275-276 Bulst.
      CiFe XVI 1960 312-313 Fiorito.
      NG IX 1962 198-199 Ventosa.
      Sophia XXXI 1963 289 Romano.

4362 BRUN J., "La mort de Socrate et la mort de Jésus".
      EThR XXXV 1960 197-204. Also Italian transl.
      "La morte di Socrate e la morte di Gesù", trad.
      di Martelli F. Ethica VIII 1969 161-167.

4363 HENNEMANN G., "Sokrates im Lichte christlicher
      Philosophen". FChrist XIV 1962 99-102.

4364 AMAND DE MENDIETA E., "L'amplification d'un thème
      socratique et stoïcien dans l'avant-dernier
      traité de Jean Chrysostome". Byzantion XXXVI
      1966 353-381.

4365 HOMMEL H., "Herrenworte im Lichte sokratischer
      Überlieferung". ZNTw LVII 1966 1-23.

4366 NOMACHI H., "Justin's View of Socrates. Early
      Christianity and Greek Philosophy, I" [in
      Japanese]. Journal of Literature and Economics
      (Hirosaki Univ.) V,2 1969.

4367 SCHWARTZ J., "Autour des 'Acta S. Apollonii'".
      RHPhR L 1970 257-261.

4368 KOUMAKIS G.C., "Das Sokratesbild in Therapeutik des
      Theodoretus und seine Quellen". Platon XXIII
      1971 337-351.

4369* BETZ H.D., Der Apostel Paulus und die sokratische
      Tradition. Eine exegetische Untersuchung zu
      seiner 'Apologie'. 2 Korinther 10-13. Beitr.
      zur hist. Theol. XLV, Tübingen, Mohr 1972
      157p.
              Rev. Erasmus XXV 1973 338-339 Bruce.
      EThR XLVIII 1973 212 Bouttier.

IX E: SOCRATES AND CHRISTIANITY

4370* CALOGERO G., Erasmo, Socrate e il Nuovo Testamento.
Discorso pronunciato nella ricorrenza del V
centenario della nascità di Erasmo di Rotterdam.
Roma, 16 novembre 1969. Accad. naz. dei
Lincei, Celebrazioni lincee XXXIV, Roma, Accad.
naz. dei Lincei 1972 20p.

For additional discussion see 4331.

IX F: SOCRATES AND LATER THINKERS

BARRÈS

4371 TRONQUART G., "Socrate et Barrès". TabR 1960 n.148
      90-101.

BERGSON

4372 LAROCK V., "Le Socrate 'oriental' de Bergson".
      Réseaux 1972 Nos.18-19 47-57.

DESCARTES

4373 PAISSE J.M., "Socrate et Descartes". BAGB 1968
      241-257; 1969 89-100.

For additional discussion of Socrates and Descartes see
      4411.

DUPRÉEL

4374 SCHUHL P.M., "Dupréel et Socrate". RIPh XXII 1968
      174-181. Reprinted p.174-181 in Eugène Dupréel,
      l'homme et l'oeuvre. Colloque de Bruxelles,

IX F: SOCRATES AND LATER THINKERS

30,31 mai-1er juin 1968. Bruxelles, Ed. de
l'Institut de Sociologie de l'U.L.B. 1968.

HAMANN

4375* HAMANN   J.G.,   Sokratische   Denkwürdigkeiten.
Aesthetica in nuce, mit. Kommentar. Hrsg. von
Jørgensen S.A.   Reclams   Universalbibliothek
926/926a, Stuttgart, Reclam 1968 191p.

4376* O'FLAHERTY J.C., Hamann's Socratic 'Memorabilia', a
transl. and comm. Baltimore, Johns Hopkins
Univ. Pr. 1967 xv&229p.

4377 O'FLAHERTY J.C., "Socrates in Hamann's Socratic
Memorabilia and Nietzsche's Birth of Tragedy: A
Comparison". p.306-329 in Philomathes. Studies
and Essays in the Humanities in Memory of Philip
Merlan, ed. by Palmer R.B. & Hamerton-Kelly R.
Den Haag, Nijhoff 1971.

HEGEL

4378 SANDVOSS E., "Hegels Antisokratismus". A&A XII 1966
156-179.

For additional discussion of Socrates and Hegel see 4411.

KANT

4379 JORDAN J.N., "Socrates' Wisdom and Kant's Virtue".
SwJP IV,2 1973 7-24.

IX F: SOCRATES AND LATER THINKERS

KIERKEGAARD

4380 ANDERSON R.E., "Kierkegaard's Theory of Communication". SpMon XXX 1963 1-14.

4381* KIERKEGAARD S., The Concept of Irony, with constant references to Socrates, transl., introd., & notes by Capel L.M. New York, Harper & Row 1966 442p.
Rev. CW LX 1966 14 Behler.
ThS XXVIII 1967 592-595 Langan.
JR XLVII 1967 171-172 Sponheim.
DownsR LXXXIV 1966 454-455 Newman.
ModS XLIV 1966-1967 285-287 Stack.
Personalist XLIX 1966 267-268 Scharlemann.
NewSt 12 Aug. 1966 234 Mairet.
TLS 23 June 1966 559.
CrossCurr XVII 1967 201 Collins.
JHI XXIX 1968 458-464 Nagley.
HeythropJ IX 1968 76-79 O'Connor.

4382 STACK G.J., "Kierkegaard: The Self and Ethical Existence". Ethics LXXXIII 1973 108-125.

NIETZSCHE

4383 GAUDEFROY-DEMOMBYNES J., "Nietzsche et Socrate". BSEN 1963 no.2 19-20.

4384* SANDVOSS E., Sokrates und Nietzsche. Leiden, Brill 1966 vi&149p.
Rev. PhilosRdschau XVII 1970 49-56 Funke.

4385* SCHMIDT H.J., Nietzsche und Sokrates. Philosophische Untersuchungen zu Nietzsches Sokratesbild. Monogr. zur philos. Forsch. LIX, Meisenheim, Hain 1969 376p.
Rev. ZPhF XXVII 1973 467-472 Rau.
NSt I 1972 441-443 Koester.
PhilosRdschau XXII 1973 294-297 Wingler.

4386 FUNKE H., "Sokrates und Nietzsche". PhilosRdschau XVII 1970 49-56.

4387 TORNAMBÈ F., "Una lezione di irrazionalismo: il guidizio di Nietzsche su Socrate". Sophia XXXIX 1971 344-347.

IX F: SOCRATES AND LATER THINKERS

4388 NIETZSCHE F., "Socrate et la tragédie. Conférence
      du 1er février 1870". NouvCom No.23 1972 55-92.

4389 LE GAL Y., "Qui est le Socrate de Nietzsche?". RSPh
      LVII 1973 35-70.

RAMUS

4390 WALTON C., "Ramus and Socrates". PAPhS CXIV 1970
      119-139.

GENERAL

4391 RIGOBELLO A., "Logicismo contemporaneo ed istanze
      socratiche". Studium(Italy) LV 1959 734-739.

4392 VELA R., "Modernità di Socrate". Sapienza XIII 1960
      246-251.

IX G: THE HISTORY OF INTERPRETATION OF SOCRATES

4393* SPIEGELBERG H. & MORGAN B.Q. eds., The Socratic
      Enigma. A Collection of Testimonies through
      twenty-four Centuries. Libr. of Liberal Arts,
      Indianapolis, Bobbs-Merrill 1964 xvi&334p.
      Rev. CW LVIII 1965 221 Urdahl.
      PhilosBks May 1965 28 Hamlyn.

4394* BOEHM B., Sokrates im achzehnten Jahrhundert.
      Studien zum Werdegange des modernen
      Persöhnlichkeitsbewusstseins. Kieler Stud. zum
      dt. Literaturgesch. IV, Neumünster, Wachholtz
      1966 318p. Reprinted from 1929 edn.
      Rev. ZKG LXXIX 1968 266-268 Hornig.

4395 BOWMAN F.P., "La confirmatio christianorum per
      Socratica dans le romantisme français". RSHum
      1966 217-226.

IX G: HISTORY OF INTERPRETATION OF SOCRATES

4396* TROUSSON R., <u>Socrate</u> <u>devant</u> <u>Voltaire,</u> <u>Diderot</u> <u>et</u>
      <u>Rousseau, la conscience en face du mythe.</u> Coll.
      Thèmes & Mythes XI, Paris, Minard 1967 154p.
      Rev. RHLF LXIX 1969 855-856 Chouillet.
      ModLJ 1969 208 Bingham.

4397 GOUHIER H., "Socrate et Caton vus par Jean-Jacques".
      StudFr 1968 no.36 412-418.

4398 CARSON   K.,   "Socrates   Observed: Three
      Eighteenth-century   Views".   DidSt XIV 1971
      273-281.

4399 NAUMANN H., "Die Gestalt des Sokrates und ihre
      Wirkungen auf die Weltliteratur". AU XII 1969,2
      64-103.

4400* RASCHINI M.A., <u>Interpretazioni</u> <u>socratiche.</u> <u>Testo</u>
      <u>per</u> <u>il</u> <u>corso</u> <u>di</u> <u>filosofia</u> <u>1o,</u> Fac. <u>di</u>
      <u>magistero, anno accademico 1968-1969.</u> Milano,
      Marzorati 1969 206p.

4401* RASCHINI M.A., <u>Interpretazioni</u> <u>socratiche,</u> <u>I.</u>
      Milano, Marzorati 1970 386p.
      Rev. VV CXII 1970 546 Olmo.
      ModS L 1972-1973 768 Sweeney.
      GM XXVII 1972 222-223 Sorge.
      RPhilos CLXII 1972 51 Namer.

For additional discussions see 4366, 4367, 4368.

X: SOCRATES' THOUGHT

Socrates' thought forms such a unity that it is
even more arbitrary and artificial to divide it
into categories than it is with Plato. The
division I have made seems to me to be a useful
starting point, as long as it is remembered that
in many cases it is no more than that, and that
a work listed under one heading may well contain
material that fits it for inclusion under a
number of others. Some cross references are
provided, but the reader might wish to consult
related sections at length. Another difficulty
in attempting to classify works on Socrates is
the close connection between his thought and
that of Plato, which makes it very difficult and
somewhat arbitrary to distinguish clearly in
every case between discussions dealing with
Plato (especially Plato's earlier thought) and
those treating Socrates. Although some cross
references are provided at the end of the
following sections, the reader might wish to
consult the sections on the corresponding areas
of Plato's thought.

A. SOCRATIC METHOD: NATURE AND GOALS;
SOCRATIC DEFINITION

4402 KANEMATSU K., "Eros as Paideia, as demonstrated by
Socrates" [in Japanese]. Otani Journal (Univ.
of Otani) XXVII,3 1958.

4403 VLASTOS G., "The Paradox of Socrates. An Essay in
Communication". QQ LXIV 1958 496-516.
Reprinted p.1-21 in The Philosophy of Socrates,
ed. by Vlastos G. (see 4621). Also in
Spanish: "La paradoja de Sócrates. Ensayo
sobre la comunicación". ROcc 1964 n.11 129-157.

4404 LUSCHNAT O., "Fortschrittsdenken und
Vollendungsstreben im Hellenismus". TheolV VI
1954-1958 (Berlin, Lettner 1959) 88-110.

4405 URWICK E.J., "The Quest of Socrates". Sunrise VIII
1959 264-268.

4406* RABBOW P., Paidagogia. Die Grundlegung der
abendländischen Erziehungskunst in der Sokratik,
hrsg. von Pfeiffer E. Göttingen, Vandenhoeck &
Ruprecht 1960 289p.
        Rev. LEC XXVIII 1960 443 Ghislain.
        RecSR XLIX 1961 290 des Places.
        Scholastik XXXVI 1961 88-89 Ennen.
        Gnomon XXXIII 1961 1-6 Rosenmeyer.
        Philoskdschau X 1962 159.
        Mnemosyne XV 1962 409-413 de Vogel.
        Gymnasium LXIX 1962 560-562 Jaekel.
        DLZ LXXXIV 1963 204-206 Saupe.
        CR XIII 1963 196-197 Wasserstein.

4407 SCHUETZ P., "Oedipus wider Sokrates".   Antaios   II
        1960 259-265.

4408 J.G., "Sokrates leraar zedenleer?".   Dialoog   I
        1960-1961 extra-nummer, 102-103.

4409 HERRMANN R.D., "Il logos socratico e il linguaggio"
        [transl. from German by Conte A.G.]. RF LII
        1961 279-284.

4410 SCHOTTLAENDER R., "Sokratischer und Sophokleischer
        Apollinismus". p.1-7 in Festschrift K. Badt
        zum siebzigsten Geburtstage. Beiträge aus
        Kunst- und Geistesgeschichte, hrsg. von
        Gosebruch M. Berlin, de Gruyter 1961.

4411 TEDESCHI F.A., "Ragione e fede in Socrate, Cartesio
        ed Hegel". Educare XII 1961 50-61.

4412 HAYASHI T., "A Problem of Human Development in
        Socrates" [in Japanese]. Tohoku Univ. (Sendai)
        Education Annual IX 1962.

4413 LICHTENSTEIN E., "Sokrates, das Bild des Erziehers".
        PaedagRdsch XVI 1962 339-345.

4414 TAGLE M.A., "Sócrates y el escepticismo".   RevUNC
        III 1962 141-150.

4415 WOŁOSZYN S., "Socratic Philosophy and its Role in
        the History of Education" [in Polish].
        p.231-245 in Problemy kultury i wychowania Zbiór
        studiów., red. Frydman E. & Kaltenberg I.
        Warszawa, PWN 1963.

4416 GORDON R.M., "Socratic Definitions and 'Moral
        Neutrality'". JPh LXI 1964 433-450.

4417 SKORPEN E., "A Commercial and a Prayer". EdForum XXVIII 1964 297-302.

4418* LIBRIZZI C., Socrate o l'educatore. 2a ed. Roma, Signorelli 1965 105p.
Rev. Sophia XXXV 1967 133 Romano.

4419* NELSON L., Socratic Method and Critical Philosophy. Selected Essays, transl. by Brown T.K. III, foreword by Blanshard B., introd. by Kraft J. New York, Dover 1965 xxii&211p. Reprint of 1949 edn. (ch.1 "The Socratic Method", p.1-43: reprint of a lecture "Die sokratische Methode", published in Abh. der Fries'schen Schule V, Göttingen 1929, no.1.)
Rev. EPh 1968 479 Deledalle.
Sapientia XXIV 1969 232-233 Argerami.

4420 HEINTEL E., "Sokratisches Wissen und praktischer Primat". p.212-223 in Kritik und Metaphysik. Studien. Heinz Heimsoeth zum achtzigsten Geburtstag, hrsg. von Kaulbach F. & Ritter J. Berlin, de Gruyter 1966.

4421* NESTLE W., Vom Mythos zum Logos. Die Selbstentfaltung des griechischen Denkens von Homer bis auf der Sophistik und Sokrates. Neudr. d. 2. Aufl., Stuttgart 1942. Aalen, Scientia-Verl. 1966 vii&580p.

4422 ANDERSON D.E., "Socrates' Concept of Piety". JHPh V 1967 1-13.

4423 NAKAMURA K., "On the Mission of Socrates in Plato's Apology 36c5-d1" [in Japanese]. HiroshimaUS XIX 1967.

4424 RUMPF H., "Die sokratische Prüfung. Beobachtungen an platonischen Frühdialogen". ZPaed XIII 1967 325-345.

4425 GRIMALDI N., "Le shamanisme socratique. Réflexion sur le langage dans la philosophie de Platon". RMM LXXIII 1968 401-429.

4426 NAGASAKA T., "Socratic Doubt" [in Japanese]. Methodos I 1968.

4427 SPEAR O. & RAMAT-GAN, "Sokrates. Wort und Verantwortung". Universitas XXIII 1968 745-752.

4428 DÉNES T., "Socrate et la valeur de la pédagogie". BAGB 1969 201-207.

4429 VOELKE A.J., "Dialectique et choix dans la pensée socratique". p.53-56 in La Dialectique. Actes du XIVe Congrès des Sociétés de Philosophie de Langue française. Nice, 1-4 sept. 1969. T.1 Paris, Presses Universitaires 1969.

4430 AUBENQUE P., "Évolution et constantes de la pensée dialectique". EPh XXIV 1970 289-301.

4431 DICKOFF J. & JAMES P., "Socrates--Still a Folk-Hero for Education?". PPES XXVI 1970 193-219.

4432 NAZZARO A.V., "Il γνῶθι σαυτόν nell'epistemologia filoniana". AFLN XII 1969-1970 49-86.

4433 VOGEL C.J. DE, "Was Socrates a Rationalist?". p.131-151 in Vogel C.J. de, Philosophia (see 4624). English transl. of a Japanese version in Greek Philosophy and Religion. Tokyo 1969.

4434 ZEPPI S., "Il problema del dialogo prima di Socrate". Cultura VIII 1970 425-434.

4435 ASMUS V.F., "The Dialectic of Socrates" [in Russian]. FilNauk 1971 No.3 83-94.

4436 CANILLI A., "Attualità dei sofisti e di Socrate". Acme XXIV 1971 47-70.

4437 CARAMELLA S., "La secolarizzazione nel pensiero di Socrate". IncCult IV 1971 319-332.

4438 LAFRANCE Y., "Communication et violence dans le dialogue socratico-platonicien". p.101-105 in La communication. Actes du XVe Congr. de l'Assoc. des Soc. de Philos. de langue française. Pensée antique et communication. Montréal, Éd. Montmorency 1971.

4439 LECHNER K., "Sokrates im Staatsdienst". Hochland LXIII 1971 567-579.

4440 PAISSE J.M., "De la sagesse socratique". BAGB 1971 353-367.

4441* RICCI M., Socrate, padre del nichilismo. Struttura logica e significato teoretico del discorso socratico. Filos. e vita VI, L'Aquila, Japadre [1971] 162p.

Rev. Logos V 1973 202-207 Casertano.

4442 ROBINSON R., "Elenchus". p.78-93 in The Philosophy
of Socrates, ed. by Vlastos G. (see 4621).
Reprinted from Robinson R., Plato's Earlier
Dialectic, 2nd edn. ch.2.

4443 ROBINSON R., "Elenchus: Direct and Indirect".
p.94-109 in The Philosophy of Socrates, ed. by
Vlastos G. (see 4621). Reprinted from Robinson
R., Plato's Earlier Dialectic, 2nd edn. ch.3.

4444 ROBINSON R., "Socratic Definition". p.65-76 in
Plato's Meno. Text and Criticism, ed. by
Sesonske A. & Fleming N. (see 1484). Also
p.110-124 in The Philosophy of Socrates, ed. by
Vlastos G. (see 4621). Reprinted from Robinson
R., Plato's Earlier Dialectic, 2nd edn. ch.5.

4445 JULIÁ V., "El método socrático". CuadFilos XII 1972
63-67.

4446 MARTIN G., "Socrates. On the Interpretation of his
Ignorance", transl. by Hartman R.D.S.
p.107-113 in Value and Valuation. Axiological
Studies in Honor of Robert S. Hartman, ed. by
Davis J.W. Knoxville, The Univ. of Tennessee
Pr. 1972.

4447 MARTIN G., "Sokrates: Das Allgemeine. Seine
Enteckung im sokratischen Gespräch". p.9-43 in
Grundprobleme der grossen Philosophen, hrsg.
von Speck J. (see 4616).

4448* MURAI M., Philosophy and Education in Socrates [in
Japanese]. Tamagawa Univ. Pr. 1972 245p.

4449 SANTAS G., "The Socratic Fallacy". JHPh X 1972
127-141.

4450 SICHÈRE B., "Socrate musicien". RMM LXXVII 1972
183-196.

4451* INATOMI E., The Educational Dialectic of Socrates
[in Japanese]. Tokyo, Fukumura 1973 217p.

4452 PAISSE J.M., "La critique, source de sagesse". BAGB
1973 519-528.

X A: SOCRATIC METHOD

For additional discussions see 162, 1052, 1061, 1067, 1098, 1234, 1249, 1337, 1346, 1350, 1356, 1504, 2660, 2729, 2731, 2742, 2750, 2761, 2787, 2798, 2806, 2821, 2822, 2828, 2829, 2836, 2842, 2844, 2853, 2890, 3048, 3081, 3599, 3923, 4189, 4345, 4365, 4421, 4425, 4465, 4466.

X B: SOCRATIC IRONY

4453 MOREAU J., "L'ironia socratica". CV XIV 1959 404-411.

4454 VERSÉNYI L., "Eros, Irony and Ecstasy". Thought XXXVII 1962 598-612.

4455 BLASUCCI S., "L'ironia di Socrate". MiscFranc LXIII 1963 429-466.

4456 BLASUCCI S., "Aspetti costruttivi dell'ironia socratica". MiscFranc LXVII 1967 38-77.

4457* BLASUCCI S., L'ironia in Socrate e in Platone. Trani, Vecchi 1969 50p.

4458 BURGE E.L., "The Irony of Socrates". Antichthon III 1969 5-17.

4459 SAUPE W., "Platon in neuer Sicht. Das Wesen der sokratischen Ironie und ihre Bedeutung für die Sozialpädagogik und Sozialethik unserer Zeit". WZPot XIII 1969 451-455.

4460 PICHT G., "Die Ironie des Sokrates". p.383-401 in Probleme biblischer Theologie. Gerhard von Rad zum 70. Geburtstag, hrsg. von Wolff H.W. München, Kaiser 1971.

4461* BLASUCCI S., Socrate. Saggio sugli aspetti costruttivi dell'ironia. Milano, Marzorati 1972 247p.
Rev. Antonianum XLVII 1972 717 Prentice.
Logos IV 1972 317-319 Martano.
Aquinas XV 1972 684-685 Composta.
BollFil VI 1972 129-130 Natali.
RRFC LXVII 1973 70-74 Alberghi.

X B: SOCRATIC IRONY

4462* BODER W., Die sokratische Ironie in den platonischen
Frühdialogen. Studien zur antiken Philos. III,
Amsterdam, Gruener 1973 viii&173p.

For additional discussions see 1951, 2710, 3057, 3081,
4118, 4221, 4381.

X C: SOCRATIC EPISTEMOLOGY

4463 STRYCKER E. DE, "De eenheid van kennis en liefde in
Socrates' opvatting over de deugd" [in Dutch
with French summary]. Bijdragen XXVII 1966
214-228. Also p.50-64 in ΦΙΛΙΑ. Wijsgerige
opstellen in vriendschap aangeboden aan Prof.
Dr. J.H. Robbers, S.J., ed. by Braun C. et
al. Nijmegen/Utrecht, Dekker & Van de Vegt
1966. Also in English translation "The Unity of
Knowledge and Love in Socrates' Conception of
Virtue". IPQ VI 1966 428-444.

4465 BLASUCCI S., "La sapienza di Socrate" [in Italian
with Latin summary]. MiscFranc LXX 1970
329-347.

4466 HAWTREY R.S.W., "Socrates and the Acquisition of
Knowledge". Antichthon VI 1972 1-9.

4467 MORI T., "Wisdom and τέχνη. On Socratic ἐπιστήμη"
[in Japanese]. Fukuoka Univ. Humanities
Journal IV,2 1972.

4468 CAHN S.M., "A Puzzle concerning the Meno and the
Protagoras". JHPh XI 1973 535-537.

4469 CAPITAN W.H., "Can Virtue be Taught?". Diotima I
1973 101-124.

For additional discussions see 1507, 1941, 2821, 3519,
3974.

4470 MARITAIN J., "Socrate et la philosophie morale". p.389-402 in Mélanges offerts à Étienne Gilson. Toronto, Pontifical Inst. of Medieval Studies and Paris, Vrin 1959.

4471 DURIĆ M.N., "Materijalni principi sokratove etike [Material principles of Socrates' Ethics]". LMS CCCLXXXIII 1959 172-176.

4472 ALLEN R.E., "The Socratic Paradox". JHI XXI 1960 256-265.

4473 BAMBROUGH R., "Socratic Paradox". PhilosQ X 1960 289-300.

4474* MONDOLFO R., Moralisti greci. La coscienza morale da Omero a Epicuro. Napoli, Ricciardi 1960 154p.
        Rev. RSF XVI 1961 111-113 de Michelis.
        GM XVII 1962 528-531 Arcoleo.
        Filosofia XII 1961 144-150 Riconda.

4475 AKARSU B., "Socrates' Conception of Virtue" [in Turkish]. FeslefeArk XIII 1962 57-73.

4476 VALCKE L., "Morale e 'demone socratico'". RIFD XL 1963 364-367.

4477 SANTAS G., "The Socratic Paradoxes". PhR LXXIII 1964 147-164. Reprinted p.49-64 in Plato's Meno. Text and Criticism, ed. by Sesonske A. & Fleming N. (see 1484).

4478 GULLEY N., "The Interpretation of 'No one does Wrong Willingly' in Plato's Dialogues". Phronesis X 1965 82-96.

4479 ROSTHAL R., "Moral Weakness and Remorse". Summary in JPh LXII 1965 661-662.

4480 THALBERG I., "The Socratic Paradox and Reasons for Action". Theoria XXXI 1965 242-254.

4481 GANTAR K., "Amicus sibi, I: Zur Entstehungsgeschichte eines ethischen Begriffs in der antiken Literatur". ZAnt XVI 1966 135-175.

X D: ETHICS AND SOCRATIC PARADOXES

4482 GIANNINI H., "Un mito acerca de la historia de Sócrates". AUChile CXXIV 1966 88-101.

4483 GRAU N.A., "Las paradojas socráticas y la utilidad de la filosofía". Humanitas XIII 1966 21-32.

4484 KAKU A., "Virtue and Wisdom in Socrates" [in Japanese]. Review of Literature (Hirosaki Univ.) II,4 1966.

4485 MOUNCE H.O., "Virtue and the Understanding". Analysis XXVIII 1967 11-17.

4486* O'BRIEN M.J., The Socratic Paradoxes and the Greek Mind. Chapel Hill, Univ. of North Carolina Pr. 1967 xiv&249p.
      Rev. AC XXXVII 1968 335-336 Joly.
      CPh LXIII 1968 218-219 Sprague.
      Cw LXI 1968 249-250 Stewart.
      LEC XXXVI 1968 277 Loriaux.
      REG LXXXI 1968 295 des Places.
      CJ LXIV 1969 178-180 Berry.
      AJPh XC 1969 484-487 Neumann.
      Phk LXXVIII 1969 559-561 Schofield.
      Augustinus XIV 1969 428 Orosio.
      Crisis XVI 1969 510 Orosio.
      Mnemosyne XXIII 1970 203 de Vries.
      CR XXI 1971 31-33 Charlton.
      PhilosQ XXI 1971 74 Adkins.
      Hermathena CXI 1971 89-90 Luce.
      RFIC C 1972 75-77 Decleva Caizzi.

4487 MULHERN J.J., "A Note on Stating the Socratic Paradox". JHI XXIX 1968 601-604.

4488 SANTAS G., "Aristotle on Practical Inference, the Explanation of Action, and Akrasia". Phronesis XIV 1969 162-189.

4489 HOULGATE L.D., "Virtue is Knowledge". Monist LIV 1970 142-153.

4490 MILLEk J.F. III, "The Socratic Meaning of Virtue". SoJP IX 1971 141-149.

4491 MUELLER W.G., "Bidrag til forståelsen af den sokratiske etik". MT 1971 No.17 44-47.

4492 SOLOMON R.C., "Aristotle, the Socratic Principle, and the Problem of Akrasia". ModS XLIX 1971 13-21.

541

4493 WALSH J.J., "The Socratic Denial of Akrasia".
p.235-263 in The Philosophy of Socrates, ed. by
Vlastos G. (see 4621). Reprinted from Walsh
J.J., Aristotle's Conception of Moral Weakness,
New York, Columbia Univ. Pr. 1963, ch.1.

4494 GAŁKOWSKI J.W., "Moral Freedom in Socrates and
Aristotle" [in Polish with French summary].
RFSE XXI,2 1973 13-30.

4495 NAKHNIKIAN G., "The First Socratic Paradox". JHPh
XI 1973 1-19.

4496 PENNER T., "Socrates on Virtue and Motivation".
p.133-151 in Exegesis and Argument, ed. by Lee
E.N. et al. (see 4608).

4497 PENNER T., "The Unity of Virtue". PhR LXXXII 1973
35-68.

4498 VOGEL C.J. DE, "Two major Problems concerning
Socrates". Th-P II 1973 18-39.

For additional discussions see 1071, 1102, 1190, 1400,
1941, 1943, 1944, 1948, 1956, 1962, 2225, 3101,
3129, 3184, 3423, 3432, 3441, 3442, 3443, 3446,
3449, 3456, 3458, 3461, 3465, 3471, 3485, 3498,
3501, 3502, 3519, 4332, 4379, 4469, 4499, 4500,
4502, 4516.

X E: POLITICAL PHILOSOPHY

4499 CREMONA A., "Filosofia del diritto e filosofia
morale in Socrate". RIFD XXXV 1958 101-104.

4500 BALLARD E.G., "Socrates' Problem". Ethics LXXI 1961
296-300.

4501 BERTMAN M.A., "Socrates' Defence of Civil
Obedience". StudGen XXIV 1971 576-582. Also in
German: "Die Argumentation des Sokrates
zugunsten des bürgerlichen Gehorsams".
Conceptus V 1971 39-45.

4502 MAHOOD G.H., "Socrates and Confucius: Moral Agents
or Moral Philosophers?". PhEW XXI 1971 177-188.

X E: POLITICAL PHILOSOPHY

4503 MARTIN R., "Socrates on Disobedience to Law". RM
     XXIV 1970-1971 21-38.

4504 WOOZLEY A.D., "Socrates on Disobeying the Law".
     p.299-318 in The Philosophy of Socrates, ed. by
     Vlastos G. (see 4621).

4505 MULGAN R.G., "Socrates and Authority". G&R XIX 1972
     208-212.

4506 WADE F.C., "In Defense of Socrates". RM   XXV
     1971-1972 311-325.

4507 JAMES G.G., "Socrates on Civil Disobedience and
     Rebellion". SoJP XI 1973 119-127.

4508 KELLY D.A., "Conditions for Legal Obligation". SwJP
     IV 1973 43-56.

4509 WENZ P.S., "Socrates on Civil Disobedience: The
     Apology and the Crito". TWA LXI 1973 103-116.

For additional discussions see 3463, 3599, 3621, 3629,
     3635, 3643, 3674, 3745, 4359.

X F: THE SOUL AND HUMAN NATURE

4510 NOUSSAN-LETTRY L., "Imagen del hombre y ser". REC
     IX 1965 19-27.

4512* INATOMI E., Eros and Death in Socrates [in
     Japanese]. Tokyo, Fukumura 1973 238p.

4513 CONCHE M., "La question de l'homme". REPh XIX 1969
     1-14.

4514 THORNTON H., "Socrates and the History of
     Psychology". JHBS V 1969 326-339.

4515 MOUNTJOY P.T. & SMITH N.W., "A Reply to Thornton's
     'Socrates and the History of Psychology'". JHBS
     VII 1971 183-186.

X F: SOUL AND HUMAN NATURE

4516 LÓPEZ CASTELLÓN E., "Cuestiones sobre antropología
     ética socrática". EstFilos XX 1971 335-356.

4517 DAMPASIS I.N., "Αἱ ἰατρικαὶ ἀπόψεις τοῦ Σωκράτους".
     Platon XXIV 1972 230-243.

For additional discussions see 1063, 1064, 1528, 3043,
3048, 3082, 3133, 3181, 4498.

X G: THEOLOGY

4518 LUETHJE H., "Sokrates und die religiöse Entwicklung
     der Menschheit". Christengemeinschaft XXXIII
     1961 25-27.

4519* CAMARERO A., Sócrates y las creencias demónicas
      griegas. Cuad. del Sur, Bahía Blanca, Inst.
      de Hum. Univ. Nac. del Sur 1968 67p.
      Rev. REC XII 1968 153-155 Larrañaga.
      RPh XLIII 1969 308 Louis.
      LEC XXXVIII 1970 381 Duhoux.

4520* HACK R.K., God in Greek Philosophy to the Time of
      Socrates. New York, Burt Franklin 1970
      vii&157p. Reprint of 1931 edn.

For additional discussions see 3084, 3923, 3967, 4239.

X H: SCIENCE

4521 FRITZ K. VON, "Die Rückwendung zur Menschenwelt.
     Die Sophisten und Sokrates". p.221-250 in Fritz
     K. von, Grundprobleme der Geschichte der
     antiken Wissenschaft (see 4591).

4522 MUNDING H., "Sokrates im Kontrast zur
     Naturwissenschaft". AU IX,4 1966 80-98.

For additional discussions see 3248, 3249, 3256.

X I: AESTHETICS

4523 STRASSNER W., "Der kunstfeindliche Sokrates". KunstWerk 1962 112-113.

4524 ELKMAN R., "A few Notes on Socrates and his Aesthetics". p.20-27 in Philosophical Essays dedicated to Gunnar Aspelin on the occasion of his sixty-fifth Birthday. Lund, Gleerup 1963.

For additional discussion see 3866.

XI: SOCRATES AND PLATO IN ANCIENT ART

4525   VERMEULE C.C., "Socrates and Aspasia. New portraits of late Antiquity". CJ LIV 1958 49-55.

4526   SCHEFOLD K., "Sokratische Wolkenverehrer". AK II 1959 21-26.

4527   RUMPF A., "Ein einzig dastehender Fall. Zur Ikonographie des Sokrates". p.93-98, tables 21-22 in Analecta archaeologica. Festschrift Fritz Fremersdorf. Köln, Der Loewe 1960.

4528   VAUGHAN M., "Graeco-Roman Head of Socrates". Conoisseur CXLVII 1961 68.

4529   CHARBONNEAUX J., "Un double hermès de Zénon et Platon". AJA LXVI 1962 269-271.

4530   CHARITONIDIS S.I., "Ἀνασκαφη Μυτιλήνης". PAAH 1962 134-141.

4531   FREL J., "Effigies Platonis nuperrime Athenis reperta". ZJKF IV 1962 69-70.

4532   KRAFT K., "Ueber die Bildnisse des Aristoteles und des Platon". JNG XIII 1963 7-50.

4533   HEINTZE H. VON, "Studien zur griechischen Porträtkunst". MDAI(R) LXXI 1964 71-103.

4534   RICHTER G.M.A., "A new Portrait of Socrates". p.267-268 in Essays in Memory of Karl Lehmann, ed. by Sandler L.F. Marsyas, Stud. in the Hist. of Art. Suppl.I, New York, New York Univ. Inst. of Fine Arts 1964.

4535   BRECKENRIDGE J.D., "Multiple portrait types". AAAH II 1965 9-22.

4536   RICHTER G.M.A., "An unfinished Portrait Herm of Socrates". p.289-291 in Studi in onore di L. Banti. Roma, L'Erma 1965.

4537   FREL J., "Plato subridens". ZJKF VIII 1966 1-3.

4538   RICHTER G.M.A., "The Portrait of Plato in Basel". AK X 1967 144-146.

4539 SALVIAT F., "Platon et Thasos. Un portrait thasien; Mnésistratos le philosophe". AFLA XLIII 1967 57-64.

4540 GAUER W., "Die griechischen Bildnisse der klassischen Zeit als politische und persönliche Denkmäler". JDAI LXXXIII 1968 118-179.

4541 KRUSE H.J., "Ein Sokratesporträt in Sfax". AA LXXXIII 1968 435-446.

4542 PETRAKOS V.C., "Ψηφιδοτὰ ἐκ Μυτιλήνης"[in Greek with French summary]. AAA II 1969 239-243.

4543 RICHTER G.M.A., "Greek Portraits on Engraved Gems of the Roman Period". p.497-501 in Hommages à Marcel Renard, éd. par Bibauw J. T.3. Coll. Latomus CIII, Bruxelles 1969.

4544 BRUYNE L. DE, "Aristote ou Socrate? À propos d'une peinture de la Via Latina". RPAA XLII 1969-1970 173-193.

4545 MINGAZZINI P., "Su due oggetti in terracotta raffiguranti Socrate". PP XXV 1970 351-358.

4546 MINGAZZINI P., "Su alcuni ritratti di Socrate". RPAA XLIII 1970-1971 47-54.

4547 BALTY J.C., "Nouvelles mosaïques paiennes et groupe épiscopal dit 'cathédrale de l'est' à Apamée de Syrie". CRAI 1972 103-127.

XII: REFERENCE

4548 "Catálogo de las obras de Platón y sus
      comentaristas". Bol. informativo de la Bibl.
      Fac. Filos. y Letras, Univ. Nac. de Tucuman
      I nov. 1958 3-26; II sept. 1959 23-35.

4549* STOCKHAMMER M., Plato Dictionary. New York,
      Philosophical Libr. 1963 xv&287p.
      Rev. BBF IX 1964 334 Ernst.
      America 18 June 1964 110 Abbot.
      LJ 1 Sept. 1964 3064 Lazenby.

4550* PLACES E. DES, Platon, Oeuvres complètes, XIV:
      Lexique, 1: A-Λ ; 2: M-Ω. Coll. G. Budé,
      Paris, Les Belles Lettres 1964 xvi&577p.
      Rev. BAGB 1964 404-405 des Places.
      GIF XVII 1964 360 Jannaccone.
      REG LXXVII 1964 343-345 Goldschmidt.
      RFIC XCIII 1965 199-201 Untersteiner.
      Biblica XLVI 1965 394 des Places.
      RPh XXXIX 1965 319 Chantraine.
      Emerita XXXIII 1965 400-402 Lens.
      CRAI 1965 87 Chantraine.
      RThPh XCVIII 1965 321-322 Schaerer.
      Mnemosyne XIX 1966 186 de Vries.
      GIF XIX 1966 163 Scivoletto.
      RSC XIV 1966 131-132 d'Agostino.
      CR XVI 1966 304-307 Robinson.
      JHS LXXXVI 1966 227-228 Brandwood.
      Gregorianum XLVII 1966 559 Orbe.
      AJPh LXXXVIII 1967 373-375 Lee.
      RHR CLXII 1967 93-94 Guillaumont.
      AC XXXVII 1968 282-285 de Strycker.

4551* RIDDELL J., A Digest of Platonic Idioms. Reprinted
      from Apology of Plato, Oxford 1867 edn., with a
      new pref. by Holwerda D. Amsterdam, Hakkert
      1967 140p.

4552* PERLS H., Lexikon der Platonischen Begriffe.
      Bern/München, Francke 1973 408p.

For additional discussions see 814, 825, 1428.

XIII: BIBLIOGRAPHY

The following section contains both normal bibliographical material and works which are critical discussions and surveys of recent literature on Socrates and Plato.

4553 MAZZANTINI C., "Platone in alcuni suoi recenti interpreti". GM XIII 1958 477-486.

4554 CHERNISS H.F., "Plato (1950-1957)". Lustrum IV 1959 5-308, V 1960 323-648.

4555 ISNARDI M., "Studi recenti e problemi aperti sulla struttura e la funzione della prima Accademia platonica". RSI LXXI 1959 271-291.

4556 VÁZQUEZ J.A., "Nuevas versiones inglesas de Platón". Philosophia(Argent) XXIII 1959 71-74.

4557 LANATA G., "Su alcuni recenti studi di estetica antica". A&R V 1960 65-78.

4558* MANASSE E.M., Bücher über Platon, II: Werke in englisher Sprache. PhilosRdschau Beih. II, Tübingen, Mohr 1961 241p.
Rev. Gnomon XXXV 1963 765-770 O'Brien.

4559 "Plato. Kroniek". Lampadion I 1960-1961 89-96; II 1961-1962 3-13.

4560 NATUCCI A., "Appunti bibliografici relativi a Platone e ad Aristotele". Physis IV 1962 379-385.

4561 PLACES E. DES, "Bulletin de la philosophie religieuse des Grecs, IV: Platon et Aristote". RecSR L 1962 605-620.

4562 WICHMANN O., "Existenziale Platondeutung". KantStud LIII 1961-1962 441-489.

4563 RUIJGH C.J., "Plato II". Lampadion VI 1965-1966 5-85.

4564 ISNARDI PARENTE M., "Studi e discussioni recenti sul Platone esoterico, l'Accademia antica e il neoplatonismo". DeHomine 1967 n.22-23 217-244. Reprinted p.113-146 in Isnardi Parente M., Filosofia e politica nelle lettere di Platone

XIII: BIBLIOGRAPHY

(see 4603).

4565 OWENS J., "Recent Footnotes to Plato". RM XX
      1966-1967 648-661.

4566 SWEENEY L., "Five Platonic Studies". ModS XLIV 1967
      375-381.

4567 YAMANO K., "Essay on recent studies of Plato" [in
      Japanese]. Riso no.409 1967.

4568 BATTEGAZZORE A., "Rassegna di recenti studi
      socratici". RFIC XCVI 1968 234-242.

4569 FREIRE A., "Bibliografia recente sobre Platão".
      RPortFil XXIV 1968 440-446.

4570 ISNARDI PARENTE M., "Gli studi platonici in Italia
      negli ultimi venti anni". CultScuola n.25 1968
      128-144.

4571 BARCENILLA A., "Veintisiete libros sobre Platón".
      Perficit II 1970 425-451.

4572 SWEENEY L., "More Books on Plato". ModS XLVII 1970
      225-237.

4573 FREIRE A., "Leitura de Platão". RPortFil Supp.
      Bibl. XLV 1971 177-184.

4574 GALLARDO M.D., "Estado actual de los estudios sobre
      los Simposios de Platón, Jenofonte y Plutarquo".
      CFC III 1972 127-191.

4575 MANSFELD J., "Moeite met Plato". Lampas VI 1973
      255-266.

4576 PRUEMM K., "Weltanschauliche Gehalte der
      griechischen Frühphilosophie bis Plato
      einschliesslich. Umriss des heutigen
      Forschungsstandes nach dem Schrifttum von
      1950-1970". Gregorianum LIV 1973 717-770.
      (p.753-767 on Plato.)

4577 SWEENEY L., "Foreign Books on Greek Philosophers:
      Socrates and Plato". ModS L 1972-1973 76-86.

For additional bibliography see 4090.

XIV: COLLECTIONS OF ARTICLES

The following books are wholly or largely comprised of articles concerned with Socrates and Plato. They are cross referenced under the articles they contain, as those articles appear in this volume.

4578* Le Néoplatonisme. Actes du Colloque de Royaumont, 9-13 juin 1969. Colloques internat. du CNRS, Sciences Humaines, Paris, Centre National de la Recherche Scientifique 1971 xiv&496p.
Rev. RSLR IX 1973 370-372 Gribomont.

4579* Zetesis. Album amicorum door vrienden en collega's aangeboden aan Prof. Dr. É. de Strycker, gewoon Hoogleraar aan de Universitaire Faculteiten Sint-Ignatius te Antwerpen ter gelegenheid van zijn vijfenzestigste verjaardag. Antwerpen/Utrecht, De Nederlandsche Boekhandel 1973 784p.

4580* ALLEN R.E. ed., Studies in Plato's Metaphysics. London, Routledge & Kegan Paul 1965 xii&452p.
Rev. CR XVI 1966 309-312 Crombie.
TLS 20 Jan. 1966 42.
NS 1966 475 Kenny.
RM XX 1966-1967 653 Owens.
CJ LXII 1967 231-232 Hoerber.
Hermathena CIV 1967 98 Luce.
JHS LXXXVIII 1968 194-195 Robinson.
Dialogue IX 1970 449 Brown.

4581* ANTON J.P. & KUSTAS G.L. eds., Essays in Ancient Greek Philosophy. Albany, State Univ. of N.Y. Pr. 1971 xlvi&650p.
Rev. CPh LXVII 298-300 Sprague.
SIF IV 1972 219-221 Preus.
Platon XXIII 1971 388 Bartzeliotis.
CR XXIII 1973 281-282 Kerferd.

4582* BAMBROUGH R. ed., New Essays on Plato and Aristotle. Intern. Libr. of Philos. and Scientific Method, London, Routledge & Kegan Paul and New York, Humanities Pr. 1965 viii&176p.
Rev. CW 1966-1967 72 Costas.
PhilosBks May 1966 2 Gulley.
RM 1965-1966 608 E.A.R.
Tablet 1966 250 Armstrong.

TLS 1966 42.
NS 1966 475 Kenny.
Ph&PhenR XXVII 1966 297-298 Novak.
Inquiry 1967 101-113 Hintikka.
PhilosQ XVII 1967 166-168 Hardie.
Philosophy XLII 1967 170-172 Robinson.
CJ LXII 1967 227-228 Hoerber.
Mind LXXVI 1967 597-598 Cross.
CR XVII 1967 30-33 Crombie.
JHS LXXXVII 1967 166 Hamlyn.
JCS XV 1967 147-150 Iwata.
PhR LXXVII 1968 512-516 Mourelatos.
JPh LXVII 1970 391-397 Moravcsik.

4583* BAMBROUGH R. ed., Plato, Popper and Politics. Some
contributions to a modern controversy.
Cambridge, Heffer 1967 viii&219p.
Rev. TLS 6 June 1968 600.
RM 1968-1969 162 R.J.B.
Listener 20 June 1968 811 Kenny.
HJ LX 1967-1968 137-139 Adcock.
REG LXXXI 1968 291 Weil.
REA LXX 1968 463-464 Schaerer.
RBPh XLVI 1968 948 des Places.
RPh XLIII 1969 131 Louis.
JHS LXXXIX 1969 166-167 Easterling.
PhilosQ XIX 1969 184-185 Cross.
RFIC XCVIII 1970 441-446 Isnardi Parente.
N&Q 1970 279 Crombie.

4584* BONITZ H., Platonische Studien. Reprographischer
Nachdruck der 3. Aufl., Berlin 1886.
Hildesheim, Olms 1968 x&323p.

4585* DIRLMEIER F., Ausgewählte Schriften zu Dichtung und
Philosophie der Griechen, hrsg. von H.
Goergemanns. Heidelberg, Winter 1970 196p.
Rev. AC XL 1971 327 Schwartz.
Emerita XL 1972 227-228 García Gual.
CR XXII 1972 233-235 Lloyd-Jones.

4586* DUERING I. & OWEN G.E.L. eds., Aristotle and Plato
in the mid-fourth Century. Papers of the
Symposium Aristotelicum held at Oxford in
August, 1957. Studia Graeca et Lat. Gothoburg.
XI, Stockholm, Almquist & Wiksell 1960 x&279p.
Rev. AC XXIX 1960 454-456 Moraux.
JHS LXXXI 1961 188 Balme.
REG LXXV 1962 581-583 Aubenque.
CR XII 1962 44-46 Kerferd.
RFIC XL 1962 304-312 Grilli.
JCS X 1962 147-153 Ono.

Gymnasium LXX 1963 141-145 Dirlmeier.
Erasmus XV 1963 621-624 Pédech.
RSF XIX 1964 219-221 Plebe.
REG LXXVII 1964 613-616 Defradas.
AGPh XLVII 1965 305-312 Furley.

4587* FESTUGIÈRE A.J., Études de philosophie grecque. Bibl. d'hist. de la philos., Paris, Vrin 1971 598p.
Rev. EPh 1971 516-517 & 1972 82-83
Moreau.

4588* FLASCH K. ed., Parusia, Festgabe für Johannes Hirschberger. Studien zur Philosophie Platons und zur Problemgeschichte des Platonismus. Frankfurt, Minerva-Verl. 1965 xi&520p.
Rev. PhJ LXXIII 1965-1966 419-422
Beierwaltes.
RecSR LIV 1966 303-304 Daniélou.
PLA XX 1967 109-115 Franz.
Laurentianum 1967 273-274 Borak.

4589* FRIEDLAENDER P., Studien zur antiken Literatur und Kunst. Berlin, de Gruyter 1969 x&703p.

4590* FRIES R. ed., The Progress of Plato's Progress. Agon Suppl. No.2. Berkeley, Univ. of California Dept. of Classics 1969 viii&75p. Papers delivered at a conference held in Santa Barbara in 1967.

4591* FRITZ K. VON, Grundprobleme der Geschichte der antiken Wissenschaft. Berlin, de Gruyter 1966 xxxvi&759p.
Rev. RSF 1972 401 Vegetti.

4592* GADAMER H.G., Platos dialektische Ethik und andere Studien zur platonischen Philosophie. Hamburg, Meiner 1968 xiv&288p.
Rev. ArchPhilos XXXII 1969 489-490
Moreau.
RIFD XLVI 1969 180-181 Romano.
PLA XXIII 1970 17-18 Steinbeck.
WJb III 1970 271-273 Heintel.
JHPh IX 1971 524 Schneider.
CR XXII 1972 103-104 Huby.
BAGB 1973 508p.

4593* GADAMER H.G., Kleine Schriften III: Idee und Sprache. Platon, Husserl, Heidegger. Tübingen, Mohr 1972.
Rev. ASSPh XXXIII 1973 221-224 Kunz.

TPh XLVIII 1973 473-474 Schmidt.

4594* GADAMER H.G. & SCHADEWALDT W. eds., Idee und Zahl.
Studien zur platonischen Philosophie. AHAW
1968,2, Heidelberg, Winter 175p.
Rev. AC XXXVIII 1969 546 des Places.
Helmantica XX 1969 403-404 Rivera de
Ventosa.
REA LXXI 1969 481-484 Moreau.
CW LXIII 1970 166 Tarán.
PLA XXIII 1970 17-20 Steinbeck.
CR XXI 1971 30-31 Gulley.

4595* GAISER K. ed., Das Platonbild. Zehn Beiträge zum
Platonverständnis. Olms Stud. I, Hildesheim,
Olms 1969 vi&330p.

4596* GAUSS H., Opuscula Philosophica aus der Werkstatt
des Philosophen. Schriften aus dem Nachlass,
hrsg. von Hebeisen A. Bern, Lang 1972.

4597* GIGON O., Studien zur antiken Philosophie, hrsg.
von Graeser A. Berlin/New York, de Gruyter 1972
vi&442p.
Rev. ArchPhilos XXXVI 1973 505 Solignac.
Angelicum L 1973 281-285 Vansteenkiste.
TPh XXXV 1973 631-632 van Straaten.

4598* GOLDSCHMIDT V., Questions platoniciennes. Bibl.
d'hist. de la philos., Paris, Vrin 1970 292p.
Rev. EPh 1971 373 École.
REG LXXXIV 1971 217-218 Moreau.

4599* HARDER R., Kleine Schriften, hrsg. von Marg W.
München, Beck 1960 vii&519p.

4600* HINTIKKA J., Tieto on Valtaa ja muita
aatehistoriallisia esseitä. Porvoo/Helsinki,
Söderström 1969 295p.

4601* HOFFMANN E., Platonismus und christliche
Philosophie. Erasmus-Bibl, Zürich,
Artemis-Verl. 1960 502p.
Rev. CW LV 1961 18 Hoerber.
PhilosRdschau IX 1961 234-235 Kuhn.
Gnomon XXXIV 1962 269-274 Wagner.
RecSR L 1962 631-632 des Places.
JHPh I 1963 99-102 Kristeller.
Gymnasium LXX 1963 457-458 Fauth.
ThLZ LXXXVIII 1963 378 Hessen.
RHPhR XLIII 1963 280 Hornus.

RHE LIX 1964 384 Mallet.

4602* HOFFMANN E., Drei Schriften zur griechischen Philosophie. Heidelberg, Winter 1964 79p.

4603* ISNARDI PARENTE M., Filosofia e politica nelle lettere di Platone. Napoli Guida 1970 223p.
Rev. BollFil IV 1970 178-179.
Logos I 1970 558-562 Casertano.
RIFD XLVIII 1971 178-179.
GM XXVIII 1973 296-300 Capecci.

4604* JAEGER W., Humanistische Reden und Vorträge. 2. Aufl. Berlin 1960.

4605* JAEGER W., Scripta Minora. 2 vols. Roma, Ed. di Storia e Lett. 1960 xxviii&416p, 568p.
Rev. RFIC XXXIX 1961 225-227 Rostagni.
RSPh LII 1968 370-372 Saffrey.

4606* KAPP E., Ausgewählte Schriften, hrsg. von Diller H. & Diller I. Berlin, de Gruyter 1968 337p.

4607* LAVELLE L., Panorama des doctrines philosophiques. Chroniques philosophiques. Paris, Albin Michel 1967 232p.

4608* LEE E.N., MOURELATOS A.P.D., & RORTY R.M. eds., Exegesis and Argument. Studies in Greek Philosophy presented to Gregory Vlastos. Phronesis Suppl. Vol. I, Assen, Van Gorcum 1973 xviii&452p.

4609* MORAVCSIK J.M.E. ed., Patterns in Plato's Thought. Papers arising out of the 1971 West Coast Greek Philosophy Conference. Synthese Historical Library VI, Dordrecht/Boston, Reidel 1973 viii&212p.

4610* NÉDONCELLE M., Explorations personnalistes. Paris, Aubier 1970 300p.
Rev. REAug XVII 1971 377.
RSR XLV 1971 103.
RecSR LXI 1973 311 Sales.

4611* OWEN G.E.L. ed., Aristotle on Dialectic. The Topics. Proceedings of the Third Symposium Aristotelicum. Oxford, Clarendon Pr. 1968 viii&346p.

Rev. PhilosQ XXII 1972 358-361 Kirwan.
Dialogue XI 1972 292-293 Gallop.
JHS XCII 1972 218-219 Rowe.
RM XXV 1971-1972 573-574 Sweeney.

4621* VLASTOS G. ed., The Philosophy of Socrates. A Collection of Critical Essays. Modern Studies in Philosophy, Garden City, N.Y., Doubleday Anchor 1971 iv&354p.
Rev. RM XXV 1971-1972 143 J.J.R.
Dialogue XI 1972 289 Shiner.
Ph&PhenR XXXII 1972 582-585 Andriopoulos.

4622* VLASTOS G., Platonic Studies. Princeton, Princeton Univ. Pr. 1973 xvi&437p.

4623* VOGEL C.J. DE, Theoria. Studies over de griekse wijsbegeerte. Assen, van Gorcum 1967 233p.
Rev. Hermeneus XXXIX 1967 16 van Straaten.

4624* VOGEL C.J. DE, Philosophia, Part I: Studies in Greek Philosophy. Assen, Van Gorcum 1970 viii&451p.
Rev. REG LXXXIV 1971 208-211 Moreau.
Helmantica XXII 1971 346 Ortall.
TPh XXXIII 1971 781-783 Smets.
CW LXV 1971 65 Ridington.
CPh LXVII 1972 298-300 Sprague.
IPQ XII 1972 633 Clarke.
PhilosQ XXII 1972 361-362 Long.
Gymnasium LXXIX 1972 110-111 Goergemanns.

4625* WEHRLI F., Theoria und Humanitas. Gesammelte Schriften zur antiken Gedankenwelt. Zürich/München Artemis-Verl. 1972 334p.

4626* WIPPERN J. ed., Das Problem der ungeschriebenen Lehre Platons. Beiträge zum Verständnis der platonischen Prinzipienphilosophie, hrsg. & mit einer Einleit., Auswahlbibliogr. & Stellenindex versehen von Wippern J. Wege der Forschung CLXXXVI, Darmstadt, Wiss. Buchges. 1972 xlviii&475p.
Rev. Philosophia II 1972 337-343 Skouteropoulos.
REA LXXIV 1972 267-270 Moreau.

4627* ZELLER E., Platonische Studien. Nachdruck der Ausg. Tübingen, Osiander 1839. Amsterdam, Rodopi 1969 vi&300p.

4612* ROBINSON R., Essays in Greek Philosophy. Oxford,
Clarendon Pr. 1969 160p.
Rev. RF LX 1969 520-522.
Ph&PhenR XXXI 1970 315 Mulhern.
TLS LXIX 1970 105.
AC XXXIX 1970 297-298 Byl.
BIEH V,2 1971 59 Alsina.
Proteus I 1970 167-168 Impara.
PhilosBks Jan. 1970 25-26 Hamlyn.
CR XXVII 1972 56-57 Easterling.

4613* ROSSI P. ed., Antologia della critica filosofica,
I: L'età antica. Bari, Laterza 1961 viii&507p.
Rev. RBPh XL 1962 1416 de Strycker.

4614* SESONSKE A. ed., Plato's Republic: Interpretation
and Criticism. Belmont, California, Wadsworth
1966 141p.

4615* SOLMSEN F., Kleine Schriften. 2 vols. Hildesheim,
Olms 1968 xviii&1068p.
Rev. Gnomon XLV 1973 737-745 Kahn.

4616* SPECK J. ed., Grundprobleme der grossen
Philosophen. Philosophie des Altertums und des
Mittelalters: Sokrates, Platon, Aristoteles,
Augustinus, Thomas von Aquin, Nikolaus von Kues.
Uni-Taschenbücher Nr. 146, Göttingen,
Vandenhoeck & Ruprecht 1972 263p.

4617* THORSON T.L., Plato, Totalitarian or Democrat?
Essays selected and introd. by Thorson T.L.
Englewood Cliffs, N.J., Prentice Hall 1963 184p.
Rev. Ethics LXXXI 1971 181-186
Meiklejohn.

4618* USENER H., Kleine Schriften. 4 vols. Nachdruck der
Ausgabe 1912-1913. Osnabrück, Zeller 1965
vi&400, 382, vi&546, vii&516p.

4619* VLASTOS G. ed., Plato. A Collection of Critical
Essays, I: Metaphysics and Epistemology.
Modern Stud. in Philos., Garden City, N.Y.,
Doubleday Anchor 1970 x&338p.
Rev. JHS XCII 1972 218-219 Rowe.
PhilosQ XXII 1972 358-361 Kirwan.

4620* VLASTOS G. ed., Plato. A Collection of Critical
Essays, II: Ethics, Politics and Philosophy of
Art and Religion. Modern Studies in Philosophy,
Garden City, N.Y., Doubleday Anchor 1971
xi&314p.

AUTHOR INDEX

AALDERS G.J.D., 1424,
1457.
ABBAGNANO N., 92, 93,
1656.
ABBAS A., 1667.
ABDEL-MASSIH E., 629.
ABEL A., 1768.
ACKRILL J.L., 1714, 2250,
2251, 2452, 2820.
ACRI F., 948, 1168, 1489,
1654.
ACTON H.B., 3649.
ADAM J., 1966.
ADAMATSU H., 4051.
ADAMIETZ J., 1094.
ADKINS A.W.H., 1963, 3160,
3432, 4272.
ADORNO F., 94, 945, 950,
1274, 1474, 2038, 3844,
4141, 4163, 4246.
ADRIANI M., 3936.
AFNAN R.M., 754, 4353.
AGARD W., 3616.
AGOGLIA R.M., 1, 3986.
AGOSTINO F. D', 690,
4119.
AICHROTH R., 2582.
AIMO M.A., 2728.
AKARSU B., 4475.
AL-NASHSHAR S., 2331.
ALAIN [pseud.], 144.
ALARCO L.F., 4331.
ALBERT K., 3778, 3937.
ALBERT-BIROT P., 1534,
1535.
ALBURY W.R., 2224.
ALDERISIO F., 318.
ALDERMAN H., 682, 2842.
ALEXANDRE M., 2, 1499.
ALFONSI L., 565, 576, 594,
2708.
ALI SAMI A., 1667.
ALLAN D.J., 358, 380.
ALLEN H.J., 879.
ALLEN M.J.B., 1876.
ALLEN R.E., 997, 1187,
1225, 1557, 1627, 2180,
2372, 2863, 2869, 2995,
3038, 4472, 4580.

ALONSO Y ALONSO P.M., 630.
ALRIVIE J.J., 2431.
ALSINA J., 208, 776.
AMADO LEVY-VALENSI E.,
2887.
AMAND DE MENDIETA E.,
4364.
AMAR M.A., 3968.
AMIRA HILMI MATAR, 1796.
AMIT M., 2209.
AMMENDOLA G., 904.
AMODEO V., 1033, 1034.
AMOROSO LIMA A., 1042.
ANAGNOSTOPOULOS G., 1135,
1142, 2821.
ANASTAPLO G., 1060.
ANAWATI G.C., 2331.
ANDERSON A., 1249, 4332.
ANDERSON D.E., 1522, 4422.
ANDERSON F.M., 651.
ANDERSON J.M., 2658.
ANDERSON R.E., 4380.
ANDERSON W., 3599.
ANDERSON W.D., 3309.
ANDERSSON T.J., 3725.
ANDIC M., 1523, 2284.
ANDREWS P.B.S., 1153.
ANGELINO G., 896.
ANNIS D.B., 4000.
ANSBRO J.J., 2101, 2103.
ANSCOMBE G.E.M., 916,
2928.
ANTON J.P., 452, 1764,
2675, 3893, 3916, 4040,
4581.
ANTUNES M., 1679.
AOKI S., 3815.
APELT O., 1486, 1973,
2313.
ARANGIO-RUIZ V., 1275,
2217.
ARAUJO M., 865.
ARCHER-HIND R.D., 1641,
2478.
ARDLEY G.W.R., 551, 2788,
3058, 3687.
ARGYLE A.W., 1069.
ARMETTA F., 3141.
ARMLEDER P.J., 1063, 2500,

1841, 3276, 3318, 4249.
CAMERER R., 2468.
CAMERON A., 574.
CAMPBELL L., 923, 2041,
2407.
CAMPBELL M., 1709.
CANCRINI A., 4151.
CANILLI A., 4436.
CANOSA CAPDEVILLE Y.,
3438.
CAPELLE A., 2313, 2416,
2432, 2435.
CAPELLE W., 101, 2570.
CAPITAN W.H., 4469.
CAPIZZI A., 212, 1957,
4252.
CAPPELLETTI A.S., 4339.
CAPPS W.H., 3938.
CAPUDER A., 4326.
CARACCIOLO A., 2615.
CARAFIDES J.L., 4329.
CARAMELLA S., 324, 4437.
CARBONARA C., 4168.
CARBONARA NADDEI M., 50,
184, 252, 3083.
CARENA C., 948.
CARLINI A., 300, 605, 777,
803, 810, 820, 946,
998, 1104, 1416, 1772,
1773, 1774, 1776, 1777,
1780, 4018.
CARMODY J., 3962.
CARRATELLO U., 569.
CARROLL K.M., 151.
CARSON K., 4398.
CARTER R.E., 3851, 4359.
CARVALHO A.P. DE, 1418.
CARVALHO J. DE, 1663.
CASERTANO G., 222.
CASINI N., 906, 909, 1159,
1653, 4310.
CASPER D.J., 2285.
CASSIN C.E., 2110.
CASTAGNA L., 910.
CASTAÑEDA H.N., 1730,
1731, 1732, 2996.
CASTELLANO A.M., 4137.
CASTILLO C., 3857.
CASTORINA E., 1201.

CATAN J., 3143.
CATTANEI G., 1353.
CAVAIGNAC E., 4344.
CAVALCANTE DE SOUZA J.,
972, 2329.
CAVARNOS C., 3876, 3894.
CAVEING M., 3306.
CAZENEUVE J., 3425.
CECCHI S., 907.
CECI G., 3729.
CEFALI V., 1033, 1034.
CELARIER J.LeR., 359,
1628.
CELENTANO L., 1106.
CELENTANO M.S., 561, 562.
CELLA S., 1165.
CELOTTI T., 1036.
CENTORE F.F., 13, 1610.
CERRI G., 28.
CHABROL H., 1649.
CHAIGNET A.E., 3099.
CHAIX-RUY J., 8, 638.
CHAMBRY E., 859, 939, 941,
942, 943, 944, 1028,
1979, 1981.
CHANCE R., 3668.
CHANG C., 753.
CHARBONNEAUX J., 4529.
CHARITONIDIS S.I., 4530.
CHATELET F., 9, 102, 1029,
2323, 3669.
CHATTE REME C., 2693.
CHAUVOIS L., 2171.
CHEN C.H., 382, 1817,
3915.
CHENE-WILLIAMS A., 1692.
CHERNISS H.F., 339, 371,
2509, 2913, 3486, 4554.
CHERRY R.S., 2516.
CHEVALIER J.M., 3307.
CHI-LU CHUNG A., 3476.
CHIEREGHIN F., 242, 1085,
2889, 3253.
CHILTON C.W., 477.
CHIRASSI COLOMBO I., 3971.
CHROUST A.H., 341, 349,
383, 384, 390, 405,
406, 412, 419, 462,
526, 818, 1531, 2120,

OKAL M., 4266.
OKSALA P., 977.
OLDEWELT H., 42.
OLIVA P., 321.
OLIVES CANALS J., 1664.
OMORI S., 3841.
OOSTHUIZEN D.C.S., 3749.
OPOCHER E., 3758.
OPRISAN M., 3605.
OPSTELTEN J.C., 3431,
    4126.
ORCIBAL J., 2580.
ORSI C., 3314.
ORTEGA A., 1444, 3873.
ORTEGA Y GASSET J., 2335,
    2336.
OSAWA K., 1852.
OSCANYAN F.S., 2226.
OSTENFELD E., 2522.
OSTWALD M., 2135.
OSWIECIMSKI S., 1214,
    1215, 4347.
OTTO W.F., 852, 853, 854,
    855, 857.
OWEN G.E.L., 368, 397,
    398, 427, 1562, 2274,
    2307, 2508, 2515, 4611.
OWENS J., 129, 635, 4565.
OZAWA K., 1765, 1855,
    3209, 3210.
PAASSEN C.R. VAN, 172.
PABON J.M., 1363, 1998.
PACI E., 2726.
PAEV M.E., 3335, 3336.
PAGLIANO M., 1236.
PAGLIARO A., 2727, 4056.
PAIOW M. see Paev M.E.
PAISSE J.M., 246, 1859,
    2811, 2937, 2987, 3091,
    3118, 3119, 3153, 3166,
    4373, 4440, 4452.
PAK Y.W., 873.
PALAIOLOGOS G.N., 591.
PALAU E., 1996.
PALEIKAT J., 840, 971,
    972.
PALGEN R., 646.
PALLAS P., 588.
PALLIS P.K., 607.

PALMEIRA P.D., 1107.
PANAGIOTOU S., 1572, 1615.
PANNWITZ R., 4213.
PANOUSSI E., 759.
PAPACOSTEA C., 978.
PAPADOPOL T., 1463.
PAPANIKOLAOU K.N., 1394,
    1927, 3606.
PAPAS C., 3775.
PAPAY J.L., 2894.
PAPOULIA B., 2839.
PAQUET L., 4112.
PARAIN B., 1573.
PARANDOWSKI J., 1289.
PARKE H.W., 4285.
PARKER G.F., 130.
PARRY A., 3451.
PARRY H., 320.
PARTEE C., 3154.
PARTEE M.H., 795, 796,
    3874, 3877, 3899, 4057.
PASOLI E., 2202.
PASQUALI G., 1417.
PATER W.A. DE, 399.
PATER W.H., 706.
PATRICIOS N.N., 3244.
PATTERSON R.L., 1686.
PATZER H., 207, 3642.
PATZIG G., 726, 891, 1255,
    2988, 3135.
PAVAN M., 1288.
PAVESE C., 1206.
PAVESE R., 2504.
PAWLOW T., 3826.
PAXSON T.D., 1261.
PAZZINI A., 3255.
PEARSON L., 3442.
PECK A.L., 1552, 2243,
    2899.
PEIPERS D., 3015.
PELTZ R., 2381.
PEMBROKE S.G., 521.
PENEDOS A. DOS, 683,
    1481.
PENNER T., 1890, 3184,
    4496, 4497.
PEPIN J., 550, 555, 584,
    3185, 3925, 4084.
PERELLI L., 568.

RADEMACHER U., 2131.
RADKAU H., 3266.
RADT S.L., 967, 1264.
RAEDER H., 45.
RAEDLE H., 1404.
RAHE H., 3952.
RAITH O., 2519.
RALFS G., 730, 3092.
RAMAGE E.S., 4351.
RAMANUJACHARI R., 2012.
RAMAROSON L., 613.
RAMAT-GAN, 4427.
RAMEIL A., 3761.
RAMIREZ CORRIA F., 3398.
RAMNOUX C., 231.
RANDALL J.H., 2661, 3662,
   3861.
RANFT H., 3554.
RANKIN H.D., 181, 198,
   718, 1384, 1707, 1716,
   2028, 2036, 2096, 2123,
   2124, 2593, 2709, 3073,
   3396, 4105.
RANKIN K.W., 1606, 1611.
RANTA J., 1335.
RAOSS M., 4322, 4325.
RASCHINI M.A., 2239, 4400,
   4401.
RAUBITSCHEK A.E., 1068,
   3427.
RAVASINI G.G., 1803.
RAVEN J.E., 46.
RAVIS G., 2957.
RE M.C. DEL, 1244, 4316.
REAGAN J.T., 1559, 2255,
   3219, 3243.
REALE G., 131, 1161, 1229,
   1233, 1273, 1488, 1657,
   1923, 4002.
REDLOW G., 3104.
REED N.H., 4058.
REES D.A., 444, 1600,
   1966, 3506.
REEVE M.D., 2403.
REEVES J.W., 877.
REFOULÉ F., 597.
REGENBOGEN O., 1804.
REGNELL H., 3402.
REGNER L., 976.

REICH E., 3156.
REICH K., 1226, 1486.
REICHE H.A.T., 400, 2706.
REIDEMEISTER K., 3279.
REIN U.G.M., 724.
REINACH J., 4309.
REINHARDT K., 2671.
REINHOLD M., 47.
REINICKE H., 3473.
REITZENSTEIN E., 4357.
RENEHAN R., 331, 1455,
   1456, 2400.
REPELLINI F.F., 1871.
REST W., 673.
REVERDIN O., 3583.
REXINE J.E., 3907.
REY ALTUNA L., 3043.
REYNEN H., 1689, 2316,
   2346, 2362, 2363, 2397,
   2603.
REZZANI M., 2552.
RICCI M., 4441.
RICH A.N.M., 486.
RICHARDS I.A., 1009, 1967.
RICHARDSON W.J., 675.
RICHELMY A., 1790.
RICHTER F., 1014.
RICHTER G.M.A., 4534,
   4536, 4538, 4543.
RICHTER L., 3299.
RICHTER P.E., 3854.
RICO M., 865.
RICOEUR P., 2875.
RIDDELL J., 1012, 4551.
RIES K., 313.
RIEZU J., 4190.
RIGOBELLO A., 1302, 3035,
   4244, 4391.
RIJK L.M. DE, 3762.
RINGBOM S., 2604.
RINTELEN F.J. VON, 2922,
   3016.
RIST J.M., 489, 490, 499,
   603, 841, 1431, 1553,
   1576, 1720, 2450, 2908,
   2958, 3074, 4289.
RITTER C., 48.
RITZEL W., 3788.
RIVAUD A., 861.

587

TOEPLITZ O., 2925.
TOMADAKIS N.V., 2607.
TONG L.K., 766.
TOPITSCH E., 3044, 3096.
TORNAMBE F., 4387.
TOTSUKA S., 77, 991, 1583.
TOUBEAU H., 163.
TOUCHARD J., 3543.
TOURLIDES G.A., 2069,
  3791.
TOURNEY G., 656.
TOVAR A., 78, 961, 2218,
  3629, 4295.
TOZZI G., 3568.
TRACY T.J., 3397, 3412.
TRAGLIA A., 560, 1317.
TRAUGOTT E., 3530.
TRAVASKIS J.R., 1893.
TREDENNICK H., 1005.
TRENCSENYI-WALDAPFEL I.,
  540.
TREPANIER E., 4029.
TREU M., 3722.
TREVASKIS J.R., 2260,
  2666, 2795.
TREVES P., 948.
TRIANTAPHYLLOPOULOS J.,
  3595, 3683.
TRIMPI W., 3879.
TRONQUART G., 4371.
TROTIGNON P., 1568, 2989,
  3213, 3455.
TROUILLARD J., 510, 1592.
TROUSSON R., 4396.
TRUEBLOOD A.S., 767.
TRUSSO F.E., 3904.
TSATSOS C.I., 3585, 3644,
  3753.
TSIRPANLIS E.C., 3097.
TSOUYOPOULOS N., 2990.
TSUMURA K., 1517, 1749,
  2290, 2770.
TSUNODA Y., 1565.
TUCKEY T.G., 1093.
TUNGA T., 2009.
TURLINGTON B., 4206.
TURNBULL R.G., 355, 2248.
TURNER E.G., 1945.
TUROLLA E., 862.

UBINK J.B., 3985.
UCHIYAMA K., 2037.
UCHTENHAGEN A., 3596.
UNGER E., 3667.
UNTERSTEINER M., 1090,
  1775, 1987.
UPHOLD W.B. JR., 593.
UPHUES K., 3028.
URMENETA F. DE, 188.
URWICK E.J., 4405.
USCATESCU J., 578.
USENER H., 1811, 4618.
UTERMOEHLEN O., 2183.
VACCARINO G., 2749.
VALASTRO F., 4210.
VALCKE L., 4476.
VALENSIN A., 147.
VALENTIN P., 3186.
VALGIMIGLI M., 900, 1032,
  1166, 1985, 1989.
VALLANDRO L., 971.
VAN DER WEY A., 3171.
VAN FRAASSEN B.C., 2270.
VANDIEST J., 4319.
VARVARO P., 79.
VASMANOLIS G.E., 2044.
VASSALIO A., 959.
VATER H., 1587.
VATIN C., 1396.
VAUGHAN M., 4528.
VAZQUEZ J.A., 4556.
VEGETTI M., 1990, 2856,
  3401, 3403, 3404, 3405.
VELA R., 3808, 4392.
VERBEKE G., 449, 2760,
  3036.
VERDENIUS W.J., 599, 824,
  1328, 1509, 1669, 1828,
  3880, 4108, 4140.
VERDROSS A., 3531, 3645.
VERENE D.P., 3830.
VERMEULE C.C., 4525.
VERNANT J.P., 2589.
VERSENYI L., 3057, 3508,
  3739, 3881, 4207, 4454.
VIANO C.A., 4017.
VICAIRE P., 938, 1651,
  1789, 3172, 3803, 3814,
  3831, 4136.